The Archaeology of Island Colonization

Society and Ecology in Island and Coastal Archaeology

UNIVERSITY PRESS OF FLORIDA

Florida A&M University, Tallahassee

Florida Atlantic University, Boca Raton

Florida Gulf Coast University, Ft. Myers

Florida International University, Miami

Florida State University, Tallahassee

New College of Florida, Sarasota

University of Central Florida, Orlando

University of Florida, Gainesville

University of North Florida, Jacksonville

University of South Florida, Tampa

University of West Florida, Pensacola

THE ARCHAEOLOGY OF
Island Colonization

Global Approaches to Initial Human Settlement

Edited by Matthew F. Napolitano,
Jessica H. Stone, and Robert J. DiNapoli

Foreword by Victor D. Thompson

UNIVERSITY PRESS OF FLORIDA

Gainesville / Tallahassee / Tampa / Boca Raton
Pensacola / Orlando / Miami / Jacksonville / Ft. Myers / Sarasota

26 25 24 23 22 21   6 5 4 3 2 1

Library of Congress Cataloging-in-Publication Data
Names: Napolitano, Matthew F., editor. | Stone, Jessica H., editor. |
   DiNapoli, Robert J., editor. | Thompson, Victor D., author of foreword.
Title: The archaeology of island colonization : global approaches to
   initial human settlement / edited by Matthew F. Napolitano, Jessica H.
   Stone, and Robert J. DiNapoli ; foreword by Victor D. Thompson.
Other titles: Society and ecology in island and coastal archaeology.
Description: Gainesville : University Press of Florida, 2021. | Series:
   Society and ecology in island and coastal archaeology | Includes
   bibliographical references and index.
Identifiers: LCCN 2020045483 (print) | LCCN 2020045484 (ebook) | ISBN
   9780813066851 (hardback) | ISBN 9780813057781 (pdf)
Subjects: LCSH: Island archaeology. | Island people—History. | Social
   archaeology—History.
Classification: LCC CC77.I84 A73 2021 (print) | LCC CC77.I84 (ebook) |
   DDC 909/.0942—dc23
LC record available at https://lccn.loc.gov/2020045483
LC ebook record available at https://lccn.loc.gov/2020045484

The University Press of Florida is the scholarly publishing agency for the State
University System of Florida, comprising Florida A&M University, Florida Atlantic
University, Florida Gulf Coast University, Florida International University, Florida
State University, New College of Florida, University of Central Florida, University
of Florida, University of North Florida, University of South Florida, and University
of West Florida.

University Press of Florida
2046 NE Waldo Road
Suite 2100
Gainesville, FL 32609
http://upress.ufl.edu

Contents

Figures

Tables

Foreword

Much like the people who made these journeys some hundreds and thousands of years ago, these authors look to the horizon, metaphorically speaking, and pose the question about what lies beyond. That is, what lies beyond the horizon of our knowledge about the nature of island colonization? How did the process of human colonization occur around the world and throughout time? Under what circumstances did the histories of these colonization events take place? What happened when groups of humans finally established settlements on these far-flung pieces of land? How were these settlements connected over what was, in some instances, vast distances of the open ocean? And, finally, what are the legacies and lessons for society at large?

The anthropological study of the initial colonization of new lands remains one of the big questions of humanity. It is a human (which includes our hominin ancestors and relatives) story of how a species who evolved in Africa went on to colonize now every possible landmass on earth. What makes this story different from other species who radiated out of homelands around the globe was that for humans, by and large, this exploration and colonization was, in no small degree, intentional, often required planning, and was at times coordinated. As humans moved into these new areas, they transformed landscapes and often brought with them other species, and in doing so, also eradicated endemic animals and plants—sometimes intentionally, sometimes unintentionally. The colonization of islands, in particular, is a unique part of this larger narrative as such events usually required specialized technology (for example, watercraft), knowledge (for example, wayfinding), and in some cases, large-scale environmental changes (for example, sea-level change). Added to this is the fact that in many of these cases, the vast expanse of oceans and seas sometimes provided little, if any, indication if lands lay beyond the vista. The nature and structure and layout of island groups, too variable to go into here, too, could also influence the timing, degree, and sustainability of colonization in a region.

All of the above points are to say that archaeologists who study the colonization of islands are met with a host of methodological challenges. These are also necessarily linked to theoretical problems, such as what constitutes the "colonization" of an island, and indeed, what exactly do we mean by the term island itself. And, finally, there is the challenge of the changing climate; human-influenced sea-level rise continues not just to wash away the record of island colonization but in some cases the whole of islands themselves. Readers will find an in-depth road map that is adeptly articulated for many of these broader theoretical and methodological issues faced by archaeologists in the first chapter by Napolitano, DiNapoli, and Stone. This work provides the more general framework that links all of the chapters in the volume together into a cohesive whole that is more than the sum of its parts, as each of the contributors to the volume works through many of the core issues identified by the editors.

This volume is the sixth book to be published in the "Society and Ecology in Island and Coastal Archaeology" series by the press. It is a landmark volume in the series as it is first to deal with the broader issue specifically of island colonization from a global perspective. In recent years, there has been a growing stream of research on the archaeology of islands and coasts to address these very issues outlined by Napolitano, Stone, and DiNapoli. This volume, however, brings together for the first time a host of scholars, both established and relatively new to the field, who present dynamic, novel, cutting-edge scholarship on the colonization of islands. The geographic (and temporal) diversity of the case studies in this volume includes work in from the Pacific, Mediterranean, Caribbean, the Indian Ocean, and others. This is also matched by the different methodological approaches used by each of the contributors to study island colonization and includes the use of aDNA, Bayesian chronological modeling, and technology studies, to name a few. What is clear from these chapters is that pushing the boundaries of our understanding of island colonization requires not just a variety of methods and ideas, but a context in which cross comparison can occur, which is one of the actual values of this volume. In reading all the case studies, one truly gets a sense of what connects them all—from Vikings, hominins, and the voyagers of Oceania. The broader themes and essential lessons come out regardless of the geographic region or methodological approach.

The idea of colonization and moving into areas of new land, to explore distant horizons—it is an idea that is still very much with us today. It does not take much imagination to connect these colonization events in the past with what the future holds for our species as we continue to try and push past the boundaries of this planet, both from within and beyond. The chapters illustrate what a complicated process this is for humans to accomplish and the consequences, good or bad, that come with striking out for new lands. And, while colonization invoked a departure of sorts, it also at the same time suggested a global connectedness that was accomplished very early on by human societies. In this sense, this volume reinforces the idea that all over the world, people from vastly different communities were able to link to one another over these huge distances to sow the seeds of a connected planet, indirectly in its beginnings and directly connected now. As Jon Erlandson says in his concluding chapter to the volume, research in these areas is well positioned to provide a substantive understanding of the long-term process under which our connected planet happened, the challenges, the success stories, and at times the failures. Such an understanding of all of these more significant issues will be critical if we are to continue to inhabit the little piece of land that we colonized so long ago in the vast black sea of the universe.

Victor D. Thompson
Series Editor

1

Introduction

The Archaeology of Island Colonization

MATTHEW F. NAPOLITANO, ROBERT J. DINAPOLI,
AND JESSICA H. STONE

The timing and drivers of colonization into previously uninhabited areas are central themes in archaeological research (for example, Anderson et al. 2010; Broodbank 2006; Dawson 2014; Fitzpatrick 2004; Leppard 2014; Rockman and Steele 2003). Questions of how, when, from where, and by whom different regions were initially settled remain important research topics as these form a baseline from which we construct explanations of the past. The intricacies of colonization are often contentiously debated, as archaeological, linguistic, paleoenvironmental, and biological perspectives can present substantially different, and sometimes conflicting, information, particularly regarding the timing of initial settlement (for example, Anderson 1994, 1995; Anderson et al. 2018; Kirch and Ellison 1994; Napolitano et al. 2019; Prebble and Wilmshurst 2009; Siegel et al. 2015). Further complicating the issue, archaeological evidence of colonization is often ephemeral and difficult to find, especially if sites are small or located along coastal margins where rising sea levels pose increasing risks for inundation (Bailey and Flemming 2008; Erlandson 2008, 2012). However, recent methodological and theoretical advances in remote sensing (see chapter 5), biomolecular studies (see chapter 8), material culture analyses (see chapters 9 and 11), experimental modeling (see chapters 5 and 12), and increased precision of chronometric dating techniques (see chapters 6 and 7) allow for increasingly detailed and fine-grained reconstructions of colonization events.

Islands provide particularly rich and unique settings to study human colonization of new landscapes, as reaching them typically involved a suite of distinct innovations and adaptations, including the use of specialized watercraft, development of maritime skills and technology (for example, wayfinding), the translocation of domesticated plants and animals, and long-distance interaction networks. Human arrival upon uninhabited islands often resulted in dramatic changes to endemic island ecosystems that were quite significant (for example, Bartlett et al. 2016; Braje et al. 2017; Cooke et al. 2017; Crowther et al. 2016a; Hofman and Rick 2018; Leppard 2017; Rick et al. 2013). In many cases, island ecosystems, which tend to be depauperate in terrestrial resources compared to continental landmasses, created unique challenges to colonizing groups, and these constraints are often more pronounced on smaller and more remote islands (for example, Fitzpatrick et al. 2016; Thomas 2019). Given these characteristics, the colonization of islands is arguably different from the settlement of uninhabited contiguous terrestrial areas and warrants specialized study.

The purpose of this volume is to highlight some of the recent work on colonization studies taking place in island regions around the world. A contribution that focuses on initial human occupation of islands from a global perspective is long overdue, as most recent works have been regionally focused and intended for a limited audience. Some notable exceptions include Fitzpatrick's (2004) *Voyages of Discovery: The Archaeology of Islands,* Anderson et al.'s (2010) *The Global Origins and Development of Seafaring,* and Rainbird's (2007) *The Archaeology of Islands,* all of which adopted global approaches to discussing island archaeologies. One of the ultimate goals of Fitzpatrick's (2004) volume was to establish island archaeology as a distinct subdiscipline. In the 17 years since it was published, island archaeology has become increasingly accepted as a distinct field of archaeological inquiry, and made significant contributions to other disciplines, as evidenced by the creation of several academic journals (see *The Journal of Island and Coastal Archaeology, Island Studies Journal, Journal of Maritime Archaeology,* among others).

Island archaeology has continued to develop in sophisticated ways both theoretically and methodologically, and has also been the subject of greater interest, particularly with regard to smaller and more remote islands that have often been overlooked in the archaeological literature (Fitzpatrick et al. 2016). More recently, islands have become a focal point in the race to mitigate the threats of sea level rise by helping to both highlight and lead efforts to protect and conserve cultural heritage, often in collaboration with island nations and descendant communities (for example, Douglass and Cooper 2020; Erlandson 2008; McCoy 2018).

The chapters in this volume provide an overview of the initial colonization of different island regions and highlight the wide variety of approaches now used to study these events and place them in a comparative perspective. Our goal is not to provide an exhaustive review of colonization events around the world (*sensu* Keegan and Diamond 1987); instead we focus on recent research and trends across different geographical areas. We have intentionally sought out different methodological and theoretical approaches to explore current debates in the study of island colonization, drive discourse, and provide comparative views across different island regions.

Understanding islands as appropriate units of analysis is also a critical component of island archaeological research. Drawing on MacArthur and Wilson's (1967) foundational work on island biogeography, islands were originally seen as ideal "laboratories" in which to examine culture change because they were conceived as discrete and isolated landforms that could be compared to one another (Clark and Terrell 1978). A major shortcoming of this approach was the assumption that islands were isolated without much, if any, ecological or social interaction. Continued archaeological research on islands has shown that only in rare circumstances were island societies truly isolated (Fitzpatrick and Anderson 2008). Now, islands are better understood as model systems (for example, DiNapoli and Leppard 2018; DiNapoli et al. 2018; Fitzpatrick and Anderson 2008; Fitzpatrick and Erlandson 2018; Kirch 2007; Vitousek 2002). This approach considers islands to be relatively isolated compared to continental-based populations, but not completely so, and that these conditions better account for the dynamic nature of human-island interactions over time in a relatively circumscribed context.

For the purposes of this book, we utilize Terrell's (1999: 240) definition of islands as "habitats surrounded by radical shifts in habitat." While we acknowledge that biogeographic islands can be defined in multiple ways, here we specifically address human colonization on landmasses surrounded by water. The biogeographic definition of islands tends to be overly restrictive as it defines islands as *never* contiguous landmasses, and that plants and animals arrive *only* by nonresident colonists (Saddler 1999: 953; Rosenzweig 1995: 211); therefore, we have chosen to take a broader interpretation. The above definition ignores how fluctuations in sea level have, at times, "created" islands that were once contiguous landforms by inundating areas of low elevation. In such a scenario, newly isolated islands are populated with endemic plants and animals.

Moreover, sea-level lowstands can reveal previously unavailable contiguous landmasses (for example, land bridges or entire islands) for occupation by immigrant plant and animal species—including humans—that would not require colonization in the biogeographic sense, especially for islands located near continental landmasses. Both processes trigger the development of productive ecological niches like shallow offshore reefs and estuarine habitats that would have been attractive for human use (for example, Dickinson 2004). For example, gradual sea-level rise off the southeastern coast of North America inundated low-lying areas and allowed for the formation of a chain of barrier islands off the coast of what is now Georgia and northern Florida (Oertel 1979; Thomas 2008). A productive estuarine marsh habitat containing hundreds of small islands, what we can think of as an expanded range (see chapter 2), developed between the mainland coast and newly formed island chain, the latter of which was quickly occupied by Archaic-age hunter-foragers (DePratter and Howard 1977; DePratter and Thompson 2013; Napolitano 2013; Thomas 2008; Thompson and Turck 2010).

The biogeographical definition of islands can also neglect to consider the human role in island building and modification. In the Ten Thousand Islands region of southwestern Florida, fisher-hunter-gatherers constructed complex "shell works"—artificial islands containing mounds, ridges, water courts, canals, and raised platforms made up of discarded mollusks—that were the proximate mechanisms or impetus for connecting people socially, politically, and ideologically (Schwadron 2017). While situating human occupation of shell islands within island colonization studies is not as clear as identifying the first human occupation of a naturally formed island, it is important to recognize the impacts that human arrival has on the surrounding environment, including the exploitation of existing landforms, the creation of new ones, and the historical ecology of long-term landscape change.

The second key concept that requires definition is colonization. While colonization may be simply defined as the point when humans first step foot on previously uninhabited islands, using this simple definition in practice can be problematic (Anderson and Sinoto 2002; Stein 2005: 7). Colonization is often used indiscriminately and applied to a number of different events ranging from evolutionary ecological concepts (see chapter 2; MacArthur and Wilson 1967) to the violent European expansion into other continents and islands around the world (chapter 4). Lipo et al. (chapter 3) argue that uses of colonization are often based on ambiguous and intuitive understandings of the assumed process whereby people "arrive to live in a new land." In this sense, they argue that establishing the needed evidence for detecting colonization in the archaeological record tends to heavily rely on plausibility, and not strictly on unambiguous empirical evidence, leading to claims that are difficult to falsify, rather than hypothesis-driven research. Lipo et al. (chapter 3) also argue that "coloniza-

Matthew F. Napolitano, Robert J. DiNapoli, and Jessica H. Stone

tion" should be viewed as an archaeological classification of time, or a kind of "temporal systematics," that requires specific archaeological data that can only be explained by the arrival of humans. Similarly, Rieth and Hamilton (chapter 7) define island colonization as the beginning of the island's archaeological record, while Cochrane (chapter 2) argues that different movement types should also be defined via explicit classification criteria. These explicit classifications or systematics approaches require archaeologists to think critically about what types of data are suitable for identifying colonization.

In the absence of direct archaeological data, proxies are often used to establish human arrival because the changes to island ecologies and biodiversity are often immediate and dramatic, even when founding populations are small (for example, Boivin et al. 2016; Braje et al. 2017; Connor et al. 2012; McWethy et al. 2014). Changes in macro- and microcharcoal concentrations may be used to infer initial landscape modification to establish an agricultural base (Burney 1997; Dodson and Intoh 1999; Gosling et al. 2020; Hunt et al. 2012; Siegel 2018; Siegel et al. 2015). Evidence for the presence of domesticated or non-native plants and animals that are closely associated with humans can also be used to confirm human presence, reconstruct potential homelands, and serve as evidence for interaction in the past (Prebble and Wilmshurst 2009). For example, barley grains found on the Faroe Islands have been used to clearly indicate human arrival and agricultural activity (Church et al. 2013). Similarly, the presence of Southeast Asian domesticates like Asian rice (*Oryza sativa*), mung bean (*Vigna radiata*), and Asian cotton (*Gossypium arboreum*) in the Comoro Islands and Madagascar have been used to infer human arrival (Crowther et al. 2016a; see also discussion in chapter 12). When compared with genetic evidence, these data indicate that the Comoros were the first point of interaction between Austronesian groups from Island Southeast Asia and Bantu-speaking groups from the African coast (Brucato et al. 2018; Hurles et al. 2005; Msaidie et al. 2011; Tofanelli et al. 2009). The remains of endemic fauna—when found modified by or in close association with humans—can also be used to both identify human arrival and document newly available resources that shift the cost and benefits of dispersal or nondispersal (chapter 2). For example, the Wairau Bar site in New Zealand contains human burials closely associated with the bones and eggs from moa (Aves: Dinornithiformes), large endemic flightless birds that went extinct within centuries of human arrival (Holdaway and Jacomb 2000; Holdaway et al. 2014). In conjunction with the presence of other extinct endemic fauna, the evidence suggests that the individuals found here likely represent one of the first generations of New Zealanders (Higham et al. 1999).

What these and other studies demonstrate is that proxy data can and have been used as important lines of evidence for both identifying the presence of humans in island environments and describing the available resources in expanded human ranges. However, proxy data must be used cautiously. In many instances, these data precede archaeological chronologies by centuries or millennia and can lead to misleading results (for example, Cañellas-Boltà et al. 2013; Kirch and Ellison 1994; Siegel et al. 2015). For example, elevated charcoal levels associated with widespread forest clearance have been used to argue that humans arrived on the Caribbean islands of Grenada and Tobago as many as 2,000 years before any archaeological evidence (Siegel et al. 2015). Even if elevated charcoal levels in the absence of secure archaeological data could be used to infer human arrival to an island, not all groups may have engaged in forest clearance immediately upon arrival to an island, especially nonagricultural groups (for example, Douglass and Zinke 2015). Taken together, these examples underscore the importance of using multiple lines of proxy evidence with archaeological data from well-stratified and rigorously dated contexts (Gosling et al. 2020; Prebble and Wilmshurst 2009; Sear et al. 2020).

Major Issues in Island Colonization Studies

How Did People Colonize Islands?

One of the most important but difficult questions to resolve in island colonization concerns *how* peoples reached islands in the past. The earliest island occupations may have simply been opportunistic given growing evidence of coastal settlement and marine resource use in Africa during the Pleistocene and subsequent dispersal(s) out of Africa (for example, Erlandson 2001; Macaulay et al. 2005; Marean et al. 2007). As watercraft technologies and wayfinding skills improved and population sizes increased, the intentionality behind such ventures likely ranged widely: from wanting to obtain food or prized resources (for example, obsidian), to adapting to population growth or limited ecological carrying capacities, to escaping persecution, among others (Anderson et al. 2010). One attempt to conceptualize how islands were colonized is Broodbank's (2006) *seagoing, seafaring,* and *voyaging. Seagoing* refers to simple water travel over relatively short distances that did not require any sophisticated technology or intentionality; *seafaring* describes the regular use of relatively sophisticated watercraft (for example, propelled by paddles or sails) over relatively long dis-

Matthew F. Napolitano, Robert J. DiNapoli, and Jessica H. Stone

tances; and *voyaging* is considered long-range and likely premeditated overwater travel that may be ideologically or economically driven (Broodbank 2006: 200). Given the almost endless range of possible mechanisms or intentions for these migrations, Cochrane (chapter 2) argues that such culture-bound, proximate mechanisms should always be considered alongside evolutionary mechanisms that sort behavioral options.

The archaeological record demonstrates a great range of variability in the ways in which island colonization was accomplished. For example, the earliest colonization of islands by the genus *Homo,* such as the presence of *H. floresiensis* on Flores or the highly debated Paleolithic settlement of some Mediterranean islands, may have been ecologically contingent, passive dispersals that were not necessarily intentional (for example, Anderson 2018; Brumm et al. 2010, 2016; Leppard 2015; Leppard and Runnels 2017; van den Bergh et al. 2016; O'Sullivan et al. 2001; see discussions in chapters 4, 10, and 12).

Many of the earliest movements of *Homo sapiens* into island environments appear to have been highly sophisticated and strategic dispersal events. Recent geospatial modeling by Norman et al. (2018), for example, suggests strategic movement of Pleistocene populations through the intervisible islands of Wallacea in settling Sahul (present-day Australia and New Guinea) (see also Bird et al. 2019). Lower sea levels in the Pleistocene meant that many of the islands in present-day Island Southeast Asia were connected as a single landmass (Sunda). Sunda and Sahul were separated by a seascape of islands, many of which are now submerged. When sea levels were at their lowest—120 m lower, around 20 kya (Lambeck and Chappell 2001; Williams et al. 2018)—reaching Sahul would have required multiple water crossings, some up to 100 km in distance (Bird et al. 2019; Kealy et al. 2016). The seafaring events that took place between what is now New Guinea and the Bismarck Archipelago circa 35–40 kya involved long water crossings and translocations of plants and lithics, which points to sophisticated maritime technology (O'Connor and Hiscock 2018). A similar argument comes from mounting evidence for a coastal migration route in the colonization of the Americas (for example, Braje et al. 2020).

Many of the largest-scale colonization events occurred in the mid- to late-Holocene with the expansion of foragers and food-producing populations in the western Pacific, Caribbean, Mediterranean, and coastal North America (for example, Fitzpatrick 2013; Gamble 2002; Leppard 2014; Thomas 2008; chapters 2, 3, 6, 7, 9, 10). These episodes resulted in the expansion of human populations into some of the most remote islands and archipelagos in the world. Both the settlement of Remote Oceania and the Norse settlement of the North Atlantic provide classic large-scale examples (for example, Rieth and Cochrane 2018; chapters 6 and 7). While similar, in some respects, to earlier colonization events, the scale of these migrations implies a high degree of planning and possibly ideological motivation. Evidence that populations brought with them a wide variety of domesticated and nondomesticated plants, animals, and insects—a process that has been termed "transported landscapes" (Kirch 1982), somewhat akin to "terraforming" (Kirch and Green 2001; Cherry and Leppard 2018)— seems to support this idea.

One of the unfortunate ironies for researchers attempting to find evidence for island colonization is that the primary mechanisms for human dispersal (that is, watercraft) are rarely preserved in the archaeological record (but see Cassidy et al. 2004; Fitzpatrick 2013; Gamble 2002; Thomas 2008: 227; Wheeler 2003). Two notable exceptions come from the Pacific, where remnants of East Polynesian sailing canoes were discovered in New Zealand (Johns et al. 2014) and Huahine in the Society Islands (Sinoto 1979). While it is well known that Native Americans occupied the Channel Islands off the California coast for at least the past 12,000 years and required watercraft to reach them, the oldest known evidence for canoes only dates to circa 3,000 years ago (Cassidy et al. 2004; Gamble 2002). Lacking archaeological evidence for watercraft, archaeologists working on islands have instead turned to a number of productive methods and conceptual frameworks for resolving patterns and processes of colonization, including experimental voyaging, computer simulations, and geographic information systems (GIS) models.

Experimental ocean traveling using traditional watercraft has been widely implemented in the Pacific, such as the famous *Kon-Tiki* expedition from South America to central East Polynesia by Heyerdahl (1950) and the ongoing Hōkūle'a project as part of the Polynesian Voyaging Society (Finney 1996). These and other experiments with replicas of traditional watercraft have provided valuable information on the possible capabilities of maritime peoples in the past and the feasibility of different migration routes. It is important to note that the degree to which these replicative experiments faithfully represent ancient water travel and technologies has been an ongoing subject of debate (for example, Anderson 2008; Cherry and Leppard 2015; Finney 2008; Holton 2004; Kaifu et al. 2019; Kirch 2008; Knapp 2008).

Another useful method for examining human movement over the seascape is the use of computer simulations, which began nearly 30 years ago and has steadily grown in popularity (for example, Irwin 1992). Like experimental voyaging, these simulations are helpful for assessing the feasibility of different dispersal routes at different times and places and can provide a valuable supplemental line of evidence for examining colonization episodes (for example, Bird et al. 2019; Bradshaw et al. 2019; Callaghan 2001, 2010; Di Piazza et al. 2007; Fitzpatrick and Callaghan 2008; Kealy et al. 2016; Montenegro et al. 2016; Slayton 2018; see also chapter 12). In particular, these studies have been useful in narrowing down possible points of origin for peoples who colonized islands, seafaring capabilities, and guiding future research. For example, when considering initial human colonization of the Caribbean, computer simulation suggests direct movement from South America to larger islands in the northern Caribbean (Cuba, Hispaniola, Puerto Rico, and the northern Lesser Antilles) that initially bypassed islands to the south, a model that is now seeing support through archaeological and chronological research (Callaghan 2010; Napolitano et al. 2019; see Fitzpatrick and Callaghan 2013 and Montenegro et al. 2016 for examples from the Pacific).

In addition to simulated voyages, the analysis of past climate regimes also can provide key insights into when certain islands were more easily colonizable. Research by Anderson et al. (2006) and Goodwin et al. (2014) in the Pacific has shown that "climate windows" (for example, periodic reversals of prevailing wind patterns) likely facilitated the Lapita expansion into Remote Oceania and later dispersals into East Polynesia (chapter 2; Montenegro et al. 2014; see also Sear et al. 2020). In the Mediterranean, Bar-Yousef Mayer et al. (2015) examined prevailing wind patterns and suggested that the initial settlers of Cyprus originated form the southern coast of Turkey, and that successful landfall was likely seasonally dependent. In these ways, computational simulations of voyaging and climatic reconstructions can help archaeologists determine the range of time and origin points that were possible in the past and distinguish which were most likely. One limitation to this approach is that simulations often have not been programmed to incorporate decision rules into voyagers, and usually involve relatively static strategies. Nonetheless, the more recent use of agent-based simulations allows researchers to more faithfully model the capabilities of maritime-oriented groups and environmental and/or climatic influences (for example, Baumann 2017; Davies and Bickler 2013).

In recent decades, archaeologists have employed increasingly sophisticated approaches to understand how people colonized islands. These studies are often interdisciplinary and incorporate ancillary datasets like sea level, bathymetric, and paleoclimate data to develop more precise models of where colonization sites may have been located, and they have helped to shed light on the scale and frequency of colonization events in ways that have not been possible until recently. One of the difficulties in identifying colonization sites is that they are often located adjacent to shorelines or in low-lying areas that were submerged as local sea levels rose. A dearth of archaeological sites that date between 65,000 and 18,000 years ago in the Ryukyu Islands, Japan, suggests that rising sea levels have obscured much of archaeological record along former coastlines (Takamiya 1996; Takamiya et al. 2019). Gusick et al. (chapter 5) demonstrate how fine-grained bathymetric modeling around California's Channel Islands improves the likelihood of finding sites that date to the early peopling of the North American Pacific Coast. When sea levels were lower approximately 10–15 kya, Santa Rosa was a "superisland" that is now called Santarosae. This phenomenon is seen in other regions like the Mediterranean—for example, the Cyclades Islands that were one island, and are now known as Cycladia; or the "mega-island" of Corsica and Sardinia, now called Corsardinia, that would have been located only a few kilometers off the coast (see chapter 10). In some cases, paleoshoreline reconstruction using bathymetric and other data sources can provide an indication of when islands may have been connected to the mainland and/or other islands (chapters 5 and 10).

When Did Colonization Occur?

As many chapters in this volume demonstrate, developing robust, accurate chronologies is one of the most important issues in island colonization studies, as establishing the timing of initial human arrival forms the beginning of the archaeological record and the baseline from which interpretations are made (for example, James et al. 1987; Rieth and Hunt 2008; Spriggs 1989). Colonization chronologies continue to be an intensely debated topic for many regions given ongoing disagreements over data reliability, taphonomy, analytical approaches, and uncertainties in different radiometric techniques, especially radiocarbon dating.

The arrival of people in Sahul, for example, has been an ongoing topic of controversy for decades with far-reaching implications for the understanding of human dispersals across Eurasia, the development of watercraft technologies, anthropogenic landscape change, and the potential role of humans in megafaunal extinction events, among others (for example, Anderson 2018; Bartlett et al. 2016; Boivin et al. 2016; Field et al. 2008; Field et al. 2013). One source of uncertainty is that the timing of these events approaches the upper limits of radiocarbon dating. For example, it is generally accepted that humans reached Sahul by circa 50 kya (Bulbeck 2007, Allen and O'Connell 2008; Hamm et al. 2016; Tobler et al. 2017), but new research from the site of Madjedbede in northern

Australia suggests colonization circa 65 kya based on optically stimulated luminescence (OSL) dating (Clarkson et al. 2017). However, some have questioned this chronology, citing uncertainties with the analytical approach and paucity of contemporaneous sites between Island Southeast Asia and Sahul; as such, skepticism for such an early movement in the region remains (for example, Allen and O'Connell 2020; O'Connell et al. 2018).

Uncertainties in radiocarbon dating have been the main source of controversy for island colonization chronologies. For decades, archaeologists have understood the potential problems introduced by radiocarbon dating long-lived plant species or specimens with significant inbuilt age, otherwise known as the "old wood" problem (Schiffer 1986). Marine shell, a common dating material in island and coastal sites, can also be problematic given several potential sources of uncertainty, such as the marine reservoir effect, hard water effects, and the "old shell" problem where fossil shells are used to make tools or inadvertently incorporated into midden deposits (Alves et al. 2018; Petchey et al. 2013; Rick et al. 2005). Furthermore, use of samples from questionable archaeological contexts (for example, surface finds) and ambiguous reporting of radiocarbon dates can lead to specious or misleading interpretations (for example, Spriggs 1989; see chapter 6). Although not unique to islands, these issues have significant implications for understanding island colonization events and interpretations of subsequent settlement histories.

In the past few decades, several "best practices" have been developed to produce increasingly reliable radiocarbon chronologies. For terrestrial samples, focusing on short-lived (<10 years old) specimens identified to the lowest taxon helps eliminate the potential error of inbuilt age (for example, Allen 2014; Allen and Huebert 2014; Rieth and Athens 2013). When anthropogenically introduced taxa are recovered, dating provides secure evidence for establishing human colonization. Church et al.'s (2013) examination of human-introduced barley grains, for example, extended the date of colonization on the Faroe Islands by 300–500 years before the ninth century large-scale Viking colonization. Measurement of local marine reservoir correction (ΔR) for marine samples is also critical, as these adjustments can shift radiocarbon calibrations by decades or even centuries (for example, DiNapoli et al. 2021; Petchey and Clark 2010; Petchey et al. 2008; Stuiver et al. 1986; Thomas et al. 2013; Ulm 2002). One extreme example is the island of Sakhalin and nearby Kuril Islands, located between the Sea of Japan and Okhotsk Sea, where the Oyashio Current contributes to a ΔR of 578 ± 50 years in addition to the global average offset (Kuzmin et al. 2007).

These improved standards for radiocarbon dating have led archaeologists to re-evaluate long-established colonization chronologies. One effective method is to apply a "chronometric hygiene" approach where radiocarbon dates are evaluated based on a set of reliability criteria (Spriggs 1989). Multiple studies have shown that careful application of these reliability criteria improves the confidence that the radiocarbon dates relate to when human activity occurred (for example, Douglass et al. 2019; Napolitano et al. 2019; Rieth and Hunt 2008; Schmid et al. 2019; chapters 3 and 6). One core strength of chronometric hygiene is that by removing potentially problematic dates from the analysis, the remaining dates represent a conservative hypothesis for colonization that is amenable to continuous testing. A notable example is Wilmshurst et al.'s (2011) chronometric hygiene study of more than 1,400 radiocarbon dates from 15 East Polynesian islands and archipelagos. The study suggested that East Polynesia, including the widely dispersed islands of Hawai'i, Rapa Nui, and New Zealand, were settled in a brief, rapid burst of exploration around 750 years ago. While a recent multiproxy study by Sear et al. (2020) has now demonstrated an earlier settlement of parts of the region (the Cook Islands), this revision to East Polynesia's colonization chronology highlights the strength of the chronometric hygiene approach in building hypotheses for initial human colonization that can be clearly and continuously tested and, importantly, falsified, as new evidence becomes available.

The application of Bayesian statistics to radiocarbon dates has led to important revisions and improved understandings of island colonization chronologies (for example, Athens et al. 2014; Bayliss 2009; Burley et al. 2015; Clark et al. 2016; Dye 2014; Napolitano et al. 2019; Reith and Athens 2019; chapters 6 and 7). A Bayesian approach is particularly useful studying island colonization because it allows for the incorporation of prior information (for example, stratigraphy), an estimate of the timing of events that are not directly dated, and the ability to deal with common problems in radiocarbon calibration, such as inbuilt age, mixed curves, large error ranges, and other sources of uncertainty (Bronk Ramsey 2009; Dye 2014; Hamilton and Krus 2018; Petchey et al. 2015; Schmid et al. 2018, 2019; chapter 6). In chapter 6, Schmid et al. combine Bayesian-modeled radiocarbon chronologies, ice core–dated tephrochronology, and textual sources to argue that the initial settlement of Iceland was more extensive and rapid than previously thought. By using a Bayesian approach, archaeologists interested in better understanding the timing of initial colonization are thus able to incorporate a wide array of chronological information and sources of uncertainty to build probabilistic, model-based estimates for the timing of human arrival. Importantly, an emphasis on transparency in publishing model data, code, and results ensures that colonization chronologies are reproducible and amenable to future revision and improvements (Bayliss 2015; Buck and Meson 2015; Hamilton and Krus 2018).

Why Did People Colonize Islands?

While the particular conditions and motivations that triggered island colonization episodes were likely unique to each group and contingent on a host of factors, archaeologists have employed a wide range of theoretical approaches ranging from broadly interpretive to empirical, model-based strategies for studying the general mechanisms that trigger these events in an attempt to compare them. Given the variety and complexities of island colonization events, what theoretical perspectives offer satisfactory explanatory mechanisms for understanding these processes at a broader scale?

Keegan and Diamond (1987: 67) introduced the term "autocatalysis" to describe the idea that the discovery of islands will lead to the belief that there are more islands waiting to discovered, which results in a persistent desire to explore seascapes. The formation of new islands or coastal morphologies themselves may also have triggered exploration that led to subsequent colonization events (chapters 2 and 10). This sort of geographic autocatalysis would have fluctuated over time depending on sea-level change, tectonic activity, and other geological factors. Lower sea levels in the remote Pacific Ocean circa 2,500 years ago, for example, led to the formation of the eastern Micronesian atolls, and the earliest evidence for human presence on these islands occurs shortly thereafter (Dickinson 2003, 2004; Poteate et al. 2016; Weisler et al. 2012). The belief that islands exist out of sight may have also been encouraged by bird flight paths, cloud formation patterns, and the appearance of smoke from fires on the horizon (Finney 1996; Gladwin 1970).

Island colonization may have also been ideological in nature. In societies that practice primogeniture, like Polynesia, non–first-born offspring, who would not be inheriting land and/or titles, may have been incentivized to seek out new land (for example, Bell 1932; Bellwood 1996). Differences in religious beliefs, exile, or disputes may also have resulted in the colonization of new islands (Anderson 2006). Similarly, seeking out new islands to colonize may have been motivated by desires to expand one's territory or economic opportunity. The Maldives, for example, are strategically located between Madagascar and Island Southeast Asia, and may have functioned as important stopover points and a trading hub when voyaging through the Malacca Straits (chapter 12).

Seasonal shifts in winds and currents may have also encouraged certain routes to be taken as well, as discussed above.

Technological innovation may have played a crucial role in allowing humans to successfully reach new islands. The "long pause" of circa 2,000 years between the settlement of West and East Polynesia may have been caused by a lack of watercraft able to successfully complete long-distance voyaging, and could have been further exacerbated in part by a prolonged sea-level highstand that may have negatively impacted island habitability (Anderson et al. 2006; Dickinson 2003; Montenegro et al. 2014). Irwin (1992) argues that the pause was required to allow for sufficient population growth before resuming colonizing ventures, and that colonization of East Polynesia was unlikely prior to the development of the double-hulled canoe.

Many of the above scenarios are considered proximate mechanisms in an evolutionary and ecological framework. Cochrane (chapter 2) argues that dispersal behavior is culturally transmitted and, as such, different types of movement behaviors, such as dispersal or range expansion, are differentially selected for, and result in distinct and predictable spatiotemporal patterns. He then evaluates this evolutionary model, using the well-known Lapita migration into Remote Oceania, and finds that the migration patterns are best explained by a model of selection-driven range expansion.

Human behavioral ecology presents another productive evolutionary framework that can be used to evaluate human colonization of islands; in particular, the approach has been useful for developing predictive models for understanding the sequence of island settlement, such as the Ideal-Free Distribution (IFD). The IFD assumes that individuals are "free" to choose the most optimal areas for habitation that will afford them the greatest fitness advantages. As such, individuals are predicted to settle the highest quality habitats first, such as large, productive islands, and as population density increases in the best habitats, second-tier habitats are then predicted to be settled (Fretwell and Lucas 1969; Giovas and Fitzpatrick 2014; Jazwa et al. 2015; Kennett et al. 2006; Sutherland 1996; Winterhalder et al. 2010). In addition to preference of some islands over others, certain parts of islands are predicted to be settled over others (see Jazwa et al. 2015; Lane 2017; Thomas 2008; Winterhalder et al. 2010).

One of the potential limitations of the IFD model is that it assumes all people have equal access to resources and equal abilities to compete for those resources, which oversimplifies the "despotic" nature of some island societies (Kennett and Winterhalder 2008: 87). To address this, Kennett and Winterhalder (2008) employed the Ideal Despotic Distribution model and argue that rapid colonization of East and South Polynesia may have been triggered by increasing population density, a decrease in suitable agricultural habitat, despotism, and increased territoriality and warfare, resulting in a "push" to groups that sought out new islands to inhabit (Kennett and Winterhalder 2008). Sear et al. (2020) have demonstrated that this population expansion was preceded by a severe drought in West Polynesia, which provides interesting support for this model.

The archaeology of island colonization is guided by questions of who, when, from where, and why. Understanding the various proximate and ultimate factors underlying why island colonization events occurred is one of the most important questions—and perhaps the most difficult—to answer. To answer these questions, archaeologists often have to look outside the discipline to consider theory-based models and multiple lines of evidence, including paleoenvironmental, paleoclimate, and paleoshoreline data, to reconstruct the conditions under which these ventures took place. Future applications of theory-based models and rigorous empirical techniques will lead to more detailed interpretations of island colonization events in ways that were not previously possible.

Island Colonization and Homelands

Identifying homelands—the various points of origin of colonizing populations—has been a central question for scholars that dates back centuries. These questions are fundamental to our understanding of early population dynamics and migration trajectories and can complement oral histories and concepts of identity in descendant communities today. Multiple approaches can be used to infer relationships and long-distance connections to homelands. Early work by anthropologists and archaeologists focused on analyzing linguistic relationships and assumed biological affinities of various groups. While linguistic analyses are still very much in use, methodological approaches have become increasingly sophisticated and have been used to develop increasingly precise chronologies for fundamental issues like the rise and spread of agriculture and migration to previously uninhabited islands (for example, Diamond and Bellwood 2003; Gray et al. 2009, 2011; Green 1999; Greenhill et al. 2010; Kirch and Green 1987, 2001; Pawley and Ross 1993).

Glottochronology, which uses lexicostatistics to date when languages shared a common origin, was once a favored method but has since been abandoned because it is now recognized that words do not change at a fixed rate (Blust 2000; Pellard 2015: 20–21). More recently, linguists began constructing phylogenetic models of language that could be applied to questions of who, how, where, and when did languages diverge and how quickly they changed. However, linguistic innovations and mixing with extant languages accelerated the rates of change, making it more difficult to track changes across space and time (Greenhill and Gray 2009; Pawley 1999; Ross 1996). These approaches have also been applied to archaeological questions as well, such as where and when did the Austronesian language family originate (Greenhill and Gray 2009: 2; Gray et al. 2009, 2011; Green 1999; Greenhill et al. 2010). The origins of the Austronesian language family, which includes 1,000–1,200 languages, are difficult to pinpoint in part because there are so many languages that appear to have spread rapidly to many different areas (Greenhill and Gray 2009). In one compelling example, the combination of archaeological and linguistic data was used to evaluate competing hypotheses of initial settlement of the Ryukyus, a group of islands along the Japanese coast. Previous attempts to reconcile archaeological and linguistic evidence were hampered by the reliance on glottochronology. Utilization of phylogenetic analyses instead shows that the archaeological and linguistic evidence independently suggests similar chronologies for the development of the Ryukyuan languages, that settlement of these islands occurred relatively quickly, and originated from a small geographic area (Pellard 2015: 25). Critics of this approach point out that linguistic and biological evolution are merely analogous and cannot be analyzed the same way because language does not evolve like biological lifeforms, and that this approach is not significantly different from lexicostatistics (Atkinson and Gray 2005; see also Terrell et al. 1997). To address these criticisms, newer applications of Bayesian phylogenetic inference have been used to strengthen these analyses (for example, Greenhill and Gray 2005; Jordan et al. 2009; Lee and Hasegawa 2011).

Advances in biomolecular techniques, including ancient DNA (aDNA), paleoproteomics, analysis of human microbiota, and improved resolution in isotopic analyses, are providing more refined information on the homelands of initial settlers at both individual and population-level scales (for example, De La Fuente et al. 2013; Fehren-Schmitz et al. 2017; Eisenhofer et al. 2019; Laffoon et al. 2013; Montgomery et al. 2014; Posth et al. 2018, Yamaoka 2009). Direct archaeological evidence in the form of human skeletal remains also have great potential for elucidating the origin of early settlers. In chapter 8, Stone and Nieves-Colón review how peopling of the Pacific Ocean has benefited significantly from genetic and genomic studies, including aDNA (see also Horsburgh and McCoy 2017; Skoglund et al. 2016; Spriggs et al. 2019). In areas where it may not be possible to conduct human skeletal analyses, the use of domesticated plants and animals can be used as proxies for human movement as part of the "commensal model" approach (Matisoo-Smith 2009; Matisoo-Smith et al. 2009; Storey et al. 2013; chapter 8).

Zooarchaeological, ethnobotanical, and artifactual evidence is also critical for resolving these issues. Given the often distinct geological composition of different islands and archipelagos, petrographic, geochemical, and isotopic analysis of nonlocal artifacts, faunal remains, and human skeletal material can also provide direct evidence for the homeland(s) of colonizing populations (for example, Dickinson and Shutler 2000; Laffoon and Leppard 2019; Weisler 1998; chapter 9). Studies of this nature are based on the fact that geological characteristics of raw materials, particularly stone and ceramic temper, vary enough within and between islands and mainland areas that nonlocal imports are readily identifiable. When these kinds of artifacts are found in early archaeological contexts, they can help infer the origin point(s) of colonizers and ongoing connections to homelands (for example, Fitzhugh 2004). Isotopic analyses of strontium ($^{87}Sr/^{86}Sr$), oxygen ($^{18}O/^{16}O$), and, more recently, lead ($^{20n}Pb/^{204}Pb$) are based on a similar rationale in that isotopic ratios present in bone or tooth enamel will reflect those present in the surrounding geology and groundwater. Because tooth enamel forms during childhood and does not remodel, the isotopic signature of enamel can be used to trace mobility over an individual's lifetime (for example, Bentley 2006; Bentley et al. 2007; Price and Gestsdóttir 2006; Wilhelmson and Ahlström 2015; Wilhelmson and Price 2017).

In chapter 9, Scott Fitzpatrick et al. review multiple lines of evidence, including provenance studies, to identify what the most parsimonious explanation is for initial settlement of the Caribbean. Until recently, there have been relatively few sourcing studies compared to other island regions for which there is evidence of long-distance interaction. But, in combination with linguistic, genetic, isotopic analyses, and the study of translocated plants and animals, evidence points exclusively to South America, particularly the Orinoco River Basin in Venezuela, as the homeland for population dispersals into the Caribbean.

As research on these subjects continues, archaeologists will develop increasingly large datasets, which will hopefully lead to increasingly detailed pictures of the past. Applications of new methods will be able to identify and distinguish past migrations to uninhabited islands from subsequent back-and-forth journeys and population admixture events with more precision than was thought possible only decades ago. As a result, reconstructions of island colonization will become increasingly complex and may also be used to better understand population movements more broadly, including maritime migrations across continental landmasses (for example, Braje et al. 2020).

Summary and Future Research

The archaeological study of islands has grown tremendously in recent decades. As research presented in this volume demonstrates, islands offer important opportunities to examine the exploratory nature of our species, including our hominin ancestors (chapters 4 and 10), the evolution of watercraft technologies and wayfinding, the role of humans in impacting their new environments (chapter 9), the ability of peoples to explore new landscapes, and understanding the motivations for those journeys (chapters 2, 3, 4, 10, 11, and 12; see also Rockman and Steele 2003). As we have discussed in this chapter, one of the critical pieces to these and many other questions is establishing when humans arrived in these islands, and this can only be achieved with detailed and robust analyses of chronologies and associated archaeological assemblages (chapters 3, 6, 7, and 9). Further, advances in methodological approaches have increased the resolution with which archaeologists can reconstruct paleolandscapes and understand the people that lived on them (see chapters 5, 8, and 12). The most cogent arguments for identifying and dating human colonization events utilize multiple lines of evidence to strengthen archaeological data (chapters 6 and 9; Anderson et al. 2018; Sear et al. 2020).

Moving forward, we see there are a number of important issues that will influence the study of island colonization and the discipline as a whole. The first is a persistent long-term problem in island archaeology: the marginalization of smaller and more remote islands due to their relative resource impoverishment, difficulties in reaching and working in these places, and a host of other issues (Fitzpatrick et al. 2016). Even for those like the Channel Islands of California, which are relatively close to the mainland and have long records of human occupation, the prevailing notion has been that they were marginal and secondarily preferable to human populations, despite evidence to the contrary (Erlandson et al. 2019; Gill et al. 2019). Other small or remote islands, like the Aleutian Islands, situated between Alaska and Russia, are logistically very difficult to access. Many island groups off the coast of Africa also tend to be studied less than other islands despite being located close to the continental mainland, although this has recently begun to change (Bailey et al. 2007; Crowther et al. 2016a, 2016b; Douglass and Zinke 2015; Douglass et al. 2019; Mitchell 2004).

Another issue is the ever-increasing threat faced by island nations from rising sea levels, which threaten a variety of cultural heritage sites as well as both known and unidentified archaeological sites (Douglass and Cooper 2020; Fitzpatrick et al. 2015; McCoy 2018; Rick and Fitzpatrick 2012; Rowland and Ulm

2012). Small and low-lying islands are particularly susceptible to these threats. Just over a decade ago, predicted rates of eustatic sea level rise by 2100 were 19–59 cm, but are now projected to be as much as 200 cm (Church et al. 2013; Storlazzi et al. 2018). If the latter prediction is accurate, many low-lying islands will be uninhabitable by the end of the century, presenting an unprecedented threat to island nations and their cultural heritage (Oppenheimer et al. 2019; Storlazzi et al. 2018). Unfortunately, even if global efforts to mitigate sea-level rise are effective, island nations still face increasing vulnerability to natural disasters and threats to local economies, food production strategies, and cultural heritage sites (for example, Kelman and West 2009; Terry and Chui 2012; Storlazzi et al. 2018). In addition to rising sea levels, increased severity and frequency of catastrophic storms, commercial development on islands, and greater demands from coastal and oceanic waters also threaten the archaeological record (for example, Church and White 2006; Erlandson 2012: 141; Gutmann et al. 2018; Knutson et al. 2010). This problem is particularly acute for island colonization sites, although early deposits can remain well preserved in cave contexts (for example, Fitzpatrick 2003; Stone et al. 2017; chapter 11). To mitigate these threats, Gusick et al. (chapter 5) stress the importance of regional approaches to understanding how archaeological sites may be individually affected by sea-level rise.

Lastly, given the uniqueness of factors that triggered colonization events and individual histories of founding populations, is there utility in comparing island colonization events? Will archaeologists be able to move past the archaeology of colonization as events and move toward a more detailed study of how the identities of colonizing groups changed over time? In addition the developing better language to approach these questions (see chapters 2 and 4), archaeologists will need to continue to work with descendant communities and continue to foster interdisciplinary collaborations and public support (Atalay 2012; Kirch 2010). Collaboration between archaeology and biological anthropology, genetics, historical linguistics, paleoecology, paleoclimatology, and Indigenous communities—incorporating oral histories, traditional ecological knowledge, and navigation and wayfinding skills—have led to a proliferation in new transdisciplinary research (for example, Horsburgh and McCoy 2017; Hviding 2003; Kirch 2010). To develop improved techniques for addressing these issues and building stronger collaborative partnerships, we must also reassess our own biases and theoretical perspectives to employ better terminology, explanatory frameworks, make our results widely available to the public, and decolonize our reconstruction of the past. It will also be productive to integrate colonization studies to the study of human dispersals across continental landmasses and nontraditional islands—like areas isolated by nonaquatic boundaries—to better understand the motivating factors associated with past human mobility (*sensu* Fitzpatrick et al. 2015: 15–16; Spriggs 2016). Looking toward the future, we see that understanding adaptations common in island colonization events around the world are relevant to future adaptations to climate change and sea-level rise. As the chapters in this volume demonstrate, ongoing archaeological field-work with increasingly sophisticated field and laboratory methods, and refined theoretical frameworks, shed new light on island colonization events around the world that can be used to inform studies of the past and issues facing island nations around the world today.

Acknowledgments

We are indebted to Cyprian Broodbank who provided extremely insightful comments on the chapters in this volume. Scott M. Fitzpatrick, Ethan Cochrane, Aletta Biersack, and Tori Byington provided very helpful feedback on earlier versions of this chapter.

References

Allen, J., and J. F. O'Connell. 2008. Getting from Sunda to Sahul. In *Islands of Inquiry: Colonisation, Seafaring and the Archaeology of Maritime Landscapes,* ed. G. Clark, F. Leach, and S. O'Connor, 31–46. Canberra: ANU E Press.

Allen, J., and J. F. O'Connell. 2020. A Different Paradigm for the Initial Colonisation of Sahul. *Archaeology in Oceania* 55(1): 1–14.

Allen, M. S. 2014. Marquesan Colonisation Chronologies and Post-Colonisation Interaction: Implications for Hawaiian Origins and the "Marquesan Homeland" Hypothesis. *Journal of Pacific Archaeology* 5(2): 1–17.

Allen, M. S., and J. M. Huebert. 2014. Short-lived Plant Materials, Long-lived Trees, and Polynesian ^{14}C dating: Considerations for [14]C Sample Selection and Documentation. *Radiocarbon* 56(1): 257–276.

Alves, M. Q., K. Macario, P. Ascough, and C. Bronk Ramsey. 2018. The Worldwide Marine Reservoir Effect: Definitions, Mechanisms, and Prospects. *Review of Geophysics* 56(1): 278–305.

Anderson, A. 1994. Palaeoenvironmental Evidence of Island Colonization: A Response. *Antiquity* 68(261): 845–847.

Anderson, A. 1995. Current Approaches in East Polynesian Colonization Research. *Journal of the Polynesian Society* 104: 110–132.

Anderson, A. 2006. Islands of Exile: Ideological Motivation in Maritime Migration. *Journal of Island and Coastal Archaeology* 1(1): 33–47.

Anderson, A. 2008. Traditionalism, Interaction, and Long-Distance Seafaring in Polynesia. *Journal of Island and Coastal Archaeology* 3(2): 240–250.

Anderson, A. 2018. Ecological Contingency Accounts for Earliest Seagoing in the Western Pacific Ocean. *Journal of Island and Coastal Archaeology* 13(2): 224–234.

Anderson, A., and Y. Sinoto. 2002. New Radiocarbon Ages of Colonization Sites in East Polynesia. *Asian Perspectives* 41(2): 242–257.

Anderson, A. A., J. H. Barrett, and K. V. Boyle. 2010. *The Global Origins and Development of Seafaring*. McDonald Institute Monographs. Cambridge: University of Cambridge.

Anderson, A. J., J. Chappell, and M. Gagan. 2006. Prehistoric Maritime Migration in the Pacific Islands: An Hypothesis of ENSO Forcing. *The Holocene* 16: 1–6.

Anderson, A., G. Clark, S. Haberle, T. Higham, M. Nowak-Kemp, A. Prendergast, C. Radimilahy, L. M. Rakotozafy, Ramilisonina, J.-L. Schwenninger, M. Virah-Sawmy, A. Camens. 2018. New Evidence of Megafaunal Bone Damage Indicates Late Colonization of Madagascar. *PloS ONE* 13(10): e0204368.

Atalay, S. 2012. *Community-based Archaeology: Research With, By, and for Indigenous and Local Communities*. Berkeley: University of California Press.

Athens, J. S., T. M. Rieth, and T. S. Dye. 2014. A Paleoenvironmental and Archaeological Model-based Age Estimate for the Colonization of Hawai'i. *American Antiquity* 79(1): 144–155.

Atkinson, Q. D., and R. D. Gray. 2005. Curious Parallels and Curious Connections—Phylogenetic Thinking in Biology and Historical Linguistics. *Systematic Biology* 54(4): 513–526.

Bailey, G. N., and N. C. Flemming. 2008. Archaeology of the Continental Shelf: Marine Resources, Submerged Landscapes, and Underwater Archaeology. *Quaternary Science Reviews* 27: 2153–2165.

Bailey, G., A. AlSharekh, N. Flemming, K. Lambeck, G. Momber, A. Sinclair, and C. Vita-Finzi. 2007. Coastal Prehistory in the Southern Red Sea Basin, Underwater Archaeology, and the Farasan Islands. *Proceedings in the Seminar for Arabian Studies* 37: 1–16.

Bartlett, L. J., D. R. Williams, G. W. Prescott, A. Balmford, R. E. Green, A. Eriksson, P. J. Valdes, J. S. Singarayer, and A. Manica. 2016. Robustness despite Uncertainty: Regional Climate Data Reveal the Dominant Role of Humans in Explaining Global Extinctions of Late Quaternary Megafauna. *Ecography* 39(2): 152–161.

Bar-Yosef Mayer, D. E., Y. Kahanov, J. Roskin, and H. Gildor. 2015. Neolithic Voyages to Cyprus: Wind Patterns, Routes, and Mechanisms. *Journal of Island and Coastal Archaeology* 10(3): 412–435.

Baumann, B. 2017. Finding Environmental Opportunities for Early Sea Crossings: An Agent-Based Model of Middle to Late Pleistocene Mediterranean Coastal Migration. Master's thesis, Geographic Information Science and Technology, University of Southern California, Los Angeles.

Bayliss, A. 2009. Rolling Out Revolution: Using Radiocarbon Dating in Archaeology. *Radiocarbon* 51(1): 123–147.

Bayliss, A. 2015. Quality in Bayesian Chronological Models in Archaeology. *World Archaeology* 47: 677–700.

Bell, F.S.L. 1932. A Functional Interpretation of Inheritance and Succession in Central Polynesia. *Oceania* 3(2): 167–206.

Bellwood, P. 1996. Hierarchy, Founder Ideology and Austronesian Expansion. In *Origin, Ancestry and Alliance*, ed. J. Fox and C. Sather, 18–40. Canberra: Australian National University.

Bentley, R. A. 2006. Strontium Isotopes from the Earth to the Archeological Skeleton: A Review. *Journal of Archaeological Method and Theory* 13(3): 135–187.

Bentley, R. A., H. R. Buckley, M. Spriggs, S. Bedford, C. J. Ottley, G. M. Nowell, C. G. Macpherson, and D. G. Pearson. 2007. Lapita Migrants in the Pacific's Oldest Cemetery: Isotopic Analysis at Teouma, Vanuatu. *American Antiquity* 72: 645–656.

Bird, M. I., S. A. Condie, S. O'Connor, D. O'Gray, C. Reepmeyer, S. Ulm, M. Zega, F. Saltre, and C.J.A. Bradshaw. 2019. Early Human Settlement of Sahul was Not an Accident. *Scientific Reports* 9(8220).

Blust, R. 2000. Why Lexicostatistics Doesn't Work: The "Universal Constant" Hypothesis and the Austronesian Languages. *Time Depth in Historical Linguistics* 2: 311–331.

Boivin, N. L., M. A. Zeder, D. Q. Fuller, A. Crowther, G. Larson, J. M. Erlandson, T. Denham, and M. D. Petraglia. 2016. Ecological Consequences of Human Niche Construction: Examining Long-term Anthropogenic Shaping of Global Species Distributions. *Proceedings of the National Academy of Sciences* 113(23): 6388–6396.

Bradshaw, C. J. A., S. Ulm, A. N. Williams, M. I. Bird, R. G. Roberts, Z. Jacobs, F. Laviano, L. S. Weyrich, T. Friedrich, K. Norman, and F. Saltre. 2019. Minimum Founding Populations for the First Peopling of Sahul. *Nature Ecology and Evolution* 3: 1057–1063.

Braje, T. J., T. P. Leppard, S. M. Fitzpatrick, and J. M. Erlandson. 2017. Archaeology, Historical Ecology and Anthropogenic Island Ecosystems. *Environmental Conservation* 44(3): 286–297.

Braje, T. J., J. M. Erlandson, T. C. Rick, L. Davis, T. Dillehay, D. W. Fedje, D. Froese, A. Gusick, Q. Mackie, and D. McLaren. 2020. Fladmark+ 40: What Have We Learned about a Potential Pacific Coast Peopling of the Americas? *American Antiquity* 85(1): 1–21.

Bronk Ramsey, C. 2009. Bayesian Analysis of Radiocarbon Dates. *Radiocarbon* 51(1): 337–360.

Broodbank, C. 2006. The Origins and Early Development of Mediterranean Maritime Activity. *Journal of Mediterranean Archaeology* 19(2): 199–230

Brucato, N., V. Fernandes, S. Mazieres, P. Kusuma, M. P. Cox, J. W. Ng'ang'a, M. Omar, M.-C. Simeone-Senelle, C. Frassati, F. Alshamali, B. Fin, A. Boland, J.-F. Deluze, M. Stoneking, A. Adelaar, A. Crowther, N. Boivin, L. Pereira, P. Bailly, J. Chiaroni, and F.-X. Ricaut. 2018. The Comoros Show the Earliest Austronesian Gene Flow into the Swahili Corridor. *American Journal of Human Genetics* 102(1): 58–68.

Brumm, A., G. M. Jensen, G. D. van den Bergh, M. J. Wormwood, I. Kurniawan, F. Aziz, and M. Storey. 2010. Hominin on Flores, Indonesia, by One Million Years Ago. *Nature* 464: 748–752.

Brumm, A., G. D. van den Bergh, M. Storey, I. Kurniawan, B. V. Alloway, R. Setiawan, E. Setiyabudi, R. Grün, M. W. Moore, D. Yurnaldi, M. R. Puspaningrum, U. P. Wibowo, H. Insani, I. Sutisna, J. A. Westgate, N.J.G. Pearce, M. Duval, H.J.M. Meijer, F. Aziz, T. Sutikna, S. van der Kaars, S. Flude, and M. J. Morwood. 2016. Age and Context of the Oldest Known Hominin Fossils from Flores. *Nature* 534: 249–253.

Buck, C. E., and B. Meson. 2015. On Being a Good Bayesian. *World Archaeology* 47: 567–584.

Bulbeck, D. 2007. Where River Meets Sea: A Parsimonious Model for *Homo sapiens* Colonization of the Indian Ocean Rim and Sahul. *Current Anthropology* 48: 315–321.

Burley, D. V., and W. R. Dickinson. 2001. Origin and Significance of a Founding Settlement in Polynesia. *Proceedings of the National Academy of Sciences* 98: 11829–11831.

Burley, D. V., and W. R. Dickinson. 2010. Among Polynesia's First Pots. *Journal of Archaeological Science* 37(5): 1020–1026.

Burley, D., K. Edinborough, M. Weisler, and J. X. Zhao. 2015. Bayesian Modeling and Chronological Precision for Polynesian Settlement of Tonga. *PLoS ONE* 10(3): e0120795.

Burney, D. A. 1997. Tropical Islands as Paleoecological Laboratories: Gauging the Consequences of Human Arrival. *Human Ecology* 25(3): 437–457.

Callaghan, R. T. 2001. Ceramic Age Seafaring and Interaction Potential in the Antilles: A Computer Simulation. *Current Anthropology* 42(2): 308–313.

Callaghan, R. T. 2010. Crossing the Guadeloupe Passage in the Archaic Age. In *Island Shores and Distant Pasts: Archaeological and Biological Approaches to Pre-Columbian Settlement of the Caribbean*, ed. S. M. Fitzpatrick and A. H. Ross, 127–147. Gainesville: University of Florida Press.

Cañellas-Boltà, N., V. Rull, A. Sáez, O. Margalef, R. Bao, S. Pla-Rabes, M. Blaauw, B. Valero-Garcés, and S. Giralt. 2013. Vegetation Changes and Human Settlement of Easter Island during the Last Millennia: A Multiproxy Study of the Lake Raraku Sediments. *Quaternary Science Reviews* 72: 36–48.

Cassidy, J. L., M. Raab, and N. A. Kononenko. 2004. Boats, Bones, and Biface Bias: The Early Holocene Mariners of Eel Point, San Clemente Island, California. *American Antiquity* 69(1): 109–130.

Cherry, J. F., and T. P. Leppard. 2015. Experimental Archaeology and the Earliest Seafaring: The Limitations of Inference. *World Archaeology* 47: 740–755.

Cherry, J. F., and T. P. Leppard. 2018. Patterning and Its Causation in the Pre-Neolithic Colonization of the Mediterranean Islands (Late Pleistocene to Early Holocene). *Journal of Island and Coastal Archaeology* 13(2): 191–205.

Church, J. A., and N. J. White. 2006. A 20th Century Acceleration in Global Sea-level Rise. *Geophysical Research Letters* 33 (1): L01602.

Church, J. A., P. U. Clark, A. Cazenave, J. M. Gregory, S. Jevrejeva, A. Levermann, M. A. Merrifield, G. A. Milne, R. S. Nerem, P. D. Nunn, A. J. Payne, W. T. Pfeffer, D. Stammer, and A. S. Unnikrishnan. 2013. Sea Level Change. In *Climate Change 2013: The Physical Science Basis. Contribution of Working Group I to the Fifth Assessment Report of the Intergovernmental Panel on Climate Change*, ed. T. F. Stocker, D. Qin, G.-K. Plattner, M. Tignor, S. K. Allen, J. Boschung, A. Nauels, Y. Xia, V. Bex, and P. M. Midgley. Cambridge: Cambridge University Press.

Church, M. J., S. V. Arge, K. J. Edwards, P. L. Ascough, J. M. Bond, G. T. Cook, S. J. Dockrill, A. J. Dugmore, T. H. McGovern, C. Nesbitt, I. A. Simpson. 2013. The Vikings Were Not the First Colonizers of the Faroe Islands. *Quaternary Science Reviews* 77(1): 228–232.

Clark, J. T., and J. E. Terrell. 1978. Archaeology in Oceania. *Annual Review of Anthropology* 7: 293–319.

Clark, J. T., S. Quintus, M. Weisler, E. St. Pierre, L. Nothdurft, and Y. Feng. 2016. Refining the Chronology for West Polynesian Colonization: New Data from the Sāmoan Archipelago. *Journal of Archaeological Science: Reports* 6: 266–274.

Clarkson, C., Z. Jacobs, B. Marwick, R. Fullagar, L. Wallis, M. Smith, R. G. Roberts, E. Hayes, K. Lowe, X. Carah. 2017. Human Occupation of Northern Australia by 65,000 Years Ago. *Nature* 547: 306.

Connor S. E., J.F.N. van Leeuwen, T. M. Rittenour, W. O van der Knaap, B. Ammann, and S. Björck. 2012. The Ecological Impact of Oceanic Island Colonization: A Palaeoecological Perspective from the Azores. *Journal of Biogeography* 39(6): 1007–1023.

Cooke, S. B., L. M. Dávalos, A. M. Mychajliw, S. T. Turvey, and N. S. Upham. 2017. Anthropogenic Extinction Dominates Holocene Declines of West Indian Mammals. *Annual Review of Ecology, Evolution, and Systematics* 48: 301–327.

Crowther, A., L. Lucas, R. Helm, M. Horton, C. Shipton, H. T. Wright, S. Walshaw, M. Pawlowicz, C. Radimilahy, K. Douka, L. Picornell-Gelabert, D. Q. Fuller, and N. L. Boivin. 2016a. Ancient Crops Provide First Archaeological Signature of the Westward Austronesian Expansion. *Proceedings of the National Academy of Sciences* 113(24): 6635–6640.

Crowther, A., P. Faulkner, M. E. Prendergast, E. M. Quintana Morales, M. Horton, E. Wilmsen, A. M. Kotarba-Morley, A. Christie, N. Petek, R. Tibesasa, K. Douka, L. Picornell-Gelabert, Z. Carah, and N. Boivin. 2016b. Coastal Subsistence, Maritime Trade, and the Colonization of Small Offshore Islands in Eastern Africa Prehistory. *Journal of Island and Coastal Archaeology* 11(2): 211–237.

Davies, B., and S. H. Bickler. 2013. Sailing the Simulated Seas: A New Simulation for Evaluating Prehistoric Seafaring. In *Across Space and Time: Papers from the 41st Conference on Computer Applications and Quantitative Methods in Archaeology*, ed. A. Traviglia, 215–233. Amsterdam: Amsterdam University Press.

Dawson, H. 2014. *Mediterranean Voyages: The Archaeology of Island Colonisation and Abandonment.* Walnut Creek, California: Left Coast Press.

De La Fuente, C., S. Flores, and M. Moraga. 2013. DNA from Human Ancient Bacteria: A Novel Source of Genetic Evidence from Archaeological Dental Calculus. *Archaeometry* 55(4): 767–778.

DePratter, C. B., and J. D. Howard. 1977. History of Shoreline Changes Determined by Archaeological Dating, Georgia Coast, United States. University of Georgia Marine Institute 337. Sapelo Island, Georgia.

DePratter, C. B., and V. D. Thompson. 2013. Past Shorelines of the Georgia Coast. In *Life among the Tides: Recent Archaeology of the Georgia Bight,* ed. V. D. Thompson and D. H. Thomas, 145–168. Anthropological Papers of the American Museum of Natural History 98. New York: American Museum of Natural History.

Diamond, J., and P. Bellwood. 2003. Farmers and Their Languages: The First Expansions. *Science* 300(5619): 597–603.

Dickinson, W. R. 2003. Impact of Mid-Holocene Hydro-Isostatic Highstand in Regional Sea Level on Habitability of Islands in Pacific Oceania. *Journal of Coastal Research* 19(3): 489–502.

Dickinson, W. R. 2004. Impacts of Eustasy and Hydro-Isostasy on the Evolution and Landforms of Pacific Atolls. *Palaeogeography, Palaeoclimatology, Palaeoecology* 213(3–4): 251–269.

Dickinson, W. R., and J. S. Athens. 2007. Holocene Paleoshoreline and Paleoenvironmental History of Palau: Implications for Human Settlement. *Journal of Island and Coastal Archaeology* 2(2): 175–196.

Dickinson, W. R., and R. Shutler, Jr. 2000. Implications of Petrographic Temper Analysis for Oceanian Prehistory. *Journal of World Prehistory* 14(3): 203–266.

DiNapoli, R. J., and T. P. Leppard. 2018. Islands as Model Environments. *Journal of Island and Coastal Archaeology* 13: 157–160.

DiNapoli, R. J., A. E. Morrison, C. P. Lipo, C. P., T. L. Hunt, and B. G. Lane. 2018. East Polynesian Islands as Models of Cultural Divergence: The Case of Rapa Nui and Rapa Iti. *Journal of Island and Coastal Archaeology* 13(2): 206–223.

DiNapoli, R. J., S. M. Fitzpatrick, M. F. Napolitano, T. Rick, J. H. Stone, and N. P. Jew. 2021. Marine Reservoir Corrections for the Caribbean Demonstrate High Intra- and Inter-Island Variability in Local Reservoir Offsets. *Quaternary Geochronology* 61(101126).

Di Piazza, A., P. Di Piazza, and E. Pearthree. 2007. Sailing Virtual Canoes across Oceania: Revisiting Island Accessibility. *Journal of Archaeological Science* 34(8): 1219–1225.

Dodson, J. R., and M. Intoh. 1999. Prehistory and Palaeoecology of Yap, Federated States of Micronesia. *Quaternary International* 59(1): 17–26.

Douglass, K., and J. Zinke. 2015. Forging Ahead by Land and by Sea: Archaeology and Paleoclimate Reconstruction in Madagascar. *African Archaeological Research* 32: 267–299.

Douglass, K., and J. Cooper. 2020. Archaeology, Environmental Justice, and Climate Change on Islands of the Caribbean and Southwestern Indian Ocean. *Proceedings of the National Academy of Sciences* 117(15): 8254–8262.

Douglass, K., S. Hixon, H. T. Wright, L. R. Godfrey, B. E. Crowley, B. Manjakahery, T. Rasolondrainy, Z. Crossland, and C. Radimilahy. 2019. A Critical Review of Radiocarbon Dates Clarifies the Human Settlement of Madagascar. *Quaternary Science Reviews* 221: 105878.

Dye, T. S. 2015. Dating Human Dispersal in Remote Oceania: A Bayesian View from Hawai'i. *World Archaeology* 47: 661–676.

Eisenhofer, R., A. Anderson, K. Dobney, A. Cooper, and L. S. Weyrich. 2019. Ancient Microbial DNA in Dental Calculus: A New Method for Studying Rapid Human Migration Events. *Journal of Island and Coastal Archaeology* 14(2): 149–162.

Erlandson, J. M. 2001. The Archaeology of Aquatic Adaptation: Paradigms for a New Millennium. *Journal of Archaeological Research* 9(4): 287–350.

Erlandson, J. M. 2008. Racing a Rising Tide: Global Warming, Rising Seas, and the Erosion of Human History. *Journal of Island and Coastal Archaeology* 3(2): 167–169.

Erlandson, J. M. 2012. As the World Warms: Rising Seas, Coastal Archaeology, and the Erosion of Maritime History. *Journal of Coastal Conservation* 6(2): 137–142.

Erlandson, J. M., and T. J. Braje. 2011. From Asia to the Americas by Boat? Paleogeography, Paleoecology, and Stemmed Points of the Pacific Northwest. *Quaternary International* 239(1–2): 28–37.

Erlandson, J. M., T. C. Rick, T. J. Braje, A. Steinberg, and R. L. Vellanoweth. 2008. Human Impacts on Ancient Shellfish: A 10,000 Year Record from San Miguel Island, California. *Journal of Archaeological Science* 35(8): 2144–2152.

Erlandson, J. M., K. M. Gill, and M. Fauvelle. 2019. Responding to Stress or Coping with Abundance? Reexamining the Marginality of the California Islands for Maritime Hunter-Gatherers. In *An Archaeology of Abundance: Reevaluating the Marginality of California's Channel Islands,* ed. K. M. Gill, M. Fauvelle, and J. M. Erlandson, 1–30. Gainesville: University Press of Florida.

Fehren-Schmitz, L., C. L. Jarman, K. M. Harkins, M. Kayser, B. N. Popp, and P. Skoglund. 2017. Genetic Ancestry of Rapanui before and after European Contact. *Current Biology* 27(20): 3209–3215.

Field, J., M. Fillios, and S. Wroe. 2008. Chronological Overlap Between Humans and Megafauna in Sahul (Pleistocene Australia-New Guinea): A Review of the Evidence. *Earth Science Reviews* 89(3–4): 97–115.

Field, J., S. Wroe, C. N. Trueman, J. Garvey, and S. Wyatt-Spratt. 2013. Looking for the Archaeological Signature in Australian Megafaunal Extinctions. *Quaternary International* 285(8): 76–88.

Finney, B. 1996. *Voyage of Rediscovery: A Cultural Odyssey through Polynesia.* Berkeley: University of California Press.

Finney, B. 2008. Contrasting Visions of Polynesian Voyaging Canoes. Comment on Atholl Anderson's "Traditionalism, Interaction and Long-Distance Seafaring in Polynesia." *Journal of Island and Coastal Archaeology* 3(2): 257–259.

Fitzhugh, B. 2004. Colonizing the Kodiak Archipelago: Trends in Raw Material Use and Lithic Technologies at the Tanginak Spring Site. *Arctic Anthropology* 41(1): 14–40.

Fitzpatrick, S. M. 2003. Early Human Burials in the Western Pacific: Evidence for a c. 3000 Year Old Occupation on Palau. *Antiquity* 77(298): 719–731.

Fitzpatrick, S. M. (ed.). 2004. *Voyages of Discovery: The Archaeology of Islands.* Westport, Connecticut: Praeger.

Fitzpatrick, S. M. 2013. Seafaring Capabilities in the Pre-Columbian Caribbean. *Journal of Maritime Archaeology* 8: 101–138.

Fitzpatrick, S. M., and A. Anderson. 2008. Islands of Isolation: Archaeology and the Power of Aquatic Perimeters. *Journal of Island and Coastal Archaeology* 3(1): 4–16.

Fitzpatrick, S. M., and R. Callaghan. 2008. Seafaring Simulations and the Origins of Prehistoric Settlers to Madagascar. In *Islands of Inquiry: Colonisation and the Archaeology of Maritime Landscapes,* ed. G. Clark, F. Leach, and S. O'Connor, 47–58. Terra Australis 29, Canberra: ANU E Press.

Fitzpatrick, S. M., and R. Callaghan. 2013. Estimating Trajectories of Colonisation to the Mariana Islands, Western Pacific. *Antiquity* 87: 840–853.

Fitzpatrick, S. M., T. C. Rick, and J. M. Erlandson. 2015. Recent Progress, Trends, and Developments in Island and Coastal Archaeology. *Journal of Island and Coastal Archaeology* 10(1): 3–27.

Fitzpatrick, S. M., V. D. Thompson, A. S. Poteate, M. F. Napolitano, and J. E. Erlandson. 2016. Marginalization of the Margins: The Importance of Smaller Islands in Human Prehistory. *Journal of Island and Coastal Archaeology* 11(2): 155–170.

Fitzpatrick, S. M., and J. E. Erlandson. 2018. Island Archaeology, Model Systems, the Anthropocene, and How the Past Informs the Future. *Journal of Island and Coastal Archaeology* 13(2): 283–99.

Fretwell, S. D., and H. L. Lucas. 1969. On Territorial Behavior and Other Factors Influencing Habitat Distribution in Birds. I. Theoretical Development. *Acta Biotheoretica* 19: 16–36.

Gamble, L. H. 2002. Archaeological Evidence for the Origin of the Plank Canoe in North America. *American Antiquity* 67(2): 301–315.

Gill, K. M., M. Fauvelle, and J. M. Erlandson (eds.). 2019. *An Archaeology of Abundance: Re-evaluating the Marginality of California's Islands.* Gainesville: University Press of Florida.

Giovas, C. M., and S. M. Fitzpatrick. 2014. Prehistoric Migration in the Caribbean: Past Perspectives, New Models and the Ideal Free Distribution of West Indian Colonization. *World Archaeology* 46: 569–589.

Gladwin, T. 1970. *East is a Big Bird: Navigation and Logic on Puluwat Atoll.* Cambridge: Harvard University Press.

Goodwin, I. D., S. A. Browning, and A. J. Anderson. 2014. Climate Windows for Polynesian Voyaging to New Zealand and Easter Island. *Proceedings of the National Academy of Sciences* 111(41): 14716–14721.

Gosling, W. D., D. A. Sear, J. D. Hassall, P. G. Langdon, M.N.T. Bönnen, T. D. Driessen, Z. R. van Kemenade, K. Noort, M. J. Leng, I. W. Croudace, A. J. Bourne, and C. N. H. McMichael. 2020. Human Occupation and Ecosystem Change on Upolu (Sāmoa) during the Holocene. *Journal of Biogeography* 47(3): 600–614.

Gray, R. D., A. J. Drummond, and S. J. Greenhill. 2009. Language Phylogenies Reveal Expansion Pulses and Pauses in Pacific Settlement. *Science* 323(5913): 479–483.

Gray, R. D., Q. D. Atkinson, and S. J. Greenhill. 2011. Language Evolution and Human History: What a Difference a Date Makes. *Philosophical Transactions of the Royal Society B: Biological Sciences* 366(1567): 1090–1100.

Green, R. C. 1996. Prehistoric Transfers of Portable Items during the Lapita Horizon in Remote Oceania: A Review. In *Indo-Pacific Prehistory: The Chiang Mai Papers,* ed. I. C. Glover, and P. Bellwood, 119–130. Vol. 2, Canberra: Australian National University.

Green, R. C. 1999. Integrating Historical Linguistics with Archaeology: Insights from Research in Remote Oceania. *Indo-Pacific Prehistory Bulletin* 18: 1–16.

Greenhill, S. J., and R. D. Gray. 2005. Testing Population Dispersal Hypotheses: Pacific Settlement, Phylogenetic Trees and Austronesian Languages. In *The Evolution of Cultural Diversity: A Phylogenetic Approach,* ed. R. Mace, C. J. Holden, and S. Shennan, 31–52. Walnut Creek, California: Left Coast Press.

Greenhill, S. J., and R. D. Gray. 2009. Austronesian Language Phylogenies: Myths and Misconceptions about Bayesian Computational Methods. In *Austronesian Historical Linguistics and Culture History: A Festschrift for Robert Blust,* ed. A. Adelaar and A. Pawley, 1–23. Canberra: Research School of Pacific and Asian Studies.

Greenhill, S. J., A. J. Drummond, and R. D. Gray. 2010. How Accurate and Robust are the Phylogenetic Estimates of Austronesian Language Relationships? *PloS ONE* 5(3): e9573.

Gutmann, E. D., R. M. Rasmussen, C. Liu, K. Ikeda, C. L. Bruyere, L. Garré, P. Friis-Hansen, and V. Veldore. 2018. Changes in Hurricanes from a 13-yr Convection Permitting Pseudo-Global Warming Simulation. *Journal of Climate* 31: 3643–3657.

Hamilton, W. D., and A. M. Krus. 2018. The Myths and Realities of Bayesian Chronological Modeling Revealed. *American Antiquity* 83(2): 187–203.

Hamm, G., P. Mitchell, L. J. Arnold, G. J. Prideaux, D. Questiaux, N. A. Spooner, V. A. Levchenko, E. C. Foley, T. H. Worthy, B. Stephenson, V. Coutlhard, C. Coulthard, S. Wilton, and D. Johnston. Cultural Innovation and Megafauna Interaction in the Early Settlement of Arid Australia. *Nature* 539: 280–283.

Heyerdahl, T. 1950. *The Kon-Tiki Expedition: By Raft across the South Seas.* Oslo: Gyldendal Norsk Forlag.

Higham, T., A. Anderson, and C. Jacomb. 1999. Dating the First New Zealanders: The Chronology of Wairau Bar. *Antiquity* 73(280): 420–427.

Hofman, C. A., and T. A. Rick. 2018. Ancient Biological Invasions and Island Ecosystems: Tracking Translocations of Wild Plants and Animals. *Journal of Archaeological Research* 26: 65–115.

Holdaway, R. N., and C. Jacomb. 2000. Rapid Extinction of the Moas (Aves: Dinornithiformes): Model, Test, and Implications. *Science* 287: 2250–2254.

Holdaway, R. N., M. E. Allentoft, C. Jacomb, C. L. Oskam, N. R. Beavan, and M. Bunce. 2014. An Extremely Low-Density Human Population Exterminated New Zealand Moa. *Nature Communications* 5: 5436.

Holton, G.E.L. 2004. Heyerdahl's Kon Tiki Theory and the Denial of the Indigenous Past. *Anthropological Forum* 14(2): 163–181.

Horsburgh, K., and M. McCoy. 2017. Dispersal, Isolation, and Interaction in the Islands of Polynesia: A Critical Review of Archaeological and Genetic Evidence. *Diversity* 9(3): 37.

Hunt, C. O., D. D. Gilbertson, and G. Rushworth. 2012. A 50,000-Year Record of Late Pleistocene Tropical Vegetation and Human Impact in Lowland Borneo. *Quaternary Science Reviews* 37: 61–80.

Hunt, T. L., and C. P. 2006. Late Colonization of Easter Island. *Science* 311: 1603–1606.

Hurles, M. E., B. C. Sykes, M. A. Jobling, and P. Forster. 2005. The Dual Origin of the Malagasy in Island Southeast Asia and East Africa: Evidence from Maternal and Paternal Lineages. *American Journal of Human Genetics* 76(5): 894–901.

Hviding, E. 2003. Between Knowledges: Pacific Studies and Academic Disciplines. *The Contemporary Pacific* 15(1): 43–73.

Irwin, G. 1992. *The Prehistoric Exploration and Colonization of the Pacific.* Cambridge: Cambridge University Press.

James, H. F. S., T. W. Stafford Jr., D. W. Steadman, S. L. Olson, P. S. Martin A.J.T. Jull, and P. C. McCoy. 1987. Radiocarbon Dates on Bones of Extinct Birds from Hawaii. *Proceedings of the National Academy of Sciences* 84: 2350–2354.

Jazwa, C. S., D. J. Kennett, B. Winterhalder. 2015. A Test of Ideal Free Distribution Predictions Using Targeted Survey and Excavation on California's Northern Channel Islands. *Journal of Archaeological Method and Theory* 23(4): 1242–1284.

Johns, D. A., G. J. Irwin, Y. K. Sung. 2014. An Early Sophisticated East Polynesian Voyaging Canoe Discovered on New Zealand's Coast. *Proceedings of the National Academy of Sciences* 111(41): 14728–733.

Jordan, F. M., R. D. Gray, S. J. Greenhill, and R. Mace. 2009. Matrilocal Residence is Ancestral in Austronesian Societies. *Proceedings of the Royal Society B* 276(1664): 1957–1964.

Kaifu, Y., C-h. Lin, A. Goto, N. Ikeya, M. Yamada, W.-C. Chiang, M. Fujita, K. Hara, T. Hawira, K. Huang, C. Huang, Y. Kubota, C. Liu, K. Miura, Y. Miyazawa, O. Monden, M. Muramatsu, Y. Sung, K. Suzuki, M. Tanaka, C. Tsang, S. Uchida, P. Wen. 2019. Paleolithic Seafaring in East Asia: Testing the Bamboo Raft Hypothesis. *Antiquity* 93(372): 1424–1441.

Kealy, S., J. Louys, and S. O'Connor. 2016. Islands under the Sea: A Review of Early Modern Human Dispersal Routes and Migration Hypotheses through Wallacea. *Journal of Island and Coastal Archaeology* 11(3): 364–384.

Keegan, W. F., and J. Diamond. 1987. Colonizations of Islands by Humans: A Biogeographical Perspective. In *Advances of Archaeological Method and Theory* 10: 49–92.

Kelman, I., and J. J. West. 2009. Climate Change and Small Island Developing States: A Critical Review. *Ecological and Environmental Anthropology* 5(1): 1–6.

Kennett, D. J., and B. Winterhalder. 2008. Demographic Expansion, Despotism and the Colonisation of East and South Polynesia. In *Islands of Inquiry: Colonisation and the Archaeology of Maritime Landscapes,* ed. G. Clark, F. Leach, and S. O'Connor, 87–96. Terra Australis 29, Canberra: ANU E Press.

Kennett, D. J., A. Anderson, and B. Winterhalder. 2006. The Ideal Free Distribution, Food Production, and the Colonization of Oceania. In *Behavioral Ecology and the Transition to Agriculture,* ed. D. J. Kennett and B. Winterhalder, 265–288. Berkeley: University of California Press.

Kinaston, R. L., R. K. Walter, C. Jacomb, E. Brooks, N. Tayles, S. E. Halcrow, C. Stirling, M. Reid, A. R. Gray, J. Spinks, and B. Shaw. 2013. The First New Zealanders: Patterns of Diet and Mobility Revealed Through Isotope Analysis. *PLoS ONE* 8(5): e64580.

Kirch, P. V. 1982. Transported Landscapes. *Natural History* 91: 32–35.

Kirch, P. V. 2007. Hawaii as a Model System for Human Ecodynamics. *American Anthropologist* 109(1): 8–26.

Kirch, P. V. 2008. Comment on Atholl Anderson's "Traditionalism, Interaction and Long-Distance Seafaring in Polynesia." *Journal of Island and Coastal Archaeology* 3(2): 260–261.

Kirch, P. V. 2010. Peopling of the Pacific: A Holistic Anthropological Perspective. *Annual Review of Anthropology* 39: 131–148.

Kirch, P. V., and J. Ellison. 1994. Palaeoenvironmental Evidence for Human Colonization of Remote Oceanic Islands. *Antiquity* 68(259): 310–321.

Kirch, P. V., and R. C. Green 1987. History, Phylogeny, and Evolution in Polynesia. *Current Anthropology* 28(4): 431–456.

Kirch, P. V., and R. C. Green. 2001. *Hawaiki, Ancestral Polynesia: An Essay in Historical Anthropology.* Cambridge: Cambridge University Press.

Knapp, A. B. 2008. Thoughts from the Mediterranean. Comment on Atholl Anderson's "Traditionalism, Interaction and Long-Distance Seafaring in Polynesia." *Journal of Island and Coastal Archaeology* 3(2): 262–264.

Knutson, T. R., J. L. McBride, J. Chan, K. Emanuel, G. Holland, C. Landsea, I. Held, J. P. Kossin, A. K. Srivastava, and M. Sugi. 2010. Tropical Cyclones and Climate Change. *Nature Geoscience* 3: 157–63.

Kuzmin, Y. V., G. S. Burr, S. V. Gorbunov, V. A. Rakov, and N. G. Razjigaeva. 2007. A Tale of Two Seas: Reservoir Age Correction Values, (R, ΔR) for the Sakhalin Island (Sea of Japan and Okhotsk Sea). *Nuclear Instruments and Methods in Physics Research Section B: Beam Interactions with Materials and Atoms* 259(1): 460–462.

Laffoon, J. E., R. Valcárcel Rojas, and C. L. Hofman. 2013. Oxygen and Carbon Isotope Analysis of Human Dental Enamel from the Caribbean: Implications for Investigating Individual Origins. *Archaeometry* 55(4): 742–765.

Laffoon, J. E., and T. P. Leppard. 2019. $^{87}Sr/^{86}Sr$ Data Indicate Human Post-Juvenile Residence Mobility Decreases over Time-Elapsed since Initial Holocene Island Colonization in the Pacific and Caribbean. *Archaeological and Anthropological Sciences* 11(5): 1757–1768.

Lambeck K., and J. Chappell. 2001. Sea Level Change through the Last Glacial Cycle. *Science* 292(5517): 679–86.

Lane, B. G. 2017. Geospatial Modelling for Predicting the Ideal Free Settlement of Rapa. *Archaeology in Oceania* 52(1): 13–21.

Lee, S., and T. Hasegawa. 2011. Bayesian Phylogenetic Analysis Supports an Agricultural Origin of Japonic Languages. *Proceedings of the Royal Society B* 278(1725): 3662–3669.

Leppard, T. P. 2014. Similarities and Diversity in the Prehistoric Colonization of Islands and Coasts by Food-Producing Communities. *Journal of Island and Coastal Archaeology* 9(1): 1–15.

Leppard, T. P. 2015. Passive Dispersal versus Strategic Dispersal in Island Colonization by Hominins. *Current Anthropology* 56(4): 590–595.

Leppard, T. P. 2017. The Biophysical Effects of Neolithic Island Colonization: General Dynamics and Sociocultural Implications. *Human Ecology* 45(5): 555–568.

Leppard, T. P., and C. Runnels. 2017. Maritime Hominin Dispersals in the Pleistocene: Advancing the Debate. *Antiquity* 91(356): 510–519.

MacArthur R. H., and E. O. Wilson. 1967. *The Theory is Island Biogeography*. Princeton: Princeton University Press.

Macaulay, V., C. Hill, A. Achilli, C. Rengo, D. Clarke, W. Meehan, J. Blackburn, O. Semino, R. Scozzari, F. Cruciani, A. Taha, N. Kassim Shaari, J. M. Raja, P. Ismail, Z. Zainuddin, W. Goodwin, D. Bulbeck, H.-J. Bandelt, S. Oppenheimer, A. Torroni, and Martin Richards. 2005. A Single, Rapid Coastal Settlement of Asia Revealed by Analysis of Complete Mitochondrial Genomes. *Science* 308(5724): 1034–1036.

Marean, C., M. Bar-Matthews, J. Bernatchez, E. Fisher, P. Goldberg, A.I.R. Herries, Z. Jacobs, A. Jerardino, P. Karkanas, T. Minichillo, P.J. Nilssen, E. Thompson, I. Watts, and H. M. Williams. 2007. Early Human Use of Marine Resources and Pigment in South Africa during the Middle Pleistocene. *Nature* 449: 905–908.

Matisoo-Smith, E. 2009. The Commensal Model for Human Settlement of the Pacific 10 Years on—What Can We Say and Where to Now? *Journal of Island and Coastal Archaeology* 4(2): 151–163.

Matisoo-Smith, E., M. Hingston, G. Summerhayes, J. Robins, H. A. Ross, and M. Hendy. 2009. On the Rat Trail in Near Oceania: Applying the Commensal Model to the Question of the Lapita Colonization. *Pacific Science* 63(4): 465–476.

McCoy, M. D. 2018. The Race to Document Archaeological Sites Ahead of Rising Sea Levels: Recent Applications of Geospatial Technologies in the Archaeology of Polynesia. *Sustainability* 10(1): 185.

McWethy, D. B., J. M. Wilmshurst, C. Whitlock, J. R. Wood, and M. S. McGlone. 2014. A High-Resolution Chronology of Rapid Forest Transitions Following Polynesian Arrival in New Zealand. *PLoS ONE* 9(11): e111328.

Mitchell, P. 2004. Towards a Comparative Archaeology of Africa's Islands. *Journal of African Archaeology* 2(2): 229–250.

Montenegro, Á., R. Callaghan, and S. M. Fitzpatrick. 2014. From West to East: Environmental Influences on the Rate and Pathways of Polynesian Colonization. *The Holocene* 24(2): 242–256.

Montenegro, Á., R. T. Callaghan, and S. M. Fitzpatrick. 2016. Using Seafaring Simulations and Shortest-hop Trajectories to Model the Prehistoric Colonization of Remote Oceania. *Proceedings of the National Academy of Sciences* 113(45): 12685–12690.

Montgomery, J., G. Vaughan, J. Buckberry, J. A. Evans, M. P. Richards, and J. H. Barrett. 2014. Finding Vikings with Isotope Analysis—The View from Wet and Windy Islands. *Journal of the North Atlantic* sp7: 54–70.

Msaidie, S., A. Ducourneau, G. Boetsch, G. Longepied, K. Papa, C. Allibert, A. A. Yahaya, J. Chiaroni, and M. J. Mitchell. 2011. Genetic Diversity on the Comoros Islands Shows Early Seafaring as Major Determinant of Human Biocultural Evolution in the Western Indian Ocean. *European Journal of Human Genetics* 19(1): 89–94.

Napolitano, M. F. 2013. The Role of Small Islands in the Foraging Economies of St. Catherines Island. In *Life among the Tides: Recent Archaeology on the Georgia Bight*, ed. V. D. Thompson and D. H. Thomas, 191–210. Anthropological Papers of the American Museum of Natural History 98. American Museum of Natural History, New York.

Napolitano, M. F., R. J. DiNapoli, J. H. Stone, M. J. Levin, N. P. Jew, B. G. Lane, J. T. O'Connor, and S. M. Fitzpatrick. 2019. Reevaluating Human Colonization of the Caribbean Using Chronometric Hygiene and Bayesian Modeling. *Science Advances* 5(12): eaar7806.

Norman, K., J. Inglis, C. Clarkson, J. T. Faith, J. Shulmeister, and D. Harris. 2018. An Early Colonisation Pathway into Northwest Australia 70–60,000 Years Ago. *Quaternary Science Reviews* 180: 229–239.

Oertel, G. F. 1979. Barrier Island Development during the Holocene Recession, Southeastern United States. In *Barrier Islands from the Gulf of St. Laurence to the Gulf of Mexico*, ed. S. P. Leatherman, 273–288. New York: Academic Press.

O'Connell, J. F., J. Allen, M.A.J. Williams, A. N. Williams, C.S.M. Turney, N. A. Spooner, J. Kamming, G. Brown, and A. Cooper. 2018. When Did *Homo sapiens* First Reach Southeast Asia and Sahul? *Proceedings of the National Academy of Sciences* 115(34): 8482–8490.

O'Connor, S., and P. Hiscock. 2018. The Peopling of Sahul and Near Oceania. In *The Oxford Handbook of Prehistoric Oceania*, ed. E. Cochrane and T. Hunt, 1–17. Oxford: Oxford University Press.

Oppenheimer, M., B. C. Glavovic , J. Hinkel, R. van de Wal, A. K. Magnan, A. Abd-Elgawad, R. Cai, M. Cifuentes-Jara, R. M. DeConto, T. Ghosh, J. Hay, F. Isla, B. Marzeion, B. Meyssignac, and Z. Sebesvari, 2019. Sea Level Rise and Implications for Low-Lying Islands, Coasts and Communities. In *IPCC Special Report on the Ocean and Cryosphere in a Changing Climate*, ed. H.-O. Pörtner, D. C. Roberts, V. Masson-Delmotte, P. Zhai, M. Tignor, E. Poloczanska, K. Mintenbeck, A. Alegría, M. Nicolai, A. Okem, J. Petzold, B. Rama, and N. M. Weyer, 321–446. Geneva: Intergovernmental Panel on Climate Change.

O'Sullivan, P. B., M. Morwood, D. Hobbs, F. Aziz, Suminto, M. Situmorang, A. Raza, and R. Maas. 2001. Archaeological Implications of the Geology and Chronology of the Sao Basin, Flores, Indonesia. *Geology* 29(7): 607–610.

Pawley, A. 1999. Chasing Rainbows: Implications of the Rapid Dispersal of Austronesian Languages for Subgrouping and Reconstruction. In *Selected Papers from the Eighth International Conference of Austronesian Linguistics, Vol. 1*, ed. E. Zeitoun and P. Jen-kuei, 95–138. Symposium Series of the Institute of Linguistics. Taipei: Academia Sinica.

Pawley, A., and M. Ross. 1993. Austronesian Historical Linguistics and Culture History. *Annual Review of Anthropology* 22: 425–459.

Pellard, T. 2015. The Linguistic Archaeology of the Ryukyu Islands. In *Handbook of the Ryukyuan Languages: History, Structure, and Use*, ed. P. Heinrich, S. Miyara, and M. Shimoji, 13–37. Berlin: De Gruyter Mouton.

Petchey, F., and G. Clark. 2010. A Marine Reservoir Correction Value (ΔR) for the Palauan Archipelago: Environmental and Oceanographic Considerations. *Journal of Island and Coastal Archaeology* 5(2): 236–252.

Petchey, F., A. Anderson, A. Hogg, A., A. Zondervan. 2008. The Marine Reservoir Effect in the Southern Ocean: An Evaluation of Extant and New ΔR Values and Their Application to Archaeological Chronologies. *Journal of the Royal Society of New Zealand* 38(4): 243–262.

Petchey, F., M. Spriggs, and F. Valentin. 2015. The Chronology of Occupation at Teouma, Vanuatu: Use of a Chronometric Hygiene Protocol and Bayesian Modeling to Evaluate Midden Remains. *Journal of Archaeological Science: Reports* 4: 95–105.

Petchey, F., S. Ulm, B. David, I. J. McNiven, B. Asmussen, H. Tomkins, N. Dolby, K. Aplin, T. Richards, C. Rowe, M. Leavesley, and H. Mandui. 2013. High-resolution Radiocarbon

Dating of Marine Materials in Archaeological Contexts: Radiocarbon Marine Reservoir Variability Between *Anadara, Gafrarium, Batissa, Polymesoda* spp. and Echinoidea at Caution Bay, Southern Coastal Papua New Guinea. *Archaeological and Anthropological Sciences* 5(1): 69–80.

Posth, C., K. Nägele, H. Colleran, F. Valentin, S. Bedford, K. W. Kami, R. Shing, H. Buckley, R. Kinaston, M. Walworth, G. R. Clark, C. Reepmeyer, J. Flexner, T. Maric, J. Moser, J. Gresky, L. Kiko, K.J. Robson, K. Auckland, S.J. Oppenheimer, A.S.V. Hill, A. J. Mentzer, J. Zech, F. Petchey, P. Roberts, C. Jeong, R. D. Gray, J. Krause, and A. Powell. 2018. Language Continuity despite Population Replacement in Remote Oceania. *Nature Ecology and Evolution* 2(4): 731.

Poteate, A. S., S. M. Fitzpatrick, W. S. Ayres, and A. Thompson. 2016. First Radiocarbon Chronology for Mwoakilloa Atoll, Eastern Caroline Islands, Micronesia. *Radiocarbon* 58(1): 169–178.

Prebble, M., and J. E. Wilmshurst. 2009. Detecting the Initial Impact of Humans and Introduced Species on Island Environments in Remote Oceania Using Palaeoecology. *Biological Invasions* 11: 1529–1556.

Price, T. D., and H. Gestsdóttir. 2006. The First Settlers of Iceland: An Isotopic Approach to Colonisation. *Antiquity* 80(307): 130–144.

Rainbird, P. 2007. *The Archaeology of Islands.* Cambridge: Cambridge University Press.

Rick, T. C., and S. M. Fitzpatrick. 2012. Archaeology and Coastal Conservation. *Journal of Coastal Conservation* 16(2): 135–136.

Rick, T. C., P. V. Kirch, J. M. Erlandson, and S. M. Fitzpatrick. 2013. Archaeology, Deep History, and the Human Transformation of Island Ecosystems. *Anthropocene* 4: 33–45.

Rick, T. C., R. L. Vellanoweth, and J. M. Erlandson. 2005. Radiocarbon Dating and the "Old Shell" Problem: Direct Dating of Artifacts and Cultural Chronologies in Coastal and Other Aquatic Regions. *Journal of Archaeological Science* 32(11): 1641–1648.

Rieth, T. M., and J. S. Athens. 2013. Suggested Best Practices for the Application of Radiocarbon Dating to Hawaiian Archaeology. *Hawaiian Archaeology* 13: 3–29.

Rieth, T. M., and E. E. Cochrane. 2018. The Chronology of Colonization in Remote Oceania. In *The Oxford Handbook of Prehistoric Oceania,* ed. E. E. Cochrane and T. L. Hunt. DOI: 10.1093/oxfordhb/9780199925070.013.010.

Rieth, T. M., and T. L. Hunt. 2008. A Radiocarbon Chronology for Sāmoan Prehistory. *Journal of Archaeological Science* 35(7): 1901–1927.

Rockman, M., and J. Steele (eds.). 2003. *The Colonization of Unfamiliar Landscapes: The Archaeology of Adaptation.* New York: Routledge.

Rosenzweig, M. L. 1995. *Species Diversity in Space in Time.* Cambridge: Cambridge University Press.

Ross, M. 1996. Contact-Induced Change and the Comparative Method: Cases from Papua New Guinea. In *The comparative Method Reviewed: Regularity and Irregularity in Language Change,* ed. M. Durie and M. D. Ross, 180–217. New York: Oxford University Press.

Rowland, M. J., and S. Ulm. 2012. Key Issues in the Conservation of the Australian Coastal Archaeological Record: Natural and Human Impacts. *Journal of Coastal Conservation* 16(2): 159–171.

Saddler, J. P. 1999. Biodiversity on Oceanic Islands: A Paleoecological Assessment. *Journal of Biogeography* 26: 75–87.

Schiffer, M. B. 1986. Radiocarbon Dating and the "Old Wood" Problem: The Case of the Hohokam Chronology. *Journal of Archaeological Science* 13(1): 13–30.

Schmid, M. M., A. J. Dugmore, L. Foresta, A. J. Newton, O. Vésteinsson, and R. Wood. 2018. How [14]C Dates on Wood Charcoal Increase Precision When Dating Colonization: The Examples of Iceland and Polynesia. *Quaternary Geochronology* 48: 64–71.

Schmid, M. M., R. Wood, A. J. Newton, O. Vesteinsson, A. J. Dugmore. 2019. Enhancing Radiocarbon Chronologies of Colonization: Chronometric Hygiene Revisited. *Radiocarbon* 61: 629–647.

Schwadron, M. 2017. Shell Works: Prehistoric Terraformed Communities in the Ten Thousand Islands, Florida. *Hunter-Gatherer Research* 3(1): 31–63.

Sear, D. A., M. S. Allen, J. D. Hassall, A. E. Maloney, P. G. Langdon, A. E. Morrison, A.C.G. Henderson, H. Mackay, I. W. Croudance, C. Clarke, J. P. Sachs, G. Macdonald, R. C. Chiverrell, M. J. Leng, L. M. Cisneros-Dozal, and T. Fonville. 2020. Human Settlement of East Polynesia Earlier, Incremental, and Coincident with Prolonged South Pacific Drought. *Proceedings of the National Academy of Sciences* 117(16): 8813–8819.

Siegel, P. E. (ed.). 2018. *Island Historical Ecology: Socionatural Landscapes of the Eastern and Southern Caribbean.* New York: Berghahn Books.

Siegel, P. E., J. G. Jones, D. M. Pearsall, N. P. Dunning, P. Farrell, N. A. Duncan, J. H. Curtis, S. K. Singh. 2015. Paleoenvironmental Evidence for First Human Colonization of the Eastern Caribbean. *Quaternary Science Reviews* 129: 275–295.

Sinoto, Y. 1979. Excavations on Huahine, French Polynesia. *Pacific Studies* 3(1): 1–40.

Skoglund, P., C. Posth, K. Sirak, M. Spriggs, F. Valentin, S. Bedford, G. R. Clark, C. Reepmeyer, F. Petchey, and D. Fernandes. 2016. Genomic Insights into the Peopling of the Southwest Pacific. *Nature* 538(7626): 510.

Slayton, E. R. 2018. *Seascape Corridors: Modeling Routes to Connected Communities across the Caribbean Sea.* Leiden: Sidestone Press.

Spriggs, M. 1989. The Dating of the Island Southeast Asian Neolithic: An Attempt at Chronometric Hygiene and Linguistic Correlation. *Antiquity* 63(240): 587–613.

Spriggs, M. 2016. Lapita and the Linearbandkeramik: What Can a Comparative Approach Tell Us about Either? In *Something Out of the Ordinary? Interpreting Diversity in Early Neolithic Linearbandkeramik and Beyond,* ed. L. Ambreutz, Fabian Haack, and D. Hoffman, 481–504. Cambridge: Cambridge Scholars.

Spriggs, M., F. Valentin, S. Bedford, R. Pinhasi, P. Skoglund, D. Reich, and M. Lipson. 2019. Revisiting Ancient DNA Insights into the Human History of the Pacific Islands. *Archaeology in Oceania* 54(1): 53–56.

Stein, G. 2005. *The Archaeology of Colonial Encounters: Comparative Perspectives.* School of American Research Seminar Series. Santa Fe, New Mexico: School of American Research Press.

Stone, J. H., S. M. Fitzpatrick, and M. F. Napolitano. 2017. Disproving Claims for Small-bodied Humans in the Palauan Archipelago. *Antiquity* 91(360): 1546–1560.

Storey, A. A., A. C. Clarke, T. Ladefoged, J. Robins, and E. Matisoo-Smith. 2013. DNA and Pacific Commensal Models: Applications, Construction, Limitations, and Future Prospects. *Journal of Island and Coastal Archaeology* 8(1): 37–65.

Storlazzi, C. D., S. B. Gingerich, A. van Dongeren, O. M. Cheriton, P. W. Swarzenski, E. Quataert, C. I. Voss, D. W. Field, H. Annamalai, G. A. Piniak, and R. McCall. 2018. Most Atolls Will be Uninhabitable by the Mid-21st Century Because of Sea-level Rise Exacerbating Wave-Driven Flooding. *Science Advances* 4(4): eaap9741.

Stuiver, M., G. W. Pearson, T. F. Braziunas. 1986. Radiocarbon Calibration of Marine Samples back to 9000 CAL YR BP. *Radiocarbon* 28(2b): 980–1021.

Summerhayes, G. 2009. Obsidian Network Patterns in Melanesia—Sources, Characterisation and Distribution. *Indo-Pacific Prehistory Bulletin* 29: 109–123.

Sutherland, W. J. 1996. *From Individual Behaviour to Population Ecology.* Oxford: Oxford University Press.

Takamiya, H. 1996. Initial Colonization, and Subsistence Adaptation Processes in the Late

Prehistory of the Island of Okinawa. *Bulletin of the Indo-Pacific Prehistory Association* 15: 143–150.

Takamiya, H., C. Katagiri, S. Yamasaki, and M. Fujita. 2019. Human Colonization of the Central Ryukyus (Amami and Okinawa Archipelagos), Japan. *Journal of Island and Coastal Archaeology* 14(3): 375–393.

Terrell, J. E. 1999. Comment on Paul Rainbird, Islands Out of Time: Towards a Critique of Island Archaeology. *Journal of Mediterranean Archaeology* 12(2): 240–245.

Terrell, J., T. L. Hunt, and C. Gosden. 1997. The Dimensions of Social Life in the Pacific: Human Diversity and the Myth of the Primitive Isolate. *Current Anthropology* 38: 155–195.

Terry, J. P., and T.F.M. Chui. 2012. Evaluating the Fate of Freshwater Lenses on Atoll Islands after Eustatic Sea-level Rise and Cyclone-Driven Inundation: A Modelling Approach. *Global and Planetary Change* 88–89: 76–84.

Thomas, D. H. 2008. *Native American Landscapes of St. Catherines Island, Georgia.* Anthropological Papers of the American Museum of Natural History 88. New York: American Museum of Natural History.

Thomas, D. H., M. C. Sanger, and R. H. Hayes. 2013. Revising the [14]C Reservoir Correction for St. Catherines Island, Georgia. In *Life Among the Tides: Recent Archaeology on the Bight*, ed. V. D. Thompson and D. H. Thomas, 25–46. Anthropological Papers of the American Museum of Natural History 98. New York: American Museum of Natural History.

Thomas, F. 2019. Atoll Archaeology in the Pacific. In *Encyclopedia of Global Archaeology*, ed. C. Smith, 1–13. New York: Springer.

Thompson, V. D., and J. A. Turck. 2010. Island Archaeology and the Native American Economies (2500 B.C. to A.D. 1700) of the Georgia Coast, USA. *Journal of Field Archaeology* 35(3): 283–297.

Tobler, R., A. Rohrlach, J. Soubrier, P. Bover, B. Llamas, J. Tuke, N. Bean, A. Abdullah-Highfold, S. Agius, A. O'Donoghue, I. O'Loughlin, P. Sutton, F. Zilio, K. Walshe, A. N. Williams, C.S.M. Turney, M. Williams, S. M. Richards, R. J. Mitchell, and E. Kowal. 2017. Aboriginal Mitogenomes Reveal 50,000 Years of Regionalism in Australia. *Nature* 544(7649): 180–184.

Tofanelli, S., S. Bertoncini, L. Castrì, D. Luiselli, F. Calafell, G. Donati, and G. Paoli. 2009. On the Origins and Admixture of Malagasy: New Evidence from High-Resolution Analyses of Paternal and Maternal Lineages. *Molecular Biology and Evolution* 26(9): 2109–2124.

Tutsumi, T. 2007. The Dynamics of Obsidian Use by the Microblade Industries of the Terminal Late Palaeolithic. *The Quaternary Research* 46(3): 179–186.

Ulm, S. 2002. Marine and Estuarine Reservoir Effects in Central Queensland, Australia: Determination of ΔR values. *Geoarchaeology* 17(4): 319–348.

van den Bergh, G. D., Y. Kaifu, I. Kurniawan, R. T. Kono, A. Brumm, E. Setiyabudi, F. Aziz, and M. J. Wormwood. 2016. *Homo floresis*-like Fossils from the Early Middle Pleistocene of Flores. *Nature* 534: 245–248.

Vitousek, P. M. 2002. Oceanic Islands as Model Systems for Ecological Studies. *Journal of Biogeography* 29(5–6): 573–582.

Walter, R., H. Buckley, C. Jacomb, and E. Matisoo-Smith. 2017. Mass Migration and the Polynesian Settlement of New Zealand. *Journal of World Prehistory* 30(4): 351–376.

Weisler, M. I. 1998. Hard Evidence for Prehistoric Interaction in Polynesia. *Current Anthropology* 39(4): 521–532.

Weisler, M. I., H. Yamano, and Q. Hua. 2012. A Multidisciplinary Approach for Dating Human Colonization of Pacific Atolls. *Journal of Island and Coastal Archaeology* 7(1): 102–125.

Wheeler, R. J., J. J. Miller, R. M. McGee, and D. Ruhl. 2003. Archaic Period Canoes from Newmans Lake, Florida. *American Antiquity* 68(3): 533–551.

Wilhelmson, H., and T. Ahlström. 2015. Iron Age Migration on the Island of Öland: Appointment of Strontium by Means of Bayesian Mixing Analysis. *Journal of Archaeological Science* 64: 30–45.

Wilhelmson, H., and T. D. Price. 2017. Migration and Integration on the Baltic Island of Öland in the Iron Age. *Journal of Archaeological Science: Reports* 12: 183–196.

Williams A. N., S. Ulm, T. Sapienza, S. Lewis, and C.S.M. Turney. 2018. Sea-level Change and Demography during the Last Glacial Termination and Early Holocene across the Australian Continent. *Quaternary Science Reviews* 182: 144–54.

Wilmshurst, J. M., T. L. Hunt, C. P. Lipo, and A. J. Anderson. 2011. High Precision Radiocarbon Dating Shows Recent and Rapid Colonization into East Polynesia. *Proceedings of the National Academy of Sciences* 108(5): 1815–1820.

Winterhalder, B., D. J. Kennett, M. N. Grote, and J. Bartruff. 2010. Ideal Free Settlement of California's Northern Channel Islands. *Journal of Anthropological Archaeology* 29: 469–490.

Yamaoka, Y. 2009. *Helicobacter pylori* Typing as a Tool for Tracking Human Migration. *Clinical Microbiology and Infection* 15(9): 829–834.

I

Theoretical Approaches

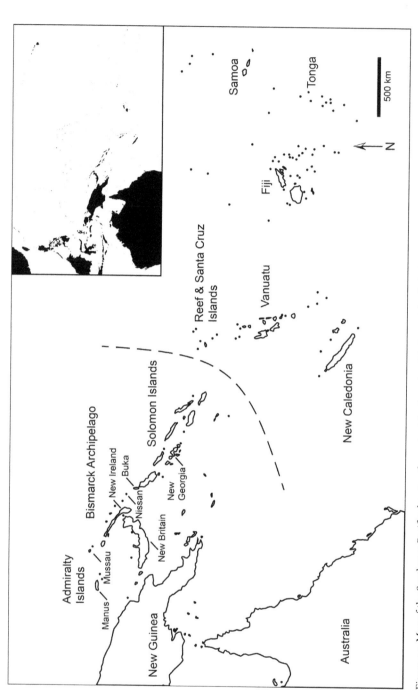

Figure 2.1. Map of the Southwest Pacific showing the major islands and archipelagos. The dashed line separates Near Oceania on the left from Remote Oceania on the right. Some small islands removed from main map for clarity.

2

Using Ecology and Evolution to Explain Archaeological Migration Signatures in the Southwest Pacific

ETHAN E. COCHRANE

This chapter outlines a program using ecological and evolutionary concepts to evaluate explanations of past human movement evidenced in the empirical archaeological record (see Cochrane 2018 for a more detailed treatment), and uses the movement of populations into the southwest Pacific Islands as a case study (Figure 2.1). Evolutionary and ecological theory, including transmission, selection, and other processes, generates expectations for the distribution of artifact classes, socionatural environments, and ecologies. This framework has been developed over the last several decades and is applicable to empirical phenomena conceptualized as exhibiting variation produced in part through both inheritance (cultural or biological) and differential persistence (for example, Atkinson and Gray 2005; Boyd and Richerson 1985; Bettinger 1991; Cavalli-Sforza and Feldman 1981; Dunnell 1980; Laland et al. 2015; Lycett 2015; Mesoudi 2011; O'Brien et al. 2016; O'Brien and Lyman 2000; Pigliucci and Muller 2010; Shennan 2002; Whiten et al. 2011). The evolutionary, ecological, and archaeological concepts used to explain population movements are developed in the next section, while subsequent sections summarize the Lapita movement to Remote Oceania and provide a testable explanation for it. The final section suggests ways that this research program can be applied elsewhere.

Evolution and Movement

Definitions and Explanatory Processes

Movement behavior is culturally transmitted, that is, passed between people; entails costs in energy, time, and other resources; and may expose individuals

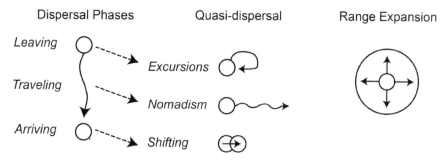

Figure 2.2. Schematic depictions of dispersal phases, corresponding quasi-dispersal types, and range expansion. The circles represent species ranges, and solid lines indicate movement (adapted from Lidicker and Stenseth [1992]).

to unfamiliar environments (Baker 1978; Bonte et al. 2012; Cox 1968; Travis et al. 2012). To explain variation in movement behavior, a first step is to define different movement types whose temporal and spatial distributions likely result from different processes (contra Anthony 1990: 897; see also Clark 1994). One movement type, *dispersal,* consists of "one-way movements of individuals away from their home ranges" (Hengeveld 1989; Lidicker and Stenseth 1992: 22). *Home range* refers to individuals' spatial span of settlement (Hengeveld 1989: 7). Three related behaviors include *nomadism* practiced by individuals without home ranges, *excursions* or short-term movements outside home ranges, and *shifting,* moving the home range by adding territory in one part, while subtracting from another (Lidicker and Stenseth 1992; Matthysen 2012). Finally, *range expansion* denotes a total spatial increase in home range, different from dispersal (Figure 2.2).

Along with defining movement types and identifying them empirically, proximate and ultimate processes are used to explain the variable frequencies of movement types within and between populations (Laland et al. 2011; Lidicker and Stenseth 1992: 24). Proximate processes or explanations focus on the events that might trigger movement and include genetic interactions, phenotypic or behavioral plasticity, and contingencies such as the behaviors of others and acute or intergeneration environmental change, such as El Niño Southern Oscillation (ENSO)–influenced wind reversals in the Pacific (Anderson et al. 2006). Ultimate processes or explanations use selection and other sorting processes, along with the differential fitness of behaviors, to explain the variable frequencies of different movement types over time and space. The subsequent

Ethan E. Cochrane

sections outline processes and related concepts that are most relevant to explanations of archaeologically recorded human movement.

Saturation Dispersal, Presaturation Dispersal, and Range Expansion

Under what conditions might the distribution of different movement types be explained by selection? Lidicker (1975), researching nonhuman animals, was the first to address this and proposed two sets of contrasting conditions to explain dispersal: saturation dispersal may occur when a population is near carrying capacity, and presaturation dispersal may occur with no such population pressure (Hamilton and May 1977; Stenseth and Lidicker 1992). The relative fitness advantage of saturation dispersal is easy to understand as nondispersal may incur increasing costs associated with competition for dwindling resources, and dispersal, while also incurring costs, can result in new environments for exploitation. If dispersal exhibits a relatively greater rate of increase than nondispersal, and dispersal outperforms nondispersal in terms of costs and benefits, then selection is the likely process accounting for variation in movement types (Johnson and Gaines 1990; Keegan 1995; compare O'Connell and Allen 2012; Travis et al. 2012).

Presaturation dispersal is less intuitive. Why would people and other organisms engage in costly behavior such as dispersal in the absence of population pressure? Presaturation dispersal is often explained by proximate triggers, and Lidicker (1975) suggests they fall into three broad categories: economic, tactical, and social. Proximate triggers are linked to particular contingent histories, and some are likely more relevant than others to human dispersal.

The characteristics of ranges can influence dispersal costs and therefore interact with both saturation and presaturation dispersal. Dispersal behavior may vary throughout a range due to a number of other factors, including behavioral plasticity, frequency-dependent influences on the distribution of behaviors, environmental variation and patchiness (Benton and Bowler 2012; Levin et al. 1984), and cooperative versus individual dispersal (Koykka and Wild 2015; Plantegenest and Kindlmann 1999; Ridley 2012).

Range expansion (see Figure 2.2) refers to continuous enlargement of a home range. Much research on range expansions considers the proximate process of climate change, as this often modifies habitat. Selection processes, however, are also used to explain range expansion (for example, Duputié and Massol 2013; Kubisch et al. 2013). If range margins comprise patchy occupied habitats, nondispersal from those habitats may outcompete dispersal. However, if the range is enlarged by climate change, for example, range expansion movement may outcompete nonmovement (Simmons and Thomas 2004).

Demographic Processes and Movement in Time and Space

Population size, structure, growth, and distribution are measures often used to describe population movements (for example, Cavalli-Sforza et al. 1994; Russell et al. 2014). Their relationships are formalized in the Fisher-Skellam model, which estimates changes in local population density based on a nonlinear population growth and a linear population dispersal function (Steele 2009). The speed of population movement is a function of rates of maximum population growth and mean movement. This is a simple model, and other concepts that increase the model's applicability include the Allee effect, and advection. The Allee effect (Allee et al. 1949; see also Courchamp et al. 1999) describes a positive correlation between growth rate and population density, such that small populations may suffer low growth rates or extinctions slowing movement. Advection is the process whereby populations preferentially move along a particular route related to a resource gradient, such that movement will be speedier along the resource gradient and slower off the gradient (for example, Grollemund et al. 2015).

Applying Evolutionary Theory of Movement to the Archaeological Record

The application of evolutionary and ecological concepts to the movement of organisms has been primarily developed in the context of plants, insects, birds, and other nonhuman animals (for exceptions, see Keegan and Diamond 1987; Winder et al. 2015). To explain the movement of human populations as evidenced in the archaeological record requires new theory and modification of previously developed concepts.

Identifying Portions of the Archaeological Record with Movement Types

Space and time are two dimensions of movement that are archaeologically measurable. Temporal and spatial variation across archaeological assemblages sharing homologous similarity defines several types of movement into *unoccupied* regions (including a null or default nonmovement type, *range*). In Table 2.1, these have been labeled using the terms discussed above and are themselves not explanations. The dimension Spatial Distribution comprises sets of categorical options that describe the spatial patterning of homologous similarity, and the options can be archaeologically identified through techniques such Kernel Density Estimation or other spatial statistics (for example, Morrison 2012) applied to assemblages when necessary. Likewise, the dimension Assemblage Chronology describes the patterning of homologous similarity over time and can be identified as synchronic or diachronic using a variety of techniques (for example,

Table 2.1. The spatial-temporal distribution of homologous artifacts and associated movement concepts

		Spatial Distribution		
		Continuous	Core-centered	Discontinuous
Assemblage Chronology	**Synchronic**	Range	Excursion	Nomadism
	Diachronic	Range expansion	Shifting	Dispersal

Source: Author.

Burley et al. 2015; Cochrane 2002b; Crema et al. 2010). Ideally, identifying a portion of the archaeological record as a particular movement type should be a quantitative exercise, the results of which can be evaluated with statistical tools. As an alternative to this approach, or to augment it, principles from comparative biogeography (for example, Brooks and McLennan 1991; Cochrane 2008; Parenti and Ebach 2009) can facilitate identification of movement types.

When artifacts are used to investigate movement into *occupied* regions, observation across multiple dimensions of archaeological variability may be required to identify movement types due to the added difficulty of distinguishing between artifact distributions resulting from human movement and distributions resulting from predominantly artifact movement, or cultural transmission of artifact manufacturing information (for example, Pétrequin 1993; Winter et al. 2012). Zedeño's (1995) work in the American Southwest provides one model for how this might be accomplished, but in the absence of archaeological observations, the construction of language phylogenies is often used to identify human movements putatively associated with artifact distributions (Gray et al. 2009; Holden 2002).

The Application of Selection and Fitness to the Archaeological Record

If selection or other sorting processes are to explain the distribution of movement behaviors in a population, two assessments must be made. First, the fitness of movement behaviors must be measured, estimated, or modeled. Madsen and colleagues' (1999) discussion of three fitness concepts—individual fitness, inclusive fitness, and fitness as a variable property of classes—is useful in this regard. Fitness as a class property is used in population genetics models and refers to the rate of increase (positive or negative) of trait classes in a population.

The rate of increase of an archaeological trait class over time or across space depends, generally, on transmission processes (Boyd and Richerson 1985; Tehrani and Riede 2008), population structure and environmental variation (Boyd and Richerson 2002; Lipo et al. 1997; Pérez-Losada and Fort 2011), innovation and trait-class frequencies (Neiman 1995), assemblage formation (Porčić 2015; Premo 2014), and feedback effects between cultural and biological transmission (O'Brien and Laland 2012; Shennan 2000). When the empirical observations to be explained are the distributions of trait classes in the archaeological record, fitness as a variable property of classes is an appropriate fitness concept.

The second assessment required to evaluate selection as an explanation requires establishing performance differences between trait classes within relevant social, technological, and natural environment contexts (for example, Cochrane 2002a; Rogers and Ehrlich 2008). Trait classes that demonstrate greater rates of increase should also perform better than alternative trait classes in a given context, if selection-driven replication is not to be mistaken for some other processes such as trait hitchhiking or pleiotropic effects (McElreath et al. 2003). Although performance differences are widely described in ancient technology studies (for example, Feathers 2006; O'Brien et al. 1994; Pierce 2005; Schiffer and Skibo 1997), the performance of different movement types in the ancient world cannot be evaluated in a laboratory, but instead must be modeled or theoretically justified (compare Shennan 2011).

An Evolutionary Hypothesis of Lapita Movement to Remote Oceania

An Empirical Description of Lapita with Reference to Movement Concepts

Ecological explanations of island colonization began in the 1960s with MacArthur and Wilson's (1963, 1967) studies of biological diversity in isolated populations, typically islands surrounded by water, but including any ecological community circumscribed by a boundary that structures immigration and extinction. MacArthur and Wilson's work was not focused solely on movement between islands, but the relationship between species diversity and environmental variables such as island size and distance between islands. MacArthur and Wilson's ideas were later used by archaeologists to understand the human colonization of islands in different world regions (Keegan and Diamond 1987), including the Pacific Islands (for example, Terrell 1976).

The biogeographic boundary between Near and Remote Oceania is pertinent to explanations of Lapita movement (Green 1991b). Near Oceania encompasses New Guinea and nearby islands and has been occupied by humans for up to 50,000 years (Summerhayes et al. 2010). The Lapita region of Remote Oceania (hereafter, simply Remote Oceania) references the archipelagos from Vanuatu to Sāmoa that were first colonized 3,000 years ago (Sheppard et al. 2015) by populations from Near Oceania who deposited Lapita pottery similar to that deposited several hundred years earlier in Near Oceania (Rieth and Athens 2019). Lapita pottery is an earthenware, intricately decorated with stamped motifs shared across sites, and without an antecedent pottery tradition in Near Oceania (see chapter 11 for purported links to Island Southeast Asia). Although Lapita pottery is unambiguous evidence of human movement to Remote Oceania, the explanation of this movement is vigorously debated, typically with reference to genetic and linguistic data (Bedford et al. 2018; Carson et al. 2013; Green 1979, 1991a; 2003; Groube 1971; Kirch 1997, 2010; Sheppard 2011; Spriggs 1984; Terrell and Welsch 1997).

Site Dates and Population Distributions

Lapita ceramics appear in the Bismarck Archipelago, without local precedent, most likely between *3535 and 3234 cal BP*[1] (Rieth and Athens 2019). After a pause, the ceramics appear with the first human colonists in Remote Oceania across the Reef/Santa Cruz Islands, Vanuatu, New Caledonia, and Fiji contemporaneously about 3000 cal BP, but skipping most of the Solomons until their appearance in the Western Solomons around 2600 cal BP (Sheppard 2011). Within 150 years of the first Lapita movement into Remote Oceania, colonists reach Tonga approximately 2850 cal BP and move quickly north up the archipelago. The oldest site in Sāmoa, and the only Lapita site, dates to approximately the same time as Tongan landfall, although likely a bit later based on comparison of the ceramic decorations. There are only a few additional archaeological sites in Sāmoa for the next several hundred years (Clark et al. 2016; Cochrane et al. 2013). This farthest eastern extent of Lapita pottery thus occurs between about 425 and 650 years after the ceramics first appear in Near Oceania. The first Remote Oceanic Lapita sites, with the possible exception of Sāmoa, all appear to be slightly earlier than the Lapita sites of the Northern and Western Solomon Islands or the New Guinea south coast, even though the Remote Oceanic sites are farther from the geographic origin of Lapita in the Bismarcks (Sheppard 2011).

Pre- and Post-Lapita Environment and Subsistence in Near and Remote Oceania

Before Lapita pottery appears in Near Oceania, populations there had a long history of hunting and gathering, mid-Holocene agriculture and arboriculture, and tuber and aroid use that began in the Pleistocene. After the appearance of Lapita in Near Oceania, these subsistence practices continue at new Lapita occupations and at locations with both pre-Lapita and Lapita deposits (Kirch 1997: 203–205; Lentfer and Torrence 2007).

A suite of domesticated Asian (mainland and island) animals appear in Near Oceania during and after the advent of Lapita pottery. Pigs (*Sus scrofa*) are rare in Near Oceanic Lapita pottery contexts, but increase in abundance over time (Kirch 1997: 211–212; Specht et al. 2013). Small amounts of dog (*Canis lupus familiaris*) bone are also found in Lapita deposits in Near Oceania, but not in the earliest phase of Lapita pottery (Manne et al. 2020; Summerhayes et al. 2019). Chickens (*Galllus gallus*) occur in Lapita contexts in the Mussau islands, but association with the earliest Lapita pottery is unclear (Specht et al. 2013).

After voyaging to Remote Oceania, Lapita populations encountered a never-before-seen world that included new plants, animals, and landscapes. The islands of Remote Oceania are generally depauperate compared to Near Oceania; however, as Remote Oceanic archipelagos had never hosted humans prior to Lapita, bird, fish, and shellfish populations were naïve to human predation and Lapita populations targeted these rich resources. Numerous archaeofaunal analyses document the focus on marine and avian resources in the first generations of Remote Oceanic Lapita (Burley 2012; Irwin et al. 2011; Nagaoka 1988; Steadman et al. 2002; Worthy and Anderson 2009). Human bone isotope studies also confirm a lesser focus on vegetable-based proteins (Valentin et al. 2010), even though plants, such as yams (*Dioscorea alata*), bananas (*Musa* spp.), and taro (*Colocasia esculenta*), which had a multimillennia history of human use in Near Oceania, were brought to Remote Oceania (Fall 2010; Horrocks and Bedford 2005; Horrocks and Nunn 2007; Horrocks et al. 2009). Lapita populations also brought domesticated animals, although their temporal and spatial distribution varies (Matisoo-Smith 2007).

The End of Lapita

Those groups who left for Remote Oceania initially maintained contact with Near Oceanic populations as evidenced by obsidian transport and the similar, intricate Lapita pottery decorations repeated on locally made pottery (Dickinson 2006) found in both regions (Figure 2.3). Lapita voyagers to different Remote Oceanic archipelagos also maintained connections for a time, as evidenced by shared pottery designs (Cochrane and Lipo 2010; Green 1979), and the transfer of Remote Oceanic volcanic glass and basalt (Clark et al. 2014; Reepmeyer et al. 2012). By approximately 2700 cal BP, this movement between

Figure 2.3. Examples of decorated Lapita ceramics from deposits in Near and Remote Oceania including (*top to bottom, left to right*): New Britain (Specht et al. 2013); Santa Cruz Islands (The University of Auckland Photographic Collection); New Caledonia (Sand et al. 1998); and Tonga (Burley and Dickinson 2010).

populations had largely stopped, both within Remote Oceania and between the regions, as evidenced by the lack of artifact transport, and the replacement of commonly decorated Lapita pottery with different, archipelago-specific styles in Remote Oceania. Lapita pottery continued to be made in Near Oceania for another 400 years (Specht and Gosden 1997; Summerhayes 2001), but the movement to Remote Oceania had ended.

The Selection and Range Expansion Hypothesis

Referencing the possibilities in Table 2.1, what movement type can be identified in the Lapita archaeological record? The diachronic character of Lapita assemblages, with the earliest Near Oceanic assemblages predating the earliest Remote Oceania assemblages, indicates that range expansion, shifting, or dispersal are possible movement types. The discontinuous spatial distribution of Lapita ceramics across Near and Remote Oceania is unavoidable due to interisland water gaps, but the evidence of Lapita design similarities and obsidian distributions indicates that assemblages distributed across Near Oceania and Remote Oceania share homologous similarity, at least for the first 200 or so years of movement. Therefore, range expansion is the relevant movement type.

Range expansion is typically explained by the proximate mechanism of climate change and demographic processes described by the Fisher-Skellam model (for example, Crozier and Dwyer 2006). Other proximate mechanisms relevant to the Lapita range expansion include social triggers and technological changes. Finally, range expansions in particular environmental contexts have also been explained by selection that accounts for the differential rate of increase of movement and nonmovement types.

Proximate Mechanisms of Lapita Range Expansion

Anderson and his colleagues (Anderson 2015; Anderson et al. 2006) have argued that the Lapita movement to Remote Oceania was triggered by the increased frequency of ENSO events and other climate phenomena. Anderson and his colleagues suggest that Lapita voyaging craft had little windward capability, but that the ENSO-influenced wind reversals would allow downwind sailing from west to east and lessen the time at sea without the need to tack over great distances. Laguna Pallcacocha (Ecuador) core data indicate an increase in ENSO frequency about 3100 cal BP, correlated with Lapita movement to Remote Oceania (Anderson et al. 2006).

Changes in sailing skills may also have been a proximate trigger. Irwin and his colleagues (Bell et al. 2015; Irwin 1989, 1992, 2008) have long argued that Lapita movement to Remote Oceania was predicated upon a search-and-return strategy, the ability to engage in open-ocean sailing beyond sight of land, and safely return to a starting point. Sailing east from Near Oceania, against the prevailing southeast trade winds, then returning safely home, requires a variety of skills, including latitude sailing, dead reckoning of position, maintaining a course, and reading weather, animal, wave, and current signs of unseen islands. Several of these skills might have been developed by Near Oceanic and Island Southeast Asian populations during the 40 millennia or more of human occupation in a "voyaging nursery . . . an island corridor which runs from Island South-east Asia to the end of the Solomon Islands" (Irwin 1989: 168) that is between northern and southern cyclone belts and within which islands, with few exceptions, are intervisible. Given that these skills would be required to sail to Remote Oceania at the speed indicated by dated Lapita deposits, it is likely that these skills coalesced within Near Oceania Lapita populations at least by approximately 3000 cal BP and also acted as a proximate trigger (see also Bell et al. 2015).

Evolutionary Mechanisms of the Lapita Range Expansion

The patchiness of habitats at range margins may promote selection-driven range expansion. Simmons and Thomas (2004) note that if the margin of a static range comprises discontinuous, occupied habitat patches, movement between patches that entails a cost may exhibit decreased fitness relative to non-movement. However, when proximate processes open new habitat, movement to unoccupied, virgin resource patches may become relatively less costly, and exhibit increased relative fitness compared to nonmovement. From Simmons and Thomas's argument, if selection explains the Lapita range expansion, we would expect both increased fitness of classes measuring human movement into Remote Oceania and discontinuous occupied habitat patches at the pre-expansion Lapita range margin.

To measure fitness as a property of classes, the relevant archaeological trait class here is a decorated Lapita ceramic deposit. In Remote Oceania these deposits identify Lapita range-expanding populations and in Near Oceania represent homologously related populations that did not expand from the original Lapita range. Based on the most recent site inventories, including the nine Caution Bay Lapita sites (Anderson et al. 2001; Bedford and Sand 2007; David et al. 2011), there are about 23 percent more spatially discrete Lapita deposits of any temporal range in Remote Oceania compared to Near Oceania (n = 132 and 102), despite the fact that the time period over which Lapita ceramics were made in Near Oceania is three times that of Remote Oceania. Simply counting deposits is a blunt measure of differential trait increase; the deposits differ in size and temporal range, and a host of processes contribute to the differences between Near and Remote Oceanic Lapita deposits (for example, research history, geomorphic processes). A better measure would be to compare deposits of similar age ranges in Near and Remote Oceania corresponding to the time of range expansion, about 3000–2800 cal BP. Using the same inventories, there are 24 temporally discrete Lapita deposits (that is, not continued deposition from an earlier non-Lapita deposit) in Near Oceania whose estimated date ranges fall within 3000 to 2800 cal BP, and there are 44 deposits in Remote Oceania, about twice as many (see also Anderson 2001: table 1). Anderson also calculated the rate at which new Lapita deposits were created in Near and Remote Oceania using the median intercepts of calibrated age ranges to place deposits in 100-year intervals. Given the (in 2001) conservative total Lapita time spans of 900 years in Near Oceania and 400 years in Remote Oceania, 9.7 Lapita deposits were established in Near Oceania per 100 years, while 23.8 Lapita deposits were established per 100 years in Remote Oceania (Anderson 2001: 17–18). The greater rate of increase of Lapita deposits in Remote Oceania relative to Near Oceania suggests selection or another sorting process is a possible explanation for the Lapita range expansion.

Were there discontinuous, occupied habitat patches at the pre-expansion Lapita range margin? This question is also difficult to conclusively answer with current paleoenvironmental and archaeological data from the Solomons (Powell 1976; Grimes 2003; Haberle 1996). Secondary forests and disturbance taxa prevailed in the region over the Holocene, and this environment may have been caused by either human activity, volcanic and other tectonic processes in the region (see for example, Dunkley 1986), or a combination of these. Grimes's (2003) detailed investigation in the western Solomons indicates large-scale forest fires after 3500 BP, likely intentionally set to promote the growth of economic plants such as breadfruit. These burning episodes are followed by periods either 1,500 or 600 years long with little charcoal deposited (Walter and Sheppard 2017:45–46), "and it is really only from 2700 cal BP, coincident with the first appearance of [Lapita] pottery, that the vegetation and sediment data can be said to clearly represent 'an anthropogenically modified landscape' (Grimes 2003: 231)" (Walter and Sheppard 2017: 60). The pre-Lapita archaeological record of the Solomons (Miller and Roe 1982; Walter and Sheppard 2017) reveals a sparsely inhabited group of islands, compared to the Near Oceanic Lapita range core in the Bismarcks. In short, the Lapita-era Solomons seem to be characterized by the discontinuous, occupied resource patches that promote selection-driven range expansion, although more paleoenvironmental work is needed to confirm this.

Simmons and Thomas (2004) also argue that individuals whose movement is explained as selection-driven range expansion will most likely be habitat generalists, as they are better able to exploit newly encountered and unfamiliar resources. Therefore, we expect that the Lapita movement to Remote Oceania will be correlated with generalist subsistence regimes that exploit a variety of newly encountered resources. The record of archaeofaunal remains (Hawkins et al. 2016; Irwin et al. 2011; White et al. 2010), fishing strategies (Butler 1988: 109), plant microfossils and animal translocations (Clark and Anderson 2001; Fall 2010; Horrocks and Nunn 2007; Horrocks et al. 2009, 2013; Matisoo-Smith 2007; Steadman et al. 2002), and human skeletal isotopes (Kinaston et al. 2016) indicate that initial Lapita populations in Remote Oceania did engage in generalist subsistence practices focused on pristine faunal resources, a spatially variable set of domesticated animals, and with less contribution from horticultural crops compared to Lapita populations in Near Oceania.

Using the Fisher-Skellam reaction-diffusion model, it should be possible to describe the demographic characteristics of Lapita populations undergoing selection-driven range expansion, including the direction of movement and variation in population density across Remote Oceania. In its most basic form, the Fisher-Skellam model predicts a linear population diffusion, but it is now clear that Lapita movement into Remote Oceania is not accurately described as a linear wave of advance from the Bismarck Archipelago to successively more eastern islands (Sheppard 2011). While the colonization dates for Vanuatu, New Caledonia, and Fiji are essentially contemporaneous at 3000–2900 cal BP, the petrography and geochemistry of the earliest Tongan Lapita pottery at approximately 2838 ± 8 BP suggest a direct colonization from Near Oceania or the Vanuatu region (Burley and Dickinson 2010), not Fiji as west-to-east linear diffusion would predict. A possible explanation may be selection promoting variation in the distances of range-expansion movements. For example, occasional very long moves, as in Lévy-flight models, are a more efficient range-expansion and foraging strategy under some conditions (Humphries and Sims 2014; Lilley 2008). Once the first Lapita populations arrive in Tonga, further colonization of the archipelago follows the expectations of advection, movement along resource gradients, as groups moved north up the island chain (Burley et al. 2015). Given that the date of the single Lapita deposit in Sāmoa, and several immediately post-Lapita plainware ceramic deposits in the Sāmoan archipelago, are contemporaneous with northern Tongan Lapita sites (Clark et al. 2016), the colonization of Sāmoa may be generally described as the last stop on the advection-influenced movement of Lapita populations from the south.

Sāmoa has a unique Lapita record, and one that should be explicable by the selection and range-expansion hypothesis. The Lapita era record of Sāmoa comprises a single Lapita deposit and a handful of immediately post-Lapita plainware ceramic deposits throughout the archipelago, contrasting with numerous Lapita and post-Lapita deposits throughout Tonga and Fiji. If Sāmoa's earliest populations were small and isolated (compare Cochrane 2013; Cochrane et al. 2016; Cochrane and Rieth 2016; Green 2002; Harris et al. 2020), the Allee effect is a possible explanation for the continuation of this demographic pattern (Courchamp et al. 1999). A reduction of cooperative interactions between individuals seems the most relevant process leading to inverse density-dependent growth.

Lastly, it is in Sāmoa that further movement ends and, at this eastern boundary of Lapita Remote Oceania, the seascape changes, with many smaller, more widely separated islands to the east, so that the costs of Lapita-era canoe voyages must rise (Di Piazza et al. 2007). Later innovations in voyaging technology and perhaps climate change may have been a proximate cause of movement to East Polynesia beginning 1000–900 cal BP. Others have suggested that processes similar to saturation dispersal, sometimes applied using the ideal free distribution, may also explain colonization of East Polynesia (Burley 2007; Kennett et al. 2006). These efforts employ ecological, proximate, or systems-based explanations and thus are only part of the answer.

Testing the Selection and Range Expansion Hypothesis

The selection and range-expansion hypothesis to explain Lapita movement to Remote Oceania is currently supported by all relevant empirical observations. While climate change and innovation in voyaging technology lowered the cost of movement for Lapita populations, selection processes related to environmental variation and demography explain the relatively greater rate of Lapita deposition in Remote Oceania. There are several observations that would refute this hypothesis: if the rate at which Lapita deposits are generated in Near and Remote Oceania is, in fact, similar, or the rate is greater in Near Oceania, then selection is not a viable explanation for the range expansion; if subsistence practices during Lapita movement are similar in Near and Remote Oceania, then support for the selection and range-expansion hypothesis is lessened; if the environment and Lapita-era demography of the eastern range margin of Near Oceania is not considerably different from the range core of the Bismarck Archipelago, then the proposal that range expansion is partly explained by environmentally based selection is questionable.

One proximate mechanism not considered here is the right of primogeniture, a possible social trigger (Lidicker 1975). Individuals who might benefit less from primogeniture—second and later sons, for example—could colonize and claim new lands and thereby gain economic power and social status (Bellwood 1996). Earle and Spriggs (2015: 522) make a similar argument based on individuals' desire for power and control of voyaging knowledge, and see "Lapita [maritime culture] as a competitive and rather accessible political forum that was the engine driving rapid colonization of the Pacific Islands." Bell et al.'s (2015) recent Bayesian model–selection analysis suggests such a social trigger was not as important as other processes in the Lapita range expansion, but perhaps future work linking variation in primogeniture processes with empirical expectations will change this.

As an alternative to the selection and range-expansion hypothesis, saturation dispersal might explain the Lapita movement to Remote Oceania. Selection-driven saturation dispersal requires a one-way movement of individuals to another home range, discontinuous with the previous one. Straightaway, this does not likely explain Lapita movement, as the Near and Remote Oceanic Lapita ranges were not discontinuous and movement appears to have been two-way. Disregarding this for the sake of illustration, saturation dispersal requires that there is increased fitness for dispersing relative to nondispersing and this is typically conceptualized in the context of ecological competition as dispersers remove themselves from competitive contexts. This leads to a relevant question: was there increased competition for resources in Near Oceania around the time of Lapita? There is, in fact, little evidence for increasing competition within Near Oceania at this time from faunal (Spriggs 1991; Steadman 2006; Steadman et al. 1999; Wickler 2001) or paleoenvironmental records (compare Pope and Terrell 2008); however, the data are very sparse. While saturation dispersal does not seem a likely alternative explanation, other research, including archaeological simulation (for example, Turchin et al. 2013) could lead to rejection of the selection driven range expansion explanation.

Conclusion

It is the use of theoretical evolutionary concepts and linked empirical evaluation that allows us to both compare research on Lapita movement to other population movements in a consistent and cumulative sense, and to generate cascading empirical implications of the explanatory processes we propose. Cumulative, in this context, means that research results are mutually compatible, and perhaps combinable in a way that leads to new insights. For example, advection is suggested in the movement of Lapita populations south to north across Tonga and perhaps into Sāmoa. This is compatible with analyses that explain Lapita assemblage decorative similarities using transmission and phylogenetic models, which also suggest cultural relatedness between southern Tonga, northern Tonga, and Sāmoa (Cochrane 2013; Cochrane and Lipo 2010).

Leaving islands and broadening to evolutionary research in other geographies can lead to global insights. For example, advection likely explains the movement of Bantu speakers from West Central Africa who followed routes privileging savannah corridors (Grollemund et al. 2015), agricultural populations moving into Europe (Silva and Steele 2014), and Paleoindians into North America (Chaput et al. 2015). Although the movement types and proximate and ultimate mechanisms need to be proposed for each case, advection may be a fundamental process in human movement, and one that can help explain and predict modern population movements as well (Abel and Sander 2014).

Note

1. Following convention, Bayesian modeled date estimates are presented in italics to distinguish these results from unmodeled dates (see also chapter 7).

References

Abel, G. J., and N. Sander. 2014. Quantifying Global International Migration Flows. *Science* 343(6178): 1520–1522.

Allee, W. C., O. Park, A. E. Emerson, T. Park, and K. P. Schmidt. 1949. *Principles of Animal Ecology.* Philadelphia: W. B. Saunders.

Anderson, A. 2001. Mobility Models of Lapita Migration. In *The Archaeology of Lapita Dispersal in Oceania,* ed. G. A. Clark, A. J. Anderson, and T. S. Vunidilo, 15–23. Canberra: Pandanus Books.

Anderson, A. 2015. Seafaring in Remote Oceania: Traditionalism and Beyond in Maritime Technology and Migration. In *The Oxford Handbook of Prehistoric Oceania,* ed. E. E. Cochrane and T. L. Hunt. Oxford: Oxford University Press.

Anderson, A., S. Bedford, G. R Clark, I. Lilley, C. Sand, G. R. Summerhayes, and R. Torrence. 2001. An Inventory of Lapita Sites Containing Dentate-Stamped Pottery. In *The Archaeology of Lapita Dispersal in Oceania,* ed. G. A. Clark, A. J. Anderson, and T. S. Vunidilo, 1–14. Canberra: Pandanus Books.

Anderson, A., J. Chappell, M. Gagan, and R. Grove. 2006. Prehistoric Maritime Migration in the Pacific Islands: An Hypothesis of ENSO Forcing. *The Holocene* 16(1): 1–6.

Anthony, D. W. 1990. Migration in Archaeology: The Baby and the Bathwater. *American Anthropologist* 92: 895–914.

Atkinson, Q., and R. D. Gray. 2005. Curious Parallels and Curious Connections—Phylogenetic Thinking in Biology and Historical Linguistics. *Systematic Biology* 54: 513.

Baker, R. R. 1978. *The Evolutionary Ecology of Animal Migration.* London: Hodder and Stoughton.

Bedford, S., and C. Sand. 2007. Lapita and Western Pacific Settlement: Progress, Prospects and Persistent Problems. In *Oceanic Explorations: Lapita and Western Pacific Settlement,* ed. S. Bedford, C. Sand, and S. P. Connaughton, 1–16. Terra Australis 26. Canberra: ANU E Press.

Bedford, S., R. Blust, D. V. Burley, M. P. Cox, P. V. Kirch, E. Matisoo-Smith, Å. Næss, A. Pawley, C. Sand, and P. Sheppard. 2018. Ancient DNA and Its Contribution to Understanding the Human History of the Pacific Islands. *Archaeology in Oceania* 53(3): 205–219.

Bell, A. V., T. E. Currie, G. Irwin, and C. Bradbury. 2015. Driving Factors in the Colonization of Oceania: Developing Island-Level Statistical Models to Test Competing Hypotheses. *American Antiquity* 80(2): 397–407.

Bellwood, P. 1996. Hierarchy, Founder Ideology and Austronesian Expansion. In *Origins, Ancestry, and Alliance: Explorations in Austronesian Ethnography,* ed. J. J. Fox and C. Sather, 19–41. Canberra: Australian National University.

Benton, T. G., and D. E. Bowler. 2012. Linking Dispersal to Spatial Dynamics. In *Dispersal Ecology and Evolution,* ed. J. Clobert, J. Baguette, T. G. Benton, and J. M. Bullock, 251–265. Oxford: Oxford University Press.

Bettinger, R. L. 1991. *Hunter-Gatherers: Archaeological and Evolutionary Theory.* New York: Plenum Press.

Bonte, D., H. Van Dyck, J. M. Bullock, A. Coulon, M. Delgado, M. Gibbs, V. Lehouck, E. Matthysen, K. Mustin, M. Saastamoinen, N. Schtickzelle, V. M. Stevens, S. Vandewoestijne, M.

Baguette, K. Barton, T. G. Benton, A. Chaput-Bardy, J. Clobert, C. Dytham, T. Hovestadt, C. M. Meier, S.C.F. Palmer, C. Turlure, and J.M.J. Travis. 2012. Costs of Dispersal. *Biological Reviews* 87(2): 290–312.

Boyd, R., and P. J. Richerson. 1985. *Culture and the Evolutionary Process.* Chicago: University of Chicago Press.

Boyd, R., and P. J. Richerson. 2002. Group Beneficial Norms Can Spread Rapidly in a Structured Population. *Journal of Theoretical Biology* 215: 287–216.

Brooks, D. R., and D. A. McLennan. 1991. *Phylogeny, Ecology, and Behavior: A Research Program in Comparative Biology.* Chicago: University of Chicago Press.

Burley, D. V. 2007. Archaeological Demography and Population Growth in the Kingdom of Tonga. In *The Growth and Collapse of Pacific Island Societies,* ed. P. V. Kirch and J.-L. Rallu, 177–202. Honolulu: University of Hawaii Press.

Burley, D. V. 2012. Exploration as a Strategic Process in the Lapita Settlement of Fiji: The Implications of Vorovoro Island. *Journal of Pacific Archaeology* 3(1): 22–34.

Burley, D. V., and W. R. Dickinson. 2010. Among Polynesia's First Pots. *Journal of Archaeological Science* 37(5): 1020–1026.

Burley, D. V., K. Edinborough, M. Weisler, and J.-x. Zhao. 2015. Bayesian Modeling and Chronological Precision for Polynesian Settlement of Tonga. *PLoS ONE* 10(3): e0120795.

Butler, V. L. 1988. Lapita Fishing Strategies: The Faunal Evidence. In *Archaeology of the Lapita Cultural Complex: A Critical Review,* ed. P. V. Kirch and T. L. Hunt, 99–116. Thomas Burke Memorial Washington State Museum Research Report 5. Seattle: Thomas Burke Memorial Washington State Museum.

Carson, M. T., H.-c. Hung, G. R. Summerhayes, and P. Bellwood. 2013. The Pottery Trail from Southeast Asia to Remote Oceania. *Journal of Island and Coastal Archaeology* 8(1): 17–36.

Cavalli-Sforza, L. L., and M. W. Feldman. 1981. *Cultural Transmission and Evolution: A Quantitative Approach.* Monographs in Population Biology. Princeton: Princeton University Press.

Cavalli-Sforza, L. L., P. Menozzi, and A. Piazza. 1994. *The History and Geography of Human Genes.* Princeton: Princeton University Press.

Chaput, M. A., B. Kriesche, M. Betts, A. Martindale, R. Kulik, V. Schmidt, and K. Gajewski. 2015. Spatiotemporal Distribution of Holocene Populations in North America. *Proceedings of the National Academy of Sciences* 112(39): 12127–12132.

Clark, G. A. 1994. Migration as an Explanatory Concept in Paleolithic Archaeology. *Journal of Archaeological Method and Theory* 1(4): 305–343.

Clark, G. R., and A. Anderson. 2001. "The Pattern of Lapita Settlement in Fiji." *Archaeology in Oceania* 36(2): 77–88.

Clark, G. R., C. Reepmeyer, N. Melekiola, J. Woodhead, W. R. Dickinson, and H. Martinsson-Wallin. 2014. Stone Tools from the Ancient Tongan State Reveal Prehistoric Interaction Centers in the Central Pacific. *Proceedings of the National Academy of Sciences* 111(29): 10491–10496.

Clark, J. T., S. J. Quintus, M. Weisler, E. St. Pierre, L. Nothdurft, and Y. Feng. 2016. Refining the Chronology for West Polynesian Colonization: New Data from the Sāmoan Archipelago. *Journal of Archaeological Science: Reports* 6: 266–274.

Cochrane, E. E. 2002a. Explaining the Prehistory of Ceramic Technology on Waya Island, Fiji. *Archaeology in Oceania* 37(1): 37–50.

Cochrane, E. E. 2002b. Separating Time and Space in Archaeological Landscapes: An Example from Windward Society Islands Ceremonial Architecture. In *Pacific Landscapes: Archaeological Approaches,* ed. T. N. Ladefoged and M. W. Graves, 189–209. Los Osos: Easter Island Foundation Press.

Cochrane, E. E. 2008. Migration and Cultural Transmission: Investigating Human Movement as an Explanation for Fijian Ceramic Change. In *Cultural Transmission in Archaeology: Issues and Case Studies*, ed. M. J. O'Brien, 132–145. Washington D.C.: Society for American Archaeology.

Cochrane, E. E. 2013. Quantitative Phylogenetic Analysis of Lapita Decoration in Near and Remote Oceania. In *Pacific Archaeology: Documenting the Past 50,000 Years*, ed. G. R. Summerhayes and H. Buckley, 17–42. University of Otago Studies in Archaeology 25. Dunedin, New Zealand: University of Otago.

Cochrane, E. E. 2018. The Evolution of Migration: The Case of Lapita in the Southwest Pacific. *Journal of Archaeological Method and Theory* 25(2): 520–558.

Cochrane, E. E., H. Kane, C. Fletcher, M. Horrocks, J. Mills, M. Barbee, A. E. Morrison, and M. M. Tautunu. 2016. Lack of Suitable Coastal Plains Likely Influenced Lapita (~2800 cal. BP) Settlement of Sāmoa: Evidence from Southeastern 'Upolu. *The Holocene* 26(1): 126–135.

Cochrane, E. E., and C. P. Lipo. 2010. Phylogenetic Analyses of Lapita Decoration Do Not Support Branching Evolution or Regional Population Structure during Colonization of Remote Oceania. *Philosophical Transactions of the Royal Society B: Biological Sciences* 365(1559): 3889–3902.

Cochrane, E. E., and T. M. Rieth. 2016. Sāmoan Artefact Provenance Reveals Limited Artefact Transfer within and beyond the Archipelago. *Archaeology in Oceania* 51(2): 150–157.

Cochrane, E. E., T. M. Rieth, and W. R. Dickinson. 2013. Plainware Ceramics from Sāmoa: Insights into Ceramic Chronology, Cultural Transmission, and Selection among Colonizing Populations. *Journal of Anthropological Archaeology* 32(4): 499–510.

Courchamp, F., T. Clutton-Brock, and B. Grenfell. 1999. Inverse Density Dependence and the Allee effect. *Trends in Ecology & Evolution* 14(10): 405–410.

Cox, G. W. 1968. The Role of Competition in the Evolution of Migration. *Evolution* 22: 180–192.

Crema, E. R., A. Bevan, and M. W. Lake. 2010. A Probabilistic Framework for Assessing Spatiotemporal Point Patterns in the Archaeological Record. *Journal of Archaeological Science* 37: 1118–1130.

Crozier, L., and G. Dwyer. 2006. Combining Population-dynamic and Ecophysiological Models to Predict Climate-induced Insect Range Shifts. *American Naturalist* 167(6): 853–866.

David, B., I. J. McNiven, T. Richards, S. P. Connaughton, M. Leavesley, B. Barker, and C. Rowe. 2011. Lapita Sites in the Central Province of Mainland Papua New Guinea. *World Archaeology* 43(4): 576–593.

Dickinson, W. R. 2006. *Temper Sands in Prehistoric Oceanian Pottery: Geotectonics, Sedimentology, Petrography, and Provenance*. Special Paper. Boulder: Geological Society of America.

Di Piazza, A., P. Di Piazza, and E. Pearthree. 2007. "Sailing Virtual Canoes across Oceania: Revisiting Island Accessibility." *Journal of Archaeological Science* 34(8): 1219–1225.

Dunkley, P. N. 1986. *The Geology of the New Georgia Group, Western Solomon Islands*. Submitted to British Geological Survey Overseas Directorate, Keyworth, Nottinghamshire, Great Britain.

Dunnell, R. C. 1980. Evolutionary Theory and Archaeology. In *Advances in Archaeological Method and Theory 3*, ed. M. B. Schiffer, 35–99. New York: Academic Press.

Duputié, A., and F. Massol. 2013. An Empiricist's Guide to Theoretical Predictions on the Evolution of Dispersal. *Interface Focus* 3(6).

Earle, T., and M. Spriggs. 2015. Political Economy in Prehistory: A Marxist Approach to Pacific Sequences. *Current Anthropology* 56(4): 515–544.

Fall, P. 2010. Pollen Evidence for Plant Introductions in a Polynesian Tropical Island Ecosystem, Kingdom of Tonga. In *Altered Ecologies: Fire, climate and human influence on terrestrial landscapes*, ed. S. G. Haberle, J. Stevenson, and M. Prebble, 253–271. Terra Australis 32. Canberra: Australia National University.

Feathers, J. K. 2006. Explaining Shell-Tempered Pottery in Prehistoric Eastern North America. *Journal of Archaeological Method and Theory* 13(2): 89–133.

Gray, R. D., A. J. Drummond, and S. J. Greenhill. 2009. Language Phylogenies Reveal Expansion Pulses and Pauses in Pacific Settlement. *Science* 323(5913): 479–483.

Green, R. C. 1979. Lapita. In *The Prehistory of Polynesia*, ed. J. D. Jennings, 27–60. Cambridge: Harvard University Press.

Green, R. C. 1991a. The Lapita Cultural Context: Current Evidence and Proposed Models. *Bulletin of the Indo-Pacific Prehistory Association* 11: 295–305.

Green, R. C. 1991b. Near and Remote Oceania: Disestablishing 'Melanesia' in Culture History. In *Man and a Half: Essays in Pacific Anthropology and Ethnobiology in Honour of Ralph Bulmer*, ed. A. K. Pawley, 491–502. Auckland: Polynesian Society.

Green, R. C. 2002. A Retrospective View of Settlement Pattern Studies in Sāmoa. In *Pacific Landscapes: Archaeological Approaches*, ed. T. N. Ladefoged and M. W. Graves, 125–152. Los Osos: Easter Island Foundation Press.

Grimes, S. L. 2003. A History of Environmental Change and Human Impact since 3750 BP in the New Georgia Group, Western Solomon Islands. PhD thesis, University of Western Australia, Perth.

Grollemund, R., S. Branford, K. Bostoen, A. Meade, C. Venditti, and M. Pagel. 2015. Bantu Expansion Shows That Habitat Alters the Route and Pace of Human Dispersals. *Proceedings of the National Academy of Sciences* 112(43): 13296–13301.

Groube, L. 1971. Tonga, Lapita Pottery, and Polynesian Origins. *Journal of the Polynesian Society* 80: 278–316.

Haberle, S. 1996. Explanations for Palaeoecological Changes on the Northern Plains of Guadalcanal, Solomon Islands: The Last 3200 years. *The Holocene* 6(3): 333–338.

Hamilton, W. D., and R. D. May. 1977. Dispersal in Stable Habitats. *Nature* 269: 578–581.

Harris, D. N., M. D. Kessler, A. C. Shetty, D. E. Weeks, R. L. Minster, S. Browning, E. E. Cochrane, R. Deka, N. L. Hawley, M. a. S. Reupena, T. Naseri, S. T. McGarvey, and T. D. O'Connor 2020). "Evolutionary history of modern Samoans." *Proceedings of the National Academy of Sciences* 117(17): 9458–9465.

Hawkins, S., T. H. Worthy, S. Bedford, M. Spriggs, G. R. Clark, G. Irwin, S. Best, and P. Kirch. 2016. Ancient Tortoise Hunting in the Southwest Pacific. *Scientific Reports* 6: 38317.

Hengeveld, Rob. 1989. *Dynamics of Biological Invasions*. New York: Chapman and Hall.

Holden, C. J. 2002. Bantu Language Trees Reflect the Spread of Farming across Sub-Saharan Africa: A Maximum-Parsimony Analysis. *Proceedings of the Royal Society of London B: Biological Sciences* 269(1493): 793–799.

Horrocks, M., and S. Bedford. 2005. Microfossil Analysis of Lapita Deposits in Vanuatu Reveals Introduced Araceae (Aroids). *Archaeology in Oceania* 40(2): 67–74.

Horrocks, M., and P. D. Nunn. 2007. Evidence for Introduced Taro (*Colocasia esculenta*) and Lesser Yam (*Dioscorea esculenta*) in Lapita-era (c. 3050–2500 cal. yr BP) Deposits from Bourewa, Southwest Viti Levu Island, Fiji. *Journal of Archaeological Science* 34: 739–748.

Horrocks, M., S. Bedford, and M. Spriggs. 2009. A Short Note on Banana (*Musa*) Phytoliths in Lapita, Immediately Post-Lapita and Modern Period Archaeological Deposits from Vanuatu. *Journal of Archaeological Science* 36(9): 2048–2054.

Horrocks, M., M. K. Nieuwoudt, R. Kinaston, H. Buckley, and S. Bedford. 2013. Microfossil and Fourier Transform InfraRed Analyses of Lapita and Post-Lapita Human Dental Calculus from Vanuatu, Southwest Pacific. *Journal of the Royal Society of New Zealand* 44(1): 17–33.

Humphries, N. E., and D. W. Sims. 2014. Optimal Foraging Strategies: Lévy Walks Balance Searching and Patch Exploitation under a Very Broad Range of Conditions. *Journal of Theoretical Biology* 358: 179–193.

Irwin, G. 1989. Against, Across and Down the Wind: A Case for the Systematic Exploration of the Remote Pacific Islands. *Journal of the Polynesian Society* 98(2): 167–206.

Irwin, G. 1992. *The Prehistoric Exploration and Colonization of the Pacific.* Cambridge: Cambridge University Press.

Irwin, G. 2008. Pacific Seascapes, Canoe Performance, and a Review of Lapita Voyaging with Regard to Theories of Migration. *Asian Perspectives* 47(1): 12–28.

Irwin, G., T. H. Worthy, S. Best, S. Hawkins, J. Carpentar, and S. Matararaba. 2011. Further Investigations at the Naigani Lapita site (VL 21/5), Fiji: Excavation, Radiocarbon Dating and Palaeofaunal Extinction. *Journal of Pacific Archaeology* 2(2): 66–78.

Johnson, M. L., and M. S. Gaines. 1990. Evolution of Dispersal: Theoretical Models and Empirical Tests Using Birds and Mammals. *Annual Review of Ecology and Systematics* 21: 449–480.

Keegan, W. F. 1995. Modelling Dispersal in the Prehistoric West Indies. *World Archaeology* 26(3): 400–420.

Keegan, W. F., and J. M. Diamond. 1987. Colonization of Islands by Humans: A Biogeographical Perspective. *Advances in Archaeological Method and Theory* 10: 49–92.

Kennett, D. J., A. Anderson, and B. Winterhalder. 2006. The Ideal Free Distribution, Food Production, and the Colonization of Oceania. In *Behavioral Ecology and the Transition to Agriculture,* ed. D. J. Kennett and B. Winterhalder, 265–288. Berkleley: University of California Press.

Kinaston, R. L., S. Bedford, M. Spriggs, D. Anson, and H. Buckley. 2016. Is There a "Lapita Diet"? A Comparison of Lapita and Post-Lapita Skeletal Samples from Four Pacific Island Archaeological Sites. In *The Routledge Handbook of Bioarchaeology in Southeast Asia and the Pacific Islands,* ed. H. Buckley and M. Oxenham, 427–461. London: Routledge.

Kirch, P. V. 1997. *The Lapita Peoples.* Cambridge: Blackwell.

Kirch, P. V. 2010. Peopling of the Pacific: A Holistic Anthropological Perspective. *Annual Review of Anthropology* 39(1): 131–148.

Koykka, C., and G. Wild. 2015. The Evolution of Group Dispersal with Leaders and Followers. *Journal of Theoretical Biology* 371: 117–126.

Kubisch, A., E. A. Fronhofer, H. J. Poethke, and T. Hovestadt. 2013. Kin Competition as a Major Driving Force for Invasions. *American Naturalist* 181(5): 700–706.

Laland, K. N., K. Sterelny, J. Odling-Smee, W. Hoppitt, and T. Uller. 2011. Cause and Effect in Biology Revisited: Is Mayr's Proximate-Ultimate Dichotomy Still Useful? *Science* 334(6062): 1512–1516.

Laland, K. N., T. Uller, M. W. Feldman, K. Sterelny, G. B. Müller, A. Moczek, E. Jablonka, and J. Odling-Smee. 2015. The Extended Evolutionary Synthesis: Its Structure, Assumptions and Predictions. *Proceedings of the Royal Society of London B: Biological Sciences* 282(1813): 20151019.

Lentfer, C. J., and R. Torrence. 2007. Holocene Volcanic Activity, Vegetation Succession, and Ancient Human Land Use: Unraveling the Interactions on Garua Island, Papua New Guinea. *Review of Palaeobotany and Palynology* 143(3–4): 83–105.

Levin, S. A., D. Cohen, and A. Hastings. 1984. Dispersal Strategies in Patchy Environments. *Theoretical Population Biology* 26(2): 165–191.

Lidicker, W. Z., Jr. 1975. The Role of Dispersal in the Demography of Small Mammals. *Small Mammals: Their Productivity and Population Dynamics* 5: 103–128.

Lidicker, W. Z., Jr., and N. C. Stenseth. 1992. To Disperse or Not to Disperse: Who Does It and Why? In *Animal Dispersal: Small Mammals as a Model,* ed. N. C. Stenseth and W. Z. Lidicker, Jr., 21–36. Dordrecht: Springer.

Lilley, I. 2008. Flights of Fancy: Fractal Geometry, the Lapita Dispersal and Punctuated Colonization in the Pacific. In *Islands of Inquiry: Colonization, Seafaring, and the Archaeology of Maritime Landscapes,* ed. G. Clark, F. Leach, and S. O'Conner, 75–86. Terra Australis 29. Canberra: Australian National University.

Lipo, C. P., M. Madsen, R. C. Dunnell, and T. Hunt. 1997. Population Structure, Cultural Transmission, and Frequency Seriation. *Journal of Anthropological Archaeology* 16(4): 301–333.

Lycett, S. J. 2015. Cultural Evolutionary Approaches to Artifact Variation over Time and Space: Basis, Progress, and Prospects. *Journal of Archaeological Science* 56: 21–31.

MacArthur, R. H. and E. O. Wilson. 1963. "An equilibrium theory of insular zoogeography." *Evolution* 17: 373–387.

MacArthur, R. and E. Wilson. 1967. *The Theory of Island Biogeography.* Princeton: Princeton University Press.

Madsen, M., C. P. Lipo, and M. Cannon. 1999. Reproductive Tradeoffs in Uncertain Environments: Explaining the Evolution of Cultural Elaboration. *Journal of Anthropological Archaeology* 18: 251–281.

Manne, T., B. David, F. Petchey, M. Leavesley, G. Roberts, K. Szabó, C. Urwin, I. J. McNiven, and T. Richards. 2020. "How long have dogs been in Melanesia? New evidence from Caution Bay, south coast of Papua New Guinea." *Journal of Archaeological Science: Reports* 30: 102255.

Matisoo-Smith, E. A. 2007. Animal Translocations, Genetic Variation and the Human Settlement of the Pacific. In *Genes, Language and Culture History in the Southwest Pacific,* ed. J. S. Friedlaender, 157–170. Oxford: Oxford University Press.

Matthysen, E. 2012. Multicausality of Dispersal: A Review. In *Dispersal Ecology and Evolution,* ed. J. Clobert, J. Baguette, T. G. Benton, and J. M. Bullock, 3–18. Oxford: Oxford University Press.

McElreath, R., R. Boyd, and P. J. Richerson. 2003. Shared Norms and the Evolution of Ethnic Markers. *Current Anthropology* 44(1): 122–129.

Mesoudi, A. 2011. *Cultural Evolution: How Darwinian Theory Can Explain Human Culture & Synthesize the Social Sciences.* Chicago: University of Chicago Press.

Miller, D., and D. Roe. 1982. The Solomon Islands National Sites Survey: The First Phase. *Indo-Pacific Prehistory Association Bulletin* 3(46–51).

Morrison, A. E. 2012. An Archaeological Analysis of Rapa Nui Settlement Structure: A Multi-Scalar Approach. PhD dissertation, University of Hawaii, Honolulu.

Nagaoka, L. 1988. Lapita Subsistence: The Evidence of Non-fish Archaeofaunal Remains. In *Archaeology of the Lapita Cultural Complex: A Critical Review,* ed. P. V. Kirch and T. L. Hunt, 17–134. Thomas Burke Memorial Washington State Museum Research Report 5. Seattle: Thomas Burke Memorial Washington State Museum.

Neiman, F. 1995. Stylistic Variation in Evolutionary Perspective: Inferences from Decorative Diversity and Interassemblage Distance in Illinois Woodland Ceramic Assemblages. *American Antiquity* 60(1): 7–36.

O'Brien, M. J., T. D. Holland, R. J. Hoard, and G. L. Fox. 1994. Evolutionary Implications of Design and Performance Characteristics of Prehistoric Pottery. *Journal of Archaeological Method and Theory* 1: 259–304.

O'Brien, M. J., and R. L. Lyman. 2000. *Applying Evolutionary Archaeology: A Systematic Approach.* New York: Kluwer Academic/Plenum.

O'Brien, M. J., M. T. Boulanger, B. Buchanan, R. A. Bentley, R. L. Lyman, C. P. Lipo, M. E. Madsen, and M. I. Eren. 2016. Design Space and Cultural Transmission: Case Studies from Paleoindian Eastern North America. *Journal of Archaeological Method and Theory* 23(2): 692–740.

O'Brien, M. J., and K. N. Laland. 2012. Genes, Culture, and Agriculture: An Example of Human Niche Construction. *Current Anthropology* 53(4): 434–470.

O'Connell, J. F., and J. Allen. 2012. The Restaurant at the End of the Universe: Modelling the Colonisation of Sahul. *Australian Archaeology* (74): 5–31.

Parenti, L., and M. Ebach. 2009. *Comparative Biogeography*. Oakland: University of California Press.

Pérez-Losada, J., and J. Fort. 2011. Spatial Dimensions Increase the Effect of Cultural Drift. *Journal of Archaeological Science* 38(6): 1294–1299.

Pétrequin, P. 1993. North Wind, South Wind: Neolithic Technical Choices in the Jura Mountains, 3700–2400 BC. In *Technological Choices*, ed. P. Lemonnier, 36–76. London: Routledge.

Pierce, C. 2005. Reverse Engineering the Ceramic Cooking Pot: Cost and Performance Properties of Plain and Textured Vessels. *Journal of Archaeological Method and Theory* 12(2): 117.

Pigliucci, M., and G. B. Muller (eds). 2010. *Evolution—The Extended Synthesis*. Cambridge: MIT Press.

Plantegenest, M., and P. Kindlmann. 1999. Evolutionarily Stable Strategies of Migration in Heterogeneous Environments. *Evolutionary Ecology* 13: 229–244.

Pope, K. O., and J. E. Terrell. 2008. Environmental Setting of Human Migrations in the Circum-Pacific Region. *Journal of Biogeography* 35(1): 1–21.

Porčić, M. 2015. Exploring the Effects of Assemblage Accumulation on Diversity and Innovation Rate Estimates in Neutral, Conformist, and Anti-Conformist Models of Cultural Transmission. *Journal of Archaeological Method and Theory* 22(4): 1071–1092.

Powell, J. M. 1976. Pollen, Plant Communities, and Prehistory in the Solomon Islands. In *Southeast Solomon Islands Cultural History*, ed. R. C. Green and M. M. Cresswell, 75–105. Bulletin 11. Wellington: Royal Society of New Zealand.

Premo, L. S. 2014. Cultural Transmission and Diversity in Time-Averaged Assemblages. *Current Anthropology* 55(1): 105–114.

Reepmeyer, C., G. R. Clark, and P. J. Sheppard. 2012. Obsidian Source Use in Tongan Prehistory: New Results and Implications. *Journal of Island and Coastal Archaeology* 7(2): 255–271.

Ridley, M. 2012. Invading Together: The Benefits of Coalition Dispersal in a Cooperative Bird. *Behavioral Ecology and Sociobiology* 66(1): 77–83.

Rieth, T. M., and J. S. Athens. 2019. Late Holocene Human Expansion into Near and Remote Oceania: A Bayesian Model of the Chronologies of the Mariana Islands and Bismarck Archipelago. *Journal of Island and Coastal Archaeology* 14(1): 5–16.

Rogers, D. S., and P. R. Ehrlich. 2008. Natural Selection and Cultural Rates of Change. *Proceedings of the National Academy of Sciences* 105(9): 3416–3420.

Russell, T., F. Silva, and J. Steele. 2014. Modelling the Spread of Farming in the Bantu-Speaking Regions of Africa: An Archaeology-Based Phylogeography. *PLoS ONE* 9(1): e87854.

Schiffer, M. B., and J. Skibo. 1997. The Explanation of Artifact Variability. *American Antiquity* 62: 27–50.

Shennan, S. 2000. Population, Culture History, and the Dynamics of Culture Change. *Current Anthropology* 41(5): 811–835.

Shennan, S. 2002. *Genes, Memes, and Human History: Darwinian Archaeology and Cultural Evolution*. London: Thames and Hudson.

Shennan, S. 2011. Descent with Modification and the Archaeological Record. *Philosophical Transactions of the Royal Society B: Biological Sciences* 366(1567): 1070–1079.

Sheppard, P. J. 2011. Lapita Colonization across the Near/Remote Oceania Boundary. *Current Anthropology* 52(6): 799–840.

Sheppard, P. J., S. Chiu, and R. Walter. 2015. Re-dating Lapita Movement into Remote Oceania. *Journal of Pacific Archaeology* 6(1): 26–36.

Silva, F., and J. Steele. 2014. New Methods for Reconstructing Geographical Effects on Dispersal Rates and Routes from Large-Scale Radiocarbon Databases. *Journal of Archaeological Science* 52: 609–620.

Simmons, A. D., and C. D. Thomas. 2004. Changes in Dispersal during Species' Range Expansions. *American Naturalist* 164(3): 378–395.

Specht, J., and C. Gosden. 1997. Dating Lapita Pottery in the Bismarck Archipelago, Papua New Guinea. *Asian Perspectives* 36(2): 175–199.

Specht, J., T. P. Denham, J. Goff, and J. E. Terrell. 2013. Deconstructing the Lapita Cultural Complex in the Bismarck Archipelago. *Journal of Archaeological Research* 22: 89–140.

Spriggs, M. 1984. The Lapita Cultural Complex: Origins, Distribution, Contemporaries, and Successors. *Journal of Pacific History* 19: 202–223.

Spriggs, M. 1991. Nissan, the Island in the Middle. Summary Report on Excavations at the North End of the Solomons and the South End of the Bismarcks. In *Report of the Lapita Homeland Project*, ed. J. Allen, and C. Gosden, 222–243. Occasional Papers in Prehistory, Vol. 20. Canberra: Australian National University.

Steadman, D. W. 2006. *Extinction and Biogeography of Tropical Pacific Birds.* Chicago: University of Chicago Press.

Steadman, D. W., J. P. White, and J. Allen. 1999. Prehistoric Birds from New Ireland, Papua New Guinea: Extinctions on a Large Melanesian Island. *Proceedings of the National Academy of Sciences* 96(5): 2563–2568.

Steadman, D. W., A. Plourde, and D. V. Burley. 2002. Prehistoric Butchery and Consumption of Birds in the Kingdom of Tonga, South Pacific. *Journal of Archaeological Science* 29(6): 571–584.

Steele, J. 2009. Human Dispersals: Mathematical Models and the Archaeological Record. *Human Biology* 81(2–3): 121–140.

Stenseth, N. C., and W. Z. Lidicker, Jr. 1992. Presaturation and Saturation Dispersal 15 Years Later: Some Theoretical Considerations. In *Animal Dispersal: Small Mammals as a Model*, ed. N. C. Stenseth and W. Z. Lidicker Jr., 201–223. Dordrecht: Springer.

Summerhayes, G. R. 2001. Far Western, Western, and Eastern Lapita: A Re-Evaluation. *Asian Perspectives* 39(1–2): 109–138.

Summerhayes, G. R., M. Leavesley, A. Fairbairn, H. Mandui, J. Field, A. Ford, and R. Fullagar. 2010. Human Adaptation and Plant Use in Highland New Guinea 49,000 to 44,000 Years Ago. *Science* 330(6000): 78–81.

Summerhayes, G. R., K. Szabó, A. Fairbain, M. Horrocks, S. McPherson, and A. Crowther. 2019. Early Lapita Subsistence: The Evidence from Kamgot, Anir Islands, New Ireland Province, Papua New Guinea. In *Debating Lapita: Distribution, Chronology, Society and Subsistence*, ed. S. Bedford and M Spriggs, 379–402. Terra Australis 52. Acton: ANU Press.

Tehrani, J. J., and F. Riede. 2008. Towards an Archaeology of Pedagogy: Learning, Teaching and the Generation of Material Culture Traditions. *World Archaeology* 40(3): 316–331.

Terrell, J. E., and R. L. Welsch. 1997. Lapita and the Temporal Geography of Prehistory. *Antiquity* 71: 548–572.

Travis, J. M. J., K. Mustin, K. A. Bartoń, T. G. Benton, J. Clobert, M. M. Delgado, C. Dytham, T. Hovestadt, S.C.F. Palmer, H. Van Dyck, and D. Bonte. 2012. Modelling Dispersal: An Eco-evolutionary Framework Incorporating Emigration, Movement, Settlement Behaviour and the Multiple Costs Involved. *Methods in Ecology and Evolution* 3(4): 628–641.

Turchin, P., T. E. Currie, E.A.L. Turner, and S. Gavrilets. 2013. War, Space, and the Evolution of Old World Complex Societies. *Proceedings of the National Academy of Sciences* 110(41): 16384–16389.

Valentin, F., H. R. Buckley, E. Herrscher, R. Kinaston, S. Bedford, M. Spriggs, S. Hawkins, and K. Neal. 2010. Lapita Subsistence Strategies and Food Consumption Patterns in the Community of Teouma (Efate, Vanuatu). *Journal of Archaeological Science* 37(8): 1820–1829.

Walter, R., and P. Sheppard. 2017. *Archaeology of the Solomon Islands*. Dunedin, New Zealand: Otago University Press.

White, A. W., T. H. Worthy, S. Hawkins, S. Bedford, and M. Spriggs. 2010. Megafaunal Meiolaniid Horned Turtles Survived until Early Human Settlement in Vanuatu, Southwest Pacific. *Proceedings of the National Academy of Sciences* 107(35): 15512–15516.

Whiten, A., R. A. Hinde, K. N. Laland, and C. B. Stringer. 2011. Culture Evolves. *Philosophical Transactions of the Royal Society B: Biological Sciences* 366(1567): 938–948.

Wickler, S. 2001. *The Prehistory of Buka: A Stepping Stone Island in the Northern Solomons*. Terra Australis 16. Canberra: Australian National University.

Winder, I. C., M. H. Devès, G.C.P. King, G. N. Bailey, R. H. Inglis, and M. Meredith-Williams. 2015. Evolution and Dispersal of the Genus *Homo*: A Landscape Approach. *Journal of Human Evolution* 87: 48–65.

Winter, O., G. R. Clark, A. Anderson, and A. Lindahl. 2012. Austronesian Sailing to the Northern Marianas, a Comment on Hung et al. (2011). *Antiquity* 86: 898–914.

Worthy, T. H., and A. Anderson. 2009. Bird, Mammal and Reptile Remains. In *The Early Prehistory of Fiji*, ed. G. Clark and A. Anderson, 231–258, Terra Australis 31. Canberra: Australian National University.

Zedeño, M. N. 1995. The Role of Population Movement and Technology Transfer in the Manufacture of Prehistoric Southwestern Ceramics. In *Ceramic Production in the American Southwest*, ed. B. J. Mills, and P. L. Crown, 115–141. Tuscon: University of Arizona Press.

3

Temporal Systematics

The Colonization of Rapa Nui (Easter Island) and the Conceptualization of Time

CARL P. LIPO, TERRY L. HUNT, AND ROBERT J. DINAPOLI

The real problem in speech is not precise language.
The problem is clear language.

Richard Feynman (1965)

All aspects of measuring the archaeological record involve numbers, and a knowledge of mathematics is essential for any counting and subsequent statistical evaluation. While we often associate mathematics with numbers, the *values* in an equation are not central to its purpose. Instead, mathematics provides a *language* that carefully distinguishes concepts and explicitly states their relations with other concepts. *Pi*, for example, is the ratio of the circumference of the circle to its radius squared. Values are then assigned to these concepts and can be explained due to the definitions and their properties. This framework uses a metaunderstanding of mathematics but the logic points to one of the reasons that mathematical structures (whether they are equations, chemical formulas, Feynman diagrams, and so on) provide the basis of language for most sciences: *explicitly defined ideas are kept distinct from empirical values*. It is this language that allows scientists to explain topics that lie outside of our common sense. Math provides the language that defines what is "true" in a conceptual sense, regardless of how we assume the world "must be" from our limited personal experiences.

Mathematics is not the only way in which logical structures are formalized and defined. In evolutionary biology and the practice of archaeology, the domain that effectively serves as math is *systematics*. For archaeologists, *archaeological systematics* is the set of rules with which units of meaning are constructed and applied in the explanation of the archaeological record. While attention is given to the role of theory, systematics forms the measurement basis for all our knowledge generation since units are needed to meaningfully describe the archaeological record. Units require theory to stipulate meaning but are also used to measure the empirical world. Thus, they provide a vital link between the empirical and the conceptual—in the same way as mathematics.

It follows then, that the greater the degree to which the process of unit construction is explicit, the more powerful the explanations that can be created. In the emergence of physics and chemistry as scientific disciplines in the late seventeenth century, it was creation of systematics that permitted researchers to go beyond medieval alchemy with its notions of fire, air, earth, and water as the basic elements.[1] In archaeology, measurable success as a discipline has come whenever we are able to incorporate explicit and meaningful units of analyses. The degree to which culture history has been an unqualified success in producing falsifiable chronologies, for example, is largely due to the degree of rigor of formation and testing of archaeological systematics (Dunnell 1986; Lyman et al. 1997). Success as a science is intrinsically linked to systematics.

In archaeological practice, systematics is limited to the construction of classes of discrete-object scale artifacts—for example, "types" of pottery or bifaces. Nevertheless, all our units, conceived at any scale and of any composition, must be considered within the context of systematics. Unlike other scientific disciplines, we lack a mathematical formalization providing an inherent means to distinguish the conceptual from the empirical. Yet, keeping units of measurement separate from the phenomena we are attempting to explain is key to science. In the case of archaeology, our work investigates classes of phenomena intrinsically linked to the past actions of our own species. In this way, our launching point for inquiry is often based on ethnocentric commonsense observations. Thus, the units share their form and meaning with their role as nouns and verbs in one's native language. Though we borrow some concepts and terms from other sciences (for example, radiocarbon), our basic units are derived from common sense. Of course, there have been attempts by some to concoct new terms that are supposed to provide conceptual tools such as Binford's (1962) "technomic" or "ideo-technic" and Schiffer's (2011) "techno-community." But these neologisms are versions of English nouns serving as fancy labels for empirical generalization that are derived from common sense. These terms are jargon, or as Service (1969) has aptly called it, "mouthtalk." With common sense providing the meanings for our basic units, it is not difficult to understand why some of our discipline struggles to produce scientific products. Fundamentally, we work under the tyranny of our native-language nouns that often make no distinction between the definition of a concept and the thing identified as a member of that concept. Our innate languages constrain our ability to construct a means of explaining the archaeological record outside of the limited realms of common sense. Thus, the use of our native language as the sole basis for justifying measurement units effectively traps us in an era analogous to prescience alchemy.

Systematics enables us to move beyond common sense. Culture historians used systematics to develop tools that allowed them to measure and track change through time and across space in the archaeological record (Dunnell 1971, 1986; Lyman et al. 1997). Modes, types, phases, traditions, and horizons are all purposefully constructed units for measuring the archaeological record across time and space.

Unfortunately, a lack of attention to systematics has progressed over time, given a general misunderstanding of the important distinction between theoretical concepts and empirical record. While the recognition of the artificial nature of unit construction was strong at the point in time in which units were built (for example, Phillips et al. 1951), over time the usefulness of the units resulted in them being treated as real (O'Brien et al. 2005). As a consequence, units are now often rationalized using common sense and ad hoc justifications. A means of avoiding this quagmire and moving forward is a renewed emphasis on unit construction and the expansion of archaeological systematics (Dunnell 1971, 1986).

One area where this issue is particularly problematic is island colonization, where our commonsense notions of how the process of initial settlement possibly occurred became conflated with measuring colonization in the archaeological record.

Here, we discuss an example of how careful construction of systematics can substantially change our understanding of the archaeological record using our research in the eastern Pacific and on Rapa Nui (Easter Island) (Figure 3.1). This example is intended to demonstrate how concepts with English language origins result in incorrect conclusions and how these can (and must) be reconstructed into meaningful and useful measurement units. It also highlights the need to consider systematics beyond the construction of classes of discrete-object scale artifacts and into the usage of more general types of nouns. In this example, we explore aspects of a unit related to time: colonization.

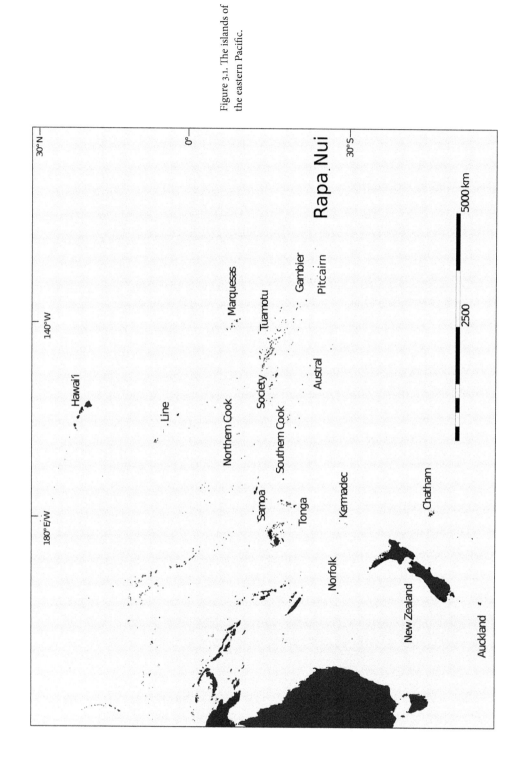

Figure 3.1. The islands of the eastern Pacific.

Units of Time

Time is a slippery dimension for archaeologists (Ramenofsky 1998). We are interested in the archaeological record because it provides information about what occurred in the past, yet the past is not directly observable. The archaeological record has two dimensions, and *only* two dimensions: form and space (Spaulding 1960). Empirically speaking, *what we study has no time dimension;* instead, it only exists in the here and now. The lack of a temporal dimension is true for all of human experience: time is removed from our senses. Instead, time exists only as a calculation we make based on sets of observations in the present. While this statement seems absurdly simple, it is vitally important for understanding the archaeological record. Temporal facts are always based on units that we construct and depend on the questions we ask. Thus, we require an understanding of "temporal systematics." To facilitate our discussion, Table 3.1 consists of a list of terms and their definitions as used in this chapter.

The crux of temporal systematics is the understanding that time can be usefully conceived as a relationship between events. Our common sense tends to distinguish between "events" and "things," where events are something "fleeting," but things are "stable." But this is an arbitrary distinction since things are only stable with respect to our point of view in time. When viewed over long stretches, we can easily see that any one "thing" has coherence over some duration, where that duration is longer than casual observation. "Things" only have coherence as identifiable discrete chunks of matter over the duration of time in which all the constituent ingredients are together. Imagine a chair: a chair only becomes a chair once the leg, seat and back are physically arranged. It no longer meets the definition of a chair once its parts are no longer physically associated. Thus, in the long-term view, things are events. We only distinguish them as "things" due to our own evolution and the scale of our lifespan (or attention span).

It is important to note that "thingness" or "eventness" are ideational classes that form a *classification,* not an empirical property (compare O'Brien and Lyman 2002). Being able to explicitly construct and manipulate this classification is critical to archaeologists because, while we deal with things, we are often interested in events. Differentiating between things and events depends solely upon common-sense conventions, so for the time being we want to talk about the units of the empirical world as *instances* or "uniquenesses" and not get tangled up in the thing-and-event stuff.

Thus, events are simply concoctions of classes, classes with a certain set of attributes that form a unique combination of features and arrangements of phenomena in time (Dunnell 1971). For example, an event might be a particular point in time at which a biface is deposited in a refuse pit. In this way, temporal units are defined on the basis of events. Events are simply configurations of classes and attributes observable in the present, but explicable in terms of time. We know time has passed, for example, by comparing sets of events. The difference between sets of events is then attributable to the passage of time.

To create units of time, we must specify the combination of classes or attribute sets that are necessarily linked to the event of interest. We are most familiar with object-scale events in which we select a set of attributes of an object to use in calculating the amount of time passed for the attributes to be as they are presently measured. Examples of these events include those measured through radiocarbon and luminescence dating. Radiocarbon-age events, for example, are identified through a classification consisting of the abundance of ^{14}C atoms within organic material relative to the ^{14}C content of the atmosphere at the time when the organism was alive. Using these attributes, we can calculate when the organism ceased respiration. Luminescence-age events, in contrast, are measured by classes that consist of the abundance of light released from crystalline forms of some minerals, the amount of ionizing radiation in the local environment, and the rate at which luminescence increases with these minerals as a

Table 3.1. Definition of terms used in the chapter

Term	Definition
Empirical unit	Any specified identified portion of the measurable world
Theoretical units	Conceptual rules for measuring the world
Object-scale events	The point in time when a set of attributes becomes physically associated with a discrete object
Aggregate-scale events	The point in time when a set of discrete objects becomes physically associated
Target event	The event of interest for the investigator (Dean 1978)
Dated event	The event that is physically measured (Dean 1978)
Commonsensical colonization	The imagined point in time that represents the arrival of people in a new location
Archaeological colonization	The first measurable observation in the archaeological record that can only be explained as the result of human activity

Source: Authors, unless otherwise indicated.

function of radiation. Using these dimensions of measurement, we can then calculate the amount of time that has passed for these samples to accumulate the measured amount of luminescence.

Less intuitive are aggregate-scale events that are composed of sets of events at lower scales (Dunnell 1971). Occupation is an example of an aggregate scale event since it consists of the set of all the events that comprise a deposit. At this scale, we must carefully define the events of interest since choices can vary from the determination of when the first member of the set was added to, when the last member of the set was added to, when the modal events became a set—or any other combination. The choice depends on the question asked. Duration is a calculated property of aggregate-scale events as are any questions related to the first measured event (that is, arrival), last event (that is, termination), and rates of change (that is, change of intensity of occupation). Infinitely more attributes of aggregate-scale events can be calculated depending on the question.

Colonization

On the Pacific Islands, one common temporal question relating to the archaeological record is, "When did human populations arrive on a particular island?" Accurate and precise answers to this question are critically important as the timing of arrival forms the basis for all other questions regarding the islands' human history (for example, Allen 2014; Anderson 1995; Burley et al. 2015; Dye 2015; Rieth and Cochrane 2018; Rieth and Hunt 2008; Sear et al. 2020; Spriggs and Anderson 1993). The question of earliest arrival is usually asked in terms of the concept of "colonization." As is unfortunately common in anthropological practice, the term "colonization" is often based on an unanalyzed, intuitive connotation referring to the process wherein people arrive to "live in a new land." Given the word's English origins, colonization is assumed to be an empirical event where a group of people leaving one location with all of their traditions and belongings travel to a new location to take up residence. The assumption that colonization is an empirical event means that it is something we can "find."

While the intuitive "living in a new land" notion appeals to an imagined (that is, *reconstructed*) set of events, colonization does not exist in the archaeological record. As a result, *commonsensical* colonization has no necessary attributes for identification. In its commonsense form, "colonization" is a concept in search of evidence with no necessary and sufficient criteria that can be specified. When conceived this way, notions of colonization tend to lead some to grasp for observations that *might* show human occupation. The determination of commonsense colonization leads to a futile search for something akin to the first human foot-print on an island beach. Is the first step of an individual onto the wet sands of the island the ultimate indicator of colonization? Or is the first cooking fire? Or is the first deposited artifact? Or the first sighting of land? Or the first house constructed? Or the first tree cut down? Or the first persistent settlement occupation? Since our research is limited to what is observable in the archaeological record, such a definition often assumes that the "real" colonization evidence is somehow missing, resulting in a quest for *imaginary* evidence of a fabricated story.

In this way, poorly defined notions used to study the archaeological record lead to assertions of mere plausibility, rather than relying upon empirical standards. Evidence is evaluated on how *plausible* it is relative to archaeological tradition and existing lore that exists about the chronology. A fragment of charcoal found below areas of clear deposits of artifactual material, for example, *could* be evidence related to early colonization. Other material might be rejected simply because it is "way too old" (that is, does not fit current thinking). However, with plausibility as the only criterion for consideration, false positives are more likely to become part of the "evidence" for colonization. Any bit of information that suggests some "reasonable" possibility of early occupation becomes the basis for making claims about colonization. As we will see shortly, due to measurement error and uncertainty, as well as choice of statistical approach, chronologies made under such conditions tend to become older, sometimes significantly so.

In the Pacific, for example, the quest for elusive "footprints" has dominated much of the discussion of colonization for the past 60 years—ever since radiocarbon dating made it possible to provide ages of organic material (for example, Heyerdahl and Ferdon 1961). Given the revolution represented by radiocarbon dating in terms of its ability to stipulate quantitative values for the degree of antiquity of materials, archaeologists enthusiastically pursued collecting and dating samples as means of specifying "colonization" dates. This enthusiasm coupled with the quest to find the "earliest" examples led to largely uncritical acceptance of samples throughout the discipline (Dean 1978). In the Pacific, this effect is demonstrated by the fact that once radiocarbon dating was introduced, arguments for the timing of human occupation of eastern Polynesia shifted from estimates of the thirteenth century AD (Buck 1938) to about 1,000 years earlier (for example, Hunt and Holsen 1991; Kirch 1986; Kirch and Ellison 1994; see Anderson 1995; Spriggs and Anderson 1993).

Archaeologically, however, our efforts at learning about the timing of the arrival of people must consist of identifying the *set of earliest observable events that can only be explained by human behavior.* Thus, "colonization" is not something

Carl P. Lipo, Terry L. Hunt, and Robert J. DiNapoli

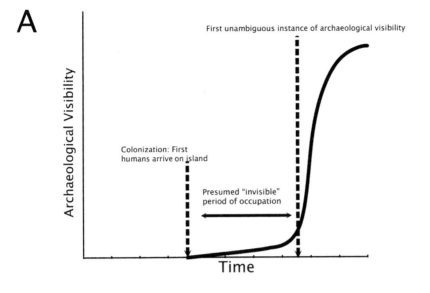

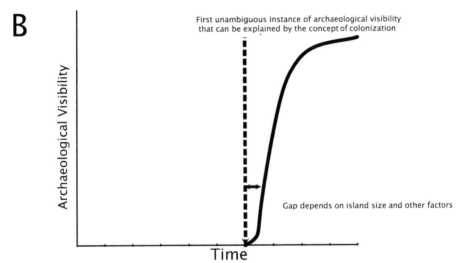

Figure 3.2. Common-sense colonization (*A*) versus archaeological colonization (*B*). Note that "invisible" period of occupation prior to archaeological visibility in the common-sense notion of colonization assumes low population–growth rates, low environmental impacts, low-density settlements, and/or large landmasses that would take significant time to result in abundant archaeological remains. From empirical evidence, none of these conditions holds true in cases when humans enter a previously unoccupied landscape. Birth rates often exceed 3% (Birdsell 1953, 1957), small populations tend to live in nucleated settlement patterns, and even large landmasses show impacts almost immediately after arrival. In the case of New Zealand (268,671 km²), e.g., human visibility took only several years to spread across the entire island (Wilmshurst and Higham 2004). In cases with far smaller islands (e.g., Rapa Nui is just 160 km²), any possible lag between "arrival" and archaeological visibility must be negligible.

that is discovered, but rather is an *explanation* for events that are defined and observed in the archaeological record. This statement simply means that we cannot look for "evidence" of colonization with the assumption that it is real and somehow "out there." Instead, we account for observations (that is, identified instances of artifact classes) that can only be explained as the result of human behavior.

Maintaining the subtle but distinctive nature of these aspects of the concept of colonization is vital. The use of commonsense colonization often assumes that the "real" colonization date must be older than the earliest archaeological evidence and thus results in an endless unfalsifiable quest for the first footprint. *Archaeological* colonization, in contrast, is associated with the identification of the earliest observations that can only be explained as the result of human activity (Figure 3.2). Based on this archaeologically defined class, the investigator begins by acquiring chronological information for the deposition of the earliest case of identified artifactual material. This conceptual approach is fundamentally distinct as it is falsifiable and amenable to continuous testing. As additional information is produced through excavations and other archaeological studies, the challenge in research is to iteratively evaluate archaeological evidence, typically with statistical modeling, in order to refine the chronology of colonization.

Uncertainty in Events

If colonization serves as a potential explanation for empirical observations (that is, a hypothesis), uncertainty comes from two primary sources: (1) linking the events we observe with the events of interest and (2) inherent measurement error. First, we must link our observations to claims about human behavior that occurred in the past. Our interest is in describing events, which are descriptions of a point in time when a set of attributes came to co-occur. In the case of colonization, we want to temporally distinguish events related to human activity. However, we cannot study human activity directly in the archaeological record. Instead, we describe phenomena in the present in terms of physical mechanisms that create them. Bridging arguments are necessary to connect these physical events with human behavior.

Consider radiocarbon ages, for example. Radiocarbon ages are determined based on the removal of an organism from the carbon cycle and the decay of ^{14}C over time. Whether that organism came to be removed from the carbon cycle (that is, died) must be reasoned through additional attributes such as physical features (for example, cut marks), association (with other artifacts), or composition (that is, non-native commensal species). Even with multiple attributes used to link a radiocarbon age with human behavior, direct relatedness cannot be guaranteed since the death of the portion of organism from which a radio-carbon age has been determined may have occurred long before the point at which the other attributes became associated. For example, the inner parts of long-lived tree species are often removed from the carbon cycle hundreds of years before they end up as fuel in an earth oven.

Dean (1978) demonstrated that we could resolve this confusion by distinguishing two kinds of events involved in establishing a "date": the *target event* and the *dated radiocarbon event*. The dated event is the point in time in which the physical attributes that are measured come together, such as the point at which the organism is removed from the carbon cycle. The target event is the event of interest to archaeologists, such as any observation that can be explainable as a consequence of human activity. These may be effectively the same event as is the case in luminescence dating where the firing of the ceramic vessel is the dated event and (often) the target event. In the case of radiocarbon ages, however, there may be a substantial difference between the two events, depending on the material used.

The second area of uncertainty in establishing the timing of an event comes from the inherent error terms involved in making measurements from *aggregate-scale events*. In the case of radiocarbon dating, there are two sources of error. The first, common to all dating techniques, comes from basic laboratory error that depends on the accumulation of imprecision of each of the measurement steps. This error is typically normally distributed and thus amenable to statistical evaluation. The second source of uncertainty, in the case of radiocarbon ages, comes from the calibration process, where calibrated ages are a function of the history of atmospheric radiocarbon and do not follow a regular distribution. There is thus a finite probability that the dated event will occur at each point in time, and we can only be 100 percent certain of the date if we consider the entire range of non-zero probabilities. For particular portions of the calibration curve, these distributions can be quite complicated and include multiple sets of possible durations (for example, Jacobsson et al. 2018; Lipo et al. 2005; Ramenofsky 1987).

The Selection of Samples

Given these sources of uncertainty, it is necessary to evaluate each dated event included in a set that meets the definition of archaeological colonization—the earliest observations that can only be explained as the result of human activity. The choice of samples used to generate the assemblage of events is perhaps the most significant step in the analysis. The better the association between the target event and the event of interest (that is, early human activity), the better the results. Including questionable dates (that is, unknown degree of divergence from target events) means that conclusions are also necessarily going to be questionable. No degree of statistical machinations can compensate for including samples that bear ambiguous association with the event of interest. Radiocarbon dates have to be carefully evaluated to ascertain that the events are appropriate for inclusion. This is not to say that any particular date is "wrong," but rather it may poorly link the dated event to the targeted event.

Such evaluation takes place whether one acknowledges it or not. It is not uncommon, for example, for researchers to reject dated events "obviously too old" on unspecified criteria. In the inclusion of materials that can be explained as related to colonization, however, particular and explicit evaluation criteria must be applied. Simply put: one must be able to definitively state the necessary and sufficient criteria used to sort dates into "acceptable" and "unacceptable."

An Example from Rapa Nui

Estimating the arrival of humans on Rapa Nui provides a useful example of the steps required for selecting samples and calculating probabilities as well as highlights the problems that emerge from commonsense notions of colonization. We initially conducted these analyses in 2006 and concluded that Rapa Nui was first colonized in the early part of the thirteenth century AD (Hunt and Lipo 2006; see also Wilmshurst et al. 2011 for the larger region). Despite attempts to invalidate our analyses (Shepardson et al. 2008), or outright rejection (for example, Bahn and Flenley 2017; Kirch 2017), our estimates of colonization have yet to be falsified (for example, DiNapoli et al. 2020; Schmid et al. 2018). Certainly, falsification of our hypotheses is possible: all that is required is at least one sample (and preferably more) that is unambiguously associated with human occupation and demonstrates earlier human presence.

The first step in evaluating colonization is to choose the samples for analyses that meet the definition of archaeological colonization. This process has to be accomplished explicitly rather than intuitively. For example, in a review of early radiocarbon dates related to the colonization of Rapa Nui, Martinsson-Wallin and Crockford (2002) reject a radiocarbon date from a sample of charcoal from Ahu Akivi by William Mulloy with an age of 2216 ± 96 BP (Mulloy and Figueroa 1978). Simply stating that the date is "questionable" (Martinsson-Wallin and Crockford 2002: 250), they eliminate it from consideration as the earliest acceptable date. No rationale is given, but it can be assumed the rejection

comes from the notion that the date is "too old" as it predates preconceived notions for colonization of the island. Following this strategy, one might argue that
"obvious" outliers can easily be excluded from analysis, but as one approaches
assumed target events, dates are accepted on tacit criteria because they appear
to "fit" or be "consistent with" other results. The reasoning is entirely circular:
"obvious" outliers simply reinforce a priori assumptions, and the a priori assumptions determine what makes an "outlier."

The use of these criteria (that is, implementing chronometric hygiene)
means that we did not include all possible samples in our original analyses; we
included those that could reliably inform us about the chronology of human
behavior. We excluded samples for which there was not a strong link between
the removal from the carbon cycle and a human-attributed event—for example,
material from unknown floral taxa (that is, the old wood problem) and samples
that contained mixed earth and charcoal. We also excluded samples of mixed
isotopic fractionation (for example, mixed charcoal and soil) that would necessarily provide a problematic relation between the dated and target events.

Significantly, we also excluded samples from marine contexts such as coral
and marine mammals. Marine samples must always be carefully considered
since old carbon in the form of dissolved carbon dioxide is sequestered in deep
water to create a global marine reservoir effect of circa 400 years, and local
offsets (ΔR) can also substantially deviate from this global average (Alves et al.
2018; Mangerud 1972; Stuiver and Braziunas 1993). Marine samples can, therefore, produce dates that are highly variable due to mixing between shallow
and deep water (Alves et al. 2018; Anderson 1995; Spriggs and Anderson 1993).
While this value can be adjusted using a ΔR correction, there can often be high
intraisland variation in ΔR, and choosing a reliable correction for some highly
mobile marine fauna (for example, sea birds, marine mammals) or samples with
mixed terrestrial/marine dietary contributions (for example, humans, commensal species) can be highly complex and difficult to resolve (for example,
Cook et al. 2015). In similar cases, such as on the Island of Hawai'i, modern
samples taken from the same bay reveal correction values that differ by several
hundred years, explained by local effects of deep water inconsistently mixed
with shallow sources (for example, Petchey 2009). Rapa Nui has a limited reef
environment and deep waters lie immediately offshore (Friedlander et al. 2013).
Consequently, there is unknown and likely substantial variability in sources of
marine carbon for certain organisms we may want to date (for example, marine
mammals). For the purposes of narrowing down the timing of archaeological
events, then, such inconsistency makes some marine samples potentially prob-

lematic. For this reason, we excluded three marine mammal (dolphin) bone/tooth samples from excavations conducted by Steadman and colleagues (1994; see also Lipo and Hunt 2016). While a marine reservoir correction has been estimated for one nearshore location on Rapa Nui (Beck et al. 2003; Burr et al. 2009), we do not know the appropriate age corrections for deep-sea, widely ranging dolphins, among others.

For a related reason, we also exclude coral dates. Beck et al. (2003: 93–111) report radiocarbon dating of 27 abraded coral artifacts, many identified as statue eye fragments, from Anakena Beach. As Beck et al. (2003: 100) correctly point out, the coral may have been collected live or used long after the death of the coral. Another problem with coral is that it secretes a hard, external skeleton as it grows. This growth can take place over 1,200 years for any particular cluster of coral (Glynn et al. 2003). Thus, some parts of coral may be significantly older than other parts, with no way of distinguishing the difference: coral death ages are likely systematically older than the manufacturing events by unknown and potentially great amounts. Thus, these coral dates must be considered ambiguous in terms of their relation to the archaeological events we seek to measure.

We also exclude lake-core sediment dates on Rapa Nui for estimating colonization events. Lake-core dates from sediments associated with changes in vegetation are often provided as evidence for early arrival of humans on Rapa Nui, but these are significantly problematic. For example, in recent publications Flenley and colleagues (for example, Butler and Flenley 2010) suggest human presence on Rapa Nui as early as AD 100 based on sediment cores taken from Rano Kau. Similarly, Cañellas-Boltà et al. (2013) and Rull (2019; Rull et al. 2013) argue for a colonization date of 400 BC based on vegetation changes in sediments from Rano Raraku lake cores.

There can be several potential problems using lake-core sediment samples for estimating colonization events. First, while coring evidence in the form of fecal biomarkers (for example, Sear et al. 2020) or commensal plants or animals (for example, Prebble and Wilmshurst 2009) would constitute reliable samples for archaeological colonization—as they are clearly related to human arrival on Rapa Nui, samples taken from cores are often argued as associated with human events, given sedimentary changes in microcharcoal, pollen, and/or other vegetation changes. Vegetation change and variation in microcharcoal, however, may not necessarily be linked to human impacts, though this is one possibility (for example, Gosling et al. 2020). More problematic in the case of Rapa Nui is the tendency for mixing to occur in the sediment profiles whereby older and younger material become associated. As Butler et al. (2004) have clearly shown, radiocarbon results from lake-core samples on Rapa Nui have produced wildly unreliable dates, explained by problems with bulk samples (that is, including unknown materials with potentially great inbuilt age), mixing of sediments and the dated constituents collected from them, and serious problems reliably relating materials dated with definitive evidence of human presence. Thus, with samples taken from Rapa Nui lake cores, there is no necessary relation between the radiocarbon and archaeological events. Instead, lake-core radiocarbon dates must be explained *in terms of* archaeological events where alternative explanations are possible or even likely. Using *only* this ambiguous lake-core evidence to infer the settlement history of Rapa Nui, as done by Flenley (for example, Butler and Flenley 2010) or Cañellas-Boltà et al. (2013), has little logical basis, as others have argued (Larsen and Simpson, 2013).

Our criteria for the analysis of Rapa Nui colonization also included dates with laboratory error terms less than 10 percent of the mean radiocarbon age. This criterion simply served to minimize the ambiguity of dates with a large degree of measurement error. As the amount of error increases, the less certain the radiocarbon age is for *any* value. In our original approach, dates with low precision limited our ability to specify any detail in the timing of colonization. Our use of 10 percent as the maximum acceptable was an arbitrary choice designed to include samples with precision great enough to contribute to resolution of the event of interest. In the case of the Rapa Nui, where our goal is to at least specify the century of colonization and where colonization has generally been thought to be no earlier than AD 500, explicitly limiting samples to those with a 10 percent maximum radiocarbon measurement error provided a restriction that ensured greater precision in our event estimation. While Hamilton and Krus (2018) argue that limiting samples to those with small error terms is not strictly necessary when using Bayesian models, especially if there are only a few dates with larger error terms, the choice of 10 percent gave us the best possible set of dates for our analyses.

Lastly, we removed dates from the Gakushuin lab, which are known to be problematic (Blakeslee 1994). Following these steps left us with 14 samples that meet all of the requirements for archaeological colonization. We distinguished these classes of samples as those that provide the most direct age estimates for defining chronology (that is, "Class 1" dates after Wilmshurst et al. [2011]).

Measuring Colonization Events

Once suitable samples are identified, decisions remain about specifying radiocarbon events to measure the timing of colonization. To convert conventional

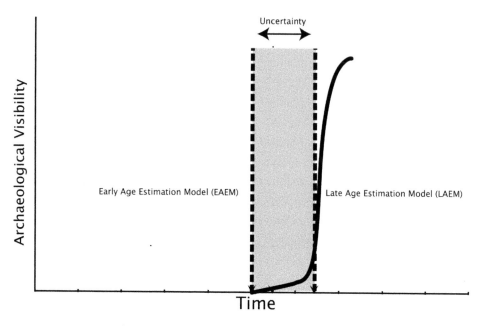

Figure 3.3. Two models for ascertaining the event of colonization. The Early Age Estimation Model (EAEM) is the point in time after which the event of colonization must have occurred. The Late Age Estimation Model (LAEM) is the point in time after which we are reasonably certain (i.e., p>0.50) that colonization has already occurred. In the case of Bayesian analysis, the process identifies range of ages that are statistically most likely to reflect the earliest date. This range is effectively the same as the EAEM.

radiocarbon ages (CRAs) into calendrical dates, the values must be calibrated, resulting in a series of time-specific probability distributions for each dated radiocarbon event. Since the values of these distributions are composed of probabilities usually not normally distributed, but reflect historically idiosyncratic ^{14}C levels in the atmosphere, it is difficult to specify the timing of the radiocarbon event with any great precision. To better specify timing, information from multiple, independently dated events can be combined and statistically analyzed to isolate a point in time when the colonization event *most likely* occurred (Figure 3.3).

Statistical Analyses

The two most common statistical approaches for estimating the colonization of Rapa Nui have been summed probability distributions of radiocarbon dates (SPD) (for example, Hunt and Lipo 2006; Lipo et al. 2016; Wilmshurst et al. 2011) and, more recently, Bayesian modeling (DiNapoli et al. 2020; Schmid et al. 2018). Shepardson and colleagues (2008; see also Contreras and Meadows 2014)

Carl P. Lipo, Terry L. Hunt, and Robert J. DiNapoli

have challenged our previous conclusions of a circa–thirteenth century colonization based on our use of SPD modeling (for example, Hunt and Lipo 2006; Wilmshurst et al. 2011; see Figure 3.4) and suggested a better statistical means for estimating colonization. In their proposed method, the probability of any date being the earliest is conditioned by the other probability distributions that are represented across all valid samples. Shepardson and colleagues use this approach for calculating the "earliest" date and find 900 AD to be more likely than our thirteenth-century conclusion. Shepardson et al. (2008) provide a useful illustration of the need to appropriately define and measure archaeological colonization rather than operate from common sense. Their problem is related to both the choice of the samples used, which do not meet the definition of archaeological colonization, and their method of estimating the point of colonization, particularly the inability to objectively account for potential outliers or large error terms. Nine out of 11 samples selected by Shepardson et al., including the 4 earliest CRAs,

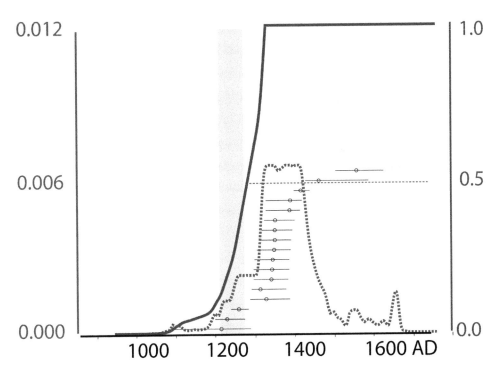

Figure 3.4. Rapa Nui colonization event as indicated by Class 1 radiocarbon ages and summed probability distribution modeling based on analyses in Hunt and Lipo (2006) and Wilmshurst et al. (2011). The gray bar indicates the area of uncertainty between the EAEM and the LAEM. For Rapa Nui, therefore, based on this analysis and the evidence used, colonization can be said to have taken place between AD 1200 and AD 1253.

derive from unidentified charcoal, and the 2 oldest CRAs have substantial error terms associated with the radiocarbon ages (>10 percent). The early values obtained through their analyses are entirely the product of the limitations of their statistical model and choice of samples: simply including values that are early, but bear unknown relations to the target events of interest, results in earlier estimates of colonization. Furthermore, their claim that "the *true* colonization date for Rapa Nui (which archaeologists will probably never know for sure) is likely to be earlier than any random, or even the earliest recovered, evidence of human occupation" (Shepardson et al. 2008: 98, emphasis added) highlights the fundamentally unfalsifiable character of commonsense notions of colonization. Defining archaeological colonization as the earliest secure and unambiguous evidence of human activity, however, results in hypotheses that are continually testable as new data and methods arise.

To address the potential statistical problems with our previous analyses raised by Shepardson et al. (2008) and others (for example, Contreras and Meadows 2014), we recently tested our previous colonization estimate by reanalyzing a suite of radiocarbon dates meeting the definition of archaeological colonization (DiNapoli et al. 2020) with a technique that is now common in the Pacific: Bayesian modeling using OxCal (for example, Athens et al. 2014; Bronk Ramsey 2009a, 2017; Burley et al. 2015; Clark et al. 2016; Dye 2015; Schmid et al. 2018; Rieth and Athens 2019).

In our model, each CRA is combined into a single unordered phase and calibrated based on prior information about other dates in the group, and the result is a 95.4 percent probability estimate for the beginning of this phase (that is, colonization). All samples were calibrated using the SHCal13 calibration curve (Hogg et al. 2013). To focus on colonization events, we chose dates sufficiently early so that the radiocarbon probabilities inform on the likelihood of earliest human arrival. Strictly speaking, this is not a necessary step. One can include dates that most likely postdate colonization, though the degree to which they help confirm the earlier portions of probability distributions is a matter of contention (Mulrooney et al. 2011). For our analyses of Rapa Nui, we arbitrarily chose dates with a CRA greater than 650 BP. This procedure simply isolates those dates that provide the most information about the earliest portion of the radiocarbon probability distributions. Given recent advancements in Bayesian modeling of radiocarbon dates, in particular the ability to objectively handle potential outliers and large error terms (for example, Bronk Ramsey 2009b; Hamilton and Krus 2018; Dee and Bronk Ramsey 2014; Schmid et al. 2018), we ran two colonization models for Rapa Nui: one that only included 9 short-lived

Carl P. Lipo, Terry L. Hunt, and Robert J. DiNapoli

plant samples, and another that also included 19 unidentified charcoal samples modeled using a Charcoal Outlier parameter (Dee and Bronk Ramsey 2014). These unidentified charcoal samples come from archaeological contexts with secure stratigraphic relationships between the sample and the target event (that is, human activity). The Charcoal Outlier model allows us to account for the other potential source of uncertainty between the dated event and the target event that Sheppardson et al. (2008) could not account for—inbuilt age.

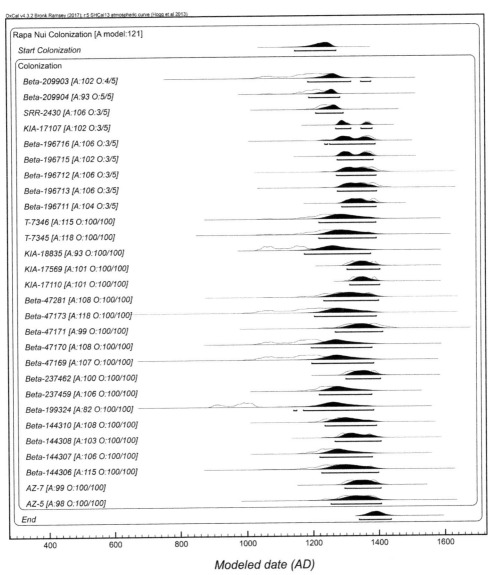

Figure 3.5. Single-phase Bayesian colonization model for Rapa Nui (figure adapted from DiNapoli et al. 2020).

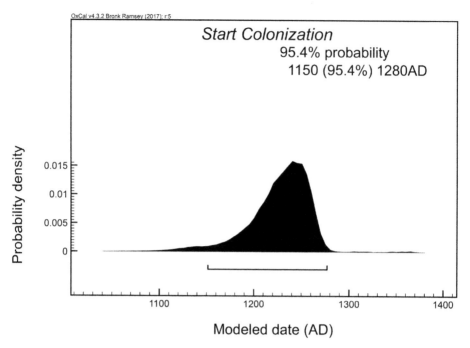

Start Colonization
95.4% probability
1150 (95.4%) 1280AD

Probability density

Modeled date (AD)

Figure 3.6. Single-phase Bayesian modeled Boundary start range for the colonization event on Rapa Nui (figure adapted from DiNapoli et al. 2020).

The results of these two models are essentially identical and suggest that the colonization event is 95.4 percent likely to have occurred between *1150 and 1280 cal AD* (Figures 3.5 and 3.6). The agreement index for each modeled date is above the commonly used threshold of 60, the model agreement is 121, and the overall agreement is 120.5. This result is consistent with the conclusions we reached with our earlier analyses (for example, Hunt and Lipo 2006; Wilmshurst et al. 2011), pointing to the fact that the current best evidence is that colonization begins sometime between the late twelfth and middle thirteenth century. This reanalysis highlights that it is crucially important that we define archaeological colonization—that is, the earliest unambiguous evidence of human activity—in selecting samples for modeling colonization.

Conclusions

The change in our understanding of the colonization event on Rapa Nui is significant. Rather than arrival in AD 700–900, humans arrived on this tiny, remote island between the twelfth and thirteenth century. Since we know that Europeans located the island in 1722, this dramatically shortens the overall precontact chronology from 1,000 years or more to only about 500. This shorter chronology, among other lines of evidence, led us to question many of the popular assumptions about Rapa Nui history, in particular, long-term population growth with overshoot, collapse, and rebound (Bahn and Flenley 1992; Diamond 1995, 2005; Puleston et al. 2017; compare Lipo et al. 2018). With a solid chronology for Rapa Nui, we now have a firm empirical understanding of the basic phenomena that must be explained. This temporal framework has led us, for example, to see that the making and transport of *moai* were associated with behavior vital to the success of communities in evolutionary and ecological terms given the environmental and social constraints of the island (for example, DiNapoli et al. 2018, 2019).

Unfortunately, unit construction is rarely considered to be of primary importance in archaeological practice, yet there is no task that is more fundamental to our ability to generating meaningful observations. While many recognize the use of classes in the measurement of artifacts, few understand how they are constructed and even fewer are aware of the need for unit construction with *all* of our nouns and verbs. The insidious nature of commonsensical notions leads us to treat English concepts as empirically discoverable, forcing us to make implicit and cryptic assumptions about what we are studying. Nowhere is the problem more acute than in the study of time. Our inability to directly observe time means that we must use conceptual units for measuring its effect on the world. Herein lies the necessity of temporal systematics.

The use of the concept of colonization in the study of humans arriving on islands across the Pacific illustrates how clarification and careful linkage of observations with meaning can produce new understandings of history. The problems illustrated in this chapter are not unique to Rapa Nui and could be usefully extended to other regions experiencing similar issues, exemplified by recent work in the Caribbean (for example, Napolitano et al. 2019), Madagascar (for example, Anderson 2019; Douglass et al. 2019), and other chapters in this volume (for example, chapters 6 and 7). With cryptic assumptions (for example, "true" colonization being earlier than the earliest evidence) and a conceptualization based on common sense, many studies of colonization have endlessly pursued elusive "footprints" that are evidence of a behavioral event. By explicitly defining the concept of colonization, we are afforded falsifiable explanations of the record with known links between hypotheses and the events we create.

Note

1. For chemistry, Robert Boyle's publication of the *The Sceptical Chymist* in AD 1661 marked the change, while physics began to shed its alchemist roots with the AD 1687 publication of Isaac Newton's *Principia Mathematica*.

References

Allen, M. S. 2014. Marquesan Colonisation Chronologies and Postcolonisation Interaction: Implications for Hawaiian Origins and the "Marquesan Homeland" Hypothesis. *Journal of Pacific Archaeology* 5(2): 1–17.

Alves, E. Q., K. Macario, P. Ascough, and C. Bronk Ramsey. 2018. The Worldwide Marine Radiocarbon Reservoir Effect: Definitions, Mechanisms, and Prospects. *Reviews of Geophysics* 56(1): 278–305.

Anderson, A. 1995. Current Approaches in East Polynesia Colonisation Research. *Journal of the Polynesian Society* 104(1):110–132.

Anderson, A. 2019. Was There Mid Holocene Habitation in Madagascar? A Reconsideration of the OSL Dates from Lakaton'i Anja. *Antiquity* 93(368): 478–487.

Athens, J. S., T. M. Rieth, and T. S. Dye. 2014. A Paleoenvironmental and Archaeological Model-based Age Estimate for the Colonization of Hawai'i. *American Antiquity* 79(1): 144–155.

Bahn, P. G., and J. Flenley. 1992. *Easter Island, Earth Island.* New York: Thames and Hudson.

Bahn, P. G., and J. Flenley. 2017. *Easter Island, Earth Island: The Enigmas of Rapa Nui,* Fourth Edition. Lanham: Rowman and Littlefield.

Beck, J. W., L. Hewitt, G. S. Burr, J. Loret, and F. T. Hochstetter. 2003. Mata Ki Te Rangi: Eyes Towards the Heavens. In *Easter Island: Scientific Exploration into the World's Environmental Problems in Microcosm,* ed. J. Loret and J. T. Tanacredi, 93–112. New York: Kluwer Academic/Plenum.

Binford, L. R. 1962. Archaeology as Anthropology. *American Antiquity* 28: 217–225.

Birdsell, J. B. 1953. Some Environmental and Cultural Factors Influencing the Structure of Australian Aboriginal Populations. *American Naturalist* 87: 171–207.

Birdsell, J. B. 1957. Some Population Problems Involving Pleistocene Man. *Cold Spring Harbor Symposia on Quantitative Biology* 22: 47–69.

Blakeslee, D. J. 1994. Reassessment of Some Radiocarbon Dates from the Central Plains. *Plains Anthropologist* 39(148): 103–210.

Bronk Ramsey, C. 2009a. Bayesian Analysis of Radiocarbon Dates. *Radiocarbon* 51(1): 337–360.

Bronk Ramsey, C. 2009b. Dealing with Outliers and Offsets in Radiocarbon Dating. *Radiocarbon* 51(3): 1023–1045.

Bronk Ramsey, C. 2017. OxCal Program, Version 4.3.

Buck, P. H. 1938. *Vikings of the Sunrise.* New York: Frederick A. Stokes.

Burley, D., K. Edinborough, M. Weisler, and J. Zhao. 2015. Bayesian Modeling and Chronological Precision for Polynesian Settlement of Tonga. *PLoS ONE* 10: e0120795.

Burr, G. S., Beck, J. W., Correge, T., Cabioch, G., Taylor, F. W., and D. J. Donahue. 2009. Modern and Pleistocene Reservoir Ages Inferred from South Pacific Corals. *Radiocarbon* 51(1): 319–338.

Butler, K. R., and J. R. Flenley. 2010. The Rano Kau 2 Pollen Diagram: Palaeoecology Revealed. *Rapa Nui Journal* 24(1): 5–10.

Butler, K., and J. Flenley. 2017. New Interpretations of Pollen Data from Rapa Nui. In *Cultural* and *Environmental Change on Rapa Nui,* ed. S. Haoa Cardinali, D. W. Ingersoll, K. B. Ingersoll, and C. M. Stevenson, pp. 74–88. New York: Routledge.

Butler, K., C. A. Prior, J. R. Flenley. 2004. Anomalous Radiocarbon dates from Easter Island. *Radiocarbon* 46(1): 395–405.

Cañellas-Boltà, N., V. Rull, A. Sáez, O. Margalef, R. Bao, S. Pla-Rabes, M. Blaauw, B. Valero-Garcés, and S. Giralt. 2013. Vegetation Changes and Human Settlement of Easter Island during the Last Millennia: A Multiproxy Study of the Lake Raraku Sediments. *Quaternary Science Reviews* 72: 36–48.

Clark, J. T., S. Quintus, M. Weisler, E. St Pierre, L. Nothdurft, and Y. Feng. 2016. Refining the Chronology for West Polynesian Colonization: New data from the Sāmoan Archipelago. *Journal of Archaeological Science: Reports* 6: 266–274.

Contreras, D. A., and J. Meadows. 2014. Summed Radiocarbon Calibrations as a Population Proxy: A Critical Evaluation Using a Realistic Simulation Approach. *Journal of Archaeological Science* 52: 591–608.

Cook, G. T., P. L. Ascough, C. Bonsall, W. D. Hamilton, N. Russell, K. L. Sayle KL, et al. 2015. Best Practice Methodology for ^{14}C Calibration of Marine and Mixed Terrestrial/Marine Samples. *Quaternary Geochronology.* 27: 164–171.

Dean, J. S. 1978. Independent Dating in Archaeological Analysis. In *Advances in Archaeological Method and Theory, Vol. 1,* ed. M. B. Schiffer. New York: Academic Press.

Dee, M. W., and C. Bronk Ramsey. 2014. High-Precision Bayesian Modeling of Samples Susceptible to Inbuilt Age. *Radiocarbon* 56(1): 83–94.

Diamond, J. 1995. Easter's End. *Discover* 9: 62–69.

Diamond, J. 2005. *Collapse: How Societies Choose to Fail or Succeed.* New York: Viking.

DiNapoli, R. J., C. P. Lipo, T. Brosnan, T. L. Hunt, S. Hixon, A. E. Morrison, and M. Becker. 2019. Rapa Nui (Easter Island) Monument (Ahu) Locations Explained by Freshwater Sources. *PLOS ONE* 14: e0210409.

DiNapoli, R. J., A. E. Morrison, C. P. Lipo, T. L. Hunt, and B. G. Lane. 2018. East Polynesian Islands as Models of Cultural Divergence: The Case of Rapa Nui and Rapa Iti. *Journal of Island and Coastal Archaeology* 13(2): 206–223.

DiNapoli, R. J., T. M. Rieth, C. P. Lipo, and T. L. Hunt. 2020. A Model-based Approach to the Tempo of "Collapse": The Case of Rapa Nui (Easter Island). *Journal of Archaeological Science* 116: 105094.

Douglass, K., S. Hixon, H. T. Wright, L. R. Godfrey, B. E. Crowley, B. Manjakahery, T. Rasolondrainy, Z. Crossland, and C. Radimilahy. 2019. A Critical Review of Radiocarbon Dates Clarifies the Human Settlement of Madagascar. *Quaternary Science Reviews* 221: 105878.

Dunnell, R. C. 1971. *Systematics in Prehistory.* New York: Free Press.

Dunnell, R. C. 1986. Methodological Issues in Americanist Artifact Classification. In *Advances in Archaeological Method and Theory,* ed. M. Schiffer, 149–207. New York: Academic Press.

Dye, T. S. 2015. Dating Human Dispersal in Remote Oceania: A Bayesian view from Hawaiʻi. *World Archaeology* 47: 661–676.

Feynman, R. 1965. New Textbooks for the "New" Mathematics. *Engineering and Science* 28(6): 9–15.

Friedlander, A., E. Ballesteros, J. Beets, E. Berkenpas, C. Gaymer, M. Gorny, and E. Sala. 2013. Effects of Isolation and Fishing on the Marine Ecosystems of Easter Island and Salas y Gómez, Chile. *Aquatic Conservation Marine and Freshwater Ecosystems* 23(23): 515–531.

Glynn, P. W., G. M. Wellington, E. A. Wieters, and S. A. Navarrete. 2003. Reef-building Coral Communities of Easter Island (Rapa Nui), Chile. In *Latin American Coral Reefs,* ed. J. Cortes, 473–494. New York: Elsevier.

Gosling, W. D., D. A. Sear, J. D. Hassall, P. G. Langdon, M.N.T. Bönnen, T. D. Driessen, Z. R. Kemenade, K. van, Noort, M. J. Leng, I. W. Croudace, A. J. Bourne, A. J., and C.N.H. McMichael. 2020. Human Occupation and Ecosystem Change on Upolu (Sāmoa) during the Holocene. *Journal of Biogeography* 47(3): 600–614.

Hamilton, W., and A. Krus. 2018. The Myths and Realities of Bayesian Chronological Modeling Revealed. *American Antiquity* 83(2): 187–203.

Heyerdahl, T., and E. N. Ferdon. 1961. *Archaeology of Easter Island*. Stockholm: Forum.

Hogg, A. G., Q. Hua, P. G. Blackwell, M. Niu, C. E. Buck, T. P. Guilderson, T. J. Heaton, J. G. Palmer, P. J. Reimer, R. W. Reimer, C.S.M. Turney, and S.R.H. Zimmerman. 2013. SHCal13 Southern Hemisphere Calibration, 0–50,000 Years cal BP. *Radiocarbon* 55(4) 1889–1903.

Hunt, T. L., and R. M. Holsen. 1991. An Early Radiocarbon Chronology for the Hawaiian Islands: A Preliminary Analysis. *Asian Perspectives* 30(1): 147–161.

Hunt T. L., and C. P. Lipo. 2006. Late Colonization of Easter Island. *Science* 311(5767): 1603–1606

Jacobsson, P., W. D. Hamilton, G. Cook, A. Crone, E. Dunbar, H. Kinch, P. Naysmith, B. Tripney, and S. Xu. 2018. Refining the Hallstatt Plateau: Short-term [14]C Variability and Small Scale Offsets in 50 Consecutive Single Tree-rings From Southwest Scotland Dendro-dated to 510–460 BC. *Radiocarbon* 60(1): 219–237.

Kirch, P. V. 1986. Rethinking East Polynesian Prehistory. *Journal of the Polynesian Society* 95(1): 9–40.

Kirch, P. V. 2017. *On the Road of the Winds: An Archaeological History of the Pacific Islands before European Contact*. Berkeley: University of California Press.

Kirch, P. V., and J. Ellison. 1994. Palaeoenvironmental Evidence for Human Colonization of Remote Oceanic Islands. *Antiquity* 68(259): 310–321.

Larsen, A., and D.F.J. Simpson. 2014. Comment to Rull et al. 2013. Challenging Easter Island's Collapse: The Need for Interdisciplinary Synergies. *Frontiers in Ecology and Evolution* 2(56): 10.3389/fevo.2014.00056.

Lipo, C. P., R. J. DiNapoli, and T. L. Hunt. 2018. Commentary: Rain, Sun, Soil, and Sweat: A Consideration of Population Limits on Rapa Nui (Easter Island) before European Contact. *Frontiers in Ecology and Evolution* 6(25): https://doi.org/10.3389/fevo.2018.00025.

Lipo, C. P, J. K. Feathers, and R. C. Dunnell. 2005. Temporal Data Requirements, Luminescence Dates, and the Resolution of Chronological Structure of Late Prehistoric Deposits in the Central Mississippi River Valley. *American Antiquity* 70(3): 527–544.

Lipo, C. P., and T. L. Hunt. 2016. Chronology and Easter Island Prehistory. In *Skeletal Biology of the Ancient Rapanui (Easter Islanders)*, ed. V. H. Stefan, G. W. Gill, 39–65. Cambridge: Cambridge University Press.

Lyman, R. L., M. J. O'Brien, and R. C. Dunnell. 1997. *The Rise and Fall of Culture History*. New York: Plenum Press.

Martinsson-Wallin, H., and S. J. Crockford. 2002. Early Settlement of Rapa Nui (Easter Island). *Asian Perspectives* 40: 244–278

Mangerud, J. 1972. Radiocarbon Dating of Marine Shells, including a Discussion of Apparent Ages of Recent Shells from Norway. *Boreas* 1: 143–172.

Mulloy, W., and G. Figueroa. 1978. *The A Kivi-Vai Teka Complex and Its Relationship to Easter Island Architectural Prehistory*. Asian and Pacific Archaeology Series 8, Social Science Research Institute. Honolulu: University of Hawaii.

Mulrooney, M. A., S. H. Bickler, M. S. Allen, and T. N. Ladefoged. 2011. High-precision Dating of Colonization and Settlement in East Polynesia. *Proceedings of the National Academy of Sciences* 108(23): E192–E194.

Napolitano, M. F., R. J. DiNapoli, J. H. Stone, M. J. Levin, N. P. Jew, B. G. Lane, J. T. O'Connor, and S. M. Fitzpatrick. (2019). Reevaluating Human Colonization of the Caribbean Using Chronometric Hygiene and Bayesian Modeling. *Science Advances* 5(12): eaar7806.

O'Brien, M. J., and R. L. Lyman. 2002. The Epistemological Nature of Archaeological Units. *Anthropological Theory* 2(1): 37–36.

O'Brien, M. J., R. L. Lyman, and M. B, Schiffer. 2005. *Archaeology as a Process: Processualism and Its Progeny.* Salt Lake City: University of Utah Press.

Petchey, F. 2009. Dating Marine Shell in Oceania: Issues and Prospects. In *New Directions in Archaeological Science,* ed. A. Fairbairn, S. O'Connor, and B. Marwick, 157–172. Canberra: Australian National University E Press.

Phillips, P., J. A. Ford, and J. B. Griffin. 1951. *Archaeological Survey in the Lower Mississippi Alluvial Valley 1940–1947.* Papers of the Peabody Museum of American Archaeology and Ethnology 25. Cambridge: Peabody Museum of American Archaeology and Ethnology.

Prebble, M., and J. M. Wilmshurst. 2009. Detecting the Initial Impact of Humans and Introduced Species on Island Environments in Remote Oceania using Palaeoecology. *Biological Invasions* 11(7): 1529–1556.

Puleston, C. O., T. N. Ladefoged, S. Haoa, O. A. Chadwick, P. M. Vitousek, and C. M. Stevenson. 2017. Rain, Sun, Soil, and Sweat: A Consideration of Population Limits on Rapa Nui (Easter Island) before European Contact. *Frontiers in Ecology and Evolution* 5(69): 10.3389/fevo.2017.00069.

Ramenofsky, A. 1987. *Vectors of Death.* Albuquerque: University of New Mexico Press.

Ramenofsky, A. 1998. The Illusion of Time. In *Unit Issues in Archaeology: Measuring Time, Space, and Material,* ed. A. F. Ramenofsky and A. Steffen, 74–84. Salt Lake City: University of Utah Press.

Rieth, T. M., and E. E. Cochrane. 2018. The Chronology of Colonization in Remote Oceania. In *The Oxford Handbook of Prehistoric Oceania,* ed. E. E. Cochrane and T. L. Hunt, 133–161. New York: Oxford University Press.

Rieth, T. M. and T. L. Hunt. 2008. A Radiocarbon Chronology for Sāmoan Prehistory. *Journal of Archaeological Science* 35(7): 1901–1927.

Rieth, T. M., and J. S. Athens. 2019. Late Holocene Human Expansion into Near and Remote Oceania: A Bayesian Model of the Chronologies of the Mariana Islands and Bismarck Archipelago. *Journal of Island and Coastal Archaeology* 14(1): 5–16.

Rull, V. 2019. Human Discovery and Settlement of the Remote Easter Island (SE Pacific). *Quaternary* 2(2): 15.

Rull, V., N. Cañellas-Boltà, A. Sáez, O. Margalef, R. Bao, S. Pla-Rabes, B. Valero-Garcés, and S. Giralt. 2013. Challenging Easter Island's Collapse: The Need for Interdisciplinary Synergies. *Frontiers in Ecology and Evolution* 1(3): 10.3389/fevo.2013.00003.

Schiffer, M. B. 2011. Archaeology as Anthropology: Where Did We Go Wrong? *The SAA Archaeological Record* 11(4): 22–28.

Schmid, M. M. E., A. J. Dugmore, L. Foresta, A. J. Newton, O. Vésteinsson, and R. Wood. 2018. How ^{14}C dates on Wood Charcoal Increase Precision When Dating Colonization: The Examples of Iceland and Polynesia. *Quaternary Geochronology* 48: 64–71.

Sear, D. A., M. S. Allen, J. D. Hassall, A. E. Maloney, P. G. Langdon, A. E. Morrison, A.C.G. Henderson, H. Mackay, I. W. Croudace, C. Clarke, J. P. Sachs, G. Macdonald, R. C. Chiverrell, M. J. Leng, L. M. Cisneros-Dozal, and T. Fonville. 2020. Human Settlement of East Polynesia Earlier, Incremental, and Coincident with Prolonged South Pacific Drought. *Proceedings of the National Academy of Sciences* 117(16): 8813–8819.

Service, E. R. 1969. Models for the Methodology of Mouthtalk. *Southwestern Journal of Anthropology* 25: 68–80.

Shepardson, B., D. Shepardson, F. Shepardson, S. Chiu, M. Graves. 2008. Re-examining the Evidence for Late Colonization on Easter Island. *Rapa Nui Journal* 22: 97–101.

Spaulding, A. C. 1960. The Dimensions of Archaeology. In *Essays in the Science and Culture in Honor of Leslie A. White*, ed. G. E. Dole and R. L. Carneiro, 437–456. New York: Crowell.

Spriggs, M. and A. Anderson. 1993. Late Colonisation of East Polynesia. *Antiquity* 67: 200–217.

Steadman, D. W., P. Vargas Casanova, and C. Cristino. 1994. Stratigraphy, Chronology, and Cultural Context of an Early Faunal Assemblage from Easter Island. *Asian Perspectives* 33(1): 79–96.

Stuiver, M and T. F. Braziunas. 1993. Modeling Atmospheric [14]C Influences and ^{14}C ages of Marine Samples to 10,000 BC. *Radiocarbon* 35: 137–189.

Wilmshurst, J. M. and T.F.G. Higham. 2004. Using Rat-gnawed Seeds to Independently Date the Arrival of Pacific Rats and Humans in New Zealand. *The Holocene* 14(6): 801–806.

Wilmshurst, J. M., T. L. Hunt, C. P. Lipo, and A. Anderson. 2011. High Precision Radiocarbon Dating Shows Recent and Rapid Initial Human Colonization of East Polynesia. *Proceedings of the National Academy of Sciences* 108(5): 1815–1820.

4

The Paleolithic Exploration of the Greek Islands and Middle Pleistocene Hominin Dispersals

The Case for Behavioral Variability over Behavioral Modernity

CURTIS RUNNELS

Until recently a scholarly consensus held that little credible evidence was to be found for a human presence on the Mediterranean islands during the Paleolithic. Reasoning from the apparent lack of physical evidence for this period, at least before the end of the Pleistocene, and basing arguments on the principles of island biogeography, some scholars—notably John Cherry (1981, 1990)— concluded that permanent island populations in the Mediterranean were only established by sedentary Neolithic agropastoralists on larger, more resource-diverse islands either during the late Pleistocene or early Holocene (Cherry and Leppard 2017). Consequently, these islands, including those in Greek waters, have generally played a minor role in the study of the Mediterranean Paleolithic (Broodbank 2006; 2013; Phoca-Cosmetatou 2011; Simmons 2012).

This was a fair position to take, at least so long as there was a lack of evidence for early Paleolithic remains on the islands, especially evidence from stratigraphic excavations that have produced unambiguous Paleolithic stone tools associated with extinct Pleistocene fauna and dated by radiometric means (Cherry and Leppard 2017; chapter 10). The perceived absence of early humans from oceanic islands appeared to be significant: oceanic islands rise from the deep-sea floor rather than shallow continental shelves and are isolated from the mainland by open water. The absence of humans on such islands would support the conclusion that Paleolithic humans were either unable to reach isolated islands or were deterred from doing so by the lack of biodiversity, water, and other resources. In the case of archaic hominins (that is, pre–*Homo sapiens sensu stricto*), it has been assumed that they lacked the cognitive and technological capacities to plan and carry out the logistically difficult open-sea crossings necessary to reach oceanic islands (Leppard 2015a, 2015b). Many scholars argue that the requisite logistical and organizational skills for planned maritime activity necessary to reach oceanic islands would be part of a complex of skills referred to as behavioral modernity, which includes the production of symbolic artifacts, mortuary ritual, specialized big game hunting, and the ability to inhabit difficult environments (Shea 2017: 108–109). The skills associated with behavioral modernity include logistical, technological, and organizational capacities, underpinned by specific neurological and cognitive structures that allow for the calculation of risk and benefit, abstraction, decision making, and communication of complex concepts (Leppard 2015a, 2015b). Behavioral modernity has been ascribed to anatomically modern humans (AMH) after about 40,000 years ago (Shea 2017: 108–109) and would not apply to archaic hominins (Leppard 2015b). Thus archaic species are usually precluded from discussion of long-distance seagoing (Cherry and Leppard 2015; Leppard and Runnels 2017). Based on these reasonable assumptions, it follows that the primary corridors for the dispersals of archaic hominins from Africa to Eurasia (roughly 1.8–0.8 million years ago) must have been restricted to terrestrial routes into Southwest Asia across the Sinai Peninsula, possibly routes across the southern quarter of the Arabian Peninsula, and the now-submerged coastal shelves of the Mediterranean (Anton and Swisher 2004; Bailey and Carrion 2008: Bar-Yosef and Belfer-Cohen 2001; Carbonell et al. 2008; Mosquera et al. 2013; Roebroeks 2006). Some modifications have been suggested to the terrestrial hypothesis, such as the Pincer model proposed by Rolland (2013) that combines the Southwest Asian routes with a crossing of the Strait of Gibraltar to the Iberian Peninsula, but these are the exceptions that prove the rule. Although it is possible that terrestrial migrations may have involved short water crossings from Africa to Spain, and from Africa to the Arabian Peninsula at the Bab el-Mandeb strait in the Red Sea, such crossings are assumed to have been possible only during glacial-isostatic marine lowstands and involved nothing more complicated than small numbers of individuals swimming or floating over small distances (Aguirre and Carbonell 2001; Lambeck et al. 2011; Scott and Gibert 2009). In my view we should be cautious in restricting behavioral flexibility to our own species, and keep an open mind about the possibility that larger scale maritime crossings may have been attempted by other hominin species (Leppard and Runnels 2017).

Recently, the question of Paleolithic humans on the Mediterranean islands, particularly in Greek waters, has been reopened. While a decade ago there seemed to be few instances of Paleolithic habitation on any Mediterranean island (Broodbank 2006), hints of a sporadic presence on a few of the Greek Islands and perhaps Cyprus have begun to emerge (Broodbank 2013; Knapp 2013). The pace of discovery has quickened as the result of the discovery of Paleolithic stone tools on a number of Greek Islands (for locations, see Figure 4.1). Lower and Middle Paleolithic artifacts have been reported from—among others—the islands of Ayios Eustratios (Kaczanowska and Kozlowski 2014); Crete (Mortensen 2008; Runnels et al. 2014a, 2014b; Strasser et al. 2010, 2011); Gavdos (Kopaka and Matzanas 2009); Kephalonia (Ferentinos et al. 2012); Lesvos (Galanidou et al. 2013; Galanidou et al. 2016); Melos (Chelidonio 2001); and Naxos (Carter et al. 2014). Additionally, sites on two of these islands are

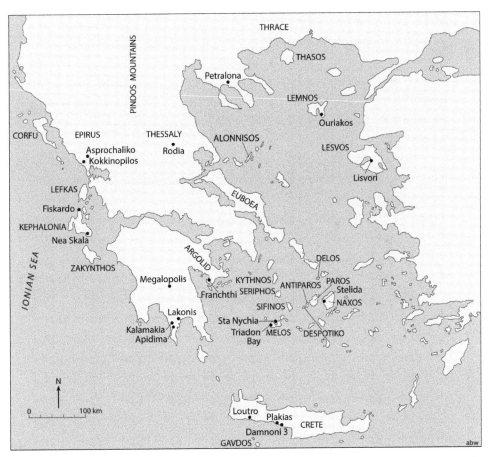

Figure 4.1. Greek Islands where Paleolithic stone tools have been recovered. (Reproduced with permission: Early Palaeolithic on the Greek Islands? *Journal of Mediterranean Archaeology* 27(2): 211–230: Figure 2, page 213: © Equinox Publishing Ltd 2014.)

currently being excavated. The site of Rodafnidia at Lisvori on Lesvos has been under investigation since 2010, and the excavations have revealed a Middle Pleistocene Acheulean site associated with a spring. The strait between Lesvos and the Turkish coast, however, is only 5.5 km, close enough to have been connected by land bridges to the mainland during marine lowstands (Galanidou et al. 2013), and the presence of Paleolithic hominins on Lesvos can be explained by the concept of species range expansion from a mainland home range, something that would have required at most a few short "hops" across small stretches of water. The site of Stelida on Naxos is a different matter. Naxos was cut off from the mainland for long, possibly discontinuous, periods of time by an unknown stretch of open sea, and as a result of local evolution in the absence of terrestrial predators, the island developed a unique endemic Pleistocene fauna that included pygmy deer (*Candiacervus* sp.), hippo (*Hippopotamus* sp.), and elephantids (Elephantidae) (Mavridis 2003; van der Geer et al. 2010). The excavations at Stelida have produced evidence for Lower, Middle, and Upper Paleolithic and Mesolithic (circa 250,000–10,000 years ago) exploitation of raw material available from an outcrop of chert. Thousands of stone artifacts, from cores to finished tools, are clustered on the surface of the site, and the excavations have detailed buried strata with stone tools of Paleolithic type (Carter et al. 2014, 2017).

Paleolithic artifacts on other islands have been found by surface survey. On Crete, nine sites containing stone tools are associated with raised marine terraces and paleosol outcrops that cluster near the mouth of the Preveli Gorge on the south coast near Plakias (Runnels et al. 2014a; Strasser et al. 2010, 2011). On the same island there are artifacts associated with Pleistocene alluvial fans at Mochlos Bay (Runnels et al. 2014b). These finds are significant because Crete was an oceanic island with its own depauperate pygmy fauna in the Pleistocene (Mavridis 2003; van der Geer et al. 2010). Both Naxos and Crete were cut off from the mainland by sea barriers sufficient to keep out terrestrial predators, and we can assume that hominins reached these islands only by using watercraft that could be propelled, steered, and navigated (Howitt-Marshall and Runnels 2016). Such watercraft had to be large enough to carry more than one individual and necessary supplies. We can also assume that multiple back-and-forth journeys between the mainland and the islands were undertaken if we are to account for the detectable archaeological signature in the form of stone tool deposits.

At present we do not know the scale of sea crossings that would have been required to reach Crete or Naxos, but based on limited marine geophysical data, some scholars estimate these distances to be relatively small, on the order of 2–5 km (for example, Lykousis 2009; Tourloukis and Karkanas 2012), while others think that multiple crossings of 10–15 km or more might have been required (Lambeck 1996; Runnels 2014; Sakelleriou and Galanidou 2016).

Debate will continue until more evidence is brought to light, but speculation about the island Paleolithic from the Aegean to the wider Mediterranean and beyond has been growing, as can be seen from the many recent publications on the subject (for example, Bednarik 2001a, 2003; Broodbank 2013; Dawson 2014; Kehoe 2016; Pydyn 2015; Sakalleriou and Galanidou 2015; Simmons 2013; Runnels 2014). Debate and speculation will serve a purpose, because if archaic hominins were making long-distance sea crossings in the Aegean during the Middle Pleistocene, it will be necessary to make significant revisions to some widely accepted models of hominin dispersals in that region, and to consider the wider significance of early seafaring for our understanding of behavioral modernity, which is limited to AMH behavior requiring the cognitive and technological capacities necessary for undertaking such behaviorally sophisticated adventures (Leppard and Runnels 2017). It should be noted that some scholars continue to withhold judgment as they await new evidence, more excavations, and better dates before they will consider any attempt to adjust their thinking on these matters (for example, chapter 10). It is not my purpose here, however, to persuade skeptical colleagues to change their minds, as the existing data have been published. While acknowledging that more data are necessary before any consensus about the nature and timing of the Paleolithic on the Greek Islands can emerge, I believe we should be free to discuss the potential implications of Pleistocene maritime activity in order to stimulate the research necessary to test new hypotheses.

Conceptual Blockbusting

My position is relevant here: I believe that archaic hominins reached the oceanic Mediterranean islands, a conclusion based primarily on the growing body of evidence from the Greek Islands in particular (Runnels 2014). This evidence prompts me to consider as a working hypothesis that there were humans on these islands in the Paleolithic, and I believe it is fair to ask questions that come from this hypothesis even if they challenge the limits of what we think is probable or possible. How were these crossings undertaken? When were they made? Why would early hominins undertake these crossings? What do these crossings tell us about their behavior? And finally, what are the implications of this sort of behavior for our understanding of hominin dispersals on a global scale? To answer these questions completely would take us far beyond the scope of the present contribution, so I focus on the concept of behavioral modernity and ask whether our investigation of pre-AMH behavior has been stymied by the behavioral modernity concept, and if a change of perspective, perhaps the adoption of a different and more appropriate vocabulary to describe archaic hominin seagoing, might enable us to chart a path for future research.

The possibility that archaic hominins engaged in intentionally planned sea crossings was scarcely considered before the discovery of *Homo floresiensis* in Indonesia (Bednarik 2001a; Brumm et al. 2010; O'Connor 2010; O'Connell et al. 2010). As noted above, most scholars assumed that large-scale movements of hominins before the emergence of AMH, and the development of the complex modalities of behavior subsumed under the rubric of behavioral modernity, were terrestrial routes from Africa to Europe and Asia. In the Mediterranean region, even when sea crossings from Africa to the Arabian Peninsula or Africa to Iberia were considered, they were portrayed as short, one-way, island-hopping ventures involving actions like swimming or the use of technologically simple floats like logs (Lambeck et al. 2011; Rolland 2013). Recently, more ambitious— and more controversial—Pleistocene sea crossings to Flores, Sulawesi, and Australia have been broached (Bednarik 1999, 2001b, 2003; Leppard and Runnels 2017; Pydyn 2015: 36–38). The narrower question that follows from the hypothesis of Paleolithic seafaring is, what kind of behavior can explain the motivations of the hominins who undertook them? Yet any discussion of early seafaring is difficult because many of the basic behavioral concepts that are implied by Paleolithic adventures on the island have not been closely examined. The use of broad terminology such as "colonization" or "occupation" has perhaps resulted in scholars talking at cross purposes because they invoke meanings, or at least connotations, that may be inappropriate for explaining early hominin behavior (see below) (Cherry and Leppard 2017; Leppard and Runnels 2017; chapter 10). Unfortunately, we cannot observe the behavior of archaic hominins, and there are no close analog species today (other than AMH) who can be used to model pre-AMH hominin behavior. The result is the persistence of ample conceptual space for speculation, although the general path has been to consider archaic hominins as too limited in cognitive and technological ability to undertake complex seafaring expeditions. A useful first step, therefore, would be to consider the suggestion made by some scholars that the narrow concept of behavioral modernity be substituted with the broader concept of behavioral variability; that can be briefly defined as "when the same stimulus evokes different response in the same subject" (Shea 2017: 108–109). In other words, there is more than one way to do something, and there are both simple and complex solutions to any problem requiring a mixed response from the problem solver, especially the tendency to repurpose "complex solutions to one set of problems to fit novel circumstances" (Shea 2017: 109). This would apply to a problem such as crossing the sea to an oceanic island like Crete. By invoking behavioral variability, we need no longer assume that archaic hominins were unable to organize, plan, or execute the sorts of sea crossings necessary to reach oceanic islands. This would open up the possibility that early hominins were able to repurpose stone tools—along with woodworking and basketry skills—to boat building, and to repurpose the basic wayfinding techniques used on land for navigation at sea, and the logistical planning necessary for resource exploitation in home ranges to the planning of expeditions (Howitt-Marshall and Runnels 2016).

If we adopt behavioral variability as a second working hypothesis, we can ask additional questions, such as what are the appropriate words for describing early sea crossings and the presence of hominins on oceanic islands in the Middle Pleistocene? To do so will require us to return to first principles. Are we talking about range expansion, migration, colonization, or something else? In many respects, the problem is so basic that it comes down to the definition of these words and the consideration of their semantic meanings (Leppard and Runnels 2017). Many terms have unrecognized connotations that make them less appropriate for discussions of early behavior, and semantic nuances may cloak differences in interpretations and explanations of phenomena leading to confusion and miscommunication. The fundamental concepts implied by the words we use must be examined if we are to enable future research. At the most basic level, we must recognize that human behavior connected with maritime activity or regional movements of any kind may be described using words that fall into two large classes: those appropriate for AMH in the last 10–20 millennia, particularly agropastoralists engaged in behavior leading to sedentary permanent inhabitation of a territory or region, and those that might apply to hunting/gathering/foraging in the Pleistocene by early hominins and AMH.

Common Terms and Concepts Applied to Paleolithic Activity on the Greek Islands

Let us consider the most common terms that are used to describe hominin activities on the Greek Islands in the early Paleolithic. The list below of 22 terms is not intended to be exhaustive. It is instead meant to provide food for thought about the vocabulary that we employ when we attempt to describe early hominin behavior. The definitions and connotations in the parentheses following each term are derived from publicly available lexicons, and have been modified when I thought it would be helpful for usage in discussions of human behavior, as distinct from that of other species of animals (see also chapter 2).

Accident (something that happens unexpectedly and unintentionally; often causing harm or injury)

Adventure (exploration of new lands; risky and potentially hazardous exploration)

Asylum (protection from harm; usually by moving to a new place to seek the protection of some greater power)

Colonization (establishing a permanent population or settlement in a new region; usually under the auspices of another power)

Curiosity (a strong impulse to learn or know something; usually something unusual or previously unknown)

Dispersal (also known as diaspora; distributing people over a large area; breaking up of a group of people to go in different directions)

Establishment (setting up a permanent residence; settling down)

Exploration (traveling to or visiting an unfamiliar or unknown area to learn about it; searching, investigation, or examination)

Habitation (living in a particular place; usually permanently)

Migration (movement of people from one place to another; when referring to human beings, migration connotes a permanent, one-way act akin to colonization)

Occupation (the possession or settlement of a territory; usually through the use of military force)

Pioneering (first explorers of a new land; usually with the intention of discovering resources in preparation for settlement)

Prospecting (looking or searching for something; more narrowly connoting minerals, gems, ores, pearls, and so on, but more broadly, any useful thing or material, including land or habitat)

Range Expansion (species expands its range to new territories; may refer to everything from small movements to long-distance dispersals)

Refuge (safe from danger or harm; having to flee from one place to another)

Robinson Crusoe Events (small-scale, short-term activity on islands [Leppard 2015a]; inconspicuous archaeologically because of stochastic effects bearing on the taphonomy and recovery of small datasets; largely invisible episodes of visitation)

Sedentism (residential settlement in one location; assumed to be permanent or semipermanent and year-round)

Settlement (establishing a residence in a land that was previously uninhabited; usually resulting in permanent communities as the result of migration or colonization)

Traverse (travel across or through an area; usually for short periods of time, with minimal stopping)

Venture (a risky journey or undertaking; dare to go somewhere that may be dangerous)

Visitation (going to see some place, often new; usually on a temporary basis)

Younger son pattern (geographic displacement of younger sons as a result of land tenure or inheritance rules; individual persons perhaps as heads of small bands leaving settled areas for new lands to seek their fortunes)

Discussion

Some words in this list—here I am thinking of examples like colonization, occupation, or migration—have connotations that have been applied rather indiscriminately to many situations, from the European colonization of Africa to the actions of animals moving from one region to another. It is unnecessarily confusing to use the same words for human behavior and the behavior of other animals, when the one may involve agency, volition, and rational decision making, and the other perhaps instinctual drives. It is equally confusing to use words with misleading or inappropriate connotations for different grades of hominins, especially when describing the behavior of archaic forms with cognitive characteristics that cannot be directly observed or reliably inferred from any existing species.

My conclusion is that it would be best to eschew terms more appropriate for describing the behavior of *Homo sapiens sensu stricto*, and to employ another vocabulary to discriminate among the different shades of behavior and motivation that we might wish to ascribe to archaic hominins. For example, the following words may better describe the actions of Lower and Middle Paleolithic hominins who engaged in maritime activity in order to reach oceanic islands:

Accident, adventure, curiosity, dispersal, exploration, pioneering, prospecting, range expansion, refuge, traversing, venturing, visitation

These words should be used in lieu of others—for example, asylum, colonization, habitation, migration, occupation, and settlement—because they have connotations connecting them with the behavior of later agropastoralists.

A new conceptual terminology can help us think about the Paleolithic on the Greek Islands in new ways. Let us consider one example. In a recent article, Leppard (2014) posits that hominins arriving on the previously unexplored oceanic islands in the Aegean might be expected to have profound impacts on the island's fauna. The endemic fauna had no experience of predators and it would have been easy for apex predators like archaic hominins to push them to extinction. As a result, the effects of hunting on the island fauna should quickly become visible in the paleontological record in the form of local extinctions and a resulting imbalance of the remaining biota that leads to turnover and ecological cascades. In Leppard's view, such effects would be proxy evidence for the presence of humans on the Greek Islands in the Paleolithic (Leppard 2014). Here is where different thinking, illustrated perhaps with a different terminology, might raise different expectations, leading us in turn to ask different questions about the paleontological record. The scenario envisioned by Leppard leading to the demise of local fauna presupposes an intrusion of hominins on a previously uninhabited island on a large scale, as implied by words such as "occupy" or "colonize." If instead we think of human presence on the island as something more like a pioneering stage of exploration or prospecting, what would the impacts on local fauna be then? Perhaps we would not imagine people spreading across Crete in a Wave of Advance and "settling" the territory, but instead imagine a few small bands of foragers who were spatially and chronologically discontinuous, and in numbers small enough to fall below the threshold capable of inducing faunal imbalances or local extinctions. If the numbers of individuals were small enough (perhaps hundreds, and certainly not thousands), and their visits were intermittent, of short duration, and confined primarily to easily accessible coastal zones, we can envisage the impact of hunting as both too local and too episodic to cause faunal extinctions. Considering the size of Crete, for example, and its topographic diversity, it would take a very long period of time for any hominin activities to have an impact on animals to a degree sufficient to be registered in the paleontological record. Crete is quite large (circa 8,336 km^2 in area), with an east-to-west range of mountain peaks up to of 2,456 m in elevation, and extremely rugged topography. The relief is dominated by steep slopes and deep intermontane valleys that make movement difficult for animals and humans alike. Even today there are animals in Crete, like the agrimi (*Capra aegagrus cretica*), or wild goat, that continue to find refuge from human predation and habitat loss. When we remember that the island was larger during periods of glacial sea-level lowstands, and had vastly larger numbers of individual animals and species than are found there now, we can imagine that hunting by Paleolithic explorers would have had only small local impacts on the fauna.

Another question emerges from this thinking. What were the first hominins to visit Crete searching for? What were their motivations for making an arduous sea crossing? We can speculate that perhaps they were searching for intangible goods such as refuge from mainland predators and other hominins, or tangible resources such as high-density pockets of animals with desired characteristics near springs or watercourses. Perhaps if we adopt the concept of behavioral diversity, we might be tempted to bring modern historical analogies into play, at least for the production of hypotheses about the kind of behavior we would connote by the use of terms like exploration and prospecting. The views of Brian Fagan, a veteran sailor and archaeologist, are particularly apt here. He details some 50,000 years of maritime adventures on a global scale, bringing his personal knowledge of oceans and sailing into play to throw light on both the challenges and the rewards for those who dared to go to sea (Fagan 2012). He profiles some of the better known episodes of early seafaring, such as the peopling of the Pacific and the Norse voyages in the North Atlantic, and some that are lesser known, like early voyaging in the Indian Ocean. These early sagas provide food for thought. Whether by land or by sea, we can imagine that incredible risks were undertaken by individuals and small groups, often made up of young men (like the Norse seafarers who explored the seaways to Iceland, Greenland, and Vinland), who sometimes covered great distances in search of adventure and fortune. Often exploration and adventure were ends in themselves. Excitement, experience, and—we hope—knowledge were perhaps among the motivations of the first to make the crossings. The knowledge gained of sailing directions and local conditions on previously unknown lands was in itself of great usefulness, especially for those who would come later and need to know the lay of the land, the best routes, and where water and food could be found. Those individuals who had taken the risks of early venturing must have been in great demand whenever other groups wanted—for whatever reason—to make the crossing.

One motivation that might be considered further may be placed under the rubric of "prospecting." Prospecting is about wealth, a notion often neglected when talking about early human travel, perhaps because in common usage today prospecting usually suggests the seeking of wealth in the form of ore bodies, particularly gold, silver, and other valuable metals. In its wider meaning, however, prospecting is searching for any useful resource: from stone for tool making and gems, minerals, salt, building stone, or metallic ores, to other resources including game, food, medicine, honey, timber, springs, furs, arable land, refuge from danger, and information—information such as the best sea lanes and mountain passes to new lands (see also chapter 12). These and other tangible and intangible forms of wealth, such as the most valuable resource of all—experience—are conceivable goals of adventurous explorers. While they were restlessly traveling to see what was new, or marvelous, or strange, I believe explorers always had their eyes open to finding whatever resources that could be of value upon their return to their points of origin.

These exercises in speculation have their usefulness because we must formulate appropriate models and appropriate terminology if we are going to ask the right questions. By rejecting a priori assumptions about the type of behavior that we think early hominins were capable of, we may begin to engage in conceptual blockbusting (Adams 2001) in order to formulate and test new hypotheses.

Conclusions

I have characterized the behavior of humans in the early Paleolithic Mediterranean as akin to familiar practices such as exploration and prospecting. These were the deeds, but what were the motivations behind them? Fagan speculates that early seafarers were motivated as much as anything else by the intangible element of adventure that is summoned up by an old Norse word: *aefintyr* [also *eventyr*] (Fagan 2012: 191, 206). *Aefintyr* means adventure or venture and it has strong connotations of restless curiosity, risk, excitement, and fear, all feelings common to those engaging in maritime voyages into the unknown. *Aefintyr* consumed Norse seafarers, according to Fagan, leading them to go to sea despite the formidable odds and the manifest dangers of doing so. Is it possible that such *aefintyr* has a genetic basis? Some scholars believe that the polymorphism DRD4-7R—popularly called the "curiosity gene"—is associated with individuals who exhibit traits of high tolerance to, and indeed an appetite for, risk taking, whether it is in high-stakes stock market gambles or extreme adventures like sailing around the world alone (Howitt-Marshall and Runnels 2016: 144). We should consider the possibility, at least as a working hypothesis, that some of the traits connoted by the word *aefintyr* could have been exhibited by archaic hominins, which would support the use of the concept of behavioral variability. If we begin to talk of archaic behavior in these terms—namely, adventure, exploration, and prospecting—we may yet find the key to the puzzle of the presence of humans on the Mediterranean islands in the Paleolithic.

References

Adams, J. L. 2001. *Conceptual Blockbusting: A Guide to Better Ideas*. New York: Basic Books.

Aguirre, E., and E. Carbonell. 2001. Early Human Expansions into Eurasia: The Atapuerca Evidence. *Quaternary International* 75(1): 11–18.

Anton, S. C., and C. C. Swisher. 2004. Early Dispersals of *Homo* from Africa. *Annual Review of Anthropology* 33: 271–296.

Bailey, G., and J. S. Carrion, 2008. Introduction: The Coastal Shelf of the Mediterranean and Beyond: Corridor and Refugium for Human Populations in the Pleistocene. *Quaternary Science Reviews* 27(23–24): 2095–2099.

Bar-Yosef, O., and A. Belfer-Cohen. 2001. From Africa to Eurasia—Early Dispersals. *Quaternary International* 75(1): 19–28.

Bednarik, R. G. 1999. Pleistocene Seafaring in the Mediterranean. *Anthropologie* 37(3): 275–282.

Bednarik, R. G. 2001a. Replicating the First Known Sea Travel by Humans: The Lower Pleistocene Crossing of Lombok Strait. *Human Evolution* 16(3–4): 229–242.

Bednarik, R. G. 2001b. The Origins of Pleistocene Navigation in the Mediterranean: Initial Replicative Experimentation. *Journal of Iberian Archaeology* 3: 11–23.

Bednarik, R. G. 2003. Seafaring in the Pleistocene. *Cambridge Archaeological Journal* 13(1): 41–46.

Broodbank, C. 2006. The Origins and Early Development of Mediterranean Maritime Activity. *Journal of Mediterranean Archaeology* 19(2): 199–230.

Broodbank, C. 2013. *The Making of the Middle Sea*. Oxford: Oxford University Press.

Brumm, A., G. M. Jensen, G. D. van den Bergh, M. J. Morwood, I. Kurniawan, F. Azia, and M. Storey. 2010. Hominins on Flores, Indonesia, by One Million Years Ago. *Nature* 464(7289): 748–752.

Carbonell, E., M. Mosquera, X. Pedro Rodriguez, J. M. Bermúdez de Castro, F. Burjachs, J. Rosell, R. Sala and J. Vallverdú. 2008. Eurasian Gates: The Earliest Human Dispersals. *Journal of Anthropological Research* 64(2): 195–228.

Carter, T., D. Contreras, S. Doyle, D. D. Mihailović, T. Moutsiou, and N. Skarpelis. 2014. The Stélida Naxos Archaeological Project: New Data on the Middle Palaeolithic and Mesolithic Cyclades. *Antiquity* 88(341): Project Gallery.

Carter, T., D. Contreras, J. Holcomb, D. D. Mihailovic, N. Skarpelis, K. Campeau, T. Moutsiou, and D. Athanasoulis. 2017. The Stélida Naxos Archaeological Project: New Studies of an Early Prehistoric Chert Quarry in the Cyclades. In *From Maple to Olive: Proceedings of a Colloquium to Celebrate the 40th Anniversary of the Canadian Institute in Greece Athens, 10–11 June 2016*, 75–103. Athens: Publications of the Canadian Institute in Greece No. 10.

Chelidonio, G. 2001. Manufatti Litici su Ciottolo da Milos (Isole Cicladi). *Pegaso: Rivista di Cultura Mediterranea* 1: 117–144.

Cherry, J. F. 1981. Pattern and Process in the Earliest Colonization of the Mediterranean Islands. *Proceedings of the Prehistoric Society* 47: 41–68.

Cherry, J. F. 1990. The First Colonization of the Mediterranean Islands: A Review of Recent Research. *Journal of Mediterranean Archaeology* 3: 145–221.

Cherry, J. F., and T. P. Leppard. 2015. Experimental Archaeology and the Earliest Seafaring: The Limitations of Inference. *World Archaeology* 47(5): 740–755.

Cherry, J. F., and T. P. Leppard. 2017. Patterning and Its Causation in the Pre-Neolithic Colonization of the Mediterranean Islands (Late Pleistocene to Early Holocene), *Journal of Island and Coastal Archaeology* 13(2): 191–205.

Dawson, H. 2014. *Mediterranean Voyages. The Archaeology of Island Colonisation and Abandonment*. Walnut Creek, California: Left Coast Press.

Fagan, B. 2012. *Beyond the Blue Horizon: How the Earliest Mariners Unlocked the Secrets of the Oceans*. New York: Bloomsbury Press.

Ferentinos, G., M. Gkioni, M. Geraga, and G. Papatheodorou. 2012. Early Seafaring Activity in the Southern Ionian Islands, Mediterranean Sea. *Journal of Archaeological Science* 39(7): 2167–2176.

Galanidou, N., J. Cole, G. Iliopoulos, and J. McNabb. 2013. East Meets West: The Middle Pleistocene Site of Rodafnidia on Lesvos, Greece. *Antiquity* 87(336): Project Gallery.

Galanidou, N., C. Athanassas, J. Cole, G. Iliopoulos, A. Katerinopoulos, A. Magganas, and J. McNabb. 2016. The Acheulian Site at Rodafnidia, Lisvori, on Lesbos, Greece: 2010–2012. In *Paleoanthropology of the Balkans and Anatolia,* ed. K. Harvati and M. Roksandic, 119–138. Tubingen, Germany: Springer.

Howitt-Marshall, D., and C. Runnels. 2016. Middle Pleistocene Sea-crossings in the Eastern Mediterranean? *Journal of Anthropological Archaeology* 42: 140–153.

Kaczanowska, M., and J. K. Kozlowski. 2014. The Aegean Mesolithic: Material Culture, Chronology, and Networks of Contact. *Eurasian Prehistory* 11(1–2): 31–62.

Kehoe, A. B. 2016. *Traveling Prehistoric Seas: Critical Thinking on Ancient Transoceanic Voyages.* Walnut Creek, California: Left Coast Press.

Knapp, A. B. 2013. *The Archaeology of Cyprus.* Cambridge: Cambridge University Press.

Kopaka, K., and C. Matzanas. 2009. Palaeolithic Industries from the Island of Gavdos, Near Neighbour to Crete in Greece. *Antiquity* 83(321): Project Gallery.

Lambeck, K. 1996. Sea-level Change and Shore-line Evolution in Aegean Greece since Upper Palaeolithic Time. *Antiquity* 70(269): 588–611.

Lambeck, K, A. Purcell, N. C. Flemming, C. Vita-Finzi, A. M. Alsharekh, and G. N. Bailey. 2011. Sea Level and Shoreline Reconstructions for the Red Sea: Isostatic and Tectonic Considerations and Implications for Hominin Migration out of Africa. *Quaternary Science Reviews* 30(25–26): 3542–3574.

Leppard, T. P. 2014. Modeling the Impacts of Mediterranean Island Colonization by Archaic Hominins: The Likelihood of an Insular Lower Palaeolithic. *Journal of Mediterranean Archaeology* 27(2): 231–254.

Leppard, T. P. 2015a. Passive Dispersal Versus Strategic Dispersal in Island Colonization by Hominins. *Current Anthropology* 56(4): 590–595.

Leppard, T. P. 2015b. The Evolution of Modern Behaviour and Its Implications for Maritime Dispersal during the Palaeolithic. *Cambridge Archaeological Journal* 25(4): 829–846.

Leppard, T. P., and C. Runnels. 2017. Maritime Hominin Dispersals in the Pleistocene: Advancing the Debate. *Antiquity* 91(356): 510–519.

Lykousis, V. 2009. Sea-level Changes and Shelf Break Prograding Sequences during the Last 400 ka in the Aegean Margins: Subsidence Rates and Palaeogeographic Implications. *Continental Shelf Research* 29(16): 2037–2044.

Mavridis, F. 2003. Early Island Archaeology and the Extinction of Endemic Fauna in the Eastern Mediterranean: Problems of Interpretation and Methodology. In *Zooarchaeology in Greece: Recent Advances,* ed. C. Gamble, P. Halstead, Y. Hamilakis, and E. Kotjabopoulou, 65–74. British School at Athens Studies 9. Athens: British School at Athens.

Mortensen, P. 2008. Lower to Middle Palaeolithic Artefacts from Loutro on the South Coast of Crete. *Antiquity* 82(317): Project Gallery.

Mosquera, M. A. Ollé, and X. P. Rodríguez. 2013. From Atapuerca to Europe: Tracing the Earliest Peopling of Europe. *Quaternary International* 295: 130–137.

O'Connell, J. F., J. Allen, and K. Hawkes. 2010. Pleistocene Sahul and the Origins of Seafaring. In *The Global Origins and Development of Seafaring,* ed. A. Anderson, J. H. Barrett, and K. V. Boyle, 57–68. Cambridge: McDonald Institute for Archaeological Research.

O'Connor, S. 2010. Pleistocene Migrations and Colonization in the Indo-Pacific Region. In *The*

Global Origins and Development of Seafaring, ed. A. Anderson, J. H. Barrett and K. V. Boyle, 41–55. Cambridge: McDonald Institute for Archaeological Research.

Phoca-Cosmetatou, N., ed. 2011. *The First Mediterranean Islanders: Initial Occupation and Survival Strategies. University of Oxford School of Archaeology Monograph 74.* Oxford: University of Oxford.

Pydyn, A. 2015. *Argonauts of the Stone Age. Early Maritime Activity from the First Migrations from Africa to the End of the Neolithic.* Oxford: Archaeopress.

Roebroeks, W. 2006. The Human Colonisation of Europe: Where are we? *Journal of Quaternary Science* 21: 425–435.

Rolland, N. 2013. The Early Pleistocene Human Dispersals in the Circum-Mediterranean Basin and Initial Peopling of Europe: Single or Multiple Pathways? *Quaternary International* 316: 59–72.

Runnels, C. 2014. Early Palaeolithic on the Greek Islands? *Journal of Mediterranean Archaeology* 27: 211–230.

Runnels, C., C. DiGregorio, K. W. Wegmann, S. F. Gallen, T. F. Strasser, and E. Panagopoulou. 2014a. Lower Palaeolithic Artifacts from Plakias, Crete: Implications for Hominin Dispersals. *Eurasian Prehistory* 11(1–2): 129–152.

Runnels, C., F. McCoy, R. Bauslaugh, and P. Murray. 2014b. Palaeolithic Research at Mochlos, Crete: New Evidence for Pleistocene Maritime Activity in the Aegean. *Antiquity* 88(342): Project Gallery.

Sakellariou, D., and N. Galanidou, 2015. Pleistocene Submerged Landscapes and Palaeolithic Archaeology in the Tectonically Active Aegean Region. In *Geology and Archaeology: Submerged Landscapes of the Continental Shelf,* ed. J. Harff, G. Bailey, and F. Lüth. Special Publications 411, 145–178. London: Geographical Society.

Scott, G. R., and L. Gibert. 2009. The Oldest Hand-axes in Europe. *Nature* 461(7260): 82–85.

Shea, J. J. 2017. *Stone Tools in Human Evolution: Behavioral Differences among Technological Primates.* Cambridge: Cambridge University Press.

Simmons, A. 2012. Mediterranean Island Voyagers. *Science* 338(6109): 895–897.

Simmons, A. 2013. *Stone Age Sailors. Paleolithic Seafaring in the Mediterranean.* Walnut Creek, California: Left Coast Press.

Strasser, T. F., E. Panagopoulou, C. N. Runnels, P. M. Murray, N. Thompson, P. Karkanas, F. W. McCoy and K. W. Wegmann. 2010. Stone Age Seafaring in the Mediterranean: Evidence from the Plakias Region for Lower Palaeolithic and Mesolithic Habitation of Crete. *Hesperia* 79: 145–190.

Strasser, T. F., C. Runnels, K. Wegmann, E. Panagopoulou, F. McCoy, C. DiGregorio, P. Karkanas, and N. Thompson. 2011. Dating Palaeolithic Sites in Southwestern Crete, Greece. *Journal of Quaternary Science* 26(5): 553–560.

Tourloukis, V., and P. Karkanas. 2012. The Middle Pleistocene Archaeological Record of Greece and the Role of the Aegean in Hominin Dispersals: New Data and Interpretations. *Quaternary Science Reviews* 43: 1–15.

van der Geer, A., M. Dermitzakis, and J. de Vos. 2010. Crete before the Cretans: The Reign of the Dwarfs. In *Evolution of Island Mammals: Adaptation and Extinction of Placental Mammals on Islands,* ed. A. van der Geer, G. Lyras, J. De Vos and M. Dermitzakis, 119–130. Oxford: Wiley-Blackwell.

II

Methodological Approaches

5

Above and Below the Waves

Advances in the Search for a Late Pleistocene Colonization of California's Islands

AMY E. GUSICK, TODD J. BRAJE, JON M. ERLANDSON,
JILLIAN MALONEY, AND DAVID BALL

The search for the First Americans has developed rapidly over the last few decades. As more archaeological data are identified, what we thought we knew about how and when the Americas were colonized has been revised, re-examined, and rewritten numerous times. This refinement in our understanding of the initial colonization of the Americas is the result of multidisciplinary research that has produced advancements in dating methods, paleoenvironmental reconstructions, and search techniques that have produced data that challenge previous theories of how and why human dispersals occur. These advancements are certainly not limited to the Americas, but reflect more widespread improvements in research techniques that look to clarify human movement and migrations, from premodern humans during the mid-Pleistocene (chapters 4 and 10) to the colonization of more distant island landmasses during the last few millennia (chapters 6 and 7). One major finding from decades of multidisciplinary research is that coastal habitats played a major role in facilitating dispersals around the globe (Erlandson and Fitzpatrick 2006; Henshilwood et al. 2001; Kirch 2017; Singer and Wyner 1982; Stiner 1999; Straus et al. 1993; Walter et al. 2000). While reasons for migrations and dispersals vary (see discussions in chapters 2, 3 and 4), one constant is that multiple lines of evidence are key to understanding these movements. From computer simulations of voyaging (chapter 12), to linguistic (chapter 9), chronometric (chapters 6 and 7), and ancient DNA data (chapter 8), island biogeography (chapter 10), and ecology (chapter 2), island and coastal researchers are producing vast amounts of multidisciplinary data that are integral for recognizing the complexity of human movements through space and time.

This is particularly true for dispersals into the Americas, where coastal regions and island landscapes have become focal points in the search for evidence of terminal Pleistocene migrations (Braje et al. 2017; Erlandson 2010, 2017; Erlandson and Braje 2015). With the more widespread acceptance of a possible Pleistocene migration along a coastal route (Braje et al. 2020), focused research efforts along the eastern Pacific shoreline have resulted in the discovery of over 100 Paleocoastal (~13,000–8,000 cal BP) archaeological sites (see Gusick and Erlandson 2019). These discoveries have been facilitated by multidisciplinary efforts to understand not only archaeological signatures, but also island biogeography, landform development, and paleoenvironmental shifts. While discovery of these terrestrial sites has driven interest toward these coastal regions, they likely represent only the tip of the iceberg for discoveries relevant to an initial occupation of the Americas. Indeed, recent efforts to advance our understanding of early coastal dispersals have gone below the waves and onto the continental shelf of the North American Pacific Coast.

Now in its early stages on the Pacific Coast of North America, precontact archaeology on the continental shelf has seen sustained research on submerged landscapes in other regions of North America for several decades (for example, Adovasio and Hemmings 2011; Dunbar et al. 1988; Evans et al. 2012; Faught 1988, 2004; Faught and Donahue 1997; Gagliano et al. 1982; Lowery and Martin 2009; Ruppe 1980). Worldwide, underwater archaeological research is widely practiced, with decades of research in numerous European regions (see Bailey et al. 2019; Benjamin et al. 2011; Gaffney et al. 2007), as well as Asia (see Hayashida et al. 2014), Africa (see Werz et al. 2014), and Oceania (see Nutley 2014). Scores of other scientists have also recognized that more extensive underwater research is necessary to answer sometimes even basic questions concerning initial or sustained habitation episodes in regions around the globe (for example, Bynoe et al. 2016; Erlandson and Fitzpatrick 2006; Felgate 2003; Gibbons and Clunie 1986; Roebroeks 2014). Within North America, submerged precontact archaeology is one of the last frontiers in First Americans research, and may rewrite what we think we know about the timing and manner of the peopling of the Americas.

That research on the eastern Pacific Coast continental shelf has been slow to develop in relation to other regions in North America and Europe may be partly due to the limited amount of offshore energy development and marine minerals extraction off the West Coast. The amount of oil and gas exploration along the North American Gulf Coast, which began in the 1940s, and interest in offshore wind energy along the Atlantic Coast over the last 15 years, has provided an abundance of geophysical survey data. Analysis of these data has identified several potential submerged landforms, some of which have been the subject of follow-up research funded by federal agencies such as Bureau of Ocean Energy Management (BOEM) and its predecessor, Minerals Management Service. Additionally, from a research perspective, there has been the assumption that the high wave energy of the Pacific Coast would have destroyed any archaeological sites on submerged landscapes. This is a regional concern, but it should not, and has not, stopped researchers from developing projects intended to better understand the dynamics of the continental shelf (Carabis et al. 2014; Dixon and Montelone 2014; Faught and Gusick 2011; Fedje and Christensen 1999; Fedje and Josenhans 2000; Gusick and Faught 2011; Gusick and Davis 2010; Mackie et al. 2013; Masters and Flemming 1983; Watts et al. 2011). These regional considerations make understanding what can—and cannot—be accomplished when conducting precontact archaeology on the continental shelf particularly important. As more and more researchers look to submerged landscapes to answer a variety of regionally pertinent research questions, it is imperative that we carefully consider best practices for underwater projects that consider regional variation.

Developing a regional methodology appropriate for the research questions being considered is a critical component for successful projects. As numerous researchers have pointed out, projects need to produce tangible results to encourage future interest and funding (for example, Erlandson and Fitzpatrick 2006: 14; Flemming 2010). This may seem obvious, but for precontact archaeology on the continental shelf, there is a general consensus that some amount of exploratory research is a necessary first step. By its nature, this type of research is considered high risk, and may not produce the desired results. However, such high-risk research cannot be what defines continental shelf archaeology. Flemming (2010: 276) noted that if we place too many expectations on finding submerged archaeological sites with underwater projects and little is discovered, then future funding could be in jeopardy. He suggests that projects should be "structured in such a way that there is a 'fail-safe' default component, plus a slightly risky 'hopeful' component, plus, if the project is big enough, a small 'blue skies wild guess' component." This sage advice should be the basis for a methodological approach for continental shelf archaeology in any region where this type of research occurs, but is particularly salient in those where underwater archaeological research is in its infancy.

The structure of a project and what defines a "fail-safe" or a "blue skies wild guess" component needs to be carefully considered within a regional context. In the North Sea region, for instance, where underwater archaeological research has been commonplace for decades, scientists have defined the structure of the remnant relict landscape in certain areas on the seabed (for example, Fitch and Gaffney 2013; Fitch et al. 2005; Gaffney et al. 2017; Tizzard et al. 2011). Research in these areas, where "hot spots" for preserved inundated cultural material may already be defined, will vary from regions such as the West Coast of the Americas where the paleoenvironment and structure of regional remnant relict landscapes are just beginning to be defined. On the West Coast, "hot spots" have not yet been defined enough to structure projects with a singular goal of finding submerged archaeological sites. There is always the possibility of a chance find, but to advance the discipline in the Americas, and other areas where submerged archaeological research is in its inception, we must first understand the complex dynamics of regional submerged continental shelves. On North America's Pacific Coast, this will require multiple lines of evidence from projects that take a broad landscape approach to help form baselines for future research, and that produce results useful to a wide variety of disciplines, thereby encouraging future funding. To achieve this level of success, we need to re-evaluate how regional underwater projects are developed.

Developing Methods

Various publications describe the methods and best practices for precontact archaeological research on the continental shelf. The majority provide universal methods that form a baseline for conducting underwater research (for example, Benjamin 2010; Faught and Gusick 2011; Gusick and Faught 2011; Masters and Flemming 1983; Muckelroy 1978; Ruppe 1988). These have both introduced the discipline of continental shelf archaeology to a wider audience and highlighted discipline-specific methods and theories that are moving underwater research from the fringe of archaeological science to a more mainstream subdiscipline. Early in the development of underwater archaeology, Ruppe (1988: 56) pointed out that "the archaeology of drowned terrestrial sites does not differ greatly from work done on dry sites," except for the scuba gear and increased atmospheric pressure. He also defined three major factors that should be considered

Amy E. Gusick, Todd J. Braje, Jon M. Erlandson, Jillian Maloney, and David Ball

when identifying and studying precontact sites on the continental shelf: "sea level change, coastal morphology, and coastal settlement patterns" (Ruppe 1988: 57). Numerous other pioneers of underwater archaeology have discussed their own methods, and nearly all include Ruppe's three factors (for example, Bailey and Flemming 2008; Benjamin et al. 2011; Dunbar et al. 1992; Evans et al. 2014; Faught 2004; Fischer 1995; Gusick and Faught 2011; Hudson 1976; Josenhans et al. 1997; Lübke 2003; Masters and Flemming 1983; Momber 2000, 2005; Skaarup 1995).

Nearly a decade ago, Benjamin (2010: 257) authored a seminal paper focused on creating a "framework for identifying appropriate variables in order to evaluate coastal regions for potential precontact underwater archaeological site discovery." Noting that the task of identifying such sites is a challenge hindered first and foremost by the sheer amount of submerged terrain around the globe, Benjamin (2010: 257) noted that a universal methodology for finding and excavating submerged precontact sites may be impossible due to the oceanographic and environmental variability of submerged terrains. This point was also stressed by Ford and Halligan (2010: 278), who provided feedback to the model based on their experiences in southern and eastern North America. They argued that deeply submerged landscapes, as opposed to shallow water and nearshore ones, typically require more intensive logistics and planning. Ultimately, sound methodologies must be at least partially based on localized research conditions. Doing so will result in a better understanding of the specific factors that may influence the efficacy of submerged sites research (Bailey and Flemming 2008; Evans et al. 2014).

Precontact Archaeology on the West Coast Continental Shelf

Regarding precontact archaeology along the continental shelf of North America's Pacific Coast, there are a number of overarching principles that should be applied when developing research plans. These principles can apply to a variety of settings around the globe, but should be considered in a regional context. It is beyond the scope of this chapter to detail all considerations, but a few of them bear repeating. Foremost is the accurate reconstruction and understanding of the paleolandscape. Prior to modeling areas of archaeological sensitivity, data should be gathered about the formation of landscapes during the Pleistocene and Holocene. Research should attempt to reconstruct areas of high biological productivity (riparian, estuarine, rocky intertidal, kelp forests, and so on), as well as features that are important for successful human habitation, such as freshwater sources, tool-quality stone outcrops, and caves and rockshelters used for shelter (Gusick and Faught 2011; Rick et al. 2013; Watts et al. 2011). Obtaining these data requires extensive background research prior to collecting initial remote sensing data. Off the Pacific Coast, there have been several large-scale geophysical surveys conducted with federal funding that produced publicly available data (for example, Johnson et al. 2015). Detailed nautical charts can provide guidance, and recent updates to relative sea-level curves are available (Clark et al. 2014; Reeder-Myers et al. 2015). Additionally, Bynoe et al. (2016) provide an often-overlooked resource for establishing a broad record of the offshore zone: extant museum collections. Their work in the North Sea utilized historical records and faunal remains—collected during activities such as trawling for fish—that had been curated at museums worldwide. Remains with sufficient provenience were used to infer general age and a coarse-grained picture of the environment associated with individual species. In regions where these types of museum collections are available, data gleaned from faunal remains can provide general insight about submerged paleolandscapes and environments.

A broad understanding of the paleolandscape includes myriad factors that have been previously detailed in the literature (for example, Benjamin 2010; Gusick and Faught 2011; Masters and Flemming 1983). One especially important factor is sea-level history. Models of paleolandscape changes through time can provide important morphological data, and paleoenvironmental reconstructions can inform about types of habitats that may have been present. However, the rate at which landscape and habitats were inundated during marine transgression is critical for modeling paleoshorelines and understanding ancient human behavior, as well as predicting the likelihood that submerged sites are preserved. Eustatic sea-level curves may be used to model Pleistocene shorelines relatively accurately in some areas (Fairbanks 1989; Peltier 2002), but many regions are impacted by a combination of tectonic, eustatic, and isostatic activity that greatly affects paleoshoreline location (Stright 1995). This is particularly true for the eastern Pacific coast, where both glacial loading and frequent tectonic activity result in paleoshoreline placement that cannot be calculated using the history of eustatic sea-level rise alone (Mackie et al. 2013). Along California's Northern Channel Islands, shorelines were submerged by marine transgression during the last glacial melting, but tectonic activity has caused a lower uplift rate than within the onshore Transverse Range province, which is an extension of these islands (Muhs et al. 2014). In the Haida Gwaii region of British Columbia, isostatic depression during the Last Glacial Maximum resulted in some inland relict shorelines, rather than deeply submerged (Clague 1983; Fedje and Chris-

Amy E. Gusick, Todd J. Braje, Jon M. Erlandson, Jillian Maloney, and David Ball

tensen 1999: 637; Josenhans et al. 1997; McLaren et al. 2007). These are just two examples that highlight the need for a detailed, local sea-level history on the eastern Pacific Coast, and elsewhere around the globe. Adding to the complication, accurate reconstructions of paleoshorelines require an understanding of the extent of marine sediment cover on the transgressive surface, the history of marine erosion, and other factors affecting the position of terrestrial sediment below the seafloor.

Most models of archaeologically sensitive inundated landscapes rely, at least in part, on terrestrial analogs. Considering the local or regional prehistory—the antiquity of human occupation, for example—can be important in narrowing initial search areas and parameters. Generalized resources necessary for human survival, such as freshwater, are universal, but the availability of freshwater sources varies tremendously along the Pacific Coast. Understanding settlement patterning during relevant time periods may also be useful for identifying other landscape features where sites on subaerial landscapes have been consistently identified. Are certain lithic outcrops targeted for exploitation? What types of habitats produce resources found in the greatest abundance in archaeological sites? Are certain landforms, such as caves, knolls, or elevated terraces, known to harbor sites from relevant time periods? Are there cultural activities that may leave unique traces on the landscape? Mackie and colleagues (2017), for example, identified a rectangular depression cut into the side of a hill on a submerged landscape in Juan Perez Sound off Haida Gwaii, British Columbia. This feature resembles the Alaskan semisubterranean houses known from terrestrial archaeological research and is approximately 1 km away from, but in the same embayment as, a stone tool recovered from a submerged landscape (Fedje and Josenhans 2000). This unique feature might have been overlooked had the researchers not been familiar with the ancient settlement patterns practiced in their research area.

While potential terrestrial analogs should be explored, these should not be used without consideration of their applicability. Ford and Halligan (2010: 278) argue for caution when using terrestrial-based models, particularly on deeply submerged landscapes. The current subaerial sites used to model cultural patterns may lie in a different landscape and environmental context than during the time period of habitation. Sites on or near the shoreline today may have been far removed from the coast prior to marine transgression. While these inland sites can still provide data with which to help guide submerged research, their context should be considered when used as an analog, particularly if the goal is to identify submerged sites that reflect a coastal resource use pattern.

Additionally, relatively rapid sea-level rise that occurred at the end of the late Pleistocene and early Holocene greatly affected the distribution of marine and terrestrial habitats along the Pacific Coast. The inundation of lowlands and coastal canyons, increased salinity of rivers, conversion of intertidal to subtidal habitats, and the creation of estuaries would have altered biodiversity and marine productivity (Kinlan et al. 2005; Scavia et al. 2002). Cultural adaptations to such changes may have resulted in unique settlement and economic patterns that may not be applicable during times of climatic stability (Ford and Halligan 2010: 278). While these considerations do not preclude the use of terrestrial analogs, they should be used cautiously in conjunction with other lines of evidence.

The importance of regionally specific methods is further highlighted when considering the different oceanographic conditions and coastal morphology present along the eastern Pacific shoreline compared to regions like the gulfs of California and Mexico, or regions like the North Sea. The Pacific Coast of North America is a tectonically active margin, characterized by a narrow and steep coastal plain and shelf with submarine canyons near the shoreline. While these features may be of special interest to archaeologists, the oceanographic conditions that accompany them can create challenges in preservation and underwater exploration. Submarine canyons would have facilitated predation of large pelagic fish that are found closer to shore in the deep water of the canyons (Glassow et al. 2008; Porcasi and Fujita 2000). This deep water also reduces wave height along the shoreline, facilitating use of watercraft in subsistence pursuits (Masters 2010). These factors may have encouraged habitation near these features, and archaeological sensitivity models may show adjacent landscapes to be ideal areas to look for archaeological sites. However, in regions where there is not a deepwater buffer, waves can be extreme and create preservation issues for sites on the continental shelf. This coastal context differs drastically from that found in the gulfs of California and Mexico, where reduced wave and tidal action and an extensive, shallow continental shelf may have encouraged rapid sedimentation during marine transgression, offering a measure of protection to sites that may have been quickly inundated. The generally high energy of the Pacific Coast requires researchers to consider the preservation potential of any possible study area (Fedje and Christensen 1999).

While the physical characteristics of the coast need to be considered during project development, also important is the inclusion of communities who have an interest in and connection to the landscape. On the Pacific Coast of North America, there are a variety of Native American communities with strong ties

Amy E. Gusick, Todd J. Braje, Jon M. Erlandson, Jillian Maloney, and David Ball

to the land and sea where their ancestors thrived. For those communities with a maritime heritage, their knowledge of the ancient land and seascape can greatly benefit project development, and any concerns about potential impacts to cultural resources must be considered. For projects subject to state and/or federal funding or regulatory actions, consultation between representatives from potentially affected Native American tribes and agency officials is not only required, but is critically important. Consultation should occur as early as possible in the planning stage of the project; efforts must be robust and meaningful and may include written communications, face-to-face meetings, and other avenues intended to open dialog between tribal representatives, agency officials, and project scientists. Sufficient time should be included in the initial project planning stage to facilitate meaningful consultation.

These considerations are not an exhaustive list of the issues to consider for continental shelf archaeology, but are some of the primary concerns when designing projects that take a landscape approach. For most of the continental shelf of western North America, we have not yet developed the necessary foundation to effectively model submerged site locations via a landscape approach (however, see Fedje and Christensen 1999; Mackie et al. 2017). As such, underwater research efforts need to focus on identifying regions where a reasonable potential exists for identifying preserved sites. Research in these regions should first focus on broad-scale mapping and data collection that can result in fine-grained integration of multiple datasets to narrow search parameters. In doing so, we can provide the "fail-safe default component" that Flemming (2010: 276) argued should be among project deliverables. While the majority of these data will come from disciplines such as geology, palynology, and marine biology, among others, they should be interpreted using a cultural framework and one that highlights the importance of a multidisciplinary approach.

Project Example: Northern Channel Islands

On the continental shelf of western North America, we are employing these standards in a multidisciplinary project focused on California's Northern Channel Islands (Figure 5.1). The first of its kind in southern California, our work addresses two pressing anthropological questions: when did humans first migrate into the Americas and how did they get here? While these questions have been central to scores of research projects on the Channel Islands, ours is the first to venture under the waves in search of submerged, precontact archaeological sites to address these questions.

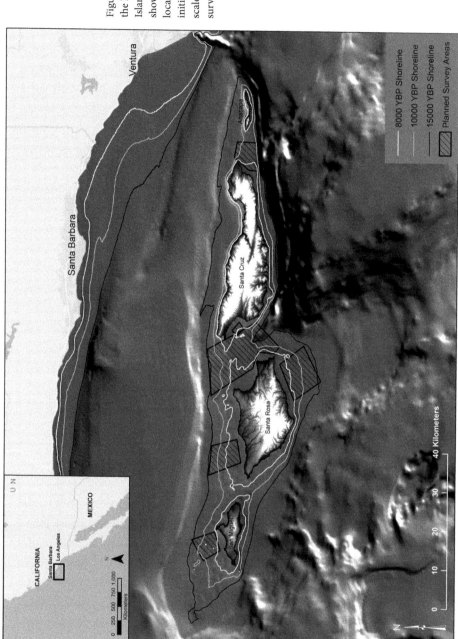

Figure 5.1. Location of the Northern Channel Islands off California showing general survey locations identified for initial broad landscape scale remote sensing surveys.

The Northern Channel Islands currently include four separate landmasses: Anacapa, Santa Cruz, Santa Rosa, and San Miguel islands. Located ~20–44 km off the mainland of California, these islands have yielded over 100 Paleocoastal sites, including four that date to 12,000 cal BP and older (Erlandson et al. 2011; Gusick and Erlandson 2019; Reeder-Meyer et al. 2015; Rick et al. 2013). While these discoveries have helped define early maritime occupation in the Americas, the most intriguing data may lie on the islands' continental shelf. Initially located only 7–8 km from the mainland coast (Reeder-Meyers et al. 2015), the four separate islands once formed a 125 km long single landmass called Santarosae (Erlandson 2016). Sea-level rise of ~100–110 m since the end of the Last Glacial Maximum inundated roughly 75 percent of Santarosae, likely submerging sites that may be key to understanding the terminal Pleistocene archaeology and historical ecology of the landmass, and illuminating the timing of a coastal migration into the Americas.

Research on the subaerial and submerged portions of Santarosae is the latest example of a broad and multidisciplinary study on the continental shelf of North America. Our work exemplifies the approach needed to form a solid foundation for submerged sites research on the Pacific Coast of the Americas. Although ongoing, the methods for this project are discussed below to show how a phased multidisciplinary approach may be the best way to tackle the complexities of understanding landscape formation, tectonic activity, sea-level rise, sedimentation, habitat shifts, and other factors relevant to submerged sites research along the vast Pacific Coast continental shelves, and elsewhere around the globe.

The current project, *Archaeological and Biological Assessment of Submerged Landforms off the Pacific Coast* (ABAS), is funded by BOEM and has numerous federal agency, university, and museum partners. Partnerships between academia and the government are ideal for conducting large-scale projects that require substantial funding. They can be designed to meet the regulatory obligations of the agency partner and fulfill the research agenda of the scientists. Offshore industry projects, like those for oil and gas or renewable energies, typically must consider multiple environmental impacts under federal regulations such as the National Environmental Policy Act and the National Historic Preservation Act, and statewide regulations like the California Environmental Quality Act, among others. Consideration of cultural resources (that is, archaeological sites), is one part of a larger effort and benefits from more extensive resources (that is, funding and data from other sciences) than are typically available for stand-alone archaeological projects. This type of academic/agency partnership has been the basis for much of the submerged precontact archaeological work conducted to date in the United States (for example, Adovasio and Hemmings 2011; Aubry and Stright 1999; Coastal Environments, Inc. 1977; Evans 2016; Evans et al. 2012; Gagliano et al. 1982; Pearson et al. 1986; Pendelton and Tobin 2002; Watts 2004); but most of this work has been in the Gulf of Mexico. The ABAS project is the largest of its kind to be funded so far by a government agency along the Pacific Coast. The goal of the project is to provide BOEM with a predictive model to improve their identification of submerged precontact sites on the Pacific Coast outer continental shelf (POCS). This will help BOEM meet its regulatory obligation to understand and avoid potential impacts to cultural resources when considering applications for offshore energy development projects. To meet this goal, our team of experts in archaeology, biology, marine geology, and predictive modeling using Geographic Information Systems (GIS) was compiled. We designed the project collaboratively and focused on four main phases: (1) data synthesis; (2) target identification/model building; (3) field investigation/model building; and (4) field investigation/ model refinement.

Data Synthesis

This first phase of the project was arguably the most important. A thorough review of the literature and available data for the region of interest helped to narrow the search area, a necessary step when considering the vast submerged Pleistocene and Holocene–aged landscapes along the Pacific Coast. All available data from previous geophysical surveys were collected and reviewed with an interdisciplinary team. It was during this phase that the archaeological record from the Northern Channel Islands was combined with geological and geomorphic seabed data to provide a robust ecological dataset. These data were reviewed by the team with the ultimate goal of collecting samples of the submerged landscape. For instance, an area that is known to have a hard substrate with no sediment cover would not be conducive to the sediment-sampling regime needed to identify landscape evolution and paleoenvironmental conditions.

One dataset that was especially important for helping narrow our initial search parameters was a predictive model developed for BOEM by ICF International, Davis Geoarchaeological Research Group, and Southeastern Archaeological Research (2013). This study modeled coastal and submerged site potential in and adjacent to the POCS off Washington, Oregon, and California. Modern bathymetry, crustal deformations, ancient stream systems, and eustatic and relative sea-level histories were used to construct a GIS-based model of areas with potential to have preserved archaeological sites (ICF International, Davis Geoarchaeological Research Group, and Southeastern Archaeological Research 2013: 1). The model predicted the landscapes on which more data should be collected to consider their feasibility for additional research and did not predict site locations. Creating a generalized model of landscape sensitivity can aid in initial phases and should be done prior to collecting any known geophysical data to narrow the datasets that need to be analyzed.

Collection of relevant datasets for the ABAS project focused on those that were publicly available, as well as those collected through research by the project collaborators and their colleagues. These data focused on a variety of information including habitat zones, seafloor character, seabed geology, faults, surficial sediment, nautical charts, fishing maps, terrestrial environmental data, geomorphology, and others.

It was during this initial phase of project planning that BOEM started the consultation process with the Santa Ynez Band of Chumash Indians (SYBCI), the only federally recognized tribe within the proposed area of study. The research team also met with representatives of non–federally recognized tribes within the study area, in order to inform them of the proposed research and identify opportunities for collaboration. Initial contacts included letters from BOEM and Channel Islands National Park informing all parties of the proposed work. We then scheduled two days of meetings at the SYBCI reservation, where a presentation was given and a question-and-answer session was held for all interested parties and the Santa Ynez Elders Council. It was during this initial consultation process that monitors were identified for our terrestrial project work, and we were able to identify a representative from SYBCI that participated in some of the offshore survey work.

Target Identification/Model Building

Once relevant datasets were gathered and analyzed, they needed to be synthesized. This included visualizations of the datasets in various software applications. ArcGIS was used as the main vehicle for model building and allowed for multiple data layers to be included in our geospatial analysis. This analysis considered previous geophysical datasets, including subbottom, bathymetric, and backscatter data. Subbottom datasets were initially compiled into IHS Kingdom Suite software (www.kingdom.ihs.com). This program allowed us to trace acoustic horizons, map and measure sediment units, generate isopach maps, map faults and paleochannels, and compare subbottom data with sediment core data, where available. Additionally, all geophysical datasets were visualized and interpreted using QPS Fledermaus software (www.qps.nl/display/fledermaus), in which subbottom data can be overlain with bathymetry and backscatter data. Analysis using this software was integral as it provided 3D visualization of the mapped sections of seafloor and sub-seafloor at a level not available in ArcGIS. By creating a "fence" diagram that overlaid the different geophysical datasets, we could highlight features such as sediment thickness, regional unconformities, faults, and other features below and at the seafloor. Integral to this step was the technical expertise of the marine geologist partners on the project. These scientists are technically trained in sonar image interpretation of seabed morphology and subbottom stratigraphy. These types of broad-scale sonar surveys are commonly conducted for marine geology research on continental shelf morphology, sediment processes, tectonics, and continental margin evolution (for example, Hill et al. 2007; Laws et al. 2019; Nordfjord et al. 2009; Le Dantec et al. 2010; Schwab et al. 2014; Klotsko et al. 2015). The findings of these studies may have implications for submerged archaeological investigations, including paleoenvironmental reconstructions and site preservation potential. A regional review of sonar data helped narrow our search area to landscapes that not only were archaeologically intriguing, but also had the geomorphic and geological context necessary for successful sample collection.

The overarching goal of this phase was to consult the previous large-scale predictive model developed for BOEM and focus on a more specific landscape for field survey. The data synthesis and analysis described above was used to narrow search areas and to identify regions where sufficient data were already collected. These data provided a general understanding of the seafloor and helped us avoid collecting data in areas already surveyed. The existing datasets were overlaid with archaeological data, and five landscapes were targeted for a broad paleolandscape field survey.

Important in all offshore projects is a contingency plan for foul weather. As such, we ranked our five main survey areas in order of importance. Our research plan included a survey of four areas, but a fifth was included in a relatively protected context in the event that we encountered high winds, dangerous waves, and rough seas (see Figure 5.1).

Field Investigation/Model Building

The field investigation phase of the project included three components: (1) a broad-scale sonar survey for submerged paleolandscape characterization; (2) a high resolution sonar survey for selection of sample sites; and (3) a terrestrial survey to fill critical gaps. The goal for this research phase was to shrink the "haystack" and identify high probability targets for testing. Depending on the depths and oceanographic conditions of the study area, this phase could include various methods for target identification. Sonar, remotely operated underwater vehicles (ROV), autonomous underwater vehicles (AUV), and/or diver surveys may be employed. For the ABAS project, the deeply submerged landscapes that were the focus for investigation required remote sensing surveys, rather than diver investigation. Even on landscapes within conventional diving limits (see Gusick and Faught 2011: 40–41), sonar, ROV, or AUV surveys should be employed during initial investigation as they can provide a broad-scale understanding of the submerged landscape. Subsequent investigation can then be tailored to use the most effective methods for fine-grained target inspection.

To conduct the broad landscape–scale survey for the ABAS project, we used a Klein 3000H (455 kHz) side scan sonar and an Edgetech 512 (0.5–16 kHz) Chirp subbottom profiler. The Chirp subbottom profiler provided submeter vertical resolution and ~40 m sub-seafloor imaging. This sonar equipment was used to capture images of large swathes of the seafloor and sub-seafloor for broadscale paleolandscape interpretations. Sonar image interpretation focused on identification of large features including fault systems, major geomorphology (that is, paleochannels, canyons, dune fields, paleoshorelines, and terraces), and transgressive surfaces that were either buried (subbottom) or visible on the seafloor (side scan). Survey line spacing and frequency of equipment varied based on the landscape and image quality. Four offshore areas were the target for these broad, paleolandscape-scale surveys: two areas within the Santa Cruz Channel, north-central Santa Rosa Island off Arlington Canyon, and off southeastern Santa Cruz Island. Initial observations and potential targets were recorded live during the survey.

After completion of the sonar survey, all data were compiled and reviewed in IHS Kingdom Suite and QPS Fledermaus software (Figure 5.2). The goal for the image interpretation was to select four 1 km^2 areas for a more targeted, second sonar survey. This follow-up survey was intended to target small sections of the landscape that were deemed to have high potential to yield paleolandscape and paleoenvironmental data during the sampling phase of the project (discussed below). The goal of the second sonar survey was to provide scientists the opportunity to select specific targets for sampling by providing high-resolution images above and below the seafloor. The four 1 km^2 study areas were surveyed using the same subbottom unit used in the first survey and a Reson 7125 (200

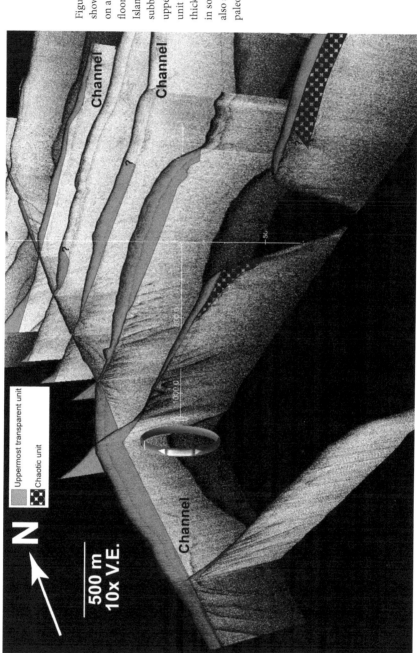

Figure 5.2. Fence diagram showing sediment units on a section of the sea floor off Santa Rosa Island imaged with a subbottom profiler. The uppermost transparent unit indicates sediment thickness, which is ~20 m in some areas. Diagram also shows possible paleochannel location.

kHz) multibeam with backscatter. The survey swath line spacing was set at 25 m with 25 percent overlap for complete coverage of the survey areas.

The terrestrial portion of this phase was designed to support the submerged research by filling in critical gaps in site identification on the Northern Channel Islands. Many of the Paleocoastal site surveys on these islands have focused on San Miguel and Santa Rosa islands (for example, Erlandson et al. 2011; Rick et al. 2013). As such, several Paleocoastal site clusters have been identified on these islands. Recent surveys on western Santa Cruz Island have identified other clusters of early sites (Erlandson et al. 2016; Gusick 2013). The growing number of Paleocoastal sites identified around the margins of the Santa Cruz Channel led Erlandson (2016) to identify a large south-facing, semiprotected paleoembayment he called Crescent Bay. Our BOEM-sponsored research has identified several additional Paleocoastal sites in this area, which has provided important insights into the paleogeography of the submerged landscape in the area.

Two of our offshore survey areas fall within the margins of Crescent Bay, where an ancient estuary, marsh habitats, a submarine canyon, and abundant freshwater may have attracted early maritime peoples. Previously known and newly recorded Paleocoastal sites also provided invaluable data on the landforms utilized by some of the earliest islanders, providing analogs that are guiding our search for similar landforms or features offshore. Our ABAS project views the submerged and subaerial landscapes as one continuous maritime landscape once available for settlement and utilization by Paleocoastal people.

This correlation between terrestrial and underwater research is a critical component to projects designed to consider a landscape approach. While numerous researchers have cautioned against terrestrial-based projects that stop at the shoreline and do not consider the entire landscape at the time of habitation, the same caution applies to research focused on the submerged terrain. A complete landscape approach may include both the submerged and subaerial paleolandscape, depending upon the time period of interest and sea-level history.

Field Investigation/Model Refinement

Having divers in the water can be the most effective way to investigate features identified during remote sensing surveys. However, on deeply submerged landscapes, dive operations to investigate and/or sample targets may not be feasible. Other options include ROV inspection with possible grab samples and sediment coring. For the ABAS project, we designed a sediment-coring regime

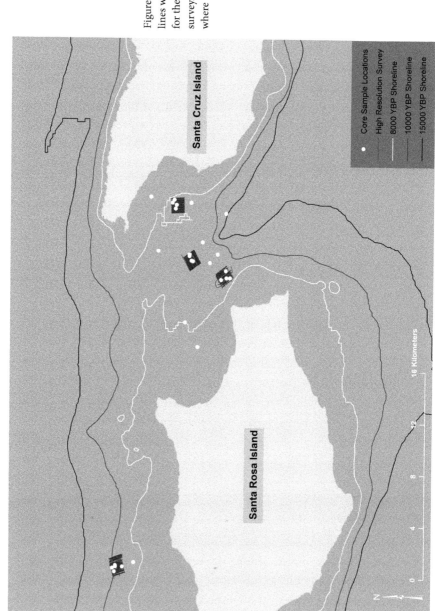

Figure 5.3. Gray boxes are track lines within the four 1 km² boxes for the high-resolution targeted survey. White dots indicate areas where cores were collected.

using a vibracore as the sampling strategy for a number of reasons. The main objective of the project was to gather data to inform on landscape and environmental evolution throughout the late Pleistocene and early Holocene. The stratigraphic sequence that can be captured from collected vibracore samples is integral not only in identifying marine sediment load, but also in collecting samples from shallow, buried terrestrial soils or estuarine sediments. It is within these sediments that we can collect material for radiocarbon dating to provide key information on a variety of issues, including the refinement of local sea-level curves. The stratigraphic sequences in these cores can also help elucidate the timeframe for the presence of key environmental features such as riparian, estuarine, and lacustrine habitats. Vibracoring also provides the opportunity to sample from different acoustic signatures identified on sonar images in an effort to ground-truth sonar image interpretation.

Selection of targets for the coring regime focused on four core locations within each of the 1 km² survey boxes (Figure 5.3). The targets for coring varied from 20 to 75 m in water depth. In the areas surrounding the Northern Channel Islands, the landscape between these depths would have been inundated from 13,000 to 7,000 years ago (Reeder-Meyers et al. 2015), providing an opportunity

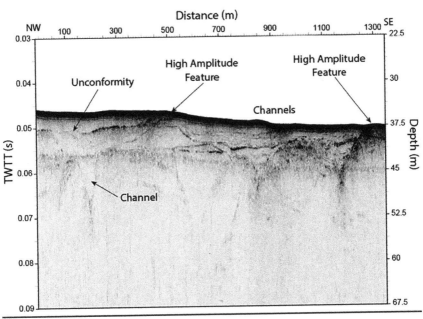

Figure 5.4. Image from subbottom profiler showing types of features and anomalies we used to select core locations. A paleochannel, changes in sediment possibly indicating lacustrine or estuary sediment, and high amplitude features that may be shell deposits are interpreted.

to understand how this marine transgression impacted local habitat and landscape development. Targets for coring were selected based on a variety of factors, including thickness of marine sediment, possible freshwater seeps, and the presence of a shallow, buried transgressive surface, acoustic signatures suggestive of estuary environments, interpreted paleochannels, and buried anomalies near freshwater sources (Figure 5.4). Core tubes were 4.5 m long and 9 cm in diameter. Collected cores were analyzed and stored at the Marine and Geology Repository at Oregon State University. Core analysis included p-wave, bulk density, and magnetic susceptibility, X-radiography, elemental geochemistry, optical imaging, and radiocarbon dating, as appropriate.

Conclusions

Data from the marine cores are not yet available, but the sonar data collected during the project have already proven useful in a number of studies on the geology of the region (Klotsko et al. 2020; Laws et al. 2019; Maloney et al. 2016; Maloney et al. 2017; Tahiry et al. 2018). The multidisciplinary approach used for the ABAS project allows for results to be realized at various stages in the process, alleviating a concern for funding agencies considering high-risk endeavors. When more data do become available from the collected cores, we do not expect there to be archaeological evidence among the findings. We do, however, expect the data to be valuable to various disciplines and form the basis for understanding late Pleistocene and early Holocene landscapes and environments of Santarosae. These data will show that those portions of the continental shelf that were part of the 75 percent of Santarosae lost to postglacial sea-level rise must be considered in studies of Paleocoastal maritime hunter-gatherers that inhabited this region, and perhaps to our understanding of the initial human colonization of the Americas. Because the earliest islanders were maritime peoples who gathered the majority of their food resources from the coastal and marine environments that were subaerial at the end of the Last Glacial Maximum, one can assume that a significant amount of the material they left behind would have been discarded near the shore, and now lies on the continental shelf surrounding the islands. These submerged landscapes may hold the key to addressing some of the region's most pressing questions about the spread of humans around the globe and ecological responses to extreme climatic conditions such as rapid sea-level rise, shifting sea surface temperatures, and dramatic habitat shifts, making this region one of the most promising for advancing research on precontact archaeology on the continental shelf in North America.

While this case study is specific to the continental shelf surrounding the Northern Channel Islands, this framework of a phased regional approach can be applied in other areas that may harbor submerged archaeological sites. There is no universal approach that will be relevant on a global scale, but one constant is the need to understand the local region, local considerations, and extent of knowledge about local paleolandscapes and archaeological history. Within this framework, submerged archaeological research can become an integral part of the anthropological discipline and expand our knowledge of a wide array of important anthropological and ecological issues.

References Cited

Adovasio, J. M., and A. Hemmings. 2011. Geoarchaeological Explorations on the Inner-Continental Shelf of the Florida Gulf of Mexico. BOEM Information Transfer Meeting, March 23, 2011, New Orleans, Louisiana.

Aubry, M. C., and M. Stright. 1999. Beneath the Waters of Time: Interior's Submerged Cultural Resource Programs. *CRM* 4: 54–56.

Bailey, G. N., and N. C. Flemming. 2008. Archaeology of the Continental Shelf: Marine Resources, Submerged Landscapes, and Underwater Archaeology. *Quaternary Science Reviews* 27: 2153–2165.

Bailey, G., N. Galanidou, H. Jöns, H. Peeters, and M. Mennenga. 2019. *The Archaeology of Europe's Drowned Landscapes.* New York: Springer.

Benjamin, J. 2010. Submerged Prehistoric Landscapes and Underwater Site Discovery: Reevaluating the "Danish Model" for International Practice. *Journal of Island and Coastal Archaeology* 5(2): 253–270.

Benjamin, J., C. Bonsall, C. Pickard, and A. Fischer (eds.). 2011. *Submerged Prehistory.* Oxford: Oxbow Books.

Braje, Todd J., T. Dillehay, J. M. Erlandson, R. G. Klein, and T. Rick. 2017. Finding the First Americans. *Science* 358(6363): 592–594.

Braje, Todd J., J. M. Erlandson, T. C. Rick, L. Davis, T. Dillehay, D. W. Fedje, D. Froese, A. E. Gusick, Q. Mackie, D. McLaren, B., and Pitblado. 2020. Fladmark+ 40: What Have We Learned about a Potential Pacific Coast Peopling of the Americas? *American Antiquity* 85(1): 1–21.

Bynoe, R., J. K. Dix and F. Sturt. 2016. Of Mammoths and Other Monsters: Historic Approaches to the Submerged Palaeolithic. *Antiquity* 90(352): 857–875.

Carabis, D., I. Cartajena, R. Simonetti, P. López, C. Morales, and C. Ortega. 2014. Submerged Paleolandscapes: Site GNL Quintero 1 (GNLQ1) and the First Evidences from the Pacific Coast of South America. In *Prehistoric Archaeology on the Continental Shelf,* ed. A. Evans, J. Flatman, and N. Flemming, 131–149. New York: Springer.

Clague, J. J. 1983. Glacio-isostatic Effects of the Cordilleran Ice Sheet, British Columbia, Canada. In *Shorelines and Isostasy,* ed. D. E. Smith and A. G. Dawson, 321–343. London: Academic Press.

Clark, J., J. X. Mitrovica, and J. Alder. 2014. Coastal Paleogeography of the California–Oregon–Washington and Bering Sea Continental Shelves during the Latest Pleistocene and Holocene: Implications for the Archaeological Record. *Journal of Archaeological Science* 52: 12–23.

Coastal Environments, Inc. (CEI). 1977. Cultural Resources Evaluation of the Northern Gulf of Mexico Continental Shelf. Submitted to Interagency Archaeological Services Office of

Archaeology and Historical Preservation, National Park Service, U.S. Department of the Interior, Baton Rouge, Louisiana.

Dixon, J. E., and K. Monteleone. 2014. Gateway to the Americas: Underwater Archeological Survey in Beringia and the North Pacific. In *Prehistoric Archaeology on the Continental Shelf,* ed. A. Evans, J. Flatman, and N. Flemming, 95–114. New York: Springer.

Dunbar, J. S., D. S. Webb, and M. K. Faught. 1988. Page/Ladson (8Je591): An Underwater Paleo-Indian Site in Northwestern Florida. *Florida Anthropologist* 41(4): 442–452.

Dunbar, J. S., D. S. Webb, and M. K. Fought. 1992. Inundated Prehistoric Sites in Apalachee Bay, Florida, and the Search for the Clovis Shoreline. In *Paleoshorelines and Prehistory: An Investigation of Method,* ed. L. L. Johnson and M. Stright, 177–246. Boca Raton, Florida: CRC Press.

Erlandson, J. M. 2010. Ancient Immigrants and Maritime Migrations. In *Migration History: Multidisciplinary Approaches,* ed. J. Lucassen, L. Lucassen, and P. Manning, 189–214. Leiden: Brill.

Erlandson, J. M. 2017. Coastlines, Marine Ecology and Maritime Dispersals in Human History. In *Human Dispersal and Species Movement: From Prehistory to Present,* ed. N. Boivin, R. Crassard, and M. Petraglia, 147–163. Cambridge: Cambridge University Press.

Erlandson, J. M. 2016. Seascapes of Santarosae: Paleocoastal Seafaring on California's Channel Islands. In *Marine Ventures: Archaeological Perspectives on Human-Sea Relations,* ed. H. B. Bjerck, H. M. Breivik, S. E. Fretheim, E. L. Piana, B. Skar, A. M. Tivoli, and J. Zangrando, 317–327. Sheffield: Equinox.

Erlandson, J. M., and T. J. Braje. 2015. Coasting out of Africa: The Potential of Mangrove Forests and Marine Habitats to Facilitate Human Coastal Expansion via the Southern Dispersal Route. *Quaternary International* 382: 31–41.

Erlandson, J. M., and S. M. Fitzpatrick. 2006. Oceans, Islands, and Coasts: Current Perspectives on the Role of the Sea in Human Prehistory. *Journal of Island and Coastal Archaeology* 1(1): 5–33.

Erlandson, J. M., K. M. Gill, M. A. Glassow, and A. E. Gusick. 2016. Three Paleocoastal Lithic Sites on Santa Cruz Island, California. *PaleoAmerica,* 2(1): 52–55.

Erlandson, J. M., T. C. Rick, T. J. Braje, M. Casperson, B. Culleton, B. Fulfrost, T. Garcia, D. Guthrie, N. Jew, D. Kennett, M. L. Moss, L. Reeder, C. E. Skinner, J. Watts, and L. M. Willis. 2011. Paleoindian Seafaring, Maritime Technologies, and Coastal Foraging on California's Channel Islands. *Science* 441: 1181–1185.

Evans, A. M. 2016. *Examining and Testing Potential Prehistoric Archaeological Features on the Gulf of Mexico Outer Continental Shelf.* Submitted to U.S. Department of the Interior, Bureau of Ocean Energy Management, Gulf of Mexico OCS Region, New Orleans, Louisiana. OCS Study BOEM 2016–015.

Evans, A. M., J. C. Flatman, and N. C. Flemming (eds.). 2014. *Prehistoric Archaeology on the Continental Shelf.* New York: Springer.

Evans, A. M., M. E. Keith, E. E. Voisin, P. Hesp, G. Cook, M. Allison, G. da Silva, and E. Swanson. 2012. *Archaeological Analysis of Submerged Sites on the Gulf of Mexico Outer Continental Shelf, U.S.* Submitted to Department of the Interior, Bureau of Ocean Energy Management, Gulf of Mexico OCS Region, New Orleans, Louisiana. OCS Study BOEM 2012–011110.

Fairbanks, R. G. 1989. A 17,000-year Glacio-eustatic Sea-level Record: Influence of Glacial Melting Rates on the Younger Dryas Event and Deep-ocean Circulation. *Nature* 324: 637–642.

Faught, M. K. 1988. Inundated Sites in the Apalachee Bay Area of the Eastern Gulf of Mexico. *Florida Anthropologist* 41: 185–190.

Faught, M. K. 2004. The Underwater Archaeology of Paleolandscapes, Apalachee Bay, Florida. *American Antiquity* 69(2): 275–289.

Faught, M. K., and J. F. Donoghue. 1997. Marine Inundated Archaeological Sites and Paleofluvial Systems: Examples from a Karst-Controlled Continental Shelf Setting in Apalachee Bay, Northeastern Gulf of Mexico. *Geoarchaeology* 12(5): 417–458.

Faught, M. K., and A. E. Gusick. 2011. Submerged Prehistory in the Americas. In *Submerged Prehistory: The Underwater Archaeology of Ancient Sites and Landscapes*, ed. J. Benjamin, C. Bonsall, and C. Pickard, 145–157. Oxford: Oxbow Books.

Fedje, D. W., and T. Christensen. 1999. Modeling Paleoshorelines and Locating Early Holocene Coastal Sites in Haida Gwaii. *American Antiquity* 64: 635–652.

Fedje, D. W., and H. Josenhans. 2000. Drowned Forests and Archaeology on the Continental Shelf of British Columbia, Canada. *Geology* 28(2): 99–102.

Felgate, M. 2003. Leap-frogging or Limping? Recent Evidence from the Lapita Littoral Fringe, New Georgia, Solomon Islands. *Oceanic Explorations: Lapita and Western Pacific Settlement*, ed. S. Bedford, C. Sand, and S. P. Connaughton, 123–140. Canberra: ANU E-Press.

Fischer, A. 1995. An Entrance to the Mesolithic World below the Ocean. Status of Ten Years' Work on the Danish Sea Floor. In *Man and Sea in the Mesolithic*, ed. A. Fischer, 371–384. Oxford: Oxbow Monograph.

Fitch, S., and V. L. Gaffney. 2013. Appendix 3 (Technical Appendix): The Application of Extensive 3D Seismic Reflection Data for the Exploration of Extensive Inundated Palaeolandscapes. In *People and the Sea: A Maritime Archaeological Research Agenda for England*, ed. F. Sturt, J. Ransley, J. Dix, J. Adams, and L. Blue. York: Council for British Archaeology.

Fitch, S., K. Thomson, and V. Gaffney. 2005. Late Pleistocene and Holocene Depositional Systems and the Palaeogeography of the Dogger Bank, North Sea. *Quaternary Research* 64(2): 185–196.

Flemming, N. 2010. Comment on Jonathan Benjamin's "Submerged Prehistoric Landscapes and Underwater Site Discovery: Reevaluating the 'Danish model' for International Practice." *Journal of Island and Coastal Archaeology,* 5(2): 274–276.

Ford, B. and J. Halligan. 2010. A North American Perspective: Comment on Jonathan Benjamin's "Submerged Prehistoric Landscapes and Underwater Site Discovery: Reevaluating the 'Danish Model' for International Practice." *Journal of Island and Coastal Archaeology* 5(2): 277–279.

Gaffney, V. L., K. Thomson, and S. Fitch (eds.). 2007. *Mapping Doggerland: The Mesolithic Landscapes of the Southern North Sea.* Oxford: Archaeopress.

Gaffney, V., R. Allaby, R. Bates, M. Bates, E. Ch'ng, S. Fitch, P. Garwood, G. Momber, P. Murgatroyd, M. Pallen, and E. Ramsey. 2017. Doggerland and the Lost Frontiers Project (2015–2020). In *Under the Sea: Archaeology and Palaeolandscapes of the Continental Shelf*, ed. G. N. Bailey, J. Harff, and D. Sakellariou, 305–319. Cham: Springer.

Gagliano, S. M., C. E. Pearson, R. A. Weinstein, D. E. Wiseman, and C. M. McClendon. 1982. *Sedimentary Studies of Prehistoric Archaeological Sites: Criteria for the Identification of Submerged Archaeological Sites of the Northern Gulf of Mexico Continental Shelf.* Submitted to the National Park Service, Division of State Plans and Grants.

Gibbons, J. R., and F. G. Clunie. 1986. Sea Level Changes and Pacific Prehistory: New Insight into Early Human Settlement of Oceania. *Journal of Pacific History* 21(2): 58–82.

Glassow, M. A., J. Perry, and P. Paige. 2008. *The Punta Arena Site: Early and Middle Holocene Development on Santa Cruz Island.* Santa Barbara Museum of Natural History Contributions in Archaeology, Santa Barbara, California.

Gusick, A. E. 2013. The Early Holocene Occupation of Santa Cruz Island. *California's Channel Islands: The Archaeology of Human-Environment Interactions.* In *An Archaeology of Abundance: Re-examining the Marginality of California's Islands*, ed. K. M. Gill, M. Fauvelle and J. M. Erlandson, 40–59. Gainesville: University Press of Florida.

Gusick, A. E., and L. G. Davis. 2010. Exploring Baja California's Submerged Landscapes. *Journal of California and Great Basin Anthropology* 30(1): 35–50.

Gusick, A. E., and J. M. Erlandson. 2019. Paleocoastal Landscapes, Marginality, and Early Human Settlement of the California Islands. In *An Archaeology of Abundance: Reevaluating the Marginality of California's Islands,* ed. K. M. Gill, M. Fauvelle, and J. M. Erlandson, 59–97. Gainesville: University Press of Florida.

Gusick, A. E., and M. K. Faught. 2011. Prehistoric Underwater Archaeology: A Nascent Subdiscipline Critical to Understanding Early Coastal Occupations and Migration Routes. In *Trekking the Shore: Changing Coastlines and the Antiquity of Coastal Settlement,* ed. N. Bicho, J. Haws, and L. G. Davis, 27–50. New York: Springer.

Hayashida, K., J. Kimura, and R. Sasaki. 2014. State and Perspectives of Submerged Sites in Japan. In *Prehistoric Archaeology on the Continental Shelf,* ed. A. Evans, J. C. Flatman, and N. C. Flemming, 275–290. New York: Springer.

Henshilwood, C. S., J. C. Sealy, R. Yates, K. Cruz-Uribe, P. Goldberg, F. E. Grine, R. G. Klein, C. Poggenpoel, K. van Niekerk and I. Watts. 2001. Blombos Cave, Southern Cape, South Africa: Preliminary Report on the 1992–1999 Excavations of the Middle Stone Age Levels. *Journal of Archaeological Science* 28: 421–448.

Hill, J. C., N. W. Driscoll, J. Brigham-Grette, J. P. Donnelly, P. T. Gayes, L. Keigwin. 2007. New Evidence for High Discharge to the Chukchi Shelf since the Last Glacial Maximum. *Quaternary Research* 68: 71–279.

Hudson, D. T. 1976. *Marine Archaeology along the Southern California Coast.* San Diego Museum of Man Papers No. 9.

ICF International, Davis Geoarchaeological Research, and Southeastern Archaeological Research. 2013. *Inventory and Analysis of Coastal and Submerged Archaeological Site Occurrence on the Pacific Outer Continental Shelf.* Submitted to U.S. Department of the Interior, Bureau of Ocean Energy Management, Pacific OCS Region, Camarillo, California OCS Study BOEM 2013–0115.

Johnson, S. Y., J. T. Johnson, and R. W. Sliter. 2015. *Seismic-reflection Profiles Offshore of Refugio Beach Map Area, California, Sheet 8.* California State Waters Map Series—Offshore of Pigeon Point, California. U.S. Geological Survey Open-File Report 1232.

Josenhans, H., D. W. Fedje, R. Pienitz, and J. Southon. 1997. Early Humans and Rapidly Changing Holocene Sea-levels in the Queen Charlotte Islands-Hecate Strait, British Columbia, Canada. *Science* 277(5322): 71–74.

Klotsko, S., M. Skakun, J. Maloney, A. E. Gusick, L. Davis, A. Nyers, and D. Ball. 2020. Geological Controls on Paleodrainage Incision and Morphology during the Last Glacial Maximum on the Cascadia Shelf in Oregon, USA. *Marine Geology.*

Kinlan, B. P., M. H. Graham, and J. M. Erlandson. 2005. Late Quaternary Changes in the Size and Shape of the California Channel Islands: Implications for Marine Subsidies to Terrestrial Communities. In *Proceeding of the Sixth California Islands Symposium, Ventura, California, December 1–3, 2003,* ed. D. K. Garcelon and C. A. Schwemm, 131–142. Arcata, California: Institute for Wildlife Studies.

Kirch, P. V. 2017. *On the Road of the Winds: An Archaeological History of the Pacific Islands before European Contact, Revised and Expanded.* Berkeley: University of California Press.

Klotsko, S., N. Driscoll, G. Kent, D. Brothers. 2015. Continental Shelf Morphology and Stratigraphy Offshore San Onofre, California: The Interplay Between Rates of Eustatic Change and Sediment Supply. *Marine Geology* 369: 116–126.

Laws, A., J. Maloney, S. Klotsko, A. E. Gusick, T. J. Braje, and D. Ball. 2019. Using High-Resolution Chirp Subbottom Data to Map Paleoshorelines: Implications for Uplift Rates and Archaeological Sites, Northern Channel Islands, California, USA. *Quaternary Research.* http://dx.doi.org/10.1017/qua.2019.34

Le Dantec, N., L. J. Hogarth, N. W. Driscoll, J. M. Babcock, W. A. Barnhardt, and W. C. Schwab. 2010. Tectonic Controls on Nearshore Sediment Accumulation and Submarine Canyon Morphology Offshore La Jolla, Southern California. *Marine Geology* 268: 115–128.

Lowery, D., and R. Martin. 2009. Archaeology of Marine Transgression: An Inundated Middle Archaic Burial in Chesapeake Bay, Maryland. *Archaeology of Eastern North America* 37: 159–173.

Lübke, H. 2003. New Investigations on Submarine Stone Age Settlements in the Wismar Bay Area. In *Mesolithic on the Move: Papers presented at the 6th International Conference on the Mesolithic in Europe, Stockholm 2000*, ed. L. Larsson, H. Kindgren, K. Knutsson, D. Loeffer, and A. Akerlund, 633–642. Oxford: Oxbow Book.

Mackie, Q., L. G. Davis, D. W. Fedje, D. McLaren, and A. E. Gusick. 2013. Locating Pleistocene-age Submerged Archaeological Sites on the Northwest Coast: Current Status of Research and Future Directions. In *Paleoamerican Odyssey Conference Companion*, ed. M. Waters and K. Graff, 133–147. College Station, Texas: Center for the Study of the First Americans.

Mackie, Q., C. Vogelaar, D. Fedje, and A. Lausanne. 2017. New Approaches to the Underwater Archaeology of Hecate Strait, British Columbia. Poster presented at the Society for American Archaeology Annual Meeting, Vancouver, B.C.

Maloney, J., T. J. Braje, A. E. Gusick, B. Ho, and D. Ball. 2016. Shallow Stratigraphy and Paleolandscapes Offshore from the Northern Channel Islands, California. Poster presented at the American Geophysical Union Annual Meeting, New Orleans.

Maloney, J., S. Klotsko, A. E. Gusick, T. J. Braje, D. Ball, L. G. Davis, and A. Nyers. 2017. Paleodrainage Morphology during Glacial Inter-glacial Cycles in the Northern Channel Islands. Poster presented at the American Geophysical Union Annual Meeting, New Orleans.

Masters, P. 2010. Comment on Jonathan Benjamin's "Submerged Prehistoric Landscapes and Underwater Site Discovery: Reevaluating the 'Danish model' for International Practice." *Journal of Island and Coastal Archaeology* 5(2): 282–284.

Masters, P. and N. C. Flemming. 1983. *Quaternary Coastlines and Marine Archaeology*. Orlando, Florida: Academic Press.

McLaren, D., Q. Mackie, D. W. Fedje, A. Martindale, and D. Archer. 2007. Relict Shorelines and Archaeological Prospection on the Continental Hinge of North Coastal British Columbia. Paper presented to the 72nd annual meeting for the Society for American Archaeology, Austin, Texas.

Momber, G. 2000. Drowned and Deserted: A Submerged Prehistoric Landscape in the Solent, England. *International Journal of Nautical Archaeology* 29(1): 86–99.

Momber, G. 2005. Stone Age Stove under the Solent. *International Journal of Nautical Archaeology* 34(1): 148–9.

Muckelroy, K. 1978. *Maritime Archaeology*. Cambridge: Cambridge University Press.

Muhs, D. R., K. R. Simmons, R. R. Schumann, L. T. Groves, S. B. Devogel, S. A. Minor, and D. Laurel. 2014. Coastal Tectonics on the Eastern Margin of the Pacific Rim: Late Quaternary Sea-level History and Uplift Rates, Channel Islands National Park, California, USA. *Quaternary Science Reviews* 105: 209–238.

Nordfjord, S., J. A. Goff, J. A. Austin Jr., and L. Schuur Duncan. 2009. Shallow Stratigraphy and Complex Transgressive Ravinement on the New Jersey Middle and Outer Continental Shelf. *Marine Geology* 266: 232–243.

Nutley, D., 2014. Inundated Site Studies in Australia. In *Prehistoric Archaeology on the Continental Shelf*, ed. A. Evans, J. C. Flatman, and N. C. Flemming, 255–273. New York: Springer.

Pearson, C. E., D. B. Kelley, R. A. Weinstein, and S. M. Gagliano. 1986. *Archaeological Investigations on the Outer Continental Shelf: A Study within the Sabine River Valley, Offshore Louisiana and Texas*. U.S. Submitted to U.S. Department of the Interior, Minerals Management Service, Reston, Virginia. OCS Study MMS 86-0119.

Peltier, W. R. 2002. On Eustatic Sea Level History: Late Glacial Maximum to Holocene. *Quaternary Science Reviews* 21: 377–396.

Pendleton, R. and C. Tobin. 2002. PaleoAucilla Prehistory Project, Report of Investigations submitted to Florida State University, Tallahassee.

Porcasi, J. F. and H. Fujita. 2000. The Dolphin Hunters: A Specialized Prehistoric Maritime Adaptation in the Southern California Channel Islands and Baja California. *American Antiquity* 65(3): 543–566.

Reeder-Myers, L. A., J. M. Erlandson, D. Muhs, and T. C. Rick. 2015. Sea Level, Paleogeography, and Archaeology on California's Northern Channel Islands. *Quaternary Research* 83: 263–272.

Rick, T. C., J. M. Erlandson, N. P. Jew, L. A. Reeder-Myers. 2013. Archaeological Survey and the Search or Paleocoastal peoples of Santa Rosa Island, California, USA. *Journal of Field Archaeology* 38: 324–331.

Roebroeks, W. 2014. Terra Incognita: The Palaeolithic Record of Northwest Europe and the Information Potential of the Southern North Sea. *Netherlands Journal of Geosciences* 93(1–2): 43–53.

Ruppe, R. J. 1980. The Archaeology of Drowned Terrestrial Sites: A Preliminary Report. In *Coes Landing, Jackson County, Florida: A Fort Walton Campsite on the Apalachicola River*, D. S. Brose, ed, 35–45. Bulletin No. 6. Tallahassee: Bureau of Historic Sites and Properties.

Ruppe, R. J. 1988. The Location and Assessment of Underwater Archaeological Sites. In *Wet Site Archaeology*, ed. B. A. Purdy, 55–68. Boca Raton, Florida: Telford Press.

Skaarup, J. 1995. Hunting the Hunters and Fishers of the Mesolithic—Twenty Years of Research on the Sea Floor South of Funen, Denmark. In *Man and Sea in the Mesolithic*, ed. A. Fischer, 397–402. Oxford: Oxbow Monograph.

Scavia, D., J. C. Field, D. F. Boesch, R. W. Buddemeier, V. Burkett, D. R. Cayan, M. Fogarty, M. A. Harwell, R. W. Howarth, and C. Mason. 2002. Climate Change Impacts on U.S. Coastal and Marine Ecosystems. *Estuaries* 25(2): 149–164.

Schwab, W. C., W. E. Baldwin, J. F. Denny, C. J. Hapke, P. T. Gayes, J. H. List, and J. C. Warner. 2014. Modification of the Quaternary Stratigraphic Framework of the Inner-continental Shelf by Holocene Marine Transgression: An Example Offshore of Fire Island, New York. *Marine Geology* 355: 346–360.

Singer, R. and J. J. Wymer. 1982. *The Middle Stone Age at Klasies River Mouth in South Africa.* Chicago: University of Chicago Press.

Stiner, M. C. 1999. Paleolithic Mollusc Exploitation at Riparo Mochi (Balzi Rossi, Italy): Food and Ornaments from the Aurignacian through the Epigravettian. *Antiquity* 73: 735–754.

Straus, L., J. L. Bischoff, and E. Carbonell. 1993. A Review of the Middle to Upper Paleolithic Transition in Iberia. *Prehistoire Europeenne* 3: 11–26.

Stright, M. J. 1995. Archaic Period Sites on the Continental Shelf of North America: The Effects of Relative Sea-level Changes on Archaeological Site Locations and Preservation. In *Archaeological Geology of the Archaic Period in North America*, ed. E. Arthur Bettis, 131–147. Geological Society of America Special Paper 297.

Tahiry, H., J. Maloney, S. Klotsko, A. E. Gusick, T. J. Braje, and D. Ball. 2018. Examining Paleodrainage Evolution since the Last Glacial Maximum, Northern Channel Islands, California, USA. Poster presented at the Geological Society of America Meeting, Indianapolis, Indiana.

Tizzard, L., P. A. Baggaley, and A. J. Firth. 2011. Seabed Prehistory: Investigating Palaeolandsurfaces with Palaeolithic Remains from the Southern North Sea. In *Submerged Prehistory: The Underwater Archaeology of Ancient Sites and Landscapes*, ed. J. Benjamin, C. Bonsall, and C. Pickard, 65–74. Oxford: Oxbow Books.

Walter, R. C., R. T. Buffler, J. H. Bruggemann, M.M.M. Guillaume, S. M. Berhe, B. Negassi, Y.

Libsekal, H. Cheng, R. L. Edwards, R. von Cosel, D. Neraudeau, and M. Gagnon. 2000. Early Human Occupation of the Red Sea Coast of Eritrea during the Last Interglacial. *Nature* 405: 65–69.

Watts, G. 2004. *Archaeological Damage from Offshore Dredging: Recommendations for Pre-Operational Surveys and Mitigation during Dredging to Avoid Adverse Impacts.* Submitted to U.S. Department of the Interior, Minerals Management Service, Herndon, Virginia. OCS Report MMS 2004–005.

Watts, J., B. Fulfrost, and J. M. Erlandson. 2011. Searching for Santarosae: Surveying Submerged Landscapes for Evidence of Paleocoastal Habitation Off California's Northern Channel Islands. In *The Archaeology of Maritime Landscapes: When the Land Meets the Sea*, ed. B. Ford, 11–26. New York: Springer.

Werz, B., H. Cawthra, J. and Compton. 2014. Recent Developments in African Offshore Prehistoric Archaeological Research, with an Emphasis on South Africa. In *Prehistoric Archaeology on the Continental Shelf*, ed. A. Evans, J. C. Flatman, and N. C. Flemming, 233–253. New York: Springer.

6

Multidisciplinary Chronological Data from Iceland Indicate a Viking Age Settlement Flood, Rather Than a Flow or Trickle

MAGDALENA M. E. SCHMID, ANDREW J. DUGMORE,
ANTHONY J. NEWTON, AND ORRI VÉSTEINSSON

Science is the knowledge of consequences,
and dependence of one fact upon another.

Thomas Hobbes (1651)

The settlement of Iceland was one of the last acts in a global story of island colonization in prehistory that involved all of earth's oceans and began deep in history. Understanding the timing and patterns of colonization in general, and the subsequent pace of environmental and cultural changes, is an intensely debated topic in island archaeology (chapters 9 and 10). Was settlement a trickle, flow, or a flood (Edwards 2012)? Debates typically revolve around the accuracy and precision of radiocarbon datasets, as some dates can be older or younger than the associated stratigraphy or archaeological material (chapter 7). Numerous attempts have been made to develop "chronometric hygiene" protocols (after Spriggs 1989; see also chapter 1) to screen data and to eliminate problematic dates. Nevertheless, the criteria used to establish robust radiocarbon chronologies vary around the world (Fitzpatrick 2006; Pettit et al. 2003; Napolitano et al. 2019; Rodríguez-Rey et al. 2015; Schmid et al. 2019; Spriggs and Anderson 1993; Waterbolk 1971).

Chronological uncertainty can lead to two unfortunate outcomes (Baillie 1991). On the one hand, when a potential trigger of change (such as an explosive volcanic eruption) is precisely dated, a range of poorly dated archaeological and ecological changes in the same general period can appear to be related to it. Such changes, however, may actually be unrelated because they occurred either long before or after the volcanic eruption, but the linkage appears possible because of poor chronological resolution. On the other hand, events that occur simultaneously or in a sequence may not be seen to be linked because the necessary chronological precision and accuracy is lacking.

While dating island colonization presents great chronological challenges, in some special circumstances it may also provide potential solutions. If multiple lines of complementary dating evidence are available, they can be used to refine our understanding of the timing of key events. Previously uninhabited islands in particular are excellent laboratories for establishing robust chronologies; they are isolated and naturally defined territories (see discussion in chapter 1). A significant case study represents the late ninth century settlement of Iceland, referred to as the *Landnám* (Old Norse: land taking). This is because initial settlement occurred on a massive scale relatively late in history, and the processes involved can be dated using several independent but complementary methods. These methods help in understanding not only the presence and absence of data, but also the spatial progression of human occupation within pristine ecosystems.

Medieval vernacular literature initially provided the framework for dating Iceland's *Landnám* to AD 870–930, which derives from the chronicle Íslendingabók written in AD 1122–1133 (Grønlie transl. 2006). A comprehensive analysis of the typology of grave goods from pagan burials carried out in the mid-twentieth century found that the assemblage had a broad "tenth century" or "Viking Age" (circa AD 800–1100) character, and was consistent with a start date for the colonization in the late ninth century (Eldjárn and Friðriksson 2016). Until recently, any Viking Age date in Iceland has tended to be considered as synonymous with *Landnám*, and the entire period has been regarded as a single, indivisible block, despite increasingly apparent variation through the growing application of both radiocarbon dating and tephrochronology, beginning in the 1970s.

Despite a long history of archaeological research on *Landnám*, only recently have multidisciplinary data been systematically collected to assess colonization as a process on a regional scale (for example, Bolender et al. 2011; Schmid 2018; Vésteinsson and McGovern 2012). The wealth of available data generated since the late twentieth century offers an excellent opportunity to provide new perspectives for understanding settlement processes. Research on the onset of *Landnám* is broadly constrained by the relationship of archaeological features to a distinctive volcanic ash (tephra) layer that is named the *Landnám* Tephra Layer (LTL)

(Figure 6.1). This tephra layer has been identified in the Greenland ice cores and has been dated to AD 877 ± 1 (Grönvold et al. 1995; Schmid et al. 2017a; Zielinski et al. 1997). The LTL was deposited just before any widespread early human activities created archaeological evidence across the island. A later ice core–dated tephra layer, the *Eldgjá* tephra of AD 939, as well as the V-Sv tephra of AD 938 ± 6 (Figure 6.1), allow the initial period of settlement to be constrained to the years AD 877–938/939 (Schmid et al. 2017a; Sigl et al. 2015). This period extends from early occupation until just after the establishment of a countrywide legal and judicial system, the Alþing, which is historically dated to AD 930 (Íslendingabók: Grønlie transl. 2006). A subsequent phase of late Viking Age settlement can be constrained by another tephra layer, the Hekla tephra of AD 1104 (Figure 6.1; Þórarinsson 1967). The end of the Viking period is more difficult to establish as the conversion to Christianity in the early eleventh century was most likely not a single countrywide event (Vésteinsson 2000); early churches had already been constructed in the late tenth century, while Viking Age settlements were abandoned or relocated some time before the H-1104 tephra was deposited (Schmid et al. 2020).

Significantly, only two turf-built enclosures or boundary walls (Jóhannesson and Einarsson 1988; Roberts et al. 2013), as well as taxa introduced by the first settlers (such as cereal-type pollen and dung-loving fungi: Schmid et al. 2017b), have so far been found immediately below the LTL (Bayesian Highest Probability Density [HPD] of AD 830–881; Schmid et al. 2017b), demonstrating that some people created structures on the island before the volcanic eruption in AD 877 (Figure 6.2). How long before AD 877 people arrived on the island is not known, and the nature of the earliest human presence is unclear. By contrast, extensive settlement after this date is confirmed by 89 archaeological sites, which occur immediately above this tephra (Figure 6.2).

Until the late 1980s, there were around 90 radiocarbon dates on material associated with early human activities in Iceland (Vilhjálmsson 1991). Some of these dates extended back to the sixth and eighth centuries, but the relationship between these dates and human activities were not always clear, which resulted in a vigorous debate about the timing of *Landnám* (for example, Hermanns-Auðardóttir 1989; Rafnsson 1990; Theodórsson 1998, 2009). Some of these radiocarbon dates were probably misleading, but it was difficult to argue the merits or limitations of individual dates in an objective manner, which is a common issue in global island archaeology (chapter 7). Recently, the accuracy and precision of *Landnám*–related radiocarbon dates in Iceland has been re-evaluated, utilizing a large dataset of 513 samples and incorporating this into a Bayesian framework (Schmid et al.

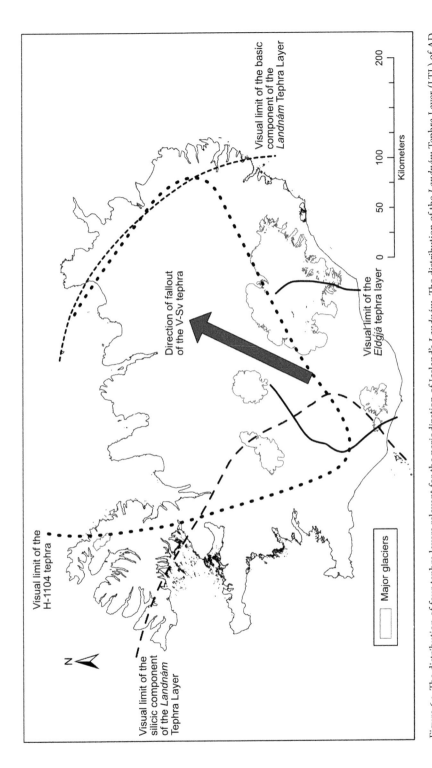

Figure 6.1. The distribution of four tephra layers relevant for the periodization of Iceland's *Landnám*. The distribution of the *Landnám* Tephra Layer (LTL) of AD 877 ±1, the *Eldgjá* tephra of AD 938 ± 6 and the Hekla tephra of AD 1104.

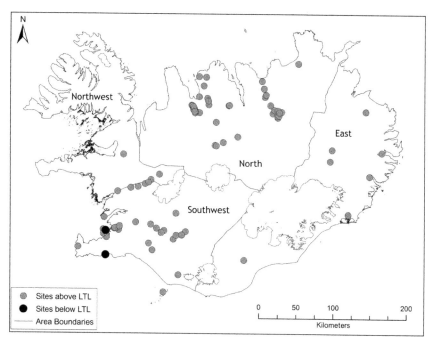

Figure 6.2. The distribution of known archaeological sites in stratigraphic relationships to the LTL (Appendix). Two archaeological sites are below the LTL (black dots), 89 settlement sites and 178 related radiocarbon dates are all above this tephra isochron (gray dots).

2018, 2019). After quality filtering, 384 radiocarbon dates from 85 archaeological sites show that the onset of widespread settlement is most likely to have occurred between AD 733 and 890. None of the 37 outliers—which individually produced dates from the sixth and eighth centuries—are from stratigraphic contexts below the LTL, and so they were all deposited after 877 AD. They are all pieces of unidentified charcoal with potentially large inbuilt ages, which may derive from burnt old wood (Sveinbjörnsdóttir et al. 2004). In contrast, 178 radiocarbon dates come from contexts above the LTL (Figure 6.2).

To sum up, multiple lines of dating evidence—radiocarbon dates, medieval literary texts, artifact typology, and ice core–dated tephrochronology—point to a widespread settlement of Iceland shortly before, but mainly after, AD 877. However, different scenarios of settlement processes in Iceland have been proposed: (1) A rapid *Landnám* settlement within 20 years (Vésteinsson and McGovern 2012); and (2) A gradual settlement process extending either over 150 years (Bolender et al. 2011; Steinberg et al. 2016), or over 300 years (Lárusson 1929).

Our aim is to assess spatiotemporal patterns of initial settlement across Iceland through a fundamental reassessment of 550 known archaeological sites in Iceland (Appendix). This data collection represents the largest assemblage of Icelandic Viking Age archaeological sites produced to date. We evaluate archaeological sites that have been dated with 18 tephra layers, associated 513 radiocarbon dates, and typologically sensitive artifacts. This synthesis explores both the archaeological evidence of early settlement and new approaches to chronology.

Typological Data

For many archaeological sites, artifact typology either provides the only available dating evidence, or complements other dating methods. In terms of chronology, there are three basic categories of artifacts found in Viking Age contexts in Iceland: (1) artifacts that either give no, or only the broadest, dating indication (for example, many stone and iron objects); (2) artifacts that provide reasonably robust "Viking Age" dates, including several types of weapons and jewelry found at 195 archaeological sites, as well as general burial practices, such as the presence of horses and various house types (for example, pit houses or halls) (Appendix Table); and (3) diagnostic artifacts that can be ascribed to a specific date or a date range of decades rather than centuries. The latter category consists of coins (at 15 sites), imported glass beads (at 42 sites), and other decorative objects (at 18 sites) with a limited period of circulation (Appendix Table). Diagnostic artifacts can provide *termini post quos* for an associated archaeological feature; however, many artifacts in Iceland show signs of long usage and may have been in circulation for some time (Batt et al. 2015; Hreiðarsdóttir 2005). So far, archaeological sites that are dated by artifact typology are primarily categorized as Viking Age or post-*Landnám* (Appendix Table). A classic example of post-*Landnám* artifacts are bead of types B and E (after Callmer 1977; Hreiðarsdóttir 2005), which are dated to AD 960–1000 (for example, at Hrísbrú; see Schmid et al. 2017b).

Archaeological Data

Here, we present a new catalogue of selected data from more than 600 field reports and academic monographs that relate to the Viking Age (AD ~800–1100) in Iceland. We focus on archaeological sites that have been investigated between the eighteenth century and 2016 (n = 550). Archaeological investigations range from large-scale open-area excavations to trenches and surface collections with dating evidence that range from excellent, through problematic, to absent. We separate archaeological sites into three basic categories: (1) settlements (n = 300); (2) burials (n = 140); and (3) assemblages or stray finds (n = 110). We define settlement sites as places where people resided and include farms, seasonally or intermittently occupied sites like shielings or iron-making facilities, and structures associated with farming in the outfields. Archaeological features typically include dwellings, animal stalls, smithies, middens, boundary earthworks, and early churches. Burials can include single or multiple internments, while assemblages are either isolated or surface finds without contextual information. These finds can represent a settlement, a burial, a hoard, or accidental loss (Eldjárn and Friðriksson 2016).

A key methodological question is the degree to which patterns that are derived from the known archaeological record reflect the spatial characteristics of the past. This is because a combination of geographical priorities and changing archaeological practices have strongly influenced the spatial characteristics of the record and the quality of the available data. Many excavators in the twentieth century did not excavate turf walls, and therefore tephra layers *in situ* below archaeological structures were not discovered. Through time, however, both archaeological excavation and the application of tephrochronology have become increasingly comprehensive, and more accurate. As most excavations in the past 20 years have been carried out in the north of the island, this area has benefited greatly from more effective uses of tephrochronology. As twentieth-century investigations conducted to older standards may underrepresent (or indeed misrepresent) the number of *Landnám* sites, distribution maps of past settlement have to be interpreted with caution as they will be biased by the intensity and quality of the research effort in different areas.

Following the medieval administrative division of Iceland into quarters, the data have been separated into four geographical areas: the southwest, the northwest, the north, and the east. The divisions mostly follow natural barriers to settlement and travel such as glaciers, interior highlands, and major rivers that were stable reference points on the landscape. Throughout this chapter, we use these geographical divisions to structure our discussion of the data. Forty-eight percent of archaeological sites are located in the north (n = 266), 28 percent are in the southwest (n = 156), 17 percent in the east (n = 91), and 7 percent in the northwest (n = 37). This distribution reflects modern archaeological fieldwork priorities and is unlikely to precisely mirror inherent archaeological contrasts. Given this caveat, we can only explore the patterns that currently exist.

The distribution of known archaeological sites is shown in Figure 6.3. The distributions are separated into 300 settlements (Figure 6.3A), 140 burials (Fig-

M.M.E. Schmid, A. J. Dugmore, A. J. Newton, and O. Vésteinsson

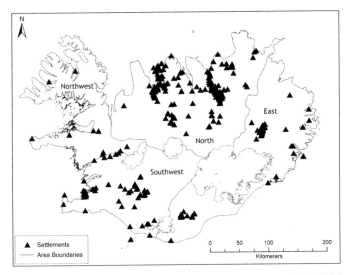

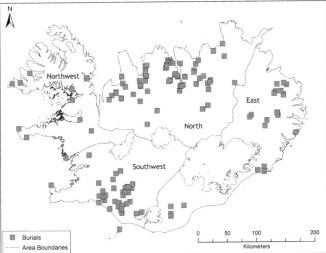

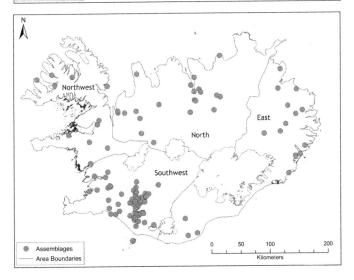

Figure 6.3. The distribution of known archaeological sites in four geographic areas in Iceland with evidence relating to the first occupation, disturbance, or presence. A: 300 settlement sites, B: 140 burials, and C: 100 assemblages or loose finds (Appendix).

ure 6.3B), and 110 assemblages (Figure 6.3C). The majority of settlements, or 60 percent, are in the north (n = 180). Similar numbers are in the southwest and east (n = 49–58), while the northwest is underrepresented (n = 13). Almost half of the burials are located in the north (n = 65), 27 percent in the southwest (n = 38), 19 percent in the east (n = 26), and 8 percent in the northwest (n = 11). More than half of assemblages were found in the southwest (n = 60), while in other areas they are relatively evenly distributed (between 13 and 21 sites).

The dates of intervention (the timing of the research activity) for the 550 sites provide evidence for the shifting of regional archaeological activity. Interventions are characterized as year(s) of (re)excavation or find accession (Appendix Table). Accession year(s) are used when excavation/find years are not known, and this primarily refers to artifact assemblages. Less than 1 percent of sites were investigated in the eighteenth century (n = 3), 16 percent in the nineteenth century (n = 89), 50 percent in the twentieth century (n = 276), and 33 percent since the year 2000 (n = 182). Ninety-six percent of burials and assemblages were discovered in the nineteenth and twentieth centuries. In contrast, 95 percent of settlements were investigated in the twentieth and twenty-first centuries. More precisely, 36 percent of settlements in the twentieth century were investigated in the southwest, while 59 percent of settlements in the twenty-first century were investigated in the north of Iceland, maximizing the quality of dating here. In the areas of most intensive fieldwork, the figures also indicate settlement density and population levels. Regional differences in burial frequencies have been explained both by taphonomic processes, discovery bias, and differences in burial practices (Vésteinsson 2011).

Archaeological Periods Based on Tephrostratigraphy

The data support a division into archaeological periods based on tephrostratigraphy described by Schmid et al. (2017a). Three consecutive periods of settlement have been identified: pre-*Landnám*, *Landnám*, and post-*Landnám*, plus a larger Viking Age group overlapping with the *Landnám* and post-*Landnám* periods (Table 6.1). The time divisions are based on 18 well-dated tephra isochrons, ranging between the ninth and seventeenth centuries, that occur within the stratigraphy of archaeological sites (after Schmid et al. 2017a: SI table 1). More precisely, tephra can be preserved *in situ* below or above archaeological features, within turf structures, or in cultural layers. Tephra layers *in situ* below archaeological features give secure *termini ante quos,* and tephra layers stratigraphically above or found within the turf of walls give secure *termini post quos* for archaeological features

Table 6.1. Three consecutive periods of the Viking Age settlement of Iceland: pre-*Landnám*, *Landnám*, and post-*Landnám*, as well as a larger Viking Age group

Period	Name of period	Description of period	Tephra correlation of deposits/dates	Age range (tephra)	Period in years
1	Pre-*Landnám*	Arrival of settlers	Below the LTL	AD pre-877	?
2	*Landnám*	Early widespread settlement	Above the LTL or below *Eldgjá*/V-Sv	AD 877–938/939	62
3	Post-*Landnám*	Late widespread settlement	Above *Eldgjá* or V-Sv	AD 938/939–1104	165
4	Viking Age	Viking Age settlement	That cannot be constrained by the LTL, *Eldgjá*, or V-Sv tephras (pre-H-1104, pre-Vj, etc.)	AD 877–1104	227

Source: After Schmid et al. 2017a.
Note: The periods are defined by four tephra layers, whose distributions are shown in Figure 6.1.

(Appendix). In particular, four tephra isochrons—the *Landnám* Tephra Layer of AD 877 ± 1, the *Eldgjá* tephra of AD 939, the V-Sv tephra of AD 938 ± 6, and the Hekla tephra of AD 1104—all anchor the broadly Viking Age archaeological record within a secure tephrochronological framework (Figure 6.1).

Eighty-four percent of settlements (n = 253) and 7 percent of burials (n = 9) are stratigraphically connected to tephra isochrons (n = 261). The distribution of tephra-dated archaeological sites in our defined geographical areas is irregular. Two archaeological sites are dated to the pre-*Landnám* period, 89 sites to the *Landnám* period, 113 sites to the post-*Landnám* period, and 78 sites can only be assigned general Viking Age dates.

There is a pattern to the regional distribution of archaeological sites that yielded scientific dates; and such dates represent the initial phase of disturbance. Definitions of the pre-*Landnám* and *Landnám* periods depend on the distribution of the LTL. This tephra layer can be identified in excavations throughout almost the entire island, although it does not form a visible layer in the northwest (Figure 6.1). Archaeological evidence is consistently found above this tephra isochron (Figure 6.2). At two sites from the southwest, structures also occur immediately below this tephra. Therefore, we argue that the numbers from the pre-*Landnám* and *Landnám* period are most likely to reflect a real pattern in the density of settlement. The post-*Landnám* period is defined by two tenth-century tephras (*Eldgjá* and V-Sv) that have a more limited distribution (Figure 6.1). The *Eldgjá* tephra is primarily associated with sites in the southwest and east, and infrequently with sites in the north (Schmid et al. 2017a). The V-Sv tephra is deposited almost exclusively to the north of Iceland and only partially to the east. It is therefore not surprising that 92 out of 113 archaeological records of early settlement that date to the post-*Landnám* period are located in the north.

The numbers of known archaeological sites from the pre-*Landnám* and *Landnám* periods could well reflect key characteristics of the overall pattern of settlement, although they only represent a minority of the actual sites. For instance, Steinberg et al. (2016) extracted 4,000 cores from modern farms in Langholt in northern Iceland. They identified 17–20 Viking Age settlements, of which 12–20 percent did not have any surface signs.

In contrast, the numbers of known archaeological sites from the post-*Landnám* period are likely to reflect both the distribution of tephra layers and field-work activities because younger archaeological features are easier to identify on the surface. Post-*Landnám* sites dated by tephrochronology are therefore more abundant in the north than the rest of the country. This highlights a key limitation of tephrochronology: its resolution crucially depends on the numbers and age of tephra layers identified. While tephrochronology provides secure *termini post quos* for archaeological remains, the time that elapsed between the deposition of the tephra and the occupation of the site is often unclear. Is an archaeological feature that is deposited above the LTL truly a site that was occupied during *Landnám*? And is a feature postdating the *Eldgjá* or V-Sv tephras in fact the earliest feature at that site? Our understanding of these issues can be improved through the assessment of radiocarbon samples.

Radiocarbon Samples

We have evaluated 513 ^{14}C samples related to the archaeological record in Iceland. We followed a new standardized protocol of outlier analysis and rejected as few dates as possible (Schmid et al. 2019). One hundred and twenty-nine samples were rejected because not enough information was available to verify their accuracy. This exclusion accounted for all the samples that were not adequately documented (for example, material types, lab numbers, or stable isotope values were not reported) or that had inbuilt ages from mixed dietary sources that could not be corrected (for example, the freshwater reservoir effect; Sayle et al. 2016). Rejection of the samples is discussed in detail by Schmid et al. (2019). The remaining, and potentially accurate, 384 dates from 85 archaeological sites are assigned to the following archaeological periods:

1. There are 37 radiocarbon samples dating between the sixth and eighth centuries (older than AD 877). Without tephra evidence we would assume that these dates represent pre-*Landnám* (for example, Reykjavík ARR-7619 is calibrated to AD 657–858).

2. There are 29 radiocarbon samples with calibrated age ranges older than AD 939; they are considered *Landnám* dates (for example, Reykjavík ARR-7614 is calibrated to AD 684–893).

3. There are 132 radiocarbon samples with calibrated age ranges younger than AD 939; they are considered post-*Landnám* dates (for example, Sveigakot SUERC-27403 is calibrated to AD 971–1149).

4. There are 186 radiocarbon samples that overlap with periods; they are considered Viking Age dates (for example, Sveigakot SUERC-27404 is calibrated to AD 879–1013).

Thirty-seven charcoal samples from the southwest produced dates between the sixth and eighth centuries, although none of them are short-lived materials or were taken from anthropogenic deposits below the LTL. Relying on single radiocarbon dates alone can, therefore, produce an inaccurate chronology for the initial colonization of Iceland. Using Bayesian statistics, we model multiple radiocarbon dates within geographic regions.

Bayesian Statistics

Bayesian statistics are routinely used to generate the most likely age ranges of archaeological events (the posterior probability: for example, chapter 7). These age ranges are achieved by modifying prior beliefs (for example, from the stratigraphy of samples, the distribution of individual dates, and the distribution of the whole dataset) with likelihoods (a specific radiocarbon dataset) (Bayliss 2009). We modeled 384 radiocarbon samples from Viking Age contexts in Iceland using the OxCal version 4.3 (Bronk Ramsey 2017), which incorporates the IntCal13 and Marine13 curves (Reimer et al. 2013). Uncertainties are presented as 95.4 percent (2 standard deviations) HPD (equivalent to a confidence level). We chose Bayesian Outlier models for our datasets, focusing on both the distribution and the prior probability of each sample, and none of the samples has to be manually removed (after Bronk Ramsey 2009; Dee and Bronk Ramsey 2014). We used the General Outlier Model for 237 short-lived taxa. Short-lived materials included grains and seeds, identified tree bark and twigs, as well as bone samples, where the δ^{13}C values reflect a

100 percent terrestrial diet, or where the $\delta^{13}C$ values enable the marine contribution to diet to be accounted for (after Ascough et al. 2012). We used the percentage of marine contribution to diet published in Schmid et al. (2019) for the samples in question (after Ascough et al. 2007). Short-lived samples are assumed to accurately date the event of interest, although a few may be outlying due to, for example, stratigraphic disturbances. It has been suggested to individually down-weigh short-lived samples in a Student's T distribution, which is flexible and accounts for extreme outliers (Bronk Ramsey 2009). This is because barley grains, for instance, are not indigenous to Iceland and must have been either grown or brought to the island by humans. Although a grain sample may not be *in situ*, it still reflects human activity. Therefore, short-lived taxa are assigned a low prior probability of outlying (p = 0.05).

We used the Charcoal Outlier model for 147 samples with inbuilt ages. Such samples are either identified heartwood of trees (inner tree rings) or unidentified charcoal that likely do not date the target event of interest (chapter 7). Each radiocarbon date is individually down-weighed in an exponential distribution. This distribution is less flexible than the Student's T, and only shifts toward the younger end to account for the inbuilt age of wood. Although such taxa are assigned a 100 percent prior probability of outlying, they are still included in the overall model (Dee and Bronk Ramsey 2014). A recent modification of this model increased its flexibility and also allows a few samples to be intrusive (the Charcoal Plus Outlier model: Dee and Bronk Ramsey 2014).

Radiocarbon dates were modeled in a Phase—an unordered group that spans a period of time. The Phase is bracketed by Boundaries, which apply to the start and end of the event in question and placed in an overall Sequence—an ordered group of an event. The use of Boundaries assumes a uniform distribution of the dataset.

We built five Bayesian Outlier models and focused on the initial start of settlement in our defined geographic areas in Iceland and compared these results with the overall start of settlement using the entire dataset. We further used the Difference function in OxCal and tested if these age ranges are different toward the age of the LTL of AD 877 ± 1. In cases where the Difference probability range overlaps with zero, the age range is considered accurate because it is consistent the age of the LTL. The five Bayesian Outlier models are:

1. The whole dataset (n = 384): The model consists of 188 short-lived materials and 147 charcoal samples. We included the percentage of marine contribution to diet for 49 bone samples. The Start Boundary

is estimated to AD 733–890, (median AD 867). There is no difference between this Boundary and the LTL (Figure 6.4a).

2. "Southwest" (n = 168): The model consists of 59 short-lived materials, 92 charcoal samples, and 17 bone samples that have marine contribution to diet. The start Boundary is estimated to AD 722–930 (median AD 874). There is no difference between this Boundary and the LTL (Figure 6.4b).

3. "Northwest" (n = 24): The model consists of six short-lived materials, 12 charcoal samples and 6 bone samples that have marine contribution to diet. The start Boundary is estimated to AD 783–957 (median AD 857). There is no difference between this Boundary and the LTL (Figure 6.4b).

4. "North" (n = 163): The model consists of 116 short-lived materials, 24 charcoal samples, and 23 bone samples that have marine contribution to diet. The start Boundary is estimated to AD 855–935 (median AD 879). There is no difference between this Boundary and the LTL (Figure 6.4b).

5. "East" (n = 29): The model consists of seven short-lived materials, 19 charcoal samples, and 3 bone samples that have marine contribution to diet. The start Boundary is estimated to AD 754–982 (median AD 880). There is no difference between this Boundary and the LTL (Figure 6.4b).

We find that accurate age ranges for the colonization of Iceland were generated using the whole dataset or different geographic areas (Figure 6.4). There are no differences between these age ranges and the LTL. The HPD for the colonization of Iceland is modeled to AD 733–890 (Figure 6.4a), and this estimate is based on radiocarbon samples that are likely derived from unequivocal basal layers at the sites in question. As none of the radiocarbon samples are from anthropogenic contexts below the LTL of AD 877 ± 1, we argue that all areas must have been settled rapidly after AD 877 and before the 890s. This shows that most sites above the LTL are indeed early settlement sites (Figures 6.1 and 6.2). We arrive at the same results discussed by Schmid et al. (2018, 2019) and find that a wide range of radiocarbon samples, including unidentified charcoal samples and the heartwood of trees, can be included in chronological models if the right priors are used: 0.05 for short-lived materials and 1 for samples with inbuilt ages. As such, relatively small datasets of 24 samples can produce both accurate and precise age ranges (for example, Model 3).

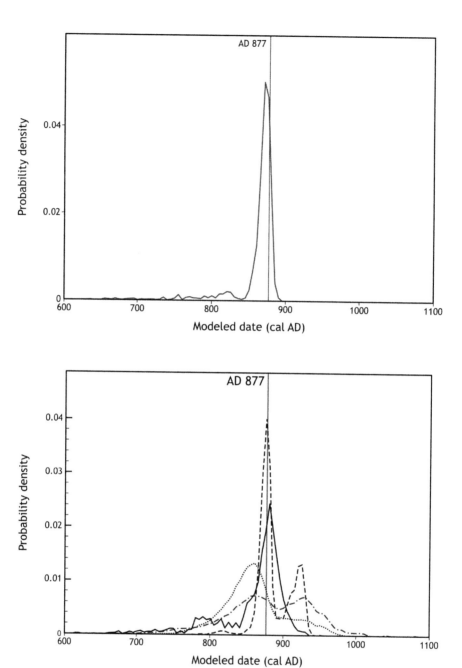

Figure 6.4. Estimated HPDs for the initial start of settlement in Iceland using Bayesian Outlier Models. *A*: all reliable ^{14}C dates (n = 384); *B*: ^{14}C dates from four geographic areas in Iceland. The solid line represents the Southwest (n = 169), dotted line represents the Northwest (n = 24), dashed line represents the North (n = 163), and the dashed and dotted line represents the East (n = 29).

Comparing Dating Evidence

We focus on comparing dated tephra layers, radiocarbon samples, and typologically diagnostic artifacts (Appendix Table). Table 6.2 demonstrates the number of archaeological sites representing each archaeological period. The numbers are based on different dating evidence: (a) tephra layers; (b) tephra and associated radiocarbon dates; (c) all radiocarbon dates without applying outlier analysis; (d) radiocarbon dates after applying outlier analysis; (e) typology; and (f) a mixture of tephra, radiocarbon, and typology. Tephra layers in Iceland produce the most robust dating evidence; thus, the chronology is mostly based on tephrochronology. In some cases, however, tephra layers only date the archaeological site to the Viking Age. Here, radiocarbon and/or typological dates may help refine the site's occupation chronology. For example, Selhagi is dated to between LTL of AD 877 and the *Hekla* tephras of AD 1104 or 1158. Two terrestrial bone samples from the site have conventional radiocarbon ages of 960 ± 45 BP (ARR-49630 of AD 991–1169) and 995 ± 45 BP (ARR-49631 of AD 970–1160) and would point to a post-*Landnám occupation*. This site is a classic example of "accumulation bias," where sparse accumulations of early site deposits were not dated but instead only the rich accumulations of late site deposits. The categorization of archaeological sites according to tephra layers (a) versus tephra layers with associated radiocarbon dates (b), however, only shows slight discrepancies at a handful of sites (Table 6.2). If tephra is not preserved or recorded at an archaeological site, we establish the age of the site with radiocarbon dates (c). The number of radiocarbon dates decreases when applying chronometric hygiene and excluding samples that are most likely not accurate (d). If tephra and radiocarbon samples are absent at an archaeological site (for example, at burials or assemblages) we date the site using typology (e). Merging all dating evidence together (tephra, radiocarbon dates, and typology) provides the most reliable chronology of archaeological sites (f), and we use these data for subsequent discussions (f).

To sum up, around half of the archaeological sites can only be dated to the Viking Age (g), while the rest can be divided into subperiods. Of these, we have 1 percent from the pre-*Landnám* period, 30 percent from the *Landnám* period, 69 percent from the post-*Landnám* period (h). Additionally, we use tephra layers to calculate the duration of archaeological periods (i): the maximum duration of the *Landnám* period is 62 years, 165 years for post-*Landnám*, and 227 years for the Viking Age. We then calculate the density of archaeological sites per archaeological period (i); strikingly, the density of sites per period yielded similar values with an average value of 1.2 sites per year (j). Finally, the density of radiocarbon dates per archaeological period has average values of 1.4 before

Table 6.2. Dating evidence of archaeological sites in Iceland using tephrochronology, radiocarbon dating (^{14}C), and typology

Period	(a) Tephra-dated sites	(b) Tephra-dated sites & associated 14C	(c) 14C dates, without applying outlier analysis	(d) 14C dates, after applying outlier analysis, stratigraphy	(e) Typology	(f) Tephra, 14C, typology	(g) % of all Viking Age sites	(h) % of subdivided sites of Viking Age period	(i) Years per period	(j) Sites/year of period (after i)	(k) 14C/year (after c)	(l) 14C/year (after d)
Pre-Landnám	2	2	37	0	0	2	less than 1%	1%	?	?	?	0
Landnám	89	81	178	66	3	84	15%	30%	62	1.35	2.53	1.06
Post-Landnám	113	118	241	132	78	189	35%	69%	165	1.15	1.46	0.80
Viking Age	78	81	57	186	237	275	50%	/	227	1.21	0.25	0.82
SUM	282	282	513	384	318	550	/	/	227	1.2	1.4	0.9
Absence of evidence	268	268	454	465	232	0	/	/	/	/	/	/

Source: Authors.
Note: The number and percentages of dated sites are categorized into four archaeological periods established in Table 6.1.

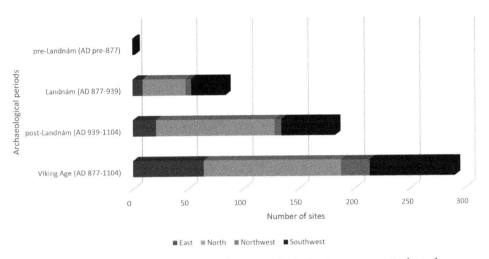

Figure 6.5. Periodization of 550 archaeological sites in Iceland. The sites are categorized into four geographic areas and are assigned four periods of settlement.

applying chronometric hygiene (k), and 0.9 after removing problematic dates (l). Although there is a relatively equal density of sites and radiocarbon dates per year, the spatial distribution of sites and dates differs; the east and northwest areas of Iceland have much lower numbers of sites than the southwest and north (Figure 6.5).

We present four distribution maps that show settlements, burials, and assemblages during the pre-*Landnám*, *Landnám*, post-*Landnám*, and Viking Age (Figure 6.6). In the pre-*Landnám* period, human activity occurred below the LTL of AD 877 ± 1. There are only two sites where evidence of settlement is dated to this period, both in the southwest of Iceland (Appendix, Figure 6.6a). In both cases the dated features are turf walls, which may have served as fences rather than supports for roofed structures, and they occur at sites that developed into permanent settlements in the *Landnám* period. Given the crucial distinction between absence of evidence as opposed to evidence of absence, it is important to contract this distribution with that of all the excavations across Iceland that have not found any early evidence of settlement (Figure 6.2).

A total of 84 archaeological sites (81 settlements, one burial, and two assemblages) are attributed to the *Landnám* period where earliest human activity occurred above the LTL of AD 877 ± 1 or below one of the tenth-century tephra (*Eldgjá* and V-Sv), where the radiocarbon dates also point to early occupation (for example, radiocarbon dates with probability curves earlier than AD 939), as well as beads that are dated to AD pre-915 and pre-950 (Appendix Table).

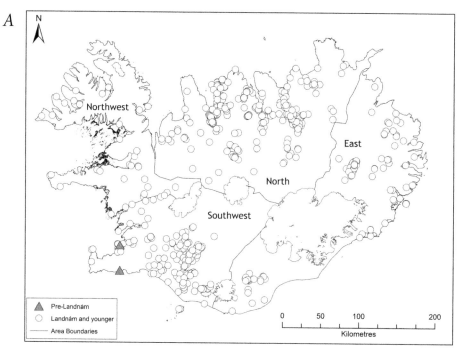

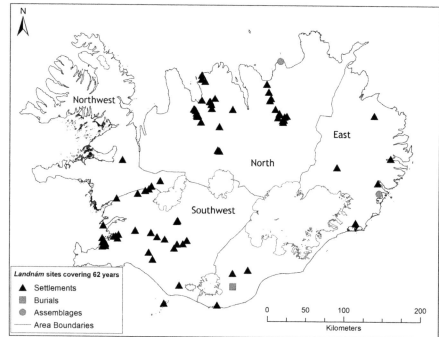

Figure 6.6. The distribution of known archaeological sites in geographic regions in Iceland. *A*: pre-*Landnám* sites (AD pre-877; the duration of this period cannot currently be established); *B*: *Landnám* sites covering 62 years; *C*: post-*Landnám* sites covering 165 years; and *D*: Viking Age sites covering 227 years.

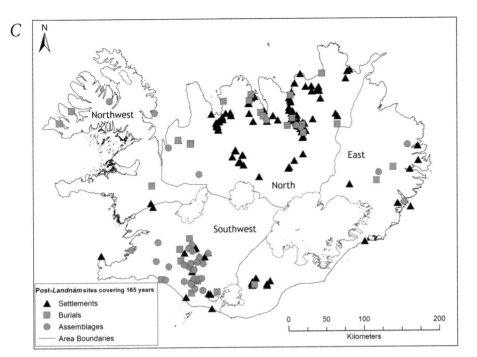

C

Post-*Landnám* sites covering 165 years
▲ Settlements
▨ Burials
● Assemblages
— Area Boundaries

Northwest
North
East
Southwest

N

0   50   100   200
Kilometers

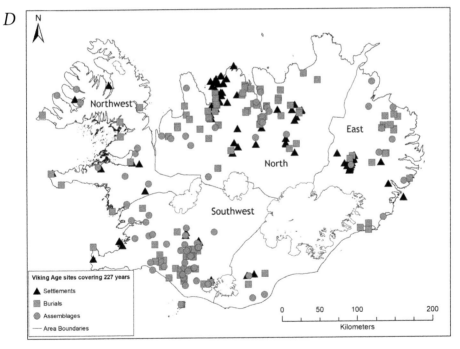

D

Viking Age sites covering 227 years
▲ Settlements
▨ Burials
● Assemblages
— Area Boundaries

Northwest
North
East
Southwest

N

0   50   100   200
Kilometers

Archaeological sites dated to this period are found across the entire island apart from the northwest peninsula—a function of the distribution of the LTL (Figures 6.1, 6.2 and 6.6b). The sites are found equally in coastal and inland areas, more or less in all inhabitable parts of the island.

The post-*Landnám* period refers to 189 sites (124 settlements, 31 burials, and 34 assemblages) where the earliest detected human activity occurred above one of the tenth-century tephras, the *Eldgjá* tephra of AD 939 or the V-Sv tephra of 938 ± 6 (Figures 6.1 and 6.6c), where the radiocarbon dates point to a late occupation (for example, radiocarbon dates with probability curves after AD 939), and where an archaeological find is dated to AD post-950 or post-960 (inferred mostly on the basis of bead production periods) (Appendix Table). Archaeological sites dated to the post-*Landnám* period have a very similar spread to the *Landnám* sites; however the majority of sites are located in the north (Fig. 6.6c).

The Viking Age period refers to 275 sites (93 settlements, 108 burials, and 74 assemblages) where human activity cannot be constrained by the LTL or a tenth-century tephra, where the calibration curve of radiocarbon samples falls within the general Viking period or where artifacts give general tenth-century or Viking Age dates (Appendix Table, Figure 6.6d).

Conclusion

Archaeological dating evidence in Iceland relies on tephrochronology, radiocarbon dating, and typology. Although each method produces dates with different precision, accuracy, and bias, each date is a piece of scientific knowledge complementing each another and should not be ignored. We demonstrate the advantages of correlating multidisciplinary datasets: the identification of tephra layers below and above archaeological features, the statistical analysis of radiocarbon datasets, as well as the categorization of typologically diagnostic artifacts in geographic areas. Until recently, all Viking Age sites were seen as evidence of one single period of colonization. The assessment of 550 archaeological sites (evidence of 300 settlements, 140 burials, and 110 assemblages) has demonstrated that 50 percent of all sites can only be assigned general Viking Age dates of 227 years (AD 877–1104). The rest of the dataset can be assigned subdivisions, of which 1 percent of the archaeological sites are, in fact, from an arrival period (pre-*Landnám* of AD pre-877), 30 percent are from an initial colonization period of 62 years (*Landnám* of AD 877–938/939), and 69 percent are from a subsequent longer settlement period of 165 years (post-*Landnám* of AD 938/939–1104). The dating of archaeological sites is primarily a function of the spatial distribution of tephra layers, 89 sites are above the LTL of AD 877 ± 1 across the country, and 113 sites are above the *Eldgjá* tephra of AD 939 or the V-Sv tephra of AD 938 ± 6 (the latter mostly in the north). Notably, the density of archaeological sites and radiocarbon dates through subdivisions of the Viking Age is fairly even (1.2 sites per year); spatial distributions, however, are not. Improved excavation techniques (for example, excavating turf walls) and increasing fieldwork intensities (for example, regional focus) in the last 25 years apply mostly to the north of Iceland. This not only creates a bias in the spatial distribution of evidence relating to colonization, but also increases the likelihood of identifying tephra layers *in situ* below archaeological features. The dating of archaeological sites using radiocarbon dating indicates that the southwest, northwest, north, and east of Iceland were settled synchronously, and soon after the volcanic eruption in AD 877 ± 1.

The evidence assembled in this paper shows that some people arrived on this island soon before the deposition of the LTL; widespread settlement, however, only happened after AD 877, and most likely before the 890s (Bayesian HPD for the colonization of Iceland is estimated to AD 733–890). This confirms previously expressed hypotheses that the island was settled in a flood, in fewer than 20 years. The data discussed in this paper clearly show that Iceland's settlement was homogeneous and continuous across the entire island. All parts of the island were occupied by the tenth century, with the exception of the interior highlands, which are still uninhabitable today. Without the successful and large-scale settlement of Iceland, an onward push to Greenland late in the tenth century would most likely not have happened, and the scale of settlement in Iceland may have been critical in providing the momentum to carry successful expansion further westward.

Acknowledgments

The authors thank the editors for the invitation to write this chapter. This chapter is based as a result of a PhD thesis from MS. MS acknowledges support from the Icelandic Centre for Research (Rannís) through grant 121153-0061. Special thanks to Adam Bunbury for his contribution to improving the manuscript.

Appendix: Viking Age Sites in Iceland

Five hundred fifty Viking Age sites in Iceland that are dated with tephrochronology, radiocarbon dating, and typology. The sites are ordered according to archaeological periods, geographic distributions, and site type (after Schmid 2018). The dating evidence refers to the earliest human presence at a site.

Appendix Table

Period[a]	Area[b]	Site characterization[c]	Site name	Excavation year(s)/Accession year(s)	Tephra below features (post-)	Tephra on top of features (pre-)	Number of 14C	Earliest Age range AD (68% probability)[d]	Typology (AD): Terminus post quem
1	SW	S	Húshólmi (Gamla Krýsuvík)	1987	—	LTL	—	—	—
1	SW	S	Reykjavík	1971–75/2001–03/2008-	—	LTL	58*	724–878 (G)	Viking Age
2	SW	S/B	Skeljastaðir	1939	LTL	H-1104	11	779–1018 (B-M)	10th–11th c.
2	SW	S	Akraland (Arnarnes)	1994–2004	LTL	K-1500	—	—	—
2	SW	S	Bessastaðir	1987–96	LTL	R-1226	3	901–996 (G)	Viking Age/post-1095 (coin)
2	SW	S	Fagridalur	1999	K-920	Eldgjá	—	—	—
2	SW	S	Gjáskógar	1942/1952/1960	LTL?	H-1104	—	—	—
2	SW	S	Göltur	1985	LTL	—	—	—	—
2	SW	S	Háls (Kolslækur)	1987–91	LTL	H-1341	4	715–962 (Ch)	—
2	SW	S	Helgadalur	2009	LTL	—	—	—	—
2	SW	S	Herjólfsdalur	1971–83	LTL	—	9	688–864 (Ch)	10th c.
2	SW	S	Heynes	1990–91	LTL	R-1226	—	—	—
2	SW	S	Hjálmsstaðir	1983–85	LTL	—	—	—	Viking Age
2	SW	S	Hofstaðir í Garðabær	1994–99	LTL	R-1226	—	—	Jelling style (Viking art)/early- mid-10th c.
2	SW	S	Hrísbrú	1999/2001–08	LTL	K-920/Eldgja?	25	886–953 (G)	Viking Age/post-960
2	SW	S	Hvaleyri	2005	—	—	2	777–946 (Ch)	—
2	SW	S	Kópsvatn	1987	LTL	—	—	—	—
2	SW	S	Leirvogstunga	2006	LTL	R-1226	—	—	—
2	SW	S	Nes II	1989/1995–96	LTL	K-1500	—	—	—
2	SW	S	Rógshólar	1939	LTL	H-1104	—	—	—
2	SW	S	Skeggjastaðir	1999/2009	LTL	K-1500	—	—	—
2	SW	S	Snjáleifartóttir	1939	LTL	H-1693	—	—	Viking Age

2	SW	S	Spöngin	1880/2005	LTL	—	—	—	Viking Age (house)
2	SW	S	Stórhólshlíð	1939	LTL	H-1104	—	—	10th–11th c.
2	SW	S	Urriðakot	2005–10	LTL	R-1226	—	—	10th–11th c.
2	SW	S	Viðey II	1986–94	LTL	—	5	723–877 (Ch)	10th c.
2	SW	S	Vogur í Höfnum	2002–03/2011	LTL	R-1226	—	—	Viking Age
2	SW	S	Þingnes by Elliðavatn	1981–86/2003	LTL	R-1226	—	—	Viking Age
2	SW	S	Þjótandi við Þjórsá	2007/2010	LTL	H-1104/H-1300?	7	889–979 (Ch)	Viking Age
2	SW	S	Þórarinsstaðir II	1945	LTL	—	—	—	1016–1035 (coin)/Viking Age
2	SW	S	Þorleifshaugur	1920/2005	LTL	—	—	—	—
2	SW	S	Þrælagarður	1986	LTL	H-1693	—	—	—
2	NW	S	Eiríksstaðir	1895/1938/1997–2002	LTL	—	3	778–967 (Ch)	?
2	NW	S	Gilsbakki in Hvítársíða	1917/1950s/2008	LTL	—	—	—	Viking Age
2	NW	S	Hallmundarhellir	1989	LTL	—	—	—	—
2	NW	S	Surtshellir (Vígishellir)	1960s/1993/2001	LTL	—	3	775–877 (B-T)	—
2	NW	S	Viðgelmir (Fljótstunga)	1993	LTL	—	4	721–869 (Ch)	950–960
2	N	S	Beinisstaðir	2007/2010	LTL	V-Sv	—	—	—
2	N	S	Efra-Gjáholt (Efra Kýrholt)	2008	LTL	H-1104	—	—	—
2	N	S	Fagrahlíð	2005	LTL	Vj	—	—	—
2	N	S	Flatatunga	2014	LTL	H-1104	—	—	—
2	N	S	Garðhús (Hólar)	2008	LTL	H-1104	—	—	—
2	N	S	Gautlandasel	1996/2010	LTL	V-Sv	—	—	—
2	N	S	Geldingaholt	after 2000	—	Vj	1	991–1016 (Ch)	—
2	N	S	Grjótgerði í Viðinesi	2008	LTL	H-1104	—	—	—
2	N	S	Hafsteinsstaðir	after 2000	LTL	Vj	1	777–950 (B-T)	—
2	N	S	Hamrar	2006	LTL	H-1158	—	—	—

continued

Period[a]	Area[b]	Site characterization[c]	Site name	Excavation year(s)/ Accession year(s)	Tephra below features (post-)	Tephra on top of features (pre-)	Number of 14C	Earliest Age range AD (68% probability)[d]	Typology (AD): Terminus post quem
2	N	S	Hamrar, Helgastaðir and Pálmholt I	2006	LTL	H-1300	—	—	—
2	N	S	Hamrar, Helgastaðir and Pálmholt II	2006	LTL	H-1158	—	—	—
2	N	S	Hof I	2008	LTL	H-1104	—	—	—
2	N	S	Hrísastaðir	2005	LTL	Vj	—	—	—
2	N	S	Hrísheimar	2001–07	LTL	V-Sv	22	724–875 (B-T)	Viking Age
2	N	S	Kálfaströnd	2012	LTL	—	—	—	—
2	N	S	Klausturhús	2008	LTL	—	—	—	—
2	N	S	Marbæli	2009	LTL	Vj	1	970–1015 (G)	—
2	N	S	Öxnadalsheiði (Skógarnes)	1962/2012	LTL	H-1104	—	—	Viking Age
2	N	S	Rauðaskriða I	2005	LTL	H-1158	—	—	—
2	N	S	Rauðaskriða II	2006	LTL	H-1300	—	—	—
2	N	S	Reynistaður (Langhúshóll)	2002	—	Vj	2	778–880 (Ch)	—
2	N	S	Rísamýri (Skiphóll)	2007	LTL	H-1104	—	—	—
2	N	S	Skútustaðir	2007-	LTL	V-Sv	18	769–874 (B-T)	Viking Age
2	N	S	Stóra Gröf	2009	LTL	Vj	2	892–962 (Ch)	Viking Age
2	N	S	Svartárkot	1897/2002	LTL	H-1104	—	—	Viking Age
2	N	S	Sveigakot	1998–2006	LTL	V-Sv	19	771–875 (B-T)	Viking Age
2	N	S	Torfgarður	2008	LTL	Vj	1	1327–1410 (B-T)	—
2	N	S	Tungukot (Tunga)	2003	LTL	Vj	—	—	—
2	N	S	Vatnsleysa (Haganes)	2015	LTL	H-1104	—	—	—
2	N	S	Ytra-Skörðugil	2005	LTL	H-1300	—	—	—
2	N	S	Þegjandadalur I	2006	LTL	H-1158	—	—	—
2	N	S	Þegjandadalur II	2006	LTL	H-1158	—	—	—

2	S	N	Þegjandadalur III	2006	LTL	H-1300	—	—	—
2	S	N	Þegjandadalur IV	2006	LTL	V-1477	—	—	—
2	S	N	Þorleifsstaðir	2007/2010	LTL	V-Sv	—	—	—
2	S	N	Þverá í Hrolleifsdal	2015	LTL	K-1262	—	—	—
2	S	N	Þyrilskot/Þyrilshóll (Máskot)	2010	LTL	V-Sv	—	—	—
2	A	N	Mánárbakki I	2005	—	—	—	—	Pre-915
2	S	E	Broddaskáli	1953/1983	LTL	—	4	904–1021 (Ch)	—
2	S	E	Geirsstaðir	1996–97	LTL?	Ö-1362	4	719–936 (Ch)	—
2	S	E	Hólmur	1997–2002	LTL	—	1	1016–1151 (Ch)	—
2	S	E	í Geirlandsheiði	2002	LTL	Eldgjá	1	899–1147 (Ch)	—
2	S	E	innan við Faxagil	1978–79	LTL	H-1158	2	776–938 (Ch)	—
2	S	E	Mjóeyri við Reyðarfjörð	2003/2007	LTL	Ö-1362	—	—	—
2	S	E	Mosholt	2013	—	Eldgjá	—	—	—
2	S	E	Syðsta Mörk (REU 18)	1990s	LTL	H-1341	2	773–878 (W-SL)	—
2	B	E	Hrífunes	1958/1981/1982/2011	LTL	Eldgjá	—	—	860–950/10th
2	A	E	Bragðavellir	1933–34	—	—	—	—	c./270–305(coin)
3	S	SW	Bergþórshvoll	1883/1885/1927–28/1931/1951	Eldgjá	—	2	901–1156 (Ch)	Viking Age–early medieval
3	S	SW	Hróðnýjarstaðir I	1983/2014	Eldgjá	H-1206	—	—	—
3	S	SW	Hrólfsstaðahellir	1871	—	—	—	—	Post-960
3	S	SW	Hrunakrókur	1988	Eldgjá	H-1104	—	—	—
3	S	SW	Hvítárholt	1963–67	LTL	H-1104	3	984–1184 (Ch)	Post-950
3	S	SW	Langanes I (REU 23)	2002	Eldgjá	H-1341	3	1024–1151 (W-SL)	—
3	S	SW	Langanes II (CP 1)	2003	Eldgjá	H-1341	3	779–970 (W-SL)	—
3	S	SW	Langanes III (CP 4)	2004	Eldgjá	H-1341	3	902–1016 (W-SL)	—
3	S	SW	Langanes IV (AS 1)	2003	Eldgjá	H-1341	3	900–1011 (W-SL)	—

continued

Perioda	Area b	Site charac-terizationc	Site name	Excavation year(s)/Accession year(s)	Tephra below features (post-)	Tephra on top of features (pre-)	Number of 14C	Earliest Age range AD (68% probability)d	Typology (AD): Terminus post quem
3	SW	S	Langanes V (AS 2)	2003	Eldgjá	H-1341	3	894–980 (W-SL)	—
3	SW	S	Markarfljót Valley (REU 17)	2003	Eldgjá	H-1341	3	893–980 (W-SL)	—
3	SW	S	Reykholt	1987–1989	LTL	—	19	776–953 (Ch)	Medieval
3	SW	S	Sámsstaðir í Þjórsárdal	1895/1971–72	Eldgjá	—	3	778–968 (Ch)	10th–11th c.
3	SW	S	Skallakot	1939/2001	Eldgjá	H-1104	—	—	10th–11th c.
3	SW	S	Stöng í Þjórsárdal	1939/1982–86/1992–93	Eldgjá	H-1104	14	718–881 (Ch)	10th–13th c.
3	SW	S	Stóraborg	1978–1990/1972	—	—	—	—	Post-950
3	SW	S	Tjaldbúð	1988	—	—	—	—	10th–11th c. (house)
3	SW	S	Útskalar	2005–06	—	—	2	993–1115 (B-T)	—
3	SW	B	Álfsstaðir	1894	—	—	—	—	Post-960
3	SW	B	Brú I	1876	—	—	—	—	10th c./post-960
3	SW	B	Gamla Berjanes	1912	—	—	—	—	10th–11th c.
3	SW	B	Gamli Húsagarður	1898	—	—	—	—	Post-960/10th c.
3	SW	B	Kápa (Steinfinnsstaðir)	1860/1883/1925/1934	—	—	—	—	10th c./post-960
3	SW	B	Miklaholt (Miklaholtshellir)	1840	—	—	—	—	Post-950
3	SW	B	Rangá (Eystri)	1818/1866/1876/1883/1954	—	—	—	—	Urnes style (Viking art)
3	SW	B	Stóra-Hof	1885	—	—	—	—	Post-960
3	SW	B	Traðarholt-Skipar	1862/1880	—	—	—	—	Post-950
3	SW	A	Ásólfsstaðir	1939 or 1950	—	—	—	—	10th–11th c.
3	SW	A	Eskiholt	1896	—	—	—	—	Post-960
3	SW	A	Flagbjarnarholt	1842	—	—	—	—	Post-1016 (coin)
3	SW	A	Foss I	1910	—	—	—	—	11th c.
3	SW	A	Gamla Akbraut (Kaldárholt)	1865/1866/2005	—	—	—	—	10th c./post-960

								Post-1016 (coin)/ Mammen style (Viking art)
3	SW	A	Gaulverjabær	1930	—	—	—	
3	SW	A	Hof í Djúpidal	1936	—	—	—	10th–11th c.
3	SW	A	Hrossatungur	1965	—	—	—	Post-1002 (coin)
3	SW	A	Járnlaugsstaðir (Harlaugsstaðir)	1864	—	—	—	Post-960
3	SW	A	Keldu (Keldnakot)	1910/1919	—	—	—	Post-960
3	SW	A	Klóarfjall	1888	—	—	—	11th c.
3	SW	A	Kóngshóll	1834/1914	—	—	—	885–980
3	SW	A	Kotmúli	1960	—	—	—	Late Viking Age
3	SW	A	Litli-Oddi	1936	—	—	—	10th–11th c.
3	SW	A	Merkihvoll	1866	—	—	—	11th c.
3	SW	A	Miðbotnar	1938	—	—	—	10th–11th c.
3	SW	A	Oddgeirshólar	1929	—	—	—	Viking Age/pre-1200
3	SW	A	Sandgil	1935	—	—	—	10th–11th c.
3	SW	A	Skipholt	2005	—	—	—	Post-950
3	SW	A	Tröllaskógur	1898/1910	—	—	—	Urnes style (Viking art)
3	SW	A	undir Árfelli	1949–50	—	—	—	10th–11th c.
3	SW	A	Viðey I	1910	—	—	—	Post-960
3	SW	A	Þingvallakirkja	1999	—	—	—	Post-1080 (coin)
3	SW	A	Þjórsárholt	1940	—	—	—	10th–11th c.
3	NW	S	Fróðastaðir	1949–50	—	—	—	10th–11th c.
3	NW	B	Hringsdalur	1950/2006–08	—	—	—	Late 10th c.
3	NW	B	Mjóidalur (Sanddalur)	1837	—	—	—	Pre-950/post-950/917–927(coin)
3	NW	B	Vatnsdalur	1964	—	6	831–986 (B-M)	Post-950/pre-980/870–930(coin)

continued

Perioda	Area b	Site characterizationc	Site name	Excavation year(s)/ Accession year(s)	Tephra below features (post-)	Tephra on top of features (pre-)	Number of 14C	Earliest Age range AD (68% probability)d	Typology (AD): Terminus post quem
3	NW	A	Ásbjarnarstaðir	1949–50	—	—	—	—	Post-960
3	NW	A	Miðhraun	1894	—	—	—	—	Post-950
3	N	S/B	Keldudalur	2002	Vj?	H-1104	22	727–938 (B-M)	860–950
3	N	S	Arnarvatnssel (Helluvað)	2010	V-Sv	V-1477	—	—	—
3	N	S	Bláskógar (Garður)	2011	V-Sv	H-1300	—	—	—
3	N	S	Brenna	2002	V-Sv	H-1104	—	—	—
3	N	S	Einarsstaðir	2012	V-Sv	K-1262	—	—	—
3	N	S	Einirlækur	1981	V-Sv	H-1104	—	—	—
3	N	S	Eystri Brú (Árbót)	2004/2011	V-Sv	H-1300	—	—	—
3	N	S	Eyvík Tjörnesi	2006	V-Sv	V-1477	—	—	—
3	N	S	Fossabrekkur	2008	Vj	H-1104	—	—	—
3	N	S	(Svaðastaðir) Fremri Fjöll	2011	V-Sv	V-1410	—	—	—
3	N	S	Gásir	2001–06	V-Sv	G-1320	5	Unknown reservoir	—
3	N	S	Geldingaættur (Hofstaðir)	2007	V-Sv	V-1477	—	—	—
3	N	S	Girðingar (Gautlönd)	2007/2010	V-Sv	H-1104/H-1158?	—	—	—
3	N	S	Glaumbær, Lower	2001–05	Vj	H-1104	5	970–1148 (B-T)	—
3	N	S	Gljúfurárgerði	2008	Vj	H-1104	—	—	—
3	N	S	Grænavatn	2007	V-Sv?	V-1477	—	—	—
3	N	S	Grasaskarð (Grænavatn)	1998/2010	V-Sv	H-1104/H-1158?	—	—	—
3	N	S	Grófargil	after 2000	Vj	H-1104	1	1014–1151 (B-T)	—
3	N	S	Hæðarnes (Goðdalir)	2003	Vj	H-1104	—	—	—
3	N	S	Hæringsbúðir	2014	Vj	H-1104	—	—	—
3	N	S	Hali (Reykjahlíð)	1994–95	LTL	H-1104	—	—	—
3	N	S	Halldórsstaðir	2008	Vj	H-1104	—	—	—
3	N	S	Hallskot (Víðar)	2010	V-Sv	H-1158	1	Unknown reservoir	—

3	N	S	Hálskot (Stóri-Háls/ Neðra-Hálskot/Stóru-Hámundarstiðir)	2010	V-Sv	V-1477	—	—	—	—
3	N	S	Hamar I	2014	Vj	H-1104	—	—	—	—
3	N	S	Hamar II	2010	V-Sv	H-1104	—	—	—	—
3	N	S	Helgastaðir	2004–05	V-Sv	H-1104	—	—	Viking Age–medieval	—
3	N	S	Hjálmarvík	2009/2012–13	V-Sv	H-1300	—	—	—	—
3	N	S	Höfðagerði (Núpar)	2002–04/2011	LTL	H-1104	—	—	—	—
3	N	S	Hofstaðir í Mývatnsveit	1908/1965/1992–2014	V-Sv	H-1104	82	776–938 (B-T)	Viking Age/10th c.	—
3	N	S	Hólakot	2008	Vj	H-1104	—	—	—	—
3	N	S	Hólakot í Seljadal	2009	V-Sv	H-1300	—	—	—	—
3	N	S	Hólar II	2011	V-Sv	H-1104	—	—	—	—
3	N	S	Höll á Hólsfjöllum	2003	V-Sv	H-1158/V-1159	—	—	—	—
3	N	S	Holt	1974	Eldgjá	H-1104	2	888–1152 (Ch)	—	—
3	N	S	Holtsmúli	2009	V-Sv	Vj	1	996–1024 (G)	—	—
3	N	S	Höskuldsstaðir í Reykjadal	2004	—	—	10	997–1147 (W-SL)	—	—
3	N	S	Hraungerði (Undirveggur)	2011	V-Sv	V-1477	—	—	—	—
3	N	S	Hraunstakkaborg	2011	V-Sv	V-1477	1	995–1185 (Ch)	10th c.	—
3	N	S	Hrauntunga (Suðurárbotnar)	1899 or 1972	—	—	—	—	—	—
3	N	S	Hraunþúfuklaustur	1970/1973	Eldgjá	H-1104	1	1035–1214 (Ch)	—	—
3	N	S	Húsatóftir	1981	V-Sv	H-1104	—	—	—	—
3	N	S	í Austurdal	2005	Vj	H-1104	—	—	—	—
3	N	S	í Vesturdal	after 2000	Vj	H-1104	—	—	—	—
3	N	S	Ingimundarhóll	1986	—	H-1104	—	—	—	—
3	N	S	Ingveldarstaðir	2011	V-Sv	H-1300	—	—	—	—

continued

Perioda	Area b	Site charac-terizationc	Site name	Excavation year(s)/ Accession year(s)	Tephra below features (post-)	Tephra on top of features (pre-)	Number of 14C	Earliest Age range AD (68% probability)d	Typology (AD): Terminus post quem
3	N	S	Ingveldarstaðir (Tóveggur)	2011	V-Sv	V-1477	—	—	—
3	N	S	Kirkjulaut (Hólar)	2011	V-Sv	V-1477	—	—	—
3	N	S	Kjartansstaðir	2009	V-Sv	Vj	1	904–993 (G)	—
3	N	S	Kúðá	2010–13	V-Sv	H-1300	1	994–1118 (Ch)	—
3	N	S	Langgarður í landi Garðs	2011	V-Sv	V-1477	—	—	—
3	N	S	Litla-Gróf	2009	V-Sv	Vj	3	900–974 (G)	—
3	N	S	Litlu-Gautlönd	2007	V-Sv	H-1300	—	—	—
3	N	S	Mánárbakki II	2002	V-Sv	H-1300	—	—	—
3	N	S	Mariugerði	2009	V-Sv	H-1300	—	—	—
3	N	S	Meðalheimur	2009	V-Sv	Vj	6	882–951 (G)	—
3	N	S	Mýnesás	2010	V-Sv	H-1104/H-1158?	—	—	—
3	N	S	Narfastaðasel	2008	V-Sv	H-1300	—	—	—
3	N	S	Narfastaðir	2006	V-Sv	H-1158	—	—	—
3	N	S	Naust	2006	V-Sv	H-1104	1	904–1021 (Ch)	950–1050
3	N	S	Nes I	2006	V-Sv	H-1158	—	—	—
3	N	S	Oddastaðir (Grænavatn)	2002	V-Sv	H-1158	—	880–970 (B-T)	—
3	N	S	Öndólfsstaðir	1970/2011	V-Sv	H-1300	—	—	—
3	N	S	Raufarhóll (Vindbelgur)	1902/2011	V-Sv	H-1104	—	—	10th c.
3	N	S	Sakka (Sökkulan)	2010	V-Sv	H-1300	—	—	—
3	N	S	Saltvík	2002–03	V-Sv	V-1477	—	—	—
3	N	S	Selhagi	1970s/2001	V-Sv	H-1300	2	991–1148 (B-T)	—
3	N	S	Selholt	2007	V-Sv	H-1300	—	—	—
3	N	S	Sellandasel	1998/2010	V-Sv	H-1104/H-1158?	—	—	—
3	N	S	Skógar III	2011–12	V-Sv	H-1104	—	—	—
3	N	S	Skuggi	2008–14	LTL	H-1104	2	990–1024 (B-T)	Turn 10th c.

3	N	S	Smiðjuskógur	1949–1950/1972	—	H-1104	1	1017–1154 (Ch)	10th c.
3	N	S	Steinbogi (Helluvað)	2002	V-Sv	H-1158	2	1035–1207 (B-T)	—
3	N	S	Steindyr	2010	V-Sv	H-1104	—	—	—
3	N	S	Stóra Gröf Ytri	2010	V-Sv	Vj	2	892–962 (Ch)	—
3	N	S	Stóra Seyla	2008	V-Sv	Vj	5	777–893 (G)	—
3	N	S	Svalbarð (Svalbarðstunga)	1986–88/2008–12	V-Sv	H-1300	—	—	—
3	N	S	Svínadalur	1919/2011	V-Sv	H-1300	1	Unknown reservoir	—
3	N	S	Sýrnes	2005	V-Sv	H-1300	—	—	—
3	N	S	Tinnársel	1982	V-Sv	H-1300	—	—	—
3	N	S	Tungufell I	2010	V-Sv	V-1477	—	—	—
3	N	S	Tungufell II	2010	V-Sv	V-1477	—	—	—
3	N	S	Unastaðasel	2014	Vj	H-1104	—	—	—
3	N	S	undir Sandmúla	1909–1974/2005	V-Sv	—	2	977–1024 (B-T)	Viking Age
3	N	S	Við Fjaðrárgljúfur	after 2000	Eldgjá	H-1206	—	—	—
3	N	S	við Kleifarhólma	2010	V-Sv	H-1104/H-1158?	—	—	—
3	N	S	Viðatóft við Másvatn	1989/2002/2011	V-Sv	H-1104/H-1158?	—	—	—
3	N	S	Þórutóftir við Laugafell	2005	V-Sv	H-1104/H-1158?	—	—	—
3	N	S	Þrælagerði	1968/2008	V-Sv	H-1158	—	—	—
3	N	S	Þverá	2005	V-Sv	H-1158	—	—	—
3	N	S	Þverá í Öxarfirði	1995	V-Sv	K-1262	—	—	—
3	N	B	Baldursheimur	1860	—	—	—	—	Post-960/11th c.
3	N	B	Daðastaðir (Kleif)	1956	—	—	—	—	Post-950/Borre style (Viking art)
3	N	B	Daðastaðir (Lyngbrekka)	1932/2004–05	V-Sv	H-1300	—	—	Late Viking Age
3	N	B	Dalvík (Brimnes I)	1909/1942	—	—	3	901–996 (B-T)	Post-950/10th c.
3	N	B	Eyjólfsstaðir	2003	—	—	—	—	10th c./955–975 (coin)
3	N	B	Gömlu Grímsstaðir	1962/2003	V-Sv	V-1477	1	892–1011 (B-M)	10th c.

continued

Perioda	Area b	Site charac-terizationc	Site name	Excavation year(s)/Accession year(s)	Tephra below features (post-)	Tephra on top of features (pre-)	Number of 14C	Earliest Age range AD (68% probability)d	Typology (AD): Terminus post quem
3	N	B	Ingiríðarstaðir	2008–15	V-Sv	H-1300	—	—	Viking Age
3	N	B	Kálfaborgará	1969	—	—	—	—	Post-950/10th c.
3	N	B	Kornsá	1879	—	—	—	—	Post-950/10th c.
3	N	B	Kumlabrekka (Geirastaðir)	2006	V-Sv	H-1104/H-1158?	—	—	Viking Age
3	N	B	Litlu Núpar	1915/2004–09	V-Sv	H-1300	1	900–1020 (B-M)	Viking Age
3	N	B	Ljótsstaðir	1958	—	—	—	—	Mammen style (Viking art)
3	N	B	Möðruvellir	1839	—	—	—	—	Urnes style (Viking art)
3	N	B	Silastaðir	1947	—	—	2	778–961 (B-T)	Post-950/10th c.
3	N	B	Ytra-Garðshorn	1952	—	—	—	—	Post-960/10th c.
3	N	A	Arnarvatn	1883/1925	—	—	—	—	11th c.
3	N	A	Eyrarland	1815	—	—	—	—	Ringerike style (Viking art)
3	N	A	Keta	1952	—	—	—	—	Post-942 (coin)
3	N	A	Stóri-Ós	1953	—	—	—	—	Post-950
3	N	A	Víðafell í Reykjadal	1867	—	—	—	—	11th c.
3	E	S	Ásmundarstaðir	1931	—	—	—	—	10th–11th c.
3	E	S	Áttahringsvogur (Papey island)	1981	—	Ö-1362	2	1030–1155 (Ch)	Viking Age
3	E	S	Fjárhóll	2011	Eldgjá	H-1206	—	—	
3	E	S	Hamar í Hamarsfirði	1949–59	—	—	—	—	10th–11th c.
3	E	S	Leiðólfsfell	after 2000	Eldgjá	H-1206	—	—	—
3	E	S	Litli-Svartinúpur	2013	Eldgjá	H-1104	—	—	—
3	E	S	Ljótarstaðir	after 2000	Eldgjá	V-1477	—	—	—
3	E	S	milli Merkurár og Sláttugils	2012	Eldgjá	H-1206	—	—	—

3	E	S	Pálstóftir	2005	V-Sv	H-1104	6	900–1012 (B-T)	Post-960 AD/1047–1066(coin)
3	E	S	Skinney í Hornafirði	1870	—	Ö-1362	—	—	10th–11th c.
3	E	S	Sómastaðagerði	2003	V-Sv	H-1206	—	—	—
3	E	S	Streyta	2014	Eldgjá	—	—	—	—
3	E	S	við Kóragil	2013	Eldgjá	—	—	—	Viking Age-medieval
3	E	S	Þórarinsstaðir I	1945	—	H-1104	2	902–1018 (Ch)	10th c./955–975 (coin)
3	E	S	Eyrarteigur	1995	—	—	—	—	Post-950
3	E	B	Granagil (Granahaugar)	1895	—	—	—	—	Post-950
3	E	B	Ketilsstaðir (Litlu Ketilsstaðir)	1938/1942	—	—	—	—	Post-950/pre-980/10th c.
3	E	B	Sturluflötur	1901	—	—	—	—	Post-960
3	E	A	Búlandsnes	1890	—	—	—	—	Post-960
3	E	A	Valþjófsstaðir I	1930	—	—	—	—	1042–1066 (coin)
3	E	A	Vestdalsheiði	2004	—	—	—	—	860–950/post-960/820–950
4	SW	S	Byggarðsvör	2004	LTL	R-1226	—	—	10th c.
4	SW	S	Einhyrningsflatir á Grænafjalli	1902/1980	—	—	—	—	—
4	SW	S	Fossárdalur II	1942/1949/1962/2005/2010	—	K-1500	1	973–1032 (Ch)	10th c.
4	SW	S	Hlíð	2005	—	H-1104	—	—	Viking Age
4	SW	S	Kópavogsþingstaður	1973–1976	—	—	3	695–976 (Ch)	—
4	SW	S	undir Lambhöfða	1895/1954/2001	—	—	—	—	Borre style (Viking art)
4	SW	S	undir Rauðukömbum	1954/2001	—	—	—	—	Viking Age (house)
4	SW	S	Þvergarður	1992	—	R-1226	—	—	Viking Age
4	SW	B	Áslákshóll	1909	—	—	—	—	Viking Age
4	SW	B	Búrfellsháls	1928	—	—	—	—	Viking Age
4	SW	B	Efri-Rauðalækur	1902	—	—	—	—	Viking Age

continued

Period[a]	Area[b]	Site charac-terization[c]	Site name	Excavation year(s)/ Accession year(s)	Tephra below features (post-)	Tephra on top of features (pre-)	Number of 14C	Earliest Age range AD (68% probability)/d	Typology (AD): Terminus post quem
4	SW	B	Fellsmúli	1888/1907/1927/1930	—	—	—	—	10th c.
4	SW	B	Galtalækur	1929	—	—	—	—	10th c.
4	SW	B	Gaukshöfði	1892	—	—	—	—	Viking Age
4	SW	B	Grafarbakki	1813	—	—	—	—	Viking Age
4	SW	B	Hábær	1914/1919/1957–58	—	—	—	—	Viking Age
4	SW	B	Hafurbjarnarstaðir	1868/1947	—	—	—	—	860–980/10th c.
4	SW	B	Hemla	1932/1937	—	—	—	—	10th c.
4	SW	B	Hólaskógur	1978	—	—	—	—	10th c.
4	SW	B	í Hraungerðishreppi (Miklaholtshellir)	Early 19th c.	—	—	—	—	Viking Age
4	SW	B	í Þjórsárdal	1864	—	—	—	—	Viking Age
4	SW	B	Kaldárhöfði	1946	—	—	—	—	10th c.
4	SW	B	Kápa á Almenningum	1860/1925/1934/1935	—	—	—	—	Viking Age (horse)
4	SW	B	Karlsnes (Skarðssel)	1932, 2004	—	—	—	—	790–845/10th c.
4	SW	B	Kolsholt	1958	—	—	—	—	Viking Age (horse)
4	SW	B	Kornhóll (Skansinn)	1968/1992	—	—	1	775–944 (B-M)	Viking Age
4	SW	B	Lækur I	1969	—	—	—	—	Viking Age (horse)
4	SW	B	Lambhagi	1922	—	—	—	—	10th c.
4	SW	B	Laufahvammur	1880–1890	—	—	—	—	Viking Age
4	SW	B	Mörk	1936	—	—	—	—	Viking Age
4	SW	B	Selfoss (Rauðholt)	1958/1962	—	—	—	—	Viking Age
4	SW	B	Skarfanes (Skarðstangi)	1989	—	—	—	—	Viking Age
4	SW	B	Skógar II	1903	—	—	—	—	10th c./Berdal style (Viking art)
4	SW	B	Snæfoksstaðir	1829	—	—	—	—	Viking Age
4	SW	B	Snartarstaðir	1938	—	—	—	—	10th c.

4	SW	B	Stóri-Klofi (Kollakot and Litli-Klofi)	1933	—	—	—	10th c.
4	SW	B	Stóri-Moshvoll	1913	—	—	—	Viking Age
4	SW	A	á Gnúpverjafrétti	1906	—	—	—	Viking Age
4	SW	A	Efstibær	1898	—	—	—	Viking Age
4	SW	A	Engidalur	1888–92 or 1944	—	—	—	Viking Age
4	SW	A	Fagriskógur	1951 or 1992	—	—	—	Viking Age
4	SW	A	Foss II	1910	—	—	—	10th c.
4	SW	A	Fossárdalur I	1949/2001	—	—	—	Viking Age
4	SW	A	Gamla Gunnarsholt (Gunnarshóll)	1866	—	—	—	Viking Age
4	SW	A	Gamli Vorsabær	1947	—	—	—	Viking Age
4	SW	A	Hestaþingshóll	1832	—	—	—	Viking Age
4	SW	A	Hrepphólar	1962	—	—	—	Viking Age
4	SW	A	Hrólfsstaðir I	1889	—	—	—	Viking Age
4	SW	A	Hvolsvöllur	1976	—	—	—	Viking Age
4	SW	A	í Rangárvallasýslu	1968	—	—	—	Viking Age
4	SW	A	Kalastaðir	1919	—	—	—	Borre style (Viking art)
4	SW	A	Knafahólar	18th c.	—	—	—	around 900
4	SW	A	Laxárdalur	1901	—	—	—	Viking Age
4	SW	A	Laxnes	1882	—	—	—	Viking Age
4	SW	A	Markhólsrúst	1945	—	—	—	Viking Age
4	SW	A	Melakot	1894	—	—	—	Viking Age
4	SW	A	Miðhús II	1921	—	—	—	Viking Age
4	SW	A	Múlakot	1888	—	—	—	Viking Age
4	SW	A	Neðra-Apavatn	1959	—	—	—	Viking Age
4	SW	A	Reyðarvatn	1915	—	—	—	885–980

continued

Perioda	Area b	Site characterizationc	Site name	Excavation year(s)/Accession year(s)	Tephra below features (post-)	Tephra on top of features (pre-)	Number of 14C	Earliest Age range AD (68% probability)d	Typology (AD): Terminus post quem
4	SW	A	Sámsstaðir	1906	—	—	—	—	Viking Age
4	SW	A	Skálabrekka	1961	—	—	—	—	Viking Age
4	SW	A	Skálatóttir	1905	—	—	—	—	Viking Age
4	SW	A	Skálhólar (Fossnes)	2000	—	—	—	—	Viking Age
4	SW	A	Steinsholt (Hólar)	1929	—	—	—	—	Viking Age
4	SW	A	Stokkseyri	1884	—	—	—	—	Viking Age
4	SW	A	Stóri-Botn	1903	—	—	—	—	Viking Age
4	SW	A	Stóri-Núpur	1927	—	—	—	—	Viking Age
4	SW	A	undir Hánni	1912	—	—	—	—	Viking Age
4	SW	A	Vatnskot	1964	—	—	—	—	Viking Age
4	SW	A	Villingaholt	1948	—	—	—	—	Viking Age
4	SW	A	Þingskálar	1868/1896	—	—	—	—	10th c.
4	SW	A	Þuríðarstaðir efri	1974/1977/1980	—	—	—	—	Viking Age
4	NW	S	Bólstaður	1931	—	—	—	—	Viking Age
4	NW	S	Grelutóttir (Grela)	1977-78	—	—	3	713-965 (Ch)	Viking Age
4	NW	S	Írskubúðir	1996/1999	—	—	1	895-1021 (Ch)	Viking Age
4	NW	S	Ísleifsstaðir	1939/2005	—	—	—	—	Viking Age (house)
4	NW	S	Orustuhvammur	1894	—	—	—	—	Viking Age
4	NW	S	Vatnsfjörður	2003-2010	—	H-1693	3	724-875 (Ch)	950-1000
4	NW	S	Ytri-Þorsteinsstaðir	1988	—	—	2	778-968 (Ch)	—
4	NW	B	Berufjörður (Hyrningsstaðir)	1898	—	—	—	—	Viking Age
4	NW	B	Breiðavík	1913	—	—	—	—	Viking Age (horse)
4	NW	B	innri-Fagridalur	1881	—	—	—	—	Viking Age
4	NW	B	Laugarbrekka	1794/1818	—	—	—	—	Viking Age (horse)
4	NW	B	Öndverðarnes	1962	—	—	—	—	10th c.

continued

4	NW	B	Rútsstaðir	1938	—	—	—	—	10th c.
4	NW	B	Strákatangi	2009/2010	—	—	—	—	Viking Age
4	NW	B	Straumfjörður	1872	—	—	—	—	Viking Age
4	NW	A	á Vestfjörðum	1888	—	—	—	—	Jelling style (Viking art)
4	NW	A	Bóndhóll	1949–50	—	—	—	—	Viking Age
4	NW	A	Glerárskógar (Ljárskógar)	1864	—	—	—	—	Borre style (Viking art)
4	NW	A	Höfði	1818	—	—	—	—	Viking Age
4	NW	A	Hróðnýjarstaðir II	1949–50	—	—	—	—	Viking Age
4	NW	A	í Norðurárdal	1865	—	—	—	—	Viking Age
4	NW	A	Kirkjubólsdalur	1891	—	—	—	—	Jelling style (Viking art)
4	NW	A	Ljárskógar	1903	—	—	—	—	Borre style (Viking art)
4	NW	A	Selárdalur	1967	—	—	—	—	Viking Age
4	NW	A	Svelgsá	1910	—	—	—	—	Viking Age
4	NW	A	Tjaldbrekka	1884	—	—	—	—	Viking Age
4	N	S	Bjarnastaðir	2014	LTL	Vj	—	—	—
4	N	S	Breiðavík í Tjörnes	2000	—	H-1158	—	—	—
4	N	S	Enni á Höfðaströnd	1935/2014	—	H-1104	—	—	Viking Age
4	N	S	Fiská (Litla Tunga)	1895	—	H-1104	—	—	—
4	N	S	Fjall	2015	—	H-1300	—	—	—
4	N	S	Fossar í Vesturdal	2004	Vj	—	—	—	Viking Age
4	N	S	Gautlönd	1855/1945/2012	—	H-1104/H-1158?	4	777–890 (B-T)	Viking Age
4	N	S	Geirmundarhólar	2015	—	H-1104	—	—	—
4	N	S	Geitakofahóll (Neðri-Ás)	2008	—	H-1104	—	—	—
4	N	S	Granastaðir	1987–91	LTL/V-Sv?	H-1104	5	770–970 (Ch)	915–980
4	N	S	Grund	2005	Vj	—	—	—	—
4	N	S	Hegranes	after 2000	—	H-1104	—	—	Viking Age-medieval

Perioda	Area b	Site characterizationc	Site name	Excavation year(s)/ Accession year(s)	Tephra below features (post-)	Tephra on top of features (pre-)	Number of 14C	Earliest Age range AD (68% probability)]d	Typology (AD): Terminus post quem
4	N	S	Helgustaðir (Bakki)	2015	—	H-1104	—	—	—
4	N	S	Hofgarðar	1972	—	H-1104	—	—	—
4	N	S	Hólar í Hjaltadal	2002–03	—	H-1104	—	—	—
4	N	S	Horngarðar	1895/1972	—	H-1104	—	—	—
4	N	S	Hrappsá (Hrafnsá-Hrappsárkot)	2013–14	—	H-1104	—	—	—
4	N	S	Illugastaðir	2015	—	H-1104	—	—	—
4	N	S	Kaldárkot	2010	—	H-1104	—	—	—
4	N	S	Kappastaðir	2015	—	Vj	—	—	—
4	N	S	Keflavík	2014	—	Vj	—	—	—
4	N	S	Klaufanes	1940	—	—	—	—	Viking Age (house)
4	N	S	Kolgrímsstaðir í Austurdal	1981	—	H-1104	—	—	—
4	N	S	Kot (Stafn)	2013–14	—	H-1104	—	—	—
4	N	S	Litli-Bakki	2015	—	Vj	—	—	—
4	N	S	Ljósavatn	1928	—	—	—	—	Viking Age (house)
4	N	S	Málmey	2012	—	H-1104	—	—	—
4	N	S	Markúsarhóll	2008	—	H-1104	—	—	—
4	N	S	Miðklif í Austurdal	1983	—	H-1104	—	—	—
4	N	S	Neðri-Ás	1997–99	—	H-1104	—	—	—
4	N	S	Nýlendi á Höfðaströnd	2013	—	H-1104	—	—	—
4	N	S	Oddsstaðir	2009	—	H-1104	3	—	Turn 10th c.
4	N	S	Páfastaðir	2009	—	Vj	—	—	—
4	N	S	Reynistaður	2001–	—	Vj	2	800–1031 (Ch)	Viking Age
4	N	S	Róðhóll	2015	—	H-1104	—	—	—
4	N	S	Sandvatnssel	1996	—	H-1300	—	—	—

4	N	S	Siglunes	2004–06	—	H-1104	—		—	—
4	N	S	Sjöundastaðir	2015	—	H-1104	—		—	—
4	N	S	Skálárkot	2015	—	H-1104	—		—	—
4	N	S	Skógargerði (Arnarstaðir)	2015	—	H-1104	—		—	—
4	N	S	Spáná	2013–14	—	H-1104	—		—	—
4	N	S	Stöng í Mývatnsveit	2002	—	H-1300	—		—	—
4	N	S	Stórhóll (Miðhús)	2012	—	H-1104	—		—	—
4	N	S	Syðra-Skörðugil	2005	—	Vj	1	Unknown reservoir	—	—
4	N	S	Tjarnarkot	2015	—	H-1104	—		—	10th c.
4	N	S	Varastaðir	1950	—	—	—		—	—
4	N	S	við Grindliskrók	2015	—	H-1104	—		—	—
4	N	S	við Viðiker	1999/2002	—	H-1104/H-1158?	—		—	—
4	N	S	Viðines	2010	—	H-1104	—		—	—
4	N	S	Þrælsgerði (Þrælagerði/Gerði)	2014	—	H-1104	—		—	—
4	N	S	Prastarstaðir	2014	—	H-1104	—		—	—
4	N	B	Austara-Land	1904 or 1905	—	—	—		—	Viking Age (horse)
4	N	B	Austarihóll	1964	—	—	—		—	10th c.
4	N	B	Björk (Öngulsstaðir)	1909	—	—	—		—	Viking Age
4	N	B	Brandsstaðir	1965	—	—	—		—	Viking Age (horse)
4	N	B	Brimnes við Dalvík	1937	—	—	—		—	9th–10th c.
4	N	B	Bringa	1937	—	—	—		—	10th c.
4	N	B	Dæli	1970	—	—	—		—	Viking Age
4	N	B	Dalvík (Böggvisstaðir)	1937	—	—	—		—	Viking Age (horse)
4	N	B	Elivogar	1954	—	—	—		—	Viking Age (horse)
4	N	B	Enni II	1934–35	—	—	—		—	Viking Age (horse)
4	N	B	Framdalir	1899	—	—	—		—	10th c.

continued

Perioda	Area b	Site characterizationc	Site name	Excavation year(s)/ Accession year(s)	Tephra below features (post-)	Tephra on top of features (pre-)	Number of 14C	Earliest Age range AD (68% probability)d	Typology (AD): Terminus post quem
4	N	B	Garðsá	1952	—	—	—	—	10th c.
4	N	B	Glaumbær	1915/2012	—	—	3	777–885 (B-T)	Viking Age (horse)
4	N	B	Gljúfurá	1868	—	—	—	—	Viking Age (horse)
4	N	B	Grafargerði	1934	—	—	—	—	Viking Age (horse)
4	N	B	Grásíða	1941	—	—	2	Unknown reservoir	10th c.
4	N	B	Grímsstaðir	1937/1952/1967	—	—	3	779–970 (B-T)	Viking Age (horse)
4	N	B	Hámundarstaðaháls (Stóru-Hámundarstaðir)	1930	—	—	—	—	Viking Age (horse)
4	N	B	Höskuldsstaðir	1873	—	—	—	—	Viking Age
4	N	B	Hrafnsstaðir	1952	—	—	1	Reservoir	10th c.
4	N	B	Hrísar	1916	—	—	—	—	10th c.
4	N	B	Kalfskinn	2003/05	—	—	—	—	Viking Age (horse)
4	N	B	Kolkuós	after 2000	—	—	—	—	10th c.
4	N	B	Kroppur	1902	—	—	—	—	Viking Age
4	N	B	Lækur II	2010	—	H-1104	—	—	Viking Age
4	N	B	Litli-Dunhagi	1963	—	—	—	—	Viking Age (horse)
4	N	B	Lómatjörn	1930/1949	—	—	—	—	Viking Age (horse)
4	N	B	Miðhóp	1941	—	—	—	—	Viking Age
4	N	B	Miklibær í Blönduhlíð	1895–96	—	—	—	—	Viking Age (horse)
4	N	B	Moldhaugar	1908	—	—	—	—	Viking Age (horse)
4	N	B	Sakka	1770	—	—	—	—	Viking Age
4	N	B	Sauðanes	1834	—	—	—	—	Viking Age
4	N	B	Skógar I	1891	—	—	—	—	Viking Age
4	N	B	Sólheimar	1956	—	—	—	—	Viking Age (horse)
4	N	B	Staðartunga	1935	—	H-1104	—	—	Viking Age (horse)
4	N	B	Stærri-Árskógur	1917	—	—	—	—	Viking Age (horse)

4	N	B	Stafn	1933	—	—	—	—	Viking Age
4	N	B	Suðurárbotnar	1947	—	1	Unknown reservoir	—	—
4	N	B	Syðra-Krossanes	1963	—	—	—	—	Viking Age (horse)
4	N	B	Syðri-Hofdalir	1951	—	—	—	—	10th c.
4	N	B	Tindar	1937	—	—	—	—	10th c.
4	N	B	Vík	1908	—	—	—	—	Viking Age (horse)
4	N	B	Ystafell	1917/1971	—	—	—	—	Viking Age (horse)
4	N	B	Ytra-Hvarf	1949	—	—	—	—	10th c.
4	N	B	Ytri-Neslönd (Neslönd)	1960	—	4	774–876 (B-T)	—	—
4	N	B	Ytri-Tjarnir	1925–26	—	—	—	—	10th c.
4	N	B	Þóreyjarnúpur	1928	—	—	—	—	Viking Age (horse)
4	N	B	Þorljótsstaðir	1869	—	—	—	—	Viking Age
4	N	B	Þúfnavellir	1948	—	—	—	—	Viking Age (horse)
4	N	B	Þverá-Auðnir	1945/1985/1999	—	1	Unknown reservoir	—	Viking Age (horse)
4	N	A	Hlaðir	1943	—	—	—	—	Viking Age
4	N	A	Hof II	1868	—	—	—	—	10th c.
4	N	A	Hólar I	1938	—	—	—	—	Viking Age
4	N	A	Hróarsstaðir	1905	—	—	—	—	Viking Age
4	N	A	í Bárðardal	1877	—	—	—	—	Viking Age (10th c.?)
4	N	A	í Kjalhrauni	1937	—	—	—	—	Viking Age
4	N	A	í Suður Þingeyarsýslu	1905	—	—	—	—	Viking Age
4	N	A	Laufás	1909/1999	—	—	—	—	Viking Age
4	N	A	Lundur	1905	—	—	—	—	Borre style (Viking art)
4	N	A	Munkaþverá	1930	—	—	—	—	Viking Age
4	N	A	Reykjavellir (Mælifell)	1865	—	—	—	—	Borre style (Viking art)
4	N	A	Tannsstaðabakki	1886	—	—	—	—	Viking Age
4	N	A	Tunguöxl á Munkaþverártungum	1895	—	—	—	—	Viking Age

continued

Perioda	Area b	Site characterizationc	Site name	Excavation year(s)/ Accession year(s)	Tephra below features (post-)	Tephra on top of features (pre-)	Number of 14C	Earliest Age range AD (68% probability)d	Typology (AD): Terminus post quem
4	N	A	við Fitjaá (Viðidalstunga)	1880	—	—	—	—	Viking Age
4	N	A	Ytri-Vellir	1900	—	—	—	—	Viking Age
4	E	S	á Vesturdal	1978–79	—	H-1158	—	—	—
4	E	S	Aðalból	1958/1978	—	H-1158	—	—	—
4	E	S	Bakkastaðir	1890/1978	LTL	H-1158	—	—	—
4	E	S	Blesatangi	1978–79	—	H-1158	—	—	—
4	E	S	Dyngja	1979	—	H-1158	—	—	—
4	E	S	Engihlið (Kirkjustaður)	1953/1983	—	Ö-1362	—	—	Viking Age
4	E	S	Erlendsstaðir	2013	—	H-1206	—	—	—
4	E	S	Geithús	1979	—	H-1158	—	—	—
4	E	S	Glúmsstaðasel	1980	—	H-1158	—	—	—
4	E	S	Goðatættur (Papey island)	1969/1989	—	Ö-1362	5	972–1183 (Ch)	Viking Age
4	E	S	Hringur	1979	—	H-1158	—	—	—
4	E	S	Hústóft	1979	—	H-1158	—	—	—
4	E	S	í Mógilshálsi	1980	—	H-1158	—	—	—
4	E	S	innan við Faxahús	1978	—	H-1158	—	—	—
4	E	S	Laugarhús	1978/1980	—	H-1158	—	—	—
4	E	S	Orrustustaðir	1985	—	H-1158	—	—	—
4	E	S	Skál	1985	—	H-1158	—	—	—
4	E	S	Sólheimar (Dalbær)	2002	—	Eldgjá?	1	970–1028 (Ch)	—
4	E	S	Steingrímsstaðir	1979	—	H-1158	—	—	—
4	E	S	Steinsgróf (Eiríksstaðir)	1979	—	H-1158	—	—	—
4	E	S	Tobbhóll	1978	—	H-1158	—	—	—
4	E	S	undir Hellisbjargi (Papey island)	1928/1989	—	Ö-1362	1	779–1025 (Ch)	Viking Age

4	E	S	undir Smjörtungufelli	1985	—	H-1158	—	—	—	—
4	E	S	Vaðbrekka	1978	—	H-1158	—	—	—	—
4	E	S	Þórisstaðir	1962 or 1980	—	H-1158	—	—	—	—
4	E	S	Prándarstaðir	1978	—	H-1158	—	—	—	—
4	E	S	Puríðarstaðasel	1978	—	H-1158	—	—	—	—
4	E	B	Álaugarey	1934	—	—	—	—	—	10th c.
4	E	B	Blöndugerði	1942	—	—	—	—	—	Viking Age
4	E	B	Brennistaðir	1950	—	—	—	—	—	10th c.
4	E	B	Brú II	1988	—	—	—	1	889–1011 (B-M)	Viking Age (horse)
4	E	B	Dalir	1895	—	—	—	—	—	10th c.
4	E	B	Einholt	1979	—	—	—	—	—	Viking Age
4	E	B	Flaga	1882	—	—	—	—	—	10th c.
4	E	B	Hóll	1998	—	—	—	—	—	Viking Age
4	E	B	Hólmur (Árnanes)	1894/1902	—	—	—	—	—	Viking Age
4	E	B	Hrólfsstaðir II	1996	—	—	—	—	—	Viking Age
4	E	B	Hrollaugsstaðir	1952	—	—	—	—	—	Viking Age (horse)
4	E	B	Kirkjubær	19th c.	—	—	—	—	—	Viking Age
4	E	B	Ormsstaðir	1966	—	—	—	—	—	10th c.
4	E	B	Rangá	1915	—	—	—	—	—	Viking Age
4	E	B	Reykjasel (Vaðbrekka)	1901/1975	—	—	—	—	—	950–960/10th c.
4	E	B	Snæhvammur	1892	—	—	—	—	—	10th c.
4	E	B	Stóra-Sandfell (Mið-Sandfell)	1982	—	—	—	—	—	10th c./Borre style (Viking art)
4	E	B	Straumur	1952	—	—	—	1	898–1021 (B-M)	10th c.
4	E	B	Surtsstaðir	1945/1949	—	—	—	—	—	Viking Age
4	E	B	Vað	1894	—	—	—	1	984–1150 (B-M)	10th c.

continued

Perioda	Area b	Site characterizationc	Site name	Excavation year(s)/ Accession year(s)	Tephra below features (post-)	Tephra on top of features (pre-)	Number of 14C	Earliest Age range AD (68% probability)d	Typology (AD): Terminus post quem
4	E	B	Valþjófsstaðir II	1800	—	—	—	—	10th c./Borre style (Viking art)
4	E	A	Arnheiðarstaðir	1890	—	—	—	—	Viking Age
4	E	A	Bær í Lóni	1932	—	—	—	—	Viking Age
4	E	A	Brekka	1906	—	—	—	—	Viking Age (horse)
4	E	A	Búland	1896	—	—	—	—	Viking Age
4	E	A	Eyjar	1927	—	—	—	—	Viking Age
4	E	A	Gil	1913	—	—	—	—	Viking Age
4	E	A	Grímsstaðir í Meðallandi	1956	—	—	—	—	Viking Age
4	E	A	Hofsborgartunga	1902	—	—	—	—	Viking Age
4	E	A	Húsey	1980	—	—	—	—	Viking Age
4	E	A	í Álftaveri	c. 1825	—	—	—	—	Viking Age
4	E	A	í Hrafnkelsdal	1900	—	—	—	—	Viking Age
4	E	A	Miðhús I	1980	—	—	—	—	Viking Age

Legend

Source: Authors.

a 1 = Pre-*Landnám* (AD pre-877); 2 = *Landnám* (AD 877–938/939); 3 = post-*Landnám* (AD 938/939–1104); 4 = Viking Age (AD 877–1104).

b E = east, N = north, NW = northwest, SW = southwest.

c A = assemblage, B = burial, S = settlement.

d Ch = charcoal (heartwood of trees or unidentified charcoal); G = charred barley grain; B-M = bone, mixed diet; B-T = bone, terrestrial diet; W-SL = wood, short-lived (identified tree bark and outer rings); reservoir = bone, inbuilt ages from unknown mixed dietary sources.

*Although the earliest occupation of the site is below the LTL, the ¹⁴C dates are on top of the LTL.

References

Ascough, P. L., G. T. Cook, M. J. Church, A. J. Dugmore, T. G. McGovern, E. Dunbar, E. Einarsson, A. Friðriksson, and H. Gestsdóttir. 2007. Reservoirs and Radiocarbon: ^{14}C dating Problems in Mývatnssveit, Northern Iceland. *Radiocarbon* 49(2): 947–961.

Ascough, P. L., M. J. Church, G. T. Cook, E. Dunbar, H. Gestsdóttir, T. H. McGovern, A. J. Dugmore, A. Friðriksson, and K. J. Edwards. 2012. Radiocarbon Reservoir Effects in Human Bone Collagen from Northern Iceland. *Journal of Archaeological Science* 39(7): 2261–2271.

Baillie, M.G.L. 1991. Suck In and Smear: Two Related Chronological Problems for the 90s. *Journal of Theoretical Archaeology* 2: 12–16.

Bayliss, A. 2009. Rolling Out Revolution: Using Radiocarbon Dating in Archaeology. *Radiocarbon* 51(1): 123–147.

Batt, C., M.M.E. Schmid, and O. Vésteinsson. 2015. Constructing Chronologies in Viking Age Iceland: Increasing Dating Resolution Using Bayesian Approaches. *Journal of Archaeological Science* 62: 161–174.

Bolender, D. J., J. M. Steinberg, and B. N. Damiata. 2011. Farmstead Reorganization at the End of the Viking Age: Results of the Skagafjörður Archaeological Settlement Survey. *Archaeologia Islandica* 9: 77–101.

Bronk Ramsey, C 2009. Dealing with Outliers and Offsets in Radiocarbon Dating. *Radiocarbon* 51(3): 1023–1045.

Bronk Ramsey, C. 2017. OxCal 4.3 manual, http://c14.arch.ox.ac.uk/oxcalhelp/hlp_contents.html.

Callmer, J. 1977. *Trade Beads and Bead Trade in Scandinavia ca. 800–1000 AD.* Lund: R. Habelt.

Dee, M., and Bronk Ramsey, C. 2014. High-precision Bayesian Modeling of Samples Susceptible to Inbuilt Age. *Radiocarbon* 56(1): 83–89.

Edwards, K. J. 2012. Was the Peopling of Iceland a Trickle, a Steady Stream or a Deluge? *Norwegian Archaeological Review* 45(2): 220–223.

Eldjárn, K. and Friðriksson, A. 2016. *Kuml og haugfé úr heiðnum sið á Ísland,* 3rd ed, A. Friðriksson. Reykjavík: Mál og menning.

Fitzpatrick, S. 2006. A Critical Approach to ^{14}C Dating in the Caribbean: Using Chronometric Hygiene to Evaluate Chronological Control and Prehistoric Settlement. *Latin American Antiquity* 17(4): 389–418.

Grønlie, Sian transl. Íslendingabók. Kristni Saga. 2006. *The Book of the Icelanders. The Story of the Conversion.* London: Viking Society for Northern Research.

Grönvold, K., K. Óskarsson, S. J. Johnsen, H. B. Clausen, C. U. Hammer, G. Bond, and E. Bard. 1995. Ash Layers from Iceland in the Greenland GRIP Ice Core Correlated with Oceanic and Land Sediments. *Earth and Planetary Science Letters* 135: 149–155.

Hermanns-Auðardóttir, M. 1989. *Islands tidiga bosättning. Studier med utgångspunkt I merovingertida-vikingatida gårdslämningar i Herjólfsdalur, Vestmannaeyjar, Island* Umeå: Studia Archaeological Universitatis Umensis.

Hreiðarsdóttir, E. Ó. 2005. Íslenskar *Perlur frá Víkingaöld: Með Viðauka um Perlur frá Síðari Öldum.* MA Thesis: University of Iceland, Reykjavík.

Jóhannesson, H., and S. Einarsson. 1988. Krýsuvíkureldar I. Aldur Ögmundarhrauns og Miðaldalagsins. *Jökull* 38: 71–85.

Lárusson, Ó. 1929. Úr Byggðarsögu Íslands. *Vaka* 3: 319–369.

Napolitano, M. F., R. J. DiNapoli, J. H. Stone, M. J. Levin, N. P. Jew, B. G. Lane, J. T. O'Connor, and S. M. Fitzpatrick. 2019. Reevaluating Human Colonization of the Caribbean Using Chronometric Hygiene and Bayesian Modeling. *Science Advances* 5: eaar5806.

Pettit, P. B., W. Davies, C. S. Gamble, and M. B. Richards. 2003. Paleolithic Radiocarbon Chronology: Quantifying Our Confidence beyond Two Half-lives. *Journal of Archaeological Science* 30: 1685–1693.

Rafnsson, S. 1990. Byggð á Íslandi á 7. og 8. Öld. Um Doktorsritgerð Margrétar Hermanns-Auðardóttur. *Árbók hins íslenzka fornleifafélags* 1989: 153–62.

Reimer, P. J., E. Bard, A. Bayliss, J. Beck, P. Blackwell, C. Bronk Ramsey, C. E. Buck, H. Cheng, R. L. Edwards, M. Friedrich, OP. M. Grootes, T. P. Guilderson, H. Haflidason, I. Hajdas, C. Hatté, T. J. Heaton, D. L. Hoffmann, A. G. Hogg, K. A. Hughen, K. F. Kaiser, B. Kromer, S. W. Manning, M. Niu, R. W. Reimer, D. A. Richards, E. M. Scott, J. R. Southon, R. A. Staff, C.S.M. Turney, and J. Van Der Plicht. 2013. IntCal13 and Marine13 Radiocarbon Age Calibration Curves 0–50,000 Years Cal BP. *Radiocarbon* 55(4): 1869–1887.

Roberts, H. M., M. Snæsdóttir, N. Mehler, and O. Vésteinsson. 2013. Skáli frá Víkingaöld í Reykjavík. *Árbók hins íslenska fornleifafélags* 2001-2002: 219–234.

Rodríguez-Rey, M., S. Herrando-Pérez, R. Gillespie, Z. Jocobs, F. Saltre, B. W. Brook, G. J. Prideaux, R. G. Roberts, A. Cooper, J. Alroy, G. H. Miller, M. I. Bird, C. N. Johnson, N. Beeton, C.S.M. Turney, and C.J.A. Bradshaw. 2015. Criteria for Assessing the Quality of Middle Pleistocene to Holocene Vertebrate Fossil Ages. *Quaternary Geochronology* 30: 69–79.

Sayle, K. L., W. D. Hamilton, G. T. Cook, P. L. Ascough, H. Gestsdóttir, and T. McGovern. 2016. Deciphering Diet and Monitoring Movement: Multiple Stable Isotope Analysis of the Viking Age Settlement at Hofstaðir, Lake Mývatn, Iceland. *American Journal of Physical Anthropology* 160(1): 126–136.

Schmid, M.M.E. 2018. *Archaeological Applications of Radiocarbon Chronologies and Statistical Models: Dating the Viking Age Settlement of Iceland (Landnám)*. PhD thesis, University of Iceland (Háskólaprent, Reykjavík December 2018). ISBN 978-9935-9385-7-2.

Schmid, M.M.E., A. J. Dugmore, A. J. Newton, and O. Vésteinsson. 2017a. Tephra Isochrons and Chronologies of Colonisation. *Quaternary Geochronology* 40: 56–66.

Schmid, M.M.E., D. Zori, E. Erlendsson, C. Batt, B. N. Damiata, and J. Byock. 2017b. A Bayesian Approach for Linking Archaeological, Paleoenvironmental and Documentary Datasets Relating to the Settlement of Iceland (*Landnám*). *The Holocene* 28(1): 19–33.

Schmid, M.M.E., A. J. Dugmore, L. Foresta, A. J. Newton, O. Vésteinsson, and R. Wood. 2018. How ^{14}C Dates on Charcoal Increase Precision when Dating Colonization: The Examples of Iceland and Polynesia. *Quaternary Geochronology* 48: 64–71.

Schmid, M.M.E., R. Wood, A. J. Newton, O. Vésteinsson, A. J. Dugmore. 2019. Enhancing Radiocarbon Chronologies of Colonization: Chronometric Hygiene Revisited. *Radiocarbon* 62(2): 629–647.

Schmid, M.M.E., A. J. Newton, A. J. Dugmore. 2020. From Sites to Regional Synthesis. Collective Chronologies of Late Viking Age and Early Christian Activities in Iceland. In *Viking Encounters*, eds. A. Pedersen and S. M. Sindbæk. Proceedings of the 18th Viking Congress, Denmark. Aarhus: Aarhus University Press.

Sigl, M., M. Winstrup, J. R. McConnell, K. C. Welten, G. Plunkett, F. Ludlow, U. Büntgen, M. W. Caffee, N. Chellman, D. Dahl-Jensen, H. Fischer, S. Kipfstuhl, C. Kostick, O. J. Maselli, F. Mekhaldi, R. Mulvaney, R. Muscheler, D. R. Pasteris, J. Pilcher, M. Salzer, S. Schüpbach, J. P. Steffensen, B. Vinther, and T. E Woodruff. 2015. Timing and Climate Forcing of Volcanic Eruptions for the Past 2,500 years. *Nature* 523: 543–562.

Spriggs, M. 1989. The Dating of the Island Southeast Asian Neolithic: An Attempt at Chronometric Hygiene and Linguistic Correlation. *Antiquity* 63(240): 587–613.

Spriggs, M., and A. Anderson. 1993. Late Colonization of East Polynesia. *Antiquity* 67: 200–217

Steinberg, J. M., D. J. Bolender, and B. N. Damiata. 2016. The Viking Age Settlement Pattern of Langholt, North Iceland: Results of the Skagafjörður Archaeological Settlement Survey. *Journal of Field Archaeology* 41(4): 389–412.

Sveinbjörnsdóttir, Á. E., J. Heinemeier, and G. Guðmundsson. 2004.[14]C Dating of the Settlement of Iceland. *Radiocarbon* 46 (1): 387–394.

Theodórsson, P. 1998. Norse Settlement of Iceland—Close to A.D. 700? *Norwegian Archaeological Review* 31: 29–38.

Theodórsson, P., 2009. Upphaf Landnáms á Íslandi 670 AD: Var Ari Fróði Sannfróður? *Skírnir* 183: 261–280.

Vésteinsson, O. 2000. *The Christianization of Iceland: Priests, Power, and Social Change 1000–1300*. Oxford: OUP Oxford.

Vésteinsson, O. 2011. A Note on the Regional Distribution of Pagan Burials in Iceland. *Archaeologia Islandica* 9: 41–49.

Vésteinsson, O., and T. McGovern. 2012. The Peopling of Iceland. *Norwegian Archaeological Review* 45(2): 206–218.

Vésteinsson, O., M. Church, A. Dugmore, T. McGovern, and A. Newton. 2014. Expensive Errors or Rational Choices: The Pioneer Fringe in Late Viking Age Iceland. *European Journal of Post-Classical Archaeologies* 4: 39–68.

Vilhjálmsson, V. Ö. 1991. The Application of Dating Methods in Icelandic Archaeology. *Acta Archaeologica* 61: 97–107.

Waterbolk, H. T. 1971. Working with Radiocarbon Dates. *Proceedings of the Prehistoric Society* 37(2): 15–33.

Zielinski, G. A., M. S. Germani, G. Larsen, M.G.L. Baille, S. Whitlow, M. S. Twickler, and K. Taylor. 1997. Volcanic Aerosol Records and Tephrochronology of the Summit, Greenland, Ice Cores. *Journal of Geophysical Research* 102(C12): 26625–26640.

Þórarinsson, S. 1967. The Eruptions of Hekla in Historical Times. In: *The Eruption of Hekla: 1947-1948*, vol. I. Societas Scientiarum Islandica, Reykjavík, pp. 1-183.

7

Improving Dating Accuracy and Precision for Mid-Late Holocene Island Colonization

TIMOTHY M. RIETH AND DEREK HAMILTON

Archaeologists have become increasingly sophisticated in their application and interpretation of radiocarbon dating for chronology building (Bayliss 2009). During the past two decades, and particularly during the last 5–10 years, Bayesian calibration modeling has been driving these improvements (Bayliss 2015; Buck and Meson 2015). Beyond the United Kingdom "homeland" for the development and application of this statistical approach (Buck et al. 1996; Whittle et al. 2011), the geographical scope for the use of Bayesian calibration modeling has been expanding such that examples can be found from archaeological sites from across the globe (see Capuzzo and Barceló 2015; Cobb et al. 2015; Marsh 2016; Napolitano et al. 2019; Wood et al. 2016; chapter 6 for a few recent examples). Applications to island archaeology, particularly in the Pacific (for example, Athens et al. 2014; Denham et al. 2012; Dye 2011, 2015; Rieth and Athens 2019), have been part of this second wave (though there are notable early examples for the region, see Anderson et al. 2001 and Buck and Christen 2000). This method of chronology building is attractive because it allows the integration of additional data beyond radiometric determinations as "informative prior" information to increase precision and accuracy (Bayliss et al. 2007). It also shifts the emphasis from individually dated events (for example, a burning event that created dated charcoal) to estimates for the beginning, end, and duration of archaeological events of interest that otherwise cannot be directly dated. Furthermore, it provides a method for investigating potential hiatuses between events, and allows for formal comparisons of sites across a region, either large or small. As such, this method is well suited to estimating island colonization.

Even with Bayesian modeling, however, the accuracy and precision of modeled calendar dates depend on several factors: (1) the shape of the calibration curve for the period under study; (2) the number of radiocarbon determinations for a given model; (3) the distribution of radiocarbon determinations in a model or modeled stratigraphic sequence; and (4) the types of dating samples. Issues regarding data and model presentations (Bayliss 2015) and model building (Hamilton and Krus 2018) are also fundamental, though we do not discuss them in detail here.

This chapter focuses on items (1), (2), and (3), namely, for any given portion of the radiocarbon calibration curve, how many independent radiocarbon determinations are needed to generate a reliable chronology for a colonization deposit, and how should these dates be distributed across a stratigraphic sequence. Our methods and results have global applicability, but we have chosen two periods of major migration in the Pacific as case studies: the Lapita colonization of Fiji, which has been dated to circa 3300–2800 cal BP (Denham et al. 2012; Nunn and Petchey 2013; Sheppard et al. 2015), and the Polynesian colonization of Hawai'i between *1010 and 820 cal BP*[1] (95 percent probability) (Athens et al. 2014).

"Lapita" is the designation for an archaeological horizon characterized by distinctive pottery, ornaments, and stone and shell tools (Kirch 1997) that appeared in the Bismarck Archipelago between *3535 and 3234 cal BP* (95 percent probability) (Rieth and Athens 2019) and expanded into the southeastern Solomon Islands, Vanuatu, New Caledonia, Fiji, and West Polynesia within one to a few centuries (Denham et al. 2012). Lapita expanded more rapidly into the southwestern and central Pacific, possibly "within at most a few generations" (Sheppard et al. 2015: 35). Explaining the causes and characteristics of this rapid migration across roughly 5,000 km requires colonization estimates of high precision and accuracy (Cochrane 2018; chapter 2). Such estimates have been hindered in large part by too few radiocarbon ages for key site deposits, failure to date complete stratified sequences, and problematic dating samples (Rieth and Athens 2019; see also Specht and Gosden 1997).

Over two millennia after Lapita migration into Remote Oceania (*sensu* Green 1991), Polynesian settlers colonized the Hawaiian Islands. The circa 2,000 year lag between the easternmost extent of Lapita settlement in the Sāmoan archipelago and renewed eastward expansion into central East Polynesia preceded another rapid dispersal across much of the region between approximately 1050 and 750 cal BP (Allen and McAlister 2013; Dye 2015; Kahn 2012; Wilmshurst et al. 2008, 2011). The history of archaeological estimates for the timing of Hawai'i's settlement, however, have been chaotic (Dye 2015; Rieth and Cochrane 2018).

Rather than a steady progression toward a more precise and accurate estimate, purported colonization dates have swung in older and younger directions by centuries to a millennium during the past 70 years. It is only relatively recently that research has shown consistent improvements in these estimates based on paleoenvironmental data (for example, Athens 1997) and Bayesian model building that couples paleoenvironmental and archaeological data (Athens et al. 2014; Dye 2011).

Though our case studies are specific to Fiji and Hawai'i, our approach and findings are relevant to other regions and time periods. Estimating the timing of island colonization at any location around the globe must address similar methodological challenges. In that respect, the simulation models presented here can be used as guides to tailor region- or island-specific models for other areas.

A Note on "Colonization"

Before proceeding, it is important to define the concept "colonization," so as to avoid confusion. From an archaeological perspective, we define island colonization as the initial creation of an island's archaeological record. Colonization is an event that is measurable through radiometric dating. Behavioral distinctions in the manner and reasons that humans migrate and establish populations in new environments (for example, Cochrane 2018; see also chapter 2) are interpretations based on characteristics of archaeological and environmental records and chronologies. For our purposes, "colonization" is synonymous with "settlement," "discovery," or "occupation," regardless of the duration of human occupancy associated with the creation of the oldest portion of an island's archaeological record (contra Graves and Addison 1996) (see chapters 2, 3, and 4 for extended discussions of this issue).

Notes on Accuracy and Precision

The accuracy of radiocarbon dating, or, the "correctness" of a calibrated date in relation to the true calendar date of the event of interest, can be affected by multiple factors. Dean's (1978: 226–228) delineation of dated (E^d), reference (E^r), and target events (E^t) is relevant—that is, the actual dated event (for example, death of plant used as fuel in a hearth) (E^d), the event that can be associated with the dated event (for example, use of a hearth) (E^r), and the broader archaeological event of interest (for example, settlement of a coastal plain) (E^t).

Considering these types of events in order, one may end up with an inaccurate radiocarbon determination if the dated event does not correspond with the target event. For example, this may occur if charcoal derived from a long-lived plant or plant part is dated (Allen and Huebert 2014; Rieth and Athens 2013), or if the dating sample is residual in the deposit of interest (that is, older material retained in a deposit). Inaccuracy may also be introduced if the reference or target events are incorrectly or poorly defined—for instance, when stratigraphy is inadequately interpreted.

For the purposes of our simulations below, we assume that there is concurrence between the dated and target events through the reference event; that is, (1) that the dating samples do not have significant inbuilt age or age offsets, or that these can be addressed with an appropriate correction value (ΔR); (2) that the archaeological stratigraphy has been correctly documented and interpreted, and; (3) that dating samples are not residual (ideally, discrete combustion features or primary burials would provide samples).

Precision, or the exactness of an estimate, is contingent on the error value of radiocarbon-dating laboratory results, the shape of the calibration curve, and calibration parameters (for example, whether or not an estimate is generated through Bayesian calibration). From a behavioral perspective, any particular event occurs at a limited and discrete point in time, such as the minutes or hours of combustion associated with the use of a hearth. Such precision is not feasible for archaeology, but precision on the order of decades—a single human generation—can be obtained with appropriate sampling and modeling (Bayliss et al. 2007). "Good" or improved precision is a value that should be addressed through problem-specific modeling, that is, by evaluating whether or not more precise values are provided as dating samples and/or model parameters are varied—as we present here.

Methods

Since the most recent estimates for the Lapita settlement of Fiji vary by centuries, we selected the period 2970–2931 cal BP for our hypothetical colonization deposit. This 40-year period bridges the Bayesian model-derived estimates of *3290–2970 cal BP* (95 percent probability) by Denham and colleagues (2012) and Sheppard and colleagues (2015) *3001–2790 cal BP* (95 percent probability). Further, the shape of the Southern Hemisphere calibration curve for these four decades is particularly amenable to precise chronological modeling, as it lacks plateaus and complex wiggles found in other portions of the calibration curve (for example, first millennium cal BC), which produce broader or multimodal calibrated probability estimates. For our Hawai'i example, we selected the period 950–911 cal BP, which falls within Athens and colleague's (2014) 95 percent and 68 percent probability estimates for colonization. This portion of the Northern Hemisphere calibration has an even, steep curve, thus resulting in more precise individual date estimates.

Having selected these periods for our hypothetical colonization deposits, we used an online random number generator (www.random.org) to select 1, 5, 10, 20, and 40 calendar dates from their spans. Through a process often referred to as back-calibration, using the R_Simulate command, radiocarbon ages were simulated from our calendar dates in OxCal v4.3 (Bronk Ramsey 2009a). An uncertainty of 30 years, which we felt is a typical error value returned by radiocarbon-dating laboratories, was applied to the simulated radiocarbon ages. These radiocarbon ages, in turn, were calibrated using single- and multiphase Bayesian models with the Southern Hemisphere curve (Hogg et al. 2013) for the hypothetical Lapita deposit, and Northern Hemisphere curve (Reimer et al. 2013) for the hypothetical Hawai'i deposit.

The single-phase models for the Lapita and Hawai'i cases rely solely on the radiocarbon determinations ("standardized likelihoods") for temporal estimates, and do not incorporate additional stratigraphic information ("informative prior beliefs") beyond that the dating samples came from the same stratum. The models assume a uniform distribution for the dated archaeological events ("uninformative prior belief"). The multiphase models include stratigraphic information in the form of a lower, dated, precultural stratum, and an overlying dated cultural layer (see Appendix for the model code). The precultural stratum for the Lapita models has a "known" date of 3040 cal BP, and the postcolonization deposit dates from 2931–2780 cal BP. For the Hawai'i models, the precolonization stratum dates to 1050 cal BP and the postcolonization deposit dates from 911–760 cal BP. The resulting estimates for the start, end, and duration of deposition were then compared to the original known calendar dates; that is, a start of 2970 cal BP, end of 2931 cal BP, and a duration of 40 years for the Fiji example, and a start of 950 cal BP, end of 911 cal BP, and a duration of 40 years for the Hawai'i example. For sensitivity analysis, each model was run six times with the R_Simulate command producing different simulated radiocarbon ages.

The "Sequence," "Boundary," "Phase," "Span," and "Difference" commands were used in the models. "Sequence" defines an order for events/groups of events. "Boundary" defines a uniformly distributed group. It is used here to calculate the beginning and end of deposition for our hypothetical colonization deposits. "Phase" is an unordered group of events. For the single-phase models, each phase includes 1, 5, 10, 20, or 40 radiocarbon determinations. The multiphase models include a precultural phase with a single radiocarbon determination; the hypothetical colonization phase with 1, 5, 10, 20, or 40 determinations; and a postcolonization phase with 1 or 5 determinations. "Span" and "Difference" are queries that give the duration of events, which in this case is the duration of the colonization deposits. The precultural and colonization phases are modeled in Sequential order (allowing for a possible hiatus), and the colonization and postcolonization phases are in Contiguous order (allowing for continuous deposition between these two periods). While the simulated models were constructed with data that represented continuous deposition, this is not always easily inferred from the archaeological record, and so we evaluated the effect of the Contiguous order structure by running the Lapita model iterations again, with the colonization and postcolonization phases modeled in Sequential order. All but four of the model runs showed good agreement between the radiocarbon determinations and model structures (A_{model} = >60) (Bronk Ramsey 2009b: 1025).

Results for the Hypothetical Lapita Deposit, 2970–2931 cal BP

Lapita Single-Phase Models

Table 7.1 presents the start, end, and duration estimates for the six runs of each Lapita single-phase model. The majority of the start and end estimates are accurate: they capture the "known" dates for the hypothetical deposit. Precision, however, is low (approximately a millennium) for the model consisting of a single radiocarbon date, as would be expected for a single data point. The addition of four more dates (n = 5) improves precision by centuries, and with 40 dates there is nearly an order of magnitude improvement over the single-date model at 95.4 percent probability range (Figure 7.1). With 40 dates, the start and end estimates have ranges of less than a century. There are inaccurate end estimates for the 68.2 percent probability range that underestimate the "known" date by a few years to over a century. The precision of the duration estimates similarly improve by about an order of magnitude, with 95.4 percent estimates of fewer than two centuries for the 40-date models. Although additional dates will likely further improve dating precision, in practical respects, 40+ dates will often exceed the budgets or suitable dating samples for most investigations.

Table 7.1. Results of the single-phase models for the hypothetical Lapita deposit

No. of Dates	Start 68.2%	Start 95.4%	End 68.2%	End 95.4%	Duration-Years 68.2%	Duration-Years 95.4%
1	3938–2935	3938–2917	3017–2148	3028–2148	0–1088	0–1705
	3938–2923	3938–2904	3017–2148	3026–2148	0–1062	0–1780
	3718–2881	3718–2875	2942–2243	2945–2243	0–905	0–1470
	3928–2905	3928–2901	2999–2153	3010–2153	0–1048	0–1765
	3938–2933	3938–2919	3021–2148	3033–2148	0–1027	0–1785
	3933–2903	3922–2895	2995–2143	3005–2143	0–1053	0–1673
5	2977–2901	3054–2874	**2926–2851**	2953–2784	0–92	0–231
	3039–2949	3132–2898	2966–2876	2998–2796	0–117	0–288
	3035–2925	3149–2885	2940–2845	2966–2731	0–154	0–365
	3058–2947	3164–2896	2959–2865	2994–2762	0–147	0–339
	3106–2941	3260–2885	**2913–2781**	2954–2636	0–301	0–559
	3052–2954	3150–2897	2967–2878	3000–2786	0–126	0–305
10	3016–2949	3081–2927 (94.2%)	2951–2880	2965–2835	0–107	0–210
	3021–2926	3078–2890	**2918–2823**	2945–2765	0–163	0–284
	3002–2947	3059–2898	2958–2888	2970–2850	0–75	0–169
	3054–2940	3118–2890	2895–2795	2935–2745	24–252	0–336
	3000–2906	3054–2886	**2923–2853**	2948–2806	0–108	0–220
	2996–2939	3041–2894	2951–2883	2962–2851	0–74	0–161
20	2995–2949	3036–2928	2952–2891	2958–2861	0–79	0–151
	3012–2961	3070–2955	2965–2916	2982–2866	0–82	0–182
	2987–2935	3026–2894	2939–2878	2951–2848	0–83	0–160
	2994–2950	3035–2928	2953–2890	2958–2861	0–80	0–152
	3020–2960	3070–2941	2937–2870	2954–2835	29–147	0–208
	3004–2957	3060–2950	2960–2910	2966–2862	0–83	0–175
40	2981–2953	3011–2938	2957–2927	2961–2881	0–48	0–114
	2993–2950	3015–2935	2948–2886	2953–2862	0–94	0–142
	3003–2959	3043–2952	2956–2908	2959–2866	0–91	0–165
	3013–2965	3045–2953	2939–2876	2953–2859	33–136	0–171
	3010–2963	3046–2953	2952–2900	2958–2866	16–112	0–170
	2999–2958	3030–2947	2950–2900	2955–2864	6–97	0–151

Source: Authors.
Note: Each model was run six times and these results are presented. Start and end estimates are cal BP. Estimates that fail to capture the true start (2970 cal BP), end (2931 cal BP), or duration (40 years) are in **bold**.

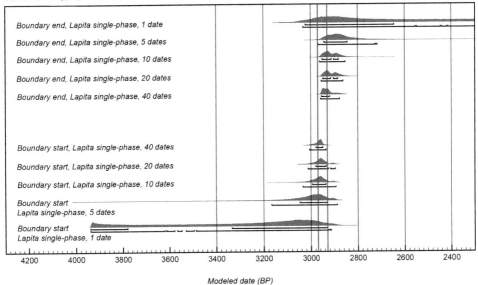

Boundary end, Lapita single-phase, 1 date

Boundary end, Lapita single-phase, 5 dates

Boundary end, Lapita single-phase, 10 dates

Boundary end, Lapita single-phase, 20 dates

Boundary end, Lapita single-phase, 40 dates

Boundary start, Lapita single-phase, 40 dates

Boundary start, Lapita single-phase, 20 dates

Boundary start, Lapita single-phase, 10 dates

Boundary start
Lapita single-phase, 5 dates

Boundary start
Lapita single-phase, 1 date

4200   4000   3800   3600   3400   3200   3000   2800   2600   2400

Modeled date (BP)

Figure 7.1. Modeled probability distributions for the start and end estimates of the single-phase Lapita models. Iterations 1–5 have 1, 5, 10, 20, and 40 radiocarbon dates, respectively. Gray lines mark the "known" start and end dates for the Lapita deposit.

Lapita Multiphase Models

The Lapita multiphase models confirm that adding stratigraphy improves precision (Tables 7.2–7.4, Figures 7.2 and 7.3). However, conversely, the inclusion of additional phases produces a greater chance of inaccurate results, particularly with the 68.2 percent probability estimates (that is, they do not capture either of the "known" start or end dates). The tendency toward inaccuracy in the end estimates seems to relate to the proportion of dates in the colonization and postcolonization phases when they are structured in a Contiguous order. Those models with 1:1 or 1:5 ratios of dates are susceptible to having end estimates that are too young as the weighting of probabilities within the model pulls the boundary to the right (that is, younger). Even at 95.4 percent probability, there is a susceptibility that the majority of the range falls beyond the "known" end date with only the left (older) tail capturing the date. Structuring the models in Sequential order substantially improves the accuracy of the end estimates and proves to be a better fit between the data and model structure (Table 7.5; Figure 7.4, compare with Figure 7.3); note that the precision does not significantly vary between the Contiguous and Sequential models (see Table 7.4), but the

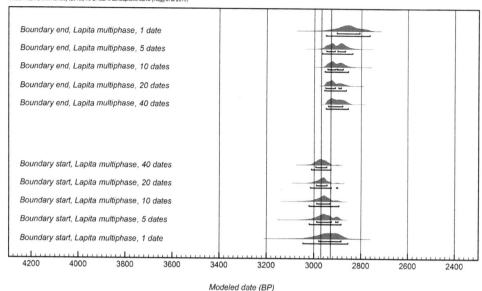

OxCal v4.2.3 Bronk Ramsey (2013); r:5 SHCal13 atmospheric curve (Hogg et al 2013)

Boundary end, Lapita multiphase, 1 date
Boundary end, Lapita multiphase, 5 dates
Boundary end, Lapita multiphase, 10 dates
Boundary end, Lapita multiphase, 20 dates
Boundary end, Lapita multiphase, 40 dates

Boundary start, Lapita multiphase, 40 dates
Boundary start, Lapita multiphase, 20 dates
Boundary start, Lapita multiphase, 10 dates
Boundary start, Lapita multiphase, 5 dates
Boundary start, Lapita multiphase, 1 date

4200   4000   3800   3600   3400   3200   3000   2800   2600   2400

Modeled date (BP)

Figure 7.2. Modeled probability distributions for the start and end estimates of the multiphase Lapita models with individual dates for the pre- and postcolonization phases (Sequential and Contiguous ordering). Iteration designations follow Figure 7.1. Gray lines mark the "known" start and end dates for the Lapita deposit.

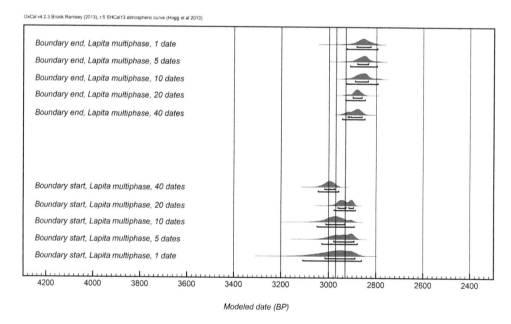

OxCal v4.2.3 Bronk Ramsey (2013); r:5 SHCal13 atmospheric curve (Hogg et al 2013)

Boundary end, Lapita multiphase, 1 date
Boundary end, Lapita multiphase, 5 dates
Boundary end, Lapita multiphase, 10 dates
Boundary end, Lapita multiphase, 20 dates
Boundary end, Lapita multiphase, 40 dates

Boundary start, Lapita multiphase, 40 dates
Boundary start, Lapita multiphase, 20 dates
Boundary start, Lapita multiphase, 10 dates
Boundary start, Lapita multiphase, 5 dates
Boundary start, Lapita multiphase, 1 date

4200   4000   3800   3600   3400   3200   3000   2800   2600   2400

Modeled date (BP)

Figure 7.3. Modeled probability distributions for the start and end estimates of the multiphase Lapita models with single precolonization date and five postcolonization dates (Sequential and Contiguous ordering). Iteration designations follow Figure 7.1. Gray lines mark the "known" start and end dates for the Lapita deposit.

Table 7.2. Results of the multiphase models (Sequential and Contiguous ordering) with one pre- and one postcolonization date for the hypothetical Lapita deposit

No. of Dates	Start 68.2%	Start 95.4%	End 68.2%	End 95.4%	Duration-Years 68.2%	Duration-Years 95.4%
1	**2958–2876**	3019–2854	**2905–2823**	2951–2777	-3-78	-3-161
	2991–2875	3085–2834	**2880–2749**	2945–2584	-3-96	-3-208
	2980–2884	3053–2853	**2916–2830**	2956–2791	-3-90	-3-181
	3009–2905	3075–2875	2943–2844	2987–2797	-3-98	-3-195
	2965–2881	3023–2858	**2923–2836**	2961–2792	-3-72	-3-154
	3048–2931	3101–2884	2955–2836	3008–2786	1–129	-3-229
5	2970–2911	3011–2881	**2930–2876**	2951–2855	-3-53	-3-122
	3008–2926	3050–2888	2931–2851	2959–2811	1–110	-2-196
	2973–2904	3002–2884	2940–2871	2957–2849	-2-53	-2-120
	2986–2904	3025–2885	2934–2863	2956–2834	-2-78	-2-160
	2982–2923	3012–2888	2947–2879	2961–2854	-2-54	-2-123
	3020–2948	3082–2924	2955–2894	2984–2846	-2-95	-2-186
10	3031–2961	3086–2941	2950–2834	2967–2834	15–145	-3-215
	3019–2956	3068–2935	2956–2881	2970–2841	2–109	-2-188
	2957–2894	2983–2883	2935–2870	2950–2855	-2-40	-2-105
	3005–2933	3035–2892	**2926–2849**	2950–2810	2–117	-2-198
	2984–2937	3013–2895	2958–2913	2964–2865	-2-49	-2-115
	2973–2902	3010–2885	**2906–2850**	2942–2826	2–89	-2-160
20	2994–2945	3031–2927 (94.1%)	2941–2884	2952–2857	1–90	-3-150
	2981–2936	3009–2865	2940–2875	2950–2859	-2-72	-2-129
	2965–2927	2985–2890	2949–2888	2954–2876	**-2-27**	-2-85
	2930–2887	**2950–2880**	**2908–2873**	2938–2860	**-2-22**	-2-59
	3000–2944	3026–2895	**2928–2856**	2945–2840	2–130	-2-162
	2992–2956	3024–2950	2962–2930	2972–2889	-2-51	-2-113
40	2984–2951	3009–2939	2955–2918	2959–2881	-3-56	-3-115
	2985–2959	3007–2955	2961–2938	2967–2915	-2-43	-2-83
	2987–2953	3016–2945	2954–2912	2958–2880	-2-68	-2-123
	3010–2965	3030–2950	2935–2875	2953–2857	37–133	-2-158
	3000–2960	3026–2945	2935–2880	2951–2863	30–120	-2-146
	2986–2946	3005–2930	2949–2886	2953–2867	-2-73	-2-125

Source: Authors.
Note: Each model was run six times, and these results are presented. Start and end estimates are cal BP. Estimates that fail to capture the true start (2970 cal BP), end (2931 cal BP), or duration (40 years) are in **bold**.

Table 7.3. Results of the multiphase models (Sequential and Contiguous ordering) with one pre- and five postcolonization dates for the hypothetical Lapita deposit

No. of Dates	Start 68.2%	Start 95.4%	End 68.2%	End 95.4%	Duration-Years 68.2%	Duration-Years 95.4%
1	3060–2924	3124–2877	**2885–2820**	2936–2793	**50–205**	1–272
	2967–2881	3031–2855	**2901–2835**	2940–2802	1–86	-3–160
	2986–2886	3064–2860	**2905–2845**	2944–2808	2–99	-3–187
	2977–2885	3167–2913	**2921–2857**	2949–2842 (94.1%)	-3–76	-3–169
	3031–2902	3107–2875	**2901–2830**	2957–2801	13–152	-3–240
	2933–2850	2995–2816	**2874–2819**	**2902–2795**	-3–63	-3–140
5	2971–2901	3018–2878	**2907–2859**	2943–2846	2–77	-3–142
	3033–2961	3089–2932	2963–2884	2990–2845	3–112	-2–191
	3092–3002	3139–2970	**2917–2849**	2960–2815	106–234	31–289
	2935–2875	2976–2861	**2885–2849**	**2920–2822**	0–61	-2–118
	3003–2902	3038–2887	**2896–2839**	2950–2815	18–131	-2–185
	2950–2884	2992–2868	**2892–2854**	2931–2837	-2–65	-2–125
10	3042–2977	3095–2948	**2881–2831**	**2916–2794**	112–208	**49–265**
	3021–2941	3054–2896	**2886–2835**	**2928–2807**	63–180	3–215
	2969–2901	3002–2886	**2896–2853**	2931–2836	7–91	-3–140
	3001–2931	3028–2892	**2901–2846**	2944–2831	5–119	-3–169
	3025–2960	3077–2932	2931–2863	2957–2840	38–155	-3–200
	3024–2948	3062–2898	**2895–2839**	2935–2815	60–178	2–214
20	3009–2958	3040–2931 (94.1%)	**2903–2847**	2944–2838	**59–156**	1–176
	3019–2965	3060–2931 (95.0%)	**2888–2846**	**2926–2830**	**83–169**	11–203
	2979–2932	3001–2893	2941–2878	2952–2867	-3 to 57	-3–111
	3034–2973	3072–2964	2969–2911	2982–2868	4–111	-3–182
	2972–2899	2993–2890	**2926–2866**	2939–2857	-3 to 67	-3–118
	2945–2891	**2965–2886**	**2901–2870**	2934–2861	-3 to 36	-3–82
40	2983–2955	3007–2950	2956–2921	2961–2881	1–60	-1–113
	3001–2963	3025–2943	**2928–2871**	2947–2856	**45–130**	2–150
	3015–2970	3044–2957	2944–2881	2955–2861	36–131	5–170
	2980–2951	3001–2934	2953–2919	2958–2876	-2–49	-2–109
	3009–2967	3033–2956	2950–2885	2956–2870	26–115	2–153
	2993–2955	3014–2933	2935–2866	2949–2852	5–122	-2–144

Source: Authors.
Note: Each model was run six times, and these results are presented. Start and end estimates are cal BP. Estimates that fail to capture the true start (2970 cal BP), end (2931 cal BP), or duration (40 years) are in **bold**.

Table 7.4. Calculation of the mean number of years in the 95.4% probability range for the start and end estimates for the Lapita single- and multiphase models (Sequential and Contiguous ordering)

No. of Dates	Single-Phase		Multiphase (Seq. & Cont.) (1 pre-, n col., 1 post-)		Multiphase (Seq. & Cont.) (1 pre-, n col., 5 post-)		Multiphase (Seq. & Seq.) (1 pre-, n col., 5 post-)	
	Start	End	Start	End	Start	End	Start	End
1	995.2	844	199.7	213.5	215.3	136	171.5	155.5
5	262	228.3	138.7	119.8	142.7	123.2	145	120.2
10	174.3	145.5	127.3	118.7	144.3	111.2	129.2	104.8
20	116.8	106.2	109.6	88.3	111.4	92	110	93.8
40	85.3	90.2	71.5	79.7	75.2	88.3	72.5	75.7

Source: Authors.
Note the improved precision with the increasing number of colonization dates and the introduction of stratigraphy.

probability ranges shift to more accurately capture the "known" end date. At 95.4 percent probability, the most precise and accurate start, end, and duration estimates are obtained with a three-phase model constructed with a single precolonization date, 40 colonization dates, and 1 postcolonization date.

Results for the Hypothetical Hawai'i Deposit, 950–911 cal BP

Hawai'i Single-Phase Models

The Hawai'i single-phase models reveal the same trend observed with the Lapita models: increasing the number of dates significantly improves accuracy and precision (Table 7.6, Figure 7.5). Improvements are most substantial with an increase from one to five dates, with the latter model providing 95.4 percent start and end estimates, with approximately 85–95 year ranges and duration estimates of slightly over a century. Subsequent doubling of the dates up to 40 continues refining the precision of the estimates, though the gains reflect diminishing returns.

Hawai'i Multiphase Models

The inclusion of additional phases to the Hawai'i models further increases precision (Tables 7.7–7.9, Figures 7.6 and 7.7). The simplest multiphase model with

Table 7.5. Results of the multiphase models (Sequential and Sequential ordering) with one pre- and five postcolonization dates for the hypothetical Lapita deposit

No. of Dates	Start 68.2%	Start 95.4%	End 68.2%	End 95.4%	Duration-Years 68.2%	Duration-Years 95.4%
1	**2965–2882**	3016–2860	**2921–2853**	2969–2826	-2-51	-2-116
	2984–2892	3039–2868	2936–2859	2988–2830	-2-57	-2-128
	2967–2891	3019–2860	**2926–2867**	2957–2840	-2-47	-2-113
	3000–2905	3059–2872	2946–2860	2996–2826	-2-68	-2-146
	3012–2902	3069–2876	2953–2856	3008–2821	-2-75	-2-157
	2969–2881	3025–2862	**2926–2848**	2981–2823	-2-53	-2-122
5	3004–2930	3050–2891	2940–2873	2966–2842	1-87	-2-163
	2973–2901	3023–2877	**2912–2854**	2943–2831	1-82	-2-157
	3010–2925	3055–2888	**2926–2857**	2951–2827	2–109	-2-189
	3048–2972	3099–2954	2990–2917	3023–2861	0–96	-2-182
	2994–2926	3021–2888	2943–2877	2965–2853	-2-60	-2-126
	2981–2926	3010–2890	2948–2893	2960–2873	-2-43	-2-98
10	3013–2959	3066–2941	2957–2896	2973–2856	3–100	-2-169
	3004–2943	3049–2900	2940–2890	2955–2865	2-89	-2-152
	3005–2960	3050–2940	2965–2906	2981–2865	-2-79	-2-150
	3015–2947	3041–2896	2938–2873	2956–2841	1–104	-2-171
	2982–2935	3011–2894	2952–2890	2960–2873	-2-50	-2-105
	2991–2903	3018–2889	**2927–2870**	2948–2844	-2-80	-2-151
20	2996–2946	3027–2898	2938–2882	2951–2858	2-91	-2-144
	2996–2957	3030–2946	2958–2917	2965–2874	1-71	-2-129
	2983–2941	3012–2897	2948–2887	2955–2868	-2-63	-2-118
	3006–2960	3045–2940	2940–2885	2954–2858	26–121	-2-162
	2995–2943	3024–2895	2935–2876	2950–2850	2-94	-2-148
	3010–2961	3045–2947	2945–2890	2956–2860	24–120	-2-162
40	**2965–2935**	2981–2894	2946–2916	2951–2881	-2-33	-2-82
	3011–2970	3037–2959	2956–2917	2965–2880	15–94	-2-142
	3001–2963	3026–2946	**2929–2875**	2949–2858	41–126	1–151
	3009–2968	3033–2954	2937–2889	2951–2868	36–120	4–154
	2993–2960	3013–2953	2954–2920	2960–2892	6-70	-2-111
	2981–2955	3002–2951	**2958–2932**	2964–2907	-2-42	-2-86

Source: Authors.
Note: Models with 1, 5, and 10 Lapita-phase radiocarbon dates were run with Sequential ordering between the Lapita and postcolonization phases since they showed the greatest prevalence of inaccurate estimates with the Contiguous ordering (see Table 7.3). Start and end estimates are cal BP. Estimates that fail to capture the true start (2970 cal BP), end (2931 cal BP), or duration (40 years) are in **bold**.

Table 7.6. Results of the single-phase models for the hypothetical Hawai'i deposit

No. of Dates	Start 68.2%	Start 95.4%	End 68.2%	End 95.4%	Duration-Years 68.2%	Duration-Years 95.4%
1	1448–924	1448–913	949–363	952–363	0–674	0–1080
	1608–933	1608–932	966–358	969–358	0–720	0–1200
	1448–922	1448–911	950–363	953–363	0–668	0–1080
	1698–962	1698–958	1039–328	1042–328	0–819	0–1350
	1643–923	1643–921	955–273	958–273	0–793	0–1269
	1638–920	1638–915	952–268	954–268	0–812	0–1365
5	955–926	987–920	931–910	950–869	**0–36**	0–104
	980–944	1029–931	**952–920**	964–882	0–48	0–132
	964–929	1008–922	931–900	950–832	0–58	0–157
	974–937	1017–928	944–909	960–862	0–52	0–144
	973–940	1012–931	**949–918**	960–886	0–41	0–109
	969–933	1015–925	934–898	955–830	0–59	0–164
10	973–940	1000–930	920–881	928–820	26–89	7–168
	967–938	990–930	931–910	950–891	8-54	0–84
	956–930	982–923	921–894	930–830	13–63	0–136
	970–935	993–930	926–905	935–878	14–64	0–101
	996–951	1031–935	924–894	933–841	33–100	8–169
	963–933	989–927	927–907	935–882	9-57	0–95
20	971–948	983–938	919–900	925–885	34–74	18–90
	965–941	975–934	917–899	925–882	29–65	13–87
	938–927	952–922	**929–916**	933–908	**0–17**	0–40
	961–937	970–929	925–906	931–896	16–52	0–66
	974–946	987–937	920–899	925–885	32–72	16–95
	970–945	982–935	925–907	930–897	24–62	9-80
40	956–938	966–932	**925–913**	930–906	16–42	6-55
	976–955	985–940	916–901	922–893	43–73	23–88
	947–933	958–929	925–911	930–905	**10-34**	0–48
	955–939	965–934	915–901	920–893	27–52	18–68
	960–940	976–936	917–905	923–897	24–56	18–73
	961–940	974–936	920–905	924–899	24–55	16–69

Source: Authors.
Note: Each model was run six times, and these results are presented. Start and end estimates are cal BP. Estimates that fail to capture the true start (950 cal BP), end (911 cal BP), or duration (40 years) dates are in **bold**.

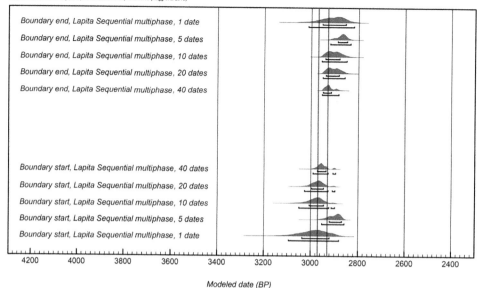

Figure 7.4. Modeled probability distributions for the start and end estimates of the multiphase Lapita models with single precolonization dates and 5 postcolonization dates (sequential ordering for all phases). Iteration designations follow Figure 7.1. Gray lines mark the "known" start and end dates for the Lapita deposit.

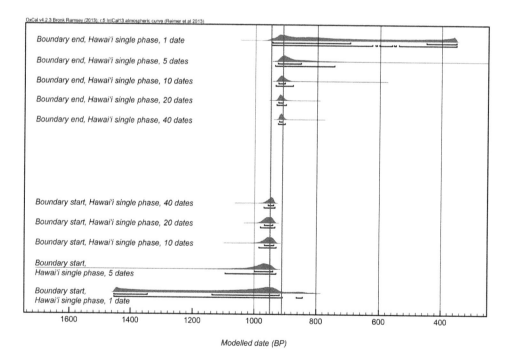

Figure 7.5. Modeled probability distributions for the start and end estimates of the single-phase Hawai'i models. Iterations 1–5 have 1, 5, 10, 20, and 40 dates, respectively. Gray lines mark the "known" start and end dates for the colonization deposit.

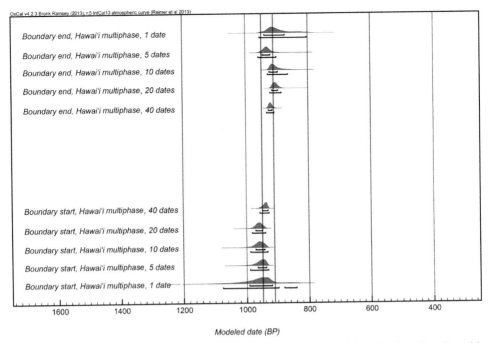

Figure 7.6. Modeled probability distributions for the start and end estimates of the multiphase Hawai'i models with individual dates for the pre- and postcolonization phases. Iteration designations follow Figure 7.5. Gray lines mark the "known" start and end dates for the colonization deposit.

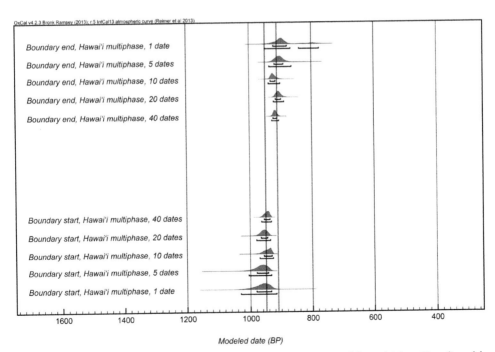

Figure 7.7. Modeled probability distributions for the start and end estimates of the multiphase Hawai'i models with single precolonization dates and 5 postcolonization dates. Iteration designations follow Figure 7.5. Gray lines mark the "known" start and end dates for the colonization deposit.

Table 7.7. Results of the multiphase models with one pre- and one postcolonization date for the hypothetical Hawai'i deposit

No. of Dates	Start 68.2%	Start 95.4%	End 68.2%	End 95.4%	Duration-Years 68.2%	Duration-Years 95.4%
1	968–915	1005–841	935–876	949–809	-2-54	-2-123
	982–937	1023–926	949–890	974–820	2-73	-2-149
	976–926	1040–856	947–897	958–831	-2-57	-2-132
	979–850	1005–814	926–789	935–761	-2-77	-2-169
	984–934	1041–920	946–887	968–809	2-80	-2-169
	985–940	1023–930	958–908	981–848	-2-58	-2-128
5	967–935	997–927	931–905	950–876	5-58	-2-105
	978–945	1004–934	**952–921**	963–896	0–46	-2-93
	991–946	1032–934	946–908	960–880	4-70	-2-133
	965–930	1004–922	926–897	934–841	6-68	-2-137
	966–936	987–929	**938–912**	955–893	2-44	-2-80
	958–929	985–922	930–905	943–872	1-48	-2-95
10	960–934	979–927	923–900	931–883	16–60	-2-86
	972–942	991–933	915–890	925–826	32–82	13–152
	990–946	1012–937	916–888	925–844	38–101	18–149
	955–931	971–925	920–895	928–878	17–58	0–85
	980–948	1000–937	911–875	919–816	**43–102**	27–171
	968–940	986–931	920–897	929–878	25–70	6–100
20	974–949	985–939	920–904	925–895	34–69	18–85
	973–952	984–941	917–900	924–887	40–71	24–89
	965–943	978–935	915–897	922–886	32–67	18–85
	953–933	965–928	925–909	930–900	11-45	1-62
	965–942	977–935	915–895	923–874	30–67	18–96
	942–928	959–925	**929–915**	933–908	-2-25	-2-45
40	964–943	974–937	925–911	929–906	21–51	12-65
	966–948	974–940	917–905	922–896	34–60	22–73
	962–945	969–939	913–900	918–893	36–61	25–71
	961–943	970–937	915–900	920–894	31–60	22–72
	948–933	960–928	**926–916**	930–909	**9-32**	1-49
	981–958	987–942	919–905	924–898	43–75	22–84

Source: Authors.
Note: Each model was run six times, and these results are presented. Start and end estimates are cal BP. Estimates that fail to capture the true start (950 cal BP), end (911 cal BP), or duration (40 years) dates are in **bold**.

Table 7.8. Results of the multiphase models with one pre- and five postcolonization dates for the hypothetical Hawai'i deposit

No. of Dates	Start 68.2%	Start 95.4%	End 68.2%	End 95.4%	Duration-Years 68.2%	Duration-Years 95.4%
1	979–935	1018–926	944–902	959–843	3-67	-2-130
	1014–941	1081–931	938–878	962–826	23–126	0–196
	978–922	1024–839	940–835	947–811	1-76	-2-143
	984–937	1026–926	939–890	961–844	10-82	-2-140
	1012–956	1039–936	941–880	979–817	22–113	-2-168
	983–936	1019–930	936–888	965–825	10-82	-2-137
5	969–937	997–930	914–884	927–825	31–83	13–142
	980–942	1012–930	926–890	936–846	24–90	2–140
	1002–951	1047–937	915–869	922–830	**50–130**	25–190
	967–935	993–926	918–887	929–849	25–80	5–126
	973–940	1001–932	936–905	951–885	5-60	-2-101
	969–935	993–928	927–899	945–867	15–69	-2-108
10	965–939	982–931	927–909	935–895	16–56	1-76
	985–948	1015–936	911–871	916–822	**44–113**	29–175
	974–943	995–934	912–874	917–819	35–99	25–163
	960–935	980–928	922–901	929–886	18–60	4-85
	966–940	987–931	920–900	929–877	25–66	9–100
	967–941	984–931	915–895	925–879	31–72	11–96
20	962–940	974–934	915–900	922–891	30–60	16–79
	970–946	980–937	920–900	926–892	33–67	17–82
	945–929	959–926	**928–915**	932–908	**3-29**	-2-47
	953–934	965–929	924–910	930–902	14–43	3-58
	967–946	978–936	921–906	927–896	28–60	14–75
	951–930	963–927	925–910	931–901	7-41	-2-55
40	969–947	976–940	916–905	922–898	34–63	22–75
	954–939	964–935	920–907	925–901	21–46	14–58
	965–945	973–938	921–908	925–900	27–56	16–69
	952–935	965–928	**925–915**	930–908	10-40	3-51
	962–942	971–936	920–907	925–900	25–53	16–66
	956–937	965–932	**925–912**	929–906	15–41	7-55

Source: Authors.
Note: Each model was run six times, and these results are presented. Start and end estimates are cal BP. Estimates that fail to capture the true start (950 cal BP), end (911 cal BP), or duration (40 years) dates are in **bold**.

Table 7.9. Calculation of the mean number of years in the 95.4% probability range for the start and end estimates for the Hawai'i single- and multiphase models

No. of Dates	Single-Phase		Multiphase (1 pre-, n col., 1 post-)		Multiphase (1 pre-, n col., 5 post-)	
	Start	End	Start	End	Start	End
1	655.5	645.8	141.7	147.8	119.8	134.5
5	85.2	96.3	73.5	74.5	73.3	84.7
10	68.3	78.2	58.2	72	58.7	62.2
20	42.3	36	40.8	36.2	38.3	29.7
40	36.2	26	35.2	24.5	34.2	23.8

Source: Authors.
Note the improved precision with the increasing number of colonization dates and the introduction of stratigraphy.

individual precolonization, colonization, and postcolonization dates removes approximately 500 years from the start and end estimates when compared to the single-phase, single-colonization date model. When compared with the single-phase model results, the benefits of the multiphase models plateau when there are 20 colonization phase dates. Unlike the Lapita models, the addition of stratigraphically linked phases does not significantly affect the accuracy of the results; for the single- and multiphase models alike, about 10 percent of the 68.2 percent estimates are inaccurate.

How Do These Results Compare to Early Deposits in Fiji and Hawai'i?

Our results indicate an area for improvements in dating Fiji's earliest archaeological deposits. The majority of the oldest known Lapita deposits in Fiji have been dated with one to a few radiocarbon determinations (Clark and Anderson 2009). Exceptions are Naigani, Naigani Island (n = 11 dates) (Irwin et al. 2011; Sheppard et al. 2015) and Bourewa,[2] Viti Levu (n = 67 dates) (Nunn and Petchey 2013). Sheppard et al. (2015) constructed a single-phase Bayesian calibration model for Naigani using 10 of Irwin et al.'s (2011) radiocarbon ages. Considering our single- and multiphase model results, their 95 percent probability estimates are likely accurate (assuming that the ΔR used for the marine shells is correct), but precision would be improved with additional dates and/or the construction of a multiphase model.

Recent redating efforts at purported early sites in Hawai'i have resulted in notably younger age estimates (Kahn et al. 2014; Kirch and McCoy 2007; Mulrooney et al. 2014). Of the nine sites considered as the earliest in the islands by Kirch (1985), Bellows Dune, O'ahu (Site O18), is the only one that has retained its position after renewed evaluation (Dye and Pantaleo 2010). More recently identified, probable early archaeological deposits from O'ahu, Maui, and Hawai'i Island have produced one to two reliable radiocarbon dates from short-lived plant taxa from secure contexts (Carson and Athens 2007; Field and Graves 2008; Morrison and Rieth 2018; see also Athens et al. 2014 and Rieth et al. 2011). Individually, dating of most of the current roster of early sites is comparable to our simplest single-phase model with one radiocarbon date. As such, additional dating samples (minimum n = 5), will justify the use of Bayesian model-based calibration and should substantially improve estimates for the beginning of deposition at individual sites. The steep shape of the calibration curve during this period is a key factor in greatly improving precision with the addition of only a few more dates.

Moving Forward: Building Better Colonization Chronologies in the Future

It goes without saying that any model that relies on poor data or a poor model structure will produce poor results. Several key observations from our models can be used as general best-practice guides for estimating the chronology of colonization events for islands across the globe, with the caveat that some of these points may be specific to the particular portions of the calibration curves examined in our Pacific case studies. (1) A single radiocarbon date for a colonization deposit of interest, with no additional stratigraphic information, should not be modeled. With a single data point, the statistical estimates for the start and end of deposition are overly imprecise (for example, a millennium for our Lapita example). In these instances, the unmodeled calibrated date is a more precise and accurate estimate, which can be used for project-specific model building and iterative planning for obtaining additional determinations. (2) Increasing the number of secure dates for the deposit/phase of interest increases accuracy and precision. (3) The addition of well-understood stratigraphy (that is, multiple model phases) can further increase accuracy and precision. This may include pre- or postcolonization geological strata such as well-dated tephra deposits (for example, Kaharoa tephra in New Zealand or various tephra of Iceland [see chapter 6]). However, the ratio of dates in each phase can affect the accuracy for certain portions of the calibration curve, as seen with 1:1 or 1:5 ratios of colonization: postcolonization dates skewing end estimates too young to be in the hypothetical Lapita models. (4) For any investigation, there may be a number of potentially suitable model structures. Simulations should be run with different models (for example, Sequential and Contiguous ordering) and the results compared to determine a best fit; the selection of a preferred model should be justified. (5) Estimates at 68.2 percent probability can be inaccurate, particularly with multiphase models. This is not surprising, since this probability range conversely means that there is a 31.8 percent probability of being incorrect. It is important to note the 95.4 percent probability range is the one that we should expect (approximately 19 out of 20 times) to encompass the correct date for our simulations. Comparisons here against the 68.2 percent range are for the benefit of evaluating the relative proximity to the mean and median of these probability distributions to the correct date, since researchers often rely on these values in place of the 95.4 percent range, perhaps because they appear to be much more precise or provide a single value in place of a range. While the 68.2 percent range is often quoted, it should only be done in addition to the full 95.4 percent probability range; and when quoted, this should only be done when this shorter range is indicative of the area under the curve where the individual probability for any given year is clearly the highest (for example, the peak of a probability that is approaching a normal distribution).

When faced with datasets that have only one or a few dates from an individual site, it is still possible to consider colonization of an island from a wider landscape perspective by constructing models that make use of all of the suitable radiocarbon dates available from sites across an island. It is also possible to combine the dating evidence for individual sites with dating estimates derived from paleoenvironmental data (for example, Athens et al. 2014), whereby dates associated with specific, unambiguous anthropogenic events are used to inform the model for island colonization.

We can never be certain that any one of the early dated sites is the initial colonizing settlement, and so these island-wide models should provide a more robust date estimate for the colonization event, as they expressly assume that we have not dated the very first event in the group (for examples, see chapters 3 and 6). It is here that the power of the Bayesian statistical approach will begin to have its most profound effect on how we understand the colonization process. As we build up increasingly robust datasets for individual sites, it becomes possible to use the individually dated settlements to investigate the tempo of colonization across the island. Similarly, the tempo of postcolonization events such as the development and change of religious architecture or agricultural systems can be examined (for example, Dye 2016). By being able to identify where the process is rapid and where it stalls, we can make more meaningful and in-depth explorations and develop more nuanced questions about such things as migration and social change, settlement and subsistence patterns, and human-environment interactions in new lands.

Conclusions

We are in the midst of a sea change in the way archaeologists approach chronology building. Visual inspection of individually calibrated radiocarbon dates and ad hoc estimations of the "true" date for a deposit or event are being surpassed by more sophisticated, and statistically defensible, Bayesian models. The ready availability of free calibration software with Bayesian modeling functions is a key factor in this transition. However, as a discipline, we run the risk of a "plug-and-play" approach (Hamilton and Krus 2018) whereby researchers insert their data into models without thoughtful consideration of the questions they are attempting to ask. This includes questioning whether or not their data are appropriate for the problem at hand, how they should go about model building, and how they should interpret their results.

We have presented a portion of the iterative approach for model building—the simulation—which can be used to assist in structuring the generation of hypotheses and data acquisition requirements for specific archaeological investigations (see Blaauw et al. 2018 for a similar exercise for simulated sediment cores, which produced comparable results). The process is integral to understanding how the number of dates made available, the area of the calibration curve we are working with, and any information about how the samples relate to one another combine to produce our results for island colonization estimates. It is, unfortunately, a part of the chronological modeling process that often seems to be neglected, or at least not reported on. The strength of the simulation stage has been shown here to not only help identify the model form and sample numbers that are ideal for the suggested archaeological chronologies, but also indicate that resolving the Lapita chronology in Fiji to a similar precision as the Polynesian colonization of Hawai'i will require more radiocarbon-dated samples. Our results indicate how island colonization estimates can be improved, though the resulting precision is dependent on not just the number of samples but the shape of the calibration curve for the particular period under investigation. We anticipate that similar modeling will provide direction for future colonization research in the Caribbean, Mediterranean, and other island regions.

Appendix: Examples of Oxcal Model Codes

The following is the code for the Hawai'i single-phase model consisting of 10 radiocarbon dates. The other single-phase models have the same structure but with varying numbers of dates. The Lapita single-phase models also have the same structure but include the code for using the Southern Hemisphere calibration curve.

```
Plot()
{
Sequence()
{
Boundary("start");
Phase()
{
Curve("IntCal13", "IntCal13.14c");
R_Simulate("date 1022, 30", 1022, 30);
R_Simulate("date 1034, 30", 1034, 30);
R_Simulate("date 1026, 30", 1026, 30);
R_Simulate("date 1005, 30", 1005, 30);
R_Simulate("date 1007, 30", 1007, 30);
R_Simulate("date 1037, 30", 1037, 30);
R_Simulate("date 1004, 30", 1004, 30);
R_Simulate("date 1015, 30", 1015, 30);
R_Simulate("date 1025, 30", 1025, 30);
R_Simulate("date 1004, 30", 1004, 30);
};
Boundary("end");
Span("duration");
};
};
```

Code for the Hawai'i multiphase model consisting of one precolonization date, 10 colonization dates, and one postcolonization date is presented below.

The other multiphase models have the same structure but with varying numbers of dates. The Lapita multiphase models also have the same structure but include the code for use of the Southern Hemisphere calibration curve.

```
Plot()
{
Sequence()
{
Boundary("start precultural");
Phase("precultural")
{
R_Simulate("date precultural", 900, 30);
};
Boundary("end precultural");
Boundary("start Poly.");
Phase()
{
R_Simulate("date 1022, 30", 1022, 30);
R_Simulate("date 1034, 30", 1034, 30);
R_Simulate("date 1026, 30", 1026, 30);
R_Simulate("date 1005, 30", 1005, 30);
R_Simulate("date 1007, 30", 1007, 30);
R_Simulate("date 1037, 30", 1037, 30);
R_Simulate("date 1004, 30", 1004, 30);
R_Simulate("date 1015, 30", 1015, 30);
R_Simulate("date 1025, 30", 1025, 30);
R_Simulate("date 1004, 30", 1004, 30);
};
Boundary("end colonization/start postcolonization");
Phase("postcolonization")
{
R_Simulate("date postcolonization 1069, 30", 1069, 30);
};
Boundary("end postcolonization");
};
Difference("span colonization", "end colonization/start postcolonization", "start
Poly.");
};
```

Notes

1. Following convention, we italicize date estimates based on Bayesian models to distinguish these results from unmodeled dates.

2. Though the high number of radiocarbon determinations provides the appearance of a well-dated site, a scattershot approach seems to have been used in dating sample selection that necessitated an involved evaluation of individual dates and model building by Nunn and Petchey (2013). Apparently several hundred square meters were excavated, and unfortunately, Bourewa seems to be an example of a project that failed to consider chronology building during the planning and implementation of fieldwork. Instead, a post hoc attempt at chronology building was made that tried to make the best of field and laboratory decisions.

References

Allen, M. S., and J. M. Huebert. 2014. Short-lived Plant Materials, Long-lived Trees, and Polynesian ^{14}C Dating: Considerations for ^{14}C Sample Selection and Documentation. *Radiocarbon* 56(1): 257–276.

Allen, M. S., and A. McAlister. 2013. Early Marquesan Settlement and Patterns of Interaction: New Insights From Hatiheu Valley, Nuku Hiva Island. *Journal of Pacific Archaeology* 4(1): 90–109.

Anderson, A., T. Higham, and R. Wallace. 2001. The Radiocarbon Chronology of the Norfolk Island Archaeological Sites. *Records of the Australian Museum, Supplement* 27: 33–42.

Athens, J. S. 1997. Hawaiian Native Lowland Vegetation in Prehistory. In *Historical Ecology in the Pacific Islands,* ed. P. V. Kirch and T. L. Hunt, 248–270. New Haven: Yale University Press.

Athens, J. S., T. M. Rieth, and T. S. Dye. 2014. A Paleoenvironmental and Archaeological Model-Based Age Estimate for the Colonization of Hawai'i. *American Antiquity* 79(1): 144–155.

Bayliss, A. 2009. Rolling Out Revolution: Using Radiocarbon Dating in Archaeology. *Radiocarbon* 51(1): 123–147.

Bayliss, A. 2015. Quality in Bayesian Chronological Models in Archaeology. *World Archaeology* 47(4): 677–700.

Bayliss, A., C. B. Ramsey, J. van der Plicht, and A. Whittle. 2007. Bradshaw and Bayes: Towards a Timetable for the Neolithic. *Cambridge Archaeological Journal* 17(1 supplement): 1–28.

Blaauw, M., J. A. Christen, K. D. Bennett, and P. J. Reimer. 2018. Double the Dates and Go for Bayes—Impacts of Model Choice, Dating Density and Quality of Chronologies. *Quaternary Science Reviews* 188: 58–66.

Bronk Ramsey, C. 2009a. Bayesian Analysis of Radiocarbon Dates. *Radiocarbon* 51(1): 337–360.

Bronk Ramsey, C. 2009b. Dealing with Outliers and Offsets in Radiocarbon Dating. *Radiocarbon* 51(3): 1023–1045.

Buck, C. E., and B. Meson. 2015. On Being a Good Bayesian. *World Archaeology* 47(4): 567–584.

Buck, C. E., and J. A. Christen. 2000. Part C: A Bayesian Calibration of Radiocarbon Determinations from the Pearl Harbor Fishponds, Hawai'i. In *Ancient Hawaiian Fishponds of Pearl Harbor: Archaeological Studies on U.S. Navy Lands, Hawai'i,* ed. J. S. Athens. Honolulu: International Archaeological Research Institute, Inc.

Buck, C. E., W. G. Cavanagh, and C. Litton. 1996. *Bayesian Approach to Interpreting Archaeological Data.* Chichester, United Kingdom: Wiley.

Capuzzo, G., and J. A. Barceló. 2015. Cultural Changes in the Second Millennium BC: A Bayesian Examination of Radiocarbon Evidence from Switzerland and Catalonia. *World Archaeology* 47(4): 622–641.

Carson, M. T., and J. S. Athens. 2007. Integration of Coastal Geomorphology, Mythology, and Archaeological Evidence at Kualoa Beach, Windward Oʻahu, Hawaiian Islands. *Journal of Island Coastal Archaeology* 2(1): 24–43.

Clark, G., and A. Anderson. 2009. Site Chronology and a Review of Radiocarbon Dates from Fiji. In *The Early Prehistory of Fiji*, ed. G. Clark and A. Anderson, 153–182. Terra Australis 31, Canberra: ANU E Press.

Cobb, C. R., A. M. Krus, and D. W. Steadman. 2015. Bayesian Modeling the Occupation Span of the Averbuch Site in the Middle Cumberland Drainage, Tennessee. *Southeastern Archaeology* 34(1): 46–56.

Cochrane, E. E. 2018. The Evolution of Migration: The Case of Lapita in the Southwest Pacific. *Journal of Archaeological Method and Theory* 25: 520–558.

Dean, J. S. 1978. Independent Dating in Archaeological Analysis. *Advances in Archaeological Method and Theory* 1: 223–265.

Denham, T., C. Bronk Ramsey, and J. Specht. 2012. Dating the Appearance of Lapita Pottery in the Bismarck Archipelago and Its Dispersal to Remote Oceania. *Archaeology in Oceania* 47(1): 39–46.

Dye, T. S. 2011. A Model-Based Age Estimate for Polynesian Colonization of Hawaiʻi. *Archaeology in Oceania* 46(3): 130–138.

Dye, T. S. 2015. Dating Human Dispersal in Remote Oceania: A Bayesian View from Hawaiʻi. *World Archaeology* 47(4): 661–676.

Dye, T. S. 2016. Long-term Rhythms in the Development of Hawaiian Social Stratification. *Journal of Archaeological Science* 71: 1–9.

Dye, T. S., and J. Pantaleo. 2010. Age of the O18 Site, Hawaiʻi. *Archaeology in Oceania* 45(3): 113–119.

Field, J. S., and M. W. Graves. 2008. A New Chronology for Pololu Valley, Hawaiʻi Island: Occupational History and Agricultural Development. *Radiocarbon* 50(2): 205–222.

Graves, M. W., and D. J. Addison. 1996. Models and Methods for Inferring the Prehistoric Colonisation of Hawaiʻi. *Indo-Pacific Prehistory Association Bulletin* 15.

Green, R. C. 1991. Near and Remote Oceania: Disestablishing "Melanesia" in Culture History. In *Man and a Half: Essays in Pacific Anthropology and Ethnobiology in Honour of Ralph Bulmer*, ed. A. Pawley, 491–502. Auckland: Polynesian Society.

Hamilton, W. D., and A. M. Krus. 2018. The Myths and Realities of Bayesian Chronological Modeling Revealed. *American Antiquity* 83(2): 187–203.

Hogg, A. G., Q. Hua, P. G. Blackwell, M. Niu, C. E. Buck, T. P. Guilderson, T. J. Heaton, J. G. Palmer, P. J. Reimer, R. W. Reimer, C.S.M. Turney, and S.R.H. Zimmerman. 2013. SHCal13 Southern Hemisphere Calibration, 0–50,000 Years Cal BP. *Radiocarbon* 55(4): 1889–1903.

Irwin, G., T. H. Worthy, S. Best, S. Hawkins, J. Carpenter, and S. Matararaba. 2011. Further Investigations at the Naigani Lapita Site (VL 21/5), Fiji: Excavation, Radiocarbon Dating and Paleofaunal Extinction. *Journal of Pacific Archaeology* 2(2): 66–78.

Kahn, J. G. 2012. Coastal Occupation at the GS-1 Site, Cook's Bay, Moʻorea, Society Islands. *Journal of Pacific Archaeology* 3(2): 52–61.

Kahn, J. G., T. M. Rieth, P. V. Kirch, J. S. Athens, and G. Murakami. 2014. Re-dating of the Kuliʻouʻou Rockshelter, Oʻahu, Hawaiʻi: Location of the First Radiocarbon Date from the Pacific Islands. *Journal of the Polynesian Society* 123(1): 67–90.

Kirch, P. V. 1985. *Feathered Gods and Fishhooks*. Honolulu: University of Hawaii Press.

Kirch, P. V. 1997. *The Lapita Peoples: Ancestors of the Oceanic World*. Cambridge: Wiley-Blackwell.

Kirch, P. V., and M. D. McCoy. 2007. Reconfiguring the Hawaiian Cultural Sequence: Results of Re-dating the Hālawa Dune Site (MO-A1-3), Molokaʻi Island. *Journal of the Polynesian Society* 116(4): 385–406.

Marsh, E. J. 2016. The Disappearing Desert and the Emergence of Agropastoralism: An Adaptive Cycle of Rapid Change in the Mid-Holocene Lake Titicaca Basin (Peru-Bolivia). *Quaternary International* 422: 123–134.

Morrison, A. E., and T. M. Rieth. 2018. *An Archaeological Perspective on Traditional Marine Subsistence and Ecology, Kaʻūpūlehu ahupuaʻa, North Kona District, Hawaiʻi.* Prepared for Kamehameha Schools. International Archaeology, LLC, Honolulu.

Mulrooney, M. A., K. S. Esh, M. D. McCoy, S. H. Bickler, and Y. H. Sinoto. 2014. New Dates From Old Samples: A Revised Radiocarbon Chronology for the Waiʻahukini Rockshelter Site (H8), Kaʻū District, Hawaiʻi Island. In *Papers in Honor of Dr. Yosihiko Sinoto,* ed. W. K. McElroy and E. Komori, 17–26. Society for Hawaiian Archaeology Special Publication 4.

Napolitano, M. F., R. J. DiNapoli, J. H. Stone, M. J. Levin, N. P. Jew, B. G. Lane, J. T. O'Connor, and S. M. Fitzpatrick. 2019. Reevaluating Human Colonization of the Caribbean Using Chronometric Hygiene and Bayesian Modeling. *Science Advances* 5: eaar5806.

Nunn, P. D., and F. Petchey. 2013. Bayesian Re-evaluation of Lapita Settlement in Fiji: Radiocarbon Analysis of the Lapita Occupation at Bourewa and Nearby Sites on the Rove Peninsula, Viti Levu Island. *Journal of Pacific Archaeology* 4(2): 21–34.

Reimer, P. J., E. Bard, A. Bayliss, J. W. Beck, P. G. Blackwell, C. Bronk Ramsey, P. M. Grootes, T. P. Guilderson, H. Haflidason, I. Hajdas, C. Hatté, T. J. Heaton, D. L. Hoffmann, A. G. Hogg, K. A. Hughen, K. F. Kaiser, B. Kromer, S. W. Manning, M. Niu, R. W. Reimer, D. A. Richards, E. M. Scott, J. R. Southon, R. A. Staff, C.S.M. Turney, and J. van der Plicht. 2013. IntCal13 and Marine13 Radiocarbon Age Calibration Curves 0–50,000 Years cal BP. *Radiocarbon* 55(4): 1869–87.

Rieth, T. M., and J. S. Athens. 2013. Suggested Best Practices for the Application of Radiocarbon Dating to Hawaiian Archaeology. *Hawaiian Archaeology* 13: 3–29.

Rieth, T. M., and J. S. Athens. 2019. Late Holocene Human Expansion into Near and Remote Oceania: A Bayesian Model of the Chronologies of the Mariana Islands and Bismarck Archipelago. *Journal of Island and Coastal Archaeology* 14(1): 5–16.

Rieth, T. M., and E. E. Cochrane. 2018. The Chronology of Colonization in Remote Oceania. In *The Oxford Handbook of Prehistoric Oceania,* ed. E. E. Cochrane and T. L. Hunt. Oxford: Oxford University Press.

Rieth, T. M., T. L. Hunt, C. Lipo, and J. M. Wilmshurst. 2011. The 13th Century Polynesian Colonization of Hawaiʻi Island. *Journal of Archaeological Science* 38: 2740–2749.

Sheppard, P. J., S. Chiu, and R. Walter. 2015. Re-dating Lapita Movement into Remote Oceania. *Journal of Pacific Archaeology* 6(1): 26–36.

Specht, J., and C. Gosden. 1997. Dating Lapita Pottery in the Bismarck Archipelago, Papua New Guinea. *Asian Perspectives* 36: 175–194.

Whittle, A., F. Healy, and A. Bayliss. 2011. *Gathering Time: Dating the Early Neolithic Enclosures of Southern Britain and Ireland.* Oxford: Oxbow Books.

Wilmshurst, J. M., A. J. Anderson, T.F.G. Higham, and T. H. Worthy. 2008. Dating the Late Prehistoric Dispersal of Polynesians to New Zealand Using the Commensal Pacific Rat. *Proceedings of the National Academy of Sciences* 105(22): 7676–7680.

Wilmshurst, J. M., T. L. Hunt, C. P. Lipo, and A. J. Anderson. 2011. High-precision Radiocarbon Dating Shows Recent and Rapid Initial Human Colonization of East Polynesia. *Proceedings of the National Academy of Sciences* 108(5): 1815–1820.

Wood, R. J. Zenobia, D. Vannieuwenhuyse, J. Balme, S. O'Connor, and R. Whitau. 2016. Towards an Accurate and Precise Chronology for the Colonization of Australia: The Example of Riwi, Kimberley, Western Australia. *PLoS ONE* 11: e0160123.

8

Stepping-stones and Genomes

Using Ancient DNA to Reconstruct Island Colonization

JESSICA H. STONE AND MARIA A. NIEVES-COLÓN

In archaeology, molecular techniques such as ancient DNA (aDNA) analysis have grown to become well-established tools for understanding research questions related to past population relationships, dispersals to new regions, and domestication of plants and animals, among others. As the field of aDNA has grown, interdisciplinary collaborations between archaeologists and geneticists have become more frequent. Although initial aDNA studies were limited in scope due to the problems posed by DNA degradation, the recent explosion of next-generation sequencing methods has improved the ability to obtain genetic material from ancient remains, especially in areas where poor preservation represents a large barrier to analysis, like the tropics. As a result, these analyses are providing a valuable new line of evidence for archaeological inquiry in a wide variety of different environments, including island systems. In this chapter, we discuss aDNA techniques, the analytical methods used for genetic/genomic analysis, and illustrate the role aDNA can play in our understanding of human mobility, especially in cases of initial settlement. We discuss how this is an especially well-suited method for island systems and how it has been used to address major questions about the colonization of the Pacific Islands.

Ancient DNA: What Is It and How Do We Get It?

Ancient DNA differs from the DNA found in modern biological samples in two important ways. First, there is very little of it, and second, it is extremely damaged (Hofreiter et al. 2001; Pääbo et al. 2004). Ancient genetic material can be obtained from biological remains such as bone, teeth, dental calculus, coprolites, hair, fabric, seeds, and other tissues (O'Rourke et al. 2000; Weyrich et al. 2015). Among these, tooth cementum, the calcified surface layer of the tooth root, and the petrous portion of the temporal bone have been identified as rich sources of endogenous DNA (that is, the DNA of the target individual) (Damgaard et al. 2015; Gamba et al. 2014; Pinhasi et al. 2015). However, preservation within these elements is quite variable and can fluctuate even between tissues from the same individual (Hansen et al. 2017; Reich et al. 2010).

Upon an organism's death, cell repair mechanisms cease to function and genetic material begins to degrade. Postmortem chemical processes such as hydrolysis and oxidation, fragment and damage DNA (Briggs et al. 2007; Dabney et al. 2013b). Decay can be accelerated by taphonomic conditions of the deposition environment, especially if the ancient remains are exposed to humidity or high temperatures, which is common for many island contexts (Adler et al. 2011; Lindahl 1993; Smith et al. 2001). Bacteria, fungi, insects, and other decomposers cause further contamination by digesting the DNA and introducing their own genetic material (Marciniak et al. 2015). Postexcavation sample treatment and storage conditions can also affect DNA preservation and introduce contamination. For example, washing specimens after excavation can both introduce contaminating DNA and simultaneously induce hydrolytic damage to endogenous DNA (Llamas et al. 2017b; Yang and Watt 2005). Thus, at the best of times, a researcher may expect an ancient sample to be mostly composed of environmental and microbial contamination (99 percent) with low quantities of poorly preserved endogenous DNA (<1 percent) (Carpenter et al. 2013). All of these characteristics make working with aDNA extremely challenging. Researchers must implement strict precautions, such as working in dedicated clean laboratories, to avoid introducing further contamination and guarantee result authenticity (Cooper and Poinar 2000; Fulton 2012; Pääbo et al. 2004).

Before the advent of next-generation sequencing (see below), most aDNA studies focused on organellar DNA, such as the mitochondrial (mtDNA) or chloroplast genomes. Organellar genomes are circular, have a uniparental inheritance pattern, and are present in high copy numbers within the cell, all factors that facilitate their recovery in degraded samples (Paijmans et al. 2013). For instance, because of their important role in energy production, between 1,000 and 10,000 mitochondria are found in mammalian cells. Each one contains a copy of mtDNA that is inherited without recombination through the maternal line (Giles et al. 1980). Although it represents a limited view of an individual's potential ancestors, analyses of mtDNA data can still provide valuable, multiscalar insights into population history, including intrasite dynamics (for example, Stone and Stoneking 1999) and peopling events (Llamas et al. 2017a; see also Paijmans et al. 2013).

In contrast to mtDNA, only one copy of nuclear DNA is present in the nucleus of eukaryotic cells. In humans, the nuclear genome is composed of 22 autosomes and 1 pair of sex chromosomes (X and Y). Nuclear DNA is inherited from both parents and recombines every generation, so it contains much more information about an individual's ancestors than mtDNA. The only exception to this pattern is the nonrecombining portion of the Y chromosome, which is inherited directly from father to son. Because of its lower copy number, recovery of nuclear DNA can be difficult. But due to the large variety of independent genetic loci that can be assessed, examining ancient nuclear genomes allows for more comprehensive analyses than possible with uniparental markers (Stoneking and Krause 2011). For example, whole-genome sequencing of archaeological individuals from Vanuatu in Remote Oceania demonstrated that differences in mtDNA and Y-chromosome ancestry patterns originally interpreted as sex-biased admixture were instead the result of changes in population structure over time (Lipson et al. 2018, Posth et al. 2018).

A variety of protocols have been developed for obtaining DNA from ancient remains. Most approaches require destructive sampling of all or part of the sample (Damgaard et al. 2015), although some nondestructive methods exist (Bolnick et al. 2012; Hofreiter 2012; Rohland et al. 2004). Currently, the most popular methods recover small fragments of DNA from pulverized bone or tooth by first digesting tissue proteins with the enzyme Proteinase K and binding the DNA to silica particles (Boessenkool et al. 2016; Dabney et al. 2013a; Glocke and Meyer 2017; Rohland and Hofreiter 2007; Yang et al. 1998).

Extracted aDNA can be amplified through the polymerase chain reaction (PCR) and subsequently sequenced with Sanger methods, which determine the sequence of a DNA fragment by copying the target DNA multiple times (Sanger et al. 1977). However, this approach is constrained by PCR inhibition, high cost, and bias toward longer DNA fragments (and concomitant loss of the more abundant and likely more informative short aDNA fragments) (Rizzi et al. 2012). In the last decade, the availability of next-generation sequencing (NGS) methods has modified the standard workflow for aDNA samples and generated genomic-scale datasets (Der Sarkissian et al. 2015). In contrast to Sanger sequencing, which can only produce data from one molecule at a time, NGS can produce sequence data from many molecules in parallel (Mardis 2008). Therefore, short, fragmented, and degraded aDNA molecules that sometimes fail to amplify with traditional PCR-based methods can now be sequenced directly with NGS (Stoneking and

Krause 2011). Due to its high-throughput and capacity to sequence short DNA fragments, the Illumina sequencing platform is currently the dominant technology used in aDNA research (Knapp and Hofreiter 2010).

Samples of aDNA are prepared for NGS by first converting the extracts into libraries, which are a collection of all the DNA fragments present in the extract (Meyer and Kircher 2010). Libraries can be sequenced directly in an approach known as shotgun sequencing; however, this is inefficient for samples with low endogenous content, because a majority of the sequence data will be from contaminant DNA (Green et al. 2010). For such samples, enrichment capture can be used to selectively target endogenous DNA molecules by using baits made from DNA or RNA sequences to target genomic regions from the organism of interest (Carpenter et al. 2013; Maricic et al. 2010). Enrichment approaches, combined with NGS, have been used to generate sequence data from a variety of ancient targets, including hominid mitochondrial genomes, commensal and pathogenic microbial genomes, and partial nuclear genomes from ancient humans, plants, and animals (Gasc et al. 2016). These strategies have also allowed for recovery of genomic aDNA from areas where such research was not previously thought possible, including tropical island contexts, where genomic data are making major contributions to our understanding of initial human settlement and subsequent population dynamics (see for example, Lipson et al. 2018; Nägele et al. 2020; Nieves-Colón et al. 2020; Schroeder et al. 2015, 2018; Skoglund et al. 2016).

Analyses of Ancient DNA Data

Once aDNA samples are sequenced, computational methods are used to process and analyze the data. Traditional sequence-processing tools rarely take into account the particularities of aDNA, such as high rates of damage, short fragments, and contamination (Pickrell and Reich 2014). Thus, novel methods have been developed, such as customized bioinformatics pipelines (Figure 8.1) (Peltzer et al. 2016; Schubert et al. 2012; Schubert et al. 2014; Seitz and Nieselt 2017) and improved statistical approaches for analyzing aDNA datasets (Mourier et al. 2012; Patterson et al. 2012; Slatkin 2016).

One of the most important advances has been the development of new approaches for distinguishing authentic aDNA from contamination. After NGS was introduced into aDNA workflows, it was discovered that ancient sequences had characteristic postmortem damage patterns (Briggs et al. 2007; Dabney et al. 2013b). The most frequent of these patterns is due to cytosine deamination, and results in increased rates of C to T and A to G changes at the 3' and 5' end of DNA reads, respectively (Figure 8.2) (Briggs et al. 2007). When observed in

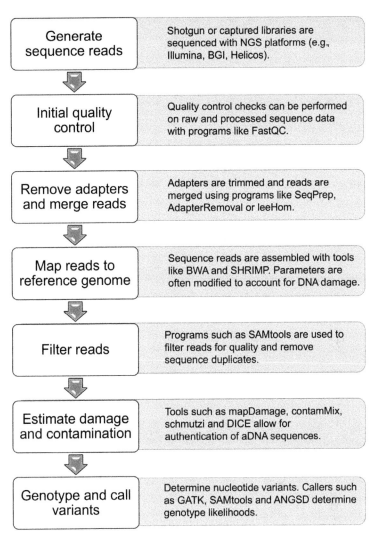

Generate sequence reads	Shotgun or captured libraries are sequenced with NGS platforms (e.g., Illumina, BGI, Helicos).
Initial quality control	Quality control checks can be performed on raw and processed sequence data with programs like FastQC.
Remove adapters and merge reads	Adapters are trimmed and reads are merged using programs like SeqPrep, AdapterRemoval or leeHom.
Map reads to reference genome	Sequence reads are assembled with tools like BWA and SHRIMP. Parameters are often modified to account for DNA damage.
Filter reads	Programs such as SAMtools are used to filter reads for quality and remove sequence duplicates.
Estimate damage and contamination	Tools such as mapDamage, contamMix, schmutzi and DICE allow for authentication of aDNA sequences.
Genotype and call variants	Determine nucleotide variants. Callers such as GATK, SAMtools and ANGSD determine genotype likelihoods.

Figure 8.1. A sample bioinformatics workflow for processing ancient DNA data.

tandem with a short fragment length distribution (<300bp), these patterns can be used to authenticate aDNA samples (Overballe-Petersen et al. 2012). Methods have also been developed to filter out modern, contaminating sequences, which do not contain these signatures (Skoglund et al. 2014); to estimate contamination rates; and to reconstruct endogenous consensus sequences from contaminated datasets (Green et al. 2008; Racimo et al. 2016; Renaud et al. 2015).

Following sequence processing and authentication, statistical analyses are used to describe genetic diversity patterns and test hypotheses of interest. These

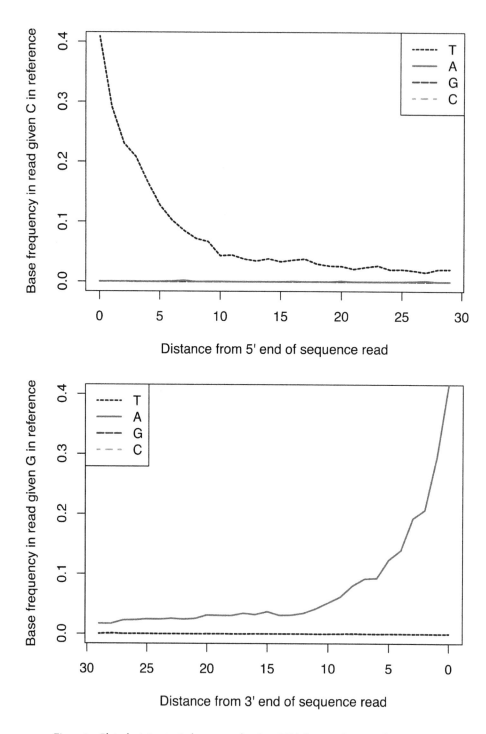

Figure 8.2. Plots depicting typical patterns of ancient DNA damage. Cytosine deamination results in increased rates of C to T transitions and A to G transitions at the 3' and 5' ends of ancient DNA sequences. Plot created with PMDtools (Skoglund et al. 2014).

can include classical population genetics approaches such as calculating diversity measures or estimating genetic distance (Nei 1987; Wright 1951). Phylogenetic approaches such as Bayesian tree inference or median networks may also be used to examine intrapopulation relationships, estimate timescales, and find shared lineages (Bandelt et al. 1999; Rieux and Balloux 2016). Other analytical approaches, especially used with genomic scale data, include principal components analyses, which describe genetic structure (Patterson et al. 2006), and genetic clustering analyses, which describe ancestry patterns (Alexander et al. 2009) (Figure 8.3). In most cases, these analyses provide a first glance at underlying genomic diversity and must be followed up with formal statistical tests or model inference. For instance, several tests have been developed to detect and date ancient admixture, including D-statistics, F-statistics, linkage disequilibrium tests, and population tree approaches (Green et al. 2010; Patterson et al. 2012; Pickrell and Pritchard 2012). Lastly, model-based approaches, which estimate the fit of several models to the observed data are also used to reconstruct migration patterns, estimate past population sizes, and date divergence events, among other inferences (Slatkin 2016; Stoneking and Krause 2011).

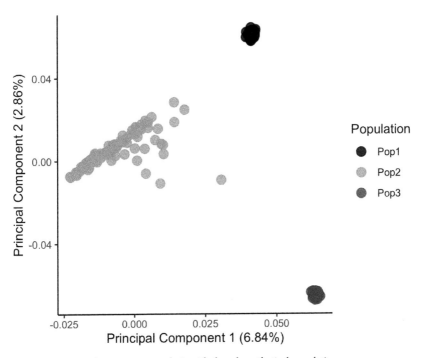

Figure 8.3. Principal components analysis with three hypothetical populations.

All of these data interpretation frameworks must take into account potential problems that can arise from combining heterochronous modern and ancient genomic datasets (Navascués et al. 2010). For instance, at present, reference panels of global human variation used for comparative analyses do not include all living populations (Popejoy and Fullerton 2016), and those that are included carry only a subset of all the genetic diversity that existed in the past. This can lead to bias when reconstructing relationships between populations, or when using data from contemporary peoples as proxies for ancient groups (Pickrell and Reich 2014). However, as obtaining aDNA data becomes easier, researchers have begun to address these issues by moving toward a population genomics approach, sampling broad geographic areas as well as multiple time points to get a full sense of population-level histories (Hofreiter et al. 2015; Pickrell and Reich 2014). These changes have made it possible to reconstruct complex demographic histories such as the initial settlement of island systems around the globe (Derbeneva et al. 2002; Ko et al. 2014; Matisoo-Smith 2015; West et al. 2017).

In island systems, aDNA data can be used to reconstruct initial colonization events and human migration dynamics. When examined in tandem with archaeological evidence, genetic data can test existing hypotheses and propose new potential scenarios for human arrival. For instance, researchers can apply theoretical population genetics models, such as the stepping-stone model, or design new models informed by archaeological findings to trace island settlement trajectories and reconstruct how and from where populations may have entered and spread through archipelagos (see chapter 9). The dynamics of island colonization can also be examined by estimating the date of arrival, the effective population size, and the directionality of migration. By comparing DNA data from different time periods or geographic regions, questions of population replacement versus continuity or the ultimate mainland origins of island peoples can also be addressed. Lastly, by also researching the genetics of domesticated and wild species that cohabitate with people, researchers can gather additional evidence for translocation events and can explore the ecological impacts of human expansion into island systems.

Case Study: The Pacific Islands

One island region where multiple lines of modern and ancient genetic evidence have contributed significantly to models of human dispersals is the Pacific Islands. As it is the last major geographic area to be settled by humans, the timing and trajectories of Pacific settlement are critical to understanding the role of

Jessica H. Stone and Maria A. Nieves-Colón

migration in human evolution. A large body of research focusing on modern human population genetics has provided great insight into these processes, but aDNA studies in the region have been somewhat limited. In some areas, ethical issues and concerns from Indigenous descendant communities have restricted genetic sampling and removal of human remains from archaeological contexts (Matisoo-Smith 2015). Additionally, the tropical environment is not conducive to the preservation of human remains or aDNA, but due to the aforementioned methodological advances, this is beginning to change (Adler et al. 2011; Smith et al. 2001).

Settlement of the Pacific

The regions known as Island Southeast Asia (ISEA) and Near Oceania stretch from the Philippines south, through Indonesia, and east of Papua New Guinea to the Solomon Islands. Due to lower sea levels in ISEA during the Pleistocene, many of today's islands were joined. As a result, both the depth and number of water gaps between landmasses were dramatically reduced and were conducive to early human settlement by mobile foraging groups as early as 65,000–55,000 years ago (Clarkson et al. 2017; O'Connell and Allen 2004; O'Connor and Hiscock 2018).

A second major wave of migration occurred around 5,000–4,000 years ago and appears to have originated out of ISEA via Taiwan (see chapter 11). These horticulturalists, often referred to as Austronesian groups based on linguistic association, continued to expand rapidly through Near Oceania west toward Madagascar and even further east into what is known as Remote Oceania, an area comprised of relatively small, isolated islands reaching across the tropical Pacific (Green 1991). The bulk of archaeological research dedicated to initial human arrival in Remote Oceania as an outgrowth of this dispersal focuses on the Lapita Cultural Complex (see chapters 2 and 7). Descendant Polynesian groups then dispersed into and across East Polynesia, including the Hawaiian Islands and Rapa Nui (Easter Island), followed by New Zealand (Bedford et al. 2006; Gosden et al. 1989; Green 1979; Kirch 1997). Interestingly, settlement of western Micronesia does not appear to be a direct result of Lapita dispersal and instead seems to have been settled directly from ISEA (Callaghan and Fitzpatrick 2008; Lum and Cann 1998, 2000; Montenegro et al. 2016).

Modern Human Population Genetics in the Pacific Region

Genetic evidence has contributed significantly to our understanding of the general trajectories and chronologies of initial settlement. Early studies utilizing frequencies of ABO blood groups, human leukocyte antigen (HLA) genetic loci, and globin genes were used to investigate distributions across the region in an effort to better understand the dispersal of mainland populations (Hill and Serjeantson 1989). These data, combined with extensive regional studies of mtDNA variation and more recent Y-chromosome and genomic studies, also lend support to the above suggestion that settlement of the Pacific occurred via two major waves of migration. Genetic signatures of the arrival of initial Papuan (non-Austronesian)–speaking groups to ISEA and Near Oceania during the Pleistocene include mtDNA and Y-chromosome haplogroups that are distinct from the East Asian and Southeast Asian–derived haplogroups associated with Austronesian speakers that first reached Remote Oceania (Friedlander et al. 2007; Kayser 2010; Merriwether et al. 2005). These Austronesian-associated mtDNA lineages include haplogroup B4a1a1a, which is often referred to as the "Polynesian Motif" and is characterized by a combination of a 9-bp deletion and additional single nucleotide polymorphisms (SNPs). This motif is found at increasingly high frequencies from ISEA eastward through the Pacific Islands and was originally thought to be evidence for an "Out of Taiwan" model of Polynesian origins (Melton et al. 1995; Redd et al. 1995). However, the distribution of the haplogroup in ISEA has raised some questions regarding this interpretation (Duggan and Stoneking 2013; Tabbada et al. 2010). Interestingly, the Y-chromosome pattern indicates that males in both Near and Remote Oceania were primarily of Melanesian origins, with a small (<25 percent) contribution of East Asian–derived haplotypes, while mtDNA indicates nearly opposite frequencies of Melanesian and East Asian ancestries. This has been attributed to matrilocal cultural patterns, but may also be due to the fact that sampling of Y-chromosome diversity has been more limited than mtDNA (Hage and Marck 2003; Underhill and Kivisild 2007). Genome-wide studies are being increasingly utilized to overcome these biases, and generally support a consensus of admixed Melanesian and Asian–derived populations with some island-specific variation. The timing of this admixture is currently unknown, but the integration of aDNA from different points in time would allow for a diachronic examination of ancestry and is one major area of focus for current research.

The Commensal Model

The majority of aDNA research in the Pacific has focused on using commensal flora and fauna as proxies for human movement. This approach, now termed the "commensal model" relies on the use of taxa that are unable to reach island environments without human intervention. Therefore, their appearance at archaeological sites serves as indirect evidence for human presence. Additionally, because these taxa are often utilized as food resources, faunal assemblages tend to be recovered in much larger numbers (Matisoo-Smith 1994, 2009). Initial studies of rats (*Rattus exulans*) demonstrated the feasibility of this approach and identified links between Polynesian and Lapita groups, as well as distinct interaction spheres within Polynesia (Matisoo-Smith et al. 1998; Matisoo-Smith and Robins 2004). Applications of this approach to pigs (*Sus scrofa*) have also been successful in identifying a regionally distinct "Pacific Clade" that could be ultimately traced back to the coast of Southeast Asia and supports Austronesian links from Asia into ISEA and Remote Oceania as part of Lapita dispersals (Larson et al. 2005). Western Micronesian pigs, however, do not possess the "Pacific Clade" and instead appear to be related to an East Asian lineage via Taiwan and the Philippines (Allen et al. 2001; Larson et al. 2005, 2007). aDNA from chickens (*Gallus gallus*) found at early Lapita sites demonstrated the introduction of at least two lineages from Southeast Asia that were also found in chicken bones from a precontact site on the Chilean coast. There has been some controversy regarding these Chilean sequences related to both possible contamination and proper radiocarbon date calibration (Gongora et al. 2008; Storey et al. 2007, 2008). However, the implication that Polynesians interacted with groups from the South American coast has been further supported by botanical evidence for South American crops on Pacific islands, including the sweet potato (*Ipomoea batatas*) and bottle gourd (*Lagenaria siceraria*), and recently, via a genome-wide study of modern Polynesian and Pacific coast Native American people (Ioannidis et al. 2020; Matisoo-Smith and Horsburgh 2012; Thomson et al. 2014). Lastly, dog (*Canis lupus familiaris*) bones have only been recovered in small amounts from Late Lapita period sites, with one exception in the Bismarcks (Manne et al. 2020). MtDNA evidence also suggests multiple small introductions to the region, including Polynesian lineages that appear to originate in Mainland Southeast Asia (Matisoo-Smith 2007; Grieg et al. 2018; Oskarsson et al. 2012; Savolainen et al. 2004).

In addition to commensal fauna, genetic analysis of commensal bacteria and modern plant domesticates, including paper mulberry (*Broussonetia papyrifera*), Polynesian Ti (*Cordyline fruticosa*), breadfruit (*Artocarpus altilis*), sweet potato (*Ipomoea batatas*), and bottle gourd have been used to infer human population movements. However, because Europeans reintroduced these taxa to many islands, data from modern plant samples may be biased by admixture (Chang et al. 2015; Clarke et al. 2006; Hinkle 2007; Muñoz-Rodriguez et al. 2018; Zerega et al. 2004). The commensal bacterium *Helicobacter pylori*, has also proven to be a useful proxy for human movement due to geographically differentiated strains, including two distinct groups in the Pacific that likely accompanied the two major initial human dispersals into the region (Moodley et al. 2009).

Human aDNA Studies

The earliest Pacific aDNA studies focused on identification of the "Polynesian Motif," as a means to authenticate aDNA and assess relationships between Lapita and East Polynesian groups (Hagelberg and Clegg 1991, 1993; Hagelberg et al. 1994). Subsequent studies with samples from the Gambier Islands in East Polynesia and historic-era Solomon Islanders demonstrated consistency between ancient and modern populations (Deguilloux et al. 2011; Ricaut et al. 2010).

With improvements in NGS technology and enrichment methods, ancient mitochondrial and nuclear genomes have now been generated from human remains dating to early settlement periods from several Pacific islands. Burials from the site of Wairau Bar in New Zealand were recovered in association with bones and eggshells of moa (Aves: Dinornithiformes), a large flightless bird that was rapidly driven to extinction shortly following human arrival. Therefore, it appears that the Wairau Bar burials represent individuals from the first generations of settlers. Results of human mtDNA analysis indicated higher diversity than expected, and suggest that Polynesian mtDNA diversity has been likely underestimated (Holdaway and Jacomb 2000; Knapp et al. 2012). More recently, genome-wide aDNA from three Lapita individuals from Vanuatu and one from Tonga demonstrated that little to no Papuan ancestry was present during initial Lapita dispersals, and admixture between the two linguistic groups occurred later than previously thought. Additional sequencing from individuals across a broader time period have demonstrated that the contribution of Papuan ancestry seen in modern Vanuatu populations instead is the result of new Papuan migrants to the archipelago by the end of the Lapita period, circa 2,400 years ago (Lipson et al. 2018; Skoglund et al. 2016). On Rapa Nui, comparisons of genome-wide data from individuals dating to pre- and post-European arrival demonstrated a lack of admixture with South American populations. Despite the island's relative proximity to the mainland and demonstrated contact between South American and Polynesian groups prior to European arrival, it appears that admixture occurred much later (Fehren-Schmitz et al. 2017).

Moving Forward

As a result of such significant improvements in NGS technology, methods are emerging for obtaining human aDNA indirectly and nondestructively through

Jessica H. Stone and Maria A. Nieves-Colón

the use of alternative sampling materials, including dental calculus and archaeological sediments. Calculus, or mineralized dental plaque, is often well-preserved in archaeological contexts and contains DNA from an individual's oral microbiome that can be sampled without destroying the tooth (De La Fuente et al. 2013; Dobney and Brothwell 1987). It has been demonstrated that the oral microbiome contains microbiota that have a rapid mutation rate and are transmitted via vertical inheritance (from parents/caregivers to offspring) at birth. Therefore, these microbial communities can serve as a proxy for population dispersals at finer scale resolutions appropriate for rapid settlement events, like that of Remote Oceania (Eisenhofer et al. 2017). Forensic science research has demonstrated that, following decomposition, DNA can persist in surrounding and nearby grave sediments (Emmons et al. 2017). Neanderthal mtDNA has been recovered from cave floor sediments, and both plant and animal DNA have been recovered from permafrost and sediments from temperate environments, including in New Zealand (Slon et al. 2017; Willerslev et al. 2003).

While the feasibility of these methods remains to be tested in humid tropical environments less conducive to DNA preservation such as the Pacific, as sequencing technology and enrichment techniques continue to improve, they may become critical for exploring ancient human genetics in areas where human remains cannot be sampled, and may facilitate new local collaborations in areas where aDNA research has not yet been possible.

Conclusions

The advent of NGS has allowed for tremendous strides to be made in aDNA research, expanding the breadth of questions that can be addressed with ancient genetic and genomic data. In the Pacific, the use of commensal plant and animal DNA, and more recently, human genomes, has shed light on the timing of population movements, admixture, and migration trajectories. However, many questions remain to be addressed. For instance, the origins of Micronesian groups are still unknown, as is the extent of possible relationships between these groups and Lapita migrants. Additionally, a lack of research in ISEA has limited our understanding of the genetics of this region and its potential as a source area for Remote Oceanic groups. Ancient DNA, especially when combined with modern genomics datasets and contextualized with archaeological and historical evidence, is beginning to provide insight into these questions and will undoubtedly continue to do so in the near future. In addition, the generation of new ancient genetic datasets may forge relationships between geneticists, archaeologists, and descendant communities in new collaborative ways that allow for researchers to answer questions Indigenous groups are interested in beyond ancestry and population history, such as those related to demography and health in both the Pacific Islands and other island regions across the globe.

References

Adler, C. J., W. Haak, D. Donlon, and A. Cooper. 2011. Survival and Recovery of DNA from Ancient Teeth and Bones. *Journal of Archaeological Science* 38(5): 956–964.

Alexander, D. H., J. Novembre, and K. Lange. 2009. Fast Model Based Estimation of Ancestry in Unrelated Individuals. *Genome Research* 19(9): 1655–1664.

Allen, M. S., E. Matisoo-Smith, and A. Horsburgh. 2001. Pacific "Babes": Issues in the Origins and Dispersal of Pacific Pigs and the Potential of Mitochondrial DNA Analysis. *International Journal of Osteoarchaeology* 11(1–2): 4–13.

Bandelt, H.-J., P. Forster, and A. Rohl. 1999. Median-Joining Networks for Inferring Intraspecific Phylogenies. *Molecular Biology and Evolution* 16(1): 37–48.

Bedford, S., M. Spriggs, and R. Regenvanu. 2006. The Teouma Lapita Site and the Early Human Settlement of the Pacific Islands. *Antiquity* 80(31): 812–828.

Boessenkool, S., K. Hanghoj, H. M. Nistelberger, C. Der Sarkissian, A. T. Gondek, L. Orlando, J. H. Barrett, and B. Star. 2016. Combining Bleach and Mild Predigestion Improves Ancient DNA Recovery from Bones. *Molecular Ecology Resources* 17(4): 742–751.

Bolnick, D. A., H. M. Bonine, J. Mata-Miguez, B. M. Kemp, M. H. Snow, and S. A. LeBlanc. 2012. Nondestructive Sampling of Human Skeletal Remains Yields Ancient Nuclear and Mitochondrial DNA. *American Journal of Physical Anthropology* 147(2): 293–300.

Briggs, A. W., U. Stenzel, P.L.F. Johnson, R. E. Green, J. Kelso, K. Prüfer, M. Meyer, J. Krause, M. T. Ronan, M. Lachmann, and S. Pääbo. 2007. Patterns of Damage in Genomic DNA Sequences from a Neandertal. *Proceedings of the National Academy of Sciences* 104(37): 14616–14621.

Callaghan, R., and S. M. Fitzpatrick. 2008. Examining Prehistoric Migration Patterns in the Palauan Archipelago: A Computer Simulated Analysis of Drift Voyaging. *Asian Perspectives* 47(1): 28–44.

Carpenter, M. L., J. D. Buenrostro, C. Valdiosera, H. Schroeder, M. E. Allentoft, M. Sikora, M. Rasmussen, S. Gravel, S. Guillen, G. Nekhrizov, K. Leshtakov, A. Moreno-Estrada, Y. Li, J. Wang, M.T.P. Gilbert, E. Willerslev, W. J. Greenleaf, and C. D. Bustamante. 2013. Pulling Out the 1%: Whole-Genome Capture for the Targeted Enrichment of Ancient DNA Sequencing Libraries. *American Journal of Human Genetics* 93(5): 852–864.

Chang, C. S., H. L. Liu, X. Moncada, X., A. Seelenfreund, D. Seelenfreund, and K. F. Chung. 2015. A Holistic Picture of Austronesian Migrations Revealed by Phylogeography of Pacific Paper Mulberry. *Proceedings of the National Academy of Sciences* 112(44): 13537–13542.

Clarke, A. C., M. K. Burtenshaw, P. A. McLenachan, D. L. Erickson, and D. Penny. 2006. Reconstructing the Origins and Dispersal of the Polynesian Bottle Gourd (*Lagenaria siceraria*). *Molecular Biology and Evolution* 23: 893–900.

Clarkson, C., Z. Jacobs, B. Marwick, R. Fullager, L. Wallis, M. Smith, R. G. Roberts, E. Hayes, K. Lowe, X. Carah, and S. A. Florin. 2017. Human Occupation of Northern Australia by 65,000 Years Ago. *Nature* 547(7663): 306.

Cooper, A., and H. Poinar. 2000. Ancient DNA: Do It Right or Not at All. *Science* 289(5482): 1139.

Dabney, J., M. Knapp, I. Glocke, M. T. Gansauge, A. Weihmann, B. Nickel, C. Valdiosera, N. Garcia, S. Pääbo, J. L. Arsuaga, and M. Meyer. 2013a. Complete Mitochondrial Genome Sequence of a Middle Pleistocene Cave Bear Reconstructed from Ultrashort DNA fragments. *Proceedings of the National Academy of Sciences* 110(39): 15758–15763.

Dabney, J., M. Meyer, and S. Pääbo. 2013b. Ancient DNA Damage. *Cold Spring Harbor Perspectives in Biology* 5(7): a012567.

Damgaard, P. B., A. Margaryan, H. Schroeder, L. Orlando, E. Willerslev, and M. E. Allentoft. 2015. Improving Access to Endogenous DNA in Ancient Bones and Teeth. *Scientific Reports* 5: 11184.

De La Fuente, C., S. Flores, and M. Moraga. 2013. DNA From Human Ancient Bacteria: A Novel Source of Genetic Evidence From Archaeological Dental Calculus. *Archaeometry* 55(4): 767–78.

Deguilloux, M. F., M. H. Pemonge, V. Dubut, S. Hughes, C. Hanni, L. Chollet, E. Conte, and P. Murail. 2011. Human Ancient and Extant mtDNA From the Gambier Islands (French Polynesia): Evidence for an Early Melanesian Maternal Contribution and New Perspectives into the Settlement of Easternmost Polynesia. *American Journal of Physical Anthropology* 144(2): 248–257.

Derbeneva, O. A., R. I. Sukernik, N. V. Volodko, S. H., Hosseini, M. T. Lott, and D. C. Wallace. 2002. Analysis of Mitochondrial DNA Diversity in the Aleuts of the Commander Islands and Its Implications for the Genetic History of Beringia. *American Journal of Human Genetics* 71(2): 415–421.

Der Sarkissian, C., M. E. Allentoft, M. C. Avila-Arcos, R. Barnett, P. F. Campos, E. Cappellini, L. Ermini, R. Fernandez, R. da Fonseca, A. Ginolhac, A. J. Hansen, H. Jónsson, T. Korneliussen, A. Margaryan, M. D. Martin, J. V. Moreno-Mayar, M. Raghavan, M. Rasmussen, M. Sandoval Velasco, H. Schroeder, M. Schubert, A. Seguin-Orlando, N. Wales, M.T.P. Gilbert, E. Willerslev, and L. Orlando. 2015. Ancient Genomics. *Philosophical Transactions of the Royal Society London B: Biological Sciences* 370(1660): 20130387.

Dobney, K., and D. Brothwell. 1987. A Method for Evaluating the Amount of Dental Calculus on Teeth from Archaeological Sites. *Journal of Archaeological Science* 14(4): 343–351.

Duggan, A., B. Evans, F. Friedlander, J. Friedlander, G. Koki, D. Merriweather, M. Kayser, and M. Stoneking. 2014. Maternal History of Oceania from Complete mtDNA Genomes: Contrasting Ancient Diversity with Recent Homogenization Due to the Austronesian Expansion. *American Journal of Human Genetics* 94(5): 721–733.

Duggan, A., and Stoneking, M. 2013. A Highly Unstable Recent Mutation in Human mtDNA. *American Journal of Human Genetics* 92(2): 279–284.

Eisenhofer, R., A. Anderson A., K. Dobney, A. Cooper, and L. S. Weyrich. 2017. Ancient Microbial DNA in Dental Calculus: A New Method for Studying Rapid Human Migration Events. *Journal of Island and Coastal Archaeology* 14(2): 149–162.

Emmons, A. L., J. M. DeBruyn, A. Z. Mundorff, K. L. Cobaugh, and G. S. Cabana. 2017. The Persistence of Human DNA in Soil Following Surface Decomposition. *Science and Justice* 57(5): 341–348.

Fehren-Schmitz, L., C. L. Jarman, K. M. Harkins, M. Kayser, B. N. Popp, and P. Skoglund. 2017. Genetic Ancestry of Rapanui Before and After European Contact. *Current Biology* 27(20): 3209–3215.

Friedlander, J., F. Friedlander, F. Reed, K., Kidd, J., Kidd, G. Chambers, R. Lea, J. Loo, G. Koki, J. Hodgson, A. Merriweather, and J. Weber. 2008. The Genetic Structure of Pacific Islanders. *PLoS Genetics* 4(1): e19.

Fulton, T. L. 2012. Setting Up an Ancient DNA Laboratory. In *Ancient DNA: Methods and Protocols,* ed. B. Shapiro and M. Hofreiter, 1–11. Totowa, New Jersey: Humana Press.

Gamba, C., E. R. Jones, M. D. Teasdale, R. L. McLaughlin, G. Gonzalez-Fortes, V. Mattiangeli, L. Domboroczki, I. Kovari, I. Pap, A. Anders, A. Whittle, J. Dani, P. Raczky, T.F.G. Higham, M. Hofreiter, D. G. Bradley, and R. Pinhasi. 2014. Genome Flux and Stasis in a Five Millennium Transect of European Prehistory. *Nature Communications* 5: 5257.

Gasc, C., E. Peyretaillade, and P. Peyret. 2016. Sequence Capture by Hybridization to Explore Modern and Ancient Genomic Diversity in Model and Nonmodel Organisms. *Nucleic Acids Research* 44(10): 4504–4518.

Giles, R. E., H. Blanc, H. M. Cann, and D. C. Wallace. 1980. Maternal Inheritance of Human Mitochondrial DNA. *Proceedings of the National Academy of Science* 77(11): 6715–6719.

Glocke, I., and M. Meyer. 2017. Extending the Spectrum of DNA Sequences Retrieved from Ancient Bones and Teeth. *Genome Research* 27(7): 1230–1237.

Gongora, J., N. Rawlence, V. Mobegi, H. Jianlin, J. Alcalde, J. Matus, O. Hanotte, C. Moran, J. Austin, S. Ulm, A. Anderson, G. Larson, and A. Cooper. 2008. Indo-Europeans and Asian Origins for Chilean and Pacific Chickens Revealed by mtDNA. *Proceedings of the National Academy of Sciences* 105(30): 10308–10313.

Gosden, C., J. Allen, W. Ambrose, D. Anson, J. Golson, R. Green, P. Kirch, I. Lilley, J. Specht, and M. Spriggs. 1989. Lapita Sites of the Bismarck Archipelago. *Antiquity* 63: 561–586.

Green, R. C. 1979. Lapita. In *The Prehistory of Polynesia*, ed. J. D. Jennings, 27–60. Cambridge: Harvard University Press.

Green, R. C. 1991. Near and Remote Oceania: Disestablishing 'Melanesia' in Culture History. In *Man and a Half: Essays in Pacific Anthropology and Ethnobiology in Honour of Ralph Bulmer*, ed. A. K. Pawley, 491–502. Auckland: Polynesian Society.

Green, R. E., J. Krause, A. W. Briggs, T. Maricic, U. Stenzel, M. Kircher, N. Patterson, H. Li, W. Zhai, M. H.-Y. Fritz, N. F. Hansen, E. Y. Durand, A.-S. Malaspinas, J. D. Jensen, T. Marques-Bonet, C. Alkan, K. Prufer, M. Mayer, H. A. Burbano, J. M. Good, R. Schultz, A. Aximu-Petri, A. Butthof, B. Hober, B. Hoffner, M. Siegemund, A. Weihmann, C. Nusbaum, E. S. Lander, C. Russ, N. Novod, J. Affourtit, M. Egholm, C. Verna, P. Rudan, D. Brajkovic, Z. Kucan, I. Gusic, V. B. Doronichev, L. V. Golovanova, C. Lalueza-Fox, M. de la Rasilla, J. Fortea, A. Rosas, R. W. Schmitz, P.L.F. Johnson, E. E. Eichler, D. Falush, E. Birney, J. C. Mullikin, M. Slatkin, R. Nielsen, J. Kelso, M. Lachmann, D. Reich, and S. Pääbo. 2010. A Draft Sequence of the Neandertal Genome. *Science* 328(5979): 710.

Green, R. E., A.-S. Malaspinas, J. Krause, A. W. Briggs, P.L.F. Johnson, C. Uhler, M. Meyer, J. M. Good, T. Maricic, U. Stenzel, K. Prufer, M. Siebauer, H. A. Burbano, M. Ronan, J. M. Rothberg, M. Egholm, P. Rudan, D. Brajkovic, Z. Kucan, I. Gusic, M. Wikstrom, L. Laakkonen, J. Kelso, M. Slatkin, and S. Pääbo. 2008. A Complete Neandertal Mitochondrial Genome Sequence Determined by High-Throughput Sequencing. *Cell* 134(3): 416–426.

Grieg, K., A. Gosling, C. J. Collins, J. Boocock, K. McDonald, D. J. Addison, M. S. Allen, B. David, M. Gibbs, C.F.W. Higham, F. Liu, I. J. McNiven, S. O'Connor, C. H. Tsang, R. Walter, and E. Matisoo-Smith. 2018. Complex History of Dog (*Canis familiaris*) Origins and Translocations in the Pacific Revealed by Ancient Mitogenomes. *Scientific Reports* 8(9130): 1–9.

Hage, P., and J. Marck. 2003. Matrilineality and the Melanesian Origin of Polynesian Y Chromosomes. *Current Anthropology* 44: 121–127.

Hagelberg, E., and J. B. Clegg. 1991. Isolation and Characterization of DNA from Archaeological Bone. *Proceedings of the Royal Society B: Biological Sciences* 244(1309): 45–50.

Hagelberg, E., and J. B. Clegg. 1993. Genetic Polymorphisms in Prehistoric Pacific Islanders Determined by Analysis of Ancient Bone DNA. *The Royal Society* 252: 163–70.

Hagelberg, E., S. Quevedo, D. Turbon, and J. B. Clegg. 1994. DNA from Ancient Easter Islanders. *Nature* 369(6475): 25.

Hansen, H. B., P. B. Damgaard, A. Margaryan, J. Stenderup, N. Lynnerup, E. Willerslev, and

M. E. Allentoft. 2017. Comparing Ancient DNA Preservation in Petrous Bone and Tooth Cementum. *PLoS ONE* 12 (1): e0170940.

Hill, A.V.S., and S. W. Serjeantson. 1989. *The Colonization of the Pacific: A Genetic Trail*. Oxford: Oxford University Press.

Hinkle, A. E. 2007. Population Structure of Pacific *Cordyline fruticosa* (Laxmanniaceae) with Implications for Human Settlement of Polynesia. *American Journal of Botany* 94(5): 828–839.

Hofreiter, M. 2012. Nondestructive DNA Extraction from Museum Specimens. In *Ancient DNA: Methods and Protocols*, ed. B. Shapiro and M. Hofreiter, 93–100. Totowa, New Jersey: Humana Press.

Hofreiter, M., J. L. Paijmans, H. Goodchild, C. F. Speller, A. Barlow, G. G. Fortes, J. A. Thomas, A. Ludwig, and M. J. Collins. 2015. The Future of Ancient DNA: Technical Advances and Conceptual Shifts. *Bioessays* 37(3): 284–293.

Hofreiter, M., D. Serre, H. N. Poinar, M. Kuch, and S. Pääbo. 2001. Ancient DNA. *Nature Reviews Genetics* 2(5): 353.

Holdaway, R. N., and C. Jacomb. 2000. Rapid Extinction of the Moas (Aves: Dinornithiformes): Model, Test, and Implications. *Science* 287(5461): 2250–2254.

Kayser, M. 2010. The Human Genetic History of Oceania: Near and Remote Views of Dispersal. *Current Biology* 20(4): R194–R201.

Ioannidis, A. G., J. Blanco-Portillo, K. Sandoval, E. Hagelberg, J. F. Miquel-Poblete, J. V. Moreno-Mayar, J. E. Rodríguez-Rodríguez, C. D. Quinto-Cortés, K. Auckland, K., Parks, K. Robson, A.V.S. Hill, M. C. Avila-Arcos, A. Sockell, J. R. Homburger, G. L. Wojcik, K. C. Barnes, L. Herrera, S. Berríos, M. Acuña, E. Llop, C. Eng, S. Huntsman, E. G. Burchard, C. R. Gignoux, L. Cifuentes, R. A. Verdugo, M. Moraga, A. J. Mentzer, C. D. Bustamante, A. and Moreno-Estrada. 2020. Native American Gene Flow into Polynesia Predating Easter Island Settlement. *Nature* 583: 572–577.

Kehlmaier, C., A. Barlow, A. K. Hastings, M. Vamberger, J. L. Paijmans, D. W. Steadman, N. A. Albury, R. Franz, M. Hofreiter, and U. Fritz. 2017. Tropical Ancient DNA Reveals Relationships of the Extinct Bahamian Giant Tortoise *Chelonoidis alburyorum*. *Proceedings of the Royal Society B: Biological Sciences* 284 (1846).

Kirch, P. V. 1997. *The Lapita Peoples*. Cambridge: Blackwell.

Knapp, M., K. A. Horsburgh, S. Prost, J. Stanton, H. R. Buckley, R. K. Walter, and E. A. Matisoo-Smith. 2012. Complete Mitochondrial DNA Genome Sequences from the First New Zealanders. *Proceedings of the National Academy of Sciences* 109 (45): 18350–18354.

Knapp, M., and M. Hofreiter M. 2010. Next Generation Sequencing of Ancient DNA: Requirements, Strategies and Perspectives. *Genes* 1(2): 227–243.

Ko, A. M., C. Y. Chen, Q. Fu, F. Delfin, M. Li, H. L. Chiu, M. Stoneking, and Y. C. Ko. 2014. Early Austronesians: Into and Out of Taiwan. *American Journal of Human Genetics* 94(3): 426–436.

Larson, G., K. Dobney, U. Albarella, M. Fang, E. Matisoo-Smith, J. Robins, S. Lowden, H. Finlayson, T. Brand, E. Willerslev, and P. Rowley-Conwy. 2005. Worldwide Phylogeography of Wild Boar Reveals Multiple Centers of Pig Domestication. *Science* 307 (5715): 1618–1621.

Larson, G., T. Cucchi, M. Fujita, E. Matisoo-Smith, J. Robins, A. Anderson, B. Rolett, M. Spriggs, G. Dolman, T. Kim, N. Thuy, E. Randi, M. Doherty, R. Due, R. Bollt, T. Djubiantono, B. Griffin, M. Intoh, E. Keane, P. Kirch, M. Li, M. Morwood, L. Pedrina, P. Piper, R. Rabett, P. Shooter, G. Van den Bergh, E. West, S. Wickler, J. Yuan, A. Cooper, and K. Dobney. 2007. Phylogeny and Ancient DNA of *Sus* Provides Insights into Neolithic Expansion in Island Southeast Asia and Oceania. *Proceedings of the National Academy of Sciences* 104: 4834–4839.

Lindahl, T. 1993. Instability and Decay of the Primary Structure of DNA. *Nature* 362: 709–715.

Lipson, M., P. Skoglund, M. Spriggs, F. Valentin, S. Bedford, R. Sing, H. Buckley, I. Phillip, G. K.

Ward, S. Mallick, N. Rohland, N. Broomandkhoshbact, O. Cheronet, M. Ferry, T. K. Harper, M. Michel, J. Oppenheimer, K. Sirak, K. Stewardson, K. Auckland, A.V.S. Hill, K. Maitland, S. J. Oppenheimer, T. Parks, K. Robson, T. N. Williams, D. J. Kennett, A. J. Mentzer, R. Pinhasi, and D. Reich. 2018. Population Turnover in Remote Oceania Shortly after Initial Settlement. *Current Biology* 28(7): 1157–1165.

Llamas, B., K. M. Harkins, and L. Fehren-Schmitz. 2017a. Genetic Studies of the Peopling of the Americas: What Insights Do Diachronic Mitochondrial Genome Datasets Provide? *Quaternary International* 444: 26–35.

Llamas, B., G. Valverde, L. Fehren-Schmitz, L. S. Weyrich, A. Cooper and W. Haak. 2017b. From the Field to the Laboratory: Controlling DNA Contamination in Human Ancient DNA Research in the High-throughput Sequencing Era. *STAR: Science & Technology of Archaeological Research* 3(1): 1–14.

Lum, J. K., and R. L. Cann. 1998. mtDNA and Language Support a Common Origin of Micronesians and Polynesians in Island Southeast Asia. *American Journal of Physical Anthropology* 105(2): 109–119.

Lum, J. K., and R. L. Cann. 2000. mtDNA Lineage Analyses: Origins and Migrations of Micronesians and Polynesians. *American Journal of Physical Anthropology* 113(2): 151–168.

Manne, T., B. David, F. Petchey, M. Leavesley, G. Roberts, K. Szabo, C. Urwin, I. J. McNiven, and T. Richards. 2020. How Long Have Dogs Been in Melanesia? New Evidence from Caution Bay, South Coast of Papua New Guinea. *Journal of Archaeological Science: Reports* 30: 102255.

Marciniak, S., J. Klunk, A. Devault, J. Enk, and H. N. Poinar. 2015. Ancient Human Genomics: The Methodology Behind Reconstructing Evolutionary Pathways. *Journal of Human Evolution* 79: 21–34.

Mardis, E. R. 2008. Next-generation DNA Sequencing Methods. *Annual Review of Genomics and Human Genetics* 9: 387–402.

Maricic, T., M. Whitten, and S. Pääbo. 2010. Multiplexed DNA Sequence Capture of Mitochondrial Genomes Using PCR Products. *PLoS ONE* 5(11): e14004.

Matisoo-Smith, E. A. 1994. The Human Colonisation of Polynesia. A Novel Approach: Genetic Analyses of the Polynesian Rat (*Rattus exulans*). *Journal of the Polynesian Society* 103: 75–87.

Matisoo-Smith, E. A. 2007. Animal Translocations, Genetic Variation and the Human Settlement of the Pacific. In *Genes, Language and Culture History in the Southwest Pacific,* ed. J. Friedlander, 157–170. Oxford: Oxford University Press.

Matisoo-Smith, E. A. 2009. The Commensal Model for Human Settlement of the Pacific 10 Years on—What Can We Say and Where to Now? *Journal of Island and Coastal Archaeology* 4(2): 151–163.

Matisoo-Smith, E. 2015. Ancient DNA and the Human Settlement of the Pacific: A Review. *Journal of Human Evolution* 79: 93–104.

Matisoo-Smith, E., and K. A. Horsburgh. 2012. *DNA for Archaeologists.* New York: Routledge.

Matisoo-Smith, E., R. M. Roberts, G. J. Irwin, J. S. Allen, D. Penny, and D. M. Lambert. 1998. Patterns of Prehistoric Human Mobility in Polynesia Indicated by mtDNA From the Pacific Rat. *Proceedings of the National Academy of Sciences* 95: 15145–15150.

Matisoo-Smith, E., and J. H. Robins. 2004. Origins and Dispersals of Pacific Peoples: Evidence From mtDNA Phylogenies of the Pacific Rat. *Proceedings of the National Academy of Sciences* 101(24): 9167–9172.

Melton, T., R. Peterson, A. J. Redd, N. Saha, A. S. Sofro, J. Martinson, and M. Stoneking. 1995. Polynesian Genetic Affinities with Southeast Asian Populations as Identified by mtDNA Analysis. *American Journal of Human Genetics* 57(2): 403.

Merriwether, D. A., J. A. Hodgson, F. R. Friedlaender, R. Allaby, S. Cerchio, G. Koki, and J. S. Friedlaender. 2005. Ancient Mitochondrial M Haplogroups Identified in the Southwest Pacific. *Proceedings of the National Academy of Sciences of the United States of America* 102(37): 13034–13039.

Meyer, M., and M. Kircher. 2010. Illumina Sequencing Library Preparation for Highly Multiplexed Target Capture and Sequencing. *Cold Spring Harbor Protocols* 6: 1–10.

Montenegro, Á., R. T. Callaghan, and S. M. Fitzpatrick. 2016. Using Seafaring Simulations and Shortest-hop Trajectories to Model the Prehistoric Colonization of Remote Oceania. *Proceedings of the National Academy of Sciences* 113(45): 12685–12690.

Moodley, Y., B. Linz, Y. Yamaoka, H. M. Windsor, S. Breurec, J. Wu, A. Maady, S. Bernhöft, J.-M. Thiberge, S. Phuanukoonnon, G. Jobb, P. Siba, D. Y. Graham, B. J. Marshall, and M. Achtman. 2009. The Peopling of the Pacific from a Bacterial Perspective. *Science* 323: 527–30.

Mourier, T., S.Y.W. Ho, M.T.P. Gilbert, E. Willerslev, and L. Orlando. 2012. Statistical Guidelines for Detecting Past Population Shifts Using Ancient DNA. *Molecular Biology and Evolution* 29(9): 2241–2251.

Munoz-Rodriguez, P., T. Carruthers, J. R. Wood, B. R. Williams, K. Weitemier, B. Kronmiller, D. Ellis, N. L. Anglin, L. Longway, S. A. Harris, and M. D. Rausher. 2018. Reconciling Conflicting Phylogenies in the Origin of Sweet Potato and Dispersal to Polynesia. *Current Biology* 28(8): 1246–1256.

Navascués, M., F. Depaulis, and B. C. Emerson. 2010. Combining Contemporary and Ancient DNA in Population Genetic and Phylogeographical Studies. *Molecular Ecology Resources* 10(5): 760–772.

Nägele, K., C. Posth, M. I. Orbegozo, Y. Chinique de Armas, S. T. Godoy, U. M. González Herrera, M. A. Nieves-Colón, M. Sandoval-Velasco, D. Mylopotamitaki, R. Radzeviciute, J. Laffoon, W. J. Pestle, J. Ramos-Madrigal, T. C. Lamnidis, W. C. Schaffer, R. S. Carr, J. S. Day, C. A. Arredondo Antúnez, A. Rangel Rivero, A. J. Martínez-Fuentes, E. Crespo-Torres, I. Roksandic, A. C. Stone, C. Lalueza-Fox, M. Hoogland, M. Roksandic, C. L. Hofman, J. Krause, and H. Schroeder. 2020. Genomic Insights into the Early Peopling of the Caribbean. *Science* 369(6502): 456–460.

Nei, M. 1987. *Molecular Evolutionary Genetics*. New York: Columbia University Press.

Nieves-Colón, M. A., W. J. Pestle, A. W. Reynolds, B. Llamas, C. de la Fuente, K. Fowler, K. M. Skerry, E. Crespo-Torres, C. D. Bustamante, and A. C. Stone. 2020. Ancient DNA Reconstructs the Genetic Legacies of Precontact Puerto Rico Communities. *Molecular Biology and Evolution* 37(3): 611–626.

O'Connell, J., and J. Allen. 2004. Dating the Colonization of Sahul (Pleistocene Australia-New Guinea): A Review of Recent Research. *Journal of Archaeological Science* 31: 835–853.

O'Connor, S., and P. Hiscock. 2018. The Peopling of Sahul and Near Oceania. In *The Oxford Handbook of Prehistoric Oceania,* ed. E. E. Cochrane and T. L. Hunt, 26–47. Oxford: Oxford University Press.

O'Rourke, D. H., M. G. Hayes, and S. W. Carlyle. 2000. Ancient DNA Studies in Physical Anthropology. *Annual Review of Anthropology* 29: 217–242.

Oskarsson, M. C. R, C.F.C. Klütsch, U. Boonyaprakob, A. Wilton, Y. Tanabe, and P. Savolainen. 2012. Mitochondrial DNA Data Indicate an Introduction through Mainland Southeast Asia for Australian Dingoes and Polynesian Domestic Dogs. *Proceedings of the Royal Society: Biological Sciences* 279 (1730): 967–974.

Overballe-Petersen, S., L. Orlando, and E. Willerslev. 2012. Next-Generation Sequencing Offers New Insights into DNA Degradation. *Trends in Biotechnology* 30(7): 364–368.

Pääbo, S., H. Poinar, D. Serre, V. Jaenicke-Després, J. Hebler, N. Rohland, M. Kuch, J. Krause, L. Vigilant, and M. Hofreiter. 2004. Genetic Analysis From Ancient DNA. *Annual Review of Genetics* 38: 645–679.

Paijmans, J. L., M.T.P. Gilbert, and M. Hofreiter. 2013. Mitogenomic Analyses From Ancient DNA. *Molecular Phylogenetics and Evolution* 69(2): 404–416.

Patterson, N., P. Moorjani, Y. Luo, S. Mallick, N. Rohland, Y. Zhan, T. Genschoreck, T. Webster, and D. Reich. 2012. Ancient Admixture in Human History. *Genetics* 192(3): 1065.

Patterson, N., A. L. Price, and D. Reich. 2006. Population Structure and Eigenanalysis. *PLoS Genetics* 2(12): e190.

Peltzer, A., G. Jäger, A. Herbig, A. Seitz, C. Kniep, J. Krause, and K. Nieselt. 2016. EAGER: Efficient Ancient Genome Reconstruction. *Genome Biology* 17(1): 60.

Pickrell, J. K., and J. K. Pritchard. 2012. Inference of Population Splits and Mixtures from Genome-wide Allele Frequency Data. *PLoS Genetics* 8: e1002967.

Pickrell, J. K., and D. Reich. 2014. Toward a New History and Geography of Human Genes Informed by Ancient DNA. *Trends in Genetics* 30(9): 377–389.

Pinhasi, R., D. Fernandes, K. Sirak, M. Novak, S. Connell, S. Alpaslan-Roodenberg, F. Gerritsen, V. Moiseyev, A. Gromov, P. Raczky, A. Anders, M. Pietrusewsky, G. Rollefson, M. Jovanovic, H. Trinhhoang, G. Bar-Oz, M. Oxenham, H. Matsumara, and M. Hofreiter. 2015. Optimal Ancient DNA Yields from the Inner Ear Part of the Human Petrous Bone. *PLoS ONE* 10(6): e0129102.

Popejoy, A. B., and S. M. Fullerton. 2016. Genomics is Failing on Diversity. *Nature* 538: 161–164.

Posth, C., K. Nägele, H. Colleran, F. Valentin, S. Bedford, K. W. Kami, R. Shing, H. Buckley, R. Kinaston, M. Walworth, G. R. Clark, C. Reepmeyer, J. Flexner, T. Maric, J. Moser, J. Gresky, L. Kiko, K. J. Robson, K. Auckland, S. J. Oppenheimer, A.S.V. Hill, A. J. Mentzer, J. Zech, F. Petchey, P. Roberts, C. Jeong, R. D. Gray, J. Krause, and A. Powell. 2018. Language Continuity Despite Population Replacement in Remote Oceania. *Nature Ecology and Evolution* 2(4): 731.

Racimo, F., G. Renaud, and M. Slatkin. 2016. Joint Estimation of Contamination, Error and Demography for Nuclear DNA from Ancient Humans. *PLoS Genetics* 12(4): e1005972.

Redd, A. J., N. Takezaki, S. T. Sherry, S. T. McGarvey, A. S. Sofro, and M. Stoneking. 1995. Evolutionary History of the COII/tRNALys Intergenic 9 Base Pair Deletion in Human Mitochondrial DNAs from the Pacific. *Molecular Biology and Evolution* 12(4): 604–615.

Reich, D., R. E. Green, M. Kircher, J. Krause, N. Patterson, E. Y. Durand, B. Viola, A. W. Briggs, U. Stenzel, P.L.F. Johnson, T. Maricic, J. M. Good, T. Marques-Bonet, C. Alkan, Q. Fu, S. Mallick, H. Li, M. Meyer, E. E. Eichler, M. Stoneking, M. Richards, S. Talamo, M. V. Shunkov, A. P. Derevianko, J.-J. Hublin, J. Kelso, M. Slatkin, and S. Pääbo. 2010. Genetic History of an Archaic Hominin Group from Denisova Cave in Siberia. *Nature* 468: 1053.

Renaud, G., V. Slon, A. T. Duggan, and J. Kelso. 2015. Schmutzi: Estimation of Contamination and Endogenous Mitochondrial Consensus Calling for Ancient DNA. *Genome Biology* 16: 224.

Ricaut, F. X., T. Thomas, M. Mormina, M. P. Cox, M. Bellatti, R. A. Foley, and M. Mirazon-Lahr. 2010. Ancient Solomon Islands mtDNA: Assessing Holocene Settlement and the Impact of European Contact. *Journal of Archaeological Science* 37(6): 1161–70.

Rieux, A., and F. Balloux. 2016. Inferences from Tip-Calibrated Phylogenies: A Review and a Practical gGuide. *Molecular Ecology* 25(9): 1911–1924.

Rizzi, E., M. Lari, E. Gigli, G. De Bellis, and D. Caramelli. 2012. Ancient DNA Studies: New Perspectives on Old Samples. *Genetics Selection Evolution* 44(1): 21.

Rohland, N., and M. Hofreiter. 2007. Ancient DNA Extraction from Bones and Teeth. *Nature Protocols* 2(7): 1756–1762.

Rohland, N., H. Siedel, and M. Hofreiter. 2004. Nondestructive DNA Extraction Method for Mitochondrial DNA Analyses of Museum Specimens. *BioTechniques* 36(5): 814–821.

Sanger, F., S. Nicklen, and A. R. Coulson. 1977. DNA Sequencing with Chain-Terminating Inhibitors. *Proceedings of the National Academy of Sciences* 74(12): 5463–5467.

Savolainen, P., T. Leitner, A. N. Wilton, E. Matisoo-Smith, and J. Lundeberg. 2004. A Detailed Picture of the Origin of the Australian Dingo, Obtained from the Study of Mitochondrial DNA. *Proceedings of the National Academy of Sciences* 101(33): 12387–12390.

Schroeder, H., M. C. Ávila-Arcos, A.-S. Malaspinas, G. D. Poznik, M. Sandoval-Velasco, M. L. Carpenter, J. V. Moreno-Mayar, M. Sikora, P.L.F. Johnson, M. E. Allentoft, J. A. Samaniego, J. B. Haviser, M. W. Dee, T. W. Stafford, Jr., A. Salas, L. Orlando, E. Willerslev, C. D. Bustamante, and M. T. P Gilbert. 2015. Genome Wide Ancestry of 17th-century Enslaved Africans from the Caribbean. *Proceedings of the National Academy of Sciences* 112(12): 3669–3673.

Schroeder, H., M. Sikora, S. Gopalakrishnan, L. M. Cassidy, P. M. Delser, M. Sandoval-Velasco, J. G. Schraiber, S. Rasmussen, J. R. Homburger, M. C. Ávila-Arcos, M. E. Allentoft, J. V. Moreno-Mayar, G. Renaud, A. Gomez-Carballa, J. E. Laffoon, R.J.A. Hopkins, T.F.G. Higham, R. S. Carr, W. C. Schaffer, J. S. Day, M. Hoogland, M. Salas, C. D. Bustamante, R. Nielsen, D. G. Bradley, C. L. Hofman, and E. Willerslev. 2018. Origins and Genetic Legacies of the Caribbean Taino. *Proceedings of the National Academy of Sciences* 115(10): 2341–2346.

Schubert, M., L. Ermini, C. D. Sarkissian, H. Jónsson, A. Ginolhac, R. Schaefer, M. D. Martin, R. Fernández, M. Kircher, M. McCue, E. Willerslev, and L. Orlando. 2014. Characterization of Ancient and Modern Genomes by SNP Detection and Phylogenomic and Metagenomic Analysis using PALEOMIX. *Nature Protocols* 9: 1056.

Schubert, M., A. Ginolhac, S. Lindgreen, J. F. Thompson, K. A. Al Rasheid, E. Willerslev, A. Krogh, and L. Orlando. 2012. Improving Ancient DNA Read Mapping against Modern Reference Genomes. *BMC Genomics* 13(1): 178.

Seitz, A., and K. Nieselt. 2017. Improving Ancient DNA Genome Assembly. *PeerJ* 5: e3126.

Skoglund, P., B. H. Northoff, M. V. Shunkov, A. P. Derevianko, S. Pääbo, J. Krause, and M. Jakobsson. 2014. Separating Endogenous Ancient DNA From Modern Day Contamination in a Siberian Neandertal. *Proceedings of the National Academy of Sciences* 111(6): 2229–2234.

Skoglund, P., C. Posth, K. Sirak, M. Spriggs, F. Valentin, S. Bedford, G. R. Clark, C. Reepmeyer, F. Petchey, D. Fernandes, Q. Fu, E. Harney, M. Lipson, S. Mallick, M. Novak, N. Rohland, K. Stewardson, S. Abdullah, M. P. Cox, F. R. Friedlander, J. S. Friedlander, T. Kivisild, G. Koki, P. Kusuma, D. A. Merriwether, F.-X. Ricaut, J.T.S. Wee, N. Patterson, J. Krause, R. Pinhasi, and D. Reich. 2016. Genomic Insights Into the Peopling of the Southwest Pacific. *Nature* 538(7626): 510.

Slatkin, M. 2016. Statistical Methods for Analyzing Ancient DNA from Hominins. *Current Opinion in Genetics & Development* 41: 72–76.

Slon, V., C. Hopfe, C. L. Weiß, F. Mafessoni, M. de la Rasilla, C. Lalueza-Fox, A. Rosas, M. Soressi, M. V. Knul, R. Miller, and J. R. Stewart. 2017. Neandertal and Denisovan DNA from Pleistocene Sediments. *Science* 356(6338): 605–608.

Smith, C. I., A. T. Chamberlain, M. S. Riley, A. Cooper, C. B. Stringer, and M. J. Collins. 2001. Not Just Old But Old and Cold? *Nature* 410: 771–772.

Stone, A. C., and M. Stoneking. 1999. Analysis of Ancient DNA from a Prehistoric Amerindian Cemetery. *Philosophical Transactions of the Royal Society B: Biological Science* 354(1379): 153–159.

Stoneking, M., and J. Krause. 2011. Learning about Human Population History from Ancient and Modern Genomes. *Nature Reviews Genetics* 12(9): 603–614.

Storey, A. A., D. Quiroz, J. Ramirez, N. Beavan-Athfield, D. Addison, R. Walter, T. Hunt, J. S. Athens, L. Huynen, and E. Matisoo-Smith. 2008. Pre-Columbian Chickens, Dates, Isotopes, and mtDNA (and Reply). *Proceedings of the National Academy of Sciences* 105: E99–E102.

Storey, A. A., J. Ramirez, D. Quiroz, D. Burley, D. Addison, R. Walter, A. Anderson, T. Hunt, J. S. Athens, L. Huynen, and E. Matisoo-Smith. 2007. Radiocarbon and DNA Evidence for a

Pre-Columbian Introduction of Polynesian Chickens to Chile. *Proceedings of the National Academy of Sciences* 104(25): 10335–10339.

Tabbada, K. A., J. Trejaut, J. H. Loo, Y. M. Chen, M. Lin, M. Mirazón-Lahr, T. Kivisild, and M.C.A. De Ungria. 2010. Philippine Mitochondrial DNA Diversity: A Populated Viaduct between Taiwan and Indonesia? *Molecular Biology and Evolution* 27 (1): 21–31.

Thomson, V. A., P. Lebrasseur, J. J. Austin, T. L. Hunt, D. A. Burney, T. Denham, N. J. Rawlence, J. R. Wood, J. Gongora, L. G. Flink, A. Linderholm, K. Dobney, G. Larson, and A. Cooper. 2014. Using Ancient DNA to Study the Origins and Dispersal of Ancestral Polynesian Chickens across the Pacific. *Proceedings of the National Academy of Sciences* 111(13): 4826–31.

Underhill, P. A., and T. Kivisild. 2007. Use of Y chromosome and Mitochondrial DNA Population Structure in Tracing Human Migrations. *Annual Review of Genetics* 41: 539–564.

West, C., C. A. Hofman, S. Ebbert, J. Martin, S. Shirazi, S. Dunning, and J. E. Maldonado. 2017. Integrating Archaeology and Ancient DNA Analysis to Address Invasive Species Colonization in the Gulf of Alaska. *Conservation Biology* 31(5): 1163–1172.

Weyrich, L. S., K. Dobney, and A. Cooper. 2015. Ancient DNA Analysis of Dental Calculus. *Journal of Human Evolution* 79: 119–124.

Willerslev, E., A. J. Hansen, J. Binladen, T. B. Brand, M.T.P. Gilbert, B. Shapiro, M. Bunce, C. Wiuf, D. A. Gilichinsky, and A. Cooper. 2003. Diverse Plant and Animal Genetic Records from Holocene and Pleistocene Sediments. *Science* 300(5620): 791–795.

Wright, S. 1951. The Genetical Structure of Populations. *Annals of Eugenics* 15: 323–354.

Yang, D. Y., B. Eng, J. S. Waye, J. C. Dudar, and S. R. Saunders. 1998. Technical Note: Improved DNA Extraction from Ancient Bones Using Silica-based Spin Columns. *American Journal of Physical Anthropology* 105: 539–543.

Yang, D. Y., and K. Watt. 2005. Contamination Controls When Preparing Archaeological Remains for Ancient DNA Analysis. *Journal of Archaeological Science* 32(3): 331–336.

Zerega, N.J.C., D. Ragone, and T. J. Motley. 2004. Complex Origins of Breadfruit (*Artocarpus altilis*, Moraceae): Implications for Human Migrations in Oceania. *American Journal of Botany* 91(5): 760–766.

III

Regional Case Studies

9

What Is the Most Parsimonious Explanation for Where Pre-Columbian Caribbean Peoples Originated?

SCOTT M. FITZPATRICK, MATTHEW F. NAPOLITANO, AND JESSICA H. STONE

The Antillean chain of islands stretches for more than 3,000 km (1,900 miles) from the coastal margins of Venezuela toward the North American continent, along a gently curving arc westward to Cuba (Figure 9.1). The scattering of these and many other islands, including the Bahamas and those lying along the continental margins, provide a backdrop for examining what was the only maritime movement of peoples in the Americas where the landmasses they were venturing to were unseeable. These seafaring events that seemed to include both small-scale explorations and larger, more expansive migrations, involved the use of dugout canoes, wayfinding techniques, and knowledge of open-water conditions (winds, currents, and seasonal variations of these) that allowed populations to not only to settle new landscapes, but also return to their homeland to initiate or maintain important social connections (Callaghan 2003, 2008; Fitzpatrick 2013, 2015; Hofman et al. 2007; Keegan and Hofman 2017).

Archaeological research in the Caribbean has long been concerned with identifying the origins of peoples who first settled the Antilles (Edwards 1969; Fitzpatrick 2015; Keegan 2000; Keegan and Hofman 2017; Rouse 1986). Many of the islands are tantalizingly close to different mainland points along the circum-Caribbean. For example, northern Cuba is only circa 150 km away from the Florida Keys, western Cuba is about 200 km from the Yucatán Peninsula, and the northern Bahamas lie 100 km east of peninsular Florida. With the exception of Trinidad and Tobago, which are in close proximity to Venezuela and each other, the next closest island in the Antilles chain to the mainland is Grenada,

Figure 9.1. Map of the Caribbean showing general origin points and directions of various cultural behaviors and manifestations.

lying 130 km north of Venezuela. The distances between these landmasses were even smaller during periods of lower sea level, with possible intervening, now-submerged islands in between. What these distances signify from a biogeographical perspective is that, at least in terms of proximity—and all things being equal—there is the possibility that cultural and/or biological contributions occurred at some point in time from all three mainland areas.

In part, historical references provide some insight into the origins of Amerindian groups inhabiting the Caribbean. At European contact in 1492, and documented in hundreds of voyages after, these islands were home to numerous vibrant cultures that spoke different dialects; practiced farming; engaged in extensive interaction networks involving the translocation of both indigenous and nonnative plants and animals and exchange of artifacts, people, and ideas; and had developed elaborate rituals accompanied by a rich materiality that included objects and raw materials such as stone, lapidary items, and metal alloys (for example, see Fitzpatrick 2013, 2015; Giovas et al. 2012; Hofman et al. 2007; Keegan 2000; Keegan and Hofman 2017; Knippenberg 2007; Wilson 2007). Despite more than half a century of archaeological fieldwork in the region, the homelands of the first Caribbean colonizers, as well as the timing and the ways in which the islands were settled, are still debated. These questions are of great significance to archaeologists working in the Caribbean, similar to other regions in the world where colonization of previously uninhabited landmasses were settled rapidly and from multiple directions (for example, the Pacific colonization of Remote Oceania, the settlement of North America or continental Europe). So, from where did these original island colonists come?

Early archaeological research prior to the widespread use of radiocarbon dating suggested that the Antilles were probably first settled from somewhere in northern South America and moved in a stepping-stone pattern northward. This population dispersal, termed "Saladoid" after the stylistically distinct pottery found at the Saladero site in the Orinoco River Basin of Venezuela (Rouse and Cruxent 1963)—and which was linked to other similar assemblages scattered across most of the Lesser Antilles and Puerto Rico—provided a seemingly robust argument for linkages between the islands and mainland South America. As scholarly inquiry into pre-Columbian settlement and lifeways continued in the Antilles through the 1950s and 1980s, it became clear that not only were there a number of other major (and probably minor) population dispersals that had occurred, but that some of these were preceramic, dated back much earlier than once thought, and may have originated from somewhere outside of South America.

Some scholars have also suggested that peoples may have colonized—or at the very least, interacted with—peoples from North America or Mesoamerica. Archaeologists have proposed that similarities in language, stone artifacts, burial customs, pottery designs, agricultural practices, and geographical proximity between Florida and the Bahamas or other islands in the Caribbean indicated some level of interaction (Helms 1988; Marquardt 1990; Rouse 1986). Likewise, Wilson et al. (1998) proposed that lithics found in Belize and Cuba were indicative of a Mesoamerican origin for early Lithic (Archaic) Age peoples. These postulations are interesting and evocative, but have been largely untested and remain hypothetical.

Over the last decade, however, there has been a tremendous increase in the number and scale of archaeological projects in the Caribbean islands, coincident with the advent of more sophisticated analytical techniques such as ancient DNA (aDNA), stable isotopes, and statistical analyses that allow us to examine some of the earlier interpretations of where Amerindian groups first came from, their temporal ranges of occupation, and the degree to which they interacted with other peoples through trade and exchange systems. In this chapter, we attempt to synthesize recent data from across various fields of study to readdress the issue of where peoples in the Caribbean may have come from, to provide what we believe is the most parsimonious explanation for island Amerindian origins. This serves to not only highlight how much has changed over the last 20 years, but also target future areas of research that could help resolve questions that still remain.

Linguistics

When Columbus arrived in 1492, there were likely dozens of different languages and dialects spoken in the Caribbean within one major language family known as Arawakan. This family of languages is thought to have begun somewhere in Western Amazonia and is now found across vast swathes of South America, comprising around 40 extant languages with an equal amount having gone extinct (Aikhenvald 2016; Walker and Ribeiro 2011). The term "Arawak" was first introduced by Daniel Brinton (1871) who suggested that a distinction be made between those speakers in the Antilles and others found on the mainland, and so he called them the "Island Arawaks." There is often confusion using these labels to differentiate between groups because peoples in the Greater Antilles (Hispaniola, Cuba, Jamaica, and Puerto Rico) are often referred to as "Arawak," while those in the southern Lesser Antilles are called "Island Carib" after the

Cariban family of languages that predominate in lowland South America. But people living in these southern islands were actually speaking an Arawakan language. The confusion stems from there being close cultural connections between these islands and the South American mainland, which may have derived from an emergence of Carib in the islands "through a new synergism of island and mainland societies" just before European contact (Keegan and Hofman 2017: 15).

Overall, it is difficult to ascertain the types of languages that existed in the ancient past in the Caribbean and many other places where societies were nonliterate and only passed down information orally. In addition, the admixture or replacement of languages over time prior to European arrival in the region, combined with the devastating effects that contact had on Indigenous populations, makes it extremely difficult to use what is known linguistically to make inferences about points of origin. However, it is clear that the languages recorded historically, and those identified since European contact, all have their roots in South America.

Archaeological and Chronometric Data

There are three primary, though very general, models that have been used to explain how people first settled different parts of the Caribbean based on archaeological and chronometric data. One suggests that Cuba and Hispaniola were colonized during what was often termed the "Lithic Age" (Rouse 1986, 1992) (now generally embedded within the broader "Archaic Age" convention) circa 7000–5000 BP from somewhere in Mesoamerica, possibly Belize or the Yucatán. This argument rests upon similarities in stone tool technologies (for example, Rouse 1992: 69; Wilson 2007; Wilson et al. 1998; but see below for a discussion about the problematic radiocarbon record on Hispaniola). Sites are identified by a suite of stone tool types and include diagnostic macroblades removed from prismatic cores (Keegan 1994: 264; Reid 2009). Another coeval dispersal from South America was associated with the Casimiroid people during the Archaic as early as circa 5000 BP (Keegan and Hofman 2017: 200–202). Similarities in ground-stone tools have been interpreted as indicating cultural connections between islands and their homelands in South America, although it is possible that ground-stone technology developed independently on multiple islands (Keegan 2010: 12). Following these early entries, there are competing models that explain how and when other islands in the region were settled later during the Ceramic Age beginning circa 2500 BP (see Fitzpatrick 2015).

The first explanations on how humans settled the Caribbean focused on some version of a "stepping-stone" model that proposed a movement northward from somewhere in South America up through the Lesser Antilles until they eventually reached Puerto Rico, at which point they stopped and did not venture further west into the rest of the Greater Antilles or north to the Bahamas (for example, Drewett 2000; Keegan 2000; Rouse 1992). However, as archaeological research progressed on many islands, it became apparent that the earliest Archaic and Ceramic Age dates were found in the northern islands (see discussion in Keegan and Hofman 2017: 53–54; also Fitzpatrick 2006, 2015; Haviser 1991; Petersen 1996). While there have been various hypotheses developed to explain this curious phenomenon (for example, the paucity of research in the southern islands compared to the north), it is generally accepted that the Windward (southern) Islands were settled later or bypassed by the first migrants.

It should be noted that recent paleoenvironmental data recovered from lake sites on several islands (Siegel 2018; Siegel et al. 2015) dated to hundreds or thousands of years before the earliest known archaeological deposits, have been used as a proxy for human activity. For instance, Siegel et al. (2015) report an increase in charcoal particles and "ethnobotanically useful" native plants with changes in vegetation on the islands of Marie Galante and Martinique that are 3,000 years before the archaeological record. However, we do not view the results of paleoenvironmental survey as convincing evidence for human colonization, as the data used in these analyses cannot be unequivocally related to local events or unambiguously related to human behavior, in part because these "anthropogenic signatures" do not derive from pollen from introduced cultigens (see also Caffrey and Horn 2015; Giovas 2016; Prebble and Wilsmhurst 2009). Further, the argument largely rests on the analysis of microcharcoal particles (typically <100 microns), despite the difficulty that other studies have shown in trying to interpret the history of fire regimes using these types of datasets, which rests on including charcoal that is susceptible to long-distance dispersal and sediment mixing (for example, Higuera et al. 2007).

The second model, the southward-route hypothesis, is an attempt to reconcile the disparity of early dates in the southern islands and couple this with other lines of evidence such as computer simulations of seafaring. This model, which incorporates the analysis of larger radiocarbon data sets, argues that in both the Archaic and Ceramic Ages there were direct movements from South America to the northern Caribbean (Puerto Rico, northern Lesser Antilles) that initially bypassed the southern Lesser Antilles (Fitzpatrick 2006, 2013; Fitzpatrick et al. 2010; Keegan 2000). Giovas and Fitzpatrick (2014) later applied an ideal-free distribution behavioral ecology model to the southward-route hypothesis and suggested that settlement location was probably influenced by the attractiveness of resources, available land, and seafaring limitations. Together, these factors suggest that dispersals were fluctuating and opportunistic, resulting in settlement of the largest and most productive islands first, followed by a gradual movement south circa 2000 BP, and again around 500 years later, resulting in the occupation of Jamaica and the Bahamas for the first time, circa 1400 BP.

In general, colonization models of the Caribbean are problematic because many of the radiocarbon dates on which they are built are reported without complete information (for example, sample material, lab number) or derive from questionable contexts (for example, surface finds, unclear provenience; Fitzpatrick 2006; Napolitano et al. 2019). A recent meta-analysis of almost 2,500 dates from the Caribbean subjected each date to chronometric hygiene (a process whereby each date is evaluated and assigned a class value), an approach used successfully in other large radiocarbon datasets to identify acceptable dates (for example, chapter 6; Fitzpatrick 2006; Hassan and Robinson 1987; Spriggs 1989; Wilmshurst et al. 2011). In this research, the most secure dates (deemed Class 1 and Class 2) were modeled using Bayesian analysis to provide modeled colonization estimated date ranges. One of the strengths of incorporating Bayesian modeling into colonization studies is that it assumes the earliest dated archaeological deposit is not necessarily the founding colony/event for that island (see chapters 6 and 7; Rieth and Athens 2019 for other studies of island colonization using Bayesian modeling). Results of this exercise demonstrate that more than 50 percent of the reported dates for the Caribbean lack critical information. Interestingly, of the 2,500 dates, only 10 were identified as Class 1 (Napolitano et al. 2019).

Bayesian analyses of only the most reliable Caribbean radiocarbon dates from 26 islands indicate that: (1) the region was settled in a series of rapid, discontinuous population dispersals from South America; (2) colonists reached islands in the northern Antilles before those in the south; and (3) the data support the southward-route hypothesis and ideal-free distribution model for colonization (Napolitano et al. 2019). Results show that Trinidad was the first Caribbean island colonized by humans at circa *8420–7295 cal BP* (95 percent highest posterior density [HPD]),[1] but, given its close proximity to mainland South America at the time, it may not have required the use of watercraft to reach and is thus considered distinct from population dispersal into the Lesser Antilles. Following Trinidad, there appear to be two periods of overlapping island colonization events: one from circa 5800 to 2500 cal BP, and a second from circa 1800 to 500 cal BP. In this model, islands in both the Greater and Lesser Antilles were colonized in the first cluster, which tentatively overlaps with what has been referred to as the "Lithic" (or early Archaic) period settlement (Keegan 2000; Wilson et al. 1998). Barbados (*5885–4440 cal BP* [95 percent HPD]) and Curaçao (*5685–4845 cal BP* [95 percent HPD]), both in the Lesser Antilles, were settled nearly coeval with or before Cuba (*5360–4675 cal BP* [95 percent HPD]) and slightly before Puerto Rico (*4655–4305 cal BP* [95 percent HPD]) and Hispaniola (*4545–3930 cal BP* [95 percent HPD]), with St. Martin having been settled circa *5275–4940 cal BP* (95 percent HPD).

This analysis suggests that those islands in the Greater Antilles, northern Lesser Antilles, and ones very close to the mainland have the earliest reliable radiocarbon chronologies. The results are also consistent with the general predictions of island biogeography in which the closest and/or largest islands are settled first (Keegan and Diamond 1987; MacArthur and Wilson 1967). These are also supported by previous chronometric hygiene analyses (Fitzpatrick 2006), seafaring simulations (Callaghan 2001), and a recent comparison of Bayesian-modeled radiocarbon dates to the ceramic chronology of Grenada (Hanna 2019). Moving forward, applications of recently obtained island-specific marine reservoir corrections (ΔR) will improve the accuracy of radiocarbon calibrations and allow for the increasingly refined colonization chronologies (DiNapoli et al. 2021; see chapter 1).

Genetic Data

More recently, the application of genetic techniques to questions related to the initial colonization of the Caribbean has shed light on our understanding of population dynamics and migration trajectories in the region (see chapter 8). Population genetics studies of modern Indigenous populations in the Greater Antilles, Aruba, Dominica, and St. Vincent reflect varying combinations of mitochondrial lineages known from mainland North and South America, as well as African and European-derived haplogroups resulting from the region's colonial history. However, the degree to which each component contributes to maternal ancestry varies between islands (Benn Torres et al. 2013, 2015; Fuller and Benn Torres 2018; Martínez-Cruzado 2010; Schurr 2010). Generally, mitochondrial DNA (mtDNA) indicates a strong relationship with groups in northern South America, yet no single South American group seems to represent a source population (Toro-Labrador et al. 2003; Vilar et al. 2014). Interestingly, Y-chromosome data indicate no Indigenous contribution to modern Caribbean groups and instead reflect a mixture of predominantly African and some European haplotypes (Mendizabel et al. 2008; Vilar et al. 2014), though the number of islands studied has been limited.

A small number of studies has been successful in isolating aDNA from Late Ceramic Age (circa post-1500 BP) skeletal remains, but unfortunately, a lack of direct radiocarbon dates on many of these individuals prevents a finer resolution reconstruction of migration events. Evidence from Hispaniola mirrors frequencies and lineages in northern South America, suggesting the area as a point of origin for early colonizers, and reflecting an overall founder effect following initial settlement (Lalueza-Fox et al. 2001). A similar study of Cuban Ciboneys yielded closely related, but distinct, lineages from those on Hispaniola that are closely related to both South American and Central American groups (Lalueza-Fox et al. 2003; Lleonart et al. 1999). Data from the Guadeloupe Archipelago in the Lesser Antilles primarily indicate strong affinities with northern South American groups, along with some Mesoamerican haplotypes that have been attributed to the migration of the Garifuna, an admixed Indigenous and West African group found on St. Vincent that was brought to Mexico via the slave trade (Mendisco et al. 2015).

With the advent of next generation sequencing (NGS) and capture technologies, the ability to obtain genomic-scale aDNA from tropical and subtropical environments like the Caribbean has improved substantially (chapter 8). The whole genome sequencing of a ~1,000 year old Taíno individual from the Preacher's Cave site on Eleuthera (Bahamas) has demonstrated genetic similarity to Arawakan-speaking groups in northern South America, as well as population continuity with present-day Puerto Rican populations (Schroeder et al. 2018). A large-scale effort to obtain mtDNA genomes and autosomal genotypes from individuals at three sites in Puerto Rico demonstrated not only population origins in Amazonian South America, but also similar diversity patterns to present-day Puerto Ricans, indicating mtDNA population continuity today (Nieves-Colón et al. 2019). Most recently, a genome-wide study of 93 individuals from across the Greater Antilles and northern Lesser Antilles dating from 3200–400 cal. BP provides evidence for at least three separate population dispersals, the latest of which involved expansions out of South America (Nägele et al. 2020).

Additionally, the use of a commensal approach, which relies on the presence of nonnative terrestrial fauna as an indirect proxy for human movement (see chapter 8), has become a common tool in island environments. In the Caribbean, however, this approach has only been applied to guinea pigs (*Cavia porcellus*) and the Bahamian hutia (*Geocapromys ingrahami*) (Kimura et al. 2016; Lord et al. 2018, 2020; Oswald et al. 2020). Genetic analysis of guinea pigs from Puerto Rico, Antigua, and Carriacou demonstrates that there were at least two different mitochondrial DNA haplotypes, and hence separate introductions: one to Carriacou (southern Lesser Antilles), and the other to Puerto Rico. The initial genetic study (Kimura et al. 2016) showed that guinea pigs in the Caribbean likely originated from northwestern South America (Colombia), but the expanded complete mitochondrial genome sequencing by Lord et al. (2018) indicates that there was a minimum of two introductions (see also Lord et al. 2020). Due to a lack of any aDNA sequences for guinea pig in South America, it is not yet possible to refine where they may have originated.

Together, these data complement both archaeological and linguistic evidence for population origins in northern South America via multiple waves of migration. However, without additional well-dated individuals from islands not yet represented in these studies, a finer resolution understanding of population relationships and migration trajectories cannot be made.

Isotopic Analyses

Stable isotope analysis is based on the assumption that "you are what you eat," and the use of carbon ($\delta^{13}C$) and nitrogen ($\delta^{15}N$) from human skeletal remains has become a standard method in bioarchaeology for evaluating diet and subsistence. The addition of oxygen ($^{18}O/^{16}O$), strontium ($^{87}Sr/^{86}Sr$), lead ($^{20n}Pb/^{204}Pb$), and others have also become increasingly useful in studies of regional human and faunal mobility (Ambrose and Krigbaum 2003; Price et al. 2002; see chapter 1).

Exchange of fauna in the Caribbean has been demonstrated with the presence of nonnative mammalian taxa throughout the region, including dog (*Canis lupus familiaris*), agouti (*Dasyprocta* sp.), deer (*Mazama* sp. and *Odocoileus virginiana*), armadillo (*Dasypus* sp.), and opossum (*Didelphis marsupialis*) (Giovas et al. 2016; Laffoon et al. 2014; see below for discussion of artifacts). $^{87}Sr/^{86}Sr$ analysis from sites in the Guadeloupe archipelago yielded evidence of nonlocal dogs associated with both local and nonlocal humans, suggesting the possibility that some migrants brought dogs with them, compared to Hispaniola where dogs have only yielded local signatures. Nonlocals from Guadeloupe could not be traced to a specific island of original residence, but are likely from the northern Lesser Antilles or one of a few small areas on Puerto Rico (Laffoon et al. 2013, 2017). $^{87}Sr/^{86}Sr$ and lead ($^{206}Pb/^{204}Pb,^{207}Pb/^{204}Pb,^{208}Pb/^{204}Pb$) analysis of agouti and opossum from the Lesser Antilles (Nevis, Carriacou, and Mustique) demonstrated strontium intraisland variability, but found problems with lead analysis due to modern contamination (Giovas et al. 2016). However, $^{87}Sr/^{86}Sr$ results also showed that both agouti and opossum samples reflected living established populations on both Carriacou and Nevis, suggesting possible captive management of these taxa during the Ceramic Age (Giovas et al. 2016).

Isotopic analyses of human tooth enamel from remains have only been conducted on a few islands in the region, but have yielded interesting information related to interisland social relationships. At Anse a la Gourde, Guadeloupe, nonlocal individuals possess a variety of $^{87}Sr/^{86}Sr$ isotopic signatures, suggesting relationships with multiple islands, and some aspects of mortuary treatment also appear to reflect these differences. However, dietary isotopic signatures are similar across both local and nonlocal individuals (Booden et al. 2008; Laffoon 2013; Laffoon and de Vos 2011). Strontium and oxygen isotopic analysis conducted on an individual from Manzanilla, Trinidad, which was found to be nonlocal, lent support to archaeological evidence for connections between the South American mainland and Trinidad as would be expected. Similarly, nonlocal signatures from an individual at El Chorro de Maíta, Cuba, were supported by nonlocal mortuary treatment, cranial modification, and dietary distinctions that may demonstrate links to Mesoamerica (Laffoon et al. 2017). Interestingly, on the island of Carriacou in the southern Lesser Antilles, variation in mortuary context does not appear to indicate a difference of residence prior to living on Carriacou (Stone et al., pers. comm.). Testing of demographic models with a regional $^{87}Sr/^{86}Sr$ data set by Laffoon and Leppard (2018) show that across the Caribbean, the presence of nonlocals varies between islands and can range from zero to over 50 percent, with an apparent decrease in mobility over time. Together, these data suggest that $^{87}Sr/^{86}Sr$ analysis is a powerful tool for elucidating regional mobility, exchange patterns, and social relationships between islands in the Caribbean, particularly when combined with other lines of evidence, such as mortuary analysis or sourcing of artifacts.

Provenance and Sourcing Studies

Pottery and stone are two major material types that are conducive to provenance study and have been used in the Caribbean to try and source artifacts to their place of manufacture and/or raw material outcrops. Pottery is the most ubiquitous artifact type in the Caribbean, and there are dozens of different kinds of stone (Knippenberg 2007) providing ample opportunity to establish provenance. Although the number of these studies is comparatively few, this has recently begun to change.

Jadeitite—a semiprecious greenstone that only occurs in four insular Caribbean locations on Hispaniola and Cuba and two locations identified in Guatemala (García-Casco 2013; Harlow et al. 2014; Tsujimori and Harlow 2012)—is of particular interest to archaeologists because it was widely used in Central America among the Aztec, Maya, and Olmec, but has rarely been found on Caribbean sites (García-Casco 2013; Harlow et al. 2006, 2019; Rodríguez Ramos 2011).

In the last few decades, the number of jadeitite objects from Caribbean archaeological sites has increased with examples from the Dominican Republic (Hispaniola) and Puerto Rico in the Greater Antilles; Antigua, St. Croix, and St. Eustatius in the northern Lesser Antilles; and San Salvador in the Bahamas, as has the number of jadeitite sources (for example, García-Casco 2013; Harlow et al. 2019; Shertl et al. 2019). On Antigua, jadeitite celts and celt fragments were recovered from Mill Reef and the Elliot's site, both of which date to the Saladoid period (circa 1700–1450 cal BP) (García-Casco 2013; Harlow et al. 2006; Rose 1987). Mineralogical and petrographic analyses indicate that the celts found on Antigua and St. Eustatius were likely sourced from Guatemala, although results were not conclusive, and an object on San Salvador was sourced to Cuba (Harlow et al. 2019). However, in each of these examples, the geological "fingerprint" is not an exact match, meaning that there is unknown mineralogical variability in jadeitite, or the raw material was procured from an unidentified source (García-Casco et al. 2013; Harlow et al. 2006, 2019). In addition to the mineralogical variability, the small sample size in each of these studies is also a limiting factor (Fitzpatrick 2015; Harlow et al. 2019). In a notable exception, the Playa Grande site in northern Hispaniola appears to be a large-scale toolmaking site with more than 100 jadeitite tools recovered. The site is located 20–30 km away from the Río San Juan Complex and represents a direct link between artifacts and the procurement site (Shertl et al. 2019).

It should be noted too that peoples in the Caribbean used many other types of materials for making artifacts, such as *guanín* (a gold-copper alloy known as *tumbaga* in the Isthmo-Colombian region of Central America), and teeth or skeletal elements from animals that originated or were translocated from South America. To date there have been no sourcing studies of *guanín*, although it does not occur naturally in the Caribbean islands and must have come from somewhere in South or Central America. Celts, pestles, grinding stones, abraders, stone balls, and stone tools, made from a variety of materials including nonlocal greenstones, basalt, diorite, gabbro, quartz crystal, and quartzite sandstone, are often found at Lucayan sites in the Bahamas (Berman 2011; Berman et al. 1999, 2013; Harlow et al. 2019). While lithic sourcing studies have shed light on long-distance exchange between islands, with the possible exception of Guatemala, there is little to evidence exchange networks at the time of colonization for many islands in the Caribbean.

Unfortunately, there has been a general paucity of published mineralogical or chemical studies on pottery in the region despite its pervasiveness. Petrographic thin-section analysis has been done sporadically and is fairly localized, having been restricted to only a few islands. These include some in the northern Lesser Antilles (Donahue et al. 1990); the Dominican Republic (Ting et al. 2016); and San Salvador in the Bahamas (Mann 1986); several studies from Carriacou (Fitzpatrick et al. 2009; Pavia et al. 2013); multi-island studies, including Carriacou, Barbados, and other islands in the Grenadines (Lawrence et al. 2016); St. Lucia (Isendoorn et al. 2008); and a PhD dissertation by Carini (1991) in which he conducted X-ray fluorescence (XRF) spectrometry, petrography, and various types of spectroscopy on assemblages from sites in Puerto Rico, St. Croix, St. Martin, Antigua, Trinidad, and Venezuela. Other studies have focused on the identification of clays and temper materials (for example, Hofman et al. 2005). While these studies have shown the usefulness of the technique in the Caribbean, there has been limited applicability for sourcing pottery to different islands, and never unequivocally to a mainland source. On Carriacou, none of the pottery appears to have been made locally, and some samples appear to come from Barbados (Pavia et al. 2013), indicating that interisland exchange of ceramics was occurring, as would be expected given the plethora of other evidence for goods, people, and so on, moving around through time (Hofman et al. 2008). In a separate study, analysis of pottery from Hacienda Grande, Puerto Rico, and Salt River, St. Croix—two sites dating to the Early Ceramic Age—demonstrates that they were manufactured from local sources and that potters on each island showed a preference for clays found in coastal plains and riverine locales (Van Thienen and Martínez Milantchí 2019). Although portable XRF (pXRF) analysis from these two sites shows a reliance on local clay sources, there are similarities in the construction technique, suggesting that recipes may have been shared between islands, perhaps through marriage or other networks of interaction (Van Thienen and Martínez Milantchí 2019).

Chemical compositional studies conducted on pre-Columbian Caribbean pottery are also few in number. Most have focused on the use of neutron activation analysis (NAA), with cases from Anguilla (Crock et al. 2008), the Dominican Republic (Conrad et al. 2008), Puerto Rico (Siegel et al. 2008), and Carriacou (Fitzpatrick et al. 2008). Less well established and rarely used techniques for pottery provenance have also been done on Amerindian figurines from the Los Roques archipelago near Venezuela (Kasztovszky et al. 2004), and pottery spanning the Early to Late Ceramic Age in Barbados from several different sites (Fitzpatrick 1996), using prompt gamma activation analysis and weak-acid extraction using inductively coupled argon plasma-emission spectrometer (ICAP-ES).

Because there have been relatively few mineralogical and compositional studies of pre-Columbian pottery in the Caribbean, there are substantial spatial and chronological gaps that have prevented archaeologists from using this artifact type to more robustly examine resource acquisition strategies (for example, clay and temper sources) and intra- and interisland or island-mainland exchange systems. To date, much of what is known about the region's population movements and interaction through pottery is still relegated to typological and stylistic inferences, though they point exclusively to South America, particularly the Orinoco River Basin in Venezuela where Saladoid and other pottery types have been found that are contemporaneous or even earlier than those in the islands.

Nonnative Plant Introductions

It is widely known that peoples living in the Caribbean prior to European contact were cultivating plants in smaller gardens and, in some cases, larger fields (see Newsom and Wing 2004; Reid 2018). It was once thought that manioc (*Manihot esculenta*) (Figure 9.2A), a tuber crop native to South America, was the primary cultigen, though an increase in micro- and macrobotanical research demonstrates that: (1) this was one of many plants introduced by Amerindians; (2) food production extends much deeper into the past than previously thought; and (3) manioc may not have been as dominant compared to other plants. What nonnative plants were translocated, when were they introduced, and can they help in determining where peoples may have originated from?

Some of the earliest evidence of plant use in the Caribbean and northern South America comes from stone tools found at the Eva 2 site in Guyana and St. John on Trinidad dating to between circa 7800 and 6000 BP. Starch grain analysis on grinding stones identified maize (*Zea mays*) (Figure 9.2B), sweet potato

(*Ipomoea batatas*) (Figure 9.2D), achira (*Canna* spp.), yams (Dioscoreaceae), legumes (Fabaceae) (Figure 9.2E), and chili pepper (*Capsicum* spp.) (Figure 9.2F), with wild plants, particularly marunguey (*Zamia* spp.) (Pagán-Jiménez et al. 2015). Despite Trinidad's proximity to the mainland, it is nonetheless indicative of the antiquity of food production in the region and its geographical scope. Other studies (for example, see Mickleburgh and Pagán-Jiménez 2012;

Figure 9.2. Various non-native plants introduced to the Caribbean: *A*, Manioc (*Manihot esculenta*) (by David Monniaux, CC BY-SA 3.0); *B*, Maize (*Zea mays*) (by inkknife_2000, CC BY-SA 2.0); *C*, Cohoba (*Anadenanthera peregrina*) (by Vojtěch Zavadil, CC BY-SA 3.0); *D*, Sweet potato (*Ipomoea batatas*) (by Melsj, CC BY-SA 4.0); *E*, Common bean (*Phaseolus vulgari*) (by PJeganathan, CC BY-SA 4.0); *F*, Chili pepper (*Capsicum annum*) (by KENPEI, CC BY-SA 3.0).

Reid 2018) indicate that Amerindians were bringing with them numerous wild plants into the Caribbean during the Archaic Age, and after circa 2500 BP, as Saladoid migrants entered the Antilles during the Ceramic Age, many more plant varieties, including both domesticates (Berman and Pearsall 2008; Newsom and Wing 2004) and psychoactive plants from South America such as tobacco (*Nicotiana rustica*) and cohoba (*Anadenanthera peregrina*) (Fitzpatrick et al. 2009; Pagán-Jiménez and Carlson 2014)—the latter of which contains the powerful mind-altering substance dimethyltryptamine (DMT) (Fitzpatrick and Merlin 2018; Figure 9.2C; see also Figure 9.4)—were introduced and became staples of ritual use or consumption (see Newsom and Wing 2004; Kaye 2018; Reid 2018). What is important to note is that all the plant varieties known to have been brought into the Caribbean by humans are of South American origin or were introduced there at some point prior to the colonization of the Antilles. To date, none appears to be indigenous to Mesoamerica or North America at any point in time before European contact.

Animal Translocations

As noted above, archaeological research demonstrates that humans translocated animals to or between various islands in the Caribbean. These included the hutia (Capromyinae)—which is native to the Caribbean islands but, with various species, moved to others (Figure 9.3A)—and numerous taxa introduced from South America, including agouti (Figure 9.3B), peccary (*Tayassu/Pecari* sp.) (Figure 9.3C), armadillo (Figure 9.3D), opossum (Figure 9.3E), guinea pig (*Cavia* sp.) (Figure 9.3F), and dog (Giovas 2017; Giovas et al. 2012; LeFebvre and de France 2014). Skeletal elements or artifacts made from deer (Giovas 2018a; Hofman et al. 2020) and pendants from jaguar (*Panthera onca*), tapir (*Tapirus terrestris*), and peccary teeth (Laffoon et al. 2014) have occasionally been found, but likely do not represent the movement of live specimens. Regardless, all of these animals and/or artifacts are found post-2000 BP during the Ceramic Age, but from where did they originate?

In their study of animal tooth pendants, Laffoon et al. (2014) used strontium ($^{87}Sr/^{86}Sr$) and oxygen ($\delta^{18}O/^{16}O$) isotope analyses to try and estimate their origins. While results were somewhat ambiguous, in that they were not able to pinpoint a source based only on the isotope signatures, they tentatively suggested that one of the two jaguar teeth originated from the Guiana Shield Region (northeastern South America); the other probably came from northwestern South America, Central America, or the Southern Lowlands of Me-

Figure 9.3. Various non-native animals introduced to the Caribbean: *A*, Demarest's (Cuban) Hutia (*Capromys pilorides*) (by Gerwin Sturm, CC BY-SA 2.0); *B*, Agouti (*Dasyprocta* sp.) (by brian.gratwicke, CC BY 2.0); *C*, Collared peccary (by Nilfanion, CC BY-SA 3.0); *D*, Armadillo (*Dasypus* sp.) (by Anrie, CC BY-SA 3.0); *E*, Opossum (*Didelphis* sp.) (by Rabipelao, CC BY 2.0); *F*, Guinea Pig (*Cavia* sp.) (by Marzper).

soamerica. Results were similarly broad for the tapir and peccary teeth, which had similar isotope values that pointed to either the Metamorphic Province of northern Central America, the Maya Mountains of Belize, or northern coastal South America.

To date, guinea pig is the only translocated animal that has satisfactorily undergone aDNA analysis (Kimura et al. 2016; Lord et al. 2018, 2020). Guinea pig is indigenous to the Amazonian highlands of South America, and so its general range is known, but not whether there were multiple introductions or from where they may have been translocated. aDNA work in conjunction with high-resolution radiocarbon dating of the Bahamian hutia—one of several species native to various islands in the Caribbean—have demonstrated the animal's presence prior to human arrival in the Bahamas, with dramatic population changes following human intervention (Oswald et al. 2020).

Overall, archaeological and genetic evidence for the presence of nonnative animals in the Caribbean points to northern South America as the source for all of the known introductions prior to AD 1492. Stable isotope analysis of jaguar, tapir, and peccary tooth pendants (Laffooon et al. 2014), while not currently capable of distinguishing the origin of these artifacts between several broad areas, is nonetheless intriguing, though the transport of smaller artifacts is on a different scale than that of live animals.

Iconographic Imagery

Artistic representations of animals and humans are common in the material culture of the Caribbean, particularly during the Ceramic Age. Ceramics are particularly notable in this regard, with numerous anthropomorphic and zoomorphic designs and appliqué on vessels (for example, Waldron 2016), but other media such as shell, coral, stone, and wood were also common (Hofman et al. 2007; Samson and Waller 2010) (for example, see Figures 9.4A and 9.4B, which are humanlike representation objects from stone used for inhaling or holding *cohoba*). While some design elements clearly show animals such as frogs, fish, birds, bats, and different mammals, it is typically not possible to identify these to the taxonomic level of species or even genera. There have been some attempts by researchers, however, to demonstrate linkages of artifacts or artistic representations to specific mainland areas based on different stylistic and visual characteristics, including the well-known early (Cedrosan) Saladoid pottery (Figure 9.4C).

One type of object that has been proffered to represent a cultural connection

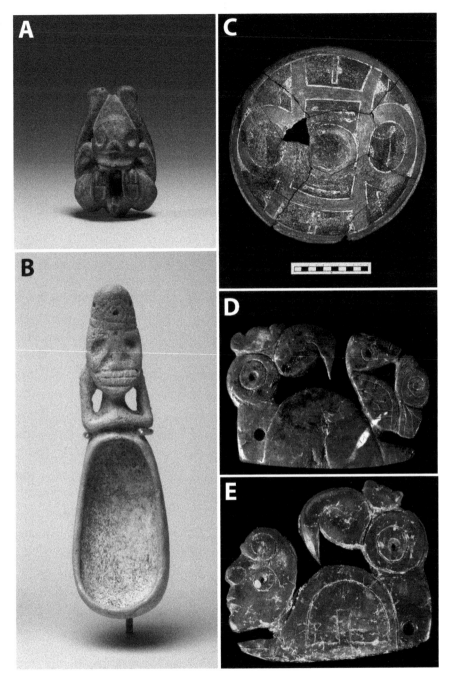

Figure 9.4. Examples of iconographic objects from the Caribbean: *A*, Cohoba Inhaler (by Walters Art Museum, CC BY-SA 3.0); *B*, Cohoba Spoon (by Brooklyn Museum); *C*, Reconstructed Cedrosan Saladoid bowl from Tecla, Guayanilla, Puerto Rico (photo by Jose Oliver); *D*, La Huecan jadeite/jadeitite bird pendant from Vieques (photo by Jose Oliver); *E*, La Huecan jadeite/jadeitite bird pendant from Vieques (photo by Jose Oliver).

to the Isthmo-Colombian region is an ornitomorphic (birdlike) pendant made from different greenstones (serpentinite, nephrite, jadeite) or calcite. These objects have been argued to represent either the Andean Condor (*Vultur gryphus*) (Chanlatte Baik 2013; Narganes Storde 1995; Rodríguez Ramos 2011, 2013) or the King vulture (*Sarcoramphus papa*) (Figures 9.4D and 9.4E). Rodríguez Ramos (2013: 161), in his discussion of possible Isthmo-Colombian and Antilles connections, notes that "[o]f particular relevance is the fact that the bird represented in Huecoid pendants is an Andean condor" and suggests that these iconographic images most closely resemble those found in Costa Rica. However, Giovas (2018b: 5) questions this interpretation, suggesting that because condors and vultures are typically associated not only with impurity and death, but also with renewal in pre-Columbian societies like the Maya, "that raptorial bird pendants may represent chimeric figures combining generalized cathartid attributes that reference the cosmological significance of the vulture-condor without need to identify a specific bird. We should thus exercise caution in over-literal interpretations of figurative elements, allowing for abstraction, the selective inclusion or exclusion of certain attributes, and the merger of multiple attributes not referable to a single species or even real animals." In addressing an Isthmo-Colombian origin or influence in design, Giovas (2018b: 5) also indicates that because the King vulture and Andean condor have overlapping ranges, "taxonomic identification cannot be used to disprove an Andean connection for the pendants," and that "nothing in these pendants allows definitive identification to a particular cathartid species . . . to adopt this approach gives primacy to Western ontologies based on Linnean taxonomy that we know from ample ethnography . . . aligns poorly with Amerindian perceptions of animals."

Nonetheless, there are a number of other examples of similar stylistic traits in artifacts, including the widespread "coffee bean eye" human motif, curly-tailed emblems found in Puerto Rico and Guadeloupe that resemble those found in Panama and Costa Rica, different lapidary and shell items, and a number of other examples of iconographic imagery that point to northwestern South America and/or parts of Central America that may have influenced Caribbean societies during the Ceramic Age (see Rodríguez Ramos 2013 for a review). There is no question that numerous iconographic representations found in the Antilles are linked to South America, and others may have their roots in the Isthmo-Colombian region. However, several issues remain that make it difficult to assign a provenance for the objects (for example, type of material, lack of study) or the ideas behind their manufacture (that is, who first developed a "style" and how was that moved somewhere else?). Because of these and other limitations, such as poor or coarse chronological associations, it is challenging, if not impossible, to ascertain whether iconographic imagery across a multitude of media originated from one location to another. As such, they remain less useful than other lines of evidence.

Seafaring Strategies and Capabilities

At European contact, many chroniclers and sailors, including Columbus himself, commented on the proficiency of Amerindian groups to travel around and between islands in canoes (for example, Columbus 1932; Lovén 1935; Mendez 1933; Shearn 2020). Many of these accounts clearly demonstrate that peoples living in the Antilles made canoes of variable sizes that were designed differently for specific purposes, and that wayfinding techniques helped seafarers navigate to specific destinations. There are differing and probably exaggerative accounts, however, as to the level of technological sophistication and seafaring capabilities of watercraft that was present at contact that are important considerations when examining colonization events.

In his review of pre-Columbian seafaring capabilities in the Caribbean, Fitzpatrick (2015) noted that there was no evidence for the use of sails, outriggers, or planking that were common features in watercraft construction in other parts of the world, with the possible exception of a washstrake being used to form the gunwale for raising the freeboard of dugouts, though this did not seem to be commonplace. This may have been the result, however, of the prevailing winds and currents in the region that both move westward and would have made eastward movement especially difficult, if not impossible in some cases without the use of the sail (see Fitzpatrick 2015). While there are very few existing artifacts or watercraft that are preserved in the archaeological record that would help in discerning what seafaring capabilities may have been (see Fitzpatrick 2013: 109–112), computer simulations have shown promise in helping to understand the strategies that Caribbean groups used to colonize and travel between mainland areas and islands.

The use of computer simulations for estimating seafaring capabilities, wayfinding strategies, and environmental influences on travel has created important avenues of inquiry in various island regions, including the Pacific (Callaghan and Fitzpatrick 2007, 2008; Davies and Bickler 2015; Di Piazza et al. 2007; Irwin 1994; Montenegro et al. 2014, 2016); Indian Ocean (Fitzpatrick and Callaghan 2008; chapter 12); areas adjacent to South America and Mesoamerica (Callaghan 2003; Callaghan and Bray 2007); and the Caribbean as a whole (Callaghan 2001, 2003, 2008; Slayton 2018). In terms of the latter, simulated seafaring has provided important complementary evidence that helps to explain where Amerindian groups in the Caribbean originated from, as well as some curious chronological disparities that currently exist in the archaeological record.

Callaghan's (2001, 2003) early research on colonization of the Antillean chain of islands, for example, challenged the prevailing notion that peoples moved northward in a stepping-stone fashion from Venezuela. Instead, he suggested that a direct route from South America to the very northern islands of the Greater Antilles or Virgin Islands was a more likely scenario given the prevailing currents and winds. He also demonstrated that these trips could have easily taken place between 7 and 10 days, well within the realm of survivability, and would have required limited navigational or wayfinding skills until land was sighted. Once the northern islands were reached, however, it would have been fairly easy to move in a southward pattern given the relatively close proximity and intervisibility between islands.

There are also a number of temporal anomalies that exist in our current understanding of when islands in the Caribbean were first colonized. As we discussed briefly in a previous section, once groups began populating the region, it appears that some islands were bypassed in favor of others, despite the apparent closeness of many islands, especially in the Lesser Antilles (Torres and Rodríguez Ramos 2008). For example, Jamaica and the Bahamas only appear to have been settled after about 1400 BP, while Puerto Rico, Hispaniola, and Cuba were settled thousands of years earlier. In addition, the Cayman Islands have no evidence for a pre-European contact occupation (Scudder and Quitmyer 1998). As Callaghan (2001) argues, there were no technological or environmental factors that would have necessitated stops at each and every island. Instead, various factors may have deterred or prevented people from stopping at islands. Volcanism (Callaghan 2008), availability of marine resources (Allaire and Mattioni 1983; Davis 2000; Hofman and Hoogland 2003) or lithic resources (Davis 2000), and avoidance of populated areas have all been suggested (see Keegan 2010: 17–18); in the case of Jamaica, challenging winds and currents may have played a role (Callaghan 2008) in preventing or dissuading settlement until more advanced canoe technologies or seafaring strategies were developed. These potential factors are not mutually exclusive and may have influenced decision making to some degree at different points in time.

Overall, an assessment of seafaring capabilities (Fitzpatrick 2015) coupled with computer simulations in the Caribbean (Callaghan 2001, 2003; Slayton

2018) suggest that open sea travel would have been easiest in the corridor be-tween mainland South America and the Greater Antilles, the trajectories of which would have differed seasonally. What still has merit is Callaghan's (2001) determination that northward travel from the Venezuelan coast to Grenada in a stepping-stone fashion up through the Lesser Antilles would have been difficult given currents and winds that bottleneck through the high islands. Alternative least-cost travel routes from Guyana into the Windward Islands modeled by Slayton (2018) also demonstrate the feasibility of reaching these islands from a far more easterly departure point, particularly during certain times of the year, and suggest that these may have been preferred routes during the Late Ceramic Age. Overall, findings from research into the origins of first Caribbean settlers (Callaghan 2001, 2003) dovetail well with radiocarbon evidence that supports the southward-route hypothesis described above (see Fitzpatrick 2006; Napoli-tano et al. 2019).

Discussion and Conclusions

How do we go about developing the most parsimonious model(s) for human colonization of the Caribbean? First, we need to consider what the most appro-priate definition of "colonization" is (see discussions in Part 1 of this volume), and second, we must decide what kinds of datasets are acceptable to address the research question. In some island regions, scholars have suggested that proxy paleoenvironmental data should supersede archaeological data or, at a mini-mum, be paired with archaeological data to satisfactorily identify colonization events. These are issues that have been debated in the Pacific for more than 20 years, but previous paleoenvironmental studies have not stood up to scrutiny, especially given that there are no archaeological sites found on any of the islands where these proxy data have been recovered that are contemporaneous (see Athens and Ward 2001, 2004; Kirch and Ellison 1994).

A recent paleoenvironmental study in the Caribbean by Siegel and colleagues (2015) has also argued that from a methodological perspective, archaeological methods are ill equipped to identify cultural deposits that have eroded, been submerged due to sea-level rise, or are now situated below volcanic deposits. We would argue, however, that in the absence of archaeological data, paleoeco-logical and paleoenvironmental proxy data are inadequate for identifying hu-man colonization events—in part, because they contain temporal uncertainties especially when age-depth modeling is used (Blaauw 2012). Even when "events" like charcoal lenses are directly dated, as in the case with the dates produced by Siegel et al. (2015), one cannot rule out how equifinality may cause similar signatures. For example, a charcoal lens may reflect a forest clearance event, yet stormwash events after a small-scale burning could redistribute charcoal fragments from older (or a series of past) fires, producing what appears to be a major forest clearance event. Studies that use proxy data to extend the date of human colonization by thousands of years, provocative as they may be, fail to explain gaps in their argument. For example, Siegel and colleagues (2015) suggest that humans who settled Grenada and Martinique spent circa 3,000 years modifying and managing the landscape before ever leaving an archaeological signature circa 2200 BP, despite archaeologists having worked on these islands for over half a century.

Further, it is important to distinguish between first human contact and semi- or permanent settlement (see chapter 2). In the former, peoples may reach islands and leave little or no trace of landfall. During this scenario, there is the possibility that biota were transferred and left behind (for example, rats), fires started, and resources acquired. But without more permanent habitation, it would be unlikely for *only* paleoenvironmental evidence to be left behind.

In the Caribbean, once an island in the Antilles is reached, others are fairly or easily visible, and it would make sense that, with all things being equal, populations would have been able to reach other islands at will. But archaeologically, this does not appear to be the case as the late colonization of the Bahamas, Jamaica, and much of the southern Lesser Antilles shows, in addition to the relatively recent (post-European arrival) occupation of the Caymans. There must be an explanation beyond that of the absence of earlier archaeological evidence that explains these anomalous patterns of colonization, though this will require further research across a broad spectrum of materials, sites, and islands to elucidate.

In this chapter, we have outlined evidence from 10 different sources of data—linguistics, archaeological and chronometric, modern and ancient DNA, isotopes, artifact provenance studies, faunal and floral studies of introduced taxa, iconographic representations, and computer modeling of seafaring—to provide what we believe is the most parsimonious explanation for where Amerindian groups likely originated from and where future research might be focused to better illuminate our understanding of these ancient diasporas. While not discussed in detail here, there is also abundant evidence for Saladoid settlement patterns in the Caribbean during the Early Ceramic Age, demonstrating clear similarities with those found in northern South America (for example, see Siegel 1996, 2010) that were intimately tied with cosmology and ceremonial space.

A review of these data here overwhelmingly supports a South American origin for peoples who settled the Caribbean at different points in time, though not necessarily from the same region. It is also possible that peoples on different islands were interacting with groups in different parts of Mesoamerica, though when and to what extent is not entirely clear.

Not every line of evidence presented here is equally useful in determining where peoples may have originated from, nor is adequate chronological data always available to provide sufficient temporal context. It should also be recognized that stylistically similar artifacts and the introduction of plants and animals may have occurred after the arrival of humans and is thus not representative of a colonizing venture. But, when these phenomena are combined, they paint a picture of provenance that is strongly indicative of South America being the place of origin for colonization of the Antilles chain of islands. Regardless of this finding, there still remains a paucity of archaeological research in northern South America (particularly Venezuela and Colombia) and the Isthmo-Colombian region as well as many islands, especially Cuba, Hispaniola, and the southern Lesser Antilles, that would help refine chronologies and provide new data sets with which to compare. Given what is currently known, it seems unlikely that Mexico or North America had substantive, or any, contribution to the peopling of the Caribbean, though many of the analytical techniques described in this paper are still in their infancy. It is quite possible that future studies using these or newly developed analyses may alter this perspective.

Note

1. Following conventional reporting standards, Bayesian modeled dates are rounded to the nearest five years and presented in italics to differentiate them from calibrated radiocarbon dates (see Hamilton and Krus 2018).

References

Aikhenvald, A. Y. 2016. *Arawak Languages*. Oxford: Oxford University Press.

Allaire, L., and M. Mattioni. 1983. Boutbois et le Godinot: Deux Gisements Acéramiques de la Martinique. In *Proceedings of the Ninth International Congress for the Study of the Pre-Columbian Cultures of the Lesser Antilles*, 27–38. Montreal: Centre de Recherches Caraibes.

Ambrose, S. H., and J. Krigbaum. 2003. Bone Chemistry and Bioarchaeology. *Journal of Anthropological Archaeology* 22(3): 193–199.

Athens, J. S., and J. V. Ward. 2001. Paleoenvironmental Evidence for Early Human Settlement in Palau: The Ngerchau Core. In *Pacific 2000: Proceedings of the Fifth International Conference on Easter Island and the Pacific*, ed. T. L. Hunt, C. P Lipo, C. M. Stevenson, G. Lee, and F. J. Morin, 164–177. Los Osos, California: Easter Island Foundation, Bearsville Press.

Athens, J. S., and J. V. Ward. 2004. Holocene Vegetation, Savanna Origins and Human Settlement of Guam. *Records—Australian Museum Supplement* 29: 15–30.

Benn Torres J., A. C. Stone, and R. Kittles. 2013. An Anthropological Genetic Perspective on Creolization in the Anglophone Caribbean. *American Journal of Physical Anthropology* 151: 135–143.

Benn Torres, J., M. G., Vilar, G. A. Torres, J. B. Gaieski, R. Bharath Hernandez, Z. E. Browne, M. Stevenson, W. Walters, T. G. Schurr, and The Genographic Consortium. 2015. Genetic Diversity in the Lesser Antilles and Its Implications for the Settlement of the Caribbean Basin. *PLoS ONE* 10(10): e0139192.

Berman, M. J. 2011. The Lucayans and Their World. In *Proceedings of the Fourteenth Symposium on the Natural History of the Bahamas,* ed. C. Tepper and R. Shaklee, 151–172. San Salvador: Gerace Research Centre.

Berman, M. J., and D. M. Pearsall. 2008. At the Crossroads: Starch Grain and Phytolith Analyses in Lucayan Prehistory. *Latin American Antiquity* 19(2): 181–203.

Berman, M. J., A. K. Sievert, and T. R. Whyte. 1999. Form and Function of Bipolar Lithic Artifacts from the Three Dog Site, San Salvador, Bahamas. *Latin American Antiquity* 10(4): 415–432.

Berman, M. J., P. L. Gnivecki, and M. P. Pateman. 2013. The Bahama Archipelago. In *The Oxford Handbook of Caribbean Archaeology,* ed. W. F. Keegan, C. L. Hofman, and R. Rodríguez-Ramos, 264–280. New York: Oxford University Press.

Blaauw, M. 2012. Out of Time: The Dangers of Aligning Proxy Archives. *Quaternary Science Reviews* 36:38–49.

Booden, M. A., G.A.M. Panhuysen, M.L.P. Hoogland, H. N. de Jong, G. R. Davies, and C. L. Hofman. 2008. Tracing Human Mobility with $^{87}Sr/^{86}Sr$ at Anse à la Gourde, Guadeloupe. In *Crossing the Borders: New Methods and Techniques in the Study of Archaeological Materials from the Caribbean,* ed. C. L. Hofman, M. Hoogland, and A. L. van Gijn, 214–225. Tuscaloosa: University of Alabama Press.

Brinton, D. 1871. The Arawakan Language of Guiana and Its Linguistic and Ethnological Relations. *Transactions of the American Philosophical Society* 14: 427–444.

Caffrey, M. A., and S. P. Horn. 2015. Long-term Fire Trends in Hispaniola and Puerto Rico from Sedimentary Charcoal: A Comparison of Three Records. *Professional Geographer* 67: 229–241.

Callaghan, R. T. 2001. Ceramic Age Seafaring and Interaction Potential in the Antilles: A Computer Simulation. *Current Anthropology* 42(2): 308–313.

Callaghan, R. T. 2003. Prehistoric Trade between Ecuador and West Mexico: A Computer Simulation of Coastal Voyages. *Antiquity* 77(298): 796–804.

Callaghan, R. T. 2008. On the Question of the Absence of Archaic Age Sites on Jamaica. *Journal of Island and Coastal Archaeology* 3(1): 54–71.

Callaghan, R. T., and W. Bray. 2007. Simulating Prehistoric Sea Contacts between Costa Rica and Colombia. *Journal of Island and Coastal Archaeology* 2(1): 4–23.

Callaghan, R., and S. M. Fitzpatrick. 2007. On the Relative Isolation of a Micronesian Archipelago during the Historic Period: The Palau Case Study. *International Journal of Nautical Archaeology* 36(2): 353–364.

Callaghan, R. T., and S. M. Fitzpatrick. 2008. Examining Prehistoric Migration Patterns in the Palauan Archipelago: A Computer Simulated Analysis of Drift Voyaging. *Asian Perspectives* 47(1): 28–44.

Carini, S. P. 1991. Compositional Analysis of West Indian Saladoid Ceramics and Their Relevance to Puerto Rican Prehistory. PhD dissertation, Department of Anthropology, University of Connecticut.

Chanlatte Baik, L. A. 2013. Huecoid Culture and the Antillean Agroalferero (Farmer-Potter) Period. In *The Oxford Handbook of Caribbean Archaeology*, ed. W. F. Keegan, C. L. Hofman, and R. T. Rodríguez Ramos, 171–183. Oxford: Oxford University Press.

Columbus, C. 1932. Fourth Voyage of Columbus. In *Select Documents Illustrating the Four Voyages of Columbus, Vol II, Second Series no. LXX*. London: Lakluyt Society.

Conrad, G. W., C. D. Beeker, C. Descantes, J. W. Foster, and M. D. Glascock. 2008. Compositional Analysis of Ceramics from La Aleta, Dominican Republic: Implications for Site Function and Organization. *Journal of Caribbean Archaeology* 2: 57–68.

Cooke, S. B., L. M. Dávalos, A. M. Mychajiliw, S. T. Turvey, and N. S. Upham. 2017. Anthropogenic Extinction Dominates Holocene Declines of West Indian Mammals. *Annual Review of Ecology, Evolution, and Systematics* 48: 301–27.

Crock, J. G., B. F. Morse, C. Descantes, J. B. Peterson, and M. D. Glascock. 2008. Preliminary Interpretations of Ceramic Compositional Analysis from Late Ceramic Age Sites in Anguilla and the Salt River Site in St. Croix. *Journal of Caribbean Archaeology* 8: 45–55.

Davies, B., and S. H. Bickler. 2015. Sailing the Simulated Seas: A New Simulation for Evaluating Prehistoric Seafaring. In *Across Space and Time: Papers from the 41st Conference on Computer Applications and Quantitative Methods in Archaeology, Perth, 25–28 March 2013*, ed. A. Traviglia, 215–223. Amsterdam: Amsterdam University Press.

Davis, D. D. 2000. *Jolly Beach and the Preceramic Occupation of Antigua, West Indies*. New Haven: Yale University Press.

DiNapoli, R. J., S. M. Fitzpatrick , M. F. Napolitano, T. C. Rick, J. H. Stone, and N. P. Jew. 2021. Marine reservoir corrections for the Caribbean demonstrate high intra- and inter-island variability in local reservoir offsets. *Quaternary Geochronology* 61(101126).

Di Piazza, A., P. Di Piazza, and E. Pearthree. 2007. Sailing Virtual Canoes across Oceania: Revisiting Island Accessibility. *Journal of Archaeological Science* 34(8): 1219–1225.

Donahue, J., D. R. Watters, and S. Millspaugh. 1990. Thin Section Petrography of Northern Lesser Antilles Ceramics. *Geoarchaeology* 5(3): 229–254.

Drewett, P. L. 2000. *Prehistoric Settlements in the Caribbean Fieldwork in Barbados, Tortola and the Cayman Islands*. London: Archetype.

Edwards, C. R. 1969. Possibilities of Pre-Columbian Maritime Contacts among New World Civilizations. In *Precolumbian Contact within Nuclear America (Southern Illinois University at Carbondale. Museum. Mesoamerican Studies)*, ed. J. C. Kelley and C. L. Riley, 3–10. Carbondale, Illinois: University Museum.

Fitzpatrick, S. M. 1996. Analysis on the Elemental Composition of Ceramics in Barbados during the Saladoid and Suazoid period. M.A. thesis, University of Montana.

Fitzpatrick, S. M. 2006. A Critical Approach to ^{14}C Dating in the Caribbean: Using Chronometric Hygiene to Evaluate Chronological Control and Prehistoric Settlement. *Latin American Antiquity* 17: 281–290.

Fitzpatrick, S. M. 2012. On the Shoals of Giants: Natural Catastrophes and the Overall Destruction of the Caribbean's Archaeological Record. *Journal of Coastal Conservation* 16(2): 173–186.

Fitzpatrick, S. M. 2013. Seafaring Capabilities in the Pre-Columbian Caribbean. *Journal of Maritime Archaeology* 8(1): 101–138.

Fitzpatrick, S. M. 2015. The Pre-Columbian Caribbean: Colonization, Population Dispersal, and Island Adaptations. *PaleoAmerica* 1(4): 305–331.

Fitzpatrick, S. M., and R. Callaghan. 2008. Seafaring Simulations and the Origin of Prehistoric Settlers to Madagascar. In *Islands of Inquiry: Colonisation, Seafaring and the Archaeology of Maritime Landscapes*, eds, G. Clark, F. Leach, and S. O'Connor, 47–58. Canberra: Australian National University Press.

Fitzpatrick, S. M., and M. Merlin. 2018. Introduction: Drugs from a Deep Time Perspective. In *Ancient Psychoactive Substances*, ed. S. M. Fitzpatrick, 1–19. Gainesville: University Press of Florida.

Fitzpatrick, S. M., M. Kappers, and C. M. Giovas. 2010. The Southward Route Hypothesis: Examining Carriacou's Chronological Position in Antillean Prehistory. In *Island Shores and Distant Pasts: Archaeological and Biological Approaches to the Pre-Columbian Settlement of the Caribbean*, ed. S. M. Fitzpatrick and A. H. Ross, 163–176. Gainesville: University Press of Florida.

Fitzpatrick, S. M., Q. Kaye, J. Feathers, J. A. Pavia, and K. M. Marsaglia. 2009. Evidence for Inter-island Transport of Heirlooms: Luminescence Dating and Petrographic Analysis of Ceramic Inhaling Bowls from Carriacou, West Indies. *Journal of Archaeological Science* 36: 596–606.

Fitzpatrick, S. M., J. A. Carstensen, K. M. Marsaglia, C. Descantes, M. D. Glascock, Q. Kaye, and M. Kappers. 2008. Preliminary Petrographic and Chemical Analyses of Prehistoric Ceramics From Carriacou, West Indies. *Journal of Caribbean Archaeology* 8: 59–82.

Fuller, H., and J. Benn Torres. 2018. Investigating the "Taíno" Ancestry of the Jamaican Maroons: A New Genetic (DNA), Historical, and Multidisciplinary Analysis and Case Study of the Accompong Town Maroons. *Canadian Journal of Latin American and Caribbean Studies* 43(1): 47–78.

García-Casco, A., and P. L. Gnivecki. 2019. Pre-Columbian Jadeitite Artifacts from San Salvador Island, Bahamas and Comparison with Jades of the Eastern Caribbean and Jadeitites of the Greater Caribbean Region. *Journal of Archaeological Science: Reports* 26: 1010830.

García-Casco, A., S. Knippenberg, R. Rodríguez Ramos, G. E. Harlow, C. Hofman, J. C. Pomo, and I. F. Blankco-Quintero. 2013. Pre-Columbian Jadeitite Artifacts from the Golden Rock Site, St. Eustatius, Lesser Antilles, With Special Reference to Jadeitite Artifacts from Elliot's, Antigua: Implications for Potential Source Regions and Long-distance Exchange Networks in the Greater Caribbean. *Journal of Archaeological Science* 40(8): 3153–3169.

Giovas, C. M. 2016. Pre-Columbian Amerindian Lifeways at the Sabazan Site, Carriacou, West Indies. *Journal of Island and Coastal Archaeology* 13(2): 161–190.

Giovas, C. M. 2017. The Beasts at Large—Perennial Questions and New Paradigms for Caribbean Translocation Research. Part I: Ethnozoogeography of Mammals. *Environmental Archaeology* 1–17.

Giovas, C. M. 2018a. Continental Connections and Insular Distributions: Deer Bone Artifacts of The Precolumbian West Indies—A Review and Synthesis with New Records. *Latin American Antiquity* 29(1): 27–43.

Giovas, C. M. 2018b. A Critical Appraisal of the Taxonomic Attribution of Raptorial Bird Pendants: Is the Condor King? Paper presented at the 27th Congress of the International Association for Caribbean Archaeology, St. Croix, U.S. Virgin Islands.

Giovas, C. M., and S. M. Fitzpatrick. 2014. Prehistoric Migration in the Caribbean: Past Perspectives, New models and the Ideal Free Distribution of West Indian Colonization. *World Archaeology* 46: 569–589.

Giovas, C. M., M. LeFebvre, and S. M. Fitzpatrick. 2012. New Records for Prehistoric Introduction of Neotropical Mammals to the West Indies: Evidence from Carriacou, Lesser Antilles. *Journal of Biogeography* 39(3): 476–487.

Giovas, C. M., G. D. Kamenov, S. M. Fitzpatrick, and J. Krigbaum. 2016. Sr and Pb Isotopic Investigation of Mammal Introductions: Pre-Columbian Zoogeographic Records from the Lesser Antilles, West Indies. *Journal of Archaeological Science* 69: 39–53.

Hamilton, W. D., and A. M. Krus. 2018. The Myths and Realities of Bayesian Chronological Modeling Revealed. *American Antiquity* 83(2): 187–203.

Hanna, J. A. 2019. Camáhogne's Chronology: The Radiocarbon Settlement Sequence on Grenada, West Indies. *Journal of Anthropological Archaeology*. 55: 101075.

Harlow, G. E., M. J. Berman, J. C. Párraga, A. Hertwig, A, García-Casco, and P. L. Gnivecki. 2019. Pre-Columbian Jadeitite Artifacts from San Salvador Island, Bahamas and Comparison with Jades of the Eastern Caribbean and Jadeitites of the Greater Caribbean Region. *Journal of Archaeological Science: Reports* 26: 101830.

Harlow, G. E., A. R. Murphy, D. J. Hozjan, C. N. de Mille and A. A. Levinson. 2006. Pre-Columbian Jadeite Axes from Antigua, West Indies: Description and Possible Sources. *The Canadian Mineralogist* 44(2): 305–321.

Harlow, G. E., S. S. Sorensen, V. B. Sisson, and G. Shi. 2014. The Geology of Jade Deposits. *Mineralogical Association of Canada, Short-Course Series* 44: 305–374.

Hassan, F. A., and S. W. Robinson. 1987. High-precision Radiocarbon Chronometry of Ancient Egypt, and Comparisons with Nubia, Palestine and Mesopotamia. *Antiquity* 61: 119–135.

Haviser, J. 1991. *The First Bonaireans*. Reports of the Archaeological-Anthropological Institute of the Netherlands Antilles, Number 9. Willemstad, Curaçao.

Helms, M. W. 1988. *Ulysses' Sail: An Ethnographic Odyssey of Power, Knowledge, and Geographical Distance*. Princeton: Princeton University Press.

Higuera, P. E., M. E. Peters, L. B. Brubaker, and D. G. Gavin. 2007. Understanding the Origins and Analysis of Sediment-Charcoal Records with a Simulation Model. *Quaternary Science Reviews* 26(13–14): 1790–1809.

Hofman, C. L., and M. L. Hoogland. 2003. Plum Piece: Evidence for Archaic Seasonal Occupation on Saba, Northern Lesser Antilles around 3300 BP. *Journal of Caribbean Archaeology* 4: 12–27.

Hofman, C. L., A.J.D. Isendoorn, and M. A. Booden. 2005. Clays Collected. Towards an Identification of Source Areas for Clays Used in the Production of Pre-Colonial Pottery in the Northern Lesser Antilles. *Leiden Journal of Pottery Studies* 21: 9–26.

Hofman, C. L., A. J. Bright, A. Boomert, and S. Knippenberg. 2007. Island Rhythms: The Web of Social Relationships and Interaction Networks in the Lesser Antillean Archipelago between 400 BC and AD 1492. *Latin American Antiquity* 18(3): 243–268.

Hofman, C. L., A. J. Bright, M. L. Hoogland, and W. F. Keegan. 2008. Attractive Ideas, Desirable Goods: Examining the Late Ceramic Age Relationships between Greater and Lesser Antillean Societies. *Journal of Island and Coastal Archaeology* 3(1): 17–34.

Hofman, C. L., L. Borck, J. Laffoon, E. Slayton, B. Scott, T. W. Breukel, C. Guzzo Falci, M. Favre, and M. Hoogland. 2020. Island Networks: Transformations of Inter-community Social Relationships in the Lesser Antilles at the Advent of European Colonialism. *Journal of Island and Coastal Archaeology*. DOI: 10.1080/15564894.2020.1748770.

Irwin, G. 1994. *The Prehistoric Exploration and Colonisation of the Pacific*. Cambridge: Cambridge University Press.

Isendoorn, A. D., C. L. Hofman, and M. Booden. 2008. Back to the Source: Provenance Areas of Clays and Temper Materials of Pre-Columbian Caribbean Ceramics. *Journal of Caribbean Archaeology* 2: 15–24.

Kasztovszky, Z., M. M. de Antczak, A. Antczak, B. Millan, J. Bermúdez, and L. Sajo-Bohus. 2004. Provenance Study of Amerindian Pottery Figurines with Prompt Gamma Activation Analysis. *Nukleonika* 49(3): 107–113.

Kaye, Q. 2018. Power from, Power to, Power over? Ritual Drug-Taking and the Social Context of Power among the Indigenous People of the Caribbean. In *Ancient Psychoactive Substances*, ed. S. M. Fitzpatrick, 149–175. Gainesville: University Press of Florida.

Keegan, W. F. 1994. West Indian Archaeology. 1. Overview and Foragers. *Journal of Archaeological Research* 2: 255–284.

Keegan, W. F. 2000. West Indian Archaeology. 3. Ceramic Age. *Journal of Archaeological Research* 8: 135–167.

Keegan, W. F. 2010. Island Shores and "Long Pauses." In *Island Shores and Distant Pasts: Archaeological and Biological Approaches to the Pre-Columbian Settlement of the Caribbean,* ed. S. M. Fitzpatrick, and A. H. Ross, 10–20. Gainesville: University Press of Florida.

Keegan, W. F., and J. M. Diamond. 1987. Colonization of Islands by Humans: A Biogeographical Perspective. In *Advances in Archaeological Method and Theory* 10, ed. M. B. Schiffer, 49–92. San Diego: Academic Press.

Keegan, W. F., and C. L. Hofman. 2017. *The Caribbean before Columbus.* New York: Oxford University Press.

Kimura, B. K., M. J. LeFebvre, H. I. Knodel, M. S. Turner, N. S. Fitzsimmons, S. M. Fitzpatrick, and C. J. Mulligan. 2016. Origin of Pre-Columbian Guinea Pigs from Caribbean Archeological Sites Revealed through Genetic Analysis. *Journal of Archaeological Science: Reports* 5: 442–452.

Kirch, P. V., and J. Ellison. 1994. Palaeoenvironmental Evidence for Human Colonization of Remote Oceanic Islands. *Antiquity* 68(259): 310–321.

Knippenberg, S. 2007. *Stone Artefact Production and Exchange among the Lesser Antilles,* Vol. 13. Amsterdam: Amsterdam University Press.

Laffoon, J. E. 2013. Paleomobility Research in Caribbean Contexts: New Perspectives from Isotope Analysis. In *The Oxford Handbook of Caribbean Archaeology,* ed. W. Keegan, C. Hofman, and R. Rodríguez Ramos, 418–435. Oxford: Oxford University Press.

Laffoon, J. E., and B. de Vos. 2011. Diverse Origins, Similar Diets: An Integrated Isotopic Perspective from Anse a la Gourde, Guadeloupe. In *Communities in Contact: Essays in Archaeology, Ethnohistory and Ethnography of the Amerindian Circum-Caribbean,* ed. C. L. Hofman and A. van Duijvenbode, 187–204. Leiden: Sidestone Press.

Laffoon, J. E., R. R. Ramos, L. C. Baik, Y. N. Storde, M. R. Lopez. G. R. Davies, and C. L. Hofman. 2014. Long-distance Exchange in the Precolonial Circum-Caribbean: A Multi-Isotope Study of Animal Tooth Pendants from Puerto Rico. *Journal of Anthropological Archaeology* 35: 220–233.

Laffoon, J. E., E. Plomp, G. R. Davies, M.L.P. Hoogland, and C. L. Hofman. 2015. The Movement and Exchange of Dogs in the Prehistoric Caribbean: An Isotopic Investigation. *International Journal of Osteoarchaeology* 25(4): 454–465.

Laffoon, J. E., M.L.P. Hoogland, G. R. Davies, and C. L. Hofman. 2017. A Multi-Isotope Investigation of Human and Dog Mobility and Diet in the Pre-Colonial Antilles. *Environmental Archaeology* 24(2: S1): 132–148.

Laffoon, J. E., T. F. Sonnemann, T. Shafie, C. L. Hofman, U. Brandes, and G. R. Davies. 2018. Investigating Human Geographic Origins Using Dual-Isotope ($^{87}Sr/^{86}Sr,^{18}O$) Assignment Approaches. *PLoS ONE* 12(2): e0172562.

Laffoon, J. E., and T. P. Leppard. 2018. $^{87}Sr/^{86}Sr$ Data Indicate Human Post-juvenile Residence Mobility Decreases over Time-Elapsed since Initial Holocene Island Colonization in the Pacific and Caribbean. *Archaeological and Anthropological Sciences* 11(5): 1757–1768.

Lalueza-Fox, C., F. Calderon, F. Calafell, B. Morera, and J. Bertranpetit. 2001. mtDNA From Extinct Tainos and the Peopling of the Caribbean. *Annals of Human Genetics* 65(2): 137–151.

Lalueza-Fox, C., M. T. Gilbert, A. J. Martinez-Fuentes, F. Calafell, and J. Bertranpetit. 2003. Mitochondrial DNA from Pre-Columbian Ciboneys from Cuba and the Prehistoric Colonization of the Caribbean. *American Journal of Physical Anthropology* 121(2): 97–108.

Lawrence, J. A., K. M. Marsaglia, and S. M. Fitzpatrick. 2016. Petrographic Analysis of Pre-Columbian Pottery from Four Islands in the Lesser Antilles and Implications for Inter-island Transport and Interactions. *Journal of Archaeological Science: Reports* 9: 663–680.

LeFebvre, M. J., and S. D. DeFrance. 2014. Guinea Pigs in the Pre-Columbian West Indies. *Journal of Island and Coastal Archaeology* 9(1): 16–44.

Lleonart, R., E. Riego, R. Rodriguez-Suarez, T. T. Ruiz, and J. de la Fuente. 1999. Analyses of DNA from Ancient Bones of a Pre-Columbian Cuban Woman and a Child. *Genetics and Molecular Biology* 22(3): 285–289.

Lord, E., C. Collins, M. J. LeFebvre, and E. Matisoo-Smith. 2018. Complete Mitogenomes of Ancient Caribbean Guinea Pigs (*Cavia porcellus*). *Journal of Archaeological Science: Reports* 17: 678–688.

Lord, E. J., C. Collins, S. deFrance, M. J. LeFebvre, F. Pigiere, P. Eeckhout, C. Eraus, S. M. Fitzpatrick, P. Healy, J. L. Garcia, E. Ramos Roca, M. Delgado, A. Sánchez Urriago, G. Alberto Peña Leon, M. Fernanda Martínez-Polanco, M. Toyne, A. Dahlstedt, K. Moore, M. Zierden, C. Laguer Diaz, C. Zori, E. J. Reitz, and E. Matisoo-Smith. 2020. Ancient DNA of Guinea Pigs Identified Multiple Domestication and Dispersal Events through Time. *Nature Scientific Reports*. doi.org/10.1038/s41598-020-65784-6.

Lovén, S. 1935. *Origins of the Tainan Culture, West Indies*. Goteborg: Elanders Bokfryckeri Akfiebolag.

MacArthur, R. H., and E. O. Wilson. 1967. *The Theory of Island Biogeography*. Princeton: Princeton University Press.

Mann, C. J. 1986. Composition and Origin of Material in Pre-Columbian Pottery, San Salvador Island, Bahamas. *Geoarchaeology* 1(2): 183–194.

Marquardt, W. H. 1990. Circum-Caribbean/Floridian Connections: A Review. Paper presented at the Southeast Archaeological Conference, Mobile, AL, November 7–10.

Martínez-Cruzado, J. C. 2010. The History of Amerindian Mitochondrial DNA Lineages in Puerto Rico. In *Island Shores and Distant Pasts: Archaeological and Biological Approaches to the Pre-Columbian Settlement of the Caribbean*, ed. S. M. Fitzpatrick, and A. H. Ross, 55–80. Gainesville: University Press of Florida.

Mendez, D. 1933. An Account, Given by Diego Mendez, of Certain Things that Occurred on the Last Voyage of the Admiral, Don Christopher Columbus. See C. Columbus 1930–1933. 2: 112–140.

Mendisco, F., M. H. Pemonge, E. Leblay, T. Romon, G. Richard, P. Courtaud, and M. F. Deguilloux. 2015. Where are the Caribs? Ancient DNA from Ceramic Period Human Remains in the Lesser Antilles. *Philosophical Transactions of the Royal Society of London. Series B: Biological Sciences* 370 (1660): 1–8.

Mendizabel, I., K. Sandoval, G. Berniell-Lee, F. Calafell, A. Salas, A. Martinez-Fuentes, and D. Comas. 2008. Genetic Origins, Admixture, and Asymmetry in Maternal and Paternal Human Lineages in Cuba. *BMC Evolutionary Biology* 8(1): 213.

Mickleburgh, H. L., and J. R. Pagán-Jiménez. 2012. New Insights into the Consumption of Maize and Other Food Plants in the Pre-Columbian Caribbean from Starch Grains Trapped in Human Dental Calculus. *Journal of Archaeological Science* 39(7): 2468–2478.

Montenegro, Á., R. T. Callaghan, and S. M. Fitzpatrick. 2014. From West to East: Environmental Influences on the Rate and Pathways of Polynesian Colonization. *The Holocene* 24(2): 242–256.

Montenegro, Á., R. T. Callaghan, and S. M. Fitzpatrick. 2016. Using Seafaring Simulations and Shortest-hop Trajectories to Model the Prehistoric Colonization of Remote Oceania. *Proceedings of the National Academy of Sciences* 113(45): 12685–12690.

Nägele, K., C. Posth, M. I. Orbegozo, Y. Chinique de Armas, S. T. Godoy, U. M. González Herrera, M. A. Nieves-Colón, M. Sandoval-Velasco, D. Mylopotamitaki, R. Radzeviciute, J. Laffoon, W. J. Pestle, J. Ramos-Madrigal, T. C. Lamnidis, W. C. Schaffer, R. S. Carr, J. S. Day, C. A. Arredondo Antúnez, A. Rangel Rivero, A. J. Martínez-Fuentes, E. Crespo-Torres,

I. Roksandic, A. C. Stone, C. Lalueza-Fox, M. Hoogland, M. Roksandic, C. L. Hofman, J. Krause, and H. Schroeder. 2020. Genomic Insights into the Early Peopling of the Caribbean. *Science* 369(6502): 456–460.

Napolitano, M. F., R. J. DiNapoli, J. H. Stone, M. J. Levin, N. P. Jew, B. G. Lane, J. T. O'Connor, and S. M. Fitzpatrick. 2019. Reevaluating Human Colonization of the Caribbean Using Chronometric Hygiene and Bayesian Modeling. *Science Advances* 5(12): eaar7806.

Narganes Storde, Y. 1995. La Lapidaria de la Hueca, Vieques, Puerto Rico. In *Proceedings of the 15th International Congress for Caribbean Archaeology*, ed. R. E. Alegría and M. Rodríguez, 141–151. San Juan: Centro de Studios Avanzados de Puerto Rico y el Caribe.

Newsom, L. A. and E. S. Wing. 2004. *On Land and Sea: Native American Uses of Biological Resources in the West Indies.* Tuscaloosa: University of Alabama Press.

Nieves-Colón, M. A., W. J. Pestle, A. W. Reynolds, B. Llamas, C. de la Fuente, K. Fowler, K. M. Skerry, E. Crespo-Torres, C. D. Bustamante, and A. C. Stone. 2019. Ancient DNA Reconstructs the Genetic Legacies of Precontact Puerto Rico Communities. *Molecular Biology and Evolution* 37(3): 611–626.

Oswald, J. A., J. M. Allen, M. J. LeFebvre, B. J. Stucky, R. A Folk, N. A. Albury, G. S. Morgan, R. P. Guralnick, and D. W. Steadman. 2020. Ancient DNA and High-Resolution Chronometry Reveal a Long-term Human Role in the Historical Diversity and Biogeography of the Bahamian Hutia. *Scientific Reports* 10: 1373.

Pagán-Jiménez, J. R., and L. A. Carlson. 2014. Recent Archaeobotanical Findings of the Hallucinogenic Snuff Cojoba (*Anadenanthera Peregrina* [L.] Speg.) in Precolonial Puerto Rico. *Latin American Antiquity* 25(1): 101–116.

Pagán-Jiménez, J. R., R. Rodríguez-Ramos, B. A. Reid, M. van den Bel, and C. L. Hofman. 2015. Early Dispersals of Maize and Other Food Plants into the Southern Caribbean and Northeastern South America. *Quaternary Science Reviews* 123: 231–246.

Pavia, J. A., K. M. Marsaglia, and S. M. Fitzpatrick. 2013. Petrography and Provenance of Sand Temper within Ceramic Sherds from Carriacou, Southern Grenadines, West Indies. *Geoarchaeology* 28: 450–477.

Petersen, J. B. 1996. Archaeology of Trants. Part 3. Chronological and Settlement Data. *Annals of the Carnegie Museum* 654: 323–361.

Prebble, M., and J. E. Wilmshurst. 2009. Detecting the Initial Impact of Humans and Introduced Species on Island Environments in Remote Oceania Using Palaeoecology. *Biological Invasions* 11: 1529–1556.

Price, T. D., J. H. Burton, and R. A. Bentley. 2002. The Characterization of Biologically Available Strontium Isotope Ratios for the Study of Prehistoric Migration. *Archaeometry* 44(1): 117–135.

Reid, B. A. 2009. *Myths and Realities of Caribbean History.* Tuscaloosa: University of Alabama Press.

Reid, B. A. (ed). 2018. *The Archaeology of Caribbean and Circum-Caribbean Farmers (6000 BC–AD 1500).* London: Routledge.

Rieth, T. M., and J. S. Athens. 2019. Late Holocene Human Expansion into Near Oceania and Remote Oceania: A Bayesian Model of the Chronologies of the Mariana Islands and Bismarck Archipelago. *Journal of Island and Coastal Archaeology* 14(1): 5–16.

Rodríguez Ramos, R. 2011. The Circulation of Jadeitite across the Caribbeanscape. In *Communities in Contact: Essays in Archaeology, Ethnohistory and Ethnography of the Amerindian Circum-Caribbean,* ed. C. L. Hofman and A. van Duijvenbode, 117–136. Leiden: Sidestone Press.

Rodríguez Ramos, R. 2013. Isthmo–Antillean Engagements. In *The Oxford Handbook of Caribbean Archaeology,* ed. W. Keegan, C. Hofman, and R. Rodríguez Ramos, 55–170. Oxford: Oxford University Press.

Rose, R. 1987. Lucayan Lifeways at the Time of Columbus. In *Proceedings of the First San Salvador Conference, Columbus and His World,* ed. D. T. Gerace, 321–340. Ft. Lauderdale, Florida: CCFL Bahamian Field Station.

Rouse, I. 1986. *Migrations in Prehistory.* New Haven: Yale University Press.

Rouse, I. 1992. *The Tainos: Rise and Decline of the People who Greeted Columbus.* New Haven: Yale University Press.

Rouse, I., and J. M. Cruxent. 1963. *Venezuelan Archaeology.* New Haven: Yale University Press.

Samson, A. V., and B. M. Waller. 2010. Not Growling but Smiling: New Interpretations of the Bared-teeth Motif in the Pre-Columbian Caribbean. *Current Anthropology* 51(3): 425–433.

Scudder, S. J., and I. R. Quitmyer. 1998. Evaluation of Evidence of Pre-Columbian Human Occupation at Great Cave, Cayman Brac, Cayman Islands. *Caribbean Journal of Science* 34: 41–49.

Schroeder, H., M. Sikora, S. Gopalakrishnan, L. M. Cassidy, P. M. Delser, M. Sandoval-Velasco, J. G. Schraiber, S. Rasmussen, J. R. Homburger, M. C. Ávila-Arcos, M. E. Allentoft, J. V. Moreno-Mayar, G. Renaud, A. Gomez-Carballa, J. E. Laffoon, R.J.A. Hopkins, T.F.G. Higham, R. S. Carr, W. C. Schaffer, J. S. Day, M. Hoogland, M. Salas, C. D. Bustamante, R. Nielsen, D. G. Bradley, C. L. Hofman, and E. Willerslev. 2018. Origins and Genetic Legacies of the Caribbean Taino. *Proceedings of the National Academy of Sciences* 115(10): 2341–2346.

Schurr, T. G. 2010. Coastal Waves and Island Hopping: A Genetic View of Caribbean Prehistory in the Context of New World Colonization. In *Island Shores and Distant Pasts: Archaeological and Biological Approaches to the Pre-Columbian Settlement of the Caribbean,* ed. S. M. Fitzpatrick, and A. H. Ross, 177–198. Gainesville: University Press of Florida.

Shearn, I. 2020. Canoe Societies in the Caribbean: Ethnography, Archaeology, and Ecology of Precolonial Canoe Manufacturing and Voyaging. *Journal of Anthropological Archaeology* 57: 101–140.

Shertl, H.-P., W. V. Maresch, S. Knippenberg, A. Hertwig, A. López Belando, R. Rodríguez Ramos, L. Speich, and C. L. Hofman. 2019. Petrography, Mineralogy and Geochemistry of Jadeite-rich Artefacts from the Playa Grande Excavation Sites, Northern Hispaniola: Evaluation of Local Provenance from the Río San Juan Complex. *Geological Society London* Special Publications 474: 231–253.

Siegel, P. E. 1996. Ideology and Culture Change in Prehistoric Puerto Rico: A View from the Community. *Journal of Field Archaeology* 23: 313–333.

Siegel, P. E. 2010. Continuity and Change in the Evolution of Religion and Political Organization on Pre-Columbian Puerto Rico. *Journal of Anthropological Archaeology* 29(3): 302–326.

Siegel, P. E. (ed.). 2018. *Island Historical Ecology: Socionatural Landscapes of the Eastern and Southern Caribbean.* New York: Berghahn Books.

Siegel, P. E., C. Descantes, J. R. Fergurson, and M. D. Glascock. 2008. Pre-Columbian Pottery in the West Indies: Compositional Change in Context. *Journal of Caribbean Archaeology* 2: 25–44.

Siegel, P. E., J. G. Jones, D. M. Pearsall, N. P. Dunning, P. Farrell, N. A. Duncan, J. H. Curtis, and S. K. Singh. 2015. Paleoenvironmental Evidence for First Human Colonization of the Eastern Caribbean. *Quaternary Science Reviews* 129: 275–295.

Slayton, E. R. 2018. *Seascape Corridors: Modeling Routes to Connect Communities across the Caribbean Sea.* Leiden: Sidestone Press.

Spriggs, M. 1989. The Dating of the Island Southeast Asian Neolithic: An Attempt at Chronometric Hygiene and Linguistic Correlation. *Antiquity* 63: 587–613.

Ting, C., B. Neyt, J. U. Hung, C. Hofman, and P. Degryse. 2016. The Production of Pre-Colonial Ceramics in Northwestern Hispaniola: A Technological Study of Meillacoid and Chicoid Ceramics from La Luperona and El Flaco, Dominican Republic. *Journal of Archaeological Science: Reports* 6: 376–385.

Toro-Labrador, G., O. R. Wever, and J. C. Martinez-Cruzado. 2003. Mitchondrial DNA Analysis in Aruba: Strong Maternal Ancestry of Closely Related Amerindians and Implications for the Peopling of Northwestern Venezuela. *Caribbean Journal of Science* 39(1): 11–22.

Torres, J. M. and R. Rodríguez Ramos. 2008. The Caribbean: A Continent Divided by Water. In *Archaeology and Geoinformatics: Case Studies from the Caribbean,* ed. B. A. Reid, 13–29. Tuscaloosa: University of Alabama Press.

Tsujimori, T., and G. E. Harlow. 2012. Petrogenetic Relationships between Jadeitite and Associated High-pressure and Low-Temperature Metamorphic Rocks in Worldwide Jadeitite Localities: A Review. *European Journal of Mineralogy* 24: 371–390.

Van Thienen, V., and M. M. Martínez Milantchí. 2019. Insights from Nondestructive Geochemical Analyses of Hacienda Grande (Puerto Rico) and Salt River (Virgin Islands) Saladoid and Ostionoid Ceramics. *Bulletin of the Peabody Museum of Natural History* 60(2): 95–102.

Vilar, M. G., C. Melendez, A. Sanders, A. Walia, J. B. Galeski, A. C. Owings, and T. G. Schurr. 2014. Genetic Diversity in Puerto Rico and Its Implications for the Peopling of the West Indies. *American Journal of Physical Anthropology* 155(3): 352–368.

Waldron, L. 2016. *Handbook of Ceramic Animal Symbols in the Ancient Lesser Antilles.* Gainesville: University of Florida Press.

Walker, R. S., and L. A. Ribeiro. 2011. Bayesian Phylogeography of the Arawak Expansion in Lowland South America. *Proceedings of the Royal Society of London B: Biological Sciences* 278(1718): 2562–2567.

Wilmshurst, J. M., T. L. Hunt, C. P. Lipo, and A. J. Anderson. 2011. High-precision Radiocarbon Dating Shows Recent and Rapid Initial Human Colonization of East Polynesia. *Proceedings of the National Academy of Sciences* 108(5): 1815–1820.

Wilson, S. M. 2006. *The Prehistory of Nevis, a Small Island in the Lesser Antilles.* New Haven: Yale University Press.

Wilson, S. M. 2007. *The Archaeology of the Caribbean.* Cambridge: Cambridge University Press.

Wilson, S. M., H. B. Iceland, and T. R. Hester. 1998. Preceramic Connections Between Yucatan and the Caribbean. *Latin American Antiquity* 9(4): 342–352.

10

The Initial Colonization and Settlement of the Mediterranean Islands

THOMAS P. LEPPARD, ALEXANDER J. SMITH, AND JOHN F. CHERRY

> The Mediterranean Sea with its various branches, penetrating far into
> the great Continent, forms the largest gulf of the ocean, and, alternately
> narrowed by islands or projections of the land and expanding to considerable
> breadth, at once separates and connects the three divisions of the Old World.
>
> *Theodor Mommsen (1911)*

The Mediterranean, pithily (yet not inaccurately) characterized by Mommsen as an inland gulf of Afro-Eurasia, has a labyrinthine, insular, midlatitude geography (Figure 10.1). The position of this gulf—at the heart of precociously early processes of domestication and state formation, and facilitating latitudinal transmission of languages, political forms, wealth, and people—has made the archaeology of the insular Mediterranean difficult to contextualize within global island archaeologies (Cherry 2004). Many of these islands were settled early, across short distances, and by farmers practicing a Neolithic lifestyle uniquely rich in cereals and animal protein, whose descendants followed very different cultural and political trajectories from their counterparts on islands in the Pacific, Caribbean, or Indian Ocean (Broodbank 2018; Leppard 2018). Yet, with the archaeology of the earliest human presence in the insular Mediterranean currently in flux, is the Mediterranean still such an outlier? Have the changes witnessed in Mediterranean island archaeology, especially with regard to initial colonization, brought its human dynamics into the mainstream?

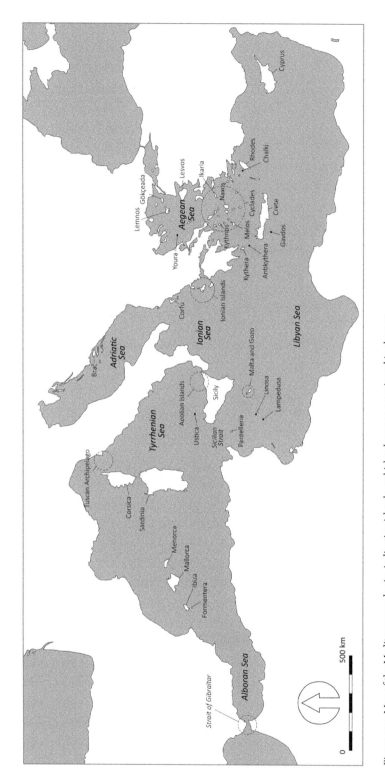

Figure 10.1. Map of the Mediterranean basin, indicating islands and island groups mentioned in the text.

How we view the pattern and process of early island colonization and settlement in the Mediterranean has, unsurprisingly, been nuanced by the steady accumulation of new data since the first syntheses were attempted (Cherry 1981, 1984, 1990); but, for reasons that we explore in this chapter, the nature of this change has been rather unexpected and the outcomes uncertain. For example, some years ago, one of us was able to sum up the situation in these terms: "By far the majority of medium- to small-size islands (e.g., throughout the Aegean) were first settled only during the Neolithic or the earlier stages of the Bronze Age, between 5,000–8,000 years ago, mainly by farming/herding groups . . ." (Cherry 2004: 240). How accurate is this statement now? Answering this question is in fact difficult: assessing any overall model of Mediterranean island colonization is clearly contingent upon how we define "settlement" and the credence given to types of data that differ radically in quality and abundance. More generally, some trends, which we might have expected to collapse under the weight of new data, have become increasingly robust; some outliers have remained resolutely "out of the stream," despite attempts to bring them into line with larger patterns; and new vistas have opened onto hitherto unappreciated fields of research.

In this chapter we consider these changes, synthesizing where possible, and noting how we might seek clarity in those areas where the data are inconclusive. We suggest that no single driving force accounts for the temporal and spatial distribution of settlement in the insular Mediterranean, although we emphasize—as we have elsewhere (Cherry and Leppard 2018a)—the continued explanatory power of island biogeographic theory, not only in terms of geometries and vectors of colonization, but also with regard to the trophic limitations that islands impose on colonists. We conclude by reflecting on how developments in the Mediterranean increasingly appear to contrast sharply with other island theaters represented in this volume, with the possible exception of the universe of islands that lie between the Malay Peninsula and Cape York, Australia (see chapter 11).

The Settlement of the Insular Mediterranean before Farming

The Lower and Middle Paleolithic of the Islands: Unsettled Business

It used to be widely accepted that the permanent settlement of the Mediterranean islands was essentially a Holocene phenomenon, with only the largest islands probably subject to periodic Upper Paleolithic to Epipaleolithic/Mesolithic exploitation (Cherry 1990; Broodbank 2006). For those scholars who were cautious about envisioning significant open-ocean travel at this early stage, it was telling that such exploitation occurred during sea-level lowstands associated with the Last Glacial Maximum (LGM). Dissenting views could be heard from some quarters (for example, Chelidonio 2001; Kopaka and Mantzanas 2009). Nonetheless, challenges to the model of an "overwhelmingly terrestrial hominin universe" (Broodbank 2014: 267) prior to the LGM were often built on dubious datasets: stray surface finds that were poorly reported and documented, datable only according to morpho-typological criteria, and that lacked stratified archaeological deposits or radiometric dates to support them. Over the last decade, this picture has either changed radically or hardly at all, depending in large part on one's perspective.

Strasser et al. (2010) reported an assemblage of quartz and quartzite-flaked artifacts from Plakias in southwestern Crete containing relatively large bifaces that, in typological terms, could conceivably pass for variations on an Acheulian industry. The assemblage was located on the modern ground surface, but its Pleistocene credentials have been supported using proxy dating of the uplifted marine terraces on which the material currently sits (Strasser et al. 2011; Sakellariou and Galanidou 2016—however, see this as flawed). Further discoveries of chipped stone artifacts with a possible Lower Paleolithic provenience followed from elsewhere on Crete (Runnels et al. 2014a), Lesvos (Galanidou et al. 2017), and Cyprus (Strasser et al. 2016), while lithic assemblages with Levallois parallels have been recorded from the Ionian Islands (Galanidou et al. 2016) and now from Stelida on Naxos (Carter et al. 2014). From this latter site, a stratigraphic sequence, with its basal component dated to the Middle Paleolithic, contained artifacts with typologically Lower and Middle Paleolithic affinities (Carter et al. 2019) (although the six infrared stimulated thermoluminescence dates, including the crucial date from LU7 [SNAP17-4], are only reported to 1σ; moreover, LU7 yielded variously 104 [Carter et al. 2019: table 1] or 106 [Carter et al. 2019: 4] artifacts, of which only three were retouched). Several of these islands have been definitively insular since the Zanclean Flood refilled the Mediterranean circa 5.33 million years ago (Garcia-Castellano et al. 2009). Accordingly, the data have been woven together to suggest that the Mediterranean, far from being such an effective barrier to hominin mobility that it drove allopatric speciation (Broodbank 2013: 82–108), was in fact a facilitator of movement between North Africa and Europe, and that, by extension, taxa including *Homo erectus, H. heidelbergensis,* and *H. neanderthalensis* were all accomplished seagoers (Howitt-Marshall and Runnels 2016; Runnels 2014; Runnels et al. 2014b; chapter 4). These data and this interpretation have been met with both support (Simmons 2014) and robust critique, including that offered by some of the present authors (Leppard 2014, 2015a; Cherry and Leppard 2015).

We do not wish to rehearse this debate here: not only has it become stale, but recent summaries have also attempted to indicate how it could be advanced with better data and a little less dogmatism (Leppard and Runnels 2017; Papoulia 2017; chapter 4). We do emphasize that the Acheulian data from Rodafnidia on Lesvos, while intrinsically interesting, shed little light on processes of island colonization, as Lesvos has intermittently formed part of the Eurasian mainland during glacial maxima (Figure 10.2) (Lykousis 2009). The same probably goes for Stelida on Naxos, an island that has been cyclically connected to and disconnected from mainland Eurasia. Carter et al. (2019) certainly report artifacts derived from a deposit dated to 198.4 ± 14.5 (1σ), corresponding to MIS 7–6; and during MIS 7, Naxos may well have been insular. But, from the perspective of parsimony of explanation, these artifacts could derive from an extant, relict population of *H. neanderthalensis*, which colonized the site via terrestrial means during the preceding severe glacial MIS 8 (during which time Naxos was continental [Lykousis 2009]), rather than indicating maritime colonization by *neanderthalensis* during MIS 7 (the undated surface finds that parallel the excavated material in typological terms are, of course, not constrained chronologically to a discrete MIS, and could as well represent activity during glacials as during interstadials). If we set these spurious data (that is, from contexts that are now insular but that were not during the period of colonization) to one side, and also note that all the other published evidence is still solely comprised of surface material dated on morpho-typological grounds, what can be said with certainty about pre-Upper Paleolithic Mediterranean island activity?

First, and most obviously, there is a preponderance of data from the eastern Mediterranean, especially from the Aegean and Ionian Seas. Why might this be the case? We could suppose that a form of geographic autocatalysis (that is, a tendency for certain configurations of islands and coasts to encourage experimental seagoing, such that continued discovery of further landmasses becomes a culturally ingrained expectation; Keegan and Diamond 1987: 67–68; Broodbank 2000: 31–32, 131–132), encouraged by the highly indented and fractal nature of the Aegean coastline—exceptional even in a Mediterranean context (Broodbank 2006: figure 3) and a feature that was clearly important in later periods—may have prompted archaic hominins into overwater forays. Yet the same tectonically driven, contorted arrangement that might drive autocatalysis has also rendered the low-seastand Aegean a very differently

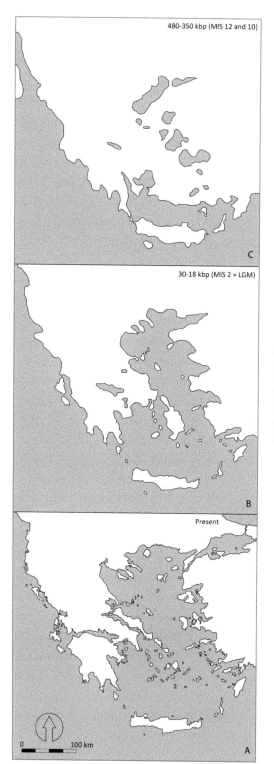

Figure 10.2. A comparison of coastlines in the Aegean basin (*A*) as they are today; (*B*) at the LGM; and (*C*) at Marine Isotope Stages 10–12. (Data for C from Lykousis [2009], by permission of the author.)

configured type of environment, in contrast to the same basin at high, inter-stadial seastands. Indeed, more so than anywhere else in the Mediterranean, the fluctuation from glacial to interstadial in the Aegean drove an unmatched dynamism in coastal geometries (Lykousis 2009; Sakellariou and Galanidou 2016). One of the immediate outcomes of this observation relates to scale. If at some points during the past several hundred thousand years Crete was separated from the palaeo-island of "Cycladia" (that is, the Cyclades united by low sea level) by only a few water gaps measured in fewer than tens of kilometers, are we in fact dealing with maritime dispersal in the sense that it has traditionally been understood (see also chapter 4)? In any case, if ar-chaic hominins did make short overwater crossings to reach Crete, or even Cyprus—though skepticism is justified concerning the single undated surface find on which this claim rests (Strasser et al. 2016)—then their anthropogenic impact on island environments seems to have been so marginal as to be unde-tectable. This might be considered unusual, knowing the types of large-scale environmental change that invasive species can cause, and even more so if these crossings were intentional and repeated (Leppard 2014). The spatial cor-relation between ephemeral data in support of an insular Lower Paleolithic, and a submarine topography that would have repeatedly created utterly novel, dense interweaves of mainland, island, and sea with each passing Marine Iso-tope Stage (Figure 10.2), is accordingly intriguing: we might be dealing with accidental strandings that might have been facilitated in such unusual and comparatively rare coastal geographies (Leppard 2015b), rather than deliber-ate and large-scale maritime movement.

The situation arguably becomes more coherent if we focus on the assem-blages that seem to be loosely within a Mousterian tradition. One insular locus appears to be the Ionian Islands (Ferentinos et al. 2012), with convincing evi-dence for Levallois flaking (Papoulia 2017: 78). Bathymetric modeling suggests that the Ionian Islands were still separated from the mainland of the Balkan Peninsula by the Ionian Sea and the Gulf of Patras during glacials, with the southern Ionians remaining insular during comparatively severe glacials such as MIS 6 (Zavitsanou et al. 2015). Indeed, a recent summary suggests that the lacunose Aegean evidence, too, has a distinctly Middle Paleolithic flavor from a technological (Papoulia 2017) and now a radiometric perspective (Carter et al. 2019)—even ignoring, for now, the question of Naxos's cyclically insular na-ture in the Middle Paleolithic. In this context, it is worthwhile to point out that Sakellariou and Galanidou (2016) would rather assign the Plakias material to a Middle than a Lower Paleolithic (that is, Acheulian) tradition. What might be emerging is a picture of the Middle Paleolithic Aegean possessed of a tortuously interdigitated mosaic of sea and coast and home to bands of Neanderthals making opportunistic short-distance hops to clearly visible landmasses. Considering the enhanced behavioral plasticity likely characteristic of *H. neanderthalensis* when compared to more archaic taxa, this model becomes increasingly cogent for explaining otherwise sparse and problematic data.

"Were the Mediterranean islands colonized during the Early-Middle Pleistocene?" is probably the wrong question. As the cyclical inundation and exposure of huge coastal plains in the Tyrrhenian, Adriatic, and especially Aegean created and annihilated hundreds of thousands of square kilometers of habitat, hominins moved into and then out of these habitats in a pump dynamic, driving dispersal in a manner comparable to such dynamics elsewhere (for example, Larrasoaña et al. 2013). In most of the Mediterranean, however, open ocean still formed a barrier to this dispersal; in this respect, we differ sharply from Runnels (chapter 4). In the large gulf lying between the Balkans and Anatolia, its mouth blocked by paleo-Crete, the intricately reticulate coastal geography seems to have permitted or encouraged infrequent, short-distance jumps to insular landmasses—probably involving Neanderthals, but less likely with more archaic species—that appear to have had minimal impact in the fossil or paleoenvironmental records. This is fascinating and complex behavior that fits well within a developing overall picture of increasingly sophisticated Neanderthal capacities (Hoffman et al. 2018; Johansson 2014; Wynn and Coolidge 2012); if this is colonization, though, it is very different from the processes that began to unfold in the aftermath of the LGM, processes that seem to be structured less by absolute biogeographic barriers and more by the intrinsic trophic limitations of islands.

The Maritime Mesolithic

Despite the precociously early advent of *Homo sapiens* around Mediterranean shores (Hublin et al. 2017), and in contrast to an increasingly complex picture of coastal and island activity involving premodern hominins (see above), Pleistocene hunting-and-gathering populations of *Homo sapiens* seem to have had little interest in the island Mediterranean. Sicily was, until recently, considered an exception to this overall trend, possessing a series of sites purportedly covering MIS 3–1, including an Aurignacian (circa 45–25 kya) and Epigravettian (circa 21–10 kya) phase from Fontana Nuova (Chilardi et al. 1996). This is now challenged on several fronts, however. The Aurignacian attribution of material from Fontana Nuova was based on typological criteria; yet AMS dates on faunal remains and human teeth found in association with the chipped stone all fall within the Holocene (Di Maida et al. 2019). Having excluded the possibility of Aurignacian settlement, we can down-date the earliest human occupation of the island to circa 21 kya and the Epigravettian. However, the most recent analysis of the tectonic history of the Strait of Messina now indicates that Sicily was connected to mainland Europe at 21.5–20 kya (Antonioli et al. 2014). Consequently, an Epigravettian phase at Fontana Nuova is most readily explained by terrestrial, not maritime, colonization at the seastand nadir associated with the glacial maximum. Elsewhere in the circum-Tyrrhenian, Sardinia and Corsica were united into "Corsardinia" during the LGM (the surface area of which island would have been around 35,000 km^2). This megaisland would have been separated from mainland Italy by only a few kilometers, with the straits that now lie between Corsica and the Tuscan Archipelago greatly narrowed by eustatic drawdown. This might in part account for the relatively early presence (circa 20 kya) of modern humans on Corsardinia, at Corbeddu Cave (Sondaar et al. 1995; for possible Final Epigravettian occupation on Sardinia, see Mussi and Melis 2002). We return below to considering the explanatory potential of island size and proximity to the mainland when it comes to accounting for patterns in settlement. Here, we simply stress (1) the absence of evidence for pre-LGM Upper Paleolithic island occupation in the Mediterranean; and (2) that among all the islands only Corsardinia now exhibits evidence for Epigravettian activity during an insular phase.

The scarcity of signs of island settlement before or during the LGM contrasts sharply with the rash of evidence for human activity on islands in the millennia after 12,000 BP, and this represents a marked change from the received model of hunter-gather exploitation of the insular Mediterranean.[1] It has been known for some time that postglacial pre-Neolithic groups were capable of accessing quite remote islands (Renfrew and Aspinall 1990). Acceptable radiocarbon dates from stratified contexts, however, remained rare until relatively recently, as did undated assemblages that nonetheless should be considered Mesolithic on morpho-typological grounds (in the Aegean, for example, tending to involve assemblages with distinctive trapezoidal microliths and an abundance of scrapers; for example, Carter 2016). As recent surveys of the data (Cherry and Leppard 2018a; Costa et al. 2003; Galanidou 2011; Martini and Tozzi 2012; Sampson 2014) have made clear, however, the island Mesolithic is now anchored with more radiocarbon dates, though not comprehensively so (see Cherry and Leppard 2018a: table 1), and appears to be an isolated, somewhat spatially restricted phenomenon.

How do these dates pattern? In general, there is a clear tendency for Meso-lithic sites to appear on large islands (larger still, prior to the stabilization of the seastand in the mid-Holocene) that are closer to the mainland (Figure 10.3). Cyprus is somewhat aberrant: certainly large, at 9,251 km^2, it is comparatively remote by Mediterranean standards, yet with very early evidence of hunter-gatherer exploitation (Ammerman 2013; Knapp 2010). This evidence might be tentatively understood within the broader context of important, but imperfectly grasped, mainland Natufian-PPNA (Pre-Pottery Neolithic A) dynamics (Bar-Yosef and Valla 2013). But generally, Mesolithic sites cluster either on the other four of the "big five" islands (Crete, Sicily, Sardinia, and Corsica), all less distant from the mainland than Cyprus during the early Holocene, or on islands that are decidedly coastal—Lemnos, Corfu, or Brač, for example. Some of these islands may have been either precariously joined to the mainland (for example, Youra, Brač), or so proximate to the mainland (for example, Ithaka, Chalki) that "seafaring" and "voyaging" are probably not appropriate terms to employ in those cases. One possible exception may be the Cyclades, where Naxos, Ikaria, and Kythnos all have evidence for Mesolithic activity. Based on bathymetric reconstructions,

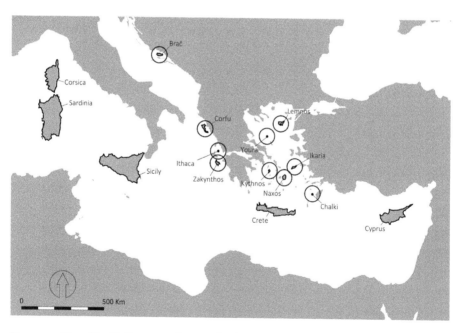

Figure 10.3. Map of the Mediterranean showing islands with evidence for a human presence between the Upper Paleolithic and Mesolithic/Epipaleolithic. (The "Big Five" and smaller islands are indicated with coasts emboldened; for emphasis, the location of smaller islands is also indicated with a circle.)

Thomas P. Leppard, Alexander J. Smith, and John F. Cherry

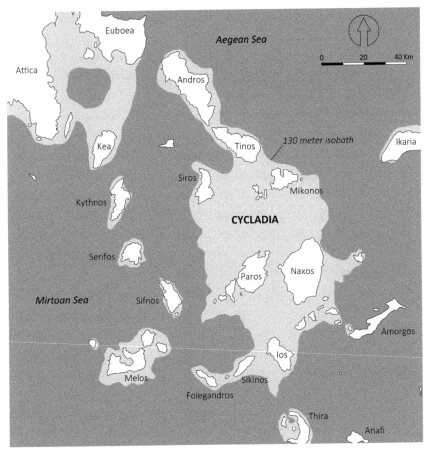

Figure 10.4. Map showing one possible reconstruction of the Cyclades at the LGM. Lighter gray shading depicts land exposed if sea level was at the current 130 m isobath. (After Runnels 2014: fig. 3; reproduced by permission of Curtis Runnels and Eliza McClennen.)

however, the palaeo-island of Cycladia (Figure 10.4) would have been rather substantial at its LGM maximal extent, perhaps even as large as Crete. There is a possibility that Mesolithic activity in the central Aegean may reflect the last vestiges of the biogeographic gravitational hold Cycladia exercised on coastal hunting-and-gathering populations. In other words, are we seeing fresh "colonization" by broad-spectrum hunter-gatherer groups, or are these relict populations clinging to traditional territories in a slowly drowning world? This observation prompts us to consider what advantages size and proximity of an island confer from the perspective of a would-be colonist.

The central tenets of island biogeographic theory, to the extent that they have been applied to the study of island colonization by humans, are well known (for example, Keegan and Diamond 1987). The Mediterranean, in fact, was a comparatively early testing ground for this application (Cherry 1981). It is quite clear that here, as in other global island theaters, MacArthur and Wilson's (1963) work continues to have explanatory power, especially in terms of island size and proximity to source population as correlating positively with "early" colonization. Keegan and Diamond (1987), for example, distilled lessons from island biogeography's emphasis on island/mainland configurations to account for patterns in global island colonization using "target-distance" or T/D ratios, calculating conspicuousness of a colonization target to a source population. Accumulating evidence for Mesolithic activity in the insular Mediterranean, however, suggests that modern humans in the early Holocene were also demonstrably capable of accessing islands that were relatively remote (for example, Cyprus or Melos), yet nonetheless expressed clear preference for certain geographic configurations. Cherry and Leppard (2018a) suggest that the depauperate nature of small islands for large-bodied mammals should in part be considered to account for this preference, as more recent work on insular trophic organization recognizes a dynamic relationship between surface area and foodweb structure (Brose et al. 2004). Small islands tend to be depauperate with regard to taxa that occupy higher trophic positions, not simply because such taxa tend to be bad at overwater dispersal, but because the range-size and caloric demands of these taxa are untenable within parameters that keep a given population viable. This argument becomes more compelling when we consider the overall trend of Upper Paleolithic exploitation limited to the largest islands, with Mesolithic exploitation also covering smaller and inshore islands; this tracks well with a general transition away from larger territories focused on hunting mobile big game during the LGM, toward strategies involving broader spectrum subsistence over smaller areas (Lubell et al. 1994; Richards et al. 2005). An Upper Paleolithic and Mesolithic preference for large islands based on their more complex foodwebs could explain both increasing activity on larger islands after the LGM, and habitual exploitation of valuable resources on remote islands (for example, Melos), in a manner that simply focusing on T/D ratios cannot.

In general, the emerging pattern for the pre-Neolithic Mediterranean might be accounted for less in terms of the ability to cross water gaps, and more in terms of the desirability of doing so. Bad places to be Upper Paleolithic bands, islands were slightly less forbidding for broad-spectrum Mesolithic hunter-gatherers, but nonetheless very limited in terms of their year-round subsistence potential (which may explain seasonal or habitual exploitation).

The trophic limitations of small, dry Mediterranean islands could only be overcome, then, by the revolution in subsistence behaviors represented by the emergence of farming.

The Settlement of the Insular Mediterranean after Farming

Neolithic Island Colonization: Size Matters?

The contours sketched by Dawson in her recent authoritative summary (2014) still mostly hold for the initial colonization of the Mediterranean islands by farming and herding populations. The overall pattern that she identifies does not, in turn, differ greatly from that noted by Cherry long ago (1981, 1984), except that cumulative percentages of islands occupied in the eastern and western Mediterranean now largely track each other over the mid- to late Holocene (Dawson 2008). What is this pattern that is so resilient?

The complex feedback dynamics of early domestication of (in particular) cereals and ungulates increasingly appear in clearer focus, but are not our immediate concern. Suffice it to note here that the Neolithic lifestyle spread discontinuously from a Southwest Asian core and into the maritime Mediterranean beyond the Levantine coast after 9,000 BC. Cyprus has the earliest dates (Knapp 2010), although these are followed by something of a gap, with no sites dated to 9,000–7,000 BC known on the southern or western Anatolian coast (Brami 2015), except for Mersin-Yumuktepe near the Gulf of İskenderun. A spate of sites, however, appears on the Aegean littoral—especially the north Aegean—in the seventh millennium BC (Çilingiroğlu 2017; Çilingiroğlu and Çakırlar 2013; Perlès et al. 2013; Reingruber and Thissen 2009), including the important, early, and somewhat aberrant (because insular) site at Knossos on Crete (Douka et al. 2017). Accumulating evidence indicates that this spread involved movements of people rather than "acculturation" of Mesolithic groups (Hofmanová et al. 2016); the sudden and drastic transition from broad-spectrum Mesolithic practices to ovicaprid-focused subsistence at Franchthi Cave (Munro and Stiner 2015, 2020) supports this. The evidence from this cave, one of the few sites in the Aegean to witness both Mesolithic and Neolithic use in stratigraphic succession, suggests a replacement model rather than cultural adoption. However, considering the late persistence of Mesolithic populations in the Aegean and the precociously early evidence for Neolithic maritime colonization[2] we might speculate about the extent to which early farmers obtained, exploited, or built upon Mesolithic peoples' conceptual geographies of waters over which their ancestors had been paddling for millennia (Broodbank 2006). In either case,

Early Neolithic settlers were clearly intimately acquainted with the Aegean islands, expressing a marked preference for Melian obsidian (Çilingiroğlu and Çakırlar 2013), and yet, excepting Crete and coastal Gökçeada (Atici et al. 2017), they completely ignored the Aegean islands as far as permanent settlement was concerned.

This pronounced preference for larger islands[3] continues as the Neolithic lurches west. Reaching the Atlantic façade of Europe at circa 5,500 BC, this sporadic and almost certainly coastally oriented process (for example, Isern et al. 2017) resulted in large numbers of Early Neolithic sites on Sardinia, Corsica, and Sicily, but none on, for example, Linosa or Ibiza (although, in the case of the latter, the Balearics as a whole seem so unusual that we discuss them separately below). Sardinia and Corsica provide exemplary case studies with which we can examine the degree to which large islands were conceptualized as suitable for Neolithic settlement (tending to focus on environmental niches best suited to rain-fed cereal agriculture), while small islands were not. Lugliè (2018) reports a total of 28 radiocarbon dates from sites on these islands that exhibit Cardial ceramics, a ware highly diagnostic of the Early Neolithic (Figure 10.5). All the dates cluster within the timeframe 5901–5074 cal BC at 95 percent confidence, and the vast majority between 5,800–5,200 BC (Lugliè 2018: table 1).[4] This arguably represents a fairly rapid infilling of the landscape, with founder settlements followed by rapid saturation of the local environment, an expansion that apparently proceeded elsewhere in the Mediterranean with equal rapidity (for example, in Thessaly in central Greece, or the Tavoliere in southern Italy). Moreover, it is clear that only sections of the landscape were subject to this process, with a pronounced Early Neolithic preference for less mountainous terrain (Figure 10.5), for example in the Campidano, in Sulcis-Iglesiente, around the Gulf of Oristano, and either side of the Strait of Bonifacio; this again recalls wider Mediterranean dynamics. Westward Neolithic expansion should be understood as structured according to preference for certain types of configuration of landscape, types that tend to be restricted to the larger islands.

While Neolithic colonists clearly exercised spatial preference with regard to settlement, the southwest Asian Neolithic package, containing cereals, pulses, and ovicaprids adapted to xeric environments, nonetheless represents the first effective subsistence means of maintaining long-term, year-round settlement on the smaller Mediterranean islands, settlement that was, if not initially the norm, demonstrably possible. The Late Neolithic of the Aegean (more or less dating to the fifth millennium BC) witnessed, for example, the appearance of a series of small settlements in the Cyclades. It is notable in this instance, however, that

Thomas P. Leppard, Alexander J. Smith, and John F. Cherry

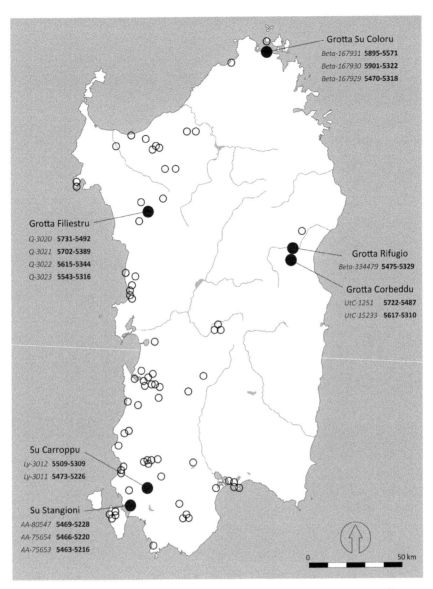

Figure 10.5. Map of Sardinia showing the distribution of Neolithic sites; those with reliable ^{14}C dates indicated with closed circles, and relevant dates cal BP presented at 95% confidence. (Data from Lugliè 2018.)

"Saliagos"-phase sites tend to be situated in niches ideal not only as anchorages, but also for exploiting rare patches of good soil. Evidence for tuna fishing (Broodbank 2000: 148), and a skew in zooarchaeological assemblages that suggests an overt reliance on aridity-adapted domesticated goats (*Capra hircus*) rather than sheep (*Ovis aries*), implies adaptation to challenging island environ-

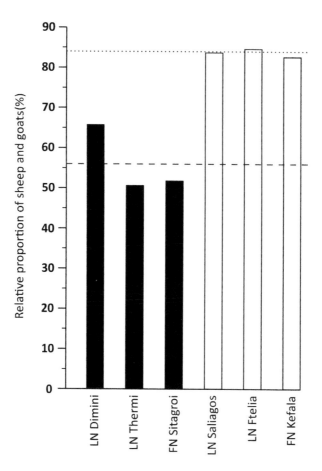

Figure 10.6. Exaggerated reliance on sheep and goats at island (open bar) vs. mainland (solid bar) sites in Greece, as measured by NISP; mean mainland value indicated by long dashes, mean island value by short dashes. (Reproduced from Leppard and Pilaar Birch 2016: fig. 3.)

ments (Figure 10.6; Leppard and Pilaar Birch 2016). Nevertheless, this challenge arguably precluded insular settlement in the central Aegean outside of the environmental sweetspots represented by Saliagos-culture villages. Comparatively early small-island settlement is also witnessed in the Tyrrhenian, where the satellites of Sicily (Ustica and the Aeolian Islands) have usually been ascribed a sixth-millennium colonization horizon (Dawson 2014: 95–107). Certainly, obsidian from Lipari was being utilized off-island in the Early Neolithic, while Impressed ware is reported from Ustica (Mannino 1998), and Stentinello ware (ascribed to the Sicilian Early Neolithic and essentially homologous with Impressed and Cardial ware), from the Aeolian Islands. Stentinello is poorly anchored in ra-

Thomas P. Leppard, Alexander J. Smith, and John F. Cherry

diocarbon terms, however, and a recent attempt to synthesize available dates placed its range at 5,600–4,000 cal BC (Freund et al. 2015), which overlaps with the earliest (Diana phase) published date for Lipari (R-180; 4313–3370 cal BC 2σ [Dawson 2014: table 4.7]). Until more dates become available for the circum-Sicilian islands, it remains the case that settlement of some may be a fifth millennium phenomenon. In any case, the Saliagos culture and the Tyrrhenian islands (which are close to the megaisland of Sicily and attractive, like Melos, because of Lipari's obsidian flows) buck the overall trend: settlement of small islands generally remained unusual from 6,500 to 3,500 BC in the Mediterranean.

As a bigger tranche of radiocarbon data becomes available from Early Neolithic island colonization, so gaps become increasingly evident, which might complicate how we view this colonization. Douka et al. (2017), having undertaken Bayesian modeling of available AMS dates from a deep trench in the Central Court at Knossos, identify a radiocarbon gap from 6,500 to 5,200 cal BC, dividing the Aceramic Neolithic from Early Neolithic 1. This could conceivably represent initial colonization "failure" (or abandonment, see Dawson 2014), followed by resettlement, but alternatively it could simply mean that occupation moved off the tell at this time. There are suggestions elsewhere, however, of similar processes. On Malta, for example, expanding suites of radiocarbon dates (Malone et al. 2019) hint at a more complex occupational history than previously supposed, including a possible hiatus in settlement in the fifth millennium BC (separating Għar Dalam, Skorba, and Żebbuġ). Neighboring Lampedusa appears to have been abandoned after ephemeral Stentinello settlement (although we repeat the foregoing caveat regarding dating: Radi 1972). On tiny Antikythera, although lacking an early Neolithic phase, Bevan and Conolly (2013) identify a similarly sporadic settlement history during the Late/Final Neolithic.

Whatever these hiatuses may index, the general pattern suggests that small-island settlement could seem either more or less attractive (dependent on locally specific changing circumstances), whereas the very largest Mediterranean islands—Sicily and Sardinia—look to have been continuously (and densely) settled after the sixth millennium BC. This reinforces the overall picture of small islands being considered less-than-prime real estate. After about 3,500 BC, it seems, this apparent disinclination was substantially overcome.

Bronze Age Waterworlds

The fourth and third millennia BC witness the final emergence of blanket island settlement. This trend is especially noticeable in the eastern Mediterranean, but it is now clear that the same is true of the western half of the basin (Dawson 2008: figure 7.4; 2014). In the Aegean, this should be understood in the context of a more general phenomenon: the essentially contemporaneous appearance of large-scale settlement in relatively marginal hinterlands and the first appearance, on both the mainland and islands, of large primate centers. In particular, the more widespread occupation of landscapes less suited to Neolithic mixed farming (Halstead 2008) might account for the expansion of settlement in the insular Aegean. As a process, this has less to do with remoteness, and more with small islands being, like uplands, less desirable niches that nonetheless grew in importance as lowland populations expanded and hints of social hierarchy emerged. Closer attention to small and habitually exploited islands in the Aegean located in proximity to comparatively larger islands (for example, Knodell et al. 2020, in the case of Naxos and Paros) will further clarify the overall picture of how both these islands came to be exploited, as well as how this exploitation relates to developing social hierarchies. Broodbank (2000) has charted in detail how these incipient social divides also made themselves felt in the islands, as systems of control over goods, knowledge, and *arcana* flourished, putting an insular spin on an otherwise general trend toward social hierarchies across the basin. More recent data, in particular the remarkable finds from Keros in the southeastern Cyclades and especially large-scale marble architecture from this site (Renfrew et al. 2012), continue to underscore this close association between insularity, access, and social power.

The Tyrrhenian islands (large and small) had already been colonized by 3,000 BC. The isolates of the Sicilian Strait (Pantelleria, Linosa, Lampedusa) were only settled in the Bronze Age, however, with the exception of Lampedusa which appears to have experienced Neolithic settlement, abandonment, and then recolonization (Radi 1972). Despite early exploitation of Pantellerian obsidian, permanent settlement only dates from the second millennium BC (Ardesia et al. 2006). This is perhaps unsurprising, since better obsidian sources lay to the north, and these islands are small, remote, and dry, even by Mediterranean standards.

More surprising is the Balearic archipelago, which was unoccupied at 3000 BC, despite the Iberian coast having witnessed Neolithicization some 2,500 years earlier and being visible from Ibiza. Indeed, despite repeated attempts to demonstrate otherwise, it has become increasingly clear that the horizon for initial settlement of Mallorca and Menorca lies in the two or three centuries after circa 2470 cal BC. This, as we have pointed out elsewhere (Cherry and Leppard 2018b), is paradoxical: the islands are distant from the mainland, but not prohibitively so. Menorca and especially Mallorca are also large; the latter covers 3,740 km² (the sixth-largest island in the Mediterranean basin), with orographic rainfall partly offsetting a prevailing parched climate. We will not reiterate here the now-overwhelming data for a later third-millennium BC colonization (Cherry and Leppard 2018b; Ramis et al. 2002). Attempts to address this paradox in terms of remoteness and difficulty of access seem untenable considering long-distance colonizing activity in deeper time elsewhere in the Mediterranean. Rather, we suggest that conditions fostering (or even necessitating) island colonization in regions farther east simply did not obtain in southwestern Europe until the terminal third millennium. Accordingly, we should contextualize this colonization within the wider socioeconomic changes evident within Western Europe at this time. Of course, it remains true that future data may alter this picture, and in fact paleoenvironmental studies hint at a curious disturbance (in the form of a vegetation successional event) in the mid-Holocene, although it may not be anthropogenic (Burjachs et al. 2017). In either case, increasingly sophisticated provenience analysis (for example, Sureda 2019) will better illuminate the vectors of initial settlement, and this in turn may allow improved understanding of this curiously late colonization episode. We note here briefly that, from the perspective offered by island biogeography, the Balearic example indicates that not only insular ecogeography, but also the relationship between continental landscapes and their populations, profoundly influences colonization dynamics.

Discussion and Conclusion

> No one wants to row who has ever sailed.
>
> *Arthur Ransome (1930)*

By the close of the third millennium BC, the overwhelming majority of the Mediterranean's islands had been settled by farming communities. Within this general settlement trend, it is possible to discern ways of living tailored to local demands, buttressing emerging cultural traditions with distinctively island flavors—whether the seabird-and-mollusc-eating *naveta*-dwellers of Formentera, tattooed marble fetishists-cum-longboat voyagers of the central Aegean, or aggrandizing *petit seigneurs* in the Sardinian interior. This florescence recalls similarly deviating trajectories in the precontact Pacific and Caribbean, both rife with divergent traditions and material cultures. The first appearance of sails

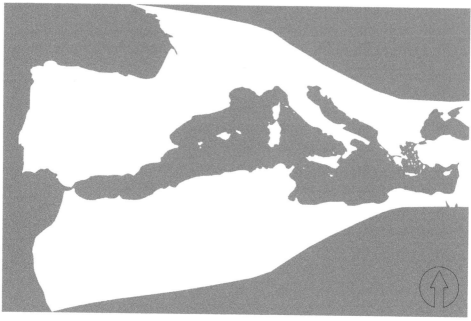

Figure 10.7. The shrinkage of the Mediterranean under the impact of sailing technology; an example of the situation in the mid-second millennium BC, with sailing technology prevalent in the east, intrusive in the center, and unknown in the west. (Reproduced from Broodbank 2010: fig. 20.3).

on the horizon brought this florescence, in the Mediterranean as much as beyond it, to a crashing halt.

We need not dwell here on the transformative nature of the introduction of large, square-rigged sailing vessels in the Mediterranean (first evidenced on the Nile in the fourth millennium, reaching the Aegean and then further west between circa 2,000 and 1,200 BC), except to emphasize that it effectively demarcated the end of a colonizing process begun several millennia before. Broodbank (2010) rightly stresses the disruptive aspect of this arrival for societies premised on short-distance, labor-intensive paddling that could carry cargoes only as large as beam, draft, and freeboard allowed. A square rig on a plank-built hull was a distance-crushing technology, revolutionary in terms of bulk transport over hitherto forbidding distances (Figure 10.7). Bypassing old centers of powers and fostering new ones, this technology—foreshadowing "globalizing" technological disruptions yet to come—remolded island societies, plugging the island Mediterranean into tightly knit ebbing-and-flowing networks of exchange and exploitation. It is possible to go too far in stressing Mediterranean connectivity (Woolf 2016); the vast majority of those living around the Mediterranean shore probably

Thomas P. Leppard, Alexander J. Smith, and John F. Cherry

never set foot in a vessel like that of the *Ulu Burun* shipwreck, a trireme, or a Roman *annona* behemoth. Nonetheless, the increasingly integrated Mediterranean of the second and then first millennium BC represents a sea change in the cultural dynamics of its islands, now more readily understood as part of a whole and less so as insular. Accordingly, this is as good a place as any to conclude a survey of these islands' early history.

Why does the foregoing matter, and what does it contribute to a wider Mediterranean archaeology? There are patterns that are now robust enough—Upper Paleolithic exploitation of the big Tyrrhenian islands, or very late colonization of the Balearics—that we can assume we have essentially grasped the spatial and temporal dimensions of real, human phenomena. This is especially true as we move into the Middle and Late Holocene. Vital here is the increasingly large radiocarbon dataset, bolstering refined (but fallible) ceramic type series. Temporal grip is important, not least as we become more aware of the complex nature of human-environment feedback dynamics after the establishment of Neolithic lifestyles, and the broader changes these feedbacks drive in biophysical systems. More generally, the emerging picture of capacity for, but reluctance to undertake, island settlement forces us to reflect more carefully on the factors behind large-scale social change in the early Mediterranean: why were certain choices about dispersal made, and what were deeper catalysts for movement? The tantalizing yet vague correlations between sudden, large-scale ruptures in mainland social organization and bursts of island colonization (for example, in the FN-EB1 Aegean, or Early Bronze western Mediterranean) seem promising avenues in which island archaeology may illuminate broader processes.

Why should island archaeologists working beyond the Strait of Gibraltar care? In terms of explicit comparanda, Broodbank (2018)—surely correctly—suggests that the archipelagos of tropical Southeast Asia provide the most instructive parallels. Both Island Southeast Asia and the Mediterranean are dense tapestries of land and sea, subject to early dispersal (including hominins outside of our own species) followed by a thick carpet of Holocene occupation built in part upon remote but attractive insular resources (whether obsidian from Melos or nutmeg from the Banda Islands). Island Southeast Asia, with its increasingly well-understood paleoanthropological record (see Rabett 2018), for example, may well provide the only possible parallels in understanding premodern maritime activity. More generally, it becomes increasingly clear that islands—unexpectedly, in terms of widely accepted models of emergent social complexity worldwide—contribute more than their fair share of examples of complex or hierarchical societies, and the Mediterranean is no exception. Nevertheless, the high temporal resolution we have over our data, coupled with a rich archaeological record, suggests that the Mediterranean should prove a robust testing ground for theories of emergent complexity both within insular environments, and beyond them.

Acknowledgments

We are grateful to the editors of this volume for their remarkable tenacity in convincing us to contribute this chapter. We would like to thank: Caroline Malone, Simon Stoddart, and Rowan McLaughlin for information regarding radiocarbon dates from FRAGSUS; Vasileios Lykousis for his kind permission to reproduce a figure; Nena Galanidou for allowing us to see a new paper prior to its publication; Gianpiero di Maida for fruitful conversations in Mettmann; and Helen Dawson for clarifying the central Mediterranean data. Leppard's work on this paper was supported by a Renfrew Fellowship jointly held between the McDonald Institute for Archaeological Research and Homerton College, University of Cambridge, support for which he is grateful and acknowledges. Smith's research is made possible by the Department of Anthropology, College at Brockport—State University of New York. Cherry expresses heartfelt appreciation for the institutional and financial support he has received, over many years, in support of his research in the Mediterranean and Caribbean islands, from the University of Cambridge, the University of Michigan, and Brown University.

Notes

1. A variety of different terms (Epipaleolithic, Mesolithic, pre-Neolithic) is used in the Mediterranean to denote periods of greater and lesser length that lie between the retreat of the northern ice sheets and the appearance of farming lifeways, terms that often implicitly connote not only temporal but cultural and behavioral units. The situation is problematic and confusing. Here, we utilize "Mesolithic" to denote that period of time that lies between the start of the Holocene at 11.7 kya and the radiocarbon-dated advent of the Neolithic around the basin; this means the Mesolithic of Portugal is longer than the Mesolithic of the Aegean. In the case of sites and assemblages dated slightly to the Pleistocene side of this boundary (for example, Ouriakos on Lemnos; Efstratiou et al. 2014), but which have strong affinities with typically Mesolithic technological complexes, it seems reasonable to use the latter term.

2. Not just of Crete but, considering the near contemporaneity in radiocarbon terms of the Early Neolithic at Ulucak and Franchthi (Brami 2015), also probably of the Balkan eastern seaboard from Anatolia.

3. Tiny Palagruža in the middle of the Adriatic, which from this perspective has no

business displaying evidence of Early Neolithic ceramics (Forenbaher and Kaiser 2011; Forenbaher 2018), should be seen as a stopover point during movements between clusters of Neolithic occupation in southern Illyria and the Italian Tavoliere.

4. This ignores Ly-2836 and Ly-2835 from Strette (whose calibrated ranges at 2σ are so broad [6393–4401 and 5976–4714 cal BC respectively] as to be suspect), and AA-65497 from Sa Punta (marine shell with no local marine reservoir correction [ΔR] reported).

References

Ammerman, A. J. 2013. Tracing the Steps in the Fieldwork at the Sites of Aspros and Nissi Beach on Cyprus. *Eurasian Prehistory* 10(1–2): 117–138.

Antonioli, F., V. Lo Presti, M. Morticelli, L. Bonfiglio, M. Mannino, M. Palombo, G. Sannino, L. Ferranti, S. Furlani, K. Lambeck, S. Canese, R. Catalano, F. Chiocci, G. Mangano, G. Scicchitano, and R. Tonielli. 2014. Timing of the Emergence of the Europe–Sicily Bridge (40–17 cal ka BP) and Its Implications for the Spread of Modern Humans. *Geological Society Special Publications* 411: 111–144.

Ardesia, V., M. Cattani, M. Marazzi, F. Nicoletti, M. Secondos, and S. Tusa. 2006. Gli Scavi nell'abitato dell'età del Bronzo di Mursia, Pantelleria (TP). *Rivista di Scienze Preistoriche* 56: 1–75.

Atici, L., S. Pilaar Birch, and B. Erdoğu. 2017. Spread of Domestic Animals across Neolithic Western Anatolia: New Zooarchaeological Evidence from Uğurlu Höyük, the Island of Gökçeada, Turkey. *PLoS ONE* 12(10): e0186519.

Bar-Yosef, O., and F. Valla. 2013. *Natufian Foragers in the Levant: Terminal Pleistocene Social Changes in Western Asia*. Ann Arbor, MI: International Monographs in Prehistory.

Bevan, A., and J. Conolly. 2013. *Mediterranean Islands, Fragile Communities and Persistent Landscapes: Antikythera in Long-Term Perspective*. Cambridge: Cambridge University Press.

Brami, M. N. 2015. A Graphical Simulation of the 2,000-year Lag in Neolithic Occupation between Central Anatolia and the Aegean Basin. *Archaeological and Anthropological Sciences* 7(3): 319–327.

Broodbank, C. 2000. *An Island Archaeology of the Early Cyclades*. Cambridge: Cambridge University Press.

Broodbank, C. 2006. The Origins and Early Development of Mediterranean Maritime Activity. *Journal of Mediterranean Archaeology* 19: 199–230.

Broodbank, C. 2010. "Ships A-sail from Over the Rim of the Sea": Voyaging, Sailing and the Making of Mediterranean Societies c. 3500–500 BC. In *The Global Origins of Seafaring*, ed. A. Anderson, J. Barrett, and K. Boyle, 249–264. Cambridge: McDonald Institute for Archaeological Research.

Broodbank, C. 2013. *The Making of the Middle Sea: A History of the Mediterranean from the Beginning to the Emergence of the Classical World*. London: Thames and Hudson.

Broodbank, C. 2014. So . . . What? Does the Paradigm Currently Want to Budge So Much? *Journal of Mediterranean Archaeology* 27: 267–272.

Broodbank, C. 2018. Does Island Archaeology Matter? In *Regional Approaches to Society and Complexity: Studies in Honor of John F. Cherry*, ed. A. R. Knodell and T. P. Leppard, 188–206. Sheffield: Equinox.

Brose, U., A. Ostling, K. Harrison, and N. Martinez. 2004. Unified Spatial Scaling of Species and Their Trophic Interactions. *Nature* 428: 167–171.

Burjachs, F., R. Pérez-Obiol, L. Picornell-Gelabert, J. Revelles, G. Servera-Vives, I. Expósito, and E.-I. Yll. 2017. Overview of Environmental Changes and Human Colonization in the

Balearic Islands (Western Mediterranean) and Their Impacts on Vegetation Composition during the Holocene. *Journal of Archaeological Science: Reports* 12: 845–859.

Carter, T. 2016. Obsidian Consumption in the Late Pleistocene–Early Holocene Aegean: Contexualising New Data from Mesolithic Crete. *Annual of the British School at Athens* 111: 13–34.

Carter, T., D. Contreras, S. Doyle, D. Mihailović, T. Moutsiou, and N. Skarpelis. 2014. The Stélida Naxos Archaeological Project: New Data on the Middle Paleolithic and Mesolithic Cyclades. *Antiquity* 88(341): Project Gallery.

Carter, T., D. Contreras, J. Holcomb, D. Mihailović, P. Karkanas, G. Guérin, N. Taffin, D. Athanasoulis, and C. Lahaye. 2019. Earliest Occupation of the Central Aegean (Naxos), Greece: Implications for Hominin and *Homo sapiens'* Behavior and Dispersals. *Science Advances* 5(10): eaax0997.

Chelidonio, G. 2001. Manufatti Litici su Ciottolo da Milos (Isole Cicladi). Nota Preliminare. *Pegaso* 1: 117–144.

Cherry, J. F. 1981. Pattern and Process in the First Colonization of the Mediterranean Islands. *Proceedings of the Prehistoric Society* 47: 41–68.

Cherry, J. F. 1984. The Initial Colonisation of the West Mediterranean Islands in the Light of Island Biogeography and Palaeogeography. In *The Deyà Conference of Prehistory: Early Settlement in the West Mediterranean Islands and the Peripheral Areas,* ed. W. H. Waldren, R. Chapman, J. Lewthwaite, and R. C. Kennard, 1–15. British Archaeological Reports, International Series 229. Oxford: British Archaeological Reports.

Cherry, J. F. 1990. The First Colonization of the Mediterranean Islands: A Reviews of Recent Research. *Journal of Mediterranean Archaeology* 3: 145–221.

Cherry, J. F. 2004. Mediterranean Island Prehistory: What's Different and What's New? In *Voyages of Discovery: The Archaeology of Islands,* ed. S. M. Fitzpatrick, 233–248. Westport, Connecticut: Praeger.

Cherry, J. F., and T. P. Leppard. 2015. Experimental Archaeology and the Earliest Seafaring: The Limitations of Inference. *World Archaeology* 47: 740–755.

Cherry, J. F., and T. P. Leppard. 2018a. Patterning and Its Causation in the Pre-Neolithic Colonization of the Mediterranean Islands (Late Pleistocene to Early Holocene). *The Journal of Island and Coastal Archaeology* 13(2): 191–205.

Cherry, J. F., and T. P. Leppard. 2018b. The Balearic Paradox: Why Were the Islands Colonized So Late? *Pyrenae* 49(1): 1–22.

Chilardi, S., D. W. Frayer, P. Gioia, and R. Macchiarelli. 1996. Fontana Nuova di Ragusa (Sicily, Italy): Southernmost Aurignacian Site in Europe. *Antiquity* 70: 553–563.

Çilingiroğlu Ç. 2017. The Aegean Before and After 7000 BC Dispersal: Defining Patterning and Variability. *Neo-Lithics* 1(16): 32–41.

Çilingiroğlu Ç., and C. Çakirlar. 2013. Towards Configuring the Neolithisation of Aegean Turkey. *Documenta Praehistorica* 40: 21–29.

Costa, L.-J., J.-D. Vigne, H. Bocherens, N. Desse-Berset, C. Heinz, F. de Lanfranchi, J. Magdeleine, M.-P. Ruas, S. Thiebault, and C. Tozzi. 2003. Early Settlement on Tyrrhenian Islands (8th millennium cal. BC): Mesolithic Adaptation to Local Resources in Corsica and Northern Sardinia. In *Mesolithic on the Move,* ed. L. Larsson, H. Kindgren, K. Knutsson, D. Loeffler, and A. Akerlund, 3–10. Oxford: Oxbow.

Dawson, H. 2008. Unravelling "Mystery" and Process from the Prehistoric Colonisation and Abandonment of the Mediterranean Islands. In *Comparative Island Archaeologies,* ed. J. Conolly and M. Campbell, 105–133. British Archaeological Reports, International Series 1829. Oxford: Archaeopress.

Dawson, H. 2014. *Mediterranean Voyages. The Archaeology of Island Colonisation and Abandonment.* Walnut Creek, California: Left Coast Press.

Di Maida, G., M. Mannino, B. Krause-Kyora, T. Zetner, T. Jensen, and S. Talamo. 2019. Radiocarbon Dating and Isotope Analysis on the Purported Aurignacian Skeletal Remains from Fontana Nuova (Ragusa, Italy). *PLoS ONE* 14(3): e0213173.

Douka, K., N. Efstratiou, M. M. Hald, P. S. Henriksen, and A. Karetsou. 2017. Dating Knossos and the Arrival of the Earliest Neolithic in the Southern Aegean. *Antiquity* 91: 304–321.

Efstratiou, N., P. Biagi, and E. Starnini. 2014. The Epipalaeolithic Site of Ouriakos on the Island of Lemnos and Its Place in the Late Pleistocene Peopling of the East Mediterranean Region. *Adalya* 17: 1–24.

Ferentinos, G., M. Gkioni, M. Geraga, and G. Papatheodorou. 2012. Early Seafaring Activity in the Southern Ionian Islands, Mediterranean Sea. *Journal of Archaeological Science* 39: 2167–2176.

Forenbaher, S. 2018. *Special Place, Interesting Times: The Island of Palagruža and Transitional Periods in Adriatic Prehistory.* Oxford: Archaeopress.

Forenbaher, S., and T. Kaiser. 2011. Palagruža and the Spread of Farming in the Adriatic. In *The First Mediterranean Islanders: Initial Occupation and Survival Strategies,* ed. N. Phoca-Cosmetatou, 99–111. Oxford: Oxbow.

Freund, K. P., R. H. Tykot, and A. Vianello. 2015. Blade Production and the Consumption of Obsidian in Stentinello period Neolithic Sicily. *Comptes Rendus Palevol* 14(3): 207–217.

Galanidou, N. 2011. Mesolithic Cave Use in Greece and the Mosaic of Human Communities. *Journal of Mediterranean Archaeology* 24: 219–242.

Galanidou, N., G. Iliopoulos, and C. Papoulia. 2016. The Palaeolithic Settlement of Lefkas. Archaeological Evidence in a Palaeogeographic Context. *Journal of Greek Archaeology* 1: 1–31.

Galanidou, N., C. Athanassas, J. Cole, G. Iliopoulos, A. Katerinopoulos, A. Magganas, and J. McNabb. 2017. The Acheulian Site at Rodafnidia, Lisvori, on Lesbos, Greece: 2010–2012. In *Paleoanthropology of the Balkans and Anatolia: Human Evolution and its Context,* ed. K. Harvati and M. Roksandic, 119–138. New York: Springer.

Garcia-Castellano, D., F. Estrada, I. Jiménez-Munt, C. Gorini, M. Fernàndez, J. Vergés, and R. De Vicente. 2009. Catastrophic Flood of the Mediterranean after the Messinian Salinity Crisis. *Nature* 462: 778–781.

Halstead, P. 2008. Between a Rock and a Hard Place: Coping with Marginal Colonisation in the Later Neolithic and Early Bronze Age of Crete and the Aegean. In *Escaping the Labyrinth: Cretan Neolithic in Context,* ed. V. Isaakidou and P. Tomkins, 229–257. Sheffield Studies in Aegean Archaeology 8. Oxford: Oxbow.

Hoffmann, D. L., D. E. Angelucci, V. Villaverde, J. Zapata, and J. Zilhão. 2018. Symbolic Use of Marine Shells and Mineral Pigments by Iberian Neandertals 115,000 Years Ago. *Science Advances* 4: eaar5255.

Hofmanová, Z., S. Kreutzer, G. Hellenthal, C. Sell, Y. Diekmann, D. Díez-del-Molino, L. van Dorp, S. López, A. Kousathanas, V. Link, K. Kirsanow, L. M. Cassidy, R. Martiniano, M. Strobel, A. Scheu, K. Kotsakis, P. Halstead, S. Triantaphyllou, N. Kyparissi-Apostolika, D. Urem-Kotsou, C. Ziota, F. Adaktylou, S. Gopalan, D. M. Bobo, L. Winklebach, J. Blöcher, M. Unterländer, C. Leuenberger, Ç. Çilingiroğlu, B. Horejs, F. Gerritsen, S. J. Shennen, D. G. Bradley, M. Currat, K. R. Veeramah, D. Webmann, M. G. Thomas, C. Papageorgopoulou, and J. Burger. 2016. Early Farmers from across Europe Directly Descended from Neolithic Aegeans. *Proceedings of the National Academy of Sciences* 113(25): 6886–6891.

Howitt-Marshall, D., and C. N. Runnels. 2016. Middle Pleistocene Sea-crossings in the Eastern Mediterranean? *Journal of Anthropological Archaeology* 42: 140–153.

Hublin, J.-J., A. Ben-Ncer, S. E. Bailey, S. Freidline, S. Neubauer, M. Skinner, I. Bergmann, A. Le

Cabec, S. Benazzi, K. Harvati, and P. Gunz. 2017. New Fossils from Jebel Irhoud, Morocco and the Pan-African Origin of *Homo sapiens*. *Nature* 546: 289–292.

Isern, N., J. Zilhão, J. Fort, and A. Ammerman. 2017. Modeling the Role of Voyaging in the Coastal Spread of the Early Neolithic in the West Mediterranean. *Proceedings of the National Academy of Sciences* 114: 897–902.

Johansson, S. 2014. The Thinking Neanderthals: What Do We Know about Neanderthal Cognition? *Wiley Interdisciplinary Review: Cognitive Science* 5: 613–620.

Keegan, W. F., and J. Diamond. 1987. Colonization of Islands by Humans: A Biogeographical Perspective. *Advances in Archaeological Method and Theory* 10: 49–92.

Knapp, A. B. 2010. Cyprus's Earliest Prehistory: Seafarers, Foragers and Settlers. *Journal of World Prehistory* 23: 79–120.

Knodell, A. D. Athanasoulis, Z. Tankosič, J. F. Cherry, T. J. Garonis, E. Levine, D. Nenova, and H. Öztürk. 2020. An Island Archaeology of Uninhabited Landscapes: Off-shore Islets near Paros, Greece (The Small Cycladic Islands Project). *Journal of Island and Coastal Archaeology* 15.

Kopaka, K., and C. Matzanas. 2009. Palaeolithic Industries from the Island of Gavdos, Near Neighbor to Crete in Greece. *Antiquity* 83(321): DOI: 10.1080/15564894.2020.1807426.

Larrasoaña, J. C., A. P. Roberts, and E. J. Rohling. 2013. Dynamics of Green Sahara Periods and Their Role in Hominin Evolution. *PLoS ONE* 8(10): e76514.

Leppard, T. P. 2014. Modeling the Impacts of Mediterranean Island Colonization by Archaic Hominins: The Likelihood of an Insular Lower Palaeolithic. *Journal of Mediterranean Archaeology* 27: 231–254.

Leppard, T. P. 2015a. The Evolution of Modern Behaviour and Its Implications for Maritime Dispersal During the Palaeolithic. *Cambridge Archaeological Journal* 25: 829–846.

Leppard, T. P. 2015b. Passive Dispersal Versus Strategic Dispersal in Island Colonization by Hominins. *Current Anthropology* 56: 590–595.

Leppard, T. P. 2018. Unique Challenges in Archipelagoes: Examples from the Mediterranean and Pacific islands. In *Island Historical Ecology: Socionatural Landscapes across the Caribbean Sea,* ed. P. Siegel, 15–33. New York: Bergahn.

Leppard, T. P., and S. Pilaar Birch. 2016. The Insular Ecology and Palaeoenvironmental Impacts of the Domestic Goat (*Capra hircus*) in Mediterranean Neolithization. In *Géoarchéologie des Îles de la Méditerranée,* ed. M. Ghilardi, F. Leandri, J. Bloemendal, L. Lespez, and S. Fachard, 47–56. Paris: CNRS Editions Alpha.

Leppard, T. P., and C. N. Runnels. 2017. Maritime Hominin Dispersals in the Pleistocene: Advancing the Debate. *Antiquity* 356: 510–519.

Lubell, D., M. Jackes, H. Schwarcz, M. Knyf, C. Meiklejohn. 1994. The Mesolithic-Neolithic Transition in Portugal: Isotopic and Dental Evidence of Diet. *Journal of Archaeological Science* 21: 201–216.

Lugliè, C. 2018. Your Path Led Trough [sic] the Sea . . . The Emergence of Neolithic in Sardinia and Corsica. *Quaternary International* 470(B): 285–300.

Lykousis, V. 2009. Sea-level Changes and Shelf Break Prograding Sequences during the Last 400 ka in the Aegean Margins: Subsidence Rates and Palaeogeographic Implications. *Continental Shelf Research* 29: 2037–2044.

MacArthur, R. H., and E. O. Wilson. 1963. An Equilibrium Theory of Insular Zoogeography. *Evolution* 17(4): 373–387.

Malone, C., N. Cutajar, T. R. McLaughlin, B. Mercieca-Spiteri, A. Pace, R. K. Power, S. Stoddart, S. Sultana, C. Bronk Ramsey, E. Dunbar, A. Bayliss, F. Healy, and A. Whittle. 2019. Island Questions: The Chronology of the Brochtorff Circle at Xaghra, Gozo, and Its Significance for the Neolithic Sequence on Malta. *Archaeological and Anthropological Sciences* 11: 4251–4306.

Mannino, G. 1998. Il Neolitico nel Palermitano e la Nuova Scoperta nell'Isola di Ustica. *Quaderni del Museo Archeologico Regionale "Antonio Salinas"* 4: 45–80.

Martini, F., and C. Tozzi. 2012. Il Mesolitico in Sardegna. In *La Preistoria e la Protostoria della Sardegna: Atti della XLIV Riunione Scientifica, Cagliari, Barumini, Sassari, 23–28 novembre 2009*, 3390406. Firenze: Istituto di preistoria e protostoria.

Mommsen, T. 1911. *The History of Rome*. Translated by W. P Dickson. London: Dent.

Munro, N. D., and M. C. Stiner. 2015. Zooarchaeological Evidence for Early Neolithic Colonization at Franchthi Cave (Peloponnese, Greece). *Current Anthropology* 56: 596–603.

Munro, N. D., and M. C. Stiner. 2020. A Zooarchaeological History of the Neolithic Occupations at Franchthi Cave and Paralia in Southern Greece. *Journal of Anthropological Archaeology* 58: 101162.

Mussi, M., and R. T. Melis. 2002. Santa Maria is Acquas e le Problematiche del Paleolitico Superiore in Sardegna. *Origini* 24: 67–94.

Papoulia, C. 2017. Seaward Dispersals to the NE Mediterranean Islands in the Pleistocene: The Lithic Evidence in Retrospect. *Quaternary International* 431: 64–87.

Perlès, C., A. Quiles, and H. Valladas. 2013. Early Seventh-Millennium AMS Dates from Domestic Seeds in the Initial Neolithic at Franchthi Cave (Argolid, Greece). *Antiquity* 87: 1001–1015.

Rabett, R. 2018. The Success of Failed *Homo sapiens* Dispersals Out of Africa and Into Asia. *Nature Ecology and Evolution* 2: 212–219.

Radi, G. 1972. Tracce di un Insediamento Neolitico nell'Isola di Lampedusa. *Atti della Società Toscana di Scienze Naturali A* 79: 197–205.

Ramis, D., J. A. Alcover, J. Coll, and M. Trias. 2002. The Chronology of the First Settlement of the Balearic Islands. *Journal of Mediterranean Archaeology* 15: 3–24.

Ransome, A. 1930. *Swallows and Amazons*. London: Jonathan Cape.

Renfrew, C., and A. Aspinall. 1990. Aegean Obsidian and Franchthi Cave. In *Excavations at Franchthi Cave, Greece. Fascicle 5*, 257–279. Bloomington: Indiana University Press.

Renfrew, C., M. Boyd, and C. Bronk Ramsey. 2012. The Oldest Maritime Sanctuary? Dating the Sanctuary at Keros and the Cycladic Early Bronze Age. *Antiquity* 86: 144–160.

Reingruber, A., and L. Thissen. 2009. Depending on [14]C Data: Chronological Frameworks in the Neolithic and Chalcolithic of Southeastern Europe. *Radiocarbon* 51: 751–770.

Richards, M. P., R. Jacobi, J. Cook, P. Pettitt, and C. Stringer. 2005. Isotope Evidence for the Intensive Use of Marine Foods by Late Upper Palaeolithic Humans. *Journal of Human Evolution* 49: 390–394.

Runnels, C. 2014. Early Palaeolithic on the Greek Islands? *Journal of Mediterranean Archaeology* 27: 211–230.

Runnels, C. N., F. McCoy, R. Bauslaugh, and P. Murray. 2014a. Palaeolithic Research at Mochlos, Crete: New Evidence for Pleistocene Maritime Activity in the Aegean. *Antiquity* 88(342): Project Gallery.

Runnels, C. N., C. DiGregorio, K. W. Wegmann, S. Gallen, T. Strasser, and E. Panagopoulou. 2014b. Lower Palaeolithic Artifacts from Plakias, Crete: Implications for Hominin Dispersals. *Eurasian Prehistory* 11(1–2): 129–152.

Sakellariou, D., and N. Galanidou. 2016. Pleistocene Submerged Landscapes and Palaeolithic Archaeology in the Tectonically Active Aegean Region. In *Geology and Archaeology: Submerged Landscapes of the Continental Shelf*, ed. J. Harff, G. Bailey, and F. Lüth, 145–178. London: Geological Society.

Sampson, A. 2014. The Aegean Mesolithic: Environment, Economy, and Seafaring. *Eurasian Prehistory* 11(1–2): 63–74.

Simmons, A. H. 2014. *Stone Age Sailors: Paleolithic Seafaring in the Mediterranean*. Walnut Creek, California: Left Coast Press.

Sondaar, P. Y., R. Elburg, G. K. Hofmeier, F. Martini, M. Sanges, A. Spaan, and H. de Visser. 1995. The Human Colonization of Sardinia: A Late-Pleistocene Human Fossil from Corbeddu Cave. *Comptes rendus de l'Académie des Sciences* 320(IIa): 145–150.

Strasser, T. F., E. Panagopoulou, C. N. Runnels, P. Murray, N. Thompson, P. Karkanas, F. McCoy, and K Wegmann. 2010. Stone Age Seafaring in the Mediterranean: Evidence from the Plakias Region for Lower Palaeolithic and Mesolithic Habitation of Crete. *Hesperia* 79: 145–190.

Strasser, T. F., C. N. Runnels, K. Wegmann, E. Panagopoulou, F. McCoy, C. Digregorio, P. Karkanas, N. Thompson. 2011. Dating Palaeolithic sites in Southwestern Crete, Greece. *Journal of Quaternary Science* 26: 553–560.

Strasser, T. F., C. N. Runnels, and C. Vita-Finzi. 2016. A Possible Palaeolithic Handaxe from Cyprus. *Antiquity* 90(350): Project Gallery.

Sureda, P. 2019. First Metallurgy in the Pithyusic Islands (Balearic Archipelago, Mediterranean Sea). *Archaeological and Anthropological Sciences* 11: 2727–2741.

Woolf, G. 2016. Movers and Stayers. In *Migration and Mobility in the Early Roman Empire,* ed. L. de Ligt and L. E. Tacoma, 438–462. Leiden: Brill.

Wynn, T., and F. L. Coolidge. 2012. *How to Think Like a Neandertal.* New York: Oxford University Press.

Zavitsanou A., D. Sakellariou, G. Rousakis, P. Georgiou, and N. Galanidou. 2015. Paleogeographic Reconstruction of the Inner Ionian Sea During Late Pleistocene Low Sealevel Stands: Preliminary Results. *Proceedings of the 11th Panhellenic Symposium on Oceanography and Fisheries:* 997–1000.

11

Human Migration from Wallacea to Oceania and the Development of Maritime Networks during the Neolithic to Early Metal Age

RINTARO ONO, ADHI AGUS OKTAVIANA, HARRY
OCTAVIANUS SOFIAN, SRIWIGATI, AND NASULLAH AZIZ

The initial colonization of Sahul (Australia and New Guinea) in Oceania represents the earliest evidence of intentional and relatively long-distance (over 80 km) seafaring by modern humans (Bird et al. 2019; Erlandson 2001; Kealy et al. 2016; Norman et al. 2018). Currently, the earliest archaeological traces of modern humans in Sahul are dated to circa 49–42 kya, but may be as old as circa 65 kya (Clarkson et al. 2017; O'Connell and Allen 2004; Summerhayes et al. 2010; Wood et al. 2016). The timing for the initial modern human migration into Sahul is still controversial, but many researchers agree that Wallacea (geographically East Indonesia and East Timor) is the point of origin. The term "Wallacea" came from Alfred Russel Wallace (1869), who voyaged through the Malay Archipelago and recognized the zoogeographic divide running between Sumatra, Java, and Borneo/Kalimantan—formerly all connected to the mainland when sea levels were lower—and Bali, Sulawesi, Maluku, Sunda, and Timor. That division, now known as the Wallace Line, is attributed to the deep sea between the two regions. Many animals, especially mammals, were unable to migrate beyond that line, resulting in a boundary for many taxa.

There are, however, a few notable exceptions of open-water travel by hominins prior to those made by *Homo sapiens* into Wallacea. Fossil remains of *Homo floresiensis* and stone tools made by *Homo erectus* on Flores Island indicate the possible presence of hominin species in Wallacea circa 800–60 kya (Morwood et al. 2004), while *Homo luzonensis* on Luzon Island in the northern Philippines suggests that another small-bodied human species similar to *H.*

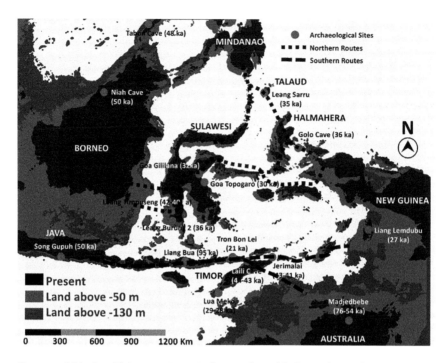

Figure 11.1. Major Late Pleistocene sites in Wallacea and possible dispersal routes by early modern humans.

floresiensis was capable of open-ocean crossings at least by circa 66 kya (Détroit et al. 2019). Although no fossil remains have been recovered, stone tools associated with megafauna dating to circa 100 kya on Sulawesi are attributed to pre–*Homo sapiens* (van den Bergh et al. 2016). These few case studies are the earliest examples of island colonization that required open-water crossings of up to circa 20 km. It was not until much later that *Homo sapiens* colonized most of the small remote islands in Wallacea and Sahul with sea crossings of circa 20–200 km during the late Pleistocene (O'Connor et al. 2011, 2019; Ono 2016; Ono et al. 2009). The earliest human colonization occurred via island(s) in Wallacea that were located next to Sahul regions in the west. For early modern human migration from Wallacea into Sahul, two major routes have been suggested: a northern route from Sulawesi to the Maluku Islands and into the region of New Guinea, and a southern route leading into northern Australia (Birdsell 1977; see Figure 11.1). Currently, the archaeological traces of early modern humans could extend to around 44–42 kya in both routes (Aubert et al. 2014, 2019; Hawking et al. 2017; O'Connor et al. 2011). Since the earliest evidence for modern humans in

Sahul now extends to 49–47 ka, there should be much earlier traces in Wallacea as well (Figure 11.1).

In Oceania, early modern humans colonized Sahul and the eastern islands to Buka in the Solomon Islands. This area is known as "Near Oceania" because each island is located within circa 80 km and visible to the other. Australia is the exception to this as it may only have been visible from the highlands on Timor Island (Norman et al. 2018). All other islands in Melanesia east of the Solomon Islands, as well as Polynesia and Micronesia, were not colonized until much later. This region, known as Remote Oceania, is made up of islands that are more remote with greater distances between them, and are often not visible to each other. The remoteness of these islands may be one factor that prevented colonization by early modern humans. Another possible factor is limited land resources (both plants and animals) on small islands, especially atolls. For example, no mammals except some bat species and no large- to middle-sized terrestrial animals except some bird species are endemic to islands in Remote Oceania. For early modern humans whose major subsistence strategy was hunting and gathering, such limited terrestrial resources could be very critical for their continuous survival in such island environments.

The second major human migration into Wallacea and Oceania was during the Neolithic, circa 4000–3000 BP. This event is significant because it marks the first human dispersal into Remote Oceania by Austronesian groups who practiced farming, animal husbandry of pig (*Sus scrofa*), dog (*Canis lupis familiaris*), and chicken (*Gallus gallus*), pottery making, and had advanced fishing and navigational technologies (for example, Bellwood 2013; Kirch 2000; Ono 2010). Recent archaeological and linguistic studies support the idea that these Austronesian-speaking peoples dispersed into Island Southeast Asia (ISEA), including Wallacea and most of Oceania, from Asia. Linguistic reconstruction of Proto-Austronesian words related to farming and fishing suggests the antiquity of plant and animal exploitation among Austronesian speakers (for example, Blust 1985, 1995). Many archaeologists and linguists (for example, Bellwood 1997, 2017; Blust 1995) believe that the ultimate origins of Austronesian subsistence strategies and material culture lie along Taiwan and the coast of ISEA, particularly around the Wallacean region in Eastern Indonesia, as is strongly advocated by Solheim's Nusantao hypothesis (for example, Solheim 1964, 1988, 2002).

Early traces of Austronesian-speaking people in Remote Oceania are found in the Mariana Islands in western Micronesia, which date to circa 3500–3200 BP, although the early chronology remains controversial (Carson 2014; Hung et al. 2011; Petchey et al. 2016; Rieth and Athens 2019). Reaching the Mariana Islands required at least a 2,000 km sea crossing from Asia, with the nearest possible homeland being the Philippine Islands, and thus demonstrates that Austronesians might have had a more advanced level of seafaring skill and maritime technology than their late Pleistocene ancestors. Settlement of the Palauan archipelago was roughly contemporaneous, at circa 3200–3000 BP (Clark 2005; Fitzpatrick 2003; Fitzpatrick and Jew 2018; Ono and Clark 2010; Stone et al. 2017). The colonization of Yap remains enigmatic, although ongoing fieldwork is beginning to address this (Napolitano et al. 2019). The other islands in Micronesia, including eastern Micronesia and most small atolls, were not colonized until much later, circa 2000 BP.

Initial Austronesian colonization of Melanesia and West Polynesia was by the so-called Lapita people, circa 3300–2500 BP, with the earliest sites in the Bismarck Archipelago dating to 3300–3100 BP. Early Lapita sites are well known for their diagnostic dentate-stamped pottery. By around 3000 BP, such Lapita sites with dentate-stamped pottery and other material culture extended east to Vanuatu, New Caledonia, and Fiji, beyond the boundary between Near Oceania and Remote Oceania (see chapters 2 and 7). By around 2800 BP, Lapita people colonized Sāmoa and Tonga in West Polynesia, and are thus considered ancestral to Polynesian people. Many of these Lapita sites also produced obsidian lithics originating from the Talasea Peninsula on New Britain Island in the Bismarck Archipelago, over 4,000 km from Fiji and West Polynesia. Such a broad distribution of obsidian from a single source, and similarly designed pottery, also indicates the possible development of long-distance interisland trade networks by Lapita people (Kirch 1997).

Surprisingly, Talasea-sourced obsidian was also excavated from Bukit Tengkorak along the eastern coast of Borneo—located circa 5,000 km away from the its source on New Britain Island—that dates to circa 3300–2000 BP (Bellwood and Koon 1989; Chia 2001; Ono 2004). This site also produced a number of red-slipped pottery sherds with a variety of decorations, although no dentate-stamped pottery was found. The discovery of the Talasea obsidian in Borneo also indicates the possible development of maritime interisland trade networks or the movement of people (and objects) between islands that spanned a much wider area between ISEA and Oceania than previously thought. Yet the total lack of dentate-stamped pottery in Bukit Tengkorak also shows that the Austronesian groups who used this site were neither Lapita people nor their direct ancestors. On the other hand, excavations in the Lallo shell midden sites along the Cagayan Valley in Northern Luzon produced dentate-stamped pottery that

R. Ono, A. Agus Oktaviana, H. Octavianus Sofian, Sriwigati, and N. Aziz

dates to circa 3800–3000 BP (Aoyagi et al. 1991, 1993; Bellwood 2017; Carson et al. 2013; Tsang et al. 2002). More recently, dentate-stamped pottery was also excavated from sites on Sulawesi that date to circa 3500–3000 BP (Anggraeni et al. 2014; Aziz et al. 2018). Our ongoing excavations at Goa Topogaro in Central Sulawesi also unearthed a large number of dentate-stamped pottery from the upper layer, although they date to 2000–1800 BP (Ono et al. 2019a). Even though these dates are younger than at other Neolithic sites—including Lapita sites—the recovery of dentate-stamped pottery in Sulawesi tentatively indicates that early Austronesian people with a dentate-stamped pottery tradition reached East Indonesia or Wallacea.

Importantly, the Bukit Tengkorak site demonstrates that not all the islands in ISEA were colonized by Austronesian groups with a dentate-stamped pottery tradition. This paper reports four archaeological sites used from the Neolithic to post-Neolithic in Wallacea to discuss early Austronesian migration into Wallacea and Oceania, and their subsistence and island adaptation strategies (Figure 11.2). Although the Neolithic colonization of Wallacea by Austronesian groups involves the arrival of people upon islands that have already been colonized

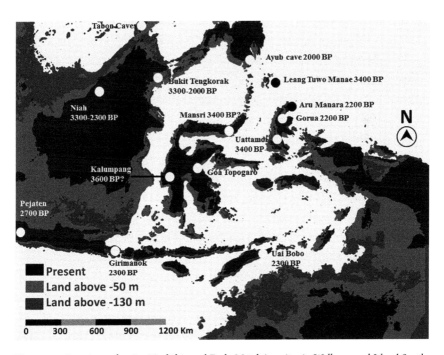

Figure 11.2. Locations of major Neolithic and Early Metal Age sites in Wallacea and Island Southeast Asia (ISEA).

by other humans, and is therefore distinct from other cases presented in this volume, we argue that the examples presented in this chapter should also be considered cases of island colonization. The arrival of Austronesian people in Wallacea and Near Oceania resulted in the introduction of a wide variety of new languages, subsistence strategies, domesticated plants and animals, and pottery traditions, among others. Additionally, successful settlement of the islands in Wallacea and Near Oceania required many of the same skills needed for initial colonization of previously uninhabited islands. The sites we report here are: (1) the Uattamdi site on Kayoa Island in Northern Maluku Islands; (2) the Aru Manara site on Morotai Island in Northern Maluku Islands; (3) the Gorua site on Halmahera Island in Northern Maluku Islands; and (4) the Goa Topogaro site in Central Sulawesi Island.

We consider both the Northern Maluku Islands and Sulawesi Island as the most significant regions in Wallacea because of their important geographic position. The Northern Malukus are located next to New Guinea, and they are the closest Wallacean islands to both Near and Remote Oceania. The current complicated linguistic distributions of Austronesian and Papuan languages in the Northern Malukus also suggest complex relationships and population movements between Wallacea and Oceania in the past (Bellwood 2019; Spriggs 1998). Located on the western edge of Wallacea, Sulawesi is the largest island (174,600 km^2) and is the only island in Wallacea where dentate-stamped pottery has been recovered.

More frequent human migrations and maritime trade networks developed in Wallacea and Oceania following the initial arrival of Austronesian people during the post-Neolithic (beginning circa 2200 BP). This is supported by linguistic evidence that demonstrates the transmigration of Austronesian and Papuan language–speaking groups in Northern and Eastern Wallacea, archaeological evidence for the expansion of similar pottery-making traditions, and later evidence for the possible spice trade between China, India, and Maluku (Bellwood 2019; Hung and Chao 2016; Miller 1969). It is also important to note that the arrival of metal (both bronze and iron) and glass objects possibly triggered additional migrations and expanded trading networks in the region (for example, Ono et al. 2017, 2018a, 2018b; Ono et al. 2019a). In this light, Wallacea is somewhat unique in that it can be considered to have witnessed a series of colonization events by circa 2000 BP. We also focus on the post-Neolithic human migration to reconstruct maritime networks and adaptations in both Wallacea and Oceania. More recently, Sulawesi, especially the southern part including Makassar/Ujung Pandang, has played an important role as a major market for maritime trade and human migration in Eastern Indonesia and Northern Australia (for example, Gerrit and Sutherland 2005; Schwerdtner and Ferse 2010).

Neolithic Human Migration and Maritime Adaptation in Wallacea and Oceania

Excavations on Uattamdi on Kayoa Island

In ISEA (including Wallacea), the number of excavated Neolithic sites is still very limited (see Figure 11.2). Among them, only three sites have been sufficiently excavated: (1) Leang Tuwo Manae, a rockshelter site in the Talaud Islands which dates to 3400–2000 BP (for example, Bellwood 1986, 1997; Tanudirjo 2001); (2) Uattamdi, a rockshelter site on Kayoa in the Northern Maluku Islands, which dates to 3500–1800 BP (for example, Bellwood 2019; Bellwood et al. 1998; Ono 2014); and (3) Karumpang, an open-air site on the southwestern part of Sulawesi, which dates to 3500–3000 BP (for example, Anggraeni et al. 2014; Bellwood 1997). As the dates suggest, use of these sites spanned the Neolithic and Early Metal Age.

In terms of Neolithic pottery, both Leang Tuwo Manae and Uattamdi produced red-slipped pottery that was primarily plain (that is, undecorated), while open-air sites in Karumpang produced red-slipped pottery with some incised and impressed decorations, and a few pieces of dentate-stamped pottery (Anggraeni et al. 2014). A number of domesticated pigs were excavated from Karumpang (Bellwood 2017), and some pig and dog bones were excavated from Uattamdi (Bellwood 2019). However, only Uattamdi produced a number of marine fish and shellfish remains, and evidence for maritime exploitation and adaptation (Bellwood 1997, 2017; Bellwood et al. 1998; Ono 2014).

Uattamdi is a complex of limestone rockshelters on a small island, with fringing coral reef developed on the western coast, where the site is located. The Uattamdi 1 site was previously excavated by Peter Bellwood and his team during the 1990s. They found a number of pottery sherds, stone tools, shell tools or ornaments, glass beads, shellfish, and fish, animal, and human bones. Human remains and glass beads were only recovered from the upper layer (Layer B), which dates to the Early Metal Age (ca. 2200–1800 BP). Pottery types show a clear difference between the Early Metal Age layer and the Neolithic layers (Bellwood 1997, 2017, 2019; Bellwood et al. 1998). Analysis of shellfish and fish remains were not fully made available until the recent publication of a monograph that details the full excavation (Bellwood 2019). Pusat Arkeologi Nasional Indonesia and Ono conducted excavations at two of the Uattamdi rockshelters in 2014 and 2015 (Ono 2014). The largest rockshelter that Bellwood excavated in the 1990s was Uattamdi 1 (Bellwood 2019). Bellwood and colleagues (1998) also report a second rockshelter next to Uattamdi 1, now named Uattamdi 2, while we found another shelter about 200 m north of Uattamdi 1 along the same limestone formation that we named Uattamdi 3. We excavated Uattamdi 1 and 3 with the goal of recovering pottery, stone and shell tools, glass beads, marine fish, shellfish, animal bones, and human remains. The previous excavations by Bellwood identified deposits over 1.2 m deep with sandy soil layers (Layer D and C) that date to the Neolithic (3400–2500 BP) and a shallower deposit (Layer B) dating to the Metal Age (2200–1800 BP) with burial jars, human remains, and glass beads (Bellwood 2019). We opened eight 1 × 1 m squares (Grid F3, 7, 8, 9, 10 and G7, 8, and E3) just next to the grids excavated by Bellwood and his team in 1994 (or 6 m trench) which are numbered as Grid E9-E4 (Figure 11.3).

Uattamdi 3 is located in a limestone formation complex with small rockshelters along the current lowland coast about 2.5 m above the current high tide level. The north mouth of Uattamdi 3 is about 5 m in length, the ceiling

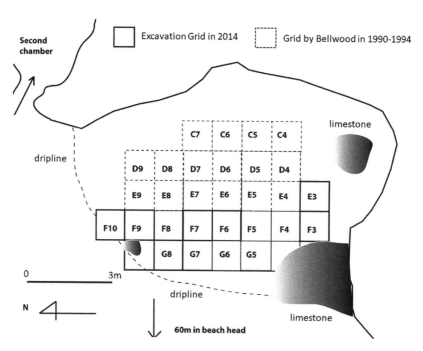

Figure 11.3. Units excavated in Uattamdi 1 by Bellwood in 1991 and 1994 and the authors in 2014.

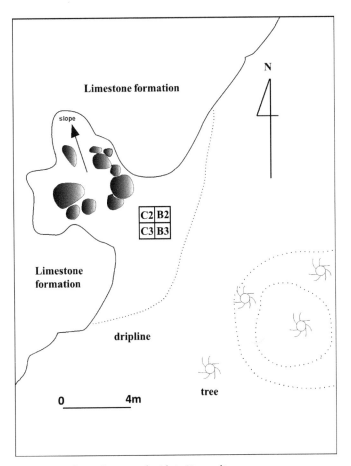

Figure 11.4. Plan and excavated grids in Uattamdi 3.

of the cave is about 6 m in height, and over 8–10 m in width from the mouth
to inner cave wall, making the inner area about 30 m² and thus wide enough
for human habitations in the past (Figure 11.4). Our excavations in Uattamdi 3
confirmed four cultural layers extending 2 m in depth like at Uattamdi 1: Layer
A, top soil; Layer B, which contained fragments of burial jars, human remains,
shells, potsherds, and a few shell ornaments in light brown sandy soil; Layer C,
which contained large quantities of plain red-slipped potsherds, marine shells,
shell ornaments or tools in dark brown to black sandy soil, and some heated
limestone fragments that may represent earth ovens; and Layer D, the lowest
layer, which contained fewer potsherds and some faunal remains including fish
and marine shells with yellowish-to-white dry beach sand. Layer E was consid-

Table 11.1. ¹⁴C dates from Uattamdi 1 and 3 (2014–2015 excavations)

Site	Lab ID	Material	Layer	Spit	¹⁴C Age (BP)	Calibrated Age	Remarks
UTMD1	PLD-29584	Human tooth	B	3	1885 ± 20	66–177 cal AD	IntCal13
UTMD1	PLD-29585	Human tooth	B	4	1920 ± 21	50–129 cal AD	IntCal13
UTMD1	PLD-29598	Charcoal	C1	3	2755 ± 25	943–831 cal BC	IntCal13
UTMD1	PLD-29593	Marine shell	C1	3	3300 ± 25	1281–1095 cal BC	Marine 13
UTMD1	PLD-29592	Marine shell	C2	5	3380 ± 25	1384–1213 cal BC	Marine 13
UTMD1	PLD-29594	Marine shell	D	5	3285 ± 25	1257–1072 cal BC	Marine 13
UTMD1	PLD-29597	Charcoal	D	8	2970 ± 25	1263–1117 cal BC	IntCal13
UTMD3	PLD-29601	Charcoal	A	3	245 ± 20	1640–1670 cal AD	IntCal13
UTMD3	PLD-29602	Charcoal	B	3	2145 ± 20	211–103 cal BC	IntCal13
UTMD3	PLD-29603	Charcoal	C	4	2885 ± 25	1130–997 cal BC	IntCal13
UTMD3	PLD-29604	Charcoal	D	5	3250 ± 25	1611–1492 cal BC	IntCal13

Source: Authors.

ered pure beach sand with no artifacts below about 200 cm in depth from the surface.

Charcoal, human and animal remains, and marine shell from Uattamdi 1 and Uattamdi 3 were radiocarbon-dated (AMS) by the Laboratory of Radiocarbon Dating at the University Museum, the University of Tokyo in Japan (Table 11.1). The date range of the lower Neolithic layers (Layer C/D) and upper Early Metal Age layer (Layer B) support the results of Bellwood's previous study (Bellwood 2019; Bellwood et al. 1998). In a comparison of our dates from Uattamdi 1 and Uattamdi 3, it appears that Uattamdi 3 is slightly older and the lowest layer (Layer D) dated to between 3600 and 3400 cal BP, but the major Neolithic layer (Layer C) dated to around 3100–3000 cal BP. Thus, when we combined the ¹⁴C dates of Uattamdi 1 by Bellwood (2019: 71), both sites could have been in use contemporaneously after 3400 cal BP. The later Neolithic layer in Uattamdi 1 was estimated to be used between around 3000 and 2500 BP by Bellwood (2019), and our new dating from Uattamdi 1 confirms the layer dated between 3200 and 2800 cal BP based on charcoal and calibrated marine shell dates. A single charcoal date from Layer C2 in Uattmadi 3 also date to around 3300–3200 cal BP.

Table 11.2. Total number of sherds from Uattamdi 1 (2014 excavation)

Number	E3	F3	F7	F8	F9	F10	G7	G8	Total
Layer A	60	18	20	41	47	25	73	20	304
Layer B	361	24	29	62	29	27	51	116	699
Layer C1	897	0	266	93	38	62	97	166	1,619
Layer C2	83	106	726	543	639	132	131	96	2,456
Layer D	3	0	65	79	10	14	78	29	278
Total	1,404	148	1,106	818	763	260	430	427	5,356

Source: Authors.

Pottery Tradition and Animal Use at Uattamdi

Potsherds are one of the major artifacts in Uattamdi. In Uattamdi 1, a total of 5,356 potsherds (14,557 g) were excavated from the 8 m² test pits (E3, F3, F7, F8, F9, F10, G7, and G8). Table 11.2 shows the total number and weights of excavated potsherds in each grid and layer. As the table shows, Layer C, a possible Neolithic layer (especially Layer C2), produced the largest numbers of potsherds in Uattamdi 1, thus the site had been used most actively during Neolithic times. It also shows that Grid E3 and F7 produced the most pottery (and other artifacts including marine shells as discussed later). Since the location of these grids are far inside the Uattamdi 1 rockshelter, it is possible that more evidence of these tools in the interior of the rockshelter may reflect taphonomic processes, as the interior is more protected.

Among the assemblage of excavated pottery from the upper layers, particularly Layer B, are parts of middle- to large-sized burial jars with various motifs and red- or black-slipped pottery, while lower layers, mainly Layers C and D, contained plain red- or black-slipped pottery (Table 11.3). As Table 11.3 shows, the total weight of excavated potsherds from Layer B is almost the same as Layers C1 and C2, while the total number of excavated potsherds from Layer B is much less than those from Layers C1 and C2 (see Table 11.2). Such a result is clearly affected by the large, heavy potsherds, which may belong to larger burial jars found in Layer B. In fact, some human remains and burial goods—mainly glass beads—were also excavated around these larger burial jar fragments in Layer A to B.

In Uattamdi 3, a total of 2,623 potsherds (12,677 g) were excavated from the 4 m² test pits (B2, B3, C2, and C3), while Grid B3 could be excavated down to

Table 11.3. Total weight of pottery from Uattamdi 1 (2014 excavation)

Weight (g)	E3	F3	F7	F8	F9	F10	G7	G8	Total
Layer A	215	143	77	91	120	147	198	35	1,026
Layer B	2,209	365	52	145	447	844	209	323	4,594
Layer C1	1,415	0	703	247	141	82	658	799	4,045
Layer C2	219	161	1,022	1,123	1,097	278	275	193	4,368
Layer D	29	0	101	122	18	46	172	36	524
Total	4,087	669	1,955	1,728	1,823	1,397	1,512	1,386	14,557

Source: Authors.

Table 11.4. Total number and weight of pottery from Uattamdi 3 (2015 excavation)

	B2		B3		C2		C3		Total	
	N	(g)	N	(g)	N	(g)	N	(g)	N	(g)
Layer A	8	25	71	196	115	411	171	596	365	1,228
Layer B	322	2,425	589	2,711	212	1,152	510	2,915	1633	9,203
Layer C	256	7,359	41	137			269	1,077	566	1,949
Layer D	4	4					45	283	49	287
Total	590	3,189	701	3,044	337	1,563	995	4,871	2,623	12,667

Source: Authors.

Layer C and Grid C2 down to Layer B only because of our limited time. Table 11.4 shows the total number and weight of excavated potsherds in each grid and layer from Uattamdi 3. Layer B is the Early Metal Age layer that produced the largest number and greatest weight of sherds, while the Neolithic layers (Layers C and D) produced fewer potsherds (Figure 11.5) when compared with the results of Uattamdi 1. Most of the sherds in the upper layers are parts of burial jars with various motifs, while sherds from lower layers are plain red-slipped vessels similar to Uattamdi 1. Uattamdi 3 did not produce any sherds possibly belonging to larger burial jars as all of the sherds belong to small- to middle-sized vessels and jars. More decorated red-slipped pottery—possibly dating to the Early Metal Age—was recovered from the Uattamdi 3 excavations, which

Figure 11.5. Neolithic and Early Metal Age pottery/jar from Uattamdi 1. *A and B*: red-slipped jar sherds from E3/ Layer B, Spit 3 (*A*: front; *B*: back); *C*: red-slipped lip with notch (E3/B/3); *D*: black-slipped sherds (E3/B/7); *E*: red-slipped sherd (E3/B/8); *F*: plain lips and lip with notch(E3/C/1).

Figure 11.6. Early Metal Age pottery/jar from Uattamdi 3. *A and B*: red-black–slipped lip (*A*: front; *B*: back); *C*: red-slipped motif sherd (B3/LayerB/2); *D*: red-slipped motif lip (B3/LayerB/2); *E*: red-slipped motif carination (B3/LayerB/3); *F*: red-slipped motif lip (B3/LayerB/3).

produced fewer Neolithic pottery sherds (Figures 11.5 and 11.6). Most of the Neolithic potsherds from Uattamdi 3 that were recovered are the plain red-slipped type.

Maritime Adaptation: Comparison between Uattamdi and Lapita Sites

Excavations from Neolithic contexts revealed over 150 species of shellfish, over 10 families of marine fish including tuna (Scombridae/*Katsuwonus* sp.), groupers (Serranidae), emperors (Lethrinidae), parrotfish (Scaridae), wrasses (Labridae), snappers (Lutjanidae), triggerfish (Balistidae), trevallies (Carangidae/*Caranx* sp.), unicorn fish (Acanthuridae), porcupinefish (Diodontidae), moray eels (Muraenidae), sweetlips (Haemuridae) and sharks (mainly Carcharhinidae), as well as sea turtle (Cheloniidae) bones. A shark tooth from a Neolithic layer in Uattamdi 3 had a drilled hole and may have been used as a tool or ornament. The previous excavation on Uattamdi 1 by Bellwood also produced 150 identified fish bones from 13 species and 545 unidentified fish bones (Hull et al. 2019: 146). Among the 13 identified species, Scaridae is the dominant family, occupying 59 percent of the total identified fish bones; other major families are Sparidae (8 percent), Lethrinidae (8 percent), and Labridae (7 percent).

Although the total number and volume of fish remains are not large, most of the tuna, mainly skipjack (*Katsuwonus* sp.), were only excavated from the Neolithic layers, and it appears that both offshore and inshore fishing took place at Uattamdi. Also, we excavated over 20 specimens of possible shellfish hook blanks made from both bivalves and gastropods, with *Nerita* sp. being the most abundant. Since there are no complete hooks, it is unclear whether they are really hooks or not, though the numbers of tuna and grouper from the site tentatively suggest that Uattamdi people practiced hook-and-line fishing.

The location of Uattamdi indicates that these Neolithic people, possibly newly migrated to the region, developed maritime skills and knowledge, and strategically selected coastal environment with large coral reefs for their initial settlements. Such migration strategies and preference for coastal settlement are also seen in the case of Lapita sites in the Pacific (Kirch 1997; see also chapter 2 for an overview). Lapita people are usually identified as early Austronesian-speaking groups originally from Asia that are associated with Neolithic material culture, including pottery and more systematic agriculture and animal husbandry practices. These groups migrated into many previously uninhabited remote islands in the Pacific, from Melanesia to Western Polynesia around 3,300 years ago (Bellwood 2005; Kirch 1997; Ono 2016).

However, Lapita culture does not appear to have developed entirely in Asia as well. One of the most diagnostic objects associated with Lapita are their pottery that include human face motifs and geometric patterns made by dentate stamping on the pottery surface, some of which is infilled with white lime. This style of decorated Lapita pottery may have originated from somewhere in ISEA since much older dentate-stamped pottery has recently been found in the Philippines and Sulawesi. The combination of a diagnostic human face motif and a mix of various patterns on one vessel is very diagnostic of Lapita pottery and supports a Southeast Asian Austronesian origin, but with the addition of elements from local island Melanesia material culture developed prior to Lapita times (Allen 2000; Green 1991; Ono 2016).

The Neolithic layers in Uattamdi produced large numbers of pottery that are primarily from plain red-slipped pots. No dentate-stamped and lime-infilled pots were discovered in our excavations or in previous studies by Bellwood (Bellwood 1997, 2019; Bellwood et al. 1998). Does this mean that the Neolithic migrants who reached Northern Maluku were a different early Austronesian group that migrated into Remote Oceania? If so, how different are they? Both groups spoke Austronesian languages, so are the stylistic differences in pottery a matter of preference? Many of these questions persist in the study of Neolithic migrations in Island Southeast Asia and Oceania.

In terms of maritime exploitation and adaptations, Lapita people appear to have more developed maritime skills (for example, fishing and seafaring). Lapita sites tend to produce more inshore fish remains similar to Uattamdi, including parrotfish, wrasses, snappers, triggerfish, groupers, emperors, unicorn fish, and porcupinefish. Although the number and volume are smaller, they also produced pelagic fish remains including tuna and barracuda (for example, Butler 1988, 1994; Green 1986; Kirch 1988, 1997, 2000; Kirch and Dye 1979; Ono 2010; Ono et al. 2019b). Furthermore, several Lapita sites produced large- to small-sized shell fishhooks and *Trochus* sp. lure shanks that could be used for offshore trolling of fast-swimming fish such as skipjack tuna (for example, Kirch 1997, 2000; Ono et al. 2019b; Szabó 2010). Lapita *Trochus* sp. lure shanks are the oldest known evidence for this type of fishhook (Ono et al. 2019b). Various sizes and styles of shell fishhooks provide further evidence of active line fishing. Most of these hooks are made from *Trochus* sp. or *Turbo* sp. shell, and the former may be originally from the *Trochus* fishhook tradition dating back to the late Pleistocene to early Holocene in southern Wallacea and Sahul region (O'Connor and Veth 2005; O'Connor et al. 2011, 2017).

The absence of shell trolling lures and a variety of fishhooks at ISEA Neolithic sites including Uattamdi implies a discontinuity between northern Wallacea and Oceania in terms of fishing technology. However, it is too early to make any conclusive statements at this stage given the small number of investigated sites and paucity of data. Nonetheless, the present information could suggest that offshore fishing techniques with trolling lures might be an innovation of Lapita fishers in Melanesia where more islands are surrounded by deep sea.

We do not have any archaeological evidence of watercraft used by Lapita people, though it has been suggested that their colonization could have been carried by outrigger canoes with a primitive Oceanic spritsail (Anderson 2000: 38). Outrigger canoes are the primary canoe types in areas where Austronesian languages are spoken, including ISEA, the Pacific, and Madagascar. Taiwan, which is considered the probable origin of Austronesian languages, is the only exception to this. It is not yet known where outrigger canoes originated, but archaeologists generally agree that long-distance voyaging could not have happened without them.

Human Migration and Maritime Networks in the Early Metal Age

In Wallacea, the Early Metal Age followed the Neolithic and is marked by the appearance of metal and glass objects around 2200–2000 cal BP. This transition corresponds to the post-Lapita age in Oceania and the initial human settlement of eastern Micronesia. The number of sites with pottery and occasional glass and metal artifacts increased dramatically both in the Northern Malukus and Sulawesi (Bellwood 2019; Ono et al. 2017, 2018a, 2018b). Historical evidence for the ancient spice trade also suggests possible development of maritime networks and human migration in and around the islands by this time (Hung and Chao 2016; Miller 1969). The complicated linguistic distributions of Austronesian and Papuan languages in the Northern Moluccas also suggest complex population relationships and movements. The arrivals of metal (bronze and iron) and glass artifacts possibly encouraged further development of active human migration and trading networks in Northern Wallacea at this time, and also more widely across ISEA. Here, we report two cases from the Northern Maluku Islands and Sulawesi based on our recent excavations for further discussions.

Northern Maluku Cases

Both the number of sites and the sheer volume of pottery recovered from sites in the Northern Maluku Islands increased dramatically during the Early Metal Age. At Uattamdi 1, use of much larger pots, identified as burial jars, increased in the Early Metal Age layer (2200–1800 cal BP) (see Table 11.1). Uattamdi 3 produced larger numbers of potsherds in the upper Early Metal Age layer than at Uattamdi 1 (see Table 11.4). The Early Metal Age layer at both sites contained fragmented human bones and teeth associated with various-sized pottery vessels and jars at both sites, which have been recognized as burial deposits and were possibly used as burial jars and containers for grave goods. The direct AMS dates on human teeth associated with these burial jars are also around 2000 cal BP (see Table 11.1). The number and variety of decorated sherds also dramatically increased in this layer, while most potsherds from the Neolithic layers at both sites are plain red-slipped. Many of these Early Metal Age sherds share strong similarities with other pottery excavated from other contemporaneous sites in and around the Northern Maluku Islands (see Figure 11.4) (Bellwood 2019; Bellwood et al. 1998).

Our excavations of the Aru Manara site on the southeastern coast of Morotai Island and the Gorua open site on the northeastern coast of Halmahera Island yielded a number of various Early Metal Age sherds dating to between 2300 and 1800 cal BP (Ono et al. 2017, 2018a, 2018b). The major types are: (1) pottery stoves (Figure 11.7A); (2) red-slipped pottery with or without incised decorations on the surface (Figure 11.7B); (3) black-ware pottery with dark brown to

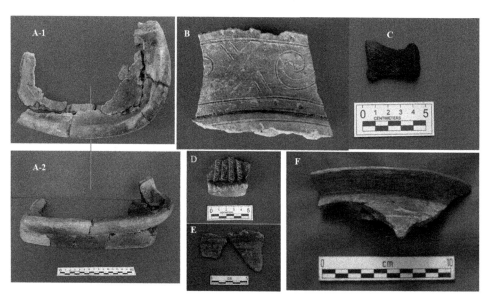

Figure 11.7. Early Metal Age pottery from Gorua site, Halmahera Island. *A-1 and A-2*: reconstructed pottery stove; *B*: red-slipped pottery with incised decorations; *C*: black-ware pottery with incised decorations; *D*: appliqué decorated pottery; *E and F*: red-slipped pottery with black color painted.

R. Ono, A. Agus Oktaviana, H. Octavianus Sofian, Sriwigati, and N. Aziz

black color on its surface (found on the inside, outside, or both sides) (Figure 11.7C); (4) appliqué-decorated pottery (Figure 11.7D); and (5) red-slipped pottery with some black painted on its surface, mainly around the rim (Figure 11.7E and 11.7F). A pottery stove is a form of portable earth oven for cooking, which could even be used on a boat at sea (Bellwood 1997; Ono 2010). The oldest dated stoves are known from the Hemudu site in China dated to around 7500–5000 BP (for example, Liu 2012), while the oldest stoves in ISEA are from Bukit Tengkorak in Borneo, one of the major Neolithic sites in the region (Bellwood 1989, 2017). A variety of pedestals or stands with triangular and oval-shaped cutouts were also excavated, but it is unknown which vessel types had these pedestals. Sharply pointed rims and possible knobs or handles with light, red-slipped surfaces were also excavated mainly from the upper layers at Gorua.

Aru Manara also produced a large number of fragmented human bones (NISP = 57,273) and teeth (n = 1,550) associated with Early Metal Age pottery, including a large red-slipped open bowl with a ring foot decorated with appliqué lizards and stamped circles with punctated central holes, as well as sherds from square, box-like vessels, one of which was decorated with appliqué anthropomorphic figures that dated to between 2150 and 1800 cal BP (Ono et al. 2017, 2018b). Similar square vessels were also excavated from the Metal Age jar burial site of Leang Buidane on Salibabu of the Talaud Islands, located about 250 km from Morotai (Bellwood 1980), and also from the contemporary site of Palawan in the Philippines (Fox 1970). The other sherds found at the site (n = 504) included 32 red-slipped and 79 decorated specimens. The latter comprised: (1) linear and curvilinear motifs created from paired, incised lines, or horizontal incised zones of simple straight-line and curvilinear incision interspersed with trademark "inverted commas"; (2) circle-stamped motifs; (3) triangular incised; and (4) triangular or round cutouts through incised pedestals (Ono et al. 2017). The linear and curvilinear incised motifs are similar to those in contemporary Moluccan assemblages at Tanjung Pinang on Morotai, as well as Buwawansi 3 and Um Kapat Papo on Gebe Island, all of which date to circa 2500–2000 BP (Bellwood 2019; Bellwood et al. 1993).

Pottery with human and zoomorphic figures are also associated with Lapita burials in Oceania (Spriggs 1990), although appliqué human figures on Lapita pots are very rare. A modeled bird's head comes from Teouma that was perhaps once attached to an early Lapita pot with dentate-stamped human figures around its lip (Bedford and Spriggs 2007: 13). There is a similar bird's head from the Lapita site SZ-8 in the Reef-Santa Cruz islands of the Southeast Solomons (Green 1979). Incised figures of possible sea turtles with human faces are also found on Lapita sherds in the Reef–Santa Cruz islands. In post-Lapita periods in Oceania, clay-modeled faces or figures of any form are very rare (Bedford and Spriggs 2007), except for a few cases such as the animal-like handles and an animal head from the Mangaasi site on Efate, Vanuatu, dated to around 2000 BP by Garanger (1971: figs. 2, 9). Mangaasi-style pottery, widely distributed in Melanesia, has incised and applied-relief decoration, including a sherd from Watom Island with stamped circles and punctate central holes (Garanger 1971: fig. 12), similar to the lizard pottery in Aru Manara.

The wider distribution of some common motifs and pottery styles in Northern Maluku and ISEA clearly indicates increased human interaction and possible development of maritime networks among the islands. In the Northern Malukus, the existence of pottery with applied-relief decorations, including a human face and lizard, suggests the development of maritime networks with the Melanesian region in Oceania from 2700 to 2000 BP. The use of large burial jars and box-type jars may also indicate possible human interaction between the Northern Maluku and Philippine Islands.

The Sulawesi Case Study

The number of Early Metal Age sites also increases on Sulawesi (for example, Bulbeck 2010), though the details of their material culture are unclear, since most of the sites have only been excavated in a very limited area or only partially contain layer(s) belonging to the Early Metal Age. In 2016, however, we excavated a large cave and rockshelter complex site named "Goa Topogaro" on the eastern coast of Central Sulawesi (see Figure 11.1) and found large numbers of fragmented human remains associated with a variety of pottery styles, including dentate-stamped pottery with lime infill, glass and shell ornaments, and metal objects.

Goa Topogaro is a massive limestone cave complex within a large doline (sinkhole) located in the hills about 3.5 km inland from the eastern coast of Topogaro village, West Morowali District. The site is a complex of three larger caves (Topogaro 1–3) and four rockshelters (Topogaro 4–7). Both the caves and rockshelters are located along the top portion of the hills about 80–100 m above the current mean sea level. All caves and rockshelters were surveyed. Topogaro 1 and 2 are the largest caves in the complex and contain a large number of artifacts including chert flakes and shellfish remains on their surfaces. Topogaro 3, located next to Topogaro 2, has a very small mouth and seems too dark and narrow for habitation (there is a possibility that it may contain burials inside, but no evidence was visible on the surface). Excavations have been ongoing since 2016 mainly at the Topogaro 1 and 2 caves, as well as the Topogaro 7 rockshelter.

AMS dates on charcoal, bone, and shell from these excavations are forthcoming (Ono et al. 2020).

Topogaro 1, the largest of the caves, contains more than 30 broken coffins with human skeletal remains on the surface in the middle to northern part of the cave floor. The cave mouth faces northwest and is 24 m wide and 25 m deep with a maximum height of about 20 m (Figure 11.8A). Surface soils are dry and contain fragments of pottery sherds, Chinese and European ceramics, chert flakes, including finely retouched tools, and shell. The presence of a number of flakes and shellfish clearly indicates that the cave had been used as a habitation or tool production site, while wooden coffins and the variety of Chinese and European ceramics show the site had been used as a burial site between 300 and 100 BP, based on AMS dates acquired from the coffin itself and some associated human teeth (Table 11.5). Our excavation in Topogaro 1 also found a possible early Metal Age burial deposit and an early- to middle-Holocene cultural layer with a number of chert flakes, bone points, and shellfish, as well as animal remains that dated between 9000 and 6000 BP. Due to the presence of limestone rocks underneath, the basal extent of the layer is unknown.

Topogaro 2 has no wooden coffins and far fewer artifacts on the surface. The mouth of Topogaro 2 faces north and its width is about 15 m, while the cave length is about 24 m and has a maximum height of about 12 m (Figure 11.8B). Our excavations in Topogaro 2 reached to 3 m below the surface and dated to around 30,000 BP (Ono et al. 2020), while the upper layers contain burials with fragmented human bones and dentate-stamped, lime-infilled potsherds. The dentate-stamped and lime-infilled pottery are recognized as a marker of early Austronesian material culture distributed from the Northern Philippines, the Mariana Islands in Western Micronesia, and many Lapita sites in Melanesia that

Table 11.5. ^{14}C dates from upper layers in Topogaro 1 and 2. Human tooth calibrated with δ^{13}C (-20.1 ± 0.3 ‰ for correction)

Lab ID	Site	Spit	Layer	Material	^{14}C Age	95% probability Cal BP (2σ)
TKA-17032	TPGR1	3	1	Charcoal	297 ± 18 BP	430–357
TKA-17033	TPGR1	7	1	Charcoal	603 ± 24 BP	652–580
TKA-17404	TPGR2-East	11	2	Human tooth	1900 ± 20 BP	1900–1810
TKA-17035	TPGR2-West	6	1	Charcoal	2274 ± 19 BP	2350–2180

Source: Stuiver and Polach 1977.

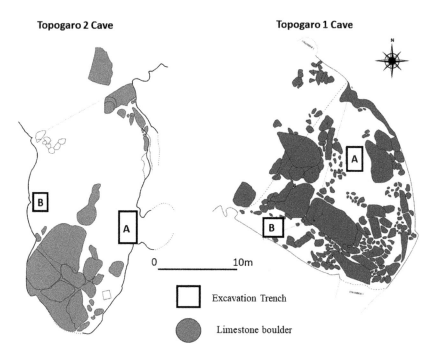

Figure 11.8. Plan and location of excavation trenches in Topogaro 1 and 2.

date circa 3700–2800 BP (for example, Anggraeni et al. 2014; Carson et al. 2013; Hung et al. 2011). However, based on the currently acquired radiocarbon dates, pottery from Topogaro 2 dates to 2300–1800 cal BP (see Table 11.5).

The decorative techniques used to make the Topogaro dentate-stamped pottery include both round-tipped (Figures 11.9A and 11.9B) and rectangular-tipped tools (Figure 11.9C and 11.9D). Surface finds in Topogaro 7 also include dentate-stamped and circle-stamped sherds with lime infilling (Figure 11.8E). The horizontal, vertical, or curved lines on the sherds are incised to make various shapes, while the inside of the shapes or boundaries between the lines are more intricately filled with dentate stamping. Filled triangles (Figure 11.9F) are one of the major motifs found in the Philippines, the Karama Valley in Sulawesi, and at early Lapita sites (for example, Anggraeni et al. 2014; Carson et al. 2013).

When comparing the common decorations seen in early dentate-stamped pottery in the Philippines, Mariana Islands, and early Lapita sites, the Topogaro dentate-stamped pots lack some commonly found early patterns, but they have more variety in design and were made with fine skills. It is now clear that dentate-stamped decorations at Lapita sites disappeared by around 2800–2700 BP,

R. Ono, A. Agus Oktaviana, H. Octavianus Sofian, Sriwigati, and N. Aziz

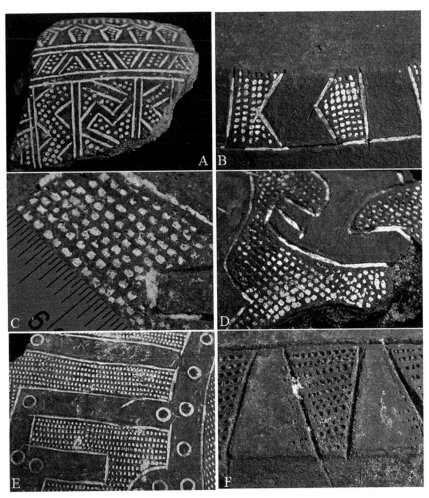

Figure 11.9. A variety of dentate-stamped, lime-infill pottery from Goa Topogaro. A: round-tipped dentate-stamp with lime infilled; B: round and rectangular-tipped dentate-stamp with lime infilled; C: rectangular-tipped, dentate-stamp with lime infilled; D: rectangular-tipped dentate-stamp with lime infilled on birdlike design; E: rectangular-tipped, dentate-stamped and circle stamps with lime infilled; F: rectangular-tipped dentate-stamp on incised triangle design.

while the Goa Topogaro dentate-stamped pottery suggests that such ceramic traditions continued in Sulawesi until at least the Early Metal Age.

Discussion

In discussions of the initial modern human migrations and colonization into Wallacea and Oceania, there are basically two important ages: (1) initial modern human migration through Wallacea or eastern Indonesia into the Sahul regions

(Australia and New Guinea); and (2) a much-later Neolithic human migration, possibly by Austronesian-speaking people, into both Near and Remote Oceania. Furthermore, a third, post-Neolithic human migration into Wallacea, particularly around the Sulawesi and Maluku regions and also into Melanesia, are important for discussions of past spice-trading networks or the complicated human and language migrations between Austronesian- and Papuan-language groups in the Maluku Islands.

Our work at Goa Topogaro along the eastern coast of Central Sulawesi could potentially be among the earliest evidence for modern human arrival in the region, as ongoing excavations demonstrate that the site extends at least 5 m below the surface, with a variety of chert and other stone tools and animal remains extending to the lowest-excavated layer. The exact dates of deep deposits are still unclear and are being dated with radiocarbon dating and optically stimulated luminescence (OSL). Preliminary radiocarbon dates from around 2.5 and 3 m depth are between 26 and 30 kya (Ono et al. 2020). Future research, including our excavation in Sulawesi, may add more detailed archaeological data for discussing the initial modern human migration into Wallacea.

Our current research contributes to a range of issues on Neolithic human migration, post-Neolithic human migration, and the possible development of maritime networks during the Early Metal Age. Based on our excavations and AMS dating of human teeth, marine shell, and charcoal from Aru Manara (Ono et al. 2017, Ono et al. 2018b), Uattamdi (see also Bellwood 2019), and Gorua (Ono et al. 2018a), it is clear now that the first human migration associated with pottery-making traditions into Uattamdi on Kayoa Island could date to circa 3400 BP, while the earliest pottery-bearing sites on Morotai to Northern Halmahera appeared after 2300–2100 BP, over 1,000 years after the first Austronesian migrations during the Neolithic age.

Our results also support the findings of Bellwood and his team in the 1990s, and we may be able to conclude that early Austronesian Neolithic people possibly skipped regions already occupied by Papuan-language groups from the early Holocene (Bellwood 2019; Bellwood et al. 1993, 1998). The burial practices at Aru Manara during the Early Metal Age used burial jars decorated with motifs similar to burials in the Philippine Islands, particularly Palawan (for example, Fox 1970) and Sulawesi, including the Talaud Islands during the late Neolithic to the Early Metal Age (for example, Bellwood 1980, 1997). Analysis of burial goods, including shell and glass ornaments, tentatively indicate that these goods were possibly brought both from China and the Indian Ocean to Morotai Island. These archaeological traces also show that human migration

R. Ono, A. Agus Oktaviana, H. Octavianus Sofian, Sriwigati, and N. Aziz

and movement, including maritime trade, were occurring in these regions and the Northern Maluku Islands around 2200 BP.

In terms of past maritime trading and post-Neolithic migration, the earliest evidence of international trade of Maluku spices comes from Han Chinese and Indian sources about 2,200 years ago (Miller 1969). Such historical sources hint at the spread of metal from mainland Southeast Asia through the islands as far as either side of Maluku starting 2300–2100 years ago. The sudden appearance of metal, including the spread of Dongson bronze drums and goods that were originally from northern Vietnam or southern China into Island Southeast Asia as far as the Maluku Islands and Bird's Head peninsula of New Guinea, mark the beginning of the spice trade. Another possible trading material were bird plumes, which were one of the major export goods from the Maluku and New Guinea regions until the twentieth century (for example, Swadling 1994).

The existence of glass ornaments in Aru Manara and the Early Metal Age layers at Uattamdi and Goa Topogaro also indicate possible trading activities by these early people in and around Northern Wallacea, possibly both via China and India. Although ongoing analysis has not yet revealed the exact origin(s) of the glass objects, it is clear that these goods were imported from outside the region, potentially from India or somewhere in Mainland Southeast Asia (Ono et al. 2017). No bronze and iron goods were excavated from Aru Manara and Uattamdi except for a small, possibly bronze fragment from the surface at Aru Manara, while Goa Topogaro produced few metal materials. The archaeological evidence in Northern Wallacea, including Northern Maluku and Sulawesi, for widespread adoption of Indonesian Metal Age–style pottery between 2200 and 1800 BP would fit in with this interpretation (see also Spriggs 1998). It is not yet known how and where such trade activities were practiced; however, the ongoing excavation indicates that these trade or exchange networks might have existed between Northern Wallacea and other Asian regions, including India, western Southeast Asia, and China.

In terms of Austronesian pottery-making traditions during the Neolithic to Early Metal Age in Wallacea, we can confirm there are some different contemporaneous traditions. During early Austronesian migrations in the Neolithic, there were at least two major pottery-making traditions that co-existed: (1) a dentate-stamped pottery tradition; and (2) a simple red-slipped pottery tradition. Excavations at Uattamdi clearly provide evidence of a Neolithic material culture that dates to 3400 BP, but the site only produced plain red-slipped pottery or pottery with very simple decorations such as notches on the rim and no decorations like dentate-stamp, circle stamp, and lime-infill. The contemporary

Leang Tuwo Manae site on the Talaud Islands, located about 500 km north from Kayoa, also produced simple plain red-slipped pottery (Bellwood 1976; Tanudirjo 2001). Similarly, only simple red-slipped pottery was excavated from Neolithic sites in the Banda Islands (Lape et al. 2018). The Bukit Tengkorak site on Borneo produced a variety of decorated pottery, mainly incised and impressed, as well as red-slipped pottery, but it had no dentate-stamped and lime-infilled types at all (Bellwood 1989, 2019; Chia 2003).

On the other hand, Goa Topogaro produced dentate-stamped, lime-infilled, and circle-stamped ceramics, but their dates are still unclear and may be younger than those of Lapita and other early Austronesian pots. Possible dentate-stamped potsherds were unearthed on the Mansiri open site in Northern Sulawesi (Aziz et al. 2018) and from the Minanga Sipakko and Kamassi sites on Karama Valley (Anggraeni 2012; Anggraeni et al. 2014). The dates of these pots are not yet known, but both sites could date to around 3500–3000 BP. As discussed in the introduction, Neolithic sites along Kagayan Valley in Northern Luzon also produced dentate-stamped pottery with lime infill that possibly date to around 3800–3000 BP. If the early dates of dentate-stamped pots in ISEA are correct, such pottery traditions with dentate-stamped, circle stamped, and lime-infilled pots could be slightly older than simple red-slipped and incised decoration pottery tradition; they all currently date after 3400 BP. In this case, the dentate-stamped pottery tradition can be considered to be part of the earliest archaeological signatures of Austronesian groups in Wallacea and Oceania since early pottery assemblages on the Mariana Islands and at Lapita sites contain pottery with dentate-stamping, circle stamping and lime infilling.

If we also include the early pottery from Taiwan and Batanes Islands, then the earliest examples of Austronesian pottery use could date to circa 4200 BP (Bellwood and Dizon 2013; Hung 2005). These early pottery traditions were also characterized by simple red-slipped and undecorated pottery. In Batanes Islands, circle-stamped pots also appeared, but not until after 3200 BP (Bellwood and Dizon 2013). Based on current archaeological evidence, Bellwood proposes that the earliest Austronesian pottery tradition is simple, undecorated red-slipped pottery that originated in Taiwan, and that this pottery tradition widely expanded with the Austronesian migration down to the Northern Maluku Islands by 3400 BP, but did not enter Oceania. More developed pottery, with dentate-stamping, circle-stamping, and lime-infilling decorations, occurred somewhere in the Philippine Islands by 3800 BP, and the Austronesian groups associated with this pottery migrated to the Mariana Islands, Sulawesi, and Melanesia by around 3500–3300 BP (Bellwood 2019: 91–92). Our new findings in both Northern Maluku and Sulawesi also support this scenario of human migration based on Neolithic pottery traditions. It should also be noted that dentate stamping disappeared by around 2500 BP in Oceania (Micronesia, Melanesia, and West Polynesia), but persisted in the Central Sulawesi region until around 1800 BP (Ono et al. 2019a).

Dentate-stamped pottery in Topogaro is associated with fragmented human bones, shell and metal ornaments, and glass beads, and thus can be recognized as Early Metal Age grave goods. In the Northern Maluku Islands, many of the Early Metal Age pottery and jars are also excavated from secondary burial sites. Both Aru Manara on Morotai Island and the Early Metal Age layer in Uattamdi sites contain a number of human bones with a variety of decorated pottery, large jars, shell ornaments, and glass beads (Ono et al. 2017, 2018a). For the decorated pottery during this age, red-slipped pottery is one of the major types used, but there are also black-ware and well-made ceramics in styles including vertical-rimmed pots, restricted bowls, and stoves in Northern Maluku Islands. Some are decorated, primarily incised and impressed motifs on their rims, and are sometimes painted with red or black color (see Figures 11.6 and 11.7).

Furthermore, at the open-air site of Gorua, red- and black-painted pottery were also used during the Early Metal Age. On a much wider scale, some red and black–painted pots have been excavated and reported from the possible late Neolithic layers on the Mariana Islands (for example, Carson 2014). The dentate-stamped and painted (red and white) pots have also been excavated from Lapita sites in Vanuatu and date to around 3000 BP (Bedford and Spriggs 2007; Bedford 2006). Although the date is not clear yet, similar dentate-stamped and painted (red and white) potsherds have recently been found at the Mansiri site in Northern Sulawesi (Aziz et al. 2018). Painted pottery with "three color ware" (black and red on a cream base) has also been found in cave sites such as Niah Cave and Luban Angin in Western Borneo dated to around 3000 BP (Bellwood 1997: 239). Thus, the findings from Gorua tentatively indicate that such pottery traditions could be more widespread from East Indonesia to Oceania since the Neolithic times.

Lastly, regarding human migration to the Northern Maluku Islands, it is still unclear who (that is, Austronesian-speaking people or Papuan-speaking people) migrated to coastal areas on Morotai and Halmahera, where they were from, or how the migration process developed during the later-Neolithic to Early Metal Age around 2300–2000 BP. Following Spriggs (1998) and others, non-Austronesian languages of the region are currently spoken on islands near Timor, Northern Halmahera, and Morotai. They are thought to be related to the languages of Western New Guinea. Whether they represent ancient language stocks present in pre-Austronesian times throughout the Maluku Islands, or are the result of more recent population movements, remains unclear, though our recent collaborative research with the Max Planck Institute for Evolutionary Anthropology in Leipzig on ancient human remains DNA from Aru Manara on Morotai confirms mitochondrial DNA (mtDNA) of these Aru Manara group show both ancient Papuan mtDNA and Austronesian mtDNA haplogroups (Oliveira et al. 2019). Similar results are also reported from the Tanjung Pinang site on Morotai Island and Uattamdi: three Tanjung Pinang skulls contain ancient Papuan mtDNA haplogroups, whereas a Tanjung Pinang skull and the Uattamdi cranium had mtDNA haplogroups associated with Austronesian-speaking populations in the Philippines and Indonesia (Bellwood 2019: 220). Although the detailed results are forthcoming, such temporal genetic evidence indicates human migration and contact by the Early Metal Age in the Northern Maluku Islands.

Our research strongly suggests the possibility that there may be at least two early Austronesian groups with different pottery-making traditions that migrated into Wallacea during the Neolithic, then some pottery styles and decorative motifs spread widely in the post-Neolithic and Early Metal Age with some modification. Further analysis of the excavated materials will provide more detail and clearer images of past human migrations into Wallacea, as well as the development of maritime networks both in Wallacea and Oceania during the Neolithic and Early Metal Ages. We hope our current research on Goa Topogaro, Central Sulawesi, will also provide more detail on the earliest modern human migration into Wallacea and Oceania, plus new insight into how humans adapt to living on islands, resource use, and technological developments.

References

Allen, J. 2000. From Beach to Beach: The Development of Maritime Economies in Prehistoric Melanesia. In *East of Wallace's Line: Studies of Past and Present Maritime Culture of the Indo-Pacific Region*, ed. S. O'Connor and P. Veth, 139–176. Modern Quaternary Research in Southeast Asia 16. Rotterdam: CRC Press.

Anderson, A. 2000. Slow Boats from China: Issues in the Prehistory of Indo-Pacific Seafaring. In *East of Wallace's Line: Studies of Past and Present Maritime Culture of the Indo-Pacific Region*, ed. S. O'Connor and P. Veth, 15–30. Modern Quaternary Research in Southeast Asia 16. Rotterdam: CRC Press.

Anggraeni, T. 2012. The Austronesian Migration Hypothesis as Seen from Prehistoric Settlements on the Karama River, Mamuju, West Sulawesi. Unpublished PhD thesis. Canberra: The Australian National University.

Anggraeni, T. Semanjuntak, P. Bellwood, and P. Piper. 2014. Neolithic Foundations in the Karama Valley, West Sulawesi, Indonesia. *Antiquity* 88(341): 740–756.

Aoyagi, Y., M. Aguilera Jr., H. Ogawa, and K. Tanaka. 1991. Excavation at Lal-lo Shell Middens 3. *Journal of Sophia Asian Studies* 9: 49–138.

Aoyagi, Y., M. Aguilera Jr., H. Ogawa, and K. Tanaka. 1993. Excavation of Hill Top Site, Magapit Shell Midden in Lal-lo Shell Middens, Northern Luzon, Philippines. *Man and Culture in Oceania* 9: 127–155.

Aubert, M., A. Brumm, M. Ramli, T. Sutikna, E. W. Saptomo, B. Hakim, M. J. Morwood, G. D. van den Bergh, L. Kinsley, and A. Dosseto. 2014. Pleistocene Cave Art from Sulawesi, Indonesia. *Nature* 514 (7521): 223–227.

Aubert, M., R. Lebe, A. A. Oktaviana, M. Tang, B. Burhan, Hamrullah, A. Jusdi, Abdullah, B. Hakim, J.-x. Zhao, I. Made Geria, P. H. Sulistyarto, R. Sardi, and A. Brumm. 2019. Earliest Hunting Scene in Prehistoric Art. *Nature* 576: 442–445.

Aziz, N. C. Reepmeyer, G. Clark, Sriwigati, and D. A. Tanudirjo. 2018. Mansiri in North Sulawesi: A New Dentate-Stamped Pottery Site in Island Southeast Asia. In *The Archaeology of Sulawesi: Current Research on the Pleistocene to the Historic Period*, ed. S. O'Connor, D. Bulbeck, and J. Mayer, 191–205. Terra Australis No. 48. Canberra: Australian National University Press.

Bedford, S. 2006. The Pacific's Earliest Painted Pottery: An Added Layer of Intrigue to the Lapita Debate and Beyond. *Antiquity* 80(309): 544-557.

Bedford, S., and M. Spriggs. 2007. Birds on the Rim: A Unique Lapita Carinated Vessel in its Wider Context. *Archaeology in Oceania* 42: 12–21.

Bedford, S., M. Spriggs, and R. Regenvanu. 2006. The Teouma Lapita Site and the Early Human Settlement of the Pacific Islands. *Antiquity* 80: 812–828.

Bellwood, P. 1976. Archaeological Research in Minahasa and the Talaud islands, Northern Indonesia. *Asian Perspectives* 19: 240–288.

Bellwood, P. 1980. The Buidane Culture of the Talaud Islands, North-Eastern Indonesia. *Bulletin of the Indo-Pacific Prehistory Association* 2: 69–127.

Bellwood, P. 1989. Archaeological Investigations at Bukit Tengkorak and Segarong, Southeastern Sabah. *Bulletin of the Indo-Pacific Prehistory Association* 9: 122–162.

Bellwood, P. 1997. *Prehistory of the Indo-Malaysian Archipelago* (revised edition). Honolulu: University of Hawaii Press.

Bellwood, P. 2005. *First Farmers: The Origins of Agricultural Societies*. Malden: Blackwell.

Bellwood, P. 2013. *First Migrants: Ancient Migration in Global Perspective*. Malden: John Wiley and Sons.

Bellwood, P. 2017. *First Islanders: Prehistory and Human Migration in Island Southeast Asia*. Oxford: Wiley Blackwell.

Bellwood, P. (ed.). 2019. *The Spice Islands in Prehistory: Archaeology in the Northern Moluccas, Indonesia*. Terra Australis 50. Canberra: Australian National University Press.

Bellwood, P., and P. Koon. 1989. Lapita Colonists Leave Boats Unburned. *Antiquity* 63: 613–622.

Bellwood, P., A. Waluyo, G. Nitihaminoto, and G. Irwin 1993. Archaeological Research in the Northern Moluccas; Interim Results, 1991 field season. *Bulletin of the Indo-Pacific Prehistory Association* 13: 20–33.

Bellwood, P., G. Nitihaminoto, G. Irwin, A. Waluyo, and D. Tanudirjo. 1998. 35,000 Years of Prehistory in the Northern Moluccas. In *Bird's Head Approaches: Irian Jaya Studies*, ed. J. C. Galipaud and I. Lilley, 233–275. Modern Quaternary Research in Southeast Asia 15. Rotterdam: Balkema.

Bellwood, P., and E. Dizon (eds.). 2013. *4000 years of Migration and Cultural Exchange: The*

Archaeology of the Batanes Islands, Northern Philippines. Terra Australis 40. Canberra: ANU E Press.

Bird, M. I., S. A. Condie, S. O'Connor, D. O'Gray, C. Reepmeyer, S. Ulm, M. Zega, F. Saltre, and C.J.A. Bradshaw. 2019. Early Human Settlement of Sahul Was Not an Accident. *Scientific Reports* 9(8220): 1–10.

Birdsell, J. B. 1977. The Recalibration of a Paradigm for the First Peopling of Greater Australia. In *Sunda and Sahul: Prehistoric Studies in Southeast Asia, Melanesia, and Australia*, ed. J. Allen, J. Golson, and R. Jones, 113–167. Academic Press: London.

Blust, R. A. 1985. The Austronesian Homeland: A Linguistic Perspective. *Asian Perspectives* 26(1): 45–68.

Blust, R. A. 1995. The Prehistory of the Austronesian-speaking Peoples: A View From Language. *Journal of World Prehistory* 9: 453–510.

Bulbeck, D. 2010. Uneven Development in Southwest Sulawesi, Indonesia during the Early Metal Phase. In *50 Years of Archaeology in Southeast Asia: Essays in Honour of Ian Glover*, ed. B. Bellina, E. A. Bacus, T. O. Pryce and J. W. Christie, 153–169. Bangkok: River Books.

Butler, V. L. 1988. Lapita Fishing Strategies: The Faunal Evidence. In *Archaeology of the Lapita Cultural Complex: A Critical Review*, ed. P. V. Kirch and T. L. Hunt, 99–115. Thomas Burke Memorial Washington State Museum Research Report 5. Burke Museum, Seattle.

Butler, V. L. 1994. Fish Feeding Behavior and Fish Capture: The Case for Variation in Lapita Fishing Strategies. *Archaeology in Oceania* 29: 81–90.

Carson, M. 2014. *First Settlement of Remote Oceania: Earliest Sites in the Mariana Islands*. Heidelberg: Springer.

Carson, M., H-C. Hung, G. Summerhayes and P. Bellwood. 2013. The Pottery Trail from Southeast Asia to Remote Oceania. *Journal of Coastal and Island Archaeology* 8(1): 17–36.

Chappell, J. 2000. Pleistocene Seedbeds of Western Pacific Maritime Cultures and the Importance of Chronology. In *East of Wallace's Line: Studies of Past and Present Maritime Culture of the Indo-Pacific Region*, ed. S. O'Connor and P. Veth, 77–98. Modern Quaternary Research in Southeast Asia 16. Rotterdam: CRC Press.

Chia, S. 2001. The Prehistory of Bukit Tengkorak, Sabah, Malaysia. *Journal of Southeast Asian Archaeology* 21: 146–159.

Chia, S. 2003. *The Prehistory of Bukit Tengkorak*. Kota Kinabalu: Sabah Museum Monograph 8.

Clark, G. R. 2005. A 3000-year Culture Sequence from Palau, Western Micronesia. *Asian Perspectives* 44(2): 349–380.

Clarkson C., Z. Jacobs, B. Marwick, R. Fullagar, L. Wallis, M. Smith, R. G. Roberts, E. Hayes, K. Lowe, X. Carath, S. A. Forin, J. McNeil, D. Cox, L. J. Arnold, Q. Hua, J. Huntley, H.E.A. Brand, T. Manne, A. Fairbain, J. Shulmeister, L. Lye, M. Salinas, M. Page, K. Connell, G. Park, K. Normal, T. Murphy, and C. Pardoe. 2017. Human Occupation of Northern Australia by 65,000 Years Ago. *Nature* 547(7663): 306–310.

Détroit, F, A. S. Mijares, J. Corny, G. Davier, C. Zanolli, E. Dizon, E. Robles, R. Grün, and P. J. Piper. 2019. A New Species of Homo from the Late Pleistocene of the Philippines. *Nature* 568(7751): 181–186.

Dizon, E. Z., and R. Santiago. 1996. *Faces from Maitum: The Archaeological Excavation of Ayub Cave*. Manila: National Museum of the Philippines.

Erlandson, J. 2001 The Archaeology of Aquatic Adaptations: Paradigms for a New Millennium. *Journal of Archaeological Research* 9(4): 287–350.

Erlandson, J., and S. Fitzpatrick 2006. Oceans, Islands, and Coasts: Current Perspectives on the Role of the Sea in Human Prehistory. *Journal of Island and Coastal Archaeology* 1(1): 5–32.

Fitzpatrick, S. M. 2003. Early Human Burials at Chelechol ra Orrak: Evidence for a 3000 Year Old Occupation in Western Micronesia. *Antiquity* 77(298): 719–731.

Fitzpatrick, S. M., and N. P. Jew. 2018. Radiocarbon Dating and Bayesian Modelling of One of Remote Oceania's Oldest Cemeteries at Chelechol ra Orrak, Palau. *Antiquity* 92(361): 149–164.

Fitzpatrick, S., and R. Callaghan. 2013. Estimating Trajectories of Colonisation to the Mariana Islands, Western Pacific. *Antiquity* 87(337): 840–853.

Fox, R. 1970. *The Tabon Caves: Archaeological Explorations and Excavations on Palawan Island, Philippines.* Monograph of the National Museum 1. Manila: Philippines National Museum.

Galipaud, J.-C., R. Kinaston, S. Halcrow, A. Foster, N. Harris, T. Simanjuntak, J. Javellel, and H. Buckley. 2016. The Pain Haka Burial Ground on Flores: Indonesian Evidence for a Shared Neolithic Belief System in Southeast Asia. *Antiquity* 90 (354): 1505–1521.

Garanger, J. 1971. Incised and Applied Relief Pottery, Its Chronology and Development in Eastern Melanesia and Extra Areal Comparisons. In *Studies in Oceanic Culture History,* ed. R. C. Green and M. Kelly, 53–67. Honolulu: Bernice Pauahi Bishop Museum.

Green, R. C. 1979. Lapita. In *The Prehistory of Polynesia,* ed. J. D. Jennings, 27–60. Cambridge: Harvard University Press.

Green, R. C. 1986. Lapita Fishing: The Evidence of Site SE-RF-2 From the Main Reef Islands, Santa Cruz Group, Solomons. In *Traditional Fishing in the Pacific: Ethnographic and Archaeological Papers from the 15th Pacific Science Congress,* ed. A. Anderson, 19–35. Pacific Anthropological Records 37. Honolulu: Bernice P. Bishop Museum.

Green, R. C. 1991. The Lapita Cultural Complex: Current Evidence and Proposed Models. In *Indo-Pacific Prehistory 1990 Volume 2,* ed. P. Bellwood, 295–304. Bulletin of the Indo-Pacific Prehistory Association 11. Auckland: University of Auckland.

Gerrit, K., and H. Sutherland. 2005. *Monsoon Traders: Ships, Skippers and Commodities in Eighteenth-century Makassar.* Leiden: Koninklijk Instituut voor Taal.

Hull, J. R., P. Piper, G. Irwin, K. Szabo, A. Oertle, and P. Bellwood. 2019. Observations on the Northern Moluccan Excavated Animal Bone and Shell Collections. In *The Spice Islands in Prehistory: Archaeology in the Northern Moluccas, Indonesia,* ed. P. Bellwood, 135–165. Terra Australis No. 50. Canberra: Australian National University Press.

Hung, H.-C., and C.-Y. Chao. 2016. Taiwan's Early Metal Age and Southeast Asian Trading System. *Antiquity* 90(354): 1537–1551.

Hung, H.-C., M. T. Carson, P. Bellwood, F. Z. Campos, P. J. Piper, E. Dizon, M.J.L. A. Bolunia, M. Oxenham, and Z. Chi. 2011. The First Settlement of Remote Oceania: The Philippines to the Marianas. *Antiquity* 85(329): 909–926.

Hung, L. Y., and C. K. Ho. 2006. New Light on Taiwan Highland Prehistory. *Bulletin of the Indo-Pacific Prehistory Association* 26: 21–31.

Irwin, G. 1992. *The Prehistoric Exploration and Colonisation of the Pacific.* Cambridge: Cambridge University Press.

Kealy, S., J. Louys, and S. O'Connor. 2016. Islands under the Sea: A Review of Early Modern Human Dispersal Routes and Migration Hypotheses through Wallacea. *Journal of Island and Coastal Archaeology* 11(3): 364–384.

Kirch, P. 1976. Ethno-archaeological Investigations in Futuna and Uvea (Western Polynesia): A Preliminary Report. *Journal of the Polynesian Society* 85(1): 27–69.

Kirch, P. 1988. *Niuatoputapu: The Prehistory of a Polynesian Chiefdom.* Seattle: Burke Museum.

Kirch, P. 1997. *The Lapita Peoples: Ancestors of the Oceanic World.* London: Blackwell.

Kirch, P. 2000. *On the Road of the Winds: An Archaeological History of the Pacific Islands Before European Contact.* Los Angeles: University of California Press.

Kirch, P., and T. Dye 1979. Ethno-Archaeology and the Development of Polynesian Fishing Strategies. *Journal of Polynesian Society* 88: 53–76.

Lape, P., E. Peterson, D. Tanudirjo, C. C. Shiung, G. A. Lee, J. Field, and A. Coster. 2018. New Data from an Open Neolithic Site in Eastern Indonesia. *Asian Perspectives* 57: 222–243.

Li, L., and X. Chen 2012. *The Archaeology of China: From the Late Paleolithic to the Early Bronze Age.* Cambridge: Cambridge University Press.

Miller, I. 1969. *The Spice Trade of the Roman Empire: 29 B.C. to A.D. 641.* Oxford: Clarendon Press.

Morwood, M. J., R. P. Soejono, R. G. Roberts, T. Sutikna, C.S.M. Turney, K. E. Westaway, W. J. Rink, J.-x. Zhao, G. D. van den Bergh, R. A. Due, D. R. Hobbs, M. W. Moore, M. I. Bird, and L. K. Fifield. 2004. Archaeology and Age of a New Hominin from Flores in Eastern Indonesia. *Nature* 431: 1087–1091.

Napolitano, M. F., S. M. Fitzpatrick, G. Clark, and J. H. Stone. 2019. New Investigations of Early Prehistoric Settlement on Yap, Western Caroline Islands. *Journal of Island and Coastal Archaeology* 14(1): 101–107.

Norman, K., J. Inglis, C. Clarkson, J. T. Faith, J. Shulmeister, and D. Harris. 2018. An Early Colonisation Pathway into Northwest Australia 70–60,000 Years Ago. *Quaternary Science Review* 180: 229–239.

O'Connell J. F., and J. Allen. 2004. Dating the Colonization of Sahul (Pleistocene Australia-New Guinea): A Review of Recent Research. *Journal of Archaeological Science* 31(6): 835–853.

O'Connor, S., and P. Veth 2005. Early Holocene Shell Fish Hooks from Lene Hara Cave, East Timor, Establish Complex Fishing Technology Was in Use in Island Southeast Asia Five Thousand Years before Austronesian Settlement. *Antiquity* 79: 1–8.

O'Connor, S., R. Ono, and C. Clarkson 2011. Pelagic Fishing at 42,000 Years before the Present and the Maritime Skills of Modern Humans. *Science* 334: 1117–1121.

O'Connor, S. Mahirta, S. C. Samper Carro, S. Hawkins, S. Kealy, J. Louys, and R. Wood. 2017. Fishing in Life and Death: Pleistocene Fish-Hooks from a Burial Context on Alor Island, Indonesia. *Antiquity* 91(360): 1451.

O'Connor, S., Mahirta, S. Kealy, C. Boulanger, T. Maloney, S. Hawkins, M. C. Langley, H. Kaharudin, Y. Suniarti, M. Husni, M. Ririmasse, D. Tanudirjo, L. Wattimena, W. Handoko, Alifah, and J. Louys. 2019. Kisar and the Archaeology of Small Islands in the Wallacean Archipelago. *Journal of Island and Coastal Archaeology* 14(2): 198–225.

Oliveira, S, K. Nägele, I. Pugach, A. Hübner, S. Carlhoff, M. Meyer, P. Bellwood, R. Ono, J. Krause, C. Posth, and M. Stoneking 2019. Austronesian-Papuan Contact in North Moluccas and Central Sulawesi. Conference presentation at the Fifth Annual Symposium of the DFG Center for Advanced Studies at the University of Tübingen, Germany (12–14th December).

Ono, R. 2004. Prehistoric Fishing at Bukit Tengkorak Rock Shelter, East Coast of Borneo Island. *New Zealand Journal of Archaeology* 24: 77–106.

Ono, R. 2010. Ethno-Archaeology and the Early Austronesian Fishing Strategies in Near-Shore Environments. *Journal of the Polynesian Society* 119(3): 269–314.

Ono, R. 2011. *Maritime Exploitation and Fishing Strategies in the Celebes Sea: An Ethno-Archaeological Study of Maritime People.* Kyoto: Kyoto University Press.

Ono, R. 2014. *Final Report of Prehistoric Human Migrations, Maritime Networks and Resource Use in Sulawesi and Maluku Islands.* Jakarta: Unpublished manuscript submitted to the Indonesian Government.

Ono, R. 2016. Human History of Maritime Exploitation and Adaptation Process to Coastal and Marine Environments: A View from the Case of Wallacea and the Pacific. In *Applied Studies of Coastal and Marine Environments,* ed. Maged Marghany, 389–426. Rijeka: InTech.

Ono, R., and G. Clark. 2010. A 2500-year Record of Marine Resource Use on Ulong Island, Republic of Palau. *International Journal of Osteoarchaeology* 22(6): 637–654.

Ono, R., S. Soegondho, and M. Yoneda. 2009. Changing Marine Exploitation during Late Pleistocene in Northern Wallacea: Shell Remains from Leang Sarru Rockshelter in Talaud Islands. *Asian Perspective* 48(2): 318–341.

Ono, R., A. Oktaviana, F. Aziz, D. Prastiningtyas, N. Iriyanto M. Ririmase, I. B. Zesse, Y. Hisa, and M. Yoneda. 2017. Development of Regional Maritime Networks during the Early Metal Ages in Northern Maluku Islands: A View from Excavated Pottery and Glass Ornaments. *Journal of Island and Coastal Archaeology* 31(1): 98–108.

Ono, R., F. Aziz, A. A. Oktaviana, M. Ririmase, N. Iriyanto, I. B. Zesse, and K. Tanaka. 2018a. Development of Pottery Making Tradition and Maritime Networks during the Early Metal Ages in Northern Maluku Islands. *AMERTA, Journal Penelitian dan Pengembangan Arkeologi* 35(2): 109–122.

Ono, R, A. Oktaviana, M. Ririmase, M. Takenaka, C. Katagiri, and M. Yoneda. 2018b. Early Metal Age Interactions in Island Southeast Asia and Oceania: Jar Burials from Aru Manara, Northern Moluccas. *Antiquity* 92(364): 1023–1039.

Ono, R., H. O. Sofian, N. Aziz, Sriwigati, A. A. Okataviana, N. Alamsyah, and M. Yoneda. 2019a. Traces of Early Austronesian Expansion to East Indonesia? New Findings of Dentate-Stamped and Lime-Infilled Pottery from Central Sulawesi. *Journal of Island and Coastal Archaeology* 14(1): 123–129.

Ono, R., S. Hawkins, and S. Bedford. 2019b. Lapita Maritime Adaptations and the Development of Fishing Technology: A View from Vanuatu. In *Debating Lapita: Chronology, Society and Subsistence,* ed. S. Bedford and M. Spriggs, 415–438. Terra Australis Series 52. Canberra: ANU Press.

Ono, R., R. Fuentes, A. Pawlik, H. O. Sofian, Sriwigati, N. Aziz, N. Alamsyah, and M. Yoneda. 2020. Island Migration and Foraging Behaviour by Anatomically Modern Humans during the Late Pleistocene to Holocene in Wallacea: New Evidence from Central Sulawesi, Indonesia. *Quaternary International* 554: 90–106.

Petchey, F. G. Clark, O. Winter, P. O'Day, and M. Litster. 2016. Colonisation of Remote Oceania: New Dates for the Bapot-1 Site in the Mariana Islands. *Archaeology in Oceania* 52(2): 108–126.

Rieth, T. M., and J. S. Athens. 2019. Late Holocene Human Expansion into Near and Remote Oceania: A Bayesian Model of the Chronologies of the Mariana Islands and Bismarck Archipelago. *Journal of Island and Coastal Archaeology* 14(1): 5–16.

Schwerdtner Máñez K., and S.C.A. Ferse. 2010. The History of Makassan Trepang Fishing and Trade. *PLoS ONE* 5(6): e11346.

Solheim, W. G. 1964. Further Relationships of the Sa Huynh-Kalanay Pottery Tradition. *Asian Perspectives* 8 (1): 196–211.

Solheim, W. G. 1988. The Nusantao Hypothesis: The Origin and Spread of Austronesian Speakers. *Asian Perspectives* 23: 167–176.

Solheim, W. G. 2002. *The Archaeology of Central Philippines: A Study Chiefly of the Iron Age and Its Relationships.* Dilman: University of the Philippines.

Spriggs, M. 1990. The Changing Face of Lapita: Transformation of a Design. In *Lapita Design, Form and Composition: Proceedings of the Lapita Design Workshop, Canberra, Australia—December 1988,* ed. M. Spriggs, 83–122. Occasional Papers in Prehistory 19. Canberra: Australian National University.

Spriggs, M. 1996. What is Southeast Asian about Lapita? In *Prehistoric Mongoloid Dispersals,* ed. T. Akazawa and E.J.E. Szathmary, 324–348. Oxford: Oxford University Press.

Spriggs, M. 1997. *The Island Melanesians.* Oxford: Blackwell Publishers.

Spriggs, M. 1998. Research Questions in Maluku Archaeology. *Cakalele* 9(2): 51–64.

Stone, J. H., S. M. Fitzpatrick, and M. F. Napolitano. 2017. Disproving Claims for Small-bodied Humans in the Palauan Archipelago. *Antiquity* 91(360): 1546–1560.

Stuiver, M., and H. A. Polach. 1977. Discussion: Reporting of ^{14}C data. *Radiocarbon* 19(3): 355–363.

Summerhayes, G. R., M. Leavesley, A. Fairbairn, H. Mandui, J. Field, A. Ford, and R. Fullagar. 2010. Human Adaptation and Plant Use in Highland New Guinea 49,000 to 44,000 Years Ago. *Science* 330 (6000): 78–81.

Swadling, P. 1994. Changing Shell Resources and Their Exploitation for Food and Artifact Production in Papua New Guinea. *Man and Culture in Oceania* 10: 127–150.

Tanudirjo, D. 2001. Islands in Between: Prehistory of the Northeastern Indonesian Archipelago. PhD dissertation. Canberra: Australian National University.

Tanudirjo, D. 2005. Long and Continuous or Short Term and Occasional Occupation? The Human Use of Leang Sarru Rockshelter in the Talaud Islands, North Eastern Indonesia. *Bulletin of Indo-Pacific Prehistory Association* 25: 15–19.

Szabó, K. A. 2010. Shell artefacts and shell-working within the Lapita Cultural Complex. *Journal of Pacific Archaeology* 1(2):115–127.

Tsang, C. H., R. Santiago, and H. C. Hung. 2002. *Fei Le Bin Lu Son Dao Bei Hai An Kao Gu Diaocha Fa Jue Bao Gao, 1996-2002 [Report in archaeological exploration in northern Luson, Philippines, 1996-2002].* Annual report for the Program of Asian and Pacific Study. Taipei: Academia Sinica.

van den Bergh G. D., B. Li., A. Brumm, R. Grün, D. Yurnaldi, M. W. Moore, I. Kurniawan, R. Setiawan, F. Aziz, R. G. Roberts, Suyono, M. Storey, E. Setiabudi, and M. J. Morwood. 2016. Earliest Hominin Occupation of Sulawesi, Indonesia. *Nature* 529(7585): 208–211.

Wallace, A. 1869. Reprinted version 1986. *The Malay Archipelago: The Land of the Orangutan and the Bird of Paradise. A Narrative of Travel with Studies of Man and Nature.* 2 vols. London: Macmillan. Oxford: Oxford University Press.

Wood, R., Z. Jacobs, D. Vannieuwenhuyse, J. Balme, S. O'Connor, and R. Whitau. 2016. Towards an Accurate and Precise Chronology for the Colonization of Australia: The Example of Riwi, Kimberley, Western Australia. *PLoS ONE.* 11(9): e0160123.

12

The Strategic Location of the Maldives in Indian Ocean Maritime Trade and Colonization

RICHARD CALLAGHAN

The chronology and pathways of colonization, migration, and trade in the Indian Ocean have interested archaeologists, historians, and linguists, among others, for a considerable amount of time. The Maldives Islands (Figure 12.1), situated off the southwest coast of India, form a chain of 27 atolls comprised of 1,190 islands. The islands trend from north 6.930° to south 0.700° latitude, across an extent of approximately 850 km. The archipelago divides the Indian Ocean into eastern and western halves geographically, as well as marking the divide between the seasonal monsoon weather patterns. The chain provides a convenient stopping place for mariners in the mid-Indian Ocean between the two monsoon patterns.

Situated similarly to the Maldives, the Chagos Archipelago also may have extended the available stopping places for mariners. The Chagos Archipelago is made up of 7 atolls forming more than 60 separate islands located about 500 km to the south of the Maldives Archipelago in the Indian Ocean. The archipelago extends from about south 4° latitude to south 8° latitude or circa 450 km. Although the Chagos Archipelago was unoccupied until the mid-eighteenth century, it was known to the people of the Maldives (Romero-Frias 1999: 19).

Here, computer simulations of voyaging are used to examine the strategic position of the Maldives Islands for trade and colonization in the Indian Ocean. This approach for studying seafaring has been used with increasing frequency globally to understand migration, colonization, and cultural interaction (for example, Avis et al. 2007; Callaghan 2001, 2003a, 2003b, 2003c; Callaghan and Fitzpatrick 2007, 2008; Irwin 1992; Levison et al. 1973; Montenegro et al. 2006, 2014, 2016). When compared to other data, the results of such simulations can

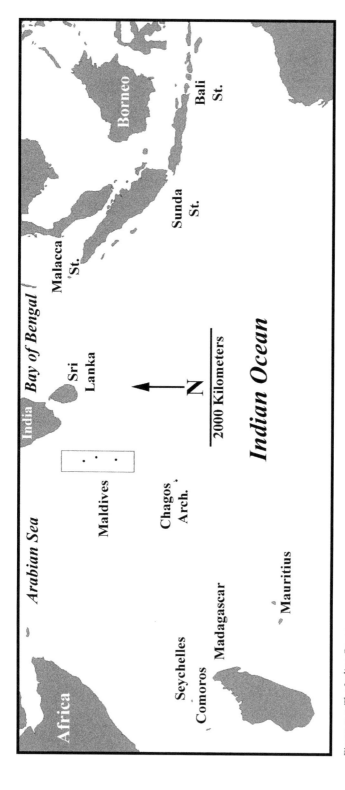

Figure 12.1. The Indian Ocean.

help develop hypotheses about the possible routes of migration, colonization, and trade in the Indian Ocean, and help demonstrate possible strategies used in maritime endeavors.

Indian Ocean Contacts and Trade

Evidence suggests that maritime travel and trade began early in the Indian Ocean. In Island Southeast Asia, human movements by sea began prior to 50,000 years ago (O'Connell et al. 2010; O'Connor 2007; O'Connor et al., 2002, 2005, 2011); chapter 11). In the western Indian Ocean, where a strong research focus is relatively recent (Boivin et al. 2013; Fuller et al. 2011), current evidence suggests maritime endeavors to be more recent. However, these movements still have considerable antiquity, and maritime adaptation along parts of the African coast may be as early as the Middle Stone Age (Boivin et al. 2013: 222). Further, there is evidence that hunter-gatherers in the region had sufficient maritime skills to navigate the difficult currents between the offshore islands and the mainland. Fuller et al. (2011: 545), while focusing on the translocation of plants and animals across the Indian Ocean, note the beginnings of maritime contacts in the northwestern Indian Ocean in the trade of obsidian from Ethiopia to Yemen from about 4000 BC. This trade expanded north into Egypt with incense and other commodities. By the end of the third millennium BC, trade had expanded to connect Africa to India. This trade appears to have been conducted by small-scale or village societies without major civilizations involved.

From about 2000 BC, at least five crops had been translocated from Africa to the drier areas of southern India, including pearl millet (*Pennisetum glaucum*), sorghum (*Sorghum bicolor*) and finger millet (*Eleusine coracana*) (Fuller et al. 2011: 246–247). The translocations were not unidirectional and by circa 1700 BC, broom millet (*Panicum miliaceum*), ultimately from China, was being grown in Sudanese Nubia. A maritime route into Africa is suggested by the absence of broom millet in Mesopotamia and Egypt at the time. Zebu cattle may also have been introduced into East Africa from India at this time, and pepper was traded from coastal south India to Africa from circa 1200 BC.

Over time, the distances and number of commodities traded around the Indian Ocean increased (Fuller et al. 2011: 548–552). By the first millennium BC, there is evidence for well-developed trade between southern India and the Malay Peninsula. Both Indian-style ceramics and stone beads are found in abundance on the Malay Peninsula, and translocated crops include many pulses used in dal in India, such as mungbean (*Vigna radiata*) and horsegram (*Macrotyloma uniflorum*). Fuller et al. (2011: 549) note the probable wild origins of several tree species from Southeast Asia that are found in South India. Areca-nut palms, along with betel nut (*Areca catechu*) and pepper leaf (*Piper betle*), used in combination as a stimulant, both originate in Southeast Asia, with citron (*Citrus medica*) and mango (*Mangifera indica*) moving in the opposite direction. Sandalwood (*Santalum album*) is another tree translocated from Indonesia to India around this time.

Many introductions were made to Africa from Southeast Asia. Bananas (*Musa paradiasiaca*), originating in New Guinea, may have been translocated to western India by about 2000 BC, and are found in Cameroon prior to 500 BC (Fuller et al. 2011: 549–550). The greater yam (*Dioscorea alata*) and taro (*Colocasia esculenta*) may have also come to Africa from Southeast Asia, but a coastal route for this dispersal seems to be contradicted by the distribution.

Boivin et al. (2013) have published an extensive summary of both plant and animal translocations around the Indian Ocean. They provide an extensive list of plants, in particular, that were transported over long distances. These are added to those discussed by Fuller et al. (2011). One of the interesting categories included are commensal plants such as weeds that were probably transported inadvertently with crop plants. As with plants, animals both domesticated and commensal were transported from all around the Indian Ocean to new locations. These connections are clear from circa 2000 BC (Boivin et al. 2013).

Boivin et al. (2013: 264–265) note a number of animals that give insights into the extent and pathways of Indian Ocean trade and contacts. Shrews are of particular interest. The Asian house shrew (*Suncus murinus*) originates in India and was spread widely around the Indian Ocean by maritime routes. Direct crossings are indicated as early as 500 BC. As an example, the pygmy shrew (*Suncus etruscus*) has also been identified as a South Asian or Southeast Asian introduction. Its introduction to Madagascar suggests a direct crossing of the Indian Ocean rather than a coastal route, given a variety endemic to Madagascar, as does the introduction of the black rat (*Rattus rattus*) from South Asia to Madagascar (Boivin et al. 2013: 249).

Prendergast et al. (2017) specifically focus on the translocation of the black rat and the chicken (*Gallus gallus*) to examine Indian Ocean contacts and trade. They used a variety of methods in their analysis, the results of which indicate an introduction from Asia to the eastern African coast in the late, mid-first millennium AD. Both species were introduced to northeastern Africa much earlier, raising the possibility of an overland route to the Swahili coast and then to offshore islands. However, no evidence is found in intervening areas supporting a maritime introduction. Interestingly, the earliest identification of both species in East Africa is in island sites, with later dates for the mainland sites. The later dates for the introduction of the chicken and black rat indicate an intensification of East African and offshore island involvement in the greater Indian Ocean trade around AD 700.

Along with plants and animals transported around the Indian Ocean, manufactured goods and technologies were moved as well (Blench 1996; Boivin et al. 2013; Fuller et al. 2011; Wood et al. 2017). Blench (1996) discusses similarities in material culture between Island Southeast Asia and East Africa, including the offshore islands, specifically those observed between musical instruments and maritime technology. Two Austronesian instruments, the leaf-funnel clarinet and the stick zither, are introductions to East Africa, while the xylophone in Indonesia appears to be of African origin. The outrigger canoe is undoubtedly of Austronesian origin and is found along the East African coast where the terminology is very similar to Malay. Further, Austronesian terms for boats and boat parts have been identified in a number of South Asian languages including Dhivehi (Maldives Islands), Sinhalese (Sri Lanka), Tamil, Hindi, and possibly some Andamanese Island languages (Fuller et al. 2011: 552). Fuller et al. (2011: 548) note ceramics and beads on the Malay Peninsula that are in the Indian style dating to the second half of the first millennium BC. There is also evidence of Indian craftworkers moving to an urban center in Thailand to locally produce stone beads and ceramics using Indian technology and style. Iron-working technology on Madagascar bears a closer resemblance to that in Southeast Asia than to Africa (Boivin et al. 2013: 254). Recently Wood et al. (2017: 879–880) conducted an analysis of glass beads from Zanzibar and found that beads were produced in Sri Lanka, South India, Southeast Asia, Syria, the Levant, and Persia.

The Maldives and the Colonization of Madagascar

Present evidence suggests that the Maldives were occupied as early as the fifth or fourth century BC with close ties to India, although the precise dating of initial occupation has not been determined. Maumoon (2002: 23–25) summarizes the history of the language of the Maldives, Dhivehi. It is closely related to the Sinhalese language of Sri Lanka, but the two languages may have had a common ancestor rather than Dhivehi being a daughter language of Sinhalese. Dhivehi does have links to earlier Indic languages as well. Buddhists found the Maldives occupied when they arrived during the first few centuries AD (Maloney 1980: 75), and the Maldivians undoubtedly were capable sailors by this time.

This is more strongly suggested by Ammianus Marcellinus (Maloney 1980: 72), who recorded a list of emissaries to Rome at that time which includes the Maldivians. A fourth-century-AD Chinese reference (Maloney 1980: 70) describes how the people of the islands were highly mobile and continually relocated as the islands rose and sank.

Woodroffe and Horton (2005) note that reconstructions of Late Holocene sea-level changes in the Indo-Pacific at the local level are not particularly reliable. However, good data do exist for the Maldives (Kench et al. 2009; Mörner 2007; Mörner et al. 2004). Katupotha (2015: figure 3) compiles the variations from these studies showing that sea levels were approximately 0.5 m above the present sea level at about 3000 BP, and diminished to present discontinuously until the current sea level was reached. Katupotha also shows that the reconstructed sea-level curves vary among the islands of the Maldives. Mörner et al. (2004) note that from 1500 to 1300 BP, the Maldives as a whole were occupied despite a 40–50 cm rise in sea level over the present. The Chinese reference to frequent relocation of Maldivians as the islands rose and sank may be indicative of the nature of many of the islands themselves. Many of the islands are coral atolls that form around volcanic islands. In time, the central volcanic portion subsides, leaving the typical ring or linear-shaped coral islands. In their discussion of past sea-level changes, Woodroffe and Horton (2005) state that, in tectonically active regions, changes in sea level can result in rapid movement of the ocean crust. Given changes in sea-level and tectonic movements, well-planned underwater investigations, such as those discussed by Gusick et al. (chapter 5), would be of value.

Forbes (1987) summarized findings from archaeological expeditions in the Maldives from the 1920s through to 1983. Excavations on the Maldives in 1922 by H.P.C. Bell (Forbes 1987: 283) in Foh Mulah Atoll (Fuvahmulah) found architectural remains that strongly resembled the third century AD Buddhist architecture at Anuradhapura in Sri Lanka. Other Buddhist architectural remains were tentatively dated to the tenth or eleventh century AD at Haddunmati Atoll, Gamu Island. A 1958 expedition to Ari Atoll, Toddu Island, recorded numerous Buddhist remains and a silver box in a coral relic-casket containing several objects, including a Roman Republican denarius of Caius Vibius Pansa. The coin was minted in Rome in 90 BC (Forbes 1987: 284). Buddhist remains were also found on many other islands and atolls in the Maldives, most of which suggest linkages to Sri Lanka. However, 1983 excavations at Machchangoli Ba Miskit, Male' (Forbes 1987: 288), recovered a series of carved marble stones suggesting Hindu influence. Marble is not found in the Maldives, but the style and material suggest a connection to Northwest India, possibly the Gujarat Kathiawad Peninsula.

The Maldives islanders led a fairly isolated life early on with a subsistence base relying on growing coconuts and fishing (Chaudhuri 1985: 18). Even building materials were derived from the sea in the form of coral blocks recovered from the sea floor. Cowrie shells are a good example of Maldives trade dating back millennia, as they had little local value to the islanders and were exchanged with India for cotton textiles and rice from early times. The shells were then traded from India to other regions. By the Islamic Period they were being traded to East Africa and the Middle East, finally by caravan to West Africa (Chaudhuri 1985: 18–19). The Maldives became the center of two large overlapping trade spheres (Chaudhuri 1985: 103) extending from East Africa to Southeast Asia.

The location of the Maldives is strategic for maritime trade in the Indian Ocean, and it became, culturally and commercially, strongly connected to both Asia and Africa after Islam was brought to the archipelago in the twelfth century. The importance of the Maldives in the Indian Ocean trade spheres is explained in the account of Tome Pires (1944: 269), written between 1512 and 1515: "Because those from Cairo and Mecca and Aden cannot reach Malacca in a single monsoon, as well as the Parsies and those from Ormuz and Rumes, Turks and similar peoples such as the Armenians, at their own time they go to the kingdom of Gujarat . . . from there they embark in March and sail direct for Malacca; on the return journey they call at the Maldives Islands." Beginning in the sixteenth century, they became increasingly important to European colonial powers.

The colonization of Madagascar provides the most significant example of the strategic importance of the Maldives. Madagascar is comprised of 587,000 km^2, making it one of the largest islands of the world. It is separated from the southeast coast of Africa by about 420 km. The Indonesian Archipelago lies some 5,600 km away at the eastern margin of the Indian Ocean. Based on archaeological and paleoenvironmental evidence, the first human colonization of Madagascar took place around 2000 BP (Dewar and Wright 1993). More recent evidence (Brucato et al. (2018: 58) suggests the eighth century AD. However, there is some evidence in the form of clearing, burning, plant introductions, and butchered extinct animal bones that may indicate a human presence as opposed to colonization (see chapters 2, 4, and 10) on Madagascar by circa 350 BC (Boivin et al. 2013: 223). This and earlier dates need more confirmation. Subsequently, the history of settlement seems to have become more complex when people from several locations around the Indian Ocean arrived, including the Near East, East Africa, South Asia, and Southeast Asia (Dewar and Wright 1993: 418).

The island of Madagascar is positioned adjacent to the mainland of Africa and may have been colonized by African hunter-gatherer-foragers in the first or second millennium BC (Burney et al. 2004; Dewar et al. 2013), but again the evidence is not strong. Subsequently, it appears to have been colonized by Austronesian speakers from the eastern side of the Indian Ocean. The Austronesian language, Malagasy, has the most speakers on the island, and is most closely related to the Maanjan language in Southeast Kalimantan (Borneo) (Dahl 1951, 1977). The connection between Malagasy and Austronesian languages was recognized in the sixteenth century if not earlier (Allibert 2008). The evidence presented by Dahl (1951, 1971) also suggests extended contact with Bantu languages of East Africa. The divergence of Malagasy from Island Southeast Asian languages seems to have occurred between 1,000 and 2,000 years ago (Dewar and Wright 1993: 419), but there was also continued contact between the two areas. Along with language connections, there are cultural ones between Madagascar and Southeast Asia, including the position of the maternal uncle in rites of passage, the association of death and the number 8, ritual association of children with a reptile and canoe burials, and secondary burials (Allibert 2008).

Evidence from genetic analysis further indicates that major migrations to Madagascar occurred from both East Africa and Indonesia (Pigache 1970). Hurles et al. (2005) analyzed mitochondrial sequence diversity, Y-chromosome polymorphisms, and mitochondrial DNA among Malagasy-speaking populations. The results show that both paternal and maternal Malagasy lineages have about equal Indonesian and African ancestry. The Y-chromosomal haplogroup that most closely matches Malagasy is from southern Kalimantan. Brucato et al. (2018) conducted analyses of genome-wide genotyping data from Madagascar, the coast of Kenya, and the Comoro Islands. The results show that, especially in the Comoros and Malagasy populations, there is an admixture with people from Island Southeast Asia. This event appears to be as early as the eighth century AD. The Comoro Islands seem to be the location of the first contact between Austronesians and East Africans. This date is in good corroboration with data from archaeology and linguistics (Brucato et al. 2018: 58). Archaeobotanical analysis indicates an Island Southeast Asian connection to Madagascar. Crowther et al. (2016) conducted archaeobotanical analysis on Madagascar, the African coast, nearshore islands, and the Comoro Islands, and found that approximately 10 percent of the flora of Madagascar has been introduced. Many of these plants are of East or Island South Asian origin, including arable weeds, spices, and staple crops. The results of the study show that Asian plants were adopted slowly on the African coast and nearshore islands, likely through commercial contacts. The patterns for the Comoros and Madagascar are quite different. The earliest archaeobotanical data date to eighth to tenth centuries AD. Asian crops make up the largest component, and the pattern suggests human colonization rather than simply commercial activities. It is suggested that Island Southeast Asia is a likely source for the Asian crops on both the Comoros and Madagascar (Crowther et al. 2016: 6638). This suggestion, based on the archaeobotanical analysis, corresponds well with ethnographic, genetic, and linguistic analysis for Madagascar (Boivin et al. 2013; Brucato et al. 2018; Crowther et al. 2016; Fuller et al. 2011; Prendergast et al. 2017; Wood et al. 2017). The Asian crops are earlier in the Comoros than Madagascar (Crowther et al. 2016: 6639), indicating that the Comoros may have been colonized from Island Southeast Asia at an earlier date.

There is a detailed description of coastal trade around the Indian Ocean from about 10° south latitude along the Somalian coast, through the Malacca Straits, and on to approximately S 5° near the east coast of Sumatra. The details of the route are found in the *Periplus of the Erythraean Sea* (Schoff 1912). The original document was likely written around AD 60 (Schoff 1912: 15) and pertains to much of the period considered here. The *Periplus* includes the seasonality of trade voyages and a description of the goods traded at each port of call. While largely a coastal route, seasons for two open-sea crossings are also given. One is for crossing the Bay of Bengal, while the other is the crossing of the Arabian Sea. The crossings are in both directions, making use of the seasonal monsoonal shifts.

More direct open-sea crossings of the Indian Ocean may have been undertaken particularly for colonization or other movements of large numbers of people. As an example, a coastal route from the Malacca Straits to the Comoro Islands northwest of Madagascar would entail a voyage of more than 6,000 nautical miles (nm), or 11,000 km. Linguistic evidence suggests continued contact between Malagasy, the westernmost member of the Malayo-Polynesian branch of the Austronesian language family, and languages on the eastern side of the Indian Ocean (Adalaar 1989) after the initial colonization of the Comoros and Madagascar, likely from Borneo. Biological evidence also suggests direct crossing as seen in the introduction of the pygmy shrew to Madagascar where the endemic variety has its closest relative to the east across the Indian Ocean (Boivin et al. 2013). Direct crossings from the Malacca Straits to Madagascar would be much shorter, around 4,000 nm or 7,500 km. The position of the Maldives and Chagos Islands between the two halves of the Indian Ocean and at the division of the monsoon shifts would make them strategic in such direct crossings in either direction.

Here, computer simulations, using wind and current data and sailing-vessel performance characteristics, are created to evaluate the possible routes traders and colonists may have used that relied on the Maldives, particularly in the earlier periods of occupation. The chain provides a convenient way station while waiting for favorable shifts in the monsoon winds, and may have played a critical role in the colonization of the Comoro Islands and Madagascar, and the east African Indian Ocean trade from early times.

The Simulation Program

The problem here is to investigate seasonality, voyage durations, and alternative migration routes in the Indian Ocean. These factors are analyzed here using a database in the Seascape simulation program of known wind and current patterns throughout the year, and performance characteristics of sailing vessels (Callaghan 1999, 2001). Several voyaging strategies can be simulated by the program. Two sailing strategies were used in the simulations of Indian Ocean seafaring with five starting points (Figure 12.1): the Bali Straits; the Sunda Straits; the north end of the Malacca Straits; Sri Lanka and; northeastern Madagascar. The first strategy is downwind sailing, also referred to as sailing before the wind. Vessels using this strategy simply sail with the wind behind them. No attempt is made to choose a particular heading. This allows a vessel to cover the maximum distance in a given time. Many of the islands of the Indian Ocean may have been discovered in this manner. The strategy is consistent with situations where voyagers are lost with no reference points, although it can be used in other situations. Although there is no recorded ethnographic information for the Indian Ocean, there is some for the Pacific regarding this strategy. The evidence is limited, but it does suggest that this is a common pattern of behavior for Polynesian sailors lost at sea and one that is adopted early (Dening 1963: 138–153).

The second strategy used in the simulations is directed sailing, where voyagers attempt to maintain a specific heading. This requires the use of vessels with some degree of windward sailing capability. From at least 2,000 years ago, vessels from Indonesia and elsewhere sailing in the Indian Ocean were capable of some windward sailing. The eighth/ninth century Javanese temple of Borobudur has a number of bas-relief carvings of vessels carrying canted rectangular sails and lug sails (McGrail 2001: 301). Some researchers (Bowen 1954: 201) classify the canted rectangular sails at Borobudur as a version of the lug sail. Lug sails are powerful rigs for sailing to windward and can be made using relatively simple technology (Bolger 1984: 42).

There are four main variables to consider when conducting downwind sailing and directed simulations: (1) current patterns; (2) wind patterns; (3) vessel type; and (4) propulsion. The mechanics of the program can be considered the program structure—examples would be defining success as a percentage of all voyages calculated and how data are selected. Parameters include whether it is a downwind or directed voyage, the starting position of the vessel, the acceptable duration at sea, and what defines a successful voyage.

Currents and winds are part of the simulation structure and cannot be changed other than by selecting a new region of the oceans of the world. Any objects, including vessels, caught in currents are affected in a 1:1 ratio, meaning that the set and speed of the current will be the same for the object. This will hold if no other forces are operating. However, if objects are floating appreciably above the water, winds will have a greater effect than the currents. Very strong currents can override this. We have very little information of how traditional voyagers used such information in wayfinding in the Indian Ocean. However, traditional navigators in Kiribati used the effect of wind on objects floating high to determine the direction of land if recent winds differed from the flow of the current (Lewis 1972: 212). The current and wind data are sourced from the U.S. Navy Marine Climatic Atlas of the World CDROM (Version l.1 1995).

The final two variables of the simulation are how the vessel is propelled and the type of vessel—these are the only two variables that can be changed by the operator, but they are used as constants in each set of experiments. New vessel types can be added to the program, while propulsion refers to drift, sail, or paddled. The shape of an object above and below the waterline will affect how it responds to the wind as well as the sail type. In this problem, however, there are many types of vessels in the Indian Ocean that could have been used, most of which have not had their performance characteristics analyzed. An Indonesian sailing vessel of some type from the relevant periods is most likely since, in some parts of Madagascar, Indonesian-style outriggers are still used (Dewar and Wright 1993: 419).

In recent years, a direct crossing of the Indian Ocean from Indonesia to Madagascar was made with a replica of a first-millennium Indonesian sailing vessel (Beale 2006). Its construction was based on one of the ships depicted at the temple of Borobudur (http:// www.borobudurshipexpedition.com/index.

htm). However, of the 11 vessels carved on the walls of Borobudur, not all are of the same design (McGrail 2001: 301). Because we do not know precisely what types of vessels were involved in migrations to Madagascar, the craft performance characteristics used in these simulations are generalized from a number of watercraft types. In their model of Pacific voyaging, Levison et al. (1973: 19) provide figures for speeds that vessels can travel under various conditions that are used here (Table 12.1). The effective craft speeds increase until 8 on the Beaufort Wind Velocity Scale. At that wind velocity, speeds begin to decline because it would be necessary to reduce sail or take the risk of capsizing. After 9 on the scale, craft speed is reduced to 0, as it is unlikely that sailing craft could survive in those force winds.

The United States Navy Marine Climatic Atlas (U.S. Navy 1995) includes data for all of the world's oceans and seas, with the exception of Arctic waters. The resolution of these data is one-degree Marsden squares (one degree of latitude by one degree of longitude). This resolution allows smaller and more variable currents to be reflected in the outcomes, as opposed to the resolution of data on pilot charts. The Marine Climatic Atlas (U.S. Navy 1995) gives compiled observations of wind and current data by month. These are then frequency-weighted and randomly selected by the program. As such, if a wind or current flowing from due east in a 1° × 1° Marsden square has been observed 45 percent of the time, then it will have a 45 percent chance of being selected. Where winds and currents have been observed flowing from due east only 5 percent of the time, they will have a 5 percent chance of being selected. The force of the winds and currents is also taken for the corresponding wind or current direction as reported in the United States Navy Climatic Atlas (U.S. Navy 1995). Both wind and current data are organized into wind and current roses with the four cardinal directions and four intercardinal directions. The selected wind and current forces operate on vessels for 24 hours and then a new selection is made (see Levison et al. 1973 for a justification of the period length). The direction and distance traveled are then combined with the speeds given by Levison et al. (1973: 19, table 1) and the parameters selected for the particular problem being analyzed.

The settings chosen by the program operator make up the parameters of the simulation. They are chosen to answer the questions of interest. There are six parameters that can be selected. They include: (1) crew strategy; (2) points of origin and destination; (3) duration of voyages; (4) performance characteristics of the type of vessel selected; (5) number of simulations; and (6) time of year.

The first parameter is the strategy used by the crew. As noted above, in this analysis, two crew strategies are investigated. The first is downwind sailing, or

Table 12.1. Beaufort wind velocity scale and effective craft speeds in knots

Beaufort Number	Description	Wind Speed	Wave Height	Effective Craft Speed
0	Calm	<1 km/h <1 knot	0.0 m	0.0 knots
1	Light air	1–5 km/h 1–3 knots	0.0–0.2 m	0.5 knots
2	Light breeze	6–11 km/h 4–6 knots	0.2–0.5 m	1.0 knots
3	Gentle breeze	12–19 km/h 7–10 knots	0.5–1.0 m	2.0 knots
4	Moderate breeze	20–28 km/h 11–16 knots	1.0–2.0 m	3.0 knots
5	Fresh breeze	29–38 km/h 17–21 knots	2.0–3.0 m	4.5 knots
6	Strong breeze	39–49 km/h 22–27 knots	3.0–4.0 m	6.0 knots
7	Moderate gale	50–61 km/h 28–33 knots	4.0–5.5 m	7.0 knots
8	Fresh gale	62–74 km/h 34–40 knots	5.5–7.5 m	6.0 knots
9	Strong gale	75–88 km/h 41–47 knots	7.0–10.0 m	4.5 knots
10	Whole gale	89–102 km/h 48–55 knots	9.0–12.5 m	0.0 knots
11	Violent storm	103–117 km/h 56–63 knots	11.5–16.0 m	0.0 knots
12	Hurricane force	≥ 118 km/h ≥ 64 knots	≥ 14.0 m	0.0 knots

Source: Based on Levison, Ward, and Webb (1972).

sailing before the wind. In this strategy, again vessels are simply sailed before the wind with no attempt to navigate, allowing close to the maximum distance to be covered in a given time. The second crew strategy, directed sailing, is one in which sailors intentionally try to sail in a specified direction. Although not necessary for the questions asked here, there is a third strategy that can be used where the direction that the crew attempts to sail in can be manually changed over the course of the simulation to circumvent obstacles or difficult wind and current patterns (Callaghan and Scarre 2009).

For the second parameter, five points of origin were chosen: (1) the Bali Straits between Bali and Java; (2) the Sunda Straits between Java and Sumatra; (3) the north end of the Malacca Straits off the northwestern tip of Sumatra; (4) just west of Sri Lanka and south of India; and (5) one point of origin off the northeastern tip of Madagascar. The first four points had Madagascar as the target land; the fifth point was used for return voyages to Indonesia.

The third parameter, the duration of the voyages, was set at 200 days, after which it was assumed the crew perished. Two hundred days would approach the maximum duration of many drift voyages in an open boat as a result of shipwreck or other misfortunes (Callaghan 2003c; Howay 1944; Levison et al. 1973: 20–21). A number of these recorded voyages covered distances of about 5,500 km over 6 to 10 weeks, and more traveled slightly shorter distances. However, the longest recorded shipwreck voyage in an open boat seems to be in the order of 15 months (Franklin 2015). The performance characteristics for the fourth parameter were the generalized ones given by Levinson et al. (1973). For the fifth and sixth parameters, respectively, 100 voyages were simulated for each of the 12 months of the year from each of the points of origin.

Survival

Although not integrated into the program in detail, it is worth considering other factors of the marine environment of the Indian Ocean in terms of survival. This is important in deciding the days' duration for survival at sea and evaluating the results. For instance, it would be wrong to set the survival duration to 200 days in an Arctic environment but correct in warm tropical waters (see McCance et al. 1956). There are three main factors impacting survival at sea: the availability of potable water, the availability of food, and surface temperature. Water is usually the major problem on long ocean voyages, as individuals are typically unable to survive longer than 10 days, given survival conditions (Lee 1965: 96, 99). Calculating the availability of water can be very difficult. Levison et al. (1973: 20) state that, "between the extremes of no water and ample water the whole range of unpredictable situations makes it impractical to construct a separate risk table for this factor" in a simulation program.

Besides what can be stored on board, there are a number of potential sources of water when at sea. Precipitation, especially in the tropics, can provide ample water if there is the means to collect it. Sails provide easy means of collecting rainwater and have even been used to collect dew and fog (Heikell 1999: 5). As an example, Bombard (1986: 61), while conducting survival experiments in the Mediterranean Sea, could at times collect nearly a half liter of water from dew. Displacement vessels have more potential for collecting precipitation than rafts, given a closed hull. Water particles will condense on many materials including matting, cloth, and leather. Many regions of the Indian Ocean are prone to afternoon showers even in the dry season (Heikell 1999: 214–215). Precipitation is not the sole source of drinking water when at sea. Many instances where water was obtained from other sources by shipwrecked sailors are cited by Lee and Lee (1980: 139–160). These sources include barnacles, fish, and teredo worms, and even blood can provide a viable substitute.

Neither of the two crew strategies simulated here, downwind sail and directed sailing, are shipwreck situations. It would then be expected that vessels be well provisioned. Many comestibles available around the lands of the Indian Ocean have considerable storability, including nuts, dried fruit, grains, and legumes (Heikell 1999: 11). At present, fish stock in the equatorial Indian Ocean are extensive, and the fish easy to catch (Heikell 1999: 18). This situation was likely even better in the past. Lee and Lee (1980: 139–160) list many sources of food available to survivors in emergency situations, and cite instances where survivors ate everything from teredo worms to nonvegetable plankton. In one report (Lee and Lee 1980: 110–111), barracuda were leaping onto a life raft, although the fish were seen as a threat more than a source of food. It is commonly reported that sharks, usually too small to be a threat, follow small vessels. Other food sources that do not require any specialized technology for capture include turtles and seabirds, which are often reported to be available in shipwreck situations.

Sea surface temperature can be the most significant factor affecting survival at sea, but it is not a major factor here. The sea surface temperatures of the equatorial Indian Ocean are between 28°C and 29°C, well above temperatures that would present a survival problem (Heikell 1999: 209; McCance et al. 1956).

Results

For downwind sailing simulations, westward progress to the Maldives was not possible from the Bali Straits or Sunda Straits (Figure 12.1). However, from April to August, vessels could reach between 88° E and 83°E, roughly 1,000 to 1,500 km or 550 to 800 nm from their origin. For downwind voyages embarking from the northern end of the Straits of Malacca, some starting in December through

March could reach as far west as 72°, the longitude of the Maldives (Figure 12.1). By simply keeping the wind at their stern and starting in November or December, vessel crews could make landfall in Sri Lanka in as little as 40 days. A particularly interesting pattern emerges for downwind sailing from the Sri Lanka position for vessels starting in January and February (Figure 12.2). Vessels passing through the Maldives and continuing south could take advantage of the winds moving both west and east. Exploiting this bifurcation, they could reach Madagascar in as little as 81 days, or Java in as little as 73 days. For downwind sailing from the Comoro Islands or the northern end of Madagascar, most vessels moved west, although a small number reached Sri Lanka, the southwest coast of India, or the northern Maldives from May through August (Figure 12.3).

The second experiment entails directed voyages and assumes the crew has some knowledge of the location they are trying to reach, and that the vessel has at least moderate windward capability. Once an initial heading is chosen, no attempt is made to change direction. Crossings of the Indian Ocean were not possible from the Bali Straits, although in June and July some vessels reached about 78° E due south of Sri Lanka, missing the Maldives by about 400 km or 215 nm. With a westward heading from the Sunda Straits, many vessels starting from December through March would reach the Maldives or Chagos Islands in 54 to 71 days (Figure 12.4).

Westward voyages from the northern end of the Malacca Straits from December through March reached the southern end of the Maldives or the Chagos Islands in 21–40 days (Figure 12.5). From the Sri Lanka position, with a southwest heading, all voyages leaving from December through March reached the Maldives and had the potential to reach Madagascar, the Comoros, the Seychelles, or East Africa in 43–61 days. Voyaging in the reverse direction from Madagascar west to east, with a heading of due east from November through April (Figure 12.6), was 100 percent successful in reaching the Maldives or the Chagos Islands. The durations were from 23 to 38 days.

Discussion and Conclusions

The Maldives, and possibly the Chagos Islands to the south, are in a strategic position for travel in both directions across the Indian Ocean for vessels using the shifting monsoon winds. Even with downwind sailing, there was success in sailing from Indonesia to the longitude of the Maldives. It would not take much navigational skill to make landfall there. None of the sets of experiments suggests voyage durations close to the survival maximum. Using the Maldives as a

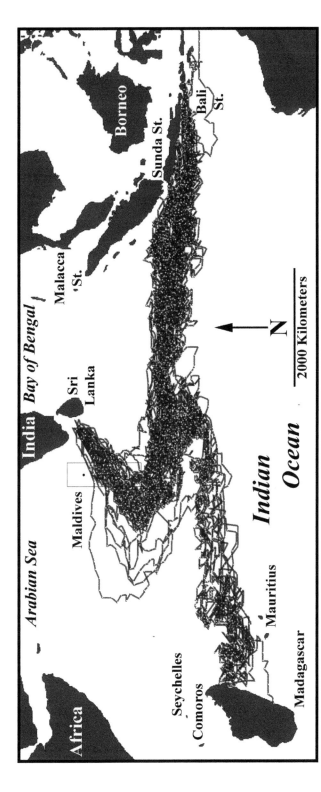

Figure 12.2. Downwind sailing from Sri Lanka in January.

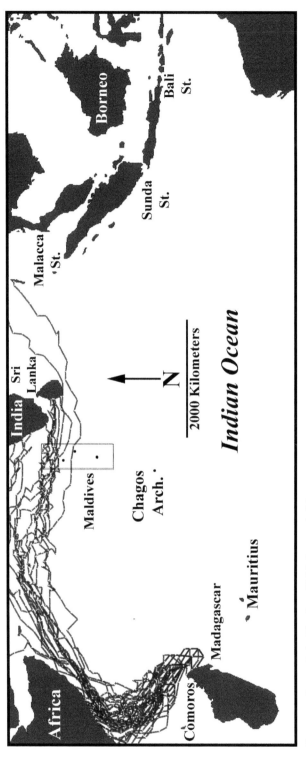

Figure 12.3. Downwind sailing from N. Madagascar in May.

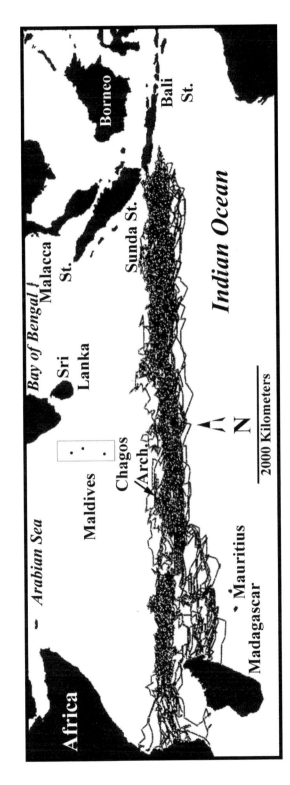

Figure 12.4. Directed sailing from the Sunda Straits in March.

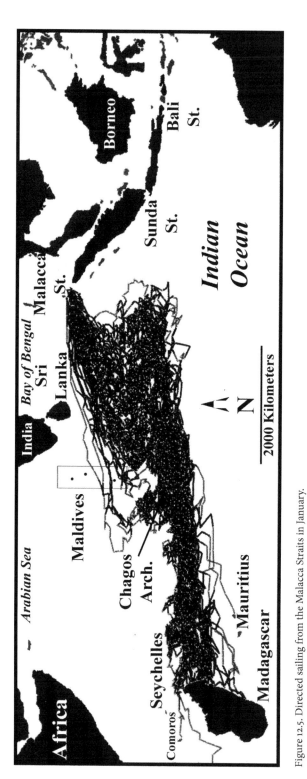

Figure 12.5. Directed sailing from the Malacca Straits in January.

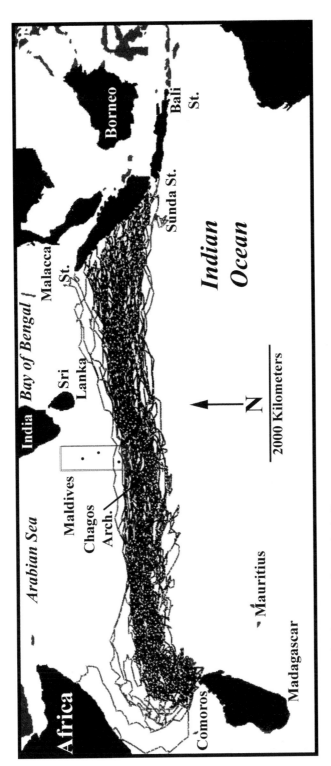

Figure 12.6. Directed sailing from N. Madagascar in April.

way station greatly enhances the use of direct ocean crossings as an alternative to coastal routes.

This is not to say that other areas around the Indian Ocean were not in strategic locations for maritime travel. Sri Lanka is an obvious example, as demonstrated by the simulation. However, much more evidence exists in historical and other sources about Sri Lanka being a key site for seagoing travel than exists for the Maldives. Many of the simulated routes to the west of Sri Lanka pass through the Maldives. In fact, even with downwind sailing in January and February, vessels from Sri Lanka could use the Maldives as a way station to sail to either Indonesia or Africa well within any survival limits. The language of the Maldives, Dhivehi, is closely relate to the Sinhalese language of Sri Lanka, but has older Indic elements that suggest strong links to Sri Lanka.

The Maldives were colonized by Buddhists and Hindus in the first few centuries AD but were already occupied. The date of the initial occupation is not known. The Chagos Islands were not permanently occupied until the mid-eighteenth century but were known to people on the Maldives. Unfortunately, the low elevation of the islands of both archipelagos and shallow soils make terrestrial archaeological recoveries difficult. A fourth-century Chinese reference to the Maldives atolls states that people there move from island to island as the islands themselves emerge and submerge. Well-planned underwater archaeological investigations may have more success at elucidating the early history of the Maldives and their strategic position in Indian Ocean trade than terrestrial excavations.

References Cited

Adalaar, K. A. 1989. Malay Influence on Malagasy: Linguistic and Culture-historical Implications. *Oceanic Linguistics* 28(1): 1–46.

Allibert, C. 2008. Austronesian Migration and the Establishment of the Malagasy Civilization: Contrasted Readings in Linguistics, Archaeology, Genetics and Cultural Anthropology. *Diogenes* 55(2): 7–16.

Avis, C., Á. Montenegro, and A. Weaver. 2007. The Discovery of Western Oceania: A New Perspective. *Journal of Island and Coastal Archaeology* 2(2): 197–209.

Beale, P. 2006. From Indonesia to Africa: Borobudur Ship Expedition. *Zanizibar International Film Festival Journal* 3: 17–24.

Blench, R. 1996. The Ethnographic Evidence for Long-Distance Contacts between Oceania and East Africa. In *The Indian Ocean in Antiquity*, ed. J. Reade, 417–438. London: Kegan Paul.

Boivin, N., A. Crowther, R. Helm, and D. Q. Fuller. 2013. East Africa and Madagascar in the Indian Ocean World. *Journal of World Prehistory* 26(3): 213–281.

Bolger, P. C. 1984. *100 Small Boat Rigs*. Camden: International Marine.

Bombard, A. 1986. *The Bombard Story*. London: Grafton Books.

Bowen, R. L., Jr. 1954. Eastern Sail Affinities, Part II. *American Neptune* 13: 185–211.

Brucato, N., V. Fernandes, S. Mazières, P. Kusuma, M. P. Cox, J. W. Ng'ang'a, O. Wainaina, M. Omar, M.-C. Simeone-Senelle, C. Frassati, F. Alshamali, B. Fin, A. Boland, J.-F. Deleuze, M. Stoneking, A. Adelaar, A. Crowther, N. Boivin, L. Pereira, P. Bailly, J. Chiaroni, and F.-J. Ricaut. 2018. The Comoros Show the Earliest Austronesian Gene Flow into the Swahili Corridor. *American Journal of Human Genetics* 102(1): 58–68.

Burney, D. A., L. Pigott Burney, L. R. Godfrey, W. L. Jungers, S. M. Goodman, H. T. Wright, and A.J.T. Jull. 2004. A Chronology for Late Prehistoric Madagascar. *Journal of Human Evolution* 47(1–2): 25–63.

Callaghan, R. T. 1999. Computer Simulations of Ancient Voyaging. *The Northern Mariner/Le Marin Du Nord* 1: 24–33.

Callaghan, R. T. 2001. Ceramic Age Seafaring and Interaction Potential in the Antilles: A Computer Simulation. *Current Anthropology* 42(2): 11–22.

Callaghan, R. T. 2003a. Comments on the Mainland Origins of the Preceramic Cultures of the Greater Antilles. *Latin American Antiquity* 14(3): 323–338.

Callaghan, R. T. 2003b. Prehistoric Trade between Ecuador and West Mexico: A Computer Simulation of Coastal Voyages. *Antiquity* 77(298): 796–804.

Callaghan, R. T. 2003c. The Use of Simulation Models to Estimate Frequency and Location of Japanese Edo Period Wrecks along the Canadian Pacific Coast. *Canadian Journal of Archaeology* 27: 62–82.

Callaghan, R. T., and S. M. Fitzpatrick. 2007. On the Relative Isolation of a Micronesian Archipelago during the Historic Period: The Palau Case Study. *International Journal of Nautical Archaeology* 36(2): 353–364.

Callaghan, R. T., and S. M. Fitzpatrick. 2008. Examining Prehistoric Migration Patterns in the Palauan Archipelago, Western Micronesia: A Computer Simulated Analysis of Drift Voyaging. *Asian Perspectives* 47(2): 28–44.

Callaghan, R. T., and C. Scarre. 2009. Simulating the Western Seaways. *Oxford Journal of Archaeology* 28(4): 357–372.

Chaudhuri, K. N. 1985. *Trade and Civilization in the Indian Ocean: An Economic History from the Rise of Islam to 1750.* Cambridge: Cambridge University Press.

Crowther, A., L. Lucas, R. Helm, M. Horton, C. Shipton, H. T. Wright, S. Walshaw, M. Pawlowicz, C. Radimilany, K. Douka, L. Picornell-Gelabert, D. Q. Fuller, and N. L. Boivin. 2016. Ancient Crops Provide First Archaeological Signature of the Westward Austronesian Expansion. *Proceedings of the National Academy of Sciences* 113(24): 6635–6640.

Dahl, O. C. 1951. *Malgache et Maanyan: Une Comparision Linguistique.* Oslo: Egede Institutett.

Dahl, O. C. 1977. La Subdivision de la Famille Barito et la Place du Malgache. *Acta Orientalia* 34: 77–134.

Dening, G. M. 1963. The Geographical Knowledge of the Polynesians and the Nature of Interisland Contact. In *Polynesian Navigation,* ed. J. Golson, 138–153. Polynesian Society Memoir 34. Wellington: Polynesian Society.

Dewar, R. E., and T. H. Wright. 1993. The Culture History of Madagascar. *Journal of World Prehistory* 7(4): 417–466.

Dewar, R. E., C. Radimilahy, H. T. Wright, Z. Jacobs, G. O. Kelly, and F. Berna. 2013. Stone Tools and Foraging in Northern Madagascar Challenge Holocene Extinction Models. *Proceedings of the National Academy of Sciences* 110(31): 12583–12588.

Forbes, A.D.W. 1987. The Pre-Islamic Archaeology of the Maldive Islands. *Bulletin de l'Ecole Française d'Extrême-Orient* 76: 281–288.

Franklin, J. 2015. *438 Days.* New York: Atria.

Fuller, D. Q., N. Boivin, T. Hoogervorst, and R. Allaby. 2011. Across the Indian Ocean: The Prehistoric Movement of Plants and Animals. *Antiquity* 85(328): 544–558.

Heikell, R. 1999. *Indian Ocean Cruising Guide*. St. Ives Cambridgeshire: Imray Laurie Norie and Wilson.

Howay, E. W. 1944. Some Lengthy Open-boat Voyages in the Pacific Ocean. *American Neptune* 4: 53–57.

Hurles, M., B. Sykes, M. Jobling, and P. Forster. 2005. The Dual Origin of the Malagasy in Island Southeast Asia and East Africa: Evidence from Maternal and Paternal Lineages. *American Journal of Human Genetics* 76: 894–901.

Irwin, G. 1992. *The Prehistoric Exploration and Colonization of the Pacific*. Cambridge: Cambridge University Press.

Katupotha, J. 2015. A Comparative Study of Sea Level Change in Maldives and Sri Lanka during the Holocene Period. *Journal of the Geological Society of Sri Lanka* 17: 75–86.

Kench, P. S., S. G. Smithers, R. F. McLean, and S. L. Nichol. 2009. Holocene Reef Growth in the Maldives: Evidence of a Mid-Holocene Sea-Level High Stand in the Central Indian Ocean. *Geology*, 37(5): 455–458.

Lee, E.C.B. 1965. *Survival at Sea*. Rome: Centro Internazionale Radio Medico.

Lee, E.C.B., and K. Lee. 1980. *Safety and Survival at Sea*. New York: Norton.

Levison, M., R. G. Ward, and J. W. Webb. 1973. *The Settlement of Polynesia: A Computer Simulation*. Canberra: Australian University Press.

Lewis, D. 1972. *We, the Navigators*. Honolulu: University of Hawaii Press.

Maloney, C. 1980. *People of the Maldive Islands*. Bombay: Orient Longman.

Maumoon, Y. 2002. *A General Overview of the Dhivehi Language*. Male, Maldives: National Centre for Linguistic and Historical Research.

McCance, R. A., C. C. Ungley, J.W.L. Crosfill, and E. M. Widdowson. 1956. The Hazards to Men Lost at Sea, 1940–44. Medical Research Council Special Report No. 291. London: Medical Research Council.

McGrail, S. 2001. *Boats of the World: From the Stone Age to Medieval Times*. Oxford: Oxford University Press.

Montenegro, Á., M.E.R. Hetherington, and A. J. Weaver. 2006. Modelling Pre-historic Trans-oceanic Crossings into the Americas. *Quaternary Science Reviews* 25(11–12): 1323–1338.

Montenegro, Á., R. T. Callaghan, and S. M. Fitzpatrick. 2014. From West to East: Environmental Influences on the Rate and Pathways of Polynesian colonization. *The Holocene* 24(2): 242–256.

Montenegro, Á., R. T. Callaghan, and S. M. Fitzpatrick. 2016. Using Seafaring Simulations and Shortest-hop Trajectories to Model Prehistoric Colonization of Remote Oceania. *Proceedings of the National Academy of Sciences* 113(45): 12685–12690.

Mörner, N.-A. 2007. Sea-Level Changes and Tsunamis, Environmental Stress Migration Overseas. The Case of the Maldives and Sri Lanka. *Internationales Asienforum* 38(34) 353–374.

Mörner, N.-A., M. Tooley, and G. Possnert. 2004. New Perspectives for the Future of the Maldives. *Global and Planetary Change* 40(1–2): 177–182.

O'Connell, J. F., J. Allen, and K. Hawkes. 2010. Pleistocene Sahul and the Origins of Seafaring. In *The Global Origins and Development of Seafaring*, ed. A. Anderson, J. H. Barret, and K. V. Boyle, 57–68. Cambridge: McDonald Institute for Archaeology Research.

O'Connor, S. 2007. New Evidence for East Timor Contributes to Our Understanding of Earliest Modern Human Colonisation East of the Sunda Shelf. *Antiquity* 81(313): 523–535.

O'Connor, S., K. Aplin, J. Pasveer, and G. Hope. 2005. Liang Nabulei Lisa: A Late Pleistocene and Holocene Sequence from the Aru Islands. In *The Archaeology of the Aru Islands, Eastern Indonesia*, ed. S. O'Connor, M. Spriggs, P. Veth, 125–162. Canberra: ANU E-Press.

O'Connor, S., R. Ono, and C. Clarkson. 2011. Pelagic Fishing at 42,000 Years Before the Present and the Maritime Skills of Modern Humans. *Science* 334(6059): 1117–1121.

O'Connor, S., M. Spriggs, and P. Veth. 2002. Excavation at Lene Hara Cave Establishes Occupation in East Timor at Least 30,000–35,000 Years Ago. *Antiquity* 76(291): 45–50.

Pigache, J. P. 1970. La Problème Anthropobiologique à Madagascar. *Taloha* 3: 175–177.

Pires, T. 1944. *The Suma Oriental of Tomé Pires: An Account of the East from the Red Sea to Japan. Written in Malacca and India in 1512–1515, and The Book of Francisco Rodrigues.* Vol. 89, ed. and trans. Armando Cortesão. London: Hakluyt Society.

Prendergast, M. E., M. Buckley, A. Crowther, L. Frantz, H. Eager, O. Lebrasseur, R. Hutterer, A. Hulme-Beaman, W. Van Neer, K. Douka, M-A. Veall, E. M. Quintana Morales, V. J. Schuenemann, E. Reiter R. Allen, E. A. Dimopoulos, R. M. Helm, C. Shipton, O. Mwebi, C. Denys, M. Horton, S. Wynne-Jones, J. Fleisher, C. Radimilahy, H. Wright, J. B. Searle, J. Krause, G. Larson, and N. L. Boivin. 2017. Reconstructing Asian Faunal Introductions to Eastern Africa from Proxy Biomolecular and Archaeological Datasets. *PLoS ONE* 12(8): e0182565.

Romero-Frias, X. 1999. *The Maldive Islanders: A Study of an Ancient Ocean Kingdom.* Barcelona: Nova Ethnographia Indica.

Schoff, W. H. 1912. *The Periplus of the Erythraean Sea.* New York: Longmans, Green.

United States Navy (U.S. Navy). 1995. *Marine Climatic Atlas of the World.* Asheville, North Carolina: National Climatic Data Center.

Wood, M., S. Panighello, E. F. Orsega, P. Robertshaw, J. T. van Elteren, A. Crowther, M. Horton, and N. Boivin. 2017. Zanzibar and Indian Ocean Trade in the First Millennium CE: The Glass Bead Evidence. *Archaeological and Anthropological Sciences* 9(5): 879–901.

Woodroffe, S. A., and B. P. Horton. 2005. Holocene Sea-level Changes in the Indo-Pacific. *Journal of Asian Earth Sciences* 25(1): 29–43.

13

Conclusion

Archaeology and Island Colonization

JON M. ERLANDSON

> The archaeology of island colonization is guided
> by questions of who, when, from where, and why.
>
> *Napolitano, DiNapoli, and Stone (chapter 1)*

As the contributors to this volume ably demonstrate, understanding the archaeology of human island colonization involves a variety of complex issues that require a diverse array of tools to decipher. Napolitano, Stone, and DiNapoli do an excellent job of framing these issues in their introductory chapter. The authors of various chapters also do a commendable job of exploring a variety of these issues and advancing our knowledge of island colonization processes on a global basis.

As Napolitano, DiNapoli, and Stone note early in chapter 1, the purpose of the current volume "is to highlight some of the recent work on colonization studies taking place in island regions around the world." In a geographic sense, the volume is a well-balanced success, with four chapters focused on islands of the Pacific (including California's Channel Islands), two on Mediterranean islands, and one each on islands of the Indian Ocean, Island Southeast Asia, the Caribbean, and the North Atlantic (Iceland).

Methodologically, too, the chapters focus on a variety of tools available to archaeologists, ranging from good old-fashioned dirt archaeology on islands, to the analysis of distinctive artifact assemblages and geochemical "sourcing," to radiocarbon dating and Bayesian analyses, the use of simulation models in the analysis of patterns in ancient voyaging and chronological databases, remote sensing and the exploration of submerged terrestrial landscapes, and DNA (modern), aDNA, and eDNA. Clearly, archaeologists working on islands around the world have much to be hopeful about in the expanding toolkit available to address a wide variety of research questions, hypotheses, and theories (see Fitzpatrick et al. 2015).

In the sections that follow, rather than comment individually on each chapter, I will discuss some of the common issues and themes raised by various authors. My intent, therefore, is not a review of the book contents per se, but a commentary I hope will provide some fitting closing thoughts to a volume that will be a valuable asset to island and coastal archaeologists (and others) worldwide.

Island Colonization and Chronological Hygiene

As many of the chapters in this volume recognize, determining the chronological onset of human colonization events and processes on various islands is critical to understanding a variety of issues. As Lipo, Hunt, and DiNapoli note in chapter 3, identifying when humans first arrived on Rapa Nui is critical because "the timing of arrival forms the basis for all other questions regarding the island's human history." Within a framework of historical ecology, of course, the initial arrival of humans or the arrival of later European colonists also represents a watershed in the ecological history of islands around the world. Determining the age of human colonization with as much accuracy and precision as possible, therefore, is crucial to understanding the climatic, environmental, and cultural contexts of maritime dispersals and settlement, the nature of human impacts to island ecosystems, the pace of extinctions on islands before and after various human colonization events, and many more issues.

There are tens of thousands of islands scattered in oceans and seas around the world, some continental in scale (Australia and Greenland), some mere specks on global maps. We now know that hominins colonized some true islands (Flores, for example) as much as a million years ago, continents such as Australia roughly 50,000 ± 5,000 years ago, and some remote islands less than a millennium ago (Rapa Nui for example) or even a few centuries ago (Christmas Island and others).

The timing of island colonization events by archaic humans may be difficult to determine with great precision and accuracy due to the nature of available dating methods and questions about whether the oldest sites have been found. Colonization events within historical times, in contrast, can often be determined with high degrees of precision due to descriptions in historical accounts and documents. As Schmid and her colleagues show in chapter 6, Iceland is a unique example, with somewhat fuzzy historic accounts of Norse and potentially pre-Norse occupations, all of which can be effectively reconciled through a careful regional analysis of site stratigraphy, tephrochronological data, and radiocarbon (^{14}C) dates analyzed with chronological hygiene and Bayesian analysis.

Elsewhere, applications of chronometric hygiene in analyses of ^{14}C dates have played an important role in refining the chronologies of many island groups, including significantly shortening the chronologies of human occupation of Rapa Nui, Hawai'i, and other islands in East Polynesia. Such hygiene is critical to island chronologies, not just for dating colonization processes, but also for correlating cultural developments with environmental changes, contact of indigenous islanders with European or American explorers, and so on. With the widespread availability of AMS ^{14}C dating, increasingly accurate calibration methods, Bayesian analysis, and other advances, archaeologists working in island settings have an opportunity to vastly improve the accuracy and precision of our chronologies. We can only accomplish such advances, however, if we rely on the systematic dating of short-lived samples (such as charred annual seeds and nuts). As Lipo, Hunt, and DiNapoli argue in Chapter 3, we should also purge our chronological analyses of old conventional ^{14}C dates run on composite samples, unidentified wood charcoal, and other samples that can suffer from significant in-built ages (such as old wood, or coral and ivory artifacts), stratigraphic mixing, or other problems (see also chapter 6). Finally, it is time to recognize that most of the ^{14}C dates in our databases that have large analytical errors (~ ± 100 years or more) were analyzed relatively early in the development of ^{14}C dating. Most of us have heard stories about labs that produced problematic dates, had relatively lax protocols, or other issues of concern. On California's Channel Islands, with a history of more than 60 years of ^{14}C dating archaeological samples, many early dates run by even reputable laboratories have been shown by recent AMS ^{14}C dating to be off by centuries or even a millennium or more. Bayesian analysis can identify these as outliers, but such dates should now be excluded as early experiments gone wrong through a combination of errors by archaeologists, geochemists, or the students who worked in many early university-based labs with too little supervision.

Archaic Humans and Island Colonization: Cautionary Tales

Twenty years ago, I wrote confidently that only *Homo sapiens* was capable of true seafaring voyages (Erlandson 2001). Today, the growing evidence for sea crossings by archaic humans in Island Southeast Asia and the Mediterranean has me on the verge of eating those words. For now, I take some solace in the fact that no clear evidence has emerged for archaic human colonization of Sahul (Australia and New Guinea), the Ryukyus, Near Oceania, the Americas, or the more remote islands and archipelagos of the Pacific, Indian, and Atlantic oceans, all of which were later settled by seafaring *Homo sapiens*. Although the voyages that colonized such distant lands still seem to separate modern wheat from archaic chaff, the Mediterranean and ISEA may hold more surprises. When it comes to archaic human voyaging, it makes sense to keep an open mind.

Colonization of true islands by archaic or modern humans requires crossing of salt water or freshwater gaps. As a result, the history of seafaring can be analyzed, in part, by tracking the presence of hominins on islands, if a colonized island was never connected to adjacent mainland areas (see Erlandson 2001). For remote oceanic islands, this is complicated only by determining when humans first arrived, using secure archaeological signatures rather than vague environmental proxies. For more continental islands, determining whether land bridges were available at critical times is essential.

The further back in time we go, of course, the more imprecise paleogeographic reconstructions become. For Norse or Polynesian seafaring and island colonization, such issues are of limited importance. For understanding the peopling of the Americas, on the other hand, detailed paleogeographic reconstructions are critical (see chapter 5). Although widely used by archaeologists, reconstructions of paleoshorelines based solely on sea-level curves and modern bathymetry are increasingly problematic, not accounting for tectonic and isostatic effects, marine erosion that accompanied sea-level fluctuations, or the amount of sediment deposited offshore since inundation.

Another California example illustrates the magnitude of variation for one 115 km long stretch of the Santa Barbara and Ventura County mainland coast. Here, the thickness of post-glacial sediments on the sea floor was mapped using seismic reflection profiles (Wong et al. 2012). From west to east, three general zones were mapped: (1) the uplifted, sediment-poor Santa Barbara shelf, with a mean sediment thickness of 3.5 m; (2) a transitional zone with a mean sediment thickness of 18.0 m; and (3) the subsiding, sediment-rich delta and shelf off the

Ventura and Santa Clara rivers, with mean sediment thicknesses of ~39 m. Off Refugio Canyon in the "sediment poor" western area, with a mean thickness of 2.7 m, sediment thickness ranged from 0 to 12 m, with thicker sediments found in nearshore delta-mouth bars fed by steep, local watersheds. Clearly, the presence of 12–39 m of sediments will significantly underestimate the location of paleoshorelines and the distances between the mainland coast and the Channel Islands—and bias modeling of ancient currents and other variables that affect human and animal dispersals.

Projecting back 125,000 or 1 million years ago, of course, only magnifies these problems, as such time scales may encompass multiple glacial-interglacial cycles of rising and falling sea levels, as well as the long-term effects of processes such as tectonics, vulcanism, sedimentation, isostatic adjustments, and so on. Nonetheless, even taking most or all of these problems into account, the evidence for maritime activity by archaic humans grows more compelling, as Curtis Runnels summarizes in chapter 4.

Islands before Humans, Islands before Europeans

One of the most compelling areas of island research in recent years has been the exploration of human impacts to island ecosystems, both terrestrial and marine. Under the rubric of historical ecology, archeologists have contributed significantly to the understanding of the importance of islands and archipelagos as hotspots of biodiversity and extinctions, as well as to conservation and restoration efforts aimed at the recovery and sustainability of endangered island species, ecosystems, fisheries, and communities (natural and cultural). Such efforts transform the discipline of archaeology from the esoteric to the essential, and island archaeologists have been in the forefront of such critical research.

As an archaeologist, I have played a role in helping identify widespread evidence that humans have significantly impacted the marine and terrestrial ecosystems of islands around the world, often for millennia, but also accelerating dramatically during the era of European colonialism, industrialization, and globalization (see Boivin et al. 2016; Erlandson and Braje 2013; Erlandson and Rick 2010; Jackson et al. 2001; Rick and Erlandson 2008; Stephens et al. 2019). Now, as we move deeper into the Anthropocene, I am increasingly interested in documenting the evidence for the long-term resilience and sustainability of island cultures around the world. As originally defined in resource management, sustainability refers to using natural resources mindfully so that the supply never runs out.

Here, the Rapa Nui story provides the clearest case of how a theoretical shift from the study of human impacts versus sustainability can affect our view of past island cultures and their interactions with the island landscapes and seascapes they lived and worked in (see chapter 3). Until Terry Hunt and Carl Lipo began their long-term research program on this iconic island, it was the poster child for the "collapse" narrative and an ancient analogy for the current process of global human ecocide. Now it seems much more likely that the collapse on Rapa Nui was the result of European contact, the transmission of Old World diseases to the indigenous Polynesian population, and other effects of colonialism. Now, the Rapa Nui story leaves us with a picture of human resilience and sustainability (albeit with some measurable ecological impacts) spanning 500 years. This alters the proverbial headline from "Collapse!" to a narrative focused once again on the amazing accomplishments of a relatively small population on a small and isolated island in the vast Pacific.

A similar narrative is emerging from our recent research on California's Channel Islands, where measurable indigenous human impacts to island fisheries and ecosystems go back 7–10 millennia or more, but where the Island Chumash and their ancestors also survived and thrived for millennia, even as their islands shrank (see chapter 5), their populations grew, and their technologies evolved. The transformation of the Channel Islands from marginal spaces for human habitation to places of abundance and sustainability has been fueled by ecological recovery of island habitats from more than 200 years of overfishing, overgrazing, and ecological devastation created by European and American colonial regimes (see Gill et al. 2019). It has also required, however, an intellectual escape from the confines of many decades of normative thinking by archaeologists (myself included) and other scholars.

Ultimately, archaeological approaches that prioritize the study of resilience and sustainability (success) among island societies—as opposed to human impacts, ecocide, and collapse (failure)—may also strengthen our cooperative relationships and collaborations with indigenous islanders around the world—key partners in the preservation, conservation, and restoration of both ecosystems and cultural heritage resources of inestimable value.

Conclusions

As the contributors to this volume on archaeological approaches to understanding the human colonization of islands have demonstrated, there is much for island archaeologists to be optimistic about. Island archaeology is emerging as a highly productive subfield in the larger field of archaeology, our knowledge base is growing, our toolbox continues to expand, our collaborative and inter-disciplinary networks are gaining momentum, and our models, methods, and theories are becoming more sophisticated.

As noted by Napolitano, DiNapoli, and Stone in their introduction, however, our optimism should be tempered by the growing number of threats to island cultures and ecosystems worldwide. These include climate change and accelerating sea-level rise, an alarming increase in the incidence and severity of coastal storms and catastrophes, associated marine erosion and habitat loss, rapid human development, overfishing, pollution, pandemics, and more. Rising seas, intensifying coastal storms, and accelerating marine erosion, of course, also lead to a worldwide acceleration in the loss of coastal archaeological sites (Erlandson 2008, 2012) sites that contain invaluable data for linking the past, present, and future of ecosystems and human communities around the world.

Rather than instilling pessimism or despair, I hope that knowledge of such destructive processes will inspire us to focus and expand our future efforts, energy, and resources. Archaeology is a powerful tool for understanding how such destructive processes have affected human communities in island and coastal settings over the *longue durée*. As a result, just as our zooarchaeological and archaeobotanical data are helping set baselines for modern conservation and restoration efforts, we are positioned to provide insights about how human societies adapted to similar challenges in the past, successfully or unsuccessfully. Island archaeologists, let us roll up our sleeves, put on our flip-flops, and get to work.

References Cited

Boivin, N., M. Zeder, D. Fuller, A. Crowther, G. Larson, J. Erlandson, T. Denham, and M. Petraglia. 2016. Ecological Consequences of Human Niche Construction: Examining Long-Term Anthropogenic Shaping of Global Species Distributions. *Proceedings of the National Academy of Sciences* 113(23): 6388–6396.

Erlandson, J. M. 2001. The Archaeology of Aquatic Adaptations: Paradigms for a New Millennium. *Journal of Archaeological Research* 9: 287–350.

Erlandson, J. M. 2008. Racing a Rising Tide: Global Warming, Rising Seas, and the Erosion of Human History. *Journal of Island and Coastal Archaeology* 3: 167–169.

Erlandson, J. M. 2012. As the World Warms: Rising Seas, Coastal Archaeology, and the Erosion of Maritime History. *Journal of Coastal Conservation* 16: 137–142.

Erlandson, J. M., and T. J. Braje (eds.). 2013. When Humans Dominated Earth: Archeological Perspectives on the Anthropocene. *Anthropocene* 4: 1–125.

Erlandson, J. M., and T. C. Rick. 2010. Archaeology Meets Marine Ecology: The Antiquity of

Maritime Cultures and Human Impacts on Marine Fisheries and Ecosystems. *Annual Reviews Of Marine Science* 2: 165–185.

Fitzpatrick, S. M., T. C. Rick, and J. M. Erlandson. 2015. Recent Progress, Trends, and Developments in Island and Coastal Archaeology. *Journal of Island & Coastal Archaeology* 10: 1–25.

Gill, K. M., M. Fauvelle, and J. M. Erlandson (eds.). 2019. *An Archaeology of Abundance: Reevaluating the Marginality of California's Islands.* Gainesville: University Press of Florida.

Glassow, M. A. 2015. Chronology of Red Abalone Middens on Santa Cruz Island, California, and Evidence aor Subsistence and Settlement Change. *American Antiquity* 80(4): 745–759.

Jackson, J. B. C., M. X. Kirby, W. Berger, K. Bjorndal, L. Botsford, B. Bourque, R. Bradbury, R. Cooke, J. Erlandson, J. Estes, T. Hughes, S. Kidwell, C. Lange, H. Lenihan, J. Pandolfi, C. Peterson, R. Steneck, M. Tegner, and R. Warner. 2001. Historical Overfishing and the Recent Collapse of Coastal Ecosystems. *Science* 293: 629–638.

Rick, T. C., and J. M. Erlandson (eds.). 2008. *Human Impacts on Ancient Marine Ecosystems: A Global Perspective.* Berkeley: University of California Press.

Stephens, L., D. Fuller, N. Boivin, T. Rick, N. Gauthier, A. Kay, C. Armstrong, T. Denham, K. Douglass, J. Driver, et al. 2019. Global Archaeological Assessment Reveals Earth's Early Transformation through Human Land Use. *Science* 365(6456): 897–902.

Wong, F. L., E. L. Phillips, S. Y. Johnson, and R. W. Sliter. 2012. Modeling of Depth to Base of Last Glacial Maximum and Seafloor Sediment Thickness for the California State Waters Map Series, Eastern Santa Barbara Channel, California. *U.S. Geological Survey Open-File Report 2012-1161 16* (http://pubs.usgs.gov/of/2012/1161/).

Contributors

Nasullah Aziz is research fellow of Balai Arkeologi Sulawesi Utara, Indonesia (the Research Office of Archaeology in North Sulawesi). His research is focused on prehistoric human adaptation to island environments in Sulawesi and Indonesia. As professional field archaeologist, he has considerable experience working in many cave and open-air sites in Sulawesi.

David Ball is the Regional Preservation Officer for the Pacific Region of the Bureau of Ocean Energy Management (BOEM). Dave joined the BOEM Gulf of Mexico Region (then Minerals Management Service) office in 1999 and transferred to the Pacific Region office in 2010. He has 30 years' experience in archaeology and has directed field research on both terrestrial and underwater archaeological sites across the United States, including inundated precontact sites, World War II shipwrecks, and deepwater shipwrecks in the Gulf of Mexico. Dave is a member of the Register of Professional Archaeologists, the International Committee on the Underwater Cultural Heritage (ICUCH) under the International Council on Monuments and Sites (ICOMOS), and has served in various roles with the Advisory Council on Underwater Archaeology (ACUA).

Todd J. Braje is professor of anthropology at San Diego State University and has worked along coastal regions in California and around the world for over 15 years. His interests center on the archaeology of maritime societies, human-environmental ecodynamics, and maritime migrations. Braje's most recent book, published in 2016, is titled, *Shellfish for the Celestial Empire: The Rise and Fall of Commercial Abalone Fishing in California.*

Richard Callaghan is professor emeritus in the Department of Anthropology and Archaeology at the University of Calgary, Canada. He has conducted archaeological and ethnological research in Western Canada, Central America,

South America, and the Caribbean. His primary research includes computer modeling of historical and archaeological problems dealing with migrations, maritime cultural contacts and interaction spheres, and voyages of discovery. His research has focused on the colonization of Palau, Madagascar, the Caribbean Islands, the Mariana Islands, and Magellan's crossing of the Pacific; the effects of the El Niño Southern Oscillation cycle (ENSO) on the Polynesian expansion across the Pacific, the avenues for the prehistoric introduction of *Gallus gallus* to Chile from Polynesia, (*Journal of Archaeological Science*), Edo period wrecks on the North West Coast of North America (*Canadian Journal of Archaeology, Archaeology Ethnology & Anthropology of Eurasia,* and Neolithic voyaging around the British Isles and the Bay of Biscay (*Oxford Journal of Archaeology*).

John F. Cherry is Joukowsky Family Professor of Archaeology and the Ancient World and Professor of Classics at Brown University in Providence, Rhode Island. His current research focuses on island archaeology in the Mediterranean and Caribbean, lithic analysis, and the Palaeolithic seafaring debate. He has codirected the Survey and Landscape Archaeology on Montserrat Project since 2010, and is also actively involved in the Mazi Archaeological Project and the Small Cycladic Islands Project, both in Greece. He is the editor or coauthor of more than a dozen books, the most recent being (with Felipe Rojas) *Archaeology for the People,* and (with Krysta Ryzewski) *An Archaeological History of Montserrat in the West Indies.* He has been coeditor of a *The Journal of Mediterranean Archaeology* since 1990.

Ethan E. Cochrane is associate professor of anthropology at the University of Auckland. He investigates the evolutionary and ecological mechanisms that shape diversity in Oceanic populations and is particularly interested in demography, material culture, and environments. He has published in several journals and is the coeditor of the *Oxford Handbook of Prehistoric Oceania.*

Robert J. DiNapoli (PhD, 2020, University of Oregon) is postdoctoral research associate in environmental studies in Harpur College at Binghamton University, New York. His research focuses on the use of human behavioral ecology and geospatial modeling to resolve questions about long-term changes in settlement patterns in the Pacific and Caribbean Islands. His research has been published in *Science Advances, PLoS ONE, Journal of Archaeological Science, Journal of Island and Coastal Archaeology, Advances in Archaeological Practice, Journal of*

Archaeological Science: Reports, Frontiers in Ecology and Evolution, Archaeology in Oceania, and *The Journal of the Polynesian Society.*

Andrew J. Dugmore is physical geographer and professor of geosciences at the University of Edinburgh. His main research interests lie in understanding human-environment interactions, environmental change over timescales from decades to millennia, and the significance of both environmental and climate change for human society. A key theme is the development and application of tephrochronology, and he recently published articles in as well as various chapters in edited volumes.

Jon M. Erlandson is emeritus professor of anthropology and Director of the Museum of Natural & Cultural History at the University of Oregon. He has written or edited more than 20 books—including the 2019 *An Archaeology of Abundance: Reevaluating the Marginality of California's Islands* (with K. M. Gill & M. Fauvelle)—and more than 300 scholarly articles. From 2005 to 2012, he also served as the founding coeditor of *The Journal of Island and Coastal Archaeology.* Although his field research has focused on the archaeology and historical ecology of California's Channel Islands, the Pacific Coast of North America, and Viking Age Iceland, Erlandson's broader theoretical interests revolve around the deep history of maritime cultures and island and coastal environments worldwide, including coastal dispersals in human history, the development of maritime technologies, and human impacts on ancient fisheries and ecosystems. In 2013 he was elected a fellow of the American Academy of Arts & Sciences.

Scott M. Fitzpatrick is professor in the Department of Anthropology and Associate Director of the Museum of Natural and Cultural History at the University of Oregon. He specializes in the archaeology of island and coastal regions, particularly the Pacific and Caribbean, with research focusing primarily on colonization events, seafaring capabilities, exchange systems, and historical ecology. He has active field projects on islands in Micronesia, the southern Caribbean, the Florida Keys, and the Oregon coast, and has published more than 130 peer-reviewed book chapters and journal articles, including recent ones in *Science, Nature Scientific Reports, Proceedings of the National Academy of Sciences,* and *Science Advances.* He is the founding coeditor of *The Journal of Island and Coastal Archaeology,* an associate editor for *Archaeology in Oceania,* and serves as an editorial board member for two other journals.

Amy E. Gusick is Associate Curator of Archaeology at the Natural History Museum in Los Angeles County. Her research is focused on island and coastal archaeology, human-environmental dynamics, the development of maritime societies, peopling of the Americas, and hunter-gatherer subsistence and settlement. Her current research projects on early human coastal migration and settlement and the effect of environmental stress on Late Pleistocene and Early Holocene maritime groups includes both terrestrial and underwater investigations.

Derek Hamilton is senior research fellow at the University of Glasgow's Scottish Universities Environmental Research Centre (SUERC). He specializes in the Iron Age archaeology of northwest Europe, radiocarbon dating, isotopic analysis, and statistical modeling. While much of his personal research is on British Iron Age societies, he is a recurrent collaborator on other time periods and places, working on all periods of European history as well as those in the Americas, Asia, and Africa. He regularly uses Bayesian statistical modeling of radiocarbon dates as a key element of his research, and coauthored a 2018 journal article, "The Myths and Realities of Bayesian Chronological Modeling Revealed" in *American Antiquity*. Currently, he is completing a handbook on *Radiocarbon Dating* for archaeologists, which traces the technique from first principles to final interpretation of the site chronology.

Terry L. Hunt is dean of the Honors College at the University of Arizona and professor in the School of Anthropology. His research centers on the human and environmental histories of the Pacific Islands, where he has conducted field research for more than four decades. He has spent the past 20 years investigating the natural and cultural history of Rapa Nui (Easter Island). In particular, his research focuses on critically evaluating the traditional "collapse" narrative for island. He is coauthor, with Carl Lipo, of *The Statues That Walked: Unraveling the Mystery of Easter Island*.

Thomas P. Leppard is assistant professor in the Department of Anthropology at Florida State University. He holds a PhD in archaeology from Brown University and has directed archaeological fieldwork in the Mediterranean, Caribbean, and Pacific. His research is concerned largely with the emergence of "complex" societies and with human ecodynamics, and has been published in journals and periodicals that include, among others, *Current Anthropology, Environmental Conservation, Human Ecology, Antiquity* and the *Journal of Field Archaeology*.

Carl P. Lipo is associate dean for Research and Programs, Director of Environmental Studies, and professor of anthropology at Binghamton University in New York. Lipo's research focuses on the application of evolutionary theory to the archaeological record, quantitative methods, remote sensing, cultural transmission models, and the study of social complexity. With Terry Hunt, he coauthored *The Statues That Walked: Unraveling the Mystery of Easter Island*, "The 'walking' megalithic statues (moai) of Easter Island," and "Weapons of war? Rapa Nui mata'a morphometric analyses."

Jillian Maloney is associate professor of geology at San Diego State University. Dr. Maloney's research is focused on marine geology, including geohazards and sediment transport processes, especially along the U.S. Pacific coast.

Matthew F. Napolitano is PhD Candidate in the Department of Anthropology at the University of Oregon. His research interests include island colonization events, adaptations to island environments, and developing high-precision chronologies for early settlement. His dissertation research looks at the early settlement of Yap, western Micronesia. He also collaborates on research projects in Palau, western Micronesia, and on St. Catherines Island, Georgia (U.S.).

Anthony J. Newton (PhD 1999, University of Edinburgh) is senior lecturer in the School of GeoSciences, University of Edinburgh. His research is centered around the application of tephrochronological research to studies of human-environmental interactions, archaeology, and earth surface processes mainly in Iceland. Recent publications can be found in the *Journal of Quaternary Science, Radiocarbon, Quaternary Geochronology,* and *Earth Surface Processes and Landforms*.

Maria A. Nieves-Colón is an affiliated researcher with the School of Human Evolution and Social Change at Arizona State University (ASU). Her research uses anthropological genetics and ancient DNA approaches to investigate human population history in the Caribbean and Latin America. Recent publications include the journal article "Ancient DNA Reconstructs the Genetic Legacies of Precontact Puerto Rico Communities" in *Molecular Biology and Evolution*. Maria holds a B.A. in Anthropology and History of the Americas from the University of Puerto Rico, Rio Piedras. She received her PhD in Evolutionary Anthropology from ASU in 2017, and from 2017 to 2019 was a

National Science Foundation Postdoctoral Fellow with joint appointments at ASU and the National Laboratory for Genomics of Biodiversity (LANGEBIO-CINVESTAV) in Guanajuato, Mexico. In 2021, she will join the faculty of the Department of Anthropology at University of Minnesota.

Adhi Agus Oktaviana is research fellow of Pustat Arkeologi Nasional, Indonesia (the National Research Centre of Archaeology), and currently a doctoral student at Griffith University, Australia. His research is focused on rock arts and behavioral development of modern humans in Indonesia and Southeast Asia.

Rintaro Ono is associate professor at the National Museum of Ethnology, Japan. His research is focused on human migration into Island Southeast Asia and the Pacific Islands, maritime adaptations, long-term exploitation of aquatic resources, and maritime trade history. He has been involved in many research projects in Japan, Indonesia, the Philippines, Malaysia, Palau, Pohnpei, and Vanuatu. He is the editor or author of several books, the most recent being (with Alfred Pawlik) Pleistocene Archaeology-Migration, Technology, and Adaptation and (with David Addison and Alex Morrison) Prehistoric Marine Resource Use in the Indo-Pacific Regions. He has been editor in chief of The Journal of Southeast Asian Archaeology (the Japanese academic journal) since 2016.

Timothy M. Rieth is manager and principal investigator at the International Archaeological Research Institute, Inc., a cultural resource management firm based in Honolulu, Hawai'i. His recent research focuses on chronology building and evolutionary ecological models of island settlement and human-environment interactions in Oceania.

Curtis Runnels is professor of archaeology, anthropology, and classical studies in the Archaeology Program and Department of Anthropology at Boston University. His research areas are the prehistoric archaeology of Greece and neighboring regions, lithic technology, and the history of archaeology. He has conducted research in Greece, Turkey, and Albania on early Paleolithic cultures, and the origins of agriculture, trade, warfare, and complex society in the Neolithic. His current research focuses on early hominin dispersals on the Greek Islands and other venues. He has authored and/or contributed to the following: Leppard, T. P., and C. Runnels, "Maritime Hominin Dispersals in the Pleistocene: Advancing the Debate," *Antiquity* 91: 510–519; Howitt-Marshall, D., and

C. Runnels, "Middle Pleistocene Sea-crossings in the Eastern Mediterranean?," *Journal of Anthropological Archaeology* 42: 140–153; and Runnels, C., "Early Palaeolithic on the Greek Islands?" *Journal of Mediterranean Archaeology* 27: 211–230).

Magdalena M. E. Schmid (PhD 2018, University of Iceland) is research associate of archaeological science at Kiel University. She specializes in the application of statistical models to improving radiocarbon dating and other methods to understand the colonization of remote islands (especially Iceland and New Zealand), the Avar migration (Hungary), as well as climate-culture interdependencies in the Southern Levant. Her work is published in *Radiocarbon, Quaternary Geochronology, The Holocene, Journal of Archaeological Science, Universitätsforschungen zur Prähistorischen Archäologie,* as well as various chapters in edited volumes.

Alexander J. Smith is assistant professor of anthropology and Director of the Museum Studies and Public History Program at the College at Brockport–SUNY (New York). His research focuses on island communities and colonial interactions in the western Mediterranean, as well as the application of various survey methodologies to island landscapes. He currently works on Sardinia (Italy) and codirects a new project looking at medieval Islamic domestic sites on Menorca (Spain). He is also the Director of Frost Town Archaeology, which investigates a late 19th-century logging village in western New York.

Harry Octavianus Sofian is research fellow of Pustat Arkeologi Nasional, Indonesia (the National Research Centre of Archaeology). His research is focused on development of archaeometallurgy in Indonesia and Southeast Asia, including microstructural and experimental archaeological analyses.

Sriwigati is research fellow of Balai Arkeologi Sulawesi Utara, Indonesia (the Research Office of Archaeology in North Sulawesi). Her research is focused on prehistoric island migration and megalithic culture in Sulawesi and Indonesia, especially in remote islands.

Jessica H. Stone (PhD, 2020, University of Oregon) is an affiliated researcher in the Department of Anthropology at the University of Oregon. She is a bioarchaeologist who specializes in the application of molecular techniques to explore the process of initial human settlement and adaptation to island and coastal environments. Her current research focuses on Micronesia and the Caribbean, and has been published in *Science Advances, Antiquity, Bioarchaeology International,* and the *International Journal of Paleopathology.*

Orri Vésteinsson is professor of archaeology at the University of Iceland. His research interests include colonization and migration in the Viking Age. He is the author and editor of numerous books and papers on Viking Age and Medieval history and archaeology of the North Atlantic.

Index

Page numbers in *italics* refer to illustrations.

Indian Ocean, the, 97, 251, 265, 316, 327–31, *328*, 333, 355; downwind sailing, 336; ethnographic evidence for marine environment of, 340–41; sea crossing, 335–36; seafaring simulation, 336–338, 341–42, *343–347*

Indonesia, 215, 293, 295, 333–34; ancestry, 334; human migration into, 297, 315, 320; pottery, 317, 319; sandalwood, 330; sea crossing, 92, 336–37, 340, 342, 348; Sulawesi, 298; xylophone, 331. *See also* Island Southeast Asia (ISEA); Translocations; Wallacea

Insects, 8, 40, 54, 208

Intentionality, and colonization, 6, 7, 92, 94, 271, 293

Iron objects, 137, 298, 309, 317

Island biogeography, 3, 4, 87, 42, 106, 233, 238, 267, 272, 275–76, 283

Island-hopping, 92

Islands: anthropogenic signatures on, 6; archaeology, 2, 3, 134, 266; endemic resources, 2, 90; habitability, 14; and hominins, 7; hopping, 92; intervisibility, 7, 46, 252; and sea-level rise, 19, 97; simulated voyages to, 9, 238, 251–53, 336–42; small, 4, 276, 278, 280–82, 295; submerged, 233; superislands or megaislands, 10, 273–75, *275*; terraforming, 8; as units of analysis, 3, 4. *See also* Caribbean; Channel Islands; Iceland; Island Southeast Asia (ISEA); Mediterranean; Pacific Islands; Remote Oceania

Island Southeast Asia (ISEA), 5, 7, 11, 13, 46, 215–17, 219, 239, 285, 295–97, *297*, 299, 308–309, 311–12, 318, 331, 334–35, 355

Isotope, 16–17; isotopic fractionation, 73; stable isotopes, 16, 142, 234, 240–41, 248; strontium, 17, 240–41, 246; studies on animals, 246, 248; studies on human bone, 44, 48. *See also* Marine Isotope Stages

Italy, 273, 278

Jadeite/jadeitite, 242, *249*

Jaguar (*Panthera onca*), 246, 248

Jamaica. *See* Caribbean

Japan, 10–11, 16

Java, 293, *294*, 336, 340, 342

King vulture (*Sarcoramphus papa*). *See* Birds

Kon-Tiki, 8

Kuril Islands, the, 11

Land: availability, 237; bridges, 3, 90, 355; inheritance, 13, 95; sighting, 46, 68, 252; wayfinding to, 337, 340

Landnám (land taking), 133–34, 136–38, 140–43, 147–50, 152; post-*Landnám*, 137, 140–43, 147–50, 152, 176. *See also* Iceland

Landscape: anthropogenic change, 5, 10, 48, 254; formation, 109, 115; inundation/infilling, 110–111, 123, 278; long-term change, 4, 116, 123; maritime, 121; reconstruction, 117; reference points, 138; relict, 108, 111; scale approach, 113, 118–19, 121; submerged, 106–7, 109, 111, *114*, 116, 119, 121, 353; survey, 118–19; transmission, 265. *See also* Transported landscapes

Language: Andamanese, 331; Austronesian, 16, 298, 308–9, 319, 334–35; Arawakan, 234–35; Bantu, 5, 51, 334–35; Cariban, 235; evolution of, 16; Maanjan, 334; Malagasy, 334; Maldives, 331, 348; of mathematics, 61; migration, 234, 316; mixing, 16; native, 63; New Guinea, 319; Papuan, 298, 309, 316; phylogenies, 15–16, 41; Ryukyuan, 16; Sinhalese, 331, 348; South Asian, 331. *See also* Glottochronology; Lexicostatistics; Linguistics

Lapidary, 233, 250

Lapita: aDNA, 218; burials, 311; chronology, 46–8, 201, 309; Cultural Complex, 215; dispersal, 181, 215, 217–18; expansion, 9, 46–9; genetic relationships, 218; hypothetical modeling, 184–85, 187, 191, 198, 200; introductions, 44; materiality, 308; migration, 14; movement of, 37, 42–43, 45; in Near Oceania, 44, 46; origin, 43; people, 296, 307, 309; post-Lapita, 43, 49, 309, 311; pottery, 43–45, *45*, 47, 49, 307, 311, 318; range, 42–43; in Remote Oceania, 44, 46; sites, 43, 47, 217, 296–97, 307–8, 313–14, 318–319; subsistence, 308; voyaging, 46, 49. *See also* Pottery; Remote Oceania

Late Glacial Maximum (LGM), 268, 270, 272–73, *275*, 276

Lexicostatistics, 15, 16

Linguistics: and archaeological data, 16, 334; association, 215; evidence for migration, 1, 43, 234–35, 240, 295, 298; evolution, 17; historical, 19; and Madagascar, 335; Northern Moluccas, 309; population mixing and, 16, 218; reconstruction, 295; relationships, 31. *See also* Glottochronology; Lexicostatistics

Society and Ecology in Island and Coastal Archaeology

EDITED BY VICTOR D. THOMPSON

The settlement and occupation of islands, coastlines, and archipelagoes can be traced deep into the human past. From the voyaging and seafaring peoples of the Oceania to the Mesolithic fisher-hunter-gatherers of coastal Ireland, to coastal salt production among Maya traders, the range of variation found in these societies over time is boundless. Yet, they share a commonality that links them all together—their dependence upon seas, coasts, and estuaries for life and prosperity. Thus, in all these cultures there is a fundamental link between society and the ecology of islands and coasts. Books in this series explore the nature of humanity's relationship to these environments from a global perspective. Topics in this series would range from edited volumes to single case studies covering the archaeology of initial migrations, seafaring, insularity, trade, societal complexity and collapse, early village life, aquaculture, and historical ecology, among others along islands and coasts.

The Powhatan Landscape: An Archaeological History of the Algonquian Chesapeake, by Martin D. Gallivan (2016; first paperback edition, 2018)

An Archaeology of Abundance: Reevaluating the Marginality of California's Islands, edited by Kristina M. Gill, Mikael Fauvelle, and Jon M. Erlandson (2019)

Maritime Communities of the Ancient Andes, edited by Gabriel Prieto and Daniel H. Sandweiss (2019)

The Archaeology of Human-Environmental Dynamics on the North American Atlantic Coast, edited by Leslie Reeder-Myers, John A. Turck, and Torben C. Rick (2019)

Historical Ecology and Archaeology in the Galapagos Islands: A Legacy of Human Occupation by Peter W. Stahl, Fernando J. Astudillo, Ross W. Jamieson, Diego Quiroga, and Florencio Delgado (2020)

The Archaeology of Island Colonization: Global Approaches to Initial Human Settlement, edited by Matthew F. Napolitano, Jessica H. Stone, and Robert J. DiNapoli (2021)